TOWARD THE YEAR
2000
WORK IN PROGRESS

THE DAEDALUS LIBRARY

Each of these volumes is available as a Beacon Paperback.

BP 247   *A New Europe?*, edited by Stephen R. Graubard

BP 248   *The Professions in America*, edited by Kenneth S. Lynn

BP 249   *The Woman in America*, edited by Robert Jay Lifton

BP 250   *Science and Culture*, edited by Gerald Holton

BP 251   *Utopias and Utopian Thought*, edited by Frank E. Manuel

BP 252   *The Contemporary University: U.S.A.*, edited by Robert S. Morison

BP 253   *The Negro American*, edited by Talcott Parsons and Kenneth B. Clark

BP 284   *Creativity and Learning*, edited by Jerome Kagan

BP 306   *Religion in America*, edited by William G. McLoughlin and Robert N. Bellah

BP 318   *Toward the Year 2000*, edited by Daniel Bell

BP 322   *Fiction in Several Languages*, edited by Henri Peyre

BP 335   *Color and Race*, edited by John Hope Franklin

BP 368   *Students in Revolt*, edited by Seymour Martin Lipset and Philip G. Altbach

BP 369   *America's Changing Environment*, edited by Roger Revelle and Hans H. Landsberg

TOWARD THE YEAR
2000
WORK IN PROGRESS

EDITED BY DANIEL BELL

BEACON PRESS   BOSTON

With the exception of "Violence" by James Q. Wilson, which
is published here for the first time, the essays in this
book appeared in the Summer 1967 issue of *Daedalus,* the
Journal of the American Academy of Arts and Sciences.

Printed in the United States of America

International Standard Book Number: 0–8070–0259–3

Second printing, December 1970

PREFACE

This volume contains the first materials to come out of the deliberations of the American Academy's Commission on the Year 2000. The story of the creation of that Commission, and of its early work, is fully described by Daniel Bell, its chairman, in his introductory essay entitled "The Year 2000—Trajectory of an Idea." Certain of the other essays and memoranda circulated in mimeographed form in loose-leaf binders for six months before consideration was given to committing the work to print in the Summer 1967 issue of *Dædalus*, the Journal of the Academy. The decision to move from the tentativeness of the typewritten sheet to the authority of the printed page was made for many reasons. It was believed that publication—first in *Dædalus*, then in this volume—would give a unique opportunity for many to share in the work of the Commission. Also, we thought that our readers would be interested to know something about the procedures which the Commission has used in its study. All agree that what is printed here is intended to be exploratory and tentative. Both the title and the organization of the materials suggest that the reader is not being offered a finished document. Rather, he is being invited to participate in an ongoing discussion, largely speculative, about which the Commission would never think to speak with a single voice.

Every effort has been made to acquaint the reader with how the Commission has gone about its work, where it stands at the moment, and what its future plans are. The book is organized in such a way as to lead the reader through the various stages of the Commission's deliberations. The phrase *work in progress*, which figures in the title, is significant. Differences have not been resolved, and consensus within the Commission has not been looked for. Many authors expect that they will alter their views in future meetings of the group. This is only a first report on its labors.

If, as Edmund Bacon suggests in his recent book *Design of Cities,* "we are in danger of losing one of the most important concepts of mankind, that the future is what we make it," the work of the Commission ought to be seen as one of many attempts to resist that possibility. Our object has not been so much to predict or prophesy as to suggest "alternative futures," among which choice is possible.

Because the study of the future cannot be said to belong rightfully to any single intellectual discipline, the Commission's membership reflects a wide range of scholarly and professional interests. These early evidences of its work necessarily concentrate on certain themes. It is to be expected that in time others will also come to be considered by the group. If the Commission continues in its present mood, however, it will never wish to make its views appear as anything more than conjecture. The Commission, believing that the study of the future is still in its infancy, is seeking to make some contribution to the advancement of such inquiries. As will be evident from what follows, a number of special working parties have now been constituted; their findings will in time be submitted to the Commission as a whole. It is probable that extensive new publication will result from these procedures.

The individual who has guided the Commission's work, providing both intellectual and personal leadership from the beginning, has been its chairman, Daniel Bell. We feel a great indebtedness to him. John Voss, the Executive Officer of the Academy, is to be thanked, for his administrative talents have helped to keep the Commission faithful to its fundamental tasks. A debt is owed Mrs. Virginia Held, who has assisted in preparing the agendas of the large meetings of the Commission as well as the smaller gatherings of the original working party. Preparation of the material in this volume was not easy. Our object has been to retain the informality of the original mimeographed documents, while altering them in such ways as to make them meaningful to those unacquainted with the Commission's work.

The Carnegie Corporation provided the funds that led to the creation of the Commission on the Year 2000. We are pleased to be able to record our continued indebtedness to that foundation.

STEPHEN R. GRAUBARD

CONTENTS

v STEPHEN R. GRAUBARD

Preface

1 DANIEL BELL

The Year 2000—The Trajectory of an Idea

Working Session One

17 Preliminary Memorandum to the Commission from the Chairman

21 Baselines for the Future

31 Alternative Futures

45 Centralization and Decentralization

56 The Need for Models

63 A Summary by the Chairman

Some Specific Problems

73 HERMAN KAHN AND ANTHONY J. WIENER

The Next Thirty-Three Years: A Framework for Speculation

101 FRED CHARLES IKLÉ

Can Social Predictions Be Evaluated?

127 DONALD A. SCHON

Forecasting and Technological Forecasting

Contents

139   MARTIN SHUBIK
Information, Rationality, and Free Choice in a Future Democratic Society

147   LEONARD J. DUHL
Planning and Predicting: Or What to Do When You Don't Know the Names of the Variables

157   HARVEY S. PERLOFF
Modernizing Urban Development

169   DANIEL P. MOYNIHAN
The Relationship of Federal to Local Authorities

177   LAWRENCE K. FRANK
The Need for a New Political Theory

185   STEPHEN R. GRAUBARD
University Cities in the Year 2000

191   HAROLD ORLANS
Educational and Scientific Institutions

200   ERNST MAYR
Biological Man and the Year 2000

205   GARDNER C. QUARTON
Deliberate Efforts to Control Human Behavior and Modify Personality

222   KRISTER STENDAHL
Religion, Mysticism, and the Institutional Church

228   ERIK H. ERIKSON
Memorandum on Youth

239   MARGARET MEAD
The Life Cycle and Its Variations: The Division of Roles

244   HARRY KALVEN, JR.
The Problems of Privacy in the Year 2000

251   GEORGE A. MILLER
Some Psychological Perspectives on the Year 2000

265   DAVID RIESMAN
Notes on Meritocracy

277   JAMES Q. WILSON
Violence

297   JOHN R. PIERCE
Communication

310   EUGENE V. ROSTOW
Thinking About the Future of International Society

315   SAMUEL P. HUNTINGTON
Political Development and the Decline of the American
System of World Order

318   ITHIEL DE SOLA POOL
The International System in the Next Half Century

Working Session Two

327   The Nature and Limitations of Forecasting

339   Four Futures

355   The Need for Normative Statements

366   A Summary by the Chairman

371   Members of the Commission on the Year 2000

372   The Working Parties

378   DANIEL BELL
Coda: Work in Further Progress

382   Notes on Contributors

387   Index

TOWARD THE YEAR 2000

WORK IN PROGRESS

DANIEL BELL

The Year 2000—The Trajectory of an Idea

TIME, SAID St. Augustine, is a three-fold present: the present as
we experience it, the past as a present memory, and the future as
a present expectation. By that criterion, the world of the year
2000 has already arrived, for in the decisions we make now, in the
way we design our environment and thus sketch the lines of constraints, the future is committed. Just as the gridiron pattern of
city streets in the nineteenth century shaped the linear growth
of cities in the twentieth, so the new networks of radial highways,
the location of new towns, the reordering of graduate-school curricula, the decision to create or not to create a computer utility as
a single system, and the like will frame the tectonics of the twenty-
first century. The future is not an overarching leap into the distance; it begins in the present.

This is the premise of the Commission on the Year 2000. It is
an effort to indicate now the future consequences of present public-
policy decisions, to anticipate future problems, and to begin the
design of alternative solutions so that our society has more options
and can make a moral choice, rather than be constrained, as is so
often the case when problems descend upon us unnoticed and
demand an immediate response.

But what began a few years ago as a serious academic enterprise—along with the Commission on the Year 2000, there is the
Futuribles project in Paris, directed by Bertrand de Jouvenel, and
the Committee on the Next Thirty Years (named with characteristic British understatement), of the English Social Science Research Council, under Michael Young and Mark Abrams—has
been seized, predictably, by the mass media and the popular imagination. The Columbia Broadcasting System has revamped its documentary program, "The Twentieth Century," into "The Twenty-
First Century," to depict the marvels of the future. *The Wall
Street Journal* has been running an intermittent series on expected

1

social and technological changes. *Time* has published a compact essay on "The Futurists: Looking Toward A.D. 2000." The theme of the year 2000 now appears repeatedly on lecture circuits and in the feature pages of newspapers. Dr. Glenn T. Seaborg, chairman of the U. S. Atomic Energy Commission, in a speech to the Women's National Democratic Club, holds out a promising future for women. "By the year 2000, housewives . . . will probably have a robot 'maid'. . . shaped like a box [with] one large eye on the top, several arms and hands, and long narrow pads on each side for moving about." Dr. Isaac Asimov foretells in a Sunday-supplement interview in *The New York Post* that by the year 2000 man will be exploring the limits of the solar system and living underground. Even the beauty industry has clambered aboard. An article on *The New York Times* women's page carries the headline: "In the Year 2000: Push-Button Beauty." The article begins enchantingly: "The chic woman of the year 2000 may have live butterflies fluttering around her hairdo . . . attracted by a specially scented hair spray. The same woman, according to predictions made at a cosmetics industry luncheon, will control her body measurements by reclining on a chaise longue with electronic bubbles that massage away problem areas. . . . She will have available silicones for filling in frown lines and wrinkles on aging faces."

All of this was probably to be expected. Much of the attention given the year 2000 is due, clearly, to the magic of the millennial number. Men have always been attracted by the mystical lure of the *chiloi,* the Greek word for a thousand from which we get our religious term *chiliasm,* the belief in a coming life free from the imperfections of human existence. Plato, in the Myth of Er which concludes *The Republic,* foretold that departed souls would return to earth after spending a thousand years in the netherworld. And the early Christian expectation of a *parousia* (prophesied in Revelation 20) placed its hopes for a Second Coming at the end of a thousand-year period. The millennial point is only thirty-three years away and within the lifetime expectation of more than three fourths of all Americans now alive.

A good deal of today's interest in the future arises also from the bewitchment of technology and the way it has transformed the world. *Time* writes portentously: "A growing number of professionals have made prophecy a serious and highly organized enterprise. They were forced into it by the fact that technology has advanced more rapidly in the past 50 years than in the previous

2

5000." And most of the images of the future have concentrated on dazzling technological prospects. The possibility of prediction, the promise of technological wizardry, and the idea of a millennial turning point make an irresistible combination to a jaded press that constantly needs to ingest new sensations and novelties. The year 2000 has all the ingredients for becoming, if it has not already become, a hoola-hoop craze.

All of this has its good side and its bad. What is bad, to begin with, is that a serious and necessary effort is in danger of being turned into a fad, and any fad trivializes a subject and quickly wears it out. A second evil is that many more expectations are aroused than can be fulfilled. There do not exist today any reliable methods of prediction or forecasting (even in technology), but some spectacular predictions are often encouraged or demanded in order to enhance the game and attract attention. As is shown in these pages, the serious effort is devoted not to making predictions, but to the more complicated and subtle art of defining alternatives. The third drawback in all this is that our major attention, reflecting an aspect of our culture, becomes concentrated on "gadgets," and breezy claims are made that such gadgets will transform our lives. (Thus, Marshall McLuhan predicts that by the year 2000 the wheel and the highway will be obsolete, having given way to hovercraft that will ride on air—a case, perhaps, of the medium creating his own medium.) Not only do people forget the predicted gadgets that failed to appear—for example, the replacement of the daily newspaper by facsimile that would come out of the television set—but the startling claims of yesterday quickly become the prosaic facts of today. Twenty-five years ago the technology magazines were filled with the coming wonders of "fractional horsepower," which would lighten all our burdens and transform our lives. And although small motors with fractions of horsepower have been developed, they have also resulted in such things as electric toothbrushes and electric carving knives.

The simple point is that a complex society is not changed by a flick of the wrist. Considered from the viewpoint of gadgetry, the United States in the year 2000 will be more *like* the United States in the year 1967 than *different*. The basic framework of day-to-day life has been shaped in the last fifty years by the ways the automobile, the airplane, the telephone, and the television have brought people together and increased the networks and interactions among them. It is highly unlikely that in the next thirty-three years (if one takes the year 2000 literally, not symbolically) the impending changes in technology will radically alter this framework. Supersonic transport will "tighten" the network and bring the world more directly into the domestic frame. The major challenges and problems already confronting our society, however—a livable physical environment, effective urban planning, the expansion of post-graduate education, the pressures of density and the reduction of privacy, the fragility of political institutions beset by many pressure groups —will extend to the end of the century. Predicting the *social* future is relatively easy, for in the Augustinian sense it is already "present expectation," just as the expectations about urbanization, education, and medical care in the volume *Recent Social Trends,* written thirty-four years ago, are "present memory."

This is not to say that substantial changes will not take place as they have been doing in the past thirty-three years. But one has to be clear about the character of such changes. In general, there are four sources of change in society, and they can be charted with differential ease. The first source of change is technology. Technology opens up many possibilities of mastering nature and transforming resources, time, and space; it also, in many ways, imposes its own constraints and imperatives. In the next thirty-three years we are likely to see great changes growing out of the new biomedical engineering, the computer, and, possibly, weather modification. Biomedical engineering, particularly its possibilities of organ transplant, genetic modification, and control of disease, promises a substantial increase in human longevity. Previous steps, principally the control of infant mortality, raised the average life expectancy; now the prolongation of life by the control of aging may be at hand. This may accentuate a tendency, already visible, in which the chief concern of a person (particularly in middle age) is not death from disease but staying young, thus strengthening the hedonistic elements in our culture. The impact of the computer will be vast. We will probably see a national information-computer-utility system, with tens of thousands of terminals in homes and offices "hooked" into giant central computers providing library and information services, retail ordering and billing services, and the like. But while the social and economic consequences will be huge, the effect will be greater on the structure of intellectual life and the character of organizations, than on the day-to-day life of the person. Weather modification, still only on the horizon, would

4

shape a control of environment men have dreamed of for thousands of years, but the working out of the economic and social arrangements, if the technology were possible, would pose some difficult problems for human civilization. In all this, one should note that "technology" is itself changing, and this may be one of the more important kinds of change in the next thirty-three years. Technology is not simply a "machine," but a systematic, disciplined approach to objectives, using a calculus of precision and measurement and a concept of system that are quite at variance with traditional and customary religious, aesthetic, and intuitive modes. Instead of a machine technology, we will have, increasingly, an "intellectual technology" in which such techniques as simulation, model construction, linear programming, and operations research will be hitched to the computers and will become the new tools of decision-making.

The second source of change, one of the most powerful engines in American society, represents the *diffusion* of existing goods and privileges in society, whether they be tangible goods or social claims on the community. This, in effect, is the realization of the promise of equality which underlies the founding of this country and the manifestation of Tocqueville's summation of American democracy: What the few have today, the many will demand tomorrow.

When diffusion begins to take rapid sway (as has recently been seen in higher education), it changes the size and scale of the servicing institution and, consequently, that institution's character. Dealing with such problems of size and scale and planning for the kind of institution we want become the urgent task of *anticipating*, not predicting, the future; for example, the university should not become a corporate entity because of the pressure of size.

A third kind of change involves structural developments in society. The centralization of the American political system in the last thirty years has marked an extraordinary transformation of American life. It is the result, in part, of our becoming a national society through the new transportation and the mass media. But it also grew out of the need for central instrumentalities first to mediate the conflicts between large functional groups and later to mobilize the society because of the demands of war. A different, more subtle structural change has been the transformation of the economy into a "postindustrial" society. The weight of the econ-

5

omy has shifted from the product sector to services; more importantly, the sources of innovation are becoming lodged in the intellectual institutions, principally the universities and research organizations, rather than in the older, industrial corporations.

The consequences of such a change are enormous for the modes of access to place and privilege in the society. They make the universities the "gatekeepers" of society. They make more urgent the husbanding of "human capital," rather than financial capital, and they raise crucial sociological questions about the relationship of the new technocratic modes of decision-making to the political structures of society.

The fourth source of change—perhaps the most important and certainly the most refractory to prediction—is the relationship of the United States to the rest of the world. In the last twenty-five years, our lives have been transformed most drastically by our participation in World War II, by our military and political posture in the Cold War, and by our relationship to the extraordinary number of new states that have emerged since 1945. The problem of *détente* in a nuclear age, the gap between rich and poor nations, the threatening role of "color" as a divisive political force, the changing balance of forces—both technological and moral—are all questions that reach from the present into the distant future.

We have begun to realize—and this is the positive side of the current interest in the year 2000—that it is possible to direct some of this change consciously, and because a normative commitment underlies any humanistic approach to social policy, we can try to widen the area of choice. Looking ahead, we realize that the rebuilding of American cities, for example, entails a thirty-five-year cycle, and one can rebuild cities only by making long-range commitments. In the process we are also forced to consider the adequacy of our political mechanisms, since Congress neither has a capital budget nor budgets money for long-range commitments. Furthermore, one must question whether a national society can sensibly be structured according to the present crazy-quilt pattern of fifty states and thousands of unwieldy municipalities.

In short, what matter most about the year 2000 are not the gadgets that might, on the serious side, introduce prosthesis in the human body or, on the lighter side, use silicones to lift wrinkles, but the kinds of social arrangements that can deal adequately with the problems we shall confront. More and more we are becoming a "communal society" in which the public sector has a greater

importance and in which the goods and services of the society—
those affecting cities, education, medical care, and the environment
—will increasingly have to be purchased jointly. Hence, the problem of social choice and individual values—the question of how
to reconcile conflicting individual desires through the political
mechanism rather than the market—becomes a potential source
of discord. The relation of the individual to bureaucratic structures
will be subject to even greater strain. The increasing centralization
of government creates a need for new social forms that will allow
the citizenry greater participation in making decisions. The growth
of a large, educated professional and technical class, with its desire for greater autonomy in work, will force institutions to reorganize the older bureaucratic patterns of hierarchy and detailed
specialization. The individual will live longer and face the problem
of renewed education and new careers. The family as the source
of primordial attachment may become less important for the child,
in both his early schooling and his emotional reinforcement. This
will be a more mobile and more crowded world, raising problems
of privacy and stress. The new densities and "communications overload" may increase the potentiality for irrational outbursts in our
society. Finally, there is the growing disjunction between the
"culture" and the "social structure." Society becomes more func-
tionally organized, geared to knowledge and the mastery of complex bodies of learning. The culture becomes more hedonistic,
permissive, expressive, distrustful of authority and of the purposive,
delayed-gratification of a bourgeois, achievement-oriented technological world. This tension between the "technocratic" and the
"apocalyptic" modes, particularly among the intellectuals, may be
one of the great ruptures in moral temper, especially in the universities.

The only prediction about the future that one can make with
certainty is that public authorities will face more problems than
they have at any previous time in history. This arises from some
simple facts: Social issues are more and more intricately related
to one another because the impact of any major change is felt
quickly throughout the national and even the international system.
Individuals and groups, more conscious of these problems as problems, demand action instead of quietly accepting their fate. Because more and more decisions will be made in the political arena
than in the market, there will be more open community conflict.
The political arena is an open cockpit where decision points are

more visible than they are in the impersonal market; different groups will clash more directly as they contend for advantage or seek to resist change in society.

For all these reasons, the society of the year 2000, so quickly and schematically outlined, will be more fragile, more susceptible to hostilities and to polarization along many different lines. Yet to say this is not to surrender to despair, for the power to deal with these problems is also present. It resides, first, in the marvelous productive capacity of our system to generate sufficient economic resources for meeting most of the country's social and economic needs. It is latent in the flexibility of the American political system, its adaptability to change, and its ability to create new social forms to meet these challenges—public corporations, regional compacts, nonprofit organizations, responsive municipalities, and the like. The problem of the future consists in defining one's priorities and making the necessary commitments. This is an intention of the Commission on the Year 2000.

Serendipity and Synergism

When I look at the diverse materials produced by the Commission on the Year 2000, and the eight "working parties" that are now considering a number of problems in detail, I am reminded of the story, perhaps apocryphal, of George Bernard Shaw's tour through the plant of *The New York Times*. In the editorial room he saw people milling about, typewriters clacking, teletype machines clattering, reporters rushing in, rewrite men taking notes over the phone, assistant editors barking orders, headlines being trimmed, proofs being corrected; in the composing rooms he saw linotype machines rattling, type being set on the stone, stories cut, bottom paragraphs thrown away, articles arbitrarily divided and sections put on "jump pages"; finally he saw the giant presses turning out the large newspaper, so neat and clean, and as he held up a copy, he remarked, "My God, you tell me all this is premeditated?"

If this question were asked of the Commission on the Year 2000, the answer would have to be "not completely." There was never a cut-and-dried plan as to where the Commission would come out. An enterprise seeking to deal with such an uncertain question as the uncertain future would necessarily be untidy in the way it started out. Not only was this premise accepted, but it was felt that such a procedure was in fact a wise one. Most books

8

or reports come to an audience neat and clean, revealing little of the uncertainty and confusion that marked the path toward a conclusion. Our feeling was that the method—the way we came to define relevant questions and relevant procedures—was as important, as a matter of self-education, as any conclusions that might be reached.

If there were no answers at the start, there was nonetheless an initial inspiration. The credit and honor for the idea of a Commission on the Year 2000 belong to Lawrence K. Frank, a distinguished social psychologist and retired foundation official who was a contributor to *Recent Social Trends,* the pioneering effort of a Commission appointed by President Hoover in 1931 to assess the rate and direction of change in our national life. In January, 1964, in a memorandum to Hudson Hoagland, then President of the Academy, Mr. Frank wrote, in part:

As large-scale transformations occur, our customary designs for living, our homes and family life, our interpersonal relations, and our social, economic, and political activities will require greater or less modification, if not supersedure. It is likely that our traditional morals and ethics and our American "character-structure" will undergo far-reaching and often radical changes. . . .

If we are to maintain a free social order in the face of the discontent and anxiety [we] will probably provoke, we must attempt the Promethean task of renewing our traditional culture and reorienting our social order as a deliberately planned process. . . .

The present situation, Mr. Frank argues, is somewhat similar to that of the eighteenth century, when such inquiring thinkers as John Locke, Adam Smith, and the French *philosophes* formulated the premises that underlie the democratic polity and market economy of the past two hundred years—rationality, mobility, the need for public information, free exchange. Today, he says, a new comprehensive political philosophy is needed that would formulate the assumptions of the pluralistic economy and the service society that is emerging. Mr. Frank proposed the creation of an Academy commission to write an "Agenda for the Year 2000" as the "first step toward meeting this urgent need for a new social philosophy."

The task of implementing the proposal fell to those who took office in the fall of 1964: Professor Paul Freund of the Harvard Law School, as President of the Academy, and John Voss, as the new Executive Officer. I was asked by Professor Freund to undertake the task of chairman.

I am not sure that I completely shared Mr. Frank's hope that we could attempt the "Promethean task" of renewing our traditional culture or articulating a new philosophy. Experience with earlier projects made me somewhat skeptical that a commission could be the vehicle of such an effort. By temperament, moreover, my concerns had been more with policy problems and with the need for adequate and rational planning to deal with them. Like many of my sociological colleagues, I was appalled by the fact that the Kennedy and Johnson Administrations had "discovered" the problems of poverty, education, urban renewal, and air pollution as if they were completely new. In typical American fashion, tremendous energy was suddenly mobilized to "solve" the problems. Although action is typical of the American style, thought and planning are not; it is considered heresy to state that some problems are not immediately or easily solvable, that it might take, as Daniel P. Moynihan argues in his famous study of the Negro family, perhaps a generation for real improvement to occur. A sense of historical time is absent from American thought, and a desire for "instant" reform or "instant" solutions is deeply ingrained in the American temper, both on the left and the right. The left wants, for example, an immediate end to poverty; the right, an immediate victory in Viet-Nam. Yet all these newly discovered American problems were, in fact, anticipated many years ago. Intelligent research and planning could have laid the groundwork for more effective programs. The real need in American society, as I saw it, was for some systematic efforts to anticipate social problems, to design new institutions, and to propose alternative programs for choice.

Thus, my own sights were more prosaic than Mr. Frank's. Yet I do feel that both perspectives gain from the interplay between them. One cannot write a new political philosophy without rooting it in some concrete problems; one cannot design new political mechanisms without becoming conscious of the philosophical assumptions behind them. The important task for any commission would be not to foreclose any area of inquiry.

In drawing up a roster for the Commission, we strove for diversity of specializations and experience—biologists, psychiatrists, economists, political scientists, government people, and scientists. A small planning group—consisting of the chairman, Leonard J. Duhl, Lawrence K. Frank, Stephen R. Graubard, Harold Orlans, Ithiel de Sola Pool, Donald A. Schon, Christopher Wright, and Dr.

Virginia Held, as rapporteur—was also created to prepare an agenda for the Commission. Several sessions were held in the fall of 1965 at Columbia University; out of these intensive discussions, a short working statement was prepared for the first plenary meeting of the Commission. At the same time, an annotated bibliography of recent major works dealing with the future and a packet of fourteen studies were sent to all members of the Commission for background use.[1]

The Commission on the Year 2000 had its first plenary session October 22-24 at the House of the Academy. The sessions were "unstructured," in that there was no effort to follow a predefined agenda or to pose specific questions for response. Following these discussions (Working Session I), the activities of the Commission were divided into two parts: considerations of hypothetical futures and methodological cautions in forecasting; and problem areas of the year 2000.

In the first sector, Herman Kahn and his associates at the Hudson Institute undertook to write for the Commission a series of papers that explore a number of "alternative worlds" (for example, the likely configurations of basic power combinations and antagonisms among the great states), and the primary trend lines or extrapolations, under different assumptions, of basic time series such as population, G.N.P., literacy, and the like. On the cautionary side, Messrs. Fred Charles Iklé, Wassily Leontief, Donald A. Schon, and Wilbert E. Moore, with the collaboration of Miss Eleanor Sheldon, produced a series of papers posing some caveats, epistemological and substantive, about forecasting in economics, social policy, and technology.

The "problem areas" were grouped under five rubrics: the adequacy of the governmental structure, the changing nature of values and rights, the structure of the intellectual institutions, the lifecycle of the individual, and the international system. Various mem-

---

1. Among these studies were the Rand Corporation "Report on a Long-Range Forecasting Study," by T. J. Gordon and Olaf Helmer, which has been a basic document for many groups that are scrutinizing the future; the massive volume by Landsberg, Fischman, and Fisher, *Resources in America's Future,* a projection to the year 2000; volumes from *World Design Science Decade 1965-1975,* prepared by Buckminister Fuller and John McHale; various studies by the National Planning Association, particularly the projections to 1975 and the study by Leonard Lecht on "The Dollar Cost of National Goals"; and "Reflections for 1985," the report of the long-range working party of the French Planning Commission.

bers of the Commission and interested colleagues were invited to write papers speculating on questions raised by the chairman. The word *speculate* was used deliberately, for individuals were requested to "think wild," if necessary, in order to deal imaginatively with the questions that were posed. About sixty papers formed the basis for the discussions at the second plenary meeting of the Commission, in February, 1966. It would have been desirable, but is beyond the limitations of space, to include all these papers in this issue of *Dædalus*. A selection of the papers is presented in part two, Some Specific Problems, and these topics are discussed further in Working Session II.

One further note for the reader: Transcripts are not always easy to read. The version that appears in this volume was edited somewhat to cut down the inevitable circumlocutions and rambling diversions that distinguish oral communication from a written text. At the same time an effort has been made to preserve the flavor of talk, as well as the often diffuse course of a conversation. As any person who has attended conferences knows, the talk of a group of thirty men, each with his own interests, prejudices, and standpoints, does not follow a linear course, like the cross-examination of a witness or the effort in a seminar to explicate an argument by sticking to a single point. There are always a number of rushing streams, at times going roughly parallel, at times intersecting, and at other times diverging. At different intervals the chairman stepped in and sought to build channels between the streams, or bridges over them, even though, on occasion, they were knocked down by one or another dissenter.

It would have been simpler, if our intention had only been to provide results and conclusions, to summarize major points as they developed during these two sessions. But this would have gone counter to our feeling that one of the valuable aspects of the enterprise is the *process* of talk itself. Out of what sometimes appear to be meanderings have come some new combinations of insights and thoughts. Many years ago, Robert K. Merton brought back into the social sciences the idea of *serendipity*, the happy circumstance in research or discourse of finding valuable or agreeable things that were not sought for in the course one originally laid out. In this transcript there are many instances of such fairy-tale gifts. But there are also examples of another process called *synergism*, which is defined neatly by Webster as the "co-operative action of discrete agencies such that the total effect is greater than the sum of the two effects taken independently." This, too, is one of the gains of the process of talk.

Yet *serendipity* and *synergism* are examples of that which may be unpremeditated and unpredictable. This is a paradox, and a chastening one, for a group that seeks earnestly to anticipate, if not to predict, the future.

WORKING SESSION ONE
OCTOBER 22–24, 1965

TO: MEMBERS OF THE COMMISSION ON THE YEAR 2000

FROM: DANIEL BELL, CHAIRMAN

DATE: OCTOBER 22, 1965

Preliminary Memorandum

THE PURPOSE of this first meeting is to define the scope of the Commission's efforts; this memorandum poses a number of questions that might guide such definition.

The impulse to the creation of the Commission came from the awareness that even though our society is becoming "future-oriented," we have no adequate mechanisms to anticipate, plan for, guide, or "invent" the future. In the last decade we have been overwhelmed by a number of fractious problems (Negro rights, poverty, pollution, urban sprawl, and so on) that, for lack of adequate foresight, have been dealt with in *ad hoc* and piecemeal fashion. Since the contours of these problems have had to be taken as "givens" (that is, the cities have sprawled, the baby bulge is already in the colleges), there has been little leeway in formulating adequate solutions. The questions, therefore, are whether we can identify sufficiently far in advance the nature of the emerging problems, whether we can indicate the kinds of data or knowledge necessary for the formulation of alternative solutions, and whether we can design new institutions or methods to cope with these problems.

In this light, there are, initially, two choices for the Commission:

1. To serve as a group concerned only with identifying a broad range of problems of the year 2000 and calling attention to the need for action.

2. To serve, in some microcosmic fashion, as a "model" planning or anticipating agency, dealing with a few problems that lie within our competence.

17

The decision between these two choices lies, I would suppose, in the way we respond to two different types of questions:

1. Whom do we want to influence—the intellectual elite or the policy-makers?

2. What is the comprehensible scope? Do we wish to concentrate primarily on the United States or on the "world scene"? Do we wish to attempt a generic forecast of the year 2000 (along the lines of the Rand study) or to take selected aspects? Do we want to concentrate on "problem areas" (for example, leisure or the aged); on structures and institutions (the organization of science, the structure of the university); or on underlying assumptions—sociological and philosophical—that may provide different perspectives than those which seem to be merely extrapolations of the present?

At the meeting of the planning group on October 9, the following list of themes was submitted. It was intended to illustrate the range of topics that might serve as the basis of the Commission's work.

1. Governmental structure: the adequacy of the existing federal-state-city structures in a "national society"; the problem of regional compacts; the distinction of public and private activities

2. Centralization and bureaucracy: in the society, in organizations, in cities

3. The influence of number: density, privacy, and interaction

4. Biological controls: genetics and personality

5. The structures of intellectual institutions

6. The adequacy of resource and energy sources

7. Population and the age balance

8. The control of the natural and human environment

9. The knowledge "explosion" and its consequences (in the curriculum of education, in the meaning of training, and so on)

10. Human capital: the location and husbanding of talent

11. The consequences of meritocracy

12. The inclusion of the Negro in the society

13. The use of leisure

14. The planning process and its varied forms

15. The state of the international system

It became clear in the discussion that these topics could be framed within four dimensions.

1. *A Bounded Problem Area.* One such example is the topic of governmental structure. One can argue that within the last decades the U. S. has become a "national society" (in polity, economy, and culture) in a way that it had not been before. Many of our current social problems arise not because of the hackneyed notions about decaying capitalism or creeping socialism, but because the interactions and repercussions of problems have had national effect so quickly. If we are becoming a national society committed to some form of directed social change, what are the functions of historic boundaries created by fifty states and tens of thousands of municipalities. Are there other social forms—regional compacts, public authorities, COMSAT-type corporations—that can take over and organize more rationally some of the functions now handled by the existing structures?

2. *Underlying Sociological Assumptions.* Many social changes, including the problem of a national society, arise out of a "change of scale," a change in the number of actors in a society, the widening of an arena, the amount of interaction. These give rise to different questions as to "optimal size" of organization, the limit to the number of problems and information that can be handled within systems, the consequences of multiple interaction, and the loss of insulating space in a mass society. These, in turn, raise value questions.

3. *Basic Philosophical Assumptions.* What will be the meaning of "democracy" and "free choice" in the twenty-first century in the light of, say, a basic assumption laid down in the eighteenth? For example, that "perfect" information available to all permits each to make rational choices according to his preferences in a self-adjusting market. Lockean and utilitarian theory provided the foundation of the political and economic institutions that were

19

adopted in the United States. What new assumptions are necessary for a service society and a free society in the twenty-first century? Assuming that some answers can be given, how are these to be implemented?

4. *The Processes of Change.* How adequate are the techniques of forecasting? What are the different strategies of change? How does one leave open options before people? (For example, is the therapeutic model an adequate one for this purpose?)

Yet these formulations should not be considered as binding on the Commission. The question of scope remains open. Should we aim for a comprehensive survey of problems, an illustrative survey, or a selection of problems treated in depth (and if so, in what kind of framework)? This is the primary question to be decided at this session.

Participants

Daniel Bell
Zbigniew Brzezinski
Karl W. Deutsch
Leonard J. Duhl
Lawrence K. Frank
Stephen R. Graubard
Charles M. Haar
Fred Charles Iklé
Herman Kahn
Wassily Leontief
Ernst Mayr
Daniel P. Moynihan
Harold Orlans
Harvey S. Perloff
John R. Pierce
Alan Pifer
Ithiel de Sola Pool
Michael Postan
Gardner C. Quarton
Roger Revelle
Eugene V. Rostow
Donald A. Schon
Martin Shubik
John Voss
Robert C. Wood
Christopher Wright
Paul N. Ylvisaker

working session one:

BASELINES
FOR THE
FUTURE

DANIEL BELL: I have the feeling that in starting something called the Commission on the Year 2000, there is a touch of extraordinary imagination and daring, and also of preposterousness. Yeats once said, "In dreams begin responsibilities." If this is going to be our dream and our responsibility, it is an appalling one.

The simple impulse behind the idea of this Commission was the question: Is it not now a fundamental responsibility for a society as interdependent as this one to try to engage in some form of systematic anticipation, some form of thinking about the future? It may well be that we are inadequate in our ability to make any specific predictions, but even so the very modest goal of simply accustoming ourselves to thinking about the future would be an important achievement.

At the planning meeting held two weeks ago some felt that this intention, while important, was quite limited. They argued that—given the fact that we are approaching a millennial symbol with the year 2000—the times required a more visionary statement. They felt that the socio-philosophical framework which has largely guided the organizations of this society is now outmoded and inadequate for the rational organization of choice. They believed that an effort should be made to think boldly of some large new framework—a philosophical view or a political theory—that would provide a guide for the new kind of society that is emerging.

If I can reconcile the way in which our discussion proceeded it was this: The effort to think about specific problems immediately ran into a consideration of underlying assumptions, while the effort to think about great issues had immediately to attend to specific problems. There was often an intermediate ground, and this was perhaps one of the more useful elements that emerged.

One problem, I feel, is the kind of expectations people have when they think about "the future." Having spent about two years reading the literature, I have concluded that the mistake a lot of people make comes from the seduction— partly from science fiction, or from books like those of H. G. Wells—that great technological breakthroughs constantly occur or that society can always be reorganized in some spectacular way. There

is an excessive concentration on the innovative and the dramatic—in technology, in biology, and the like. My own conclusion is that while such large changes are possible, they are often the most unpredictable. In speaking with scientists and engineers, one gets the sense that even such inventions as the transistor or the laser were not really predictable; and while it is sometimes very useful to look for the great innovative things, it may be misleading.

This is particularly so if our sights are set realistically—not symbolically—on the year 2000. The more significant *social* changes (not political) arise from diffusion of existing things—of privileges and goods—from the few to the many. Following diffusion there is a change of scale and a change of institution. If one takes a look at higher education today the critical social factor is not anything technically innovative but the fact that in 1939, 14 per cent of the youth group went to college, and today the figure reaches 42 per cent. It is the change in magnitude that creates the new problem.

More and more people are coming into society and, as claimants, are making effective demands on it. The nature of diffusion and change of scale can alert us to many similar problems. The very nature of urbanism is an instructive example. The major urban problems—crowding, lack of privacy, noise, lack of planning—are not new. What is new is the scale, the fact that so many more people are now living within urban civilization.

It is a change of scale in terms of space and time, as well as simply in number. The United States has probably had more labor violence, and to some extent more class war, than almost any country in Europe, measured by whatever indicator you take—number of troops called out, number killed, and so forth. Yet in the simple geographical sense this violence took place largely at the peripheries of society, whereas in Europe much of it took place at the center—for example, in Paris. Today in the United States the insulation of space has largely disappeared; everything immediately gets pushed to the center, and everything gets pushed there faster.

Turning, however, to the problems at hand, there are four kinds of considera-

22

tions for the Commission: first, the identification of concrete problems of the future; second, the philosophical implications of these issues; third, the underlying structural changes which may come about; and fourth, the nature of the planning process itself. How do people become aware of all these elements and begin to plan for them? What are the kinds of things involved in the planning process? How can its techniques be effective? What feedback processes are needed?

But at this first session, it may be wiser to throw the floor open for more general discussion, to tap the range of interests, and even the range of skepticism among us. Out of these we would then try to shape the nature of the Commission's inquiry.

ERNST MAYR: Reading through the literature that was sent to us, I had the feeling that it could be divided into two parts—the literature written by technologists, engineers, and resource planners, and the literature of persons more concerned with the movement of ideas, of underlying conceptual problems of mankind, of Man (spelled with a capital "M"). The resources, the technology, and the engineering engage a lot of people already, and are comparatively well in hand. What is rather neglected is the far more difficult, more intangible business of thinking about our values and our visions. I hope we can leave such things as the technology of traffic alone and concentrate on the broader issues.

HERMAN KAHN: It is true that there is a good deal of technological extrapolation, of "hard data"; but it is done very unimaginatively and almost without attention to innovations that you know are going to occur. At the Hudson Institute we have just started trying to look at the "quality of life" to lay out some of the aspects of what Europe, the United States, Latin America, and Japan might look like in the year 2000. And one has to be aware of cultural differences. Europeans' hours of work may be decreased to thirty or thirty-five hours a week, with two or three months vacation a year. I can imagine Europeans working very hard for their vacations and arranging their lives around their avocations. When you ask a European what he does, instead of saying he is a clerk, he is likely to say, "I'm a motor driver," or "I'm a bicyclist," or "I'm a mountain climber." Europeans care very much how they use their skills; they have the ideal of the gentleman, of the man who trains himself to do things that are useless in the American value system. You cannot imagine half the people in the United States doing something like that. The psychiatrists and teachers will work some eighty hours a week, laboring for mankind; a very large alienated group, working thirty or forty hours a week, is not going to be satisfied. These people are achievement-oriented, work-oriented, and really cannot say: "I'm the best swimmer in the county or the best climber."

I suggest that in talking about the future we lay out such descriptions. In so doing we should deal with styles of life. You can say, "That's nonsense," or you can say, "That's rather interesting, why don't we follow it up." But we should lay out some panoramas of the year 2000 to get an integrated picture.

MARTIN SHUBIK: We probably have reasonable predictive methods in technology, so that we can envisage how the roads would look if there were 120 million automobiles. On the other hand, we have social critics who write fine scenarios of the brave new world. I suggest that we need to address ourselves to the area between the two. Those who limit themselves to the technological aspects of the future often address themselves to the wrong problem, while the social critics, even when they define the right problem, know little about the technology to deal with it.

Since traffic has been mentioned, let me offer some notions of how a social analysis can modify a technological problem. Suppose we put a high tax on privately owned automobiles in the United States and a low one on leased or rented automobiles. Suppose for the sake of argument we had mammoth networks of Hertz companies (or whatever you want to call them) which would deliver an automobile to your doorstep in five minutes; the individual would have a standard credit card which merely punched the number of automobile hours that he used per week. Under such circumstances we would have very different patterns of use, although the technology would remain the same.

The problem is not automobile ownership, but convenient transportation; convenient transportation and the ownership of a private automobile can easily be confused if a society equates the two. There are many technological problems to which the people interested in technical coefficients have the solutions in terms of that particular game or framework. But their frameworks may very easily be wrong. I feel that we would be well advised to direct ourselves to the area of gearing the sociological imagination to the technological imagination.

ITHIEL POOL: I would like to concur with Martin Shubik, but also to express the hope that we will not neglect technological prognoses. Because we can do so much better on these, they provide a useful basis for predicting nontechnological developments too. When I looked at the Rand Delphi predictions, I was struck by the difference between the predictions made by the science panel and those made by the other panels. The nonscience panels essentially predicted that whatever was recently happening was going to continue, only a little more so. If there had been a relaxation of Cold War tensions, they predicted that there would be more; if there had been nuclear proliferation, then they predicted there would be some more; if there had been some population growth, then there would be more. All the predictions of a nontechnological kind merely extended current trends into the future. Among the technological predictions, however, were some rather startling ones that probably contained the causes of reversals of most of the simple trend projections in the nontechnological field. For example, I recall one prediction of genetic control. This kind of quantum change in the conditions of human life would leave the simple extrapolations that were made in all other fields in considerable doubt. If we do not link our technological expectations to our nontechnological ones, the scope of imagination that we will be able to apply in our prognoses will be distinctly limited.

KARL DEUTSCH: As an exercise, I have tried to imagine that this group had met in 1765 and had tried to predict the year 1800, or in 1865 and had tried to predict the problems of 1900. In jotting down, with the vision of hindsight, some of the problems in the first period, 1765 to 1800, certain extremes became apparent. A major energy source—steam power—was harnessed; a major scientific breakthrough occurred in quantitative chemistry; major political revolutions occurred in America and in France; there were major cultural renaissances; political equality became a major issue; and a major transformation of warfare occurred through the rise of mass armies. A certain number of evils, such as torture as part of normal juridical processes, began to disappear, and slavery came under attack, but new evils appeared with the rise of industrial distress and child labor. Between 1865 and 1900 we get another new energy source—electricity—and the combustion engine, the peak of the railroad age, and the full triumph of industrialization; labor unions and socialist parties, unheard of in 1865, appear; social equality and welfare, rather than political equality, became the new issues; imperialism and colonialism have their heyday in these thirty-five years; chattel slavery disappears and is even suppressed in Central Africa; serfdom goes out; industrial distress, tuberculosis, and suicide become some of the major evils of the time as then discussed.

If I try to project this and make a guess for the period between 1965 and 2000, I find that we can state our problems under five headings. The first: *The Technological Changes.* We will have major new energy sources, presumably nuclear, but perhaps also something as unexpected as electricity was in 1865. Automation and information technology will be fully implemented. We will see the triumph of the computer comparable only to the triumph of the railroad in the past century, or the triumph of the automobile in the first half of this century. We will probably see the beginning of interplanetary transportation, and a stream of scientific information coming from laboratories in outer space. This will give us knowledge comparable to what the microscope supplied at the end of the nineteenth century.

The second is *Psychological and Sociological Problems.* In the advanced and rich countries we will see a preoccupation with quality of life and leisure, and in the poor countries a demand for more food, machinery, medicine, and freedom from poverty. The gap between the two could tear the world apart in a deadly conflict. We will have to hand over economic growth itself to automatic machinery in order to develop automatic factories to make more factories. If we can automate not just production but economic growth, mankind can have its goods and also worry about leisure. If we do not do that, somebody will have to produce the capital goods that a world population of six billion people will need at the turn of the century. We will in any case also have by the end of the century severe maintenance problems; as we get more and more capital equipment, we will need more and more people to service and maintain them, and we are not getting these people.

The main problem in this second group, a sociological and psychological one, will be the socialization of adolescence. In the eighteenth century, grade-school education was thought of for the first time and introduced; from 1865 to 1900 grade-school education triumphed, and high-school education began to spread. In the period before us, college education will probably become standard in advanced countries, and high-school education standard in the developing countries.

The third group is the *Political Problems.* The advanced countries will become overwhelmingly urban. Through reapportionment people will become much more equally represented, and this will also come about through the decline in educational differences. The difference between illiterate and literate is qualitatively greater than the difference between senior college and junior college, or even between senior college and high school. It will, therefore, be much harder to maintain gross inequalities in political representation. Moreover, if the content of people's heads becomes more valuable, governments will find it more expedient to treat them with some respect and some consideration. This is likely to make people less expendable than they used to be.

We may get a permeation of criminal jurisprudence with the concepts and techniques of mental health. Since mental health is receiving huge amounts of re-

search money, we will get from the resultant psychopharmacological findings all kinds of other methods—a technological development—which by that time will begin to merge with our criminal jurisprudence system.

We may also get a growth of the public sector of the economy in non-Communist countries from the present level of roughly 30 per cent in advanced countries to anywhere between 40 and 50 per cent. This does not mean that the government will keep it all, but the government may distribute half of the national income. If there is anything to the law of declining marginal utility, we may find that people fight much less severely for marginal units of income when all of them are getting richer. Labor conflicts in advanced countries will become even less violent than they are now; resistance to high income taxes will become less and less desperate because people do not really mind giving up marginal proportions of their income if their income is high enough. This may mean a decline in resistance against an international income tax to be collected in the advanced countries in a way comparable to that by which Massachusetts and Connecticut are now being taxed for the benefit of New Mexico and Mississippi. We may get, therefore, an international transfer payment problem.

This brings me to the fourth problem: *Economy and Demography.* We will have six billion people in the world. With recent annual growth rates of 4 per cent in the total income of the world, we may easily have a quadrupling of world income from 1,800 billion dollars for the more than 3 billion people living now to 7,200 billion dollars for the six billion population that may be expected in 2,000 A.D. (and remember how misleading an average is here), from the present figure of $600 per capita to $1,200 per capita by the end of the century. The present range of per-capita national products, however, is from less than $100 to $3,000. If the transfer payments do not get anywhere, by the end of the century the range may be from $200 in the very poor countries to $6,000 in the very rich. I expect that the tendency toward declining marginal utility, however, may make the rich countries quite contented with $5,000 per capita, and it may, therefore, be possible to make available very major amounts of capital for the developing countries.

This leads finally to the fifth heading: *The International Question*. We may find a greater willingness on the part of the advanced countries to use as much as 5 per cent and conceivably even 10 per cent of their income for the economic development of the backward countries—perhaps 5 per cent about halfway through the period and 10 per cent by the end of the century. At the moment advanced countries are employing less than 2 per cent of their income for economic development elsewhere.

Just as evils such as chattel slavery and child labor disappeared in earlier periods, we may see the disappearance of organized preparations for all-out war, although this does not mean that we will not have all sorts of limited troubles. If we cut the arms burdens of the world by the end of the century from roughly 8 or 10 per cent of world income, which they are today, to 4 or 5 per cent, it might be possible to transfer that much to capital formation; this would in turn add another per cent to the growth rate of world income, given even a fairly conservative estimate of a capital output ratio.

We may have new evils—in the socialization of adolescence, in finding meaningful occupations, in the problems of a society suffering from information overload. Labor might be so expensive that maintenance will be deferred and equipment, neighborhoods, and houses neglected. This may then be combatted by automated maintenance procedures and a cultural emphasis on caring for things or for people. The English responded to the ugliness of the incipient industrial age and the "dark satanic mills" by a nationwide effort to keep the brass and silver polished, by stressing the appearance of care, of maintenance, of concern, of solicitousness. A response similar to the British reaction to the severe onslaught of early industrialization may become worldwide.

MARTIN SHUBIK: I gather from your division of the world into developed and underdeveloped countries that you do not expect national boundaries to change.

KARL DEUTSCH: I would expect most national boundaries not to change and the nation state to be the main social engine for getting things done by the end of our century. I would expect two things not to change before 2000: the reproductive habits of most of the peasant populations of Asia and Africa, and the national habits of most people everywhere. I would expect both of these to change sometime in the middle of the next century.

HERMAN KAHN: Why would you not expect the reproductive habits to change?

KARL DEUTSCH: It is extremely difficult to make a peasant change his habits about anything, and we have no good social technology for making large numbers of peasants change their habits. The Russians worked with hideous human cost and very brutal methods to collectivize—something that did not involve everyday marital habits. I would say collectivization was easy compared to changing marital life or imposing change in Central Africa.

ROGER REVELLE: I disagree with Karl Deutsch. In many less developed countries a widespread need to limit the family's size is felt. This need has arisen because infant and child mortalities are being reduced. There is nothing more erroneous than to think that the Indian peasant, for example, is stupid. To survive in an Indian village, a person must be shrewd and very much concerned with his self-interest. Indian villagers have shown their ability to change very rapidly in other things. When, for example, they were moved into the Punjab in the middle of the last century, the peasants adopted new kinds of agriculture in these new lands with great skill and effectiveness. I would guess that a marked decline in birth rates in many countries now depends mainly on adequate organization. You need to get knowledge and equipment of the right kinds to the peasants.

KARL DEUTSCH: I would not contradict Roger Revelle; I would only suggest that one should take learning speeds into account. We know when people learned to grow potatoes and how long it took them; we know when people learned to grow maize and how long it took them; we know how long it took people to accept smallpox vaccinations in different countries in the nineteenth century. As soon as we have more knowledge of this sort, there will be much better models for a forecast.

LEONARD DUHL: Reverting to my profession as a therapist, I would like to comment on the discussion. There has been a great deal said about technology, predictions, and the good things we are going to have. Yet I have heard little comment on what the process of development is, on what processes are involved in getting people to change, or on how we can start building new institutions and new ways of coping with problems at this very moment.

More and more people are flexing their muscles and are demanding a say about their future. This may well overturn all our predictions, because these people would rather have what *they* want than what all the technologists and scientists may desire. Thus, we must concern ourselves with the vital issue of how we are going to get these people involved in the processes of decisions—of decision-making.

When a patient comes to a therapist reporting a current crisis, he usually asks for help in reaching a certain goal. If the therapist were a planner, he would probably sit down and outline five steps for the patient to take. If, however, the therapist simply gives a patient five steps to follow, nothing will happen. He must first teach the patient the step-by-step process of assimilating new information, of reconceptualizing the world, of looking toward generalized goals, and of thinking about how certain immediate steps may be directed toward these generalized goals. Thus, even if *we* begin with technology and its potential as a generalized goal, the very act of coping with it will force people to see and to conceptualize the wider social processes essential to achieving that goal.

JOHN PIERCE: Most of the changes in the last thirty-five years that have affected my life and the lives of the people around me have been in part due to technological advances that were unforeseen and in part due to rapid adaptation —almost in spite of our institutions and

our government—by the people themselves to things that they wanted. They wanted television when it came along; they may not have wanted some other things. They wanted a mobile home, and 15 per cent of our new individual housing is mobile. In some ways life is different because people have preferred one thing to something else—be it fretwork or pre-Raphaelite painting. This makes me feel that predicting the future is rather hopeless, but it does bring up one point. If people would stay as flexible as they have been in adapting to things, and if institutions would be a little more flexible and apply fewer brakes upon things, perhaps we would get into the future less painfully.

DANIEL BELL: There is, though, one complication with that assumption—that all purchases are made by individuals. But one can divide goods into two kinds: those owned by individuals and those which are bought communally. People adapt quickly when it is a matter of individual goods, but there are other kinds of things that cannot be purchased in this way. You can buy your own suit, but not your share of clean air. Increasingly our new problems arise because certain actions must be undertaken collectively—for example, steps to eliminate air and water pollution. Certain goods must be purchased communally. Today we have few adequate mechanisms to realize social choices. The problem for the next thirty-five years is not the individual adapting to his own new wants or needs, but how to do this as a community.

STEPHEN GRAUBARD: I wonder whether the element of want has been that significant in the last thirty-five years. The two things that have most changed our lives during this period were not wanted in 1930—neither as an individual nor as a social want. One was the sudden realization that we were militarily vulnerable, that a certain kind of security which we had come to believe in as our natural right did not exist. This has altered our lives in every dimension: the obligations that were put upon us, taxes, the whole structure of academic life. The other was the great expansion of the Federal Government and federal power.

The extent to which the state now concerns itself with and is an agency for change would have been inconceivable in 1930.

FRED IKLÉ: We should keep in mind, without being pedantic about it, the distinction between predictions about values and predictions about things other than values—let me call these facts. Values are the things that matter to us. If you peruse a history written in the Middle Ages, you read about pestilences, plagues, the monster born when the king died, the battles fought, and so on. For us it is a dreary recital as these things are not so important to us. We should realize that in making our predictions we may be selecting things which we feel will be important in the future but which may not jibe at all with what people in the year 2000 will find important. We find that many past predictions are wrong not only about what would or would not happen, but also in their selection of what is important.

A different question is what we *want* to have happen; this goes into the issue of social engineering. In some of the extrapolations Karl Deutsch has made, there are both extrapolations about facts and extrapolations about human values. One of the dominant themes is that egalitarianism, a trend observed in the past, will continue in the future. This may be right, but it falls into the trap that Ithiel Pool criticized—that in making our predictions we political scientists simply extend present trends into the future. But these are modified in many ways, particularly by technology and even more so by changes in what people may want when new technologies are available.

HAROLD ORLANS: In much of our thinking on social development we operate on the assumption that whatever is technically possible will in fact develop. Yet we have to recognize that we may want to forestall certain possible technological developments deliberately on grounds of the social good. In *Science* not long ago Freeman Dyson wrote an article in which he deplored the cutting off of funds for the Orion project, which was to develop means of using baby atom bombs in the back of a space vehicle as an economical means of space propulsion. He was dismayed because never before in history, he said, had a technology that was possible been rejected. This man spends a great deal of his life in attempting to control technology in nuclear bans and arms control, but when it was a technology that was a personal hobby, he could not understand why no one else would support it.

DANIEL P. MOYNIHAN: Clearly one of the most powerful forces right now in politics is the diffusion of middle-class attitudes concerning participation: "I want to take part," "I want to help decide," "I want to be heard." These are animating more and more people, but perhaps the number of people who can be heard is limited. What changes are going to be self-defeating? What would we like to see remain unchanged, and what changes will turn out to produce a sort of I've-been-cheated feeling because the whole society cannot change in response to the individual's expectations?

ROBERT WOOD: I would protest somewhat the distinction between the diffusive and the innovative processes. I think one shrewd point of departure would be to recognize that the physical sciences have had their day for a while, that there is an innovative turn to the life sciences, and that most of our problems will come from the new advances in genetics, pharmacology, artificial organs, and medicine. The diffusion will come from the ways in which we try to grapple with life-science problems.

ERNST MAYR: This is, of course, a current trend. Alvin Weinberg of Oak Ridge recently commented that this was obviously the beginning of the century of biology. We have to an extraordinary extent controlled child mortality and infectious diseases; this in turn has led to the population explosion.

But not only biological-control problems are involved here. There is mankind as a whole. When Leonard Duhl talks with a patient, he tries to help him reconceptualize the world for himself. This, I think, is one of the most important things that faces us. To what extent should we face up to a reconceptualization of this world? We can extrapolate from the past in technological affairs, in economic matters, or in political actions; even if we are wrong, nobody will particularly object. But when we come to reconceptualization, we will be stepping on somebody's toes in anything we do.

Take, for example, the word *equality*. This term appeared in the period when the Western world was rebelling against feudalism; it meant equality before the law, equality of opportunity, and the like. By now equality has unfortunately acquired all sorts of meanings that are neither contained in the original concept nor particularly good for mankind. Biologically speaking, every person is genetically different from every other. The late J. B. S. Haldane who was, as you know, a Marxist (and nobody could accuse him of having been a racist or Fascist or Nazi) harped on the theme that we will never have true equality of opportunity until we realize the genetic differences between individuals. He said that until mankind faced up to the very unpleasant problem of the genetic nonidentity of man, it would never find an adequate solution to the problems it confronted. This would necessitate a reconceptualization of some of the things that we have always believed in.

LAWRENCE FRANK: I am disturbed by the frequency with which the problem is seen as that of predicting or creating a special institution or mechanism for doing something. My historical understanding indicates that ideas have been the most effective agents of change. Two hundred years ago the beginning of the American republic was not predicted; it came about because certain new ideas challenged old ones. Adam Smith's conception of free enterprise directly challenged and led to the supersedure of the old arrangement which limited production and wages. This led to the overthrow of the mercantile system. The Lockean conception of representative government largely displaced the dominant political structure. I would plead for an imaginative grasp of the possibilities of ideas, of concepts—of which the biological are a very important part. For example, people might realize that contraception is an attempt to complete the biological evolution of the human, making it possible for sexual intercourse to be not simply an instinctive, coercive, organic act, but a human relation.

KARL DEUTSCH: We should think quite carefully about the possible long-range psychological changes we might expect. Between 1765 and 1800 there was a major psychological change—the shift from rationalism to romanticism, from following convention to self-expression. Between 1865 and 1900, you get a split in the Western consciousness—a shift from traditionalism to more science, on the one hand, and to more violence, on the other. We have some studies, by David Potter and others, of the changes in the American character under the influence of increased material abundance. We have, of course, David Riesman's notions about the shift to other-directedness, and some of our most valuable work could be done here.

In evaluating alternatives we should consider which alternatives are most likely to increase the autonomy of people. Throughout the world, student self-government, on the American model, is becoming somewhat more frequent than the nineteenth-century authoritarian school. In very many parts of the world, something like the American parent-teacher associations, the American county agent, and other devices have appeared. You can see village councils working in India, Pakistan, and other places. On the other hand, one can use the technology of the future to put in more and more loud speakers, fewer and fewer microphones, and more and more great leaders.

At the moment we are developing machines for teaching people knowledge that is already fixed. We can, however, imagine that psychologists in the year 2000 would use a trainer by which an individual could learn how to make rapidly the decisions needed to keep a conference from foundering or to get through a committee meeting. We could also imagine that parents would have a session with the trainer just before their children reached adolescence; the machine might say go back, this parental response to your youngster's behavior does not work; try another one; and it would tell you quickly when you had found a response which usually works. These technological devices might be used to increase the autonomous capabilities of people to a very considerable degree.

The nineteenth-century ideal of equal treatment of children in schools was to give them more chairs with right-hand writing surfaces. It was then discovered, both by biologists and statisticians, that about one child in ten is left-handed. Real equality is to give right-handed children the right-handed writing chairs, and the left-handed children the left-handed writing chairs. Only if we know the extent to which we are dealing with statistical distributions of inequalities can we develop an art of government that will respond to the statistical distributions of human differences. This would, of course, also involve a substantial increase in the steering and self-steering capabilities of government.

ALTERNATIVE FUTURES

DANIEL BELL: In opening this second session, I would like to sketch some "hypothetical futures" about the world, or America, in the year 2000 so that we can have some baselines for discussion. Let me begin first with the world of 2000 as it appears in the Rand study. The predictions are that the world population will be about 5.1 billion, 65 per cent greater than the 1963 population. New food sources will have been opened up by large-scale ocean farming and fabrication of synthetic proteins. Controlled thermonuclear power will be a source of energy. New raw materials will be derived from the oceans. Regional weather control will be past the experimental stage. General immunization against bacterial and viral diseases will be available. Primitive forms of artificial life will have been generated within the laboratory. The correction of hereditary defects will be possible. Automation will have advanced further—from many menial robot services to sophisticated, high-IQ machines. A universal language will have been evolved through automated communication. On the moon there will be mining and manufacturing of propellant materials. Men will have landed on Mars and permanent unmanned research stations will have been established in outer space, while on earth commercial global ballistic transport will have been instituted. Weather manipulation for military purposes will be possible. Effective anti-ICBM defense in the form of air-launched missiles will have been developed.

Some of these elements appeared in the speculations Karl Deutsch made earlier about the advanced countries where he would expect control of nuclear power, the extension of information technology to encompass tasks now performed by skilled labor, interplanetary travel and transportation, extension of the GNP so that there will be a problem of leisure and use of time. He anticipates the breakdown of service industries, the socialization of the adolescent, great egalitarianism on the political level in terms of demands of excluded groups in the society, and problems created by new pharmacological devices. He expects the public sector to grow to roughly 40 or 50 per cent of the GNP, and diminution of such conflicts as those between labor and capital because of the diminishing marginal utility of some of the goods available.

At the working party meeting, Stephen Graubard also portrayed a hypothetical future, sketching a number of problems. Because men will live longer, the life cycle will become more and more of a problem as people do not pursue simply one career, but go through different career cycles. The diminished influence of the family upon various groups in the society may be a problem. People will be more mobile and live in a more crowded world. Interaction with remote parts of the world will be common. There will be greater consciousness of mass communication. The problem of indecisiveness about what to educate for will increase; people will be unaware or insecure in their ability because of the many new tasks confronting them. A blunting of the definition of what is social and what is anti-social behavior, and of the many distinctions that have characterized society so far, such as age grading, may cause difficulties.

From my own work, I would like to present a set of propositions about the postindustrial society—that of the twenty-first century. The key institutions of the nineteenth and mid-twentieth centuries have been, primarily, industrial institutions or organizations for the production of goods. The key values have derived primarily from the business firm, from the entrepreneurs within the business firm, from the managers of the business firm, or from policies in the society to facilitate their work. The major social problems—the relationship of industry to government and particularly the relationship of industry to labor—derived from the primacy of the business firm in the society. I would assume that in a post-industrial society, where many of the problems of production tend to be fairly routinized, the major new institutions of the society will be primarily intellectual institutions. These could be research corporations of various kinds—nonprofit

corporations, scientific laboratories, mixed corporations in terms of partnerships like COMSAT; universities, particularly scientific institutions; different kinds of regional compacts for the organization of different problems. These will tend to be the primary institutions of the society insofar as they are the major innovative institutions. No single kind may dominate, though perhaps the universities may be the strongest because so many problems get thrown at them, and they are immediately available for the kinds of tasks that were not there before. Before 1940, the major social forms were the government, the universities, and industry; after 1945, fifty or so major nongovernmental, nonindustrial, nonuniversity institutions emerged as new sources of change—Argonne, Brookhaven, Lincoln Lab attached to M.I.T., Jet Propulsion Lab attached to Cal Tech. This new social form was generated primarily by defense needs. New needs for services, research, and planning, particularly in domestic affairs, may in their own way generate different social forms in the next forty years. But these will be primarily research and intellectual institutions.

The Rand predictions with their strong emphasis on technology, Karl Deutsch's picture of the balance of technology and economics, Stephen Graubard's sketch of the problems of the life cycle and the individual's view of himself, and my own view of a postindustrial society give us some baselines of what the hypothetical future may be.

It may well be that the actual future, the year 2000, will in no way look the way we are hypothetically assuming it will. But then we would have a means of ascertaining what intervened to create a decisive change. In effect, we are setting up a kind of controlled experiment, a "prospective experiment," and allowing our heirs to match our "as ifs" with reality.

Assuming, however, that the future moves in the direction of these "hypothetical futures," I foresee several large areas of problems. First, what will this mean in the light of some of our received values, our basic values? There is at the moment a consensus about certain base values, although there is disagreement as to which come first and their exact weights. Some of these futures clearly pose problems for the kinds of values we hold. They pose problems for public policy in terms of what government may be called upon to do, and they pose problems for the individual in terms of his own psyche. The question that Lawrence Frank has been enjoining us to look at is in many ways crucial. What kinds of things will we come more and more to accept as part of the communal enterprise? In what ways will we have to forego various kinds of *individual* decisions in moving in this kind of world? Already, of course, one foregoes all kinds of rights, by such simple things as traffic laws or zoning, that were available, at least theoretically, one hundred years ago. The problem is clearly more acute in this dense, crowded society where greater stress is put on doing things through communal or governmental institutions because the very needs are so great. What does this mean to the individual and, as a corollary, what is the meaning of free choice, when so many choices are essentially or necessarily group rather than individual?

Many more demands for group action may cause a very important shift in the way an individual proceeds in the world. Ernst Mayr earlier questioned what equality would mean in such terms—equality at a variety of different levels, the whole question of genetic distribution. Eugene Rostow is very much interested in the effects a world of this kind would have on the shape of intelligence. How will national intelligence change when more and more people who have been excluded come into a society? What does this do to the whole level of national intelligence? What does it do to the development of talent. What will the emergence of a meritocracy—in which people earn a position in society largely by intellectual achievement—do to a political process based primarily on representation of interests and group interests as seen in their particular ways. Is merit to be the sole principle of status and achievement in the society? Michael Young speculates in *The Rise of the Meritocracy* about England in the year 2000. The society is in turmoil because the lower classes cannot stand the psychological burdens of having their inferiority exposed; at the lower end of the scale, they have no leaders who can control them and act as their spokesmen the way the Labour Party leaders have done for the last hundred years or so, making accommodations for them. The lower classes can only engage in outbursts, and so the meritocracy is in the end destroyed. Whether this is a valid picture or not is open to debate, but it is at least a relevant question.

Again in the realm of values, there is the problem of the nature of work. What becomes important in filling out people's hours in a "double class" system where there is a large area of intellectual work and large areas where people are excluded from work in which they use thought, where they are unable to relate themselves to a work process? It has been said that work is the chief means of binding us to reality, and it does seem to have this kind of ballast. What happens, then, in a society where work becomes less important to many people, and intellectual work becomes concentrated in a very small minority?

What is the nature of property in this kind of society? I would commend to you a very interesting article in *The Yale Law Journal* of April, 1964, by Charles Reich called "The New Property." He raises a whole series of questions, some involving the nature of civil liberties. He shows that we have new forms of property in terms of contracts, franchises, and tender systems—all of which involve a different conception of property than the simple possession of *things* in the old-fashioned way. What will the nature of property be in a hypothetical future in this society?

In a second realm—the public policy based upon this hypothetical future—I would assume that the baseline is the national society. There has been a distinct centralization of society, a centralization occasioned, in part, by demands for mobilization for national security, by the demands of disadvantaged groups for new social rights, and by the society's need to manage economic problems that are now national in scope. If the national society is the fundamental baseline, we face the problem of whether the governmental structure is adequate to handle the kinds of problems predicted for this hypothetical future. The relation of centralization to decentralization and the definition of regional or subnational units may be more pressing. There may be growing resentment that so many things have become centralized and therefore seem farther away from people. This raises the question of the nature of so-called participatory democracy.

The hypothetical future clearly involves the expansion of numbers and raises the question of optimal size of organization. Organizations may grow because of and in response to the market; in old terms, there is a natural limit in their ability to produce for a market. By what methods do you determine the optimal size of an organization when the market becomes less important as a means of check—particularly when you have governmental organizations, governmental bureaucracies, and universities.

Where people live is another problem. Increasingly Americans are living away from the geographical center because of the decline of agriculture, and more and more around the rims, the coastlines and the borderlines of the country. What sorts of problems come up in public policy because of this kind of spatial arrangement?

Thirdly, there is the whole range of questions of what the future situation will mean in the social-psychological realm. A number of people have been speculating about the relation of the adolescent to society. Reading the Beat literature, the poetry of people like Ginsberg, or some of the science-fiction things, one gets the impression that the technological world excludes many young people. It is a world they can neither manipulate nor master. They feel that technology now controls nature and the environment. Many of these people retreat into the distance, use hallucinatory drugs, withdraw to a private sphere of irrationality. Leonard Duhl has suggested that in the future as the world becomes more rationalized and controlled one of the major functions of the family may be providing a place where people can still play out their infantile feelings and indulge irrational fantasies.

Finally, one can look at both the hypothetical future and these different consequences and problems—problems of values, of public policy, of the individual—in terms of some new conceptualizations, new ways of grouping these problems. In

this respect, one can consider them in terms of underlying dimensions, such as *density, number,* and *interaction,* and see the ways in which new problems are generated by this fantastic multiplication.

One of the things in sociology which has always impressed me is the analysis by Durkheim of social change and "mass society." In the nineteenth century and earlier, Russia, China, and the United States were all segmental societies. Each village essentially recapitulated every other village; there were few complementary relationships and little interaction. Once you begin to get high interaction—increased division of labor, increased specialization, multiple interaction—everything increases exponentially, and a mass society is created. Mass communication, for example, dumps every problem immediately into the hands of the President. How many minutes a day does a man have to look at how many problems? The President must shift gears constantly, from the appointment of a judge in Massachusetts to the war in Viet-Nam. In our own lives we feel more and more harassed by the increasing number of things to which we have to respond. I once tried to speculate to some extent on what this means experientially. When the Constitution under which we are governed was laid down in 1789, there were 800,000 males in the United States; New York City, when Washington was President, held 30,000 persons. If you think of how many people each of them *knew* and how many each of them *knew of,* and then think of how many people each of us *knows* and those we have to *know of,* you get a sense of the extraordinary experiential differences in the ways in which people confront their lives.

The meaning of privacy, both personal and spatial, obviously assumes a very different dimension. What are the consequences when we are no long insulated by space? Many people feel disoriented about the world, and seek explanations in the manifest actions of government. Yet the underlying elements of size, density, number, and interaction shape experiences in ways that individuals are often unaware of.

I would hope at this session that we could get some agreement about the kinds of hypothetical futures we face, so that we could then proceed, either through working parties, or some other device, to undertake some more detailed scrutiny of the problems.

FRED IKLÉ: I am somewhat disturbed by the possible direction our exercise might take if we focus too much on a single baseline prediction. The Rand prediction already looks a little foolish; the anti-ICBM is not for the year 2000 but for 1967. The population for the year 2000 has a different projection, probably more like seven or eight billion rather than five billion. This has happened to many other predictions that have matured enough to be judged. The problem of servicing equipment which Karl Deutsch described might be solved by importing labor; West Germany is now importing one third of its labor force. We have a big pool of possible labor we could import from Latin America. But redistribution of wealth may not get started, even in so small a way as Karl Deutsch projected, because we do not have an international political mechanism comparable to the domestic one by which Massachusetts pays for Mississippi. The United Nations or whatever you postulate is not strong enough to bring this about. We may have more international feeding programs but that would be all. This would not change the economic development picture for the poor nations. The birth rate may not decline below a certain level, not because we do not have the means or the education to curb it, but because people like to have four children. This would mean that we would continue to have a substantial population increase. Russell Baker once wrote in *The New York Times* that in the past we have had the two-car family but in the future we may have the two-family family. People have two children when they are in their twenties; when they are forty, they find it lonely around the house—the children are in college, working, or married—so they have another two children. This doubles your rate of increase.

Above all, however, we have left out something which has dominated 90 per cent of the writing of the last two thousand years—which would have dominated to a large extent the predictions made in 1775, and to a lesser extent those made

in 1865—the field of religion and theology. Men have always held some conception of a sacred realm. What will be the nature of religious feelings a generation or two hence?

ZBIGNIEW BRZEZINSKI: I should like to address myself to the problems of political change. I think we accept the idea of a vast expansion in social regulation. It may take such forms as legislation for the number of children, perhaps even legislation determining the sex of children once we have choice, the regulation of weather, the regulation of leisure, and so forth. This poses major problems for political organization and decision-making; it will fundamentally change the role of groups—informal pluralism—in political systems and affect the relationship between the political system and society. All in all, this might lead to a collapse of the democratic ideal of a self-directing society. It poses a special relevance to the American political system, which, while evolving very flexibly and pragmatically, nonetheless is increasingly based on assumptions that are becoming irrelevant to our age.

I was strikingly reminded of this when I was looking at the *Goals for Americans* document [The Report of the President's Commission on National Goals (Englewood Cliffs, N. J., 1960)] prepared a few years ago. In a sense it was a conservative document projecting, in terms of the long future, goals and assumptions very much derived from the distant past. I was even more struck when I compared that document to the program the 22nd Party Congress adopted in the Soviet Union which projected ideals and conceptions of the future for the year 1985. Here, too, in a society dedicated to revolutionary change, the projection was inherently conservative in form with merely a marginal adjustment of present trends. There were no fundamental departures even in social organization or, more importantly—and this was true of both documents—in political organization.

This poses the generalized danger of the political system increasingly becoming a conservative instrumentality, a conservative institution, in relation to social change. It also poses the questions: How can such political systems adjust effectively to very rapid change, and what kind of a political system is perhaps more effective in adjusting?

It might seem that the Soviet political system is more effective than the American in adjusting because it is highly bureaucratized; it is a directed political system of the kind which is likely to emerge with the technological and biological changes we anticipate. Hence, it will require, perhaps, less fundamental change in the relation between the political system and the society than might be the case in the United States. But going beyond that, I wonder whether such a projection would not overlook the fact that a great deal of the change will be unanticipated, explosive, unpredictable change. This raises the further question of which of the two systems is less effective as a conservative institution; this might be the most important way of judging the ability of political systems to adjust to change. A political system that is less effective in maintaining itself and less efficient as a self-contained unit might be more adaptable than a political system which, on the face of it, appears to be more efficient, more integrated, and more directed. In that respect, looking into the future, it might be easier for the American political system to shift, when faced with unpredictable, explosive change, from an instrumental, adjusted kind of political system into a new, directed system that is already directed and already bureaucratized.

I would like to suggest at least two basic changes that will be of fundamental importance to the American political system. One is the revolution of the concept of representation. This seems to be moving increasingly in the direction of functional representation, the generalized theory of representation based largely on the predominance of lawyers and generalists giving way to technological, functional specialization. This, in turn, will fundamentally alter the pattern of legislation. Legislation will cease to be a canceling out and balancing of interests, and will become something far more abstracted, involving the weighing of inter-relationships within the society and within the technological processes.

Such weighing will have to be done by some body other than that which involves functional representation; by some sort of computing and planning agency out-side the legislative process. The legislative process will have to adjust to such changes, and this will in turn pose fundamental problems for the maintenance of the kind of Executive to which we have become accustomed. The expansion of the functions of the Presidency, including the expansion of the personal role of the President, may become something far more symbolic. The President will not be able to adjust effectively and inter-relate all of the functional specialized interests that will evolve. Such political problems cannot be solved or meaningfully analyzed by people concerned only with the political system. Unlike economists and technologists, political scientists have not produced any meaningful analyses of change, largely because the political system has become over the last two hundred years a highly conservative institution in relation to social change.

HARVEY PERLOFF: I think a good bit can be learned by stating where we are and trying to think of the future in terms of the actions and reactions we are likely to encounter. Looking at the picture today, the organizations that dominate the scene are the nation and the private corporation, the nation being the organizational unit for public policy and the private corporation, at least in the Western world, being the productive, innovative agency. For much of the world, and especially for some of the new countries, the nation is incapable of organizing the kinds of public policies that are needed. For example, the very small countries of Africa are basically nonviable. Various reactions to this nonviability are conceivable. One would be reversion to continuing internal conflict to divert attention from the public policy incapacity; another would be for several nations to organize on a regional basis forming a Common Market. Thus, the year 2000 might very well be dominated by political units that do not look at all like the nations of today.

The same sort of argument applies to the corporation. While it has served the advanced Western countries, it may not be the major productive unit of the future. It does not seem to fit the need for effective innovative units in the under-developed world nor their political and cultural requirements. There will very likely be a whole series of experiments to devise a new innovative organizational productive unit short of the government. These are the kinds of changes that are likely to be much more dominant in certain areas of the world than most of those mentioned thus far.

WASSILY LEONTIEF: I find the notion of a challenge and a response coming into our discussions. Without any fundamental innovations, straight quantitative growth by itself will prompt all kinds of adjustments. Although it is rather simplistic and naïve, I think it is quite useful to investigate the probable consequences of processes already operative in society. In metropolitan areas, for instance, certain adjustments will have to take place. If we were all to project our own trends and to determine whether they would be able to coexist, we would discover that they could not. Since this procedure is somewhat boring, we are inclined to introduce new autonomous factors which would provide additional problems of adjustment; of these, technological development is the most obvious.

We could organize our discussion by trying to identify the problems of adjustment that will result just from simply *extrapolating* the forces that operate already—the fact, for example, that natural resources do not increase so fast as the population and the demand for them, or that the population growth is much faster in the less developed countries than in the more developed countries. We could then identify what appear to be some *autonomous* forces that create additional possibilities and adjustments.

LAWRENCE FRANK: In all our thinking we are largely governed by certain assumptions that very often we do not make explicit. Each of the problems raised thus far is subject to a different formulation depending upon the assumptions of the different disciplines involved. Should we not be more critically aware of these assumptions which, if they remain undiscovered, are going to lead to confusion and conflict? For example, we use the eighteenth-century metaphor "social forces." This has become completely meaningless today. What do we mean by it? We are not thinking of large-scale forces that act at a distance. A society

is made up of individuals who are guided by values, assumptions, aspirations, and feelings. These beliefs and expectations, translated into the various economic, political, social, religious, and other patterns and uses of social symbols, direct our social life and provide the dynamic operations that are recorded by these symbols. Let us not be misled by outworn figures of speech and similes patterned upon the older celestial mechanics.

EUGENE ROSTOW: I did a little statistical analysis on my pad, jotting down some numbers: The time span between 1965 and 2000 is exactly the same as that between 1930 and 1965, 1895 and 1930, and 1860 and 1895. If we look at these spans starting with 1860, several classes of changes immediately appear dominant—series of changes, for example, in the concept of the accepted scale and scope of the social unit. In 1860 the dominance of the nation over regions and states began to be asserted and the Marshallian concept of the nation emerged. In 1895, our flirtation with manifest destiny and foreign policy began, bringing to an end the period of American isolation. Nineteen-thirty brought world-wide economic collapse and the extensive involvement of the United States in the world economy, as well as the reawakening, after the clash of 1914, of the awareness of America's involvement in and responsibility for the world balance of power.

Are we talking about an American society or a world society? What assumptions do we have to make about the structure and shape of world society in the next thirty-five years, arising out of necessity or otherwise? How, for example, can you have a world in which the Northern Hemisphere is short of labor and the Southern Hemisphere is underemployed? Some kind of osmosis is obviously going to take place between these two worlds—these two sets of markets—either through the migration of capital or the migration of people, or both. The problem may completely change.

We might look at the future by asking what will be the prevailing notion of the scale and scope of the organizing social unit? How, for example, will that prevailing notion emerge—through war, through agreement, or through acceptance of necessity?

Another category of changes that strikes me as significant after glancing back at the period from 1860 to 1965 is the deep change in the prevailing concept of social justice—changes in the relationship of man to man, of man to society, and of society to man. Striking elements in this process are the emergence of the welfare state from voluntary spontaneous notions of charity, the worldwide consequences of the socialist movement, and the persuasive power this movement has had on political life with the spread of universal voting simply because of its inherent appeal to our inner value systems. What changes can we anticipate during the next thirty-five years in our notions of social justice? A colossal revolution of this kind is now going on in this country. We read in the papers of a jury in the South refusing to convict a man who murders a Negro or a civil rights worker. This residual resistance shocks the national conscience. But the race problem, in its many aspects, cannot be solved easily. Underlying factors impede rapid social change. But change will come, nevertheless.

I want now to come to a third category—the relationship of the political system and the social order to technological change. Zbigniew Brzezinski spoke of political systems as being a conservative force in relation to social changes induced by technological developments. I do not know whether he considers conservatism a pejorative or a positive word, or merely a factually descriptive one, or whether he thinks that the political system should be abandoned as an intermediary trying to guide and direct the consequences of technological change. He seems to suggest that politics inhibits historical and social change originating in the technological sector, and that this is somehow a mistake; that existing devices of representation—devices for providing human control over the processes of change—are inadequate or totally negative and need replacement by systems of functional representation.

This area deserves considerable attention on our part. How and in terms of what values do we want political systems to control processes of change that originate in other areas? Functional representation, which we normally associate with syndicalism and with modern Fascist developments, has proved to be neither an attractive nor an adequate substitute for political systems based on a notion of the equality of man—one man, one vote. Have political systems of the old type already proved themselves inadequate, or should they be preserved, adapted, and utilized to control this process?

Society is not an aggregate of individuals alone. No matter how much we stress individuality, society is a complicated composite of mores and customs, and custom resists directed social change imposed by bureaucracies. Nothing can make the southern jury convict if it does not believe the murder of a Negro or a civil rights worker to be a crime. We can say that we are going to replace the jury system, but are we really going to do it? Do we want to replace it? Do we want to have people convicted of murder by acts of executive authority, without juries?

DONALD SCHON: When Wassily Leontief began to talk about challenge and response, I was not sure whether he was talking about the process of historical change or the process of discussion. I think both points of view are interesting. The forecasts and prophecies of the past have been handled in various ways. Traditionally their specific predictions are ignored; we do not look back to see if they were right or not. Occasionally—with H. G. Wells, for example—we look back and say they were right. Sometimes prophecies, when they are uttered by the right people, become self-fulfilling and make themselves right.

I have the feeling that the specific content of what we say—whether we are right—is not terribly important; we will certainly be wrong. Our process is more interesting than our product. The more interesting questions concern the ways in which our society can use the results of such deliberations. If predictions are going to be wrong, how can they be organized so that they are wrong effectively? By what methods can you compensate in flexibility for what you lose in accuracy?

As Lawrence Frank underlined in his comments, we can talk about equality, individuality, and freedom of choice; about prosperity, progress, and the technological program. We can use every term in our kit bag of eighteenth-century ethical tools, but each turns out to be inadequate. We can ask what equality or social justice is going to be like in the year 2000, or we can try to determine whether we are going to be confronted with a process in which such terms have no referents. The emphasis would then fall on how you develop values for the *process of change* itself, and how you retain a sense of self-respect when you are uncertain and changing. This is difficult not only for an individual, which is close to Leonard Duhl's point, but also for a society. The 1964 elections and Goldwaterism represent one means of confronting an uncertain situation in which you have more information than you can handle. You can either go back to the last stable state or revolt against it; you can retreat into mindlessness or anxiety and oscillation; you can struggle to develop concepts and values for a process that changes and is radically unlike anything in the past.

It seems to me that these process issues are the key. How do you take the thirty people sitting around this table, each of whom could stand and talk brilliantly for three days about the year 2000, and make out of this process something more than a series of individual interventions? How does one bring the uses of intelligence into the service of the future? How does one convince a refractory and intractable government of the need to plan?

HERMAN KAHN: I have had the exhilarating experience of selling at least three sorts of changes to the U. S. government, which at first we thought could not be done. I had felt that bureaucracies could not be moved; nowadays I have very much the opposite feeling. If you have a persuasive case, you would be startled at how readily you can move large bureaucracies. But why should we expect the bureaucrats to agree to something if a group like this cannot reach a consensus? A bureaucrat, after all, has less time, less interest, and less inclination to arrive at an agreement.

As Dan Bell has pointed out, looking at the diffusion process or at current tendencies is a good way to get at the future. Some of these tendencies are, however, incompatible. By jumping to a picture of the year 2000 and asking how you have gotten there, you may learn a lot about current tendencies.

With the exception of Eugene Rostow, I do not think anybody here has yet raised very seriously the questions of national security, international order, internal order, and the question of material goods. Let us assume that it does not take much time or effort to worry about internal order, international order, national security, or material goods. I submit that the main motives for our going to school would then disappear. There would be no incentives. Achievements—big factories, roads, and so forth —would lose their appeal. People would be more interested in skiing. There would be a sense of relaxation; nothing much is going to happen, but if it does, it won't affect me very much. There would also be a kind of rejection. The world *alienation* is often misused, but it is useful. Karl Deutsch has suggested that people will be well educated and that the government will be concerned with their opinions. I disagree. People will not be interested in the government, even though the government may spend a lot of time trying to get them interested. No one will care, because it will not make any difference.

ITHIEL POOL: Herman Kahn is right in his dissent. Karl Deutsch referred to the growth of the national public sector up to around one half of the GNP, and Zbigniew Brzezinski referred to the growth of managerial government. References have been made to weather control, crowding, urbanization. We have been assuming too readily a society in which social control becomes a more dominant and individuality a less dominant feature. Clearly there are tendencies toward a centrally, rationally planned society; but these are more than offset by opposite tendencies. A number of developments, such as weather control, that have been asserted to reinforce the tendency toward social control simply create a more predictable environment; they do not impose any more demands on the individual than the environment already does in its unpredictable state. Other factors operate to foster individuality. The rapidity of change in society calls for a very high degree of flexibility in personal behavior. The increase of leisure leaves

39

a larger sector of life for self-expression. The growth of the computer can, as the Soviets are very much aware, make economic units of a somewhat larger size efficient, but it can just as easily be a major instrumentality in making units of a smaller size efficient, and it can thus be a factor for decentralization.

On balance, I see no reason to expect a growth in the degree of centralization of social control growing out of the development in our domestic life. On the other hand, the growing split in living standards and conditions between the successfully organized, usually called the developed, societies and those that are underdeveloped is likely to be a very dominant factor in determining the character of life in the developed societies, particularly in the United States; out of these international tensions centralization of social controls may well follow.

DANIEL BELL: I am a little unclear why you see this as a counter-tendency to centralized social control.

ITHIEL POOL: Because, in the first place, I am assuming nuclear diffusion.

DANIEL BELL: If you have an increase in international tension and hostile postures, you will have to have more mobilized societies to deal with these kinds of things.

ITHIEL POOL: Yes, the external threat will be tremendous because of nuclear diffusion. Underdeveloped countries will have enough technology to organize political action to achieve their goals. The growth of communications will certainly make any discrepancy between the well-off and the deprived societies known. Peasants will no longer be unaware of the discrepancies. Karl Deutsch talked about the possibility of wealth sharing; I would regard defense by the rich of their status and attack on the rich by the poor as more probable. And with such conflicts there may come the establishment of central social controls, with all their military and emotional and nationalistic consequences.

LEONARD DUHL: One of the really critical problems we are going to have to face is how to live with the differences encountered in a fantastically pluralistic society. How do you live with the anxiety of not really comprehending the thinking of people around you?

CHRISTOPHER WRIGHT: I doubt that we shall get much agreement on baselines. In fact, the desire to predict or foresee the future may be part of a scapegoat operation which assumes that if we guess wrongly or are given misinformation about the future, we shall not be held responsible for what we do. But the problems of the year 2000 will be very close to the basic problems of today. If we could learn how to cope with today's problems on a less *ad hoc* basis, we would have the mechanisms for coping with those of the year 2000. I do not think it is meaningless to ask what kinds of mechanisms, processes, or concepts we need to develop in order to cope with the world today.

WASSILY LEONTIEF: To retort to Christopher Wright, my feeling is that there is indeed a very great justification for looking ahead. One of the troubles with day-to-day political decisions, even those on very important matters, is that they are often derived from analysis of only the immediate situation.

DANIEL BELL: We have with us a guest, Professor Michael Postan of the University of Cambridge, who is a member of the *Futuribles* group, directed by Bertrand de Jouvenel in Paris, which has published more than a hundred studies of conjectures. Mr. Postan.

MICHAEL POSTAN: In this conference there are people interested in technological changes and others interested in changes in the sphere of politics and society. The discussion appears focused on the coherence of the two—on those technological changes that are either induced by or induce political and social changes and on those social changes that give direction to technological progress. If we can agree that our primary issue is that of coherence, we must reconcile ourselves to neglecting political phenomena not clearly linked to technological processes and technological phenomena that neither induce political and social change, nor are induced by it. Among the social and political changes that are bound to have fundamental technological consequences are the movements of the frontier between public and private expenditure. Whatever is mentioned here—be it transport, consumption of goods, or the shape of things to come in the technological field—depends on whether the effective demand comes from society or from individuals. Any changes in public squalor and private affluence will depend on this. Among the technological changes that will induce social changes is, of course, automation.

DANIEL BELL: The preliminary studies of the President's Commission on Technology, Automation and Economic Progress [*Technology and the American Economy: Report of the President's Commission* (Washington, 1966)] report that the economic impact of automation seems to have been exaggerated, at least if one takes the rate of productivity as the criterion. While the rate has increased in the last decade, it is not unmanageable through sound fiscal policy. A recent book by Herbert Simon called *The New Shape of Automation* puts the issue in the best perspective. Calling himself a technological radical but an economic conservative, he makes a simple distinction that most people have not made. On the technology side, he feels that large-scale changes are in the offing because of the possibility of using computers as problem-solving machines; this will have consequences for the structure of management and the universities. But Mr. Simon does not think that the economic consequences will be so drastic as people assume. At least on the *aggregate* level, automation will not have the disruptive employment effects that people expect.

MICHAEL POSTAN: Automation's quantitative effect on employment may not be great, but it will have considerable effect on the structure of employment.

ERNST MAYR: In our discussion we have assumed that everything is in flux but man; only man remains unchangeable. I question whether this is a correct assumption. Two kinds of changes have, for instance, affected the dairy cow during the last thirty years. Some of the changes have made the dairy cow's genetic

program perform more effectively—improving food conditions, for example (this includes everything that was called nurture in the Victorian days). The other changes have been within the genetic program itself—through breeding, genetic improvement, animal husbandry, and so forth.

But what if we look at nurture and breeding in relation to man? We can make and already have made considerable advances in the translation of the genetic program. All improvements in public health, nutrition, and housing are of this kind. We are, however, still way behind in providing some elements of the social environment that would permit an improvement in the human genetic program.

Every once in a while a biologist is asked about the possible changes in the genetic program, whether he thinks eugenics is good or possible. If we are interested only in the next thirty-five years, we need not mention the word *eugenics* again. Nothing of consequence will be done in thirty-five years. On the other hand, we have been talking about planning, which depends on getting the right facts and then associating them properly. When you deal with questions in economics or the physical sciences, you can generally get your facts—even though they may not always be complete or completely right. Getting proper facts in the biological sciences is most difficult. Teams all over the world are working on schizophrenia, the most common mental illness, and there still is no basic agreement. Some people say it is strictly a genetic condition, while others maintain that it is entirely environmentally induced. About 50 per cent of all the hospital beds in the United States are taken up by schizophrenics, and yet we do not know the facts.

If somebody were to tell me to go ahead and plan eugenics, I would throw up my hands in despair. I could do nothing because we simply do not have the facts. We know evolution has occurred in the past. In a period of 400,000 or 500,000 years the human brain shot up from 500 cc. to 1500 cc. under very strong selective pressures. But in the last hundred thousand years there has been no visible change in the measurable cubic content of the skull capacity. Something

41

has stopped this process, and we have reached a plateau. Now a utopian, and in my more hopeful moments I am a utopian, might think it would be wonderful if we could get back onto that slope again, hoping to have, eventually, descendants a little less foolish than we are. If we have such hopes and wishes, we would have to start learning far more about genetics right now. We do know, on the basis of many, many tests, that intelligence has about a 30 to 50 per cent genetic component in it.

Realizing how little we know about the genetics of human achievements and of the best human qualities, we should pay far more attention to the kinds of knowledge that we would have to have if someday we want to do something in genetics.

GARDNER QUARTON: Even though there is some relatively uniform biological mechanism that we will probably understand someday, the number of interacting factors in the relationship of genetics to human behavior is so great that conducting controlled experiments becomes an enormously complex problem. It will not be resolved for many generations. It is only a very remote possibility that we will be changing people's lives in the test tube within the near future.

ERNST MAYR: I agree. I would also like to say that the least desirable aim of all would be to make man homogeneous. Nothing leads more rapidly to extinction than genetic uniformity or homogeneity. If we do any human genetic planning, we must at all times arrange it so that the maximum genetic variability is maintained. Equality in education means setting up our school systems in such a way that each person receives the school's optimal for his individual abilities and eventually finds a job in which he can be reasonably happy and make a maximum contribution. When we deal with biological man, we must recognize this total variability; there is no biological future for any species without it. We must incorporate it in our planning.

KARL DEUTSCH: I was struck by Fred Iklé's comment that a good prediction does not just say A will happen, but that

it is the most likely thing and that the most likely alternatives, if A does not happen, are contingencies B and C. If, for example, we had two notions about whether people in the year 2000 will be more resistant to or more tolerant of being taxed for the distribution of wealth, we might be able to correlate these notions with examples from economic history. The French nobility was quite spirited in their resistance at one time, while other elites in other countries were quite willing to go along with it.

STEPHEN GRAUBARD: Earlier I felt that there was a good deal of disagreement around this table about the future of the nation state. Harvey Perloff's comments, for example, differ substantially from Karl Deutsch's. In the definition Michael Postan has given there is, however, a way of treating not only the nation state but many other phenomena. A great many things that were thought to be private in 1865 did, rather unexpectedly, become public by 1900. This change was the consequence of certain military happenings and certain intellectual currents. It had to do with the defeat by Germany of certain powers and the establishment of a new kind of state in Europe; the influence of Darwinian thought and the arrival of socialism and new concepts of social justice.

It is apparent that sometime in the early-twentieth century a great change occurred in the conception of what is public and what is private. We have now reached yet another plane in this development; it might be very useful to extrapolate from the present situation what, in fact, the situation in the year 2000 might be. What was public and what was private were very precisely delineated in 1865. Today they are becoming increasingly difficult to differentiate. What is a public institution; what is a private institution? What is the public interest; what is the private interest? This problem is likely to be enormously significant in the next thirty-five years. Here again it is not so much a matter of predicting but of formulating the alternatives that we imagine exist for us in this period.

ROBERT WOOD: Though I subscribe to the confusion of public and private, I think you can go further and talk about the decay of institutions and the rise of systems. When a missile does not go up at Cape Kennedy, how do you fix the responsibility? Is the fault General Dynamic's or M.I.T.'s or the Pentagon's? When you look at what makes a metropolitan area run, taking an example from my own field of urban affairs, you discover that public and private are completely mixed. Couplings and relationships become more important than formal organizations.

STEPHEN GRAUBARD: When Karl Deutsch spoke of the kinds of changes that occurred in the two thirty-five-year periods in earlier centuries, he was really describing changes that can be subsumed under the general category of public versus private. You can talk about an increase of state power, but you can also talk about the intellectual currents, the social needs that provide the justification for that increase of state power. John Stuart Mill started out his great book on political economy entirely on behalf of private agencies doing most things; by the time he arrived at his third edition, however, he gave the state a far greater role than he had previously assumed to be necessary. The same problem confronts us today in education or transportation. How do we justify the state's becoming the chief regulator or provider of these services, and what are the likely consequences of that happening? On the other hand, what other alternatives are there?

ROBERT WOOD: The concepts of private and public sector can be misleading when one assumes a set of reasonably rigid institutional administrative processes. There are important mutations in the character of the response by each to societal and technological problems.

LAWRENCE FRANK: This discussion emphasizes the need for formulating a political theory or theories for the emerging Service State. We have today no general policy or theoretical statement of what functions and responsibilities should be established and administered so that the government will be responsive to and congruent with the lives we must lead in our urbanized, technological civilization, or "post civilization." Who will formulate

at least the principles and state the dimensions for such a new political theory?

CHARLES HAAR: We have been looking for some levers with which to discuss problems like the nature of man, war and peace, depression and social forces, and the corporation. Although I am doubtful that the public-private distinction was clear in 1865, Stephen Graubard's suggestion was an attempt to give us a kind of conceptual leverage. It might be useful if we tried to set down guidelines for the decision-maker as to what is public and what is private. Just raising the question is not adequate.

LEONARD DUHL: I sense a need to get relatively concrete. We could select one particular field—health, for example —and determine the implications of its present policies and their probable evolution, taking into account changes in technology and so forth. If we do not become concrete, we are going to become overwhelmed by anxiety.

GARDNER QUARTON: I agree with this; my anxiety has been increasing. In addition to picking an area, however, you must also decide whether you want to talk about the future and what might happen, or about the methodology of using predictions.

LAWRENCE FRANK: As a veteran of many conferences, I have found comfort in a statement by Proust—"that each individual can find lucidity only in those ideas which are in the same state of confusion."

KARL DEUTSCH: Since there is genetic nonidentity among men, some of us are uncomfortable with abstractions and others live a little better on the slopes up there. If we tried to work only on health or economics or technology, we would have no idea of the society in which this particular health, economic, or technological program was going to work. The historian looking back three thousand years is perfectly capable of seeing in ancient Athens a highly individualistic culture, involved with problems of power rivalry and a precarious economy. You can say in three sentences what you think, rightly or wrongly, were the essential problems, although it would take many scholars many years to write a good study of Athenian civilization. We are trying to do this forward rather than backward. We need to have a rough sketch of what the general configuration of the future might be, and what the general alternatives are. We also need sketches of the crucial sectors or alternatives in particular fields. Could we have a division of labor?

EUGENE ROSTOW: I am fascinated that the psychiatrists are so much more anxious than the rest of us. I want to offer a word of comfort to the chair. The people at this table represent different interests and skills; it is naturally going to take us a little time—because of the natural history of conversations involving thirty people—to probe our way to some sense of consensus. Professor Hoyle once commented that if you had brought together all the wisest people in medicine in 1890 and asked them to predict the most important discovery or invention that would occur in the field of medicine in the next fifteen years, not one would have mentioned the X-ray. Lenin and Hitler did more to change the base of the world and the destiny of man during the last hundred years than anyone else. We cannot predict what strange rogue events are going to seize power in disorganized situations, but we might note the importance of such phenomena.

DANIEL BELL: I think that we have here an effort to get a coherence out of thirty different minds moving in different directions.

HAROLD ORLANS: There are those who take a philosophical or theoretical approach, and those who take an empirical or pragmatic one.

DANIEL BELL: Well, it may be a split in temperament or in focus. From whatever starting point, each has to learn to accept the grounds of the other. The real problem is how do we mesh the two approaches.

CENTRALIZATION AND DECENTRALIZATION

DANIEL BELL: If I read the temper of the group correctly, there is a readiness to discuss some concrete problems. I would propose, as a start, the adequacy of the political structure in the year 2000. Perhaps this reflects my bias as a sociologist, but I believe that the way you create structures affects the behavior of people; that the constraints of structure shape actions, even those of people who kick over the traces in reaction. The question of the adequacy of the political structure would allow us to deal with the questions raised by Eugene Rostow on the size and scope of the social unit to deal with appropriate problems; with the questions raised by Zbigniew Brzezinski of the "conservative" nature of the political system; with the needs raised by Leonard Duhl for the government itself to begin to embody planning mechanisms; and with the relevant problems of the distinction between the public and private and the kinds of participation one can have in government. If, for example, we begin to think more in "systems" terms, what role is there for local participation? Should the site of a jetport be determined by a local community or by the requirements of the transportation system? What of the relation of government to universities? Many liberals accept government regulation of business; but what of similar regulation of universities? If the government is going to appropriate large sums of money for education and science, does it have a right to set standards in the way, say, the Securities and Exchange Commission sets standards for business, or to set vocational goals by increasing student subsidies in order to encourage entry into "socially desirable" occupations? Who is to set educational and science policy?

Pat Moynihan has observed that in the last three or four years the government has begun to feel confident about its short-run predictions, particularly in the economic sphere. The Council of Economic Advisers is able to make longer-run estimates of its revenue budgets, and so one knows more accurately how much money will be available for government spending. And yet, we may be moving too self-confidently with the idea that cost-effectiveness and cost-benefit analysis will provide rational guides for spending procedures. When the National Commission on Automation sent out some inquiries on the feasibility of setting up social accounts to complement economic accounts, Wassily Leontief replied that we did not realize how inadequate the sources of our information are. In considering the adequacy of the political structure, the adequacy of our information, our social accounting, and our planning abilities may be as relevant as any discussion of federal-state relations or other formal administrative problems.

We would want, also, to discuss the creation of new social forms—not-for-profit corporations, regional compacts, and the like—which could introduce a new flexibility into government. And this, in turn, leads into the broad questions of the philosophy of the Service State, the limited or expanded role of the individual and his rights, and the relationship of centralization to decentralization. If, in a national society, so much has to be done at the "center," what is left for the local community? Can we assume that such matters as policy, funding, and standards are set by the Federal Government, while operations are distributed throughout other levels of government?

Thus, I propose political structure and planning mechanisms as a concrete topic, and have sought to define some dimensions of the problem. I would be interested to see if other frameworks can be worked into this one.

HARVEY PERLOFF: At the outset you must break the problem down to international, national, regional, and local kinds of problems. The question of the coherence between science and technology is a useful frame. Transportation systems are, of course, among the technological developments that have a direct impact on cities. This technological element immediately has a political and social response. We are ill-equipped governmentally to plan and use such tech-

nological developments to achieve social aims. The governmental structure we have today does, however, enable separate interest groups to achieve their ends in a direct way. For example, a high-income group can form its own government in outlying areas and be sure that there is no need to be taxed for expenditures for the poor. Other groups can so arrange the governmental structure that by capturing the large industrial plants within a given area they can see to it that no one has to pay taxes except those particular plants. Others guarantee that they do not have to cope with very difficult problems—for example, by having no Negroes in their community.

I think a change is going to come rather quickly because of the new political power of the nonwhite and poor groups, and possibly because of a new morality on the part of the rich and the white. There are many alternatives to the present governmental structure, but so far the proposals that have been made in reaction to it have not been very successful because they have run counter to some strong interests.

One can conceive of an effort that would call for the creation of new cities specifically geared to setting up governments that can achieve certain social ends. If, for example, housing were built, with public assistance, to encompass a range of incomes, you would automatically have a certain number of poor people and nonwhites built into the community. The size of the governmental unit could be such that people could participate in the governmental process. This would be a conscious act to achieve a given social end. The community could be made so attractive that people would be willing to give up their present more limited advantages to achieve these other more attractive advantages—be they excellent, publicly provided recreational facilities or a beautiful lake, or whatever. You could arrange in advance to have excellent education for the nonwhite and poor groups so that certain of the problems that people worry about simply would not eventuate.

LAWRENCE FRANK: In order to get a more dynamic model, I suggest that we supplement, if not replace, the more or less static spatial models of political structures with a model of a communications network, with a number of different channels. This would help us to recognize that organization is not an entity or a tangible thing, but a complex of activities and operations that are carried on through the different communication channels and may be viewed in terms of dynamic processes.

DANIEL BELL: You are perfectly right. I have never conceived of government structure as something static, simply as some organizational arrangement.

Is the new planned town of Reston, Virginia, the kind of thing you have in mind, Harvey?

HARVEY PERLOFF: No. It did not start with the concept of achieving political and social ends. I am not, however, suggesting merely the "New Town" idea, but the use of technical possibilities in order to achieve social and political ends. Today Negroes move into suburban communities composed more or less exclusively of wealthy or middle-class people, and these people feel threatened and cheated. When a town or city is initially planned to achieve social ends, people would move into new communities knowing from the very beginning that they were going to include minority groups and poorer people. The planning process would involve, as a matter of course, a variety of approaches to achieve the major social and political goals.

HAROLD ORLANS: In our comments there are both utopian notions and realistic ones. Somehow utopia seems a little more realistic when you move into completely fresh land with a fresh population—as if the people had no previous history, and no political, economical, or practical factors were operative in this new place. This, of course, is silly.

HARVEY PERLOFF: Maybe, but this is merely a way of shortcutting a lot of things. You could quite easily have a "New Town in-town" where you would organize the renewal, the public-housing, and the transportation programs in order to achieve the New Town ideas. Without any major physical changes, you could achieve the same social and political ends; you do not have to use entirely new areas.

PAUL YLVISAKER: I suggest that the weakest link in the governmental mechanism is the bureaucratic element. We keep accepting the medieval concepts that Roosevelt made popular in our society—first you define a problem and muster a legislative majority, then you put a bureaucracy into the field to do the job. Kennedy carried on this process; Johnson is carrying it on today. But our society is not so amenable to the bureaucrat as the medieval one was.

We have perfected every other part of the chain. The foundations and the universities are quick to perceive problems in the future. The legislatures have adapted very well, particularly the national legislature, and are very receptive to statements of problems. The offices of the Joe Clarks and the Mayor Lindsays are staffed by case workers taking telephone calls from all their constituents. There is lightning-like communication on problems. Recently, the Judiciary has been a kind of advance guard. Some of the judiciaries, in the states particularly, are not so good, but these are local problems. As to the Executive, the Johnsons and the Kennedys have learned instinctively that the role of the public executive in our society is to define problems, to state them so that the nation can act. Thanks to the Negro, we have developed a fourth branch of American government —the March. This provides a needed feedback.

What is less known is how to get the job done once the problem has been defined, and the consumers, the legislators, the judges, and the President have been alerted. The bureaucrat does not really know how to function in our society. The business bureaucrat is coming closer to knowing, but, with very few exceptions, he is not emerging in the governmental sector. As old-line bureaucrats and old-line advisers to the prince, we have perpetuated certain myths—especially the theory of public administration that maintains that everything must focus on the top of the chain of command, and then by a series of regulations and hierarchical processes you get a job done. This ignores the reciprocal nature of modern power.

How are you going to perfect the bureaucratic function and the performance of public jobs in the next thirty-five years? Some people have talked about the centralization of power, but I think this is all wet. The first job of an executive now is somehow to muster, through the incentive device or whatever, some consensus. He trades *quid pro quo* with the state governments, the industrialists, and the Congressional leaders. The decentralization, the dispersion, of his power is constantly taking place. Do you not produce more inflexibility as you continue to trade away?

DANIEL BELL: You are probably right that in order to get things done you must have trade-offs. The operating problem is, however, somewhat different from the structural one. One needs centralization in order to define policy, to get money, to explore ramifications for the whole society. But once you have policy, funding, and standards, how do you decentralize operations?

PAUL YLVISAKER: Two different kinds of power are involved. One—the old medieval power in which one could act unilaterally—is not being centralized. But the other—the ability to influence by inducing co-operation or compliance —is increasing at both the national and the international levels. A very smart executive today has the best intellectuals working for him; he has a monopoly of the mystique that used to be confined to the bureaucracy.

Harvey Perloff's conception of how to handle the arrangements of cities is rather medieval. He wants to design rational planning processes, to draw relatively static solutions. The Homesteading Act had a touch of genius; it set certain ground rules, certain parameters, and then let society go to it. We may not be able to repeat this practice in an urban age, but we are going to have to come up with an analogue. You must establish ground rules and parameters consistent with some concept of where society should be going, and still maintain freedom and decentralization.

I think there will be a trend over the next fifty years back to stabilization. For example, Japanese society closed itself at a certain point; Greek society regarded change as evil. Elements in our system are now propelling us in the direction of change, mobility, and freedom, but a

psychological insecurity is present even among our young. The composition of the population will change over time. When the discrepancy between the haves and the have-nots increases, when we join forces with the Soviet Union and with other developed countries, we may go toward a stabilization psychology. That stabilization psychology will draw together power that has been dispersed, and we may return to a medieval practice of government again, to stability and stasis.

ROBERT WOOD: We do have a process leading to the defining of national goals, the national recognition of needs; but when national programs are carried out, they go through various half-way houses. The process of goal recognition or of setting standards is primarily carried on through persuasive techniques rather than by fiat from the hierarchy. Every major national program of interest today is a non-national program in application. Programs for Appalachia, urban problems, poverty, new cities, and health are geared to particular regions and particular areas. Unfortunately, when bureaucracies organized on national bases are dealing with problems which vary greatly in their local manifestations, administration is very difficult, and confusion is a constant risk. The mechanisms being developed under several domestic programs, for example, suffer from precisely such confusion. People have forgotten that they should be using and developing new techniques—like research and development, invention, the mixing of the public and private sectors, incentive systems, the idea of power as reciprocal—and are just going through the old ritual dance of the medieval bureaucrat.

DANIEL BELL: Until now the economic market mechanism has co-ordinated society; decisions have been made by individuals vis-à-vis one another. The political arena is a very different kind of "market"; it works, in part, through bargaining among different groups. But as a system becomes more complex, there are, of course, greater problems in co-ordination. How do you get a policy that is "more" than bargaining? The economic market has no "consciousness." But in the political arena, we can see the visible points of decision-making, and this become a greater focus for conflict, and there is an acute consciousness of the ramifications of decisions. There is, thus, a conflict between "political" and "rational" decision-making.

It would also be a mistake to assume that decentralization is taking place generally in the United States. Because the process is becoming more conscious, the need for co-ordination is greater. At some point one must go to the central source of co-ordination for decisions, and you thereby increase central power. But we do have to find modes of decentralization—especially for operations.

WASSILY LEONTIEF: The argument is twofold. Most issues arise when the short-range private interests of those affected by a decision conflict with the wider, long-range interests of the planners. The argument for people deciding their own fate on the local level is that they know more about it. But knowledge is transmittible, and we can learn about other people's positions even though we may not be immediately involved. Very often outsiders do a much better job in preserving the public interest than insiders. People outside the agricultural sector, for example, often deal more satisfactorily with agricultural problems than those within it.

PAUL YLVISAKER: One advantage of the dollar has been that it is a convertible currency. The vote has not been a convertible currency in the United States. It has remained a vote on agriculture, on education, and so forth. Johnson is becoming the first President with a convertible vote—on urban affairs, on beauty, on land, on everything.

MARTIN SHUBIK: There is a long history of log-rolling in this country. A dam appearing in Mississippi is very often correlated with a hospital going up in the State of Washington. This is the vote used as a convertible currency. According to one set of definitions, economics may be viewed as the study of the distribution and allocation of scarce, individually held resources, while politics is the distribution and allocation of scarce, jointly held resources. For the first kind of distribution, we use the market "pricing mechanism" and for the second, the voting mechanism. The pricing mechanism has nice properties when units of ownership are small. You can meet certain criteria of optimal efficiency and at the same time keep power blocs from meeting head on in an attempt by each to get 70 per cent of the same cake. This is no longer true when there is an increasing number of jointly owned resources.

Swapping five fancy marbles for a penknife is a legitimate economic transaction. On the other hand, taking a tax reduction in one area of my political bailiwick for voting for a school in yours is somehow not quite acceptable, even though it is one of the natural ways of making the vote convertible currency.

DANIEL P. MOYNIHAN: Is there reason to suppose that we are going to be rich enough in the year 2000 so that much of the desperate economic conflict of our past life will disappear? As resources become plentiful, the conflict over scarce resources will dwindle. There need not be any poor; the rich can get rich beyond the utility of richness. If this happens, the political system will be asked to do different things than it has been doing in the past; it might, for example, serve to keep people very busy—in the same way that church activities and vocations do today. Many of the traditional disadvantages in the American political structure—the diffusion of power, the multiplicity of jurisdictions, the fourteen hundred governments that Robert Wood found in the New York metropolitan area—might be ideally suited to a society in which the middle-class ideal of participation is diffused. George Bernard Shaw's comment on marriage could well apply to the political structure: It is popular because it combines the maximum of temptation with the maximum of opportunity. American governmental arrangements could provide the maximum opportunity for the temptation of participating in government. Each jurisdiction will become more involved; there will be more committees; every assemblyman will form task forces.

PAUL YLVISAKER: At one time the church and the state had a monopoly on talent. Very few people outside these sectors could rouse and defeat their bureaucracy. Today philanthropy is part of the governmental process; its technique of action through grants, rather than hierarchy, is characterizing every one of the new domestic programs. There is a spontaneous generation of bureaucracies to which the government makes allocations of money; these can be both public and private. We must invent other new links between the decision-making process on national problems and the capacity to act.

CHRISTOPHER WRIGHT: By concentrating on the distribution of power as a kind of currency, we have neglected power in the sense of new ideas, information, and analysis. To say that people on the local scene have this kind of power more than do people on the national scene is to miss the point, particularly with respect to the future. The power of ideas and the capacity to see how ideas relate to a particular situation must be continually recreated. The problem of distribution will take care of itself, since power in this sense will only be relevant to a particular locale and will not be fungible.

DONALD SCHON: The various agencies of the Federal Government are identified with problems which in general are thirty years old. The Agriculture Department is really even older than that, going back to the period of agricultural scarcity and the need for productivity. There are still seventy thousand agricultural-extension agents in the field. The Labor Department goes back to the labor problems of the thirties; and the Small Business Administration to a period in the forties when we began to worry about the little entrepreneur. In the Bureau of Standards, for example, a million dollars is spent each year testing cement, even though thousands of little laboratories in the United States are perfectly capable of doing it. If you examine the roots of this program, you discover tentacles that connect with the cement companies, the Congressmen in whose district the employees work, and the government agencies that have traditionally used the services of this group and do not trust the private cement companies.

Within the bureaucracy, heads keep coming in and getting chopped off. These heads are in contact with the power sources of the Executive and are given tasks to do, but they are not attached to the instruments doing the task. These instruments have their own continuing informal communities—lots of good minds and talent—that try to do what they think is appropriate under the cover of heads that keep getting chopped off.

How can you create self-destroying organizations—organizations that destroy themselves when their task is completed? One way to do this is to have an Executive that really takes on the form of the modern corporation. The various autonomous, semiattached units could be spun off, destroyed, or sold when the need for them has disappeared.

DANIEL BELL: All these agencies were originally set up as public remedies against private abuses, and in most cases, usually out of liberal impulses. Today these have become transmogrified, as in the case of cement testing. The problem now is to set up new agencies that will deal with other abuses, many of which are *public* abuses. How do you keep these sufficiently flexible and fluid so that whatever is set up as a new kind of structure does not itself go through the same process as the old one?

DANIEL P. MOYNIHAN: I think this is wrong. The things we are talking about have already happened. A wholly new bureaucracy has not been created in domestic affairs since the New Deal; most of the growth of government during the last twenty years has been overwhelmingly at the state and local level. A small new bureaucracy was created to run the poverty program, but President Roosevelt would have established a department of some kind. Federal employment tends to be down every year, not up. The process of utilizing the diversity of the American governmental structure is already well under way. Grants-in-aid to other government levels is almost the automatic form in which new federal expenditures take place.

EUGENE ROSTOW: You are merely using the old bureaucratic principles and concepts at a lower level; people at the federal level do not have to assume the responsibility. It is a much worse bureaucracy.

LEONARD DUHL: The most impressive groups in Washington—in terms of getting things done—have nothing to do with the bureaucracies. They are what some of us used to call the "guerrillas"; periodically they meet informally and then separate. The poverty program was created by a group which just happened to be sitting in one senator's office. The group later disappeared, dissipated. The current group [Fall, 1965] which, to me, is really the most intriguing in Washington, and which has absolutely no bureaucratic base is made up of ex-Peace Corps staff people. They have now wandered all over government, forming a sort of nucleus at Bill Moyers' headquarters. They somehow connect and reconnect, no matter what their agency affiliation. This group is really pulling all the power in the government.

None of the members of such groups are really interested in creating a bureaucratic power structure. A few have made the mistake of trying to get into bureaucratic power positions and have had their heads cut off.

CHARLES HAAR: Many large private corporations have the same problems as the governmental bureaucracies—old departments, old appointees, out-dated jobs. I wonder why Paul Ylvisaker took issue with Harvey Perloff.

PAUL YLVISAKER: I was using his statement as a launching pad, and it is not really fair because he has not even shot back yet.

HARVEY PERLOFF: Everything you have said is very interesting and pertinent. It is another issue, however, and we should deal with both. The question of size, of scale, is very important in many kinds of public purposes or functions. Certain of New York's problems arise because of numbers. The same things come out differently, in various fields, depending upon the numbers involved. I was struck by a report prepared on Greater London which showed that size of governmental units is directly related to capacity to carry out different public functions. The report proposed that most

of the local governments be restructured because they could not effectively carry out local functions; it called for a reduction in size for some and an increase for others.

Because of many changes—social, political, economic, and technological—the Federal Government is being called upon to solve metropolitan problems simply because there are no other means of solving them. This is very difficult not only for the Federal Government but also for the local people. There are governmental arrangements that would permit us to achieve certain highly valuable social goals, but they need to be consciously developed. We need to create certain kinds of arrangements that would allow greater interchange between bureaucrats and different interest groups. We know a good deal about the poor groups in inner-city areas—about, for example, the inadequacy of the planning for jobs and for better educational opportunities. Having discovered this, it does not seem very bright to use methods that have proved to be ineffective in the past. Instead of revising existing governmental structures, it might possibly be more effective to start with new kinds of physical, technological structures, where government would fit in because of the nature of the structure. You cannot create a "New Town in-town" without creating new political forms. I suggest this procedure not as any kind of "final" solution but merely as a way of playing through the idea of using technological possibilities in order to achieve social and political ends.

ZBIGNIEW BRZEZINSKI: The discussion seems to be centering on problems of 1965, not of the year 2000. Perhaps we can relate these current problems to the future by discussing the relationship of the political system to social change. Eugene Rostow earlier challenged me to explain what I meant by saying the government is conservative. The government is conservative in relation to change because it generates essentially post-crisis management institutions. In order to create pre-crisis management institutions, in a setting which we could call political-democratic, we will have to increasingly separate the political system from society and begin to conceive of the two as separate entities. The two became enmeshed because the political structure did not keep up with social and economic change. Change in the political system comes about only through the merging of the political system and society. Increasingly we may see the negation of this tendency; social, economic, and technological change may precipitate the separation of the political system from society. In some respects France under de Gaulle is a relevant model. French society, which still remains libertarian, democratic, and pluralistic, is being separated from the political system, which is increasingly technical in orientation and self-contained. The intellectual in this political system is more and more the functional specialist and no longer a generalist.

DANIEL BELL: Do you think such a system is democratic?

ZBIGNIEW BRZEZINSKI: The political system is not democratic, but the society remains so. Part of the trouble today is that it is very difficult to anticipate problems in a democratic political system because of the close meshing between the political system and society.

DANIEL BELL: In what sense do you mean that the society is democratic?

ZBIGNIEW BRZEZINSKI: In a libertarian, negative sense; democratic not in terms of exercising fundamental choices concerning policy-making, but in the sense of maintaining certain areas of autonomy for individual self-expression.

DANIEL BELL: There seems to be here a real confrontation between Paul Ylvisaker and Zbigniew Brzezinski. Paul wants to extend the areas of participation, making this central to the ways in which change would proceed, while Zbigniew maintains the political system should become professional and oriented to managing problems. In Ylvisaker's view, bureaucracy should be broken up and other institutions, more responsive to the people, created. Brzezinski wants to safeguard fundamental liberties, but feels the political system would work better—presumably be more rational, flexible, and even more responsive—if

participation in processes other than representation were reduced.

ZBIGNIEW BRZEZINSKI: In the present political setting in the United States, you could not implement the long-range and far-reaching reforms that are being undertaken in French agriculture, for example. You could not even have the kind of work that is being done in Paris by the Commission on the Year 1985.

DANIEL BELL: I would argue this. While I think your example may be relevant to France, I do not see how it could be grafted onto the American political structure.

PAUL YLVISAKER: I agree. This is completely alien to my conception of what should be and what will be in this country.

LAWRENCE FRANK: We should perhaps ask what additions and improvements should be provided for communications between the electorate and the government and ask whether the frequency of opinion polls may be devaluating the formal election procedures. Moreover, we might ask whether elections should always be in terms of choosing individuals. Except for referenda on special issues, this choice largely engrosses our attention and provokes our strong reactions, but it may or may not be relevant to the questions of government that are to be decided.

DANIEL BELL: You could have a national referendum on various issues using the telephone and the computer. People would simply buzz *yes* or *no* answers, and the volume would decide the question. Is that the sort of political system you want?

LAWRENCE FRANK: When we ask people to reply to a question, especially in an opinion poll, we often get answers that are biased or distorted by the way the questions are presented. As we are realizing in science, it is not the answers, but the questions we raise and how we formulate them that are crucial. So many of the choices and decisions to be made by people are either trivial or misleading and only occasionally relevant to and expressive of the issues that will largely govern their lives.

STEPHEN GRAUBARD: I have been impressed by an idea on which Daniel Bell and Paul Ylvisaker are essentially in accord—that you may have both a spinning-off and a centralization of authority. In this connection I particularly think of federal aid to higher education. How are these institutions going to be transformed by such help? Analogies could perhaps be drawn from the Federal Government's intervention into defense. In the end, certain decisions will and can only be made in Washington. But Washington can, in turn, give new strength to all sorts of agencies that did not originate in, but are the beneficiaries of its intervention. Washington would have some influence on them, but not control over them; they are not its creatures.

PAUL YLVISAKER: If we have a national communications system, the best actors are sometimes going to be in positions of power. It is no accident that the Ronald Reagans are now becoming political figures. I would consider carefully the ways in which this system might operate and the dangers. You are giving elements of power in areas like defense to groups who face no effective consumer complaint mechanism. Is it time the United States had a citizens' advice bureau? The cities are already getting five-percenter types who know all the federal grants and can consolidate and manipulate them. As soon as every city in the United States becomes as sophisticated as New Haven about how to get all the money out of Washington, the federal budget is going to be multiplied by a factor of ten.

Also, how do you criticize performance? How do you tell whether you are getting your money's worth if you allocate money to a loose system of bureaucracies? You may be getting just a perpetuation of the Farm Bureau. We must develop measures of performance, although I am frankly at a loss as to what some of these measures might be. The old methods, such as having the Inspector General go around the country to police urban renewal, are clearly not effective.

MICHAEL POSTAN: One need not inevitably have new centralized power to do some of these things. In England, for instance, new forms of local self-government are emerging on a functional basis. There are governmental subsidies to the arts or the universities, and functional self-government with respect to these particular spheres.

DANIEL BELL: It may be that British precedents are not applicable here. It has been said that when you increase government in Russia, it leads to more brutality; when you increase government in England, it leads to more decency; and when you increase it in America, it leads to more corruption.

LEONARD DUHL: The planning process is beginning to teach skills which enable people to get involved in a new way. The poor, for example, are learning how to use the money they are given.

One of the current problems in evaluating all of these efforts is that you really have no *outside* observers. For an example, there is a very close relationship between the National Institutes of Health and the scientific community. The scientists serving on advisory councils and the various study sections reviewing grants include a significant percentage of the leaders in the medical research field. Obviously, although rigid controls have been established to prevent conflicts of interest, these advisers may be the very recipients of grant funds. Similarly, through their professional organizations as well as through voluntary groups, they may push for more support of a broad range of research. These scientists, thus, are playing multiple roles—as grantors, grantees, and even as lobbyists. You end up with a magnificent circle. It thus becomes quite impossible to confront the system and to tell NIH, for example, that it is going off on a tangent, that it does not further the over-all health policies of the United States. Perhaps we need a parallel institution of confronters on every level—national and local.

EUGENE ROSTOW: Does responsibility for the failure of democratic government in adapting our society to the flow of change rest with the democratic political machinery, the bureaucracy, or the legislative or executive branches, or does it reside with the intellectuals, the experts,

53

because they have not provided the ideas? In many cases it is demonstrably the latter. By and large the most important problem in the future will be the quality of our innovative and creative strength in all spheres of intellectual life. In the field of education, the obstructive habits of an entrenched bureaucracy are very important, of course, but fundamentally the failure is a failure of ideas, a lack of imagination and innovation.

I would like to comment on a remark that Pat Moynihan made—that the fundamental historical function of politics has been to mediate and settle controversies about economic affairs. I think this overemphasizes the importance of economics. The biggest political problem in the history of the United States has been the Negro question and all its manifestations. The Fourth Republic in France collapsed over Algeria which was not an economic problem at all, but one of those insoluable human and political problems.

In many of these areas, we must be careful not to lose sight of our most important single issue—the quality of intellectual life. Sometimes the over-involvement of experts is dangerous. We have very scarce resources in this field, as well as in a good many other fields. If these scarce resources become excessively involved in creating new mechanisms, they may not be able to create new ideas.

ZBIGNIEW BRZEZINSKI: I very much agree. I would, however, like to move beyond this and ask where innovation in recent years has been most effective in the United States. Where has it been most imaginative? I would say that it has been most effective and imaginative in technology, in defense, in foreign policy on a broad level, in developing foreign programs—in areas of public policy that are the least susceptible to domestic pressure. Domestic policies are the least effective. The Federal Government's most imaginative domestic institution, the one which comes closest to what I would call a pre-crisis management institution, is the Supreme Court. The Supreme Court is one of the least "democratic" institutions in the Federal Government. This has some bearing on the point I was making earlier—namely, the difficulty of mobilizing energy for the purpose of anticipating

effectively the legislative and social problems in a mass democratic society.

HARVEY PERLOFF: I think you have not given us enough credit. There are quite a few areas where conflict has been resolved—the area of labor and management, for example. Not so long ago we had bloody strikes through which few people gained. Progress has been made, in part, because many things that had previously been handled by confrontations are now handled by bureaucracies that function in a certain way. In labor-management relations we have achieved a set of arrangements to resolve the conflicts and solve problems. Contrast these with the struggles that went on about cutting wages in order to solve economic problems during the Depression. As we got more information about the common elements of gain, we could see large areas where labor and management could profit by working together. Who, for example, wants to worry about problems like sewerage? Let a bureaucracy take care of them.

DANIEL BELL: What you say is true. The bureaucratization of labor-management relations is an effort to achieve stability in a situation of conflict. But the problem of initiating change is somewhat different. The kinds of models that are very important for the labor-management situation are not models for handling change.

HARVEY PERLOFF: What is to be changed, for example, in the Negro problem? Levels of living must be raised and racial conflicts resolved. You must be aware of the kind of change you want. Do you want change for its own sake or because of an inadequate situation? If you want to change an inadequate situation, the labor-management situation does provide a model for resolving conflict. The same elements are present in the problems of the Negro, the city, or the nation generally, or in international conflicts. We are trying to find out what are the areas of common ground on which we can get agreement. Increasing these areas is in itself a very important change. You do not want to have change continuously in this regard, of course, if the resolution is satisfactory to both parties.

The elements of communication and information become very critical in all of these things.

LEONARD DUHL: You have a paradox, though. You did want to bureaucratize things; you did want someone to take over the sewers. The bureaucracy has taken over the sewers, yet it is not really solving the problems of modern sewers. In a sense we do need something else now.

PAUL YLVISAKER: The same is true for labor. Labor and management have been solving their problems, but labor has not solved the entrance of the minorities, and we are in for a crisis. It is also true for education. The children who have the most promise and potential and are best capable of dealing with life are kept longest in preparatory shelters. The children with the least promise hit the streets at age fourteen. We spend all the money on the children who can do it, and have no institutions, except the courts, for those who cannot and are over fourteen. We have a bureaucracy for education, but what has it done about preschooling, about Negro education, about vocational education?

MARTIN SHUBIK: It would be rather interesting to look at the United States at this moment, thirty-five years back, and thirty-five years ahead, using three categories—individually owned or controlled assets and decisions, private corporate assets and decisions, and governmental assets and decisions. We could then ask whether there has been any significant change in the distribution of assets among these three sectors and whether we expect much further change. The split at the present moment is probably about a third, a third, and a third. If we conclude that thirty-five years from now 50 per cent of all assets will be held by governmental bodies, 30 per cent by corporate bodies, and only 20 per cent by private individuals, we are obviously moving much more of the control of our state into the political process as opposed to the economic-allocation process.

DANIEL BELL: We have explored, so far, some of the dimensions of the problem of political structure. If I read our previous discussions correctly, there are four other broad areas under which most of our concerns can be subsumed. These are the changing nature of values and rights (the problems of equality, of privacy, of choice, of property); the structure of intellectual institutions (the knowledge explosion, the nature of the university); the life cycle of the individual (the problems of careers, of alienated youth); and the international system (rich and poor nations, nationalism, and so forth). Perhaps we can touch on some of these questions at the concluding session, and on the question of what models we can create to order these problems.

THE
NEED
FOR
MODELS

DANIEL BELL: This is our final session, and we come back to the question of baselines and forecasts. I would like to know of any omissions in the list of problems we have set forth; I would like to see some discussion of methodology and of the relevant distinctions we have to make; and some notions of how all of this is to be put together—in short, what models of analysis are available to us.

DANIEL P. MOYNIHAN: I have been surprised to find that it is not generally known how the population in this country is shifting. We all agree there will be more people in this country, but it is not just more people; it is relatively more of some people and fewer of others. We have grown up in a world where one person in ten is Negro. Today one person in six under the age of one is Negro. A country in which one person in six is Negro is different from a country in which the ratio is one in ten, and most Negroes live in the rural South.

ROGER REVELLE: The Natural Resources Planning Commission on the United States predicted in 1935 that there would be 165 million people in the United States by 1990, instead of the 190 million we actually had in 1965. The man who organized these reports pointed out that this figure would be true only if the low birth rates of the 1930's continued. Everybody bought his prediction, paying no attention to the rider. In the case of the Negroes, I would think current growth rates might be very temporary. Our birth rate has gone down a lot in the last few years; this is a kind of wave that sweeps through society, and it is very likely to affect Negroes somewhat later than whites. Right now there is a higher birth rate among Negroes than among white people, but this may last only for a few years. The white birth rate has been going down very fast, but the Negro birth rate is also decreasing.

GARDNER QUARTON: The individual and his life cycle could be treated in a social-science context or in very different ways. It would be possible to think, as Lawrence Frank suggested, more in terms of what an individual life would be like in an introspective sense. I have no difficulty seeing the relationship between changes in institutions and changes in the life of an individual. The problem of the richness of an individual life, however, requires a type of thinking that is a little different from the usual sociological-demographic way of approaching things.

LEONARD DUHL: Individuals and families will have to be able to cope with a whole series of alternative futures. This raises a round of questions as to how people deal with change on many different levels, and what happens when people break down—not just medically, but because they are unable to cope with the system. How do you repair them? What happens to those people you cannot repair, those who cannot go on? Do you relegate the aged to hospitals, to private communities like Leisure World, to veritable prisons?

FRED IKLÉ: I see a prime distinction between the substantivists and the methodologists. I find myself rather alone on the methodologists' side, but I do think it is important to consider how we predict the future. We are all familiar with the self-fulfilling prophecy—the Chairman of the Federal Reserve Board predicts that the market will go down and the market goes down; or the self-defeating prophecy—predicting a population explosion and working to prevent it. There is a third thing to be added—self-defeating social engineering.

The National Planning Association group working in the late 1940's finally managed to convince the government that something should be done about the proliferation problem, and something was done in 1953: the Atoms for Peace program. The Israelis are far ahead in this area because of the Atoms for Peace program. Or consider the nuclear test ban. According to the hypothesis developed by Morton Halpern, Khrushchev

gave nuclear aid to China to bring China into the nuclear test ban. There are indications—and the French are spreading the rumors—that the French have given similar information to Great Britain to get Great Britain into the nuclear test ban. Both of these actions resulted in further proliferation. Thus, there was an Oedipus parent effect.

But we should spend some time on the question of the methodolgy of prediction and not concentrate solely on the substance.

DANIEL BELL: Is this methodology or consequences? Your illustration is of consequences. There is always the problem that what you say is going to have both progressive and regressive consequences. How do you build in guards against these regressive consequences?

HAROLD ORLANS: Fred Iklé's example may not be a very good one. There was nothing we could conceivably have done that would have forestalled proliferation by more than a year or two.

HERMAN KAHN: But Fred Iklé has made a very valid point. If you "describe" the future world and are wrong, your responsibility is less than if you had made policy recommendations. If you make policy recommendations, you ought to review them at least once or twice. To guard against this self-defeating effect, you can go over the material and ask how it might be wrong. The predictions made at Rand during its heyday may have been wrong, but the people who made them had systematically thought of all objections and were almost never surprised by outsiders raising new objections. It takes time, energy, and interest to think of where you may be wrong. The Atoms for Peace program was predicted by experts in the field to be proliferative, but the people who were pushing the program never bothered to check this possibility. If they had debated this subject, they might have changed their minds. It is perfectly possible for people to examine a series of ideas to determine what is wrong with it.

GARDNER QUARTON: We ought to deal not only with the question of self-fulfilling prophecy, but also with the ways in which plans are not used, with the extent to which people do not know either how to think or to plan.

ROGER REVELLE: I understand how you can think about the problem of the underdeveloped world, but I cannot understand how you think about it in human terms. In India, for example, people will probably be somewhat worse off—socially, economically, and physically—thirty-five years from now. The same thing may be true in Africa. This is not a question of the international system, but of human relationships and values. We might ask what can be done so that such a prediction will not come true. If one had looked at Chile, for example, in 1930, what would its future have looked like? One might have said that it had quite a bright future, that it might become another Sweden. Its population was thought to be largely European, with a high proportion from Northern Europe. It turns out, however, that the annual per-capita income in Chile is about $400, and its future looks bleak. What happened between 1930 and 1965 to give rise to this very bad situation? What could have been done in 1930 to prevent this from happening? Chile does not have a comparative advantage in any economic sense. There is nothing they can make that other people cannot make cheaper, more easily, and better; the price of everything they sell is going down. The nitrate business disappeared in World War I, and the only real export was copper for a very long time. In a small country like Chile one would have to have developed technical skills to offset such a trend.

MARTIN SHUBIK: I have recently spent half a year in Chile, and I cannot agree with Roger Revelle's remarks. Chile seems to have a rather good supply of natural resources, although it seems to be mismanaging them.

FRED IKLÉ: In reading an old document, *Recent Social Trends,* which dates from the 1930's, I was first struck by the excellence in methodology and then by the similarity between its projections and those of today. I found missing in it only the subject of adolescents and beatniks.

DANIEL BELL: I know *Recent Social Trend,* and many of our problems—urbanism, education, and the like—are prefigured there. There is, however, a point at which something new does appear—a change in scale does produce a very different kind of situation. The methodology of Ogburn [the research director of that President's Commission] was extrapolative; he was only interested in time series. This was the main limitation of the volumes.

FRED IKLÉ: We might well spend time thinking about how we can improve the art of prediction, otherwise we will do it the same way it was done thirty-five years ago.

DONALD SCHON: If we do produce a set of views of the future, let us also design a process for their use. If we are not willing to do that, then we should not allow ourselves the luxury of making statements to appear in academic journals.

HERMAN KAHN: I really think this is wrong in two important ways. We cannot, in a committee which meets only three times, exchange views on papers and also get a program of action. I do agree that it is important to influence the government, but there is an important difference between 1930 and 1965. It is very easy to influence the government today.

DANIEL BELL: I think Donald Schon is knocking down an open door, as the Russian proverb says. If it were a matter of recommending some concrete policy—such as the reorganization of the poverty program or the devising of a population program—his point would be well taken. But we have been enjoined to consider alternative futures. This society, like most societies, has not yet come around to making the idea of speculating about the future respectable. It has been respectable in the past only in the art of science fiction, which is already outside a sense of responsibility. A number of years ago when Olaf Helmer of Rand suggested the idea of long-range forecasting, everybody hooted at him. Suddenly we realize that we must deal with these things. In this Commission I want to be a *luft-*

mensch—someone who lives on air, rises high, and has his kicks in an intellectual way.

PAUL YLVISAKER: I like the *luftmensch* idea, but I wonder if we are as air-borne as we might be, and if we have tested our model enough. The composition of this group is not terribly rounded; we do not have young enough people here. A huge component of the population that has already declared its character is not represented. We talk about them as parents do, but you cannot have them represented in that way.

Further, we are accepting in our model the age of accelerating change, and we are accelerating it. We are talking about getting more people and more institutions change-oriented, yet at the same time we talk about the casualty rate of accelerating change. Should we test the model by asking how we can slow Americans down, or whether the process will slow down?

DANIEL P. MOYNIHAN: If there has been one real break in the continuity of American government, it has been in our ability to make short-range predictions and in our willingness to bet on them. When we drew up the 1960 Democratic Platform, it was merely a list of ideas. We held open meetings throughout the country at which anybody could propose anything. We would dismiss questions about a program's cost as demonstrating a typical "Republican" callousness to human needs. When we sat down to draft the 1964 Platform, however, we worked with a set of economic projections in front of us: The GNP will go from here to there during the next four years; revenues to the Federal Government will go from here to there; the increment for on-going programs will be such and such; the remainder will be somewhere around 5.5 billion dollars in discretionary income for each of the next four years. We had to spend the money; there was no intention of bringing on a fiscal drag. This year already that projection has gone up from 5.5 billion to 5.6 billion. And, in the end, we produced a platform that was not only expansive but seriously intended.

At the meeting of the Joint Committee of Economic Reports this summer [1965], internal revenues were projected to go from 120 billion to 170 billion in 1970; you can define the social policies of the American government in terms of how we use that 50 billion dollars. Things become much more concrete in these terms.

Another instance of forecasting: in 1961 there were more men out of work than at any time since the Great Depression, and there was great popular apprehension about the economy, centering on Robert Theobald's position. Moreover, the unemployment problem did not respond to Kennedy's early economic policies. Even so, the Bureau of Labor Statistics people said there was no indication in their productivity figures that automation would bring wholesale elimination of jobs. In the end, it turned out that they knew more about it than did the alarmists.

One of the most important events of the future will be the further development of forecasting techniques. The methodology of applying forecasting will mean the difference between saying we will do whatever we can, and saying we will do four or five billion dollars' worth. A proper part of our predictions about the future would be forecasting the ways in which we are going to use the art of prediction.

DANIEL BELL: The phrase *the art of forecasting* is very poor. Most forecasting is simple extrapolation of time series. In the *Futuribles* project, we came to distrust using extrapolation for anything but the barest kind of baseline. This is why we hunted around for words like *conjecture, anticipation, prevision*—words that emphasize the "openness" of dealing with the future. Demographic predictions today give a high, low, and middle range under various assumptions and specifications. The same is true for government predictions about who will go to college. Such figures are interesting because they are based on alternative assumptions—in the education forecasts some predictions are straight-line extrapolation, others are predicted on the proportion of sons' repeating their fathers' experience, still others on the sons' going beyond the fathers' aspirations, on ethnic group differences, and so on. One then has to make further judgments as to which are the relevant assumptions.

So far as I know, there is very little

literature on the art of "combination" forecasting as against the extrapolation kind. Most work in economic forecasting is being done along the lines of the Brookings model, yet the people at Brookings are suddenly saying that they need some sociological data and other things. They have discovered the narrow limitations of the econometric model.

HAROLD ORLANS: You must remember that these are short-range forecasts.

DANIEL BELL: But how you say it also counts. Robert Waelder, the psychoanalyst, once told a story about a sultan who asked a soothsayer to predict his future. The soothsayer looked at the globe and said, "Sire, I have great news. *All your relatives will die before you.*" And the sultan said, "Kill that man." Then he called in another soothsayer. This soothsayer looked into the globe and said, "Sire, I have great news for you. *You will outlive all your relatives.*" And the sultan said, "Reward that man." The predictions are exactly the same, but the tone is different.

There are some *Futuribles* papers on the methodology of forecasting that it might be well to translate, especially Michael Massenet's paper. You can use sorting devices or logical devices; you can see what happens when you use certain models. There are no formal, methodological canons; there are no real accepted ones for very specific problems. We may know more when James Tobin and Robert Solow finish their model of long-range economic forecasting. But for the kind of effort we are starting, one gains more by a simple speculative leap, with a self-consciousness of where one started from.

MARTIN SHUBIK: I would interpret the sultan story in another sense. The greater degree of sophistication in some problems that we are dealing with comes, I think, in the first soothsayer's statement and not in the second's. If you want to get some NIH or Veterans' Administration people unhappy, do not ask how many lives we are going to save this year, but how many people we want to kill in the hospital system. Because certain problems happen to be fundamental moral or ethical problems, we have lovely self-decep-

tive ways of never looking at them. When we talk about the various old-age programs, we never face the question of whether or not society can afford to pay between $20,000 and $50,000 a year for a nonproductive ninety-year-old, using crude measures of what society calls productive. Since resources are limited, somebody must make a value judgment in regard to them. The short-term economic models are, in fact, rotten for our purposes. James Tobin and Robert Solow are addressing themselves to different problems. It is lovely to be Galbraithian and talk about worlds of abundance, but this is nonsense. Even if per-capita expenditure for health, education, and welfare were a million dollars, there would still be an allocation problem. To use Tobin's models on long-range projections does them an injustice simply because they do not have the sociological variables.

FRED IKLÉ: The differences among alternative scenarios relate to the problem of values and predictions. If we had a perfect art of prediction and knew what the year 2000 would be like, we would not be here. If we had no values, we would not be here because we would not care. As Daniel Moynihan pointed out, the 1960 Democratic Platform was looking for values whereas the 1964 Platform was based on sound projections. We are looking for something between the two.

LAWRENCE FRANK: We live by memories and expectations, and today we do not need criteria derived from past performance, but those that will help people to make the choices and decisions that now press for consideration. Too exact or too narrow range of choice deprives people of the opportunity to accept new possibilities that are becoming available or will be open in the years ahead. We are repeatedly being threatened by individuals and groups that have "the answers" and ready panaceas for all our troubles. Let us remember that these are usually proposals generated by our present difficulties and frustrations and not imaginative provisions for the future. For a free society we must keep open not only the possibility but the obligation to make choices and decisions predicated upon the values and aspirations we cherish and must continually strive to attain.

DANIEL P. MOYNIHAN: A society in which the short-range forecasts are good will probably act differently than one in which there are none, or in which they are undependable.

ROGER REVELLE: In the so-called natural sciences the test of a hypothesis is the ability to make a forecast—by hypothesis we mean that we have found what we believe is a causal relationship between processes or events. What precisely is meant by a model? Have any of these social or economic models been tested by hindcast?

LAWRENCE FRANK: One of the most fruitful political and social models was the Declaration of Independence, which did not prescribe how to deal with specific problems but rather stated some basic policies that were capable of elaboration and application and that, thereby, were policies for the development of a new nation. Almost two hundred years later, we can still admire and celebrate this statement, but we must revise and reformulate the aims and goals they sought if we are to carry on their aspirations.

ROGER REVELLE: That is a very different model.

LAWRENCE FRANK: Theirs was an expression of general policies and a model of what a free society should and could be, and they left to their successors its implementation through a variety of plans and programs, institutions and new practices. I suggest that we face a similar situation calling for a new formulation of aims and policies to guide those who must struggle with the practical problems and applications presented by an industrialized society and the development of a Service State.

DANIEL BELL: The economic models Martin Shubik mentioned try to specify the causal relationships between a number of variables in quantitative terms, then make predictions and see to what extent they have been modified. The kind of thing Lawrence Frank is talking about would not come under the head of a model in the analytic sense, but it does provide a boundary line of possi-

bilities. We have taken the word *model* from another science and to an extent have obscured what we are doing. We are not simply trying to describe what is going to be in the sense of specifying causal relationships, but to consider what can be.

In any situation, people can judge better when they have some comparisons before them. One of the earliest criticisms made of the variety of studies on worker satisfaction was that the researchers would often ask a man with no alternative experience whether he liked his job. People will stay on the farm if they know nothing else. Will they stay, however, if they have been to the city, to Paris?

We must keep telling people that there are alternative combinations possible, that there is nothing fixed and determinate about the future. We want them to choose if they can, and to get mechanisms which allow us to intervene and change to a different path if that seems to be necessary.

MARTIN SHUBIK: We are using the word *model* in two very standard ways—the normative and the behavioristic. Behavioristic models, such as the econometric ones, do not have any value judgments in them *per se*, and econometricians working on them are usually interested in the standard problems of measurement as in the physical sciences, except that they are measuring social phenomena. By keeping control variables constant, you should be able to predict the behavior of the system. If we assume that we can cure cancer, we can predict what will happen to the health of the population. When you apply these behavioristic models to politics, you may also wish to introduce control variables. When you do that, you are in fact introducing value judgments.

On the other hand, the Declaration of Independence is a normative structure which in and of itself may be axiomatized. The document neither stands nor falls on empirical testing.

ROGER REVELLE: At the present time the carbon dioxide content of the air is increasing by about a quarter of a per cent a year. By the year 2000 we will have about 25 per cent more carbon dioxide in the air than we had in 1900.

This statement is based entirely on statistics; if you extrapolate statistical trends, you will find this increase. I might go further and say that the statistical trends are the result of the trends in fuel combustion which in turn are economic trends. We can then ask what this will do to the climate. Here there is a range of possibilities because we do not perfectly understand climatic processes. If the causal relations are such and such, the air temperature will probably rise by a few tenths of a degree throughout the world. If, on the other hand, the causal relationships are different, the temperature may rise by three or four degrees. These are hypotheses based upon assumed relations. We can also have a normative model: what you want to have happen to the climate. We might want the climate to remain as it is now or as it was ten or fifteen years ago, in which case we would have to invent ways to make countervailing changes in the climate to offset changes caused by carbon dioxide.

I think then we have three levels of forecasting: the projection of trends without asking any questions about relationships; hypotheses based upon an understanding of the relationships; and desires about what ought to happen but in the realm of what is possible.

DANIEL BELL: I would like to close with a parable, a Talmudic one, since I am so fond of these, as my friends know.

There was once a rabbi who had the reputation for knowing what was in a man's mind by reading his thoughts. A wicked boy came to see him and said: "Rabbi, I have in my hand a small bird. Is it alive, or is it dead?" And the boy thought to himself: If he says it is dead, I will open my hand and let it fly away; if he says it is alive, I will quickly squeeze it and show him it is dead. And the boy repeated the question: "Rabbi, I have in my hand a small bird. Is it alive, or is it dead?" And the rabbi gazed steadily at him, and said, quietly: "Whatever you will; whatever you will."

A Summary by the Chairman

Some Common—or Loosely Agreed Upon—Assumptions

To SAY that there were some common, or loosely agreed upon, assumptions is not to say that we all agreed upon these points, or that there was a coherent framework of either intentions or approaches. This summary is an effort to indicate the points of convergence of the various views that were expressed. Curiously, there was little discussion of values or of priorities. An implicit agreement may underlie our purpose, but I suspect that the differences among us will emerge only when the Commission's direction becomes more fully articulated.

I have grouped these assumptions under three headings: *Intentions, Methodologies,* and *Reconceptualizations* and stated them in schematic form.

Intentions of the Commission

1. *To sketch hypothetical futures.* The emphasis is on the plural not only because a single projection may be wrong, but because a preoccupation with only one picture may foreclose alternative paths that might be socially desirable. Thus, we would seek to sketch "alternative futures" and to deal with problems that might emerge in the light of these alternative possibilities.

2. *To allow us to come to better decisions.* By anticipating future problems, we might be able to plan for these, pose alternative policies, design stand-by institutions, and strengthen the decision-making process.

3. *To measure social performance.* In anticipating possibilities (for example, future capacities and new technologies), we can set up standards of performance in many areas in order to see whether they can be met, to identify shortfalls, and to call attention to remedial needs.

4. *To forestall developments.* Not all change is desirable. We would want to decide on what should not be changed (from "open spaces" to a "work ethic"), and to see in the light of possible futures which developments should or could be forestalled. Under this heading, and in the broadest sense, we might include nuclear proliferation, fragmented international economic regions, and other issues that were but briefly mentioned.

5. *To write a new political theory.* The political tradition from John Locke to Adam Smith paved the way for a new society in which representative government and the free market economy served as the framework for a system of individual decision-making based on self-interest and rational choice. Can one write a new political theory (descriptive and normative) that deals with a service state and a society characterized by a new mixture of individual and communal—public and private—decision-making units?

6. *To explicate the "planning process."* In an older language, how do we enhance "self-consciousness" and "self-determination"? This process is to be explored on two "levels": in the Commission itself—to see how new ideas and new options are created among ourselves by our own effort to clarify "alternative futures"; in the society—to see whether and how new mechanisms can be created and a sophistication developed which keep the future open so that new alternatives may always be allowed, and new options pursued.

Methodologies

While less attention was paid, formally, to methodologies of envisaging the future, a number of points were raised *en passant.* These are combined here along with those that are discussed in materials previously distributed to the Commission.

1. *Projections*

a. Extrapolations. These are simply the projections of individual time series (demographic, occupational, national product) under varying assumptions.

b. Forecasting models. These are combinations of series, mathematically expressed, that make assumptions about future expectations. Examples of these are the Brookings econometric model of quarterly economic projections, and the Tobin-Solow long-range forecasting model now being developed.

c. Cybernetic models. These are forecasting models that try to build in, either on a stochastic or a more determinate basis, some anticipated or actual feedbacks so as to allow for continual readjustments. There are few such large-scale social models in existence, though Soviet economists and mathematicians are now drafting such cybernetic models for the Soviet economy.

d. The Delphi technique. As exemplified by the Rand study, this is essentially a "panel technique" in which a group of experts makes predictions in specific areas. These results are then "fed back" repeatedly to the individuals in order to clarify the agreements and disagreements among the panel members.

2. *The identification of innovations.* On the assumption that some major innovative item will force the restructuring of organization or methods of intellectual work, or reorganize markets, efforts should be made to identify such possible changes. In the past, such efforts have concentrated upon the implications of new products, like the transistor or the computer. One can, however, think conceptually of new social forms, like the not-for-profit corporation, or new doctrines, like the revolutions in military technology and doctrines of strategy, that have been socially innovative.

3. *The specification of diffusions.* Most social change, it has been argued, proceeds less from giant new innovations than from diffusions of existing techniques or, more importantly, of privileges. In effect, what has often been the property of the few becomes the claim of the many. Thus, the changes in the character of higher education proceed not only from the new role of research, but equally from the fact that what was once restricted to a few is now open to the many. In consequence, the "change of scale" is the element that creates the problem.

4. *Selective models.* Any comprehensive theory of social change has to take into account an enormous number of variables. For our limited purposes, it has been suggested that we study simply the influence of a selected number of variables that, more than

any others, seem to be determinative of change in the society. In the discussion during the weekend, a number of individuals suggested at one time or another that technology be taken as the starting point, and that ramifications of changes created by technology be the major areas of study. There were, in a sense, four aspects, each overlapping somewhat with the others, that were singled out for explication:

a. The notion of considering technology autonomous and charting the adjustment to a major technological advance. More broadly, the idea of singling out a specific item as the autonomous variable produced the example of the relationship of natural resources to population and demands. It was suggested that the expansion of natural resources would not come so rapidly as the increase in population and demand, and that this would be a major source of problems for the year 2000. (A by-product of this discussion produced the judgment that the "scarcest" natural resource, in terms of increasing cost in the next decade or more, would be "clean air." So much for the textbook example in economics that air is the only "free good.")

b. More generally, the discussion produced the suggestion that the basic methodology concentrate on those technological changes that induce social change (for example, automation) and those social decisions that will have technological consequences (spending for space, sciences, the military, and so forth).

c. Ecologies of change. Only some combinations of technology and social structure fit together, only some are flexible and realizable. Any methodology, therefore, ought to concentrate on selecting those "ecologies" or bounded units that exemplify such relationships.

d. It was pointed out, more as a caution than as a specific methodology, that most models of change assume the introduction of a new element and some determinate consequence, which can then be charted. But change actually proceeds on the basis of "action and reaction," and consequences often "react back" and change the original variable itself. Social change should be regarded, therefore, as a series of stages that exemplifies such a process. On a more formal basis, stochastic models might be introduced to set the limits of such action and reaction.

5. *The therapeutic model.* While borrowed from the psychiatric situation, the therapeutic model has surprising relevance in many problem-solving situations, as sophisticated business managers, for example, might attest. Its simple caution is not to accept the situation as given or as defined by the client, but to keep open a range of generalized goals. Individuals may define a problem in terms of the difficulties they encounter in reaching a solution, only to find on analysis that the problem has been falsely put or that some other problem is actually at stake. By emphasizing self-scrutiny, feedback, and re-evaluation of means and goals, the model by its simple common sense warns against the premature "closure" of a definition or the foreshortening of perspective.

Reconceptualizations

Forecasts are organized in some conceptual framework, and various time series serve as indicators of the conceptualized phenomenon. But one can significantly miss the identification of a relevant social process if one takes existing definitions or concepts as given. In the discussion, it was argued that a number of crucial concepts or distinctions would have to be redefined so that the new shape of a social process or the outlines of an emerging social problem might be understood more adequately. The following terms were ones that received some attention in the discussion.

1. *The national society.* It was pointed out that many problems now arise because for the first time the U. S. has become a genuinely national society. The growing interdependence of the economy and the polity, and the new role of government in fiscal policy give a new dimension to the range of problems that must be brought to a political center for decision. All this poses a question about existing federal-state-local relationships.

2. *The scope and size of the social unit.* This is a more abstract formulation of the term noted above. It was pointed out that in the last two hundred years, because of new means of transportation and communication, the scope and size of the governmental and regulative units of society have increased. The formulation, however, allows one to pose a general, normative question: What is the scope and size of social units appropriate to certain kinds of

problems and social relations. Along one axis is the question of *centralization* and *decentralization;* along another, the question of what is or should be *public* and what is or should be *private.*

3. *Number-density-interaction.* A modern mass society is characterized not only by increasing number, but by even more frequent interaction between persons and between organizational units, all of which results in an increasing social and psychic density. A whole series of problems issues from this dimension of change. For example:

> a. The span of comprehension. George A. Miller argues in an article, "The Magical Number Seven, Plus or Minus Two—Some Limits on Our Capacity for Processing Information," that there are limits to the number of different "bits" a human channel can encompass at one time. More generally, there is the organizational problem of how many individuals can report to another, the levels of organization, and so forth. One specific—and terrifying—illustration is the number of problems that automatically flow to Washington, as a political center, from all over the world, and the multifarious issues which the President has to confront in "real time."
>
> b. The loss of insulating space. It has been observed that the U. S. has escaped some of the political holocausts of European society, despite its higher incidence of violence—labor violence, for example—in part because such violence takes place at the perimeter of the society and not at the political center, as it does in, say, France. The loss of "insulating space" because of modern mass communication allows us to respond more directly to social issues, but it may also in other circumstances set off chain reactions disruptive to the democratic process. In effect, society is becoming more permeable.
>
> c. Privacy. This is a more personal dimension of the loss of insulating space. What is the meaning of privacy in a highly urbanized, highly interactive society?

4. *Systems analysis.* An emphasis on linked interaction focuses attention on the need to identify relevant relationships and the determinate consequences and effects of social actions. For example, the oyster has been disappearing from the Delaware Bay. Investi-

gation has shown that this is due to a parasite brought into the area by the advancing ocean waters, an advance caused by industry's withdrawing fresh water at a faster rate than that at which the rivers flow into the bay. Here one has a change in ecological balance because of "unanticipated consequences" of economic activity. In a different illustration, it has been pointed out that if one looked at the automobile primarily as a means of efficient transportation, rather than, perhaps, as a status symbol, it would be more rational to replace private ownership with a system of national and regional car-rental systems that could "reallocate" cars where they were needed. In a similar way, the transportation problems of the Northeast might be handled better by a combination of auto, bus, rail, and air transport based on a systems analysis of the movements of numbers of persons to distant or intermediate points and the volumes of freight over designated distances.

5. *Costs.* Today our calculus of costs is set forth in individual terms, and we have few ways of knowing what the social costs of a change may be, and how these costs are distributed. One needs a broader definition of costs and some system of social accounts to complement the system of economic accounts; these would provide a more accurate measure of social progress, social welfare, and social needs.

6. *Equality.* Our notions of equality are conceived of in terms of social and legal equality. (As Rousseau put it in *The Social Contract:* "The fundamental compact substitutes . . . a moral and legal equality, to make up for that natural and physical difference which prevails among individuals, who, though unequal in personal strength and mental abilities, become thus all equal by conventions and right.") But the idea of equality today, particularly with the new discoveries in biology, raises a series of questions about genetic distribution and genetic variability. As Ernst Mayr has observed, equality assumes some common identity of man, yet it may be useful to seek for genetic variability as one of the ways of keeping man adaptive to natural circumstances. How can one plan at the same time for equality and for genetic variability, which may imply special treatment? In a different vein, what social consequences ensue if a society is organized largely on the basis of pure distribution of talent, as a "meritocracy"?

November 25, 1965

SOME SPECIFIC PROBLEMS

HERMAN KAHN AND ANTHONY J. WIENER

The Next Thirty-Three Years:
A Framework for Speculation

THE PACE at which various technological, social, political, and economic changes are taking place has reduced the relevance of experience as a guide to public-policy judgments. Scientists, engineers, and managers who deal directly with modern technology and who are also interested in broad policy issues often overestimate the likely social consequences of technological development and go to extremes of optimism or pessimism, while those more oriented to the cultural heritage often bank too heavily on historical continuity and social inertia. The problem, of course, is to sort out what changes from what continues and to discern what is continuous in the changes themselves.

At the Hudson Institute we have used three interrelated devices to facilitate making systematic conjectures about the future.[1] We first identify those long-term trends that seem likely to continue. These include, for example, the world-wide spread of a more or less secular humanism, the institutionalization of scientific and technological innovation, and continuous economic growth. We have, in this paper, identified a "multifold trend" consisting of thirteen interrelated elements.

We then cluster significant events by thirty-three-year intervals, starting with 1900, in order to see which combinations give rise to new clusters, to define the qualitative changes in the combination of trends, and to identify emergent properties, such as the increasing self-consciousness of time and history.

Finally, we have attempted to construct significant baselines, statistical where possible, to project key variables in society—population, literacy, Gross National Product, energy sources, military strength, and the like. These variables and their growth rates tend both to furnish and to constrain the possibilities for any society. By selecting extrapolations of current or emerging tendencies that

73

grow continuously out of today's world and reflect the multifold trend and our current expectations, we create a "surprise-free" projection—one that seems less surprising than any other specific possibility. Consistent with this projection we describe a "standard world" and several "canonical variations" that form the likely worlds of the future.

In this paper we shall seek to illustrate these methods and to provide some brief examples of some of our conclusions.

I

The Basic Multifold Trend

The basic trends of Western society, most of which can be traced back hundreds of years, have a common set of sources in the rationalization and secularization of society. For analytic purposes, we shall separate these basic trends into thirteen rubrics, though obviously one might wish to group them into fewer and more abstract categories or to refine the analysis by identifying or distinguishing many more aspects. As basic trends, these elements seem very likely to continue at least for the next thirty-three years, though some may saturate or begin to recede beyond that point.

There Is a Basic, Long-Term, Multifold Trend Toward:

1. Increasingly Sensate (empirical, this-worldly, secular, humanistic, pragmatic, utilitarian, contractual, epicurean, or hedonistic) cultures
2. Bourgeois, bureaucratic, "meritocratic," democratic (and nationalistic?) elites
3. Accumulation of scientific and technological knowledge
4. Institutionalization of change, especially research, development, innovation, and diffusion
5. World-wide industrialization and modernization
6. Increasing affluence and (recently) leisure
7. Population growth
8. Decreasing importance of primary occupations
9. Urbanization and (soon) the growth of megalopolises
10. Literacy and education
11. Increased capability for mass destruction
12. Increasing tempo of change
13. Increasing universality of these trends.

A Framework for Speculation

Speculations about the future have ranged from the literary speculations of Jules Verne and Edward Bellamy to the humanistic and philosophical writing of Jacob Burckhardt, Arnold Toynbee, and Pitirim Sorokin. Although the observations and philosophical assumptions have differed greatly, some of the empirical observations or contentions have had much in common. Thus when Sorokin finds a circular pattern of Idealistic, Integrated, and Sensate cultures, his categories bear comparison to what Edward Gibbon noted of Rome on a more descriptive level. If both the more theoretical and the more empirical observations are treated merely as *heuristic metaphors*, regardless of their authors' diverse intentions, they may suggest possible patterns for the future without confining one to too narrow or too rigid a view. Metaphoric and heuristic use of these concepts broadens the range of speculations; one can then pick and choose from these speculations as the evidence is developed. Nevertheless, in using concepts this way, there is an obvious risk not only of superficiality and oversimplification but also of excessive or premature commitment to some idiosyncratic view. In this paper we shall illustrate only a few elements of the multifold trend.

The Increasingly Sensate Culture

The use of the term *Sensate*, derived from Pitirim Sorokin, is best explained in contrast with Sorokin's other concepts: "Integrated" (or Idealistic), "Ideational," and "Late Sensate."[2] One can characterize Ideational art by such terms as transcendental, supersensory, religious, symbolic, allegoric, static, worshipful, anonymous, traditional, and immanent. Idealistic or Integrated art can usually be associated with such adjectives as heroic, noble, uplifting, sublime, patriotic, moralistic, beautiful, flattering, and educational, while Sensate art would be worldly, naturalistic, realistic, visual, illusionistic, everyday, amusing, interesting, erotic, satirical, novel, eclectic, syncretic, fashionable, technically superb, impressionistic, materialistic, commercial, and professional. Finally, there are tendencies toward what would be called Late Sensate, characterized as underworldly, expressing protest or revolt, over-ripe, extreme, sensation-seeking, titillating, depraved, faddish, violently novel, exhibitionistic, debased, vulgar, ugly, debunking, nihilistic, pornographic, sarcastic, or sadistic.

Sensate, of course, does not intend a connotation of sensual or

75

sensational; a word such as *worldly, humanistic,* or *empirical* would have been equally useful for our purposes.

Within a culture there is a considerable congruence or convergence among the various parts. If, for example, a culture is Sensate in art or in systems of truth, it tends to be Sensate in systems of government and family as well. While a high culture may seem vividly defined to an outside observer and appear to be pervasive in a society, the situation may be much more complicated. For example, in Cromwellian England the majority of the people actually rejected Puritan values, although this rejection might have been almost invisible to the visitor. Values are often enforced as well as exhibited by an elite. The degree of unity and pervasiveness of any particular culture is, in fact, a crucial issue, as is the question of the importance of the visible elites as opposed to the less visible, but perhaps more influential ones. In the United States today, for example, there is clearly a strong split between a large group of intellectuals and the government on many issues. Public-opinion polls seem to indicate that although these intellectuals hold a "progressive" consensus and dominate discussion in many serious journals, they are not representative of the country. In particular, the high culture can be thought of as secular humanist, and the public as more religious and less humanist.

Western culture as a whole is clearly Sensate and possibly entering a Late Sensate stage. The Sensate trend goes back seven or eight centuries, but its progress has not been uninterrupted. The Reformation, the Counter-Reformation, the Puritan era in England, some aspects of the later Victorian era, and to some degree such phenomena as Stalinism, Hitlerism, and Fascism—all represented, at least at the time, currents counter to the basic trend of an increasingly Sensate culture. Nevertheless, the long-term, all-embracing Sensate trend expanded from the West and now covers virtually the entire world. Whether this will continue for the next thirty-three or sixty-six years is an open question. If the obvious implications of the description of Late Sensate culture are valid, the long-term tendencies toward Late Sensate must stabilize or even reverse if the system is not to be profoundly modified.

Bourgeois, Bureaucratic, "Meritocratic," Democratic (and Nationalistic?) Elites

By *bourgeois* we mean holding economic values and ideologies of the kind that characterized the new middle classes that emerged from the breakup of feudal society—values of personal and family achievement, financial prudence, economic calculation, commercial foresight, and "business" and professional success as a moral imperative. (The emergence of "bourgeois" elites in this sense is vividly described in such works as Max Weber's *The Protestant Ethic* and R. H. Tawney's *Religion and the Rise of Capitalism*.) Though Karl Marx and Friedrich Engels might have been surprised, it is now clear that these values can, and perhaps must, also be present in socialist or Communist economies, especially if they are industrialized and "revisionist." By *democratic* we mean having a popular political base; this can also be totalitarian or tyrannical in the classical sense, provided it is not merely imposed from above and that there is some economic mobility and relative equality in access to opportunity. Bureaucratic and meritocratic administrations also characterize modern industrial societies, whether capitalist or Communist.

Bourgeois democracy tends to rest on some form of "social contract" concept of the relationship between the people and their government. The people "hire" and "fire" their governments, and no group has theocratic (Ideational) or aristocratic (Integrated) claims on the government. Clearly, democratic government is also an expression of democratic ideology—it is sustained by the idea of the consent of the governed. The idea is contractual; and the factors of sacredness, occultness, or charisma are restricted.

Nationalistic values are also associated with the rise of the middle class. Kings used nationalism to gain allies among the middle class against the nobles, the church, the emperor, or enemy states. The nationalist idea later involved a recognition that the people (the nation) have the contractual right to government of (and by) their own kind and eventually to self-government—or that the right to govern has to be justified as representing the will of the people and serving the general welfare. Even the totalitarian nationalism of Mussolini, Hitler, Stalin, and the Japanese officer corps usually made its basic appeal to and found its greatest response in the middle class (or, in the case of the Japanese, the agrarian middle class).

One can argue that the long-term nationalist trend is on the decline today, at least in what might be thought of as the NATO area, though this remains in many ways an open issue. (The West European nations could conceivably become more nationalist in the future, and a European political community might emerge that would be nationalist in the sense that "Europe" becomes the "nation.") In any case, Late Sensate culture carries implications of cosmopolitanism and pacifism and lack of particularist ethics or loyalties, except on a shifting, contractual basis. Nevertheless, it is probably safe to argue that over the next thirty-three years nationalism will increase in most of the underdeveloped and developing worlds, at least in the minimal sense that modern systems of public education and mass communication will integrate even the most peripheral groups into the common language and culture.

Science and Technology

In order to provide a quick impression of science and technology (with an emphasis on technology) in the last third of the twentieth century, we list one hundred areas in which technological innovation will almost certainly occur.

Each item is important enough to make, by itself, a significant change. The difference might lie mainly in being spectacular (for example, transoceanic rocket transportation in twenty or thirty minutes, rather than supersonic in two or three hours); in being ubiquitous (widespread use of paper clothes); in enabling a large number of different things to be done (super materials); in effecting a general and significant increase in productivity (cybernation); or simply in being important to specific individuals (convenient artificial kidneys). It could be argued reasonably that each of these warrants the description technological innovation, revolution, or breakthrough. None is merely an obvious minor improvement on what currently exists.

We should note that the one hundred areas are not ordered randomly. Most people would consider the first twenty-five unambiguous examples of progress. A few would question even these, since lasers and masers, for example, might make possible a particularly effective ballistic missile defense and, thus, accelerate the Soviet-American arms race. Similarly, the expansion of tropical agriculture and forestry could mean a geographical shift in economic and military power, as well as a dislocation of competitive industries. Nevertheless, there probably would be a consensus among readers that the first twenty-five areas do represent progress—at least for those who are in favor of "progress."

The next twenty-five areas are clearly controversial; many would argue that government policy might better restrain or discourage innovation or diffusion here. These "controversial areas" raise issues of accelerated nuclear proliferation, loss of privacy, excessive governmental or private power over individuals, dangerously vulnerable, deceptive, and degradable overcentralization, inherently dangerous new capabilities, change too cataclysmic for smooth adjustment, or decisions that are inescapable, yet at the same time too complex and far-reaching to be safely trusted to anyone's individual or collective judgment.

The last fifty items are included because they are intrinsically interesting and to demonstrate that a list of one hundred items of "almost certain" and "very significant" innovation can be produced fairly easily.[3]

One Hundred Technical Innovations Likely in the Next Thirty-Three Years

1. Multiple applications of lasers and masers for sensing, measuring, communicating, cutting, heating, welding, power transmission, illumination, destructive (defensive), and other purposes

2. Extremely high-strength or high-temperature structural materials

3. New or improved super-performance fabrics (papers, fibers, and plastics)

4. New or improved materials for equipment and appliances (plastics, glasses, alloys, ceramics, intermetallics, and cermets)

5. New airborne vehicles (ground-effect machines, VTOL and STOL, superhelicopters, giant supersonic jets)

6. Extensive commercial application of shaped charges

7. More reliable and longer-range weather forecasting

8. Intensive or extensive expansion of tropical agriculture and forestry

9. New sources of power for fixed installations (for example, magnetohydrodynamic, thermionic, and thermoelectric, radioactive)

10. New sources of power for ground transportation (storage-battery, fuel-cell propulsion or support by electromagnetic fields, jet engine, turbine)

11. Extensive and intensive world-wide use of high-altitude cameras for mapping, prospecting, census, land use, and geological investigations

12. New methods of water transportation (large submarines, flexible and special-purpose "container ships," more extensive use of large automated single-purpose bulk cargo ships)

13. Major reduction in hereditary and congenital defects

14. Extensive use of cyborg techniques (mechanical aids or substitutes for human organs, sense, limbs)

15. New techniques for preserving or improving the environment

16. Relatively effective appetite and weight control

17. New techniques in adult education

18. New improved plants and animals

19. Human "hibernation" for short periods (hours or days) for medical purposes

20. Inexpensive "one of a kind" design and procurement through use of computerized analysis and automated production

21. Controlled super-effective relaxation and sleep

22. More sophisticated architectural engineering (geodesic domes, thin shells, pressurized skins, esoteric materials)

23. New or improved uses of the oceans (mining, extraction of minerals, controlled "farming," source of energy)

24. Three-dimensional photography, illustrations, movies, and television

25. Automated or more mechanized housekeeping and home maintenance

26. Widespread use of nuclear reactors for power

27. Use of nuclear explosives for excavation and mining, generation of power, creation of high-temperature/high-pressure environments, or for a source of neutrons or other radiation

28. General use of automation and cybernation in management and production

29. Extensive and intensive centralization (or automatic interconnection) of current and past personal and business information in high-speed data processors

30. Other new and possibly pervasive techniques for surveillance, monitoring, and control of individuals and organizations

31. Some control of weather or climate

32. Other (permanent or temporary) changes or experiments with the over-all environment (for example, the "permanent" increase in C-14 and temporary creation of other radioactivity by nuclear explosions, the increasing generation of CO_2 in the atmosphere, projects Starfire, West Ford, Storm Fury, and so forth)

33. New and more reliable "educational" and propaganda techniques for affecting human behavior—public and private

34. Practical use of direct electronic communication with and stimulation of the brain

35. Human hibernation for relatively extensive periods (months to years)

36. Cheap and widely available or excessively destructive central war weapons and weapons systems

37. New and relatively effective counterinsurgency techniques (and perhaps also insurgency techniques)

38. New kinds of very cheap, convenient, and reliable birth-control techniques

39. New, more varied, and more reliable drugs for control of fatigue, relaxation, alertness, mood, personality, perceptions, and fantasies

40. Capability to choose the sex of unborn children

41. Improved capability to "change" sex

42. Other genetic control or influence over the "basic constitution" of an individual

43. New techniques in the education of children

44. General and substantial increase in life expectancy, postponement of aging, and limited rejuvenation

45. Generally acceptable and competitive synthetic foods and beverages (carbohydrates, fats, proteins, enzymes, vitamins, coffee, tea, cocoa, liquor)

46. "High quality" medical care for underdeveloped areas (for example, use of referral hospitals, broad-spectrum antibiotics, artificial blood plasma)

47. Design and extensive use of responsive and super-controlled environments for private and public use (for pleasurable, educational, and vocational purposes)

48. "Nonharmful" methods of "overindulging"

49. Simple techniques for extensive and "permanent" cosmetological changes (features, "figures," perhaps complexion, skin color, even physique)

50. More extensive use of transplantation of human organs

51. Permanent manned satellite and lunar installations—interplanetary travel

52. Application of space life systems or similar techniques to terrestrial installations

53. Permanent inhabited undersea installations and perhaps even colonies

54. Automated grocery and department stores

55. Extensive use of robots and machines "slaved" to humans

56. New uses of underground tunnels for private and public transportation

57. Automated universal (real time) credit, audit, and banking systems

58. Chemical methods for improved memory and learning

59. Greater use of underground buildings

60. New and improved materials and equipment for buildings and interiors (variable transmission glass, heating and cooling by thermoelectric effect, electroluminescent and phosphorescent lighting)

61. Widespread use of cryogenics

62. Improved chemical control of some mental illness and some aspects of senility

63. Mechanical and chemical methods for improving human analytical ability more or less directly

64. Inexpensive and rapid techniques for making tunnels and underground cavities in earth or rock

65. Major improvements in earth moving and construction equipment generally

66. New techniques for keeping physically fit or acquiring physical skills

67. Commercial extraction of oil from shale

68. Recoverable boosters for economic space launching

69. Individual flying platforms

70. Simple inexpensive video recording and playing

71. Inexpensive high-capacity, world-wide, regional, and local (home and business) communication (using satellites, lasers, light pipes, and so forth)

72. Practical home and business use of "wired" video communication for both telephone and television (possibly including retrieval of taped material from libraries or other sources) and rapid transmission and reception of facsimiles (possibly including news, library material, commercial announcements, instantaneous mail delivery, other printouts)

73. Practical large-scale desalinization

74. Pervasive business use of computers for the storage, processing, and retrieval of information

75. Shared-time (public and interconnected) computers generally available to home and business on a metered basis

76. Other widespread use of computers for intellectual and professional assistance (translation, teaching, literary research, medical diagnosis, traffic control, crime detection, computation, design, analysis, and, to some degree, as a general intellectual collaborator)

77. General availability of inexpensive transuranic and other esoteric elements

78. Space defense systems

79. Inexpensive and reasonably effective ground-based ballistic missile defense

80. Very low-cost buildings for home and business use

81. Personal "pagers" (perhaps even two-way pocket phones) and other personal electronic equipment for communication, computing, and data-processing)

82. Direct broadcasts from satellites to home receivers

83. Inexpensive (less than $20), long-lasting, very small, battery-operated television receivers

84. Home computers to "run" the household and communicate with outside world

85. Maintenance-free, long-life electronic and other equipment

86. Home education via video and computerized and programmed learning

87. Programmed dreams

88. Inexpensive (less than 1 cent a page) rapid, high-quality black and white reproduction; followed by colored, highly detailed photography reproduction

89. Widespread use of improved fluid amplifiers

90. Conference television (both closed-circuit and public communication systems)

91. Flexible penology without necessarily using prisons (by use of modern methods of surveillance, monitoring, and control)

92. Common use of individual power source for lights, appliances, and machines

93. Inexpensive world-wide transportation of humans and cargo

94. Inexpensive road-free (and facility-free) transportation

95. New methods for teaching languages rapidly

96. Extensive genetic control for plants and animals

97. New biological and chemical methods to identify, trace, incapacitate, or annoy people for police and military uses

98. New and possibly very simple methods for lethal biological and chemical warfare

99. Artificial moons and other methods of lighting large areas at night

100. Extensive use of "biological processes" in the extraction and processing of minerals

World-wide Industrialization, Affluence, and Population Growth

Many people—Kenneth Boulding, Peter Drucker, and John Maynard Keynes, for example—have pointed out that until the last two or three centuries no large human society had ever produced more than the equivalent of $200 per capita annually. With industrialization, mankind broke out of this pattern. By the end of this century, we expect that the nations of the world might be divided into the following five classes:

1. Preindustrial	$50 to $200 per capita
2. Partially industrialized or transitional	$200 to $600 per capita
3. Industrial	$600 to perhaps $1,500 per capita
4. Mass-consumption or advanced industrial	Perhaps $1,500 to something more than $4,000 per capita
5. Postindustrial	Something over $4,000 to $16,000 per capita

We shall consider partially industrialized societies as being in a transition stage, without assuming that they will necessarily continue to industrialize. Those countries we call industrialized are roughly in the condition of interwar America or postwar Europe.

Many preindustrial or partially industrialized societies may also, of course, have dual economies—for example, northern and southern Italy. This problem, now defined in terms of urban and rural differences, may, by the year 2000, be most critical in the six most populous, least developed countries: China, India, Pakistan, Indonesia, Brazil, and Nigeria. These now contain, and in the future will probably continue to contain, about half of the world's population; they are now preindustrial, but presumably will be partially industrialized by the end of the century.

Problems caused by great development in major cities and less in lesser cities and rural areas are already evident in these countries. Despite important differences in average development, one can argue that most great cities today have achieved startlingly similar conditions of modernization, and are at least "twentieth century." Rio de Janeiro, Bangkok, and Athens have many of the virtues and problems of the major cities of the United States: twentieth-century slums, computers, labor displaced by automation, great universities, skilled craftsmen, a trend toward tertiary and quaternary occupations, startlingly similar price structures for many commodities and activities.

The post-World War II period has seen the emergence of the mass-consumption society, first in the United States and then in Western Europe and Japan. Japan, although it has less than $1,000 per capita, is by every superficial appearance a mass-consumption society today, while the Soviet Union, with a per-capita income of around $1,500, seems far short of that condition. Similarly $4,000 per capita will probably be sufficient for transition to a postindustrial economy for the Scandinavian countries or Great Britain, while countries with more ambitious goals in terms of world power (the U.S.S.R.), stronger traditions of economic striving (West Germany), or higher expectations of productive affluence (the U. S.) will not become postindustrial until higher levels of affluence have been reached.

The chart below indicates a rather impressionistic, but not wholly unreasonable economic ranking for the nations of the world in the year 2000. The figures express national populations in millions, and the total world population is estimated at 6.4 billion. On the whole, the descriptions are optimistic, but we would not care to defend in detail the specific rank order we have suggested. The numbers identifying each group correspond roughly to the levels of income of the previous table.

If this scenario is realized, the year 2000 will find a rather large island of wealth surrounded by "misery"—at least relative to the developed world and to "rising expectations." But even the poor countries will, for the most part, enjoy great improvements over their traditional standards of living. The postindustrial and industrial societies will contain about 40 per cent of the world's population, and more than 90 per cent of the world's population

Economic Groupings in the Standard World

(5) *Visibly Postindustrial*

U. S.	320
Japan	120
Canada	40
Scandinavia & Switzerland	25
France, W. Germany, Benelux, Great Britain	215
	720

(3) *Mature Industrial*

¼ of Latin America	150
⅓ of Arab World	100
½ of East & S.E. Asia	200
Miscellaneous	50
	500

(5) *Early Postindustrial*

Italy	60
Soviet Union	350
E. Germany, Poland, Czechoslovakia	135
Israel	5
Australia, New Zealand	25
	575

(2) *Large & Partially Industrialized*

Brazil	200
Pakistan	230
China	1,300
India	1,000
Indonesia	220
Nigeria	150
	3,100

(4) *Mass-Consumption*

Spain, Portugal, Austria, Yugoslavia, Albania, Greece, Bulgaria, Hungary, Ireland	125
Turkey	75
Mexico, Argentina, Colombia, Venezuela, Chile	300
Taiwan, S. Korea, Hong Kong, Malaysia, etc.	120
	620

(1&2) *Preindustrial or Small & Partially Industrialized*

Rest of Africa	350
⅔ Arab World	200
Rest of Asia	160
Rest of Latin America	40
	750

will live in nations that have broken out of the historical $50-$200 per-capita range. Yet at the same time the absolute gap in living standards between countries or sectors of countries with developed economies and those at preindustrial levels will have widened abysmally.

Urbanization, Literacy, and Education

The United States in the year 2000 will probably see at least three gargantuan megalopolises. We have labeled these—only half-frivolously—"Boswash," "Chipitts," and "Sansan." Boswash identifies the megalopolis that will extend from Washington to Boston and contain almost one quarter of the American population (something under 80 million people). Chipitts, concentrated around the Great Lakes, may stretch from Chicago to Pittsburgh and north to Canada—thereby including Detroit, Toledo, Cleveland, Akron, Buffalo, and Rochester. This megalopolis seems likely to contain more than one eighth of the U. S. population (perhaps 40 million people or more). Sansan, a Pacific megalopolis that will presumably stretch from Santa Barbara (or even San Francisco) to San Diego, should contain more than one sixteenth of the population (perhaps 20 million people or more). These megalopolises will all be maritime. Boswash is on an extremely narrow strip of the North Atlantic coast; Chipitts, on Lake Erie and the southern and western shores of Lake Michigan and Lake Ontario; Sansan, on an even more narrow strip on the West Coast.

While all three will be recognizably American in culture, they will most likely be quite distinguishable sub-cultures. Sansan will presumably provide an informal "Bar-B-Q" culture, which has sometimes been called "wholesome degeneracy," and will include large and self-conscious, alienated, New Left, "hip," and bohemian groups. Chipitts, recently the site of successful architectural and urban-renewal programs, will probably still have traces of both the "Bible belt" and Carl Sandburg's "raw and lusty vitality." Boswash will, of course, be "cosmopolitan"—the home of New York liberals, Boston bankers, tired or creative intellectuals in publishing, entertainment, and the arts, and political Washington.

The three megalopolises should contain roughly one half of the total United States population, including the overwhelming majority of the most technologically and scientifically advanced, and prosperous intellectual and creative elements. Even Sansan will have a larger total income than all but five or six nations. Study of the United States in the year 2000 may largely be of Boswash, Chipitts, and Sansan.

Such structures will be typical of other countries as well. Thus, most of southeastern England is likely to be one megalopolis, though in this case it may be called a conurbation. The Japanese will no doubt coin or borrow a word for the Tokyo-Osaka strip. Nevertheless, although between 80 and 90 per cent of the developed world's population will be urbanized by the end of the century, most people will still live in more traditional urban areas.

Suburbia, then as now, will be a special kind of low-density urban living, quite different from rural patterns.

Decreasing Importance of Primary Occupations

Closely related to current trends toward very large urban agglomerations are the declining importance of primary and secondary occupations, and the growing importance of what are normally called tertiary occupations, though we shall distinguish between tertiary and quaternary occupations. (The primary occupations are, of course, fishing, forestry, hunting, agriculture, and mining. Secondary occupations are concerned with processing the products of a primary occupation. A tertiary occupation is a service rendered mostly to primary and secondary occupations. Quaternary occupations render services mostly to tertiary occupations or to one another.) There will undoubtedly be a large shift to quaternary occupations. Since these occupations are heavily concentrated in the government, the professions, the nonprofit private groups, and the like, this implies—in conjunction with others things—a shift from the private business enterprise as the major source of innovation, attention, and prominence in society. The lessening emphasis on primary occupations will be accompanied by a lessened dependence on access to inexpensive or convenient raw materials (rather than a situation of desperate shortages of usable or available raw materials). This, in turn, will make many factors of geography and location less crucial for the nation as a whole.

II

Some Perspectives on Change

A second way of looking at the future is to identify the relevant clusters of events that have marked off different time periods in man's history. One can thus seek to identify the constants of each time, the secular trend lines, and the "turning points" of an era. For our purpose we begin by considering what a "surprise-free" projection might have been like in 1900 or 1933.

The Year 1900

One world (Western-dominated), though with many unassimilated, traditional cultures

Industrial, colonial, or "protected" societies

Declining United Kingdom and France—rising Germany, United States, Russia, and Japan

Parliamentary government and Christianity

Basic feeling in almost all classes of the white race (and in many nonwhite) of optimism, security, progress, order; a belief in the physical and moral supremacy of Western culture, and in rational and moral domestic and foreign politics; and, perhaps most important of all, a relative absence of guilt feelings

Intellectual acceptance of the ideas of Adam Smith, Darwin, and the Enlightenment

It is interesting to note that the only two non-Western countries that had successfully begun to industrialize by 1900, Japan and Russia, did so more to serve their national security than to increase their standard of living. Except possibly for Turkey, Iran, Thailand, Ethiopia, and some Latin American countries, every nation that had failed to industrialize by 1900 was either a colony, a protectorate, or a *de facto* dependency. Thus, successful industrialization was widely perceived as a matter of national independence, if not of national survival. Today these incentives are greatly reduced.

In 1900 it was clear that the two established powers of Western Europe—Great Britain and France—were losing in power relative to Germany, the United States, Japan, and Russia. One can think of Britain and France as "core" powers of the West, Germany (or at least Prussianized Germany) as "semiperipheral," the United States as "fully peripheral," and Russia and Japan as either fully peripheral or new "mixtures."

The Parliamentary ideal was widely accepted, and Christianity was almost everywhere triumphant or on the rise in 1900. National self-satisfaction, optimism, and faith in the future of most Western or Westernized people are, to modern eyes, perhaps the most striking characteristics of the year 1900—and ones which were soon to disappear in the tragic futilities of World War I and its aftermath.

The Period 1900-1933

The first third of the twentieth century brought some surprises:

Russo-Japanese War

La Belle Époque (1901-1913)

World War I (Europe devastated)

Five major dynasties (Hohenzollern, Hapsburg, Manchu, Romanov, and Ottoman) dethroned

Emergence of the United States as leading world power

Loss of European (and democratic) morale and prestige

Rise of Communism and the Soviet Union

Great Depression

Rise of Fascist ideologies and various dictatorships

Impact of new intellectual concepts (those of Bohr, de Broglie, Einstein, Freud, and Schroedinger)

The Period 1933-1966

The next third of a century experienced still more unexpected changes and disturbing events:

Continued growth of Fascism and Communism

World War II—Europe again devastated

Mass murders and forced population movements on extraordinary scale before, during, and after World War II

Intense, nationalistic competition in the development and application of radically new technologies for peace and war

Decolonization

The Cold War and neutralism in the Third World

Emergence of two super-powers (U. S. and Soviet Union); five large powers (Japan, West Germany, France, China, United Kingdom); three intermediate powers (India, Italy, Canada)

Rise and decline of Italy, Canada, and India

Decline and re-emergence of Europe

Decline and re-emergence of Japan

Reunification and centralization of China

Post-Keynesian, post-Marxian, and perhaps postcommunal and sophisticated "development" economics

Emergence of mass-consumption societies

"Second" industrial revolution

Chinese achieve nuclear status

In looking at this sixty-six-year kaleidoscope, an Indian national is quoted as saying:

For us in Asia there have been two epochal events in this century. The first was Japan's defeat of Russia in 1905. The second was China's atom bomb. . . . Asia and India are learning the uses of power in the modern world. The first lesson was taught by Japan in 1905. It demonstrated that an Asian country could master the West's weapons and use them to defeat the West. The second lesson was taught by China. It demonstrated that Asia could equal the West even in advanced military technology.[4]

To Asia—or some Asians—the century began with a nonwhite nation's successfully beating a white nation on its own ground, thus proving that Europe's supremacy was not necessarily permanent, and the second third of the century ended with the acquisition of nuclear weapons by a nonwhite nation. Both of these events were thought at the time to be of crucial and world-wide significance. It is said that during the first decade of the century there were Africans who did not know what Russia and Japan were, and yet knew that a nonwhite people had defeated a white nation.

Most of these items would probably not have been predicted by any individual or policy research group "speculating about the next thirty-three years" in either 1900 or 1933. Probably the great divide was World War I. Preceded by the thirteen years that are still known as *la belle époque,* these years were, for almost all the civilized world, an unprecedented era of sustained growth. While some of the period's glory has been dimmed by the passing of time and comparison with the post-World War II era of growth, the years are still remembered nostalgically. Not only did World War I terminate *la belle époque,* but it shattered the moral and political structure of Europe. The effective triumph of democracy over despotism (or at least unenlightened monarchy) might have created a situation of high morale, but the cost of the war had been too high—particularly the seeming senselessness of many of the tactics, the moral effect of various revisionist and antiwar writers, and the disillusionment with the postwar settlement. The loss of European morale and prestige following 1918 was both grave and world-wide. The pessimism that seized the West was reflected in the popularity of such an author as Spengler. Although many Europeans expected the Russians or Asians to succeed to the West's power, an aberrant of Western culture, Nazism, came perilously close to conquering all of Europe. While Fascism and Nazism are no doubt heretical to the Western tradition, they are products of Western culture and result from identifiable and historically continuous religious, ideological, cultural, and structural forces within

91

Western societies—trends that were emphasized by the pessimism and frustration that resulted from World War I.

Despite the widespread belief that poverty creates instability and messianic totalitarian movements such as Communism and Fascism, the four nations closest to catching up with or passing the advanced industrial powers—Japan, Russia,[5] Germany, and Italy—provided the serious instability of the first half of this century. This may turn out to be the prototype of some possibilities in the next sixty-six years as well. While poverty and preindustrial economies are not themselves indicia of stability, neither is industrialization or Westernization.

In the first third of the century, many new theories were, at least intellectually, profoundly upsetting. The self-assured, rationalistic, moralistic, and mechanically-minded Victorians were told, in effect, that solid matter is mostly empty; that time is relative and that perfectly accurate clocks run at different speeds; that the world is governed by the probabilistic laws of wave mechanics, rather than by simple deterministic "cause and effect" as suggested by Newtonian Mechanics[6]; and, finally, that a good deal of what passes for rational behavior is actually motivated by unconscious impulses and feelings of a socially unacceptable or reprehensible character. What is most striking is that these radical shifts in *Weltanschauung* were managed with so little disruption.

Perhaps the most significant aspect of the middle third of the twentieth century has been the sustained economic growth achieved in the post-World War II era. This has raised the real possibility of world-wide industrialization and of the emergence in more advanced industrial nations of what has been called a post-industrial culture. Some of this economic growth clearly derives from a growing sophistication in governmental economic policies. As even the "classical" economist Milton Friedman recently said, "We are all Keynesians today, and we are all post-Keynesians as well." If this were not true, and the postwar world had been marked by the same violent swings between prosperity and depression as the interwar world, we would not now take such a sanguine view of future economic prospects. Today it is widely believed that, except possibly for China, almost all the Communist and capitalist governments are coming to understand how to keep their economies reasonably stable and growing; both the capitalists and the Marxists are, in this sense, "revisionist."

While we reject the so-called convergence theory, in which it is argued that Communism and capitalism will come to resemble each other so closely that they will be practically indistinguishable, it is clear that they are borrowing from each other—with the Marxists, however, doing more of the explicit borrowing. The current governmental success in economics and planning is a major cause of the emergence of mass-consumption societies in Western Europe, the United States, Japan, and Australia, and is one reason why such societies can be expected to emerge rapidly in the Soviet Union and Eastern Europe.

It is still an open question, however, whether the same thing can be achieved in communal societies (such as China is striving to be) and in the less developed nations generally. But at least two groups of less developed nations are now doing so well economically that it is reasonable to think of them as undergoing a kind of "second" industrial revolution. Thus, those parts of Europe that were left behind by the industrial revolution, or which were "transplanted," are now beginning to catch up.

Even more impressive are the growth rates in the Sinic cultures of the world outside China (including Malaysia and perhaps the Philippines, but possibly not Thailand). These countries seem able to sustain growth rates of about 8 per cent, except for the Philippines with 5 per cent. Wherever the Chinese and their culture have gone in the world, they have done well, except in China. Until about 1800, China was, except for periodic interregna, an eminent culture in the world. It may once again be coming out of an interregnum, but whether or not it will achieve its "normal" status must now be judged unlikely or at best an open question.

The second third of the twentieth century ended with two super-powers, five large powers, three intermediate powers, and about 120 small powers. This structure and hierarchy seems likely to characterize the next decade or two as well. In fact, listing Japan and West Germany as the two largest of the five "large" powers is even more appropriate for the mid-seventies than for today.

The Last Third of the Twentieth Century

Continuation of long-term multifold trend

Emergence of postindustrial society

World-wide capability for modern technology

Need for world-wide zoning ordinances and other restraints

High (1 to 10 per cent) growth rates in GNP per capita

Increasing emphasis on "meaning and purpose"

Much turmoil in the "new" and possibly in the industrializing nations

Some possibility for sustained "nativist," messianic, or other mass movements

Second rise of Japan

Some further rise of Europe and China

Emergence of new intermediate powers: Brazil, Mexico, Pakistan, Indonesia, East Germany, Egypt

Some decline (relative) of U. S. and Soviet Union

A possible absence of stark "life and death" political and economic issues in the "old nations"

Except for the possible emergence of what we call, following Daniel Bell, the postindustrial society,[7] the listing is "surprise-free": It assumes the continuation of the multifold trend, but excludes precisely the kinds of dramatic or surprising events that dominated the first two thirds of the century. More specifically, the "surprise-free" projection rules out *major changes in the old nations* that might be caused by such possibilities as invasion and war; civil strife and revolution; famine and pestilence; despotism (persecution) and natural disaster; depression or economic stagnation; the development of "inexpensive" doomsday or near-doomsday machines and nuclear "six-gun" weapons technology; resurgence of Communism or a revival of Fascism along with a racial, North-South, rich-poor, East-West dichotomy; an economically dynamic China, with 10 per cent annual growth rate, and a politically dynamic U. S., Soviet Union, Japan, or Brazil; development of the U. N. or other worldwide organizations, and possible regional or other multinational organizations; new religious philosophies or other mass movements, and a psychologically upsetting impact of the new techniques, ideas, and philosophies.

If the basic long-term multifold trend continues or is accelerated during the next thirty-three years, and there are no surprising but not-impossible disruptions of the sort listed above, then a postindustrial society seems likely to develop in the affluent parts of the world.

In a postindustrial world, per-capita income is about fifty times that in a preindustrial society. Most "economic" activities are tertiary and quaternary rather than primary or secondary; business firms are, consequently, no longer the major source of innovation. There is an effective floor on income and welfare, and efficiency is not a primary consideration. There is widespread cybernation, a typical "doubling time" for social change of three to thirty years, and a common technological foundation for a world society. Work-oriented, achievement-oriented, advancement-oriented values and "national interest" values erode, and Sensate, secular, humanistic, perhaps self-indulgent, criteria become central, as do the intellectual institutions. Continuing education is widespread, and there is rapid improvement in educational techniques.

III

The Standard World and Its Canonical Variations

So far, we have been dealing with trends or clusters of "traits." To make any significant assumptions, we would want to combine the most likely predictions into a more or less coherent whole and specify them in more detail. This we would call our least improbable "alternative future," or our "Standard World."

One problem of long-range speculation is that the curve of probabilities often seems very flat—that is, no particular course of events seems more likely than another. In order to avoid the dilemma of Buridan's ass, we must make almost arbitrary choices among equally interesting, important, and plausible possibilities. If we are to explore any predictions at all, we must to some extent "make them up." The most salient of the projections we can make is one that is "surprise-free"; nevertheless it would be very surprising if in any thirty-three-year period the real world did not produce many political and technological surprises.

For the skeptical reader this "surprise-free" projection may be useful chiefly as a norm for comparison and disagreement. Although the "surprise-free" projection is similar in spirit to the "naïve projection" of the economist, which assumes a continuation of current tendencies, it is more complex because it includes the implications of whatever empirical and theoretical considerations affect current expectations. (For example, a "naïve" projection of world population to 2000 would be about 7.2 billion, but our "surprise-free" projection would be 6.4 billion.)

Each of the major alternatives to the Standard World that we have constructed fits into one of three categories: more "integrated," more "inward-looking," or in greater "disarray." The models in these categories envisage, respectively:

1. A relatively peaceful, relatively prosperous world with a relatively high degree of consultation among nations, with arms control and political co-ordination or even integration among all, or almost all, the "major" or minor powers

2. Almost as peaceful and prosperous a world but with little arms control or general co-ordination

3. A relatively troubled and violent world, but one in which no large central wars have occurred

The following are eight canonical variations:

I. More integrated
   A. Stability-oriented
   B. Development-oriented

II. More inward-looking
   A. With an eroded Communist movement
   B. With an eroded democratic morale and some Communist dynamism
   C. With a dynamic Europe or Japan

III. Greater disarray
   A. With an eroded Communist movement
   B. With a dynamic Communist movement and some erosion of democratic morale
   C. With a dynamic Europe or Japan

By focusing attention on each of the above possibilities in turn, we get a sense of comparative structures and of a range of possibilities, while remaining within or fairly close to the "surprise-free" projections. Yet it should be clear that only a Procrustean theory could attempt to define the next ten to fifteen years (much less the next thirty-three) in terms of such single themes. The reality undoubtedly will be one in which one theme alternates with another, or in which there is a dialectical contention among political trends or open conflict. But for our standardized and canonical contexts (and for some but not all of the scenarios that illustrate them) we assume that there is little fluctuation from simple secular trends.

In these projections we assume that the ten major powers (which we have divided into the categories "super," "large," and "intermediate") develop more or less according to the figure below.

One might have wanted to assume that the "Integrated World" develops more rapidly and with smaller disparities in income than the "Inward-Looking World," and that this in turn develops more rapidly than the "Disarray World." While this is reasonable, it is not by any means inevitable.

The figure shows how the ten largest nations compared in GNP and population in 1965 (numerals in circles), and the points they seem most likely to reach by the year 2000 (numerals in ellipses). The numerals identifying each country are in the order of our "best estimate" for 2000 GNP, although the differences among Canada, Italy, and India are not significant. The ellipses indicate a range of reasonable uncertainty for each year-2000 projection. In 1965, for example, the U. S. had a GNP of about $692 billion (by U. N. definition), a population of about 195 million, and a per-capita GNP of about $3,560. By the year 2000, its GNP could reach nearly $4,000 billion (almost the top of the chart) with more than $15,000 per-capita GNP; or, assuming a much lower growth rate, the GNP could be less than $1,500 billion and GNP per capita under $5,000. The range in population estimates is narrower. Our "best estimate" is for a GNP close to the top of the "reasonable range" and for a relatively moderate population growth. (Our report contains more detailed figures.) The ellipses for India and China slope backward because they are more likely to achieve relatively high GNP growth if they can limit population. We have labeled the GNP per-capita groups in terms of the classes discussed above.

Finally, we separate the 135 nations of the world into two classes—"old" (about 55) and "new" (about 80). "Old" nations are those that have had a relatively continuous existence at least since World War I; "new" nations are for the most part post-World War II creations or ancient countries recently emerged from colonial status. (Thus we consider West Germany to be an old nation; East Germany and China, newly integrated; Taiwan and India, newly independent; Egypt, new.) We assume—again in all worlds, and for the 1967-2000 period as a whole—the fulfillment of certain widespread current expectations of more or less sustained economic growth among all the major (and most minor) nations, and more or less sustained (but usually slackening) population growth. We also assume that except in periods of actual war or great crisis there will be freedom of the seas, with foreign commerce moving freely without explicit reliance on national naval or other military power. We assume that there will be few and minor frontier

FIGURE 1
"SURPRISE-FREE" PROJECTIONS
FOR THE TEN MAJOR COUNTRIES

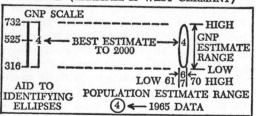

changes, if any, in the old nations, chiefly because of general conditions of political stability or inertia rather than because of the balance—or lack of balance—of local military situations. We assume that most of the old nations will not be called on to use military power to advance their national interests—at least in any simple or direct way. Obviously nations may nonetheless experience benefits (or disutilities) from military power—for example, from their ability implicitly or explicitly to protect (or threaten) various other nations. Some small nations may obtain security benefits (or disutilities) from having sizable national military forces—for example, from being a more valuable ally or feeling freer to accept or reject offers of protection by larger nations. But by and large, for *most* of the old nations and many of the new, national security is assumed to be "free"—derived from the general condition of stability rather than from a nation's own efforts.

Of course, this stability, if it exists or is to continue, will be maintained in part by the willingness of various nations, especially the U. S. and the U.S.S.R., to intervene judiciously when situations arise that threaten the general equilibrium. Presumably the balance could be tipped by one of these nations trying either too hard or not hard enough—by intervening too readily in an attempt to control events or by failing to check forces tending to instability.

To go beyond the year 2000, we can speculate briefly on world society in the first third of the next century. We expect the rise of new great powers—perhaps Japan, China, a European complex, Brazil, Mexico, or India. There will be new political, perhaps even "philosophical," issues, and a leveling-off or diminishing of some aspects of the basic long-term multifold trend, such as urbanization. The postindustrial and industrial worlds will have been largely realized, as will population control, arms control, and some kind of moderately stable international security arrangement, though probably not a "world government." In the industrializing world, disorder, ideology, and irrational movements will probably continue to play disruptive, though geographically confined roles. In the U. S. and Western Europe, there will presumably be either a return to certain Hellenic or older European concepts of the good life, or an intensified alienation and search for identity, values, meaning, and purpose, a search made necessary and facilitated by the unprecedented affluence and permissiveness of the postindustrial economy.

References

1. These and related issues are taken up in some detail in our volume for the Working Papers of the Commission, *The Next Thirty-Three Years: A Framework for Speculation,* to be published in October, 1967, by the Macmillan Company as *Toward the Year 2000: A Framework for Speculation.*

2. Pitirim A. Sorokin, *Social and Cultural Dynamics,* Vol. 4 (New York, 1962), pp. 737 ff.

3. In compiling this list we have received useful suggestions from Jane Kahn, John Menke, Robert Prehoda, and G. Harry Stine.

4. As quoted by Harrison E. Salisbury in *The New York Times,* August 18, 1966.

5. From 1890 to 1914 (except for the years of the Russo-Japanese War—1904 and 1905), Russia grew in GNP at an average rate of 8 per cent and was thus, in some ways, undergoing a very successful industrialization.

6. Of course, many physicists now believe that the world is deterministic, but that there are unknowable "hidden variables." In the early days of quantum mechanics and the uncertainty principle, however, many philosophers seized upon the latter as allowing for, or being identical with, free will and thus providing a belated and unexpected answer to the mechanists and determinists of the eighteenth and nineteenth centuries.

7. For a discussion of some features of the postindustrial society as Daniel Bell has used the term, see his "Notes on the Post-Industrial Society," *The Public Interest,* Numbers 6 and 7 (Winter and Spring, 1967).

FRED CHARLES IKLÉ

Can Social Predictions Be Evaluated?

How CAN we tell a good prediction from a bad one? Unless we
have some way of gauging the quality of predictions, all our efforts
to forecast, conjecture about, or anticipate the future must remain
essentially dilettante. Without some criteria for evaluating our predictions, we will be unable to detect whether or not our work
concerning the future is making any progress.

Intuitively, of course, we have some feeling for judging the
worth of predictions. We have to think about the future whenever
we deliberately choose among alternative courses of action, and
evidently we manage to sort out these predictive thoughts more
or less to our satisfaction. Furthermore, all branches of science
help by enabling us—way beyond the capacity of our intuition—
to make specific statements that will come true in the future.
Indeed, for the physical scientist qua scientist, future verification
is essentially the criterion of a successful prediction. But for the
social scientist, this will not quite do. And for the man of action
or the man with a "social conscience," verification is, of course, not
what he is after. Besides, the criterion of verification will not serve
to separate the wheat from the chaff—one can make many trivial, useless, boring, or even harmful predictions that will turn out
to be true.

The first thing to recognize in judging the worth of predictions
—or in answering the question as to what we are trying to accomplish when we predict—is that predictions can serve quite
different purposes. The erroneous presumption is often made that
all predictions have just one purpose according to which they can
be evaluated: to guide our actions regarding the future or, more
precisely, to describe the consequences of a course of action and of
some of its alternatives so that we can shape the future more to

101

our liking. If this is indeed the purpose of statements about the future, I shall call them *guiding predictions*. These predictions are essential for any effort to plan for or to shape the future, and understanding of them is sharpened if they are contrasted with statements about the future that have other purposes.[1]

Predictions to Overcome Indecision: To Help Buridan's Ass

Medieval philosophers have pondered the question why Buridan's ass, equidistant between two equal heaps of hay, would not die of hunger since nothing in the objective situation would tell it whether to turn left or right. More often than we realize, we find ourselves in the position of Buridan's ass: We face several courses of action, of which we only know that they are better than inaction, but among which we cannot find the preferred choice because their consequences (considering their utility *and* probability) look indistinguishable.

If we are fully aware of the nature of our dilemma, we flip a coin—that is, we do not pretend that head or tail will "predict" the better course of action. We admit that we have merely chosen a random device or some other trick to overcome our indecision. After this gambit has done its work, we sometimes begin to feel better and more confident about our choice because we begin to re-evaluate the alternatives, as if we wanted to prove that our choice was right. This is the interesting process that psychologists have studied under the name of "cognitive dissonance." Their studies show that in certain circumstances people tend to reduce discrepancies between their behavior and what they know by distorting what they know. A person who has chosen among alternatives that seemed equally attractive to him tends to suppress or modify information that suggests his choice was wrong. He will inflate the data that make the chosen alternative look preferable and belittle the advantages of the rejected alternative that he belatedly discovers.[2] (Perhaps this description does not fit all personality types; a morose, self-accusing person will act in the opposite way.)

If we are less aware of the nature of our dilemma, we will try to make a prediction rather than flip a coin. Such a "Buridan's-ass prediction" differs from a "guiding prediction" in that its worth depends primarily on its capacity to overcome our indecision. Where there is no discernible difference between alternative futures, the "Buridan's-ass prediction" has to invent one; where there are only trivial differences, this prediction has to focus on the trivia as if they mattered. One might say, somewhat naïvely, that the "Buridan's-ass prediction" does not have to be true because it has to fake a difference where there is none. I qualify by "somewhat naïvely," since it may be impossible to indicate what would make such a prediction true or false. If the reduction of cognitive dissonance takes over, the prediction that served to overcome our indecision will often turn out to be "true" in the sense that we will feel—after the predicted time has come—that the world is more to our liking than it probably would have been had we chosen one of the alternative courses of action. Thus, it looks to us as if the prediction was "probably true."

There are, however, situations where we can discriminate between a true and a false "Buridan's-ass prediction" (or between a lucky and an unlucky flip of the coin for overcoming our indecision). If someone has some cash to invest and arrives at the "guiding prediction" that automobile shares will go up, but cannot choose between Chrysler and Ford shares, he may flip a coin or ask a soothsayer. When the time comes for him to sell his shares, he can obviously tell whether or not the soothsayer was right. This is one of these rare situations where the outcomes from hypothetical alternative actions can be clearly reconstructed and where there is only one way of assigning values to these outcomes. Contrast with this the flipping of a coin to decide whether one should buy a Chrysler or a Ford car. Regardless of how one later feels about the purchased car, one will never know for sure how one would have fared with the alternative.

In our personal lives, the random gambit for overcoming indecision (such as flipping a coin) is less effective in making us feel confident and happy about our choice than a "Buridan's-ass prediction." One can believe of the latter that it is "probably true," and this belief will strengthen one's motivation to reduce cognitive dissonance. The ancient Greeks and Romans were not more naïve than we are—they were wiser—by paying a little money to a soothsayer so that he would flip the coin for them or do some equivalent hocus-pocus.

But "Buridan's-ass predictions" can also be carried too far. It is often better to recognize that one must make a random choice, than to focus on trivial differences or to fake a difference between alternatives whose merit is indistinguishable. We all know the person who never buys the house he needs and can well afford, as he keeps looking for the discriminating prediction that would indicate which among his acceptable options is best. In government and in other large organizations (where it seems a bit unbecoming to flip a coin), one must be on guard not to waste time and scarce analytical skills on such fake predictions. For the last few years there has been an increasing emphasis in the United States Government on the systematic analysis of policy choices and cost-benefit studies. This highly promising development might become discredited if it got diverted to problems that affect the evaluation of alternative programs only trivially. This new analytical approach to government decisions (and the predictions that are part of it) aims not to pick the optimum out of some diffusely different options, but to design alternatives that are clearly better.[8]

Predictions for the Purpose of Entertainment or Spiritual Edification

A large number of statements about the future that look like "guiding predictions" are actually predictions for entertainment or spiritual edification. By keeping this distinction clearly in mind we can get both better guidance and better entertainment.

One form of prediction for entertainment is the *guessing game*. Here someone guesses about something he cannot know for sure but that can clearly be verified before the game is over. Since the guess has no relevance for the players' actions (except that they may play the game for money), it does not matter what is being guessed so long as the guess can be verified before too long. The most diverse topics will do: the cards that lie face down on the table, the next bride of a movie star, the winner in the World Series, the plurality in the next Presidential elections.

Let us note the main differences between "guiding predictions" and "guessing-game predictions." First, what matters for the game is *who* turns out to be right, while the choice of subject about which the predictions are being made is rather unimportant. For guidance, on the other hand, it does not matter much *whose* prediction is being used (as long as it is helpful), while the choice of subject is enormously important. Second, the more certain we are about the predicted future the less entertaining the "guessing-game prediction," but the better the "guiding prediction." Third, the guessing game cannot be finished without unequivocal verification,

104

whereas it is not necessary that a "guiding prediction" be verified. The "guiding prediction" has served its purpose if it has helped us to choose that course of action which makes the future more to our liking. We do not have to determine afterwards whether or not the prediction was "true." Indeed, as is shown in the example about the Chrysler and Ford car, it is often impossible to ascertain whether a "guiding prediction" was "true," since we cannot reconstruct the consequences of alternative courses of action that nobody has taken.

The *futuristic novel* is another form of prediction for entertainment. Its requirements are quite different from those of the guessing game. What matters here is whether the reader finds the future realization of the tale plausible or at least possible; later verification is quite unnecessary for entertainment. This category characterizes H. G. Wells' novels, nearly all of the social predictions that reach beyond the year 2000 (exceptions are demographic forecasts), and even some of the current writings regarding the less distant future. How do we tell a good prediction of this kind from a bad one? We do so exactly the same way as we tell a good novel from a bad one.[4]

Before we delegate the evaluation of all futuristic novels to the literary critic, however, we must recognize that they can serve some of the functions of "guiding predictions." They can suggest future possibilities that a less literary approach might overlook, and they can trace connections between more detailed forecasts. For instance, H. G. Wells in *The World Set Free*, published in 1914 before the outbreak of World War I, writes about "atomic bombs" that would be used in a war in the 1950's and describes how this war began (somewhat accidentally) because "the world still . . . fooled around with the paraphernalia and pretensions of war" even though "it was a matter of common knowledge that man could carry in a handbag an amount of latent energy sufficient to wreck half a city."[5] Wells got this idea from reading Frederick Soddy's *The Interpretation of Radium* (1909), a popular version of earlier scientific papers by Soddy and Ernest Rutherford. This source, however, suggested only that the enormous energy contained in uranium would someday be "unlocked"; it remained for Wells to combine this prediction with his expectation that the current international order—or lack of it—would make the unlocked atom important as a weapon for future wars.

The futuristic novel, by tracing connections between more detailed forecasts and by drawing a coherent picture, serves a function similar to the "artist's renditions" in textbooks on ancient history that help us literally *to see* the past. (Of course, the futuristic novel, just like the artist's rendition, might also give a misleading picture.)

Futuristic novels also impinge on "guiding predictions" by stimulating us to like or dislike certain alternative futures; they add what Francis Bacon called "the colors of good and evil" to what would otherwise be bland possibilities. These "colors" presumably reflect the author's values. Thus, George Orwell's *1984* might have made some of us more aware that we want to avoid various trends toward totalitarian socialism or toward government control of news. Many of H. G. Wells' novels, on the other hand, might have induced his readers to see merit in a united world welfare state and to become apprehensive of developments toward another war— whether it be the stalemated trench warfare and the fighting with "flying machines" predicted in Wells' *Anticipations* (1902), or the "atomic bombs" predicted in *The World Set Free*, or the incident at Danzig mentioned in *The Shape of Things to Come* (1933) that would start World War II.[6]

Lastly, we sometimes want predictions for our *spiritual edification* rather than for simple entertainment. When we are in this mood, we like to know where society is headed, not to guide our actions but to satisfy our "philosophical" curiosity. This is the same curiosity that makes us read cosmological predictions about the universe billions of years hence.

Even in talking about the not so distant year 2000, we may be influenced by and catering to this spiritual yearning. From Monday to Saturday we make predictions regarding the year 2000 because we want to shape the future more to our liking, but on Sunday we may predict the year 2000 not to decide where we *should* go, but because we "just like to know" where we are going. To be sure, the more convincing this prediction seems to us, the better will our spiritual curiosity be satisfied. But it does not matter for these Sunday predictions whether or not the future they prophesy will at all resemble the real future. What matters on Sunday is that our predictions satisfy our spiritual needs *on that day*.

I am using the fuzzy word *spiritual* advisedly, for as soon as we examine what we were after on Sunday in the cold light of logical positivism on Monday morning, we discover that we did not really know what we wanted as we tried to predict our future. On the one hand, we were driven by our yearning for ultimate things, our desire to round off infinity with an ending, our longing for a purpose of history—that is, we were asking unanswerable questions. On the other hand, we simply wanted to know the end of a suspense story in which we had become engrossed—any exciting and not too implausible outcome would have sufficed.

I am belaboring this point because of its importance for the improvement of social predictions. If we fail to separate "guiding predictions" from this "spiritual edification," we will be careless in the selection of what we predict and will neglect to relate our predictions to our choices. So many of the current writings on the future are nothing but collections of random predictions that, while intriguing to read and satisfying to our curiosity, make no difference at all for what we will do.

First Step in "Guiding Predictions": How We Can Have Some Knowledge About the Future.

Daniel Bell has written that "few persons today would declare with confidence that something is unknowable."[7] If one interpreted this proposition more broadly than Bell probably meant it, one would have to disagree. Among the predictions that can be made most confidently and that are most confidence-inspiring are certain predictions that something is unknowable. Certain predictions can be "absolute" because they are logically true; they deduce from the meaning of certain premises that certain conclusions, which apply to the future, inevitably follow.

For four thousand years mathematicians have tried to solve the quadrature of the circle, until Ferdinand Lindmann proved in 1882 that the problem, as posed, cannot be solved. This was tantamount to predicting that it will not be solved. It was a useful prediction, since it saved further mathematicians from wasting their time on this problem. A parallel can be found in the history of the idea of a perpetual motion machine.

Not all these predictions are so definitive. For over two thousand years, philosophers have tried to find answers to metaphysical questions. Some fifty years ago, Ludwig Wittgenstein started to show that most of these questions cannot be meaningfully answered.[8] Wittgenstein and his followers have not succeeded in convincing everyone. Some people still try to answer metaphysical questions, in part, because there can be disagreement as to what is "meaningful."

107

Logically (or analytically) true predictions can take other forms. They can link a conditional premise to futuristic conclusions. For instance, given the assumption that (living) space is finite, the death rates of the world population will eventually have to become equal to or higher than the birth rates.[9] Such a prediction is not so trivial as it sounds. It narrows the argument about our choices. If one accepts the premise that living space is finite, one cannot deny that a population policy (either passive or active) that fails to bring birth rates down is a policy that must bring the death rate up again—if not in the short run, then *certainly* in the long run. In this connection it is worth noting that given the present or projected mortality of the rich countries, the birth rates will have to come down close to two children per mother. This is a long way from the most optimistic goals of current population policies in the poor countries. And the population policies of the rich countries, of course, are only partly directed—if at all—toward closing the gap between birth and death rates.

"Guiding predictions" that are not logically true must be based on the assumption that the regularities we have observed in the past will obtain in the future. In other words, the epistemological basis of such predictions is the same as that of inductive knowledge in general. Saying this does not explain everything, for the philosophers' analysis of induction is still an unfinished task with many annoyingly refractory problems.

In order to describe any observation that we have not yet made, we assume that it belongs to a class of observations that we have sampled in the past (or that it is a composite of such observations). Induction not only serves to foretell what we will observe if we are around at a certain time in the future, but also what we will observe if we move to our left or right, or if we dig into certain records of the past. In foretelling such observations we do not, of course, rely on induction alone, but try to use, where we can, theories and empirical laws. By doing so, we reduce at one stroke our sampling requirements since we deductively tie together a great mass of relevant observations.

This rudimentary explication of scientific reasoning—for which I must apologize—serves to bring out four points that are somewhat less elementary:

1. Some predictions can be based, almost exclusively, on logical truths. Hence, they can be as certain as the most certain

propositions we can name, *contrary to the allegation that nothing can be predicted with certainty.*[10] Indeed, they can be more certain than many statements about the present or past.

2. Other predictions are based primarily on induction (with the assistance, if we are lucky, of theories and laws). Deduction and induction, of course, do not distinguish the methodology of prediction from scientific method in general. Hence we have not yet identified procedures that justify our talking of a "science of prediction." In particular, trends, cycles, and analogies—about which some writers on prediction make so much ado—are used for propositions about unobserved phenomena, regardless of whether the phenomena are invariant with time or, if they vary, whether they are located in the past, present, or future. For instance, propositions about the unobserved temperature of interior layers of the earth (invariant within our time) can be based on the observed *trend* according to which temperature increases with increasing depth.

The philosophy of science and the analytic philosophy of history have a great deal to say regarding the reasoning and methods we use for making social predictions. Recognizing this will save us fom dilettante discussions of cycles, fluctuations, unique events, extrapolations, and so forth.

3. In making predictions, however, we rely on additional ways of thinking that do not exhibit the logical structure of deduction or induction. By saying what these ways of thinking do not represent, I may group highly diverse things together; if I tried to sort them, however, I would go beyond the scope of this essay. What I have in mind here are such mental abilities as placing single events into useful classes without explicitly knowing the principle of classification, estimating the likelihood of an event without explicitly considering relative frequencies, and selecting and integrating regularities from inarticulate experiences without being conscious of the process of selection and integration.

Looked at from the psychological viewpoint, these mental processes are the very building blocks of thinking and cognition.[11] Looked at from the epistemological viewpoint, these processes make up a form of knowledge that is distinct from the knowledge traditionally analyzed by logicians and philosophers of science, a form of "tacit knowing" in Michael Polanyi's apt term.[12] Looked at by the modern statistician, these processes furnish one of his basic inputs: the "subjective" probabilities that he always takes as given and beyond further analysis. To put it crudely, this modern (so-called Bayesian) approach to statistical inference starts out with one's initial judgment as to the probability of the occurrence of an event (or of the truth of a hypothesis) and then modifies this probability in the light of further observations.

I have stressed that the epistemological basis of prediction, to the extent that it consists of inductive and deductive reasoning, is indistinguishable from the basis of scientific knowledge in general. This also obtains for the reliance on "tacit knowledge," except that "tacit knowledge" often plays a more conspicuous role in predictions (especially in those about social phenomena) than in scientific propositions about past, present, or temporally invariant phenomena. To put it more colloquially: The role of "common sense" or "intuition" leaps to the eye in social predictions, whereas it is buried more deeply in propositions of the "exact" sciences.

Finally, to conclude this first step in "guiding predictions," I can pass quickly over two features that distinguish social predictions (more precisely, predictions about phenomena alterable by human action) from other predictions, since these features have been dealt with so well by many other authors. One feature is the self-fulfilling or self-defeating effect—that is, the response to a prediction may enhance or nullify the predicted event. Of course, this effect stems from the fact that predictions can guide (or misguide) the actions of people for whom they describe some aspect of their potential future. To the extent that this effect is a disturbance rather than the very purpose of prediction, the predictor must try to correct for it.

As Herbert Simon has shown, we can make this correction conceptually, though practically we often lack the requisite data. Assume, for instance, that we wish to predict election pluralities but expect that some voters will switch to the "underdog" (or to the winner) depending on the plurality announced in our prediction. If we can estimate how this switching varies with the plurality predicted by us, we can adjust for its effect with a simple mathematical procedure so that our published prediction will come out right.[13] An analogous procedure to correct for self-fulfilling or self-defeating effects can be thought up for predictions that give the probability of a unique event.

The second feature peculiar to *social* predictions is most helpful to the predictor. Quite simply, it is the fact that people think about their deliberate efforts before they act and often talk about or otherwise reveal these thoughts. Hence, the predictor can use these advance signals while trying to foresee whether anything might induce or force the actor to abandon his project. For all political prediction this is as fundamental as it is banal. Hundreds of intelligence analysts search the utterances of political leaders for cues as to what these leaders intend to do next.

Second Step: Relating Predictions to Action

As soon as we relate "guiding predictions" to their purpose, a body of principles becomes relevant that is not to be found anywhere else in scientific activity. These principles are the subject of decision theory (and if our future can be importantly affected by an opponent, some game theory may also be relevant).[14] Now, I can say a little more in answer to my initial question as to how we can tell a good prediction from a bad one.

To put it broadly: A "guiding prediction" for the year 2000 should not attempt to describe our world in the year 2000, but should evaluate the consequences of our alternative courses of actions. Such a prediction can omit as irrelevant any aspect of the future whose consequences for us do not depend on our choice of actions.[15] In other words, it should omit those features of the future that we cannot shape more to our liking or render more or less tolerable, whatever we do. This exclusion does not exempt many features about which we care. (It exempts, of course, all the things that we expect will neither please nor hurt us.) For instance, should we predict that the climate will become warmer by the year 2000 and yet conclude that we can do nothing to prevent this, we would still have many choices among remedial measures. It is the consequences of these remedial measures (not only the unalterable climatic change) that our "guiding predictions" ought to predict.

Having explained what kind of predictions are irrelevant for our guidance, I still have not offered any criteria for telling the

111

good predictions among the relevant ones. Intuitively how to rank predictions seems obvious, and, indeed, in principle this ranking can be defined: A given set of predictions is better for us than another set *if* the future turns out to be more to our liking after we have been guided by this first set than it would have turned out had we been guided by the second set.

Alas, this definition is much less precise than its crinkled language may suggest. First, it discriminates predictions from hindsight only, whereas we would like to pick out the good predictions while they still can be of use to us. Moreover, even with hindsight we usually find it difficult to reconstruct how our future would have turned out had we been guided by some alternative prediction (compare the example of choosing between a Ford and a Chrysler car). Second, apart from the difficulty of predicting how various aspects of the future will differ depending on our policy, we also have to determine which of these variants is "more to our liking."

Furthermore, there is the question as to what it means "to be guided" by a set of predictions. In real life situations, we cannot deduce our ("rational") choices from a manageable set of predictions without first making some enormous abstractions. To arrive at these abstractions, we must rely on our "tacit knowledge" or judgment. One way of visualizing the kind of explicit decision problems that decision theory can handle is a so-called contingency table. In such a table, the columns are possible future states of the world that we wish to influence, the rows are alternative courses of actions among which we must choose, and the cell entries describe the value of the outcome in the event that we have chosen a particular action, and one of the specified states of the world has occurred. The abstractions are many, but the most striking one is that such a table selects just a few states of the world and a few courses of action, and tells nothing about how this selection has been made. That decision theory *presupposes* such abstractions is, of course, fully recognized by the experts, though not always by the laymen.

Once we have made the necessary abstractions, decision theory can help us not only in sorting out our choices, but also in improving the "guiding predictions" that precede our choices. It can advise us, for instance, on the following questions:

1. How to calculate our next decision from a network of inter-connected decision- and outcome-forks. (For example,

whether to choose A or B when, if we choose A, there is a one-third chance that X will happen, a two-thirds chance that Y will happen, and if X happens then. . . .)

2. How much money and time we should spend on the acquisition of new data to improve our predictions.

3. How much we should spend (or sacrifice) to enable ourselves to defer some choices until we know the future better. (The design of flexible institutions is one such procedure.)

Third Step: Predicting Our Values

Our values change. In 1985 we may prefer another alternative for the year 2000 than we did in 1965. This may in part be due to the fact that in 1985 we can see new consequences, say for the year 2010, of the alternative futures in 2000. We can look further ahead and discover that we would rather travel on a different road than the one which initially appeared preferable. Decision theory can help us with this problem; it shows us how to estimate whether we should defer our decision until 1985, and how much we should now pay for retaining the option to change our direction later on. For instance, a common procedure in the allocation of funds for applied research is to back several competing approaches. This permits one to postpone the choice of a particular technique until one knows more about one's future needs and technology.

Other changes in our preferences, however, are not attributable to new foresight but rather to new insights into our likes and dislikes. As long as we have to cope with just a few narrow issues on which our preferences might change, and as long as we do not feel attached to our present values on these issues, we can still use the principle of deferred decision. For instance, we can rent furniture if we are concerned about our unpredictably changing tastes in furniture. An example relevant to the year 2000 is the program for preserving wilderness areas. Even if we assume that those who favor commercial exploitation of wilderness areas outnumber those today who want to preserve these areas, we have good indications that these preferences might change. Since it is much easier to convert wilderness into an exploited area than the reverse, the principle of deferred decision argues for the retention of wilderness areas.

But more profound difficulties arise for our "guiding predic-

113

tions" from the fact that not just some isolated values keep changing, but a great many interconnected ones, including some to which we now feel strongly attached. Moreover, many of our variable values masquerade as "objective facts." I shall try to clarify this problem by using an analogy from historiography.

John Dewey claimed that all history is necessarily written from the standpoint of the present. And as Morris Cohen put it:

> No historian conscious of his task can avoid the problem of evaluation. The historian must have a point of view in selecting his material, a point of view that determines what is important and what is unimportant in the confused maze of human events.[16]

Sociologists concerned with social change also share this problem. They have recently rediscovered how difficult it is to measure social change, not just because statistics are lacking, but because we do not know what should be measured. (That we do not know what to measure accounts in part for the lack of statistical data.[17])

My observations about historiography and descriptive sociology also apply to social predictions. Indeed, it would be a fascinating exercise to sift through past predictions with the attitude of a historiographer—that is, to write a "predictography."[18] Nostradamus' prophecies evolved around plagues, monsters, and local dynastic quarrels, projecting the "violent tenor of life" that Johan Huizinga found characteristic of the Middle Ages. Edward Bellamy, in 1888, looked at the future in the light of the socialist ideals of the 1880's. H. G. Wells straddled at least two styles of "predictographies": the nineteenth-century technological optimism of the Crystal Palace expositions and the end-of-this-world experience of World War I. And what about the Commission on the Year 2000 of the American Academy of Arts and Sciences, as it met in 1965-66? The agenda of its predictions was almost identical with the agenda of President Johnson's "Great Society" as enunciated the year before. This marked tendency to select our topics for predictions from among our concerns of the most recent past should give us pause.

The historiography (or "predictography") problem of selecting for importance and giving meaning to a conglomeration of data is not the same as the problem of projecting inductive inferences backwards (or forwards) in time. Even if we obtained as much data about the future as the historians have about the past, we would still be as uncertain in our interpretations of the future as the historians are in their interpretations of the past. Hence, the difficulty of predicting our future has two components. One is what I called the first step in "guiding predictions": the problem of how we can foretell observations that we will be able to make at a later date—that is, the problem of the incomplete, or incompletely understood, regularity of the universe. If this were all a predictor need worry about, he could turn Leopold von Ranke's ambition into the future tense and try to show *"wie es eigentlich sein wird"* (without ignoring, of course, possible self-fulfilling and self-defeating effects of his predictions).

But the predictor, just like the historian, faces a second problem —that of interpreting his predicted data by giving them "a meaning." In particular, "guiding predictions" are incomplete unless they evaluate the desirability of the predicted aspects of alternative futures. If we assume that this desirability is to be determined by our future rather than our present preferences (I shall later reexamine this assumption), then we have to predict our values *before* we can meaningfully predict our future. Or rather, since our values will be affected by the future state of the world, we may face what mathematicians call a problem of iteration: We have to shift from evaluation to prediction and back to evaluation.

It depends on the particular domain chosen, whether it is easier to predict the raw aspects of the future or their "meaning" and desirability. Let me call the first component "data-prediction," the prediction of relatively[19] value-free data; and the second component, "value-prediction," the prediction of the "meaning" that future phenomena will have for us, or, to put it differently, the prediction of our preferences among these phenomena or of our future ways of looking at them. Four examples illustrate all four possible combinations of a high vs. a low predictability of the first and the second component:

1. *The School Board.* A school board wants to predict whether it should take some action to avoid overcrowding in next year's classes. Its "data-predictions" are trivial demographic estimates of the number of teachers and pupils next year, plus an engineering estimate of how many classrooms will be completed in the new building under construction. Its "value-predictions" are indices of crowding, using various pupil-teacher and pupil-classroom ratios. The predictability of both the data-component and the value-component are high.

2. *The Weatherman.* A meteorologist tries to advise us, for our trip to Paris in July, whether or not we should reserve a room that is air-conditioned. His "data-predictions" are the temperature, humidity, and perhaps a few other items for the specific days in July. His "value-predictions" are indices of our comfort based on these data (such as are now used in some day-to-day weather forecasts). The predictability of the former is miserably low; of the latter it is perfect.

3. *The Perfume-Maker.* A chemist tries to predict whether a not yet existing synthetic chemical will make a valuable perfume. His "data-predictions"—the specific weight, boiling point, and volatility of the chemical—are pretty good. But the predictability of the value-component—the odor-*Gestalt* of his new chemical—is almost nil.

4. *The Academic Committee on Technological Change.* A committee of learned men tries to predict the social impact of technological change. The data-component of its predictions are future industrial employment statistics, per-capita energy figures, costs of various machines, performance characteristics of computers, and so forth. By and large, this component has a rather low predictability. But the "value-predictions" of such a committee . . . what are they? Recently, a committee that met on just this question was unable to find an answer.[20]

I have deliberately chosen my four examples to mix up the domains of the physical and the social sciences. The predictability of the school board's problem, lying primarily within the social-science domain, is *high* both in its data- and value-component. But the social-science problems of the committee on technological change have *low* predictability in both components (particularly in the value-component). By contrast, the weatherman and the perfume-maker, who tinker mostly within the physical sciences, have trouble with *only* the first or the second component, respectively. Incidentally, this way of looking at predictions in different domains of science provides a useful corrective to the common view that predictions in the physical sciences are more accurate than predictions in the social sciences.

We can make many useful "guiding predictions" without having to ponder about their value-component because we can safely re-

gard the values as constant. For instance, should we reach the conclusion that in the year 2000 the U. S. population will not get their
teeth properly fixed unless we now start training more dentists, we
need not predict any change in our dislike of tooth decay. For less
pedestrian "guiding predictions," however, we may mislead ourselves badly if we assume constant values. Our next generation may
not only pursue different goals, but may judge the importance of
things differently. What looks like an important trend to us may be
ignored by our children even though it developed exactly as we
predicted. And what we ignored as being trivial—even though we
could have forseen how it would change—may become one of the
most critical issues.

Today, for instance, almost everyone who makes predictions
about the next few decades emphasizes the future exploits in outer
space. This seems like a safe prediction, since our boys now are so
interested in outer space. But how do we know that by the year
2000 people will not look at a new space exploit by NASA in the
same way that we now look at the completion of a new dam in
Oklahoma by the Corps of Engineers: The contractors and NASA
will be keenly interested, but our grown-up boys may not even
notice the event buried in the back sections of their newspaper.

Today we reject such an "unscientific" view of the world. We
believe that the giant engineering effort on outer space cannot but
have wide repercussions on science and technology and, hence,
alter the lives of us all. Indeed, nearly all contemporary predictions are nothing but variations of a theme—the theme that
scientific knowledge will further accumulate, and technology will
become more powerful, more pervasive, and more elaborate. I
must admit this theme convinces me too. Yet, I wonder if we are
not seeing the world from a rather narrow perspective, somewhat
like the medieval scribes who saw their past, present, and future
only in terms of religious and ecclesiastical events. While we find
it well-nigh impossible to visualize our future without further technological developments, we can nonetheless visualize that the
march of science might not turn out to be the cumulative enterprise that we had thought. Thomas S. Kuhn argues in his essay on
scientific revolutions that the cumulativeness of science is partly a
myth created by our textbooks, which refer only to those pieces of
the work of past scientists that can easily be viewed as contributions to current scientific positions.[21]

One can imagine other changes in our values and interests that

117

could make our current predictions for the year 2000 look badly out of focus. For example, a few decades ago the view prevailed that demographic "stagnation" was bad; yet today many people favor a stable, or nearly stable population. Economic stagnation, on the other hand, is still felt to be bad. Perhaps in the year 2000, more of us will favor John Stuart Mill's "stationary state," not only in the demographic sphere but also in much of the economic sphere (though not in culture).[22] If this happens, economic growth will be smaller than we now project on the basis of the current trade-off between more goods and more leisure. By the same token, people will *care* less about economic growth. Thus, our predictions regarding economic growth will not only be rather inaccurate, but they will describe what, by the year 2000, will be quite an uninteresting feature.

The influence of the present social environment upon the views and knowledge of man has long been recognized. In its somewhat old-fashioned way, sociology of knowledge has dealt with this problem. What concerns me here is that we be aware of this influence in trying to evaluate our "guiding predictions." Embedded in these predictions are today's preferences as to what is desirable and today's biases as to what is interesting.

Some Errors in Predicting

My original question—how we can tell a good prediction from a bad one—still defies a clear answer. Nonetheless, certain rules of thumb emerge, and some gross errors in predicting can now be identified.

To begin with, we must not confound the different purposes of predictions. When we need a "Buridan's-ass prediction," we should not demand that it really resolve our ignorance about the hypothetical outcomes resulting from possible choices in our dilemma. This kind of prediction helps us to choose not by resolving our ignorance but by resolving our indifference. Sometimes, when we face such a choice, we can fully accept the fact that we must decide between different routes without having any epistemological grounds for discrimination. At other times, we can overcome our points of indecision more easily by pretending that we are predicting which route is likely to be better for us. Neither the flipping of the coin in the former case nor the soothsaying in the latter has to be correlated with the *praedicendum* to serve our purpose.[23]

Likewise, we should be discerning enough to recognize when predictions are merely meant to entertain. As long as this entertainment pleases us, we can enjoy it without worrying whether the predictions are "accurate" or will come "true." Accuracy and coming true, after all, are irrelevant criteria for the worth of entertainment, and we should not confuse "guiding predictions" with a guessing game. It is only if we are playing the guessing game that we have to find out precisely *whose* prediction is right, and we wish to reject obvious predictions. For guidance, the obvious, easy to predict, can be of greatest value.

If we want to make "guiding predictions" rather than entertain, accuracy is no longer irrelevant, even though it may be difficult to judge. As said above, for the first step in "guiding predictions" we have to infer from past observations to future ones, using theories and empirical laws from all branches of science as much as we can. Second, we should not overlook the usefulness of logically true predictions. Third, we also have to rely on common sense (or "tacit knowledge") to place single events into classes, to estimate the likelihood of an event without having explicit frequency observations, and so forth. Fourth, the greater the role of this tacit reasoning, the more we must beware of the distorting effect of our emotions.[24] Since the error of wishful thinking has been advertised so much, we must also guard against overcompensating for it. Some predictors indulge in "prophylactic pessimism." They try to avoid disappointment by reasoning against their desires whenever their inferences are tacit enough to permit this.

Intuitive judgments play a particularly decisive role when we have to assign weights to various pieces of evidence in order to use them as samples for our *praedicendum*. (For example, how much weight should one give to the Greek civil war in making predictions about the war in Viet-Nam?) In this slippery, intuitive process, our emotions can sway our thinking. One common distortion is to give excessive weight to the most recent evidence.

In addition to distorted inferences about the future, "guiding predictions" leave room for other types of errors. These arise in what I called the second and third steps: in relating prediction to action, and in the prediction of our values. One common mistake is to ignore alternatives. If we predict only one future state of the world or only one version of a social problem, we usually exceed our capacity for making inferences about the future but leave unused our capacity to plan simultaneously for several alternatives.

Decision theory shows how we can develop a program of action to take account of several alternative futures. By allocating our resources among the alternatives, we avoid putting all our eggs into one basket and will do better in the long run than if we had considered only a single, most likely future.

There are other mistakes in relating prediction to action. Some predictions imply such a horrible course of action that we experience a failure of nerve and find ourselves unable to go through with the indicated choice. This might be called the "non-Freudian Oedipus effect." Oedipus' parents did not have the nerve to make sure that their son would be killed. By deliberately or subconsciously keeping the probability of their son's death significantly below one, they left a probability significantly above zero that their chosen course of action would lead back to the very contingency they wanted to avoid.

The way in which we predict the possibility of a thermonuclear war seems to be affected both by the emotional distortions of our inferences (wishful thinking or its reverse) and by this "Oedipus effect." The interaction of these effects creates wide swings in our estimates of the probability of war. For this reason, the idea of such a probability is very dubious indeed. Initially, wishful thinking makes us estimate the probability of nuclear war exceedingly low; then we notice this and correct for it; upon which we discover how unpleasant our lives would become if we acted as if we believed our higher estimate; hence we switch back again to a lower probability.

In a recent study based on predictions by a panel of experts, the estimated probabilities of nuclear war were so high that the panel could not have taken them seriously as "guiding predictions."[25] If these predictors had acted in accordance with their estimates, they would have had to rearrange their personal lives or at least lobby actively for a change in national defense policies (a vast increase in civil defense or deterrence measures). There is, however, also evidence that a panel of predictors can estimate their country's future involvement in a major war with astonishing accuracy (at least for the pre-nuclear era). In a poll taken in the New York area in April, 1937, 62 per cent of the respondents predicted another great European war would start between 1939 and 1945, and 73 per cent predicted the United States would not remain neutral.[26]

Finally, another error in predicting social phenomena is to pay attention to just those matters that are bothering us now. In our selection of topics for prediction, we tend to be swayed by our troubles of the recent past. We make the mistake of focusing our predictions where our shoe hurts. If we have been hurt particularly badly, our predictions will look backwards to our old pain for a long time. The Great Depression of the 1930's had a depressing effect on all social predictions; this cast a longer shadow into the future than the real dislocations of the Depression itself. On a number of issues, our predictions are only now recovering from the Great Depression. Thus, the volume *Recent Social Trends*, written just before the worst years of the Depression, takes a view of the future in many ways closer to our current agenda for predictions than the planning and forecasting done for some twenty years following the Depression. For instance, the committee findings in this volume speak of the "problems arising from the inventions in the field of communications" which break down "regional isolation all over the world"; "the problems presented by increasing leisure"; the problem of "the development of distant peoples for whose welfare the United States has assumed a degree of responsibility."[27] (Today we call them "less developed" instead of "distant.")

Predicting for or Against Social Change?

The truism that contemporary society is changing far more rapidly than societies in the past does not necessarily mean that our future is less predictable than was the future of our grandfathers. To be sure, technology will bring vast social changes (quite apart from the cataclysmic possibility of nuclear war). But in other respects, modern technology makes our lives more predictable—at least in industrialized countries—because it protects us from the vagaries of nature. Moreover, modern science has improved our ability to predict with precision and to prevent calamities that can be foreseen only as possibilities. This is true even for the oft-maligned social sciences. An impressive illustration is the pessimism expressed in the *Recent Social Trends* study (1929-32), regarding the impossibility of predicting economic depressions, let alone controlling them.[28]

How will the quality of our social predictions change as a result of future developments in science and technology? The problem of predicting the outcome of games may serve as a partial analogy. In chess, we can predict the outcome of an end game. By means of a computer this prediction can be carried somewhat further and done faster, but a modern computer is far too slow to predict the outcome of a complete chess game, although the game is analyzable in theory so that the winning strategy could be deduced from its rules. If we wish to predict a ball game, however, we do not know how to analyze it completely even in theory, much less in practice— what with the "random" effects of the players, the air currents affecting the ball, and so forth. Even vastly improved computers would not make a ball game deterministic, as they would a chess game. Predicting for society adds one more level of complexity. In the ball game we know from the outset what we wish to predict, since the method of scoring remains constant; but this is not the case for social predictions.

Some of the things I have said about prediction may serve to clarify a certain role of *conservatism*. Since we can make better choices the more we can say about the future, it is advantageous for us to keep our future more predictable by imposing controls on the rate of change. Thus, the conservatism of a society has somewhat the same function as the reliability of individuals. As Bertrand de Jouvenel puts it, "the network of reciprocal commitments traps the future and moderates its mobility."[29]

We are in a quandary, however, if we predict that our society might alter certain values to which we feel strongly attached. The anti-utopias, such as Evgenii Zamiatin's *We* and Aldous Huxley's *Brave New World,* have highlighted this question. In these stories the people are made happy; it is only the predictors and decision-makers of today who do not like these futures. If we let our choice of actions be guided entirely by the predicted future tastes of society, we would want to move into these worlds of tranquilized happiness. Still, we would have to choose which variant utopia to make our goal. Karl Popper is right in upbraiding the Marxists and their "unholy allies" for pretending that they know ("scientifically"—to boot) the new society into which we should move.[30]

It has been reported that General de Gaulle is anxious to stop the growth of integrated European institutions and to loosen the bonds of NATO while he is still in power, fearing that those after him might share the values of the "integrationists" in Brussels. Similarly, Mao is said to be worried that the next generation of leaders in Peking will be seduced into "revisionism" and begin to like it. From the point of view of their own political values, these two statesmen are the truly great conservatives of our age.

The real contrast to a conservative is not a radical or revolutionary who knows where he is going and reveals his conservative colors as soon as he gets halfway, but the man who wants change for its own sake. Most of us are still old-fashioned Faustians in that we want to be both. We want to predict so that we can better *conserve* our world and protect our values, and we constantly want *change*, since we enjoy desiring new goals. When it comes to predicting our goals, we are perpetual "revisionists," for we know that we can only follow the light at the prow of our ship.[31]

REFERENCES

1. For brevity I shall use the term *social prediction* for any statement describing people and political organizations at a future date. Some authors do not like to use the word *prediction* in this wider sense because they feel it conveys too much certainty. *Prevision* and *conjecture* have been suggested as alternatives. See Chapter 3 of Bertrand de Jouvenel's highly stimulating book, *The Art of Conjecture* (New York, 1967).

2. Leon Festinger, *A Theory of Cognitive Dissonance* (Evanston, Ill., 1957); J. W. Brehm and A. R. Cohen, *Explorations in Cognitive Dissonance* (New York, 1962).

3. This has long been pointed out in the texts on systematic policy analysis. See, for example, Herman Kahn and I. Mann, *Techniques of Systems Analysis* (Rand Corporation RM-1829-1; 1957), pp. 133, 142-43; and Albert Wohlstetter, in *Analysis for Military Decisions*, ed. E. S. Quade (Chicago, 1964), pp. 147-48.

4. A note on the criterion of plausibility: When a novel regarding the present includes events most readers would consider to be impossible, it is called a "romance" by the literary taxonomists. Similarly, when a futuristic novel seems improbable, we call it "science fiction" or "social utopia" rather than prediction. In either case, there is no clear dividing line.

5. H. G. Wells, *The World Set Free* (London, 1914), p. 104.

6. "War came at last in 1940," wrote Wells in 1932. "The particular incident that led to actual warfare in Europe was due to a Polish commercial traveller, a Pole of Jewish origin," who accidentally started a fight with some Nazis in Danzig. "For eight years now [by 1940] the German mind had been working up a fight over the Corridor, and the rearmament of Germany, overt and secret, had been going on." (*The Shape of Things to Come* [New York, 1933], pp. 191-92.) Apart from this passage, however, the ideas of this novel were not borne out by later events.

7. Daniel Bell, "Twelve Modes of Prediction—A Preliminary Sorting of Approaches in the Social Sciences," *Dædalus* (Summer, 1964), p. 865.

8. "Most of the propositions and questions to be found in philosophical works

are not false but nonsensical. Consequently, we cannot give any answer to questions of this kind, but can only establish that they are nonsensical. Most of the propositions and questions of philosophers arise from our failure to understand the logic of our language. (They belong to the same class as the question: Whether the good is more or less identical than the beautiful?) And it is not surprising that the deepest problems are in fact not problems at all." (Ludwig Wittgenstein, *Tractatus Logico-Philosophicus* [London, 1961], p. 37.)

9. Strictly speaking, this prediction is not completely analytically (logically) true. It starts from the empirical fact (not an analytical truth) that birth rates in nearly all areas of the world presently exceed death rates, and it adds the stated assumption that living space is finite. Implied in this assumption is the premise that people will not shrink in size to adapt an expanding population to a finite space. If one likes these word games, one can finesse this logically true prediction in various ways—for instance, by specifying the extent to which space travel might alter the limits of "living space."

10. Compare the quotation from Daniel Bell *supra* and Bertrand de Jouvenel's assertion: "Only probable statements can be uttered regarding the future." ("Political Science and Prevision," *American Political Science Review*, Vol. 59 [1965], p. 29.) I am only claiming here that logically true predictions are *more* certain than predominantly nonanalytic statements regarding the past, present, or future. Just how certain logically true predictions are is a question for the specialist on *a priori* knowledge.

11. Jerome S. Bruner, J. J. Goodnow, and G. A. Austin, *A Study of Thinking* (New York, 1956). Also M. W. Shelly and G. L. Bryan, eds., *Human Judgments and Optimality* (New York, 1964), especially Part 5.

12. Michael Polanyi, "Tacit Knowing: Its Bearing on Some Problems of Philosophy," *Reviews of Modern Physics*, Vol. 34 (1962), pp. 601-16; and "The Logic of Tacit Inference," *Philosophy*, Vol. 41 (1966), pp. 1-18. Olaf Helmer and Nicholas Rescher use the term *intrinsic expertise* to describe this tacit knowledge if it represents the professional judgment of experienced and learned men. ("On the Epistemology of the Inexact Sciences," *Management Science*, Vol. 6 [1959], pp. 25-52.) Helmer and Rescher are correct in stressing that predictions do not have the same logical structure as explanations. It seems unfortunate, in view of their many eminent contributions to philosophy of science, that C. G. Hempel and P. Oppenheim gave this futile thesis of the identity of predictions and explanations so much weight. This thesis merely amounts to a rather narrow definition of *prediction*. (Compare, Israel Scheffler, "Explanation, Prediction, and Abstraction," *The British Journal for the Philosophy of Science*, Vol. 8 [1957], pp. 293-309.)

13. Herbert Simon, *Models of Man* (New York, 1957), pp. 79-87.

14. Decision theory is only about twenty years old, apart from some forerunners. Yet, before the decision-theorist came along, people tried to follow more or less the same principles in making deliberate choices. The

decision-theorist seeks to make the application of these principles more coherent and free from error. The literature in this area has grown rapidly; see Paul Wasserman and Fred S. Silander, *Decision-Making: An Annotated Bibliography, Supplement 1958-1963* (Ithaca, N. Y., 1964).

15. Given various simplifying abstractions, it is possible to make a formalized statement as to what kinds of predictions are irrelevant. Various types of "irrelevance" of economic forecasts are described by Franco Modigliani and Kalman J. Cohen, *The Role of Anticipations and Plans in Economic Behavior and Their Use in Economic Analysis and Forecasting* (Urbana, Ill., 1961), pp. 20-27.

16. Morris R. Cohen, *The Meaning of Human History* (La Salle, Ill., 1947), p. 80. An excellent survey of this problem is given by William H. Dray, *Philosophy of History* (Englewood Cliffs, N. J., 1964), Chapter 3.

17. See Eleanor Bernert Sheldon and Wilbert E. Moore, "Toward the Measurement of Social Change: Implications for Progress," *Economic Progress and Social Welfare*, ed. Leonard H. Goodman (New York, 1966); and Albert D. Biderman, "Social Indicators and Goals," *Social Indicators*, ed. Raymond A. Bauer (Cambridge, 1966). Also the important book by Oscar Morgenstern, *On the Accuracy of Economic Observations* (2d ed.; Princeton, N. J., 1963).

18. Some work in this direction has been done; for instance, Jean Meynaud, "A Propos des Spéculations sur l'Avenir," *Révue Francaise de Science Politique*, Vol. 13 (1963), pp. 666-88.

19. Data—any data—are difficult (or impossible?) to extricate completely from values. As Abraham Kaplan put it: "Data have meaning and this word 'meaning,' like its cognates 'significance' and 'import,' includes a reference to values." (*The Conduct of Inquiry* [San Francisco, 1964], p. 385.)

20. Some of the unsolved questions of this committee (as clarified by the editor of its report) were: How can technological change be measured? Can automation be operationally defined? Eli Ginzberg, *Technology and Social Change* (New York, 1964), p. 144.

21. Thomas S. Kuhn, *The Structure of Scientific Revolutions* (Chicago, 1962), p. 137.

22. John Stuart Mill, in his eloquent chapter, "Of the Stationary State" (*Principles of Political Economy*, IV, 6), argues against universal population growth and never-ending economic growth, but maintains that "a stationary condition of capital and population" does not imply a "stationary condition of human improvement."

23. Bertrand de Jouvenel, in his interesting justification of ancient augury, overlooks this purpose by seeking to justify augury exclusively with the possibility that the hocus-pocus and the *praedicendum* are correlated. De Jouvenel, *The Art of Conjecture*, pp. 89-90.

24. A number of studies have investigated the effect of people's preferences on their intuitive ("subjective") probability estimates. A study now thirty years old is still worth reading: Douglas McGregor, "The Major Determinants of the Prediction of Social Events," *Journal of Abnormal and Social Psychology*, Vol. 33 (1938), pp. 179-204. A more recent article is by Ward Edwards, "Utility, Subjective Probability, Their Interaction and Variance Preferences," *Journal of Conflict Resolution*, Vol. 6 (1962), pp. 42-51.

25. T. J. Gordon and Olaf Helmer, *Report on a Long-Range Forecasting Study* (The Rand Corporation, P-2982; 1964). Incidentally, the fact that people tend to weigh the most recent events excessively seems reflected by the extent to which this panel lowered the twenty-five-year probability of a major war between June, 1963, and January, 1964. (Why should this twenty-five-year probability be substantially lower after the nuclear test ban, given that the sample of events in the previous eight years included both the Cuban missile crisis and the 1955 "Geneva spirit"?) Some of the vagaries of estimated probabilities of war are described by Albert Wohlstetter, "Technology, Prediction, and Disorder," *Bulletin of the Atomic Scientists* (October, 1964), pp. 14-15.

26. Hadley Cantril and M. Sherif, "The Prediction of Social Events," *Journal of Abnormal and Social Psychology*, Vol. 33 (1938), pp. 364-89.

27. *Recent Social Trends in the United States.* Report of the President's Research Committee on Social Trends (New York, 1933), pp. xxvii, li, xli.

28. *Ibid.*, pp. xxix-xxx.

29. Bertrand de Jouvenel, *The Art of Conjecture*, p. 45.

30. Karl Popper, *The Poverty of Historicism* (New York, 1961), p. 70.

31. This is an expanded revision of "On the Epistemology of Social Predictions." The original version (distributed to the Commission on the Year 2000) was published in French in *Analyse et Prévision* (July, 1967). I am indebted to Bernard Cazes, Edmund Leites, and Paul Keckskemeti for critical comments.

DONALD A. SCHON

Forecasting and Technological Forecasting

DURING THE last five years, and particularly in the last two, there
has been among government, private industry, and the intellectual
community at large a wave of interest in technological forecasting
that itself constitutes a trend of no mean interest.[1] This trend
raises a number of questions:

What do we mean by technological forecasting?

How is it related to forecasting *per se?*

To what extent is technological forecasting feasible?

What are its limits or constraints?

To what extent is it currently practiced?

To what use is it put? To what use should it be put?

How do our objectives in undertaking it indicate what our approach to it should be?

Technological Forecasting

By "technological forecasting" I mean the forecasting of technological change. The technology that changes is the set of tools
and techniques—"hard," as in the case of new machine tools, or
"soft," as in the case of new computer programs or methods of
work—by which we extend human capability. It is useful to divide
the process of technological change into three stages: invention,
the creation of a new product or process; innovation, the introduction of that product or process into use; and diffusion, the
spread of the product or process beyond first use. A technological
forecast, therefore, is the forecast of the invention, innovation, or
diffusion of some technology. It simply asserts either that an inven-

127

tion not yet made will come to be made; that an existing invention will come into use at a certain time and in a certain manner; or that some technology, already in use, will spread at a certain rate and in a certain direction. A technological projection is a conditional assertion that one or more of these propositions will be true *if* certain other conditions are met (for example, that numerically controlled knitting machines will come into heavy use in the U. S. apparel industry if the growth of the market for knit goods continues at the present rate). Technological forecasting, in this limited sense, is practiced relatively infrequently and is of little interest to potential users inside or outside the U. S. Federal Government.

What *is* of interest, and what frequently passes for technological forecasting, is the forecasting of something else—industrial growth, for example, or employment—of which technological change is one component. A great many organizations, as diverse as industrial corporations, banks, investment firms, labor unions, and government agencies, undertake such forecasts and are very much interested in their results. Research on forecasting methodology, in this sense, is very much on the increase. Such forecasts might be called technology-related.

In fact, technological change is so closely linked to social and economic factors that no prediction about the one can be made without assumptions, implicit or explicit, about the other. An apparently nontechnological economic forecast rests on the assumption that there will be no economically significant technological change counter to the forecast. But technological change may be, and in many forecasts of the greatest interest is, of relatively minor importance to what is being predicted. For the most part, therefore, I will be talking simply about forecasting, with the understanding that all of it is in some degree related to technological change.

Most technological forecasts concern themselves with invention or the diffusion of existing inventions. There are few occasions when an effort is made to predict the first use of an invention without attempting to predict some aspect of its diffusion as well.

Predictions of invention fall generally into the category of informed opinion, based on grasp of a complicated field and offered as though the field had a life of its own. In the simplest cases, these are simply presented as one man's opinion, as in Dennis Gabor's *Inventing the Future*.[2] In other cases, opinions are pooled or averaged, as in a recent Rand Corporation study.[3] In the U. S. Air Force effort, Project Forecast, opinions are gathered from experts about development of new physical phenomena—effects or materials—and their implications for possible future systems (aircraft, for example) are worked out more or less systematically.

A number of writers on technological change—notably Buckminster Fuller, Ralph Lenz of the U. S. Air Force, and Robert Ayres of the Hudson Institute—have developed approaches to the forecasting of invention based on "envelope curve" analysis. In this sort of analysis, certain technological parameters—for example, engine thrust-to-weight ratio, maximum transport speed, or operating energy of particle accelerators—are plotted over long periods of time (1800 to 1960, in the case of maximum speeds). It is then assumed, as a first approximation, that the growth curve may be extrapolated to some future time (for example, the year 2000), and that the necessary inventions will be made and applied so as to make that growth possible. Lenz, for one, has claimed that it is useful to extrapolate from such envelope curves in most instances in terms of continued *logarithmic* growth, and to deviate from this assumption only when persuasive reasons are found for doing so. Ayres treats envelope curves as big "S-curves" made up of many smaller ones, where decrease in the rate of growth occurs as the curve approaches upper limits of physical possibility.

Envelope curve analysis is not, strictly speaking, a forecast of invention but, rather, of the effects of sequential inventions on some engineering parameter. Its predictive use depends on choice of parameter and on estimation of the place in the curve, in relation to the present, at which a leveling-off will occur, or, in Lenz's terms, on the correctness of the assumption that engineering parameters tend generally to grow logarithmically. Deviation from an extrapolated curve can always be explained, however, on the ground that the wrong parameter was chosen for analysis.

Most technological forecasts do not forecast invention. They assume invention—in fact, they usually start with invention already introduced—and go on to predict the rate or direction of diffusion. There is some reason for this. In general, the time-period of diffusion is so long (from fifteen to twenty years in most instances, depending on the character of the technology and the circumstances of its introduction) that if we are concerned with *doing* something about technological change, we have little reason to be interested in any technology that has not already been brought into use. In his report to the Automation Commission, "An Investigation of the Rate of Development and Diffusion of Technology in Our Modern Industrial Society," Frank Lynn points out that there is no reason to be concerned with "technological early warning systems" since, technologically speaking, the future is already here. The radical decrease in the time-period required for widespread diffusion during the last two hundred years (thirty-seven years for the total development of technologies introduced in the early-twentieth century; fourteen years, on average, for those introduced after World War II) does not significantly change this finding. There is no more reason to suppose that diffusion periods will decrease indefinitely than there is to suppose that engineering parameters will increase indefinitely.

There are a number of approaches to forecasting rate and direction of diffusion of technology. One approach analyzes historical diffusion curves (some measure of use—dollar volume, number of units in use, or the like—plotted against time). It then goes on to identify characteristic curve-shapes,[4] or to formulate conditions governing rate of diffusion.[5] Either approach *could* be used to forecast diffusion, again assuming that the technology in question acted as though it had a life of its own, but neither, to my knowledge, has been much used in this way.

A second approach tackles diffusion of technology on an industry-by-industry, or even product-by-product, basis.[6] Ordinary industrial market forecasts are undertaken for the sake of assessing the effect of technological diffusion on, for example, manpower, industrial growth, or corporate profits.

Studies of this kind usually take an eclectic approach. It is assumed that rate and direction of diffusion are functions of total market available over time, or total potential applications. These are seen as varying with some features of the user community—rate of growth of population, rate of growth of user industries, and so forth. There may also be an effort to take into account the number of units already introduced, the rate at which they have been introduced, the percentage of untapped market remaining, the capacity of producers to make the new unit, the economics of introduction of the unit, competitive pressures for its introduction, competing technologies, and characteristic trends of users with respect to the replacement of capital equipment. These are only a few of the factors that may be and often are relevant. In addition, there are problems about defining potential markets and about identifying potentially competitive technologies. There is often invention in the choice of potential application, and forecast of the rate and direction of diffusion of a particular technology implies forecasts of the new technologies with which it may compete and of the rate and direction of *their* diffusion. Unanticipated events—shifts in corporate or government policy, wars, changes in consumer preference—may affect forecasts adversely. Moreover, it is hard to confirm such forecasts. In the case of market forecasts, there is a special problem about confirmation since action taken on the basis of the forecast may influence the trends forecasted. In general, efforts at forecasting of this sort attempt to juggle variables in an intuitive manner, to *Gestalt* the process, rather than to present themselves as applications of rigorous theory.

Depending on the criteria chosen for accuracy, on the time span of the forecast, and on the degree of technological novelty involved, a forecast of this kind has a greater or lesser chance of succeeding. For example, forecasts of the rate and direction of diffusion of synthetic fibers over the next five years have a high probability of being accurate to plus or minus 15 per cent. Forecasts of the rate and direction of diffusion of numerically controlled production equipment over the next ten years have a much smaller chance of being right within that margin of error. The probability of a technological forecast is directly proportional to the allowable margin of error and inversely proportional to time-span.

The diffusion of technology takes place in a complex economy and, more broadly still, in a total, complex culture. The most interesting approaches to forecasting technological diffusion are those that attempt to locate diffusion in these contexts.

It is possible to deal with technological diffusion at a very high level of aggregation and abstraction. While productivity (taken roughly as Gross National Product divided by the number of workers working) is a function of many factors in addition to technological change, change in productivity can be taken as an index of at least one kind of technological change. Projections of national productivity, such as those undertaken by the Bureau of Labor Statistics are in this sense projections of technological change. In comparison to the diffusion of particular technologies, it is possible to be relatively accurate about forecasting national productivity. It is reasonably safe to say, for example, that national productivity will increase, on the average, by 2.5 to 3.5 per cent per year over the next ten years. Small differences and deviations from the average can, however, be of critical importance with respect to the uses to which such forecasts may be put. Again, productivity projections are *Gestalt* processes that combine productivity trend extrapolation, consideration of output and manpower trends, and trends in demand for goods and services, capital investment, and the like.

At a lower level of abstraction and aggregation, efforts are now under way to adapt the techniques of input-output economic analysis to projection of technological diffusion. Wassily Leontief of Harvard and Marshall Wood of the National Planning Association, for example, are attempting to incorporate changing, as opposed to static, input-output coefficients in models of the national economy. These changing coefficients would reflect changes in production processes significantly dependent on the introduction of new technology. Models of this kind would be used to provide more accurate projections of economic development and of diffusion of production process technologies through repeated processes in which economic change is fed back to influence projection of technological diffusion. In his current work, Wood concentrates on technological change in the form of introduction of new capital equipment. He views this introduction as a function of average age of existing equipment and of demand for industrial output relative to existing capacity. The productivity of available new equipment in particular industrial fields would then be fed into the model in order to permit projections of change in process coefficients.

Forecasting

There is no social or economic forecasting to which technological change is not possibly relevant. Many kinds of forecast are actually of interest to government and to other institutions, and many more are of potential interest. These are most easily grouped according to the uses to which they are put.

All forecasts are used principally for planning; in the Federal Government the planning may be either for specific programs or for broad policies. Those concerned with program and policy planning can be grouped as follows: use of natural resources; industrial growth and development; economic growth and development, both national and regional; manpower supply and demand; research and development.

132

In spite of their various uses, most of these forecasts share a common methodological approach. Certain baseline trends—growth of national product, labor force, productivity—are taken as basic and extrapolated to some future time. These trends are then modified by other quantitatively described trends or qualitative judgments covering other factors. Considerations of technological change usually enter forecasts as judgmental factors of this kind, modifying a basic trend in output, productivity, or the like. In forecasting demand for manpower in specific industrial occupations, for example, it is customary to make a basic analysis by projecting demand in those industries first for goods and services, and then for productivity. The analyst modifies this baseline projection by such considerations as projections of retirement rate or restructuring of jobs through technological change.

Again, forecasts become more interesting and more nearly convincing as they become more nearly complete. The efforts by Resources for the Future to predict trends in the nation's use of natural resources gain in credibility because they juxtapose trends in resource utilization throughout the economy as a whole. Predictions of the future use of aluminum in automobile engine blocks must be tested against predictions of the use of steel for the same purpose; these comparative projections must stand up in the light of projected production methods, costs, and properties for both metals.

Methodological Problems

It will be useful here to outline some of the practical and theoretical obstacles to effective forecasting. These apply, in varying degrees, both to forecasts generally and to technological forecasts in particular.

Efforts at forecasting are plagued by a lack of appropriate, uniform, complete, credible, and timely data. Because there are no formats for standard data or mechanisms for collection and analysis, there is little reliable, uniform, credible data, for example, about the economic and process characteristics of new production equipment. Moreover, as producers are unwilling to reveal information they consider proprietary, there is an inability or unwillingness to generate such data in the first place. Getting the data in time may be as critical as getting it at all, as when we attempted in 1965 to make forecasts to 1975 on the basis of 1958 data.

There is currently no adequate theory that spells out the necessary and sufficient conditions for technological change; nor is there any particularly promising candidate. Technological change cannot be well understood, and certainly not anticipated, if one assumes that it behaves as though it had a life of its own. Any instance of technological change can best be understood as an event in a total socio-economic-technical system. We know enough about such systems to understand that they are characterized by large numbers of interdependent variables. These variables change according to differential rates, and small rate changes may be highly significant for the system as a whole. Because the system is characterized by dynamic feedback, it is in complex ways self-controlling.

Efforts at understanding technological change are now fragmented. Economists tend to look at a small number of relevant factors, such as trends in output and in demand relative to capacity; technologists and students of technology often view technology as though it had a life of its own; and sociologists tend to relate it to the characteristics of social systems. There is, to my knowledge, no effort being made to develop a more nearly complete theory.

In the absence of adequate theory, forecasting—including technological forecasting—relies on the projection of trends related to a small number of variables, modified qualitatively by intuitive judgments. Such forecasts or projections always make us ask whether the future, for those few variables, will be like the past. We can observe rates of increase in productivity over the last twenty-five years, for example, and make trend projections into the future. Such projections, however, are always open to these questions: Will the productivity trend in the short-term future exhibit rates of increase that have held only on the average for long periods in the past? Will these average rates of increase continue to hold, or will they shift? Will manufacturing productivity, for example, behave as it has on the average for the last ten years, or will it change so as to approximate the long-term curve for agricultural productivity? With respect to manufacturing productivity, what kind of a curve are we on and where are we on that curve?

There are special problems about the prediction of *rate* of change, such as rate of diffusion. There is a lack of information as a basis for rate projections. Characteristically, predictions of rate of diffusion tend to be optimistic for the short term and pessimistic for the long.

When we come to anticipate the effects of the interaction of trends—for example, the rates of expansion in automotive use of steel and aluminum—we are in the position of the weather forecaster who is able to predict movement of fronts with reasonable accuracy, but lacks adequate means of anticipating the outcome of their collision.

Is it possible, in principle, to have an adequate theory of technological change, assuming that such a theory presents necessary and sufficient conditions of technological change and permits prediction with a high probability of accuracy? There is a special problem about any theory that presumes to permit prediction of invention. In one sense, a prediction of invention *is* invention, and the prediction fulfills itself. To claim that a theory permits prediction of invention is to claim that a theory permits invention. On the other hand, the prediction of invention may mean only prediction of some characteristic of invention (such as "numerically controlled textile machinery") or an objective of invention ("an increase of 50 per cent in thrust-to-weight ratio for aircraft engines") without specifying the means for accomplishing it. Predictions of this kind hinge on judgments about such factors as technical feasibility, cost, willingness, and alternative research routes. They share, consequently, the problems of any theory that claims prediction concerning the future states of complex socio-economic-technical systems.

It is by no means clear that such systems are rational and convergent and lend themselves to theories from which accurate predictions can be drawn. If we act as though they are, our behavior rests on an ungrounded methodological assumption. The observation that certain patterns have held historically provides no basis for assuming future rationality when the very matter at issue is whether the future of social systems will be like their past.

Moreover, there are many different ways of looking at technological change. We may, for example, see it as being conditioned by response to competition; controlled by the need to curve-fit available labor supply; or precipitated by increased demand or the wishes of a corporate executive. Taken singly, these alternate ways of looking at technological change may be useful in particular situations. When we attempt to apply them together to a specific forecasting problem, they confront us with more information than we can handle.

We operate always from within the most deeply held assumptions—what Marshall McLuhan calls the "spell"—of our own society. Those who looked toward the future in the eighteenth and nineteenth centuries operated under a mechanistic, visually oriented bias that is apparent to us now. Do we not operate under a similar cultural spell the nature of which we will perceive only as we emerge from it? Our technology—the subject of our predictions—also helps to determine the theories under which we make predictions, since it provides the metaphors out of which our theories are made. Perhaps most importantly, our cultural assumptions determine what we think *relevant* to predict.

Forecasts may function as self-fulfilling or self-defeating prophecies, particularly when a prominent public institution such as the government makes them. There is evidence, for example, that predictions made in the 1950's concerning imminent shortages of scientists and engineers produced a change in patterns of enrollment in graduate schools of science and engineering that has, in turn, produced surpluses. Any prestigious public utterance of this kind about the future is likely to affect people's behavior. Alleged predictions become performative. This is a kind of uncertainty principle in the realm of social systems.

Attitudes Toward Forecasting

In the light of such considerations, many writers maintain that forecasting, technological or otherwise, is either impossible or undesirable. Others, less concerned with the dangers of self-fulfilling prophecy than with methodological inadequacies, assert that significant forecasting is premature. They claim that years will have to be spent working out theories of social development, and technological change in particular, before we can begin to talk about meaningful forecasts.

But there is a second view; although it admits the weakness of current forecasting methodology, it emphasizes the ways in which the conduct of public and private programs requires planning and forecasting as necessary ingredients. If managers must make policy and program decisions that will have future impact—such as decisions about long-range federal policies or about investment in research and development or in productive capacity—they base their decisions on forecasts. Decisions about investments in research and development imply forecasts about the relative utility of alternative technical routes. Decisions about educational and training curricula imply certain assumptions about future requirements for skill and knowledge. Such forecasting assumptions are often unavoidable in the sense that even the decision *not* to make them carries with it the implicit assumption that relevant present conditions will not change within the range of the forecast.

It should be noted that not all decisions are of this kind, only those that suffer from being made after the fact rather than before the fact. The decision to provide welfare payments and unemployment insurance, for example, rests on certain broad assumptions about the future, but these assumptions have very little specificity. The decision would not necessarily be unwise, even if the occasion for making a payment never arose. Except within very broad limits, the success of the policy does not depend on the government's anticipating how many people will request such payments, or when or where they will do so. On the other hand, training and counseling programs are designed to act in anticipation of future events and rest, implicitly or explicitly, on assumptions about future employment requirements. Decisions about policies and programs should be made with an eye to the kinds of forecasts that successful implementation would require. If a program or policy requires accurate, specific, long-range forecasts, that is a strike against it.

Nevertheless, there are many program and policy decisions, in government and out of it, that rest unavoidably on assumptions about the future, including assumptions about technological change. We should, therefore, address ourselves to the forecasting task as explicitly and intelligently as possible. This implies, from what has been said above, that we see forecasts as tools or aids for decision rather than as assertions about the future. We must look to forecasting tools, in their present state, for insights rather than for answers, and guard against the public use of forecasts as self-fulfilling prophecies. We should seek to improve forecasting methodology by determining data requirements and improving data availability, and by developing more complete theories of the socio-economic-technical systems in which we are interested. We should also try to merge the currently specialized professional approaches to technological change, regarding it as only one component of a complex socio-economic system. Furthermore, we should devote more attention to testing and confirming or disconfirming those forecasts that have been made and are now being made.

There is a tendency among those interested in forecasting to concentrate on the methodology rather than its use. Our approach should be to begin with potential use and user requirements, and to move on from there to relevant methodology.

Still, there is no guarantee that technological change, within the economic and cultural context, is a rational and convergent system. The complexity of interacting trends, the cultural spell that determines our sense of predictive relevance, the self-fulfilling character of public forecasts—all confront the forecaster with more information than he can handle. His response to this may take the form of a new rationalism, a drive toward ever more complex simulations of real-world processes. Or it may take the form of increasing concern for and skill in the *process* by which insights about the future can be used and unanticipated events responded to.

Our increasing sense of need for planned response to change drives us in both directions. It requires increasingly sophisticated simulations of social and technological processes that we can use effectively only in existential ways. And it requires fleet-footed reaction to the unanticipated—a strategy of flexible response, in which tools for the provision of insight play a major role.

REFERENCES

1. One of the signs of the times was the establishment in 1966 of an Inter-agency Task Force, which I headed, addressed to the role of the U.S. Federal Government in technological forecasting. I have drawn this paper from the work of that task force and from subsequent reflection in connection with the Commission on the Year 2000.

2. Dennis Gabor, *Inventing the Future* (New York, 1964).

3. T. J. Gordon and Olaf Helmer, *Report on a Long-Range Forecasting Study* (The Rand Corporation, 0-2982; 1964).

4. Everett M. Rogers, *Diffusion of Innovations* (New York, 1962).

5. Edward Mansfield, "Technical Change and the Rate of Imitation," *Econometrica* (October, 1961).

6. Approaches of this kind have been taken by the Bureau of Labor Statistics in its "36 Industry" study; by Corplan Associates, in its studies of industries in the Chicago area; in the Bureau of Labor Statistics' study of numerical controls; and in Peter Haase's study of three industries for the Department of Labor: "Technology and Manpower in the Health Service Industry, 1965-1975"; "Technology and Manpower in Design and Drafting, 1965-1975"; "Technology and Manpower in the Telephone Industry, 1965-1975" (U.S. Department of Labor, 1966).

MARTIN SHUBIK

Information, Rationality, and Free Choice in a Future Democratic Society

UNDERLYING THE concepts of the free market and the democratic voting process are some implicit models of man both as a rational, informed individual and as a decision-maker with an important freedom of choice. The rational utilitarian man, the Invisible Hand, and the democratic vote may be regarded as forming a trinity for an economic and political faith in a free-enterprise democracy.

Changes in society and in knowledge have caused us to question all of these concepts. The behavioral sciences, especially psychology and economics, and to some extent political science, sociology, and anthropology, have provided new tools with which one may examine them.

What are the economic and political values that a democratic society wishes to foster and preserve? What conditions must be imposed on institutions designed to obtain and maintain these values? What assumptions have been made implicitly or explicitly in current doctrines concerning the role and the nature of the individual?

Numbers, communication, the growing importance of joint property and services, as well as the speed of change in knowledge and information, force a reconsideration of our concepts. In terms of the democratic state and its citizens, we must re-examine power, equality, freedom of choice, ownership, centralization, "fair shares for all," "to each according to his needs, from each according to his ability," and many other appealing yet ill-defined words and slogans.

Both implicitly and explicitly much of our economic and political thought draws upon the peculiarly rationalistic basis of utilitarianism. Rational economic man in the economists' model is someone who knows what he wants, what his choices are, what his resources are. His value system is assumed to be well defined; his cool, consistent mind quickly and costlessly scans the myriads of alternatives facing him. His flawless discernment enables him to spy subtle differences in quality. He even calculates the value differences between the "giant economy size" and the regular pack. Many an economist realizes, however, that this is not so; that gaps in information exist; that *homo economicus* is not always certain of his desires. Yet it has been felt that the utilitarian model of the maximizing man with complete information is a good approximation. How good an approximation and of what are questions that remain to be answered. As technology grows, markets expand, and societies grow in size, the individual's share of the knowable decreases drastically. More and more the question becomes: How much should one pay for information the worth of which cannot be evaluated until it has been obtained?

Given clear preferences and complete knowledge, rational behavior amounts to following a consistent plan of action toward one's goals. The optimal program may be very complex, but it is well defined. Modern decision theory, economics, psychology, and game theory recognize, as a basic case, clearly motivated individual choice under conditions of complete information. It is also recognized that two unfortunate facts of life remove us from the relative simplicity of this basic case. The first concerns man as an information processor and the second the conflict of individual with group preferences.

Man lives in an environment about which his information is highly incomplete. Not only does he not know how to evaluate many of the alternatives facing him, he is not even aware of a considerable percentage of them. His perceptions are relatively limited; his powers of calculation and accuracy are less than those of a computer in many situations; his searching, data processing, and memory capacities are erratic. As the speed of transmission of stimuli and the volume of new stimuli increase, the limitations of the individual become more marked relative to society as a whole. *Per se* there is no indication that individual genius or perceptions have changed in an important manner for better or worse in the last few centuries, but the numbers of humans, the size of the body of knowledge, and the complexity of society have grown larger by orders of magnitude.

Perhaps the eighteenth and nineteenth centuries will go down as the brief interlude in which the growth of communications and knowledge relative to the size of population, speed of social and political change, and size of the total body of knowledge encouraged individualism and independence. By its very success, this brought about the tremendous need for and growth of knowledge reflected in the research monasteries, colleges of specialists, and cloisters of experts of the twentieth century's corporate society.

Dr. Johnson observed that there were two types of knowledge: knowing something oneself or knowing who knows it. In bureaucracies it is often said pejoratively that "it is not what you know but whom you know." Both of these observations are reasonable in terms of a world in which the gathering and evaluation of information is costly. As the number of individuals, things, and concepts grows, it becomes more and more difficult to maintain a constant relative level of information. The languages of signs, sounds, and motions provide us with methods of coding vast amounts of information in a compact manner. An experience shared can often be called to view at a glance by those who shared it. Yet even with our ingenuity for coding, the overload grows, especially if we wish to maintain values that stress individual men not as small component parts of the social intelligence, but as individuals.

If we believe that our political and economic values are based on the individual who understands principles, knows what the issues are, and has an important level of knowledge and understanding of his fellow citizens, then the twentieth and twenty-first centuries pose problems never posed before. Quantitative change has brought important qualitative distinctions. Specifically, how viable is the jury system for cases with technical evidence? How close must we move to formalizing concepts of statistical justice where the costs and time in the process, together with impersonal probabilities of being caught, become more important considerations than the case itself?

In spite of growth in communications, has there been any considerable change in the number of individuals that a person can get to know well? Since spatial distribution has changed, the individual may select his friends from a larger set. Yet regardless of the growth of modern science and the speeds of transportation, an evening with a friend, except for the transportation factor, will still call for the same amount of time to be expended in the twenty-first century as in the nineteenth. It has been suggested that 7! (5,040) citizens is the optimum size for the city state. Span of control literature suggests 7 as the largest span. George A. Miller's "magical number 7 ± 2" discusses the data-processing implications of this number.[1]

Taking a few crude calculations we observe that if half a day a year is needed to maintain contact with a relatively good friend, then there is an upper bound of seven hundred people with whom we could have much personal interaction. How many cases can the judge handle? How many patients can the psychiatrist treat? Is personal interaction becoming a luxury that modern mass society cannot afford, or are there new social forms and institutions that will foster and preserve it?

In voting do we have criteria other than a blind faith in the "stolid common sense of the yeomen"? The growth in the size of the electorate and in the numbers and complexities of issues is only exceeded by the torrents of writings in which the public may be buried if it so chooses. In the jungle of municipal politics, even the well-educated and relatively more articulate part of the population is woefully under-informed. At what point does a division of labor become a division of values and of social responsibilities?

The second fact of life that limits any simple view of individual rational men with freedom of choice, who wisely select actions so that their private welfare coincides with the public welfare, is that, given the preferences of all, market mechanisms and voting procedures will only succeed if very special conditions prevail (even assuming complete information). These conditions were indicated in writings from Adam Smith onwards. They call for certain technical properties to hold for the production processes in society; it is necessary to consider that the preferences of the individual are either completely independent of the welfare of others or subject to very strict limitations (such as being identical). Furthermore, the conditions go against intensive specialization, as many individuals are needed in all walks of life in order to avoid the dangers of monopolization. It is doubtful that conditions for the smooth functioning of the price system were ever applicable to the majority of the economy of any society; in general, they do not hold. As the size of the population and cities grows and as modern communication and information technologies weld previously independent groups together, the chances for the conditions to hold become even more diminished.

The aggregation of individual wants and powers into social wants and powers is one of the central problems of political science, economics, and sociology. We are currently in the position where we need to, and may be able to, answer certain fundamental questions concerning the possibility of constructing institutions to satisfy desired properties for the relation between the individual and his society. In particular, we are at least able to formulate in several different ways concepts such as equality, centralization, and power, and to ask if it is at least logically possible to discover methods for making diverse aims of a society consistent. It is neither obvious nor true that there may be any institutions that enable our desires for decentralization, dispersion of power, and equality (or equity) of distribution to be simultaneously satisfied.

These casual comments should be taken merely as preliminary and somewhat disjointed notes calling for the rethinking of some of our models of political and economic man so that they fit the pattern of the uncertain decision-maker acting under severely restricted conditions of information embedded within a communication system upon which he is becoming increasingly more dependent. His freedom of scope is limited by the powers of others; as these powers become more numerous and technology permits quicker communication, his actions become more deeply intertwined with those of others. Given our view of man, and for the moment assuming no great biological changes, we need to explore the arithmetic of economics and politics for the restrictions on the societies of the future.

Where will we be in the year 2000 or 2100 is far more a problem in control and anticipation than in prediction. Man has succeeded so far because of his incredible flexibility and adaptability. Now that he has learned to control fantastic sources of energy and to create devices in the form of computers and communication equipment that promise to aid his intellectual and organizational abilities, his power to manipulate the future has grown tremendously.

Knowledge has grown, and our abilities to analyze have increased. Has there been a like increase in either individual or social wisdom? Additions to human power without like additions to wisdom could set up the conditions for the destruction of civilization. The case has not yet been proved in either direction. Whether this society will destroy itself or not cannot be answered even with the proliferation of modern weaponry.

We may not be able to specify sufficient conditions to guarantee the preservation of values and of man. It is possible, however, to consider some necessary conditions. These involve a thinking-through of a political economy for the modern world. We need to touch upon conceptual problems dealing with measurements and the logic of society's control of itself, and to re-examine both the values to be preserved in our society and the role of modern technology in the attainment of its goals.

Problems are often complex and cannot be explained in a few sentences. The market mechanism is not sufficient to solve the problems of optimum allocation in our society. The voting mechanism in combination with the price system may provide a way, though not necessarily an optimal one, for the achievement of society's goals. Our beliefs and desires may call for a preservation of both the market and voting mechanisms at the federal, state, municipal, and corporate levels. Nevertheless, many modifications are possible. The period from 1930 to the present can be characterized by a tremendous growth in the means and measures of economic control. National income accounting, input-output tables, gross national income figures, and other monetary measures came to the fore. The next thirty years must be characterized by the development of social statistics and measures for the control of the services and joint processes of society. What are the measures by which to judge the performance of the police, education, social services, justice, and so forth? Such measures will undoubtedly be complex and subject to dangerous misinterpretation. (For example, how are the police to be credited for crime prevention?) Because of the difficulties involved in constructing suitable measures, it may easily require decades of devising and revising the appropriate indices and processes for obtaining them.

Compulsory levels of sanitation and education are not regarded by any except a small minority as limitations on freedom. Does this also hold for the draft, Medicare, taxation, or fluoridation of the water supply? In the next few years, birth control and possibly even genetic control must be considered seriously. The nature of government for a multi-billion-person world (and, eventually, planetary system) is neither quantitatively nor qualitatively the same as that required for an isolated New England village. What freedoms do we intend to preserve? Perhaps it would be more accurate to ask: What new concepts of freedom do we intend to attach the old names to?

The purely academic economic, social, or political theorist may claim that we can scarcely define values, can hardly measure them, and cannot compare them. Only the Philistine or the administrator

144

faced with the problem dares to ask the question, "What price should we pay to increase the safety level for an astronaut?" In spite of themselves, the behavioral sciences have been forced to become applied sciences. Measurements have been and will be made that many claim are impossible. Even the crudest approximation provides a guide for behavior where a decision *has* to be made.

The influence of the high-speed digital computer upon society cannot be underestimated. If we wish to preserve even modified democratic values in a multi-billion-person society, then the computer, mass data processing, and communications are absolute necessities. It must be stressed again that they are necessary, but not sufficient. Using an analogy from the ballet, as the set becomes more complex and the dancers more numerous, the choreography required to maintain a given level of co-ordination becomes far more refined and difficult. The computer and modern data processing provide the refinement—the means to treat individuals as individuals rather than as parts of a large aggregate.

The treatment of an individual as an individual will not be an unmixed blessing. Problems concerning the protection of privacy will be large. Once established, the universal identification number will mean a great release from the drudgery of having to use a dozen cards to establish one's credit rating. A computer check of central files could supply the individual with an extensive dossier whenever he needed it. It could, however, also supply the dossier to others unless appropriate checks on availability are established.

Devices on automobiles or other property may be invented in order to keep track of their use. This would enable societies to enforce tax schemes for the use of joint assets that are closely related to individual use—such as parking space and roads. Computers would do the accounting, meter reading, and billing. Once more we are confronted with questions concerning privacy. At what point do we wish to stop "Big Brother" from watching our every move?

Voting patterns could change by use of the "instant referendum." With the availability of a computer console as a standard consumer good as commonly available as a television set, it would be feasible to present the electorate with the opportunity to vote directly and immediately on a variety of issues. Not only could they be asked to vote, but they could be supplied with information by direct library interrogation prior to casting their vote.

Computer and other modern information technology can make it possible to preserve or even to extend the treatment by society of

145

the individual as an individual. His own memory and internal data processing may not change, but information technology will increase by several orders of magnitude his ability to obtain information and to store and retrieve it externally.

The growth of numbers of people, amounts of knowledge, and speed of change in technology work against the individual being in a position to exercise free, reasonably well-informed, rational, individual choice concerning much of his destiny. The advent of computing and communications devices to aid both in the obtaining and analysis of information has provided the possibility of preserving and possibly extending the individual's freedom. Technology is necessary, but it is not enough. Sophisticated devices and sophisticated measures and methods for the co-ordination of behavior in a complex free society may call for a sophisticated society with sophisticated individual members. If we wish to preserve and extend our freedoms, to permit the growth of world population to tens of billions, to increase the world's standard of living, to explore and possibly colonize space, then the next changes may well have to be within ourselves.

REFERENCES

1. George A. Miller, "The Magical Number Seven, Plus or Minus Two—Some Limits on Our Capacity for Processing Information," *Psychological Review*, Vol. 63, No. 2 (1956), pp. 81-97.

LEONARD J. DUHL

Planning and Predicting: Or What to Do When You Don't Know the Names of the Variables

FORECASTING WAS once an honorable occupation for seers and magicians. In more recent times we have tried to take it out of the area of magic; it may now range from an educated guess to a genuine attempt to find methods that make accurate prediction possible. Essentially, forecasting is a kind of game, even though it has become a very serious game with business and government alike pouring enormous amounts of money into attempts to predict the consequences of given sets of policies, actions, decisions. It would be advantageous if we could truthfully say, "Business and government alike are pouring enormous amounts of money into attempts *to learn how to predict* the consequences. . . ." In some instances, the second version would be correct, but not in all, and most certainly not in enough instances.

Some forms of prediction are feasible now. We can predict with reasonable accuracy what kinds of people will succeed in certain types of jobs. Even the number of tests that must be used for this kind of prediction has been reduced to a manageable lower limit. It is possible to predict within varying margins the probability of sales going up or down in certain consumer areas at certain times of the year. The variables for that sort of analysis have become available to us out of experience, hunch, and some research. Given reasonably good conditions for weather forecasting and a knowledge of the current economic state of the nation, we can predict approximately how many people will die in automobile accidents over a Labor Day weekend. We cannot predict with any reasonable accuracy, however, what the long-range effects of large-scale automation are going to be on the economic and cultural patterns of the nation, although it is now possible to begin observing and even measuring certain kinds of indicators. In an area as broad as this we are still *speculating*.

147

We can predict well in situations that involve few—and identifiable—variables and with which we have had many experiences. But in most areas of social planning, we cannot even extrapolate with reasonable reliability how a single policy statement on housing will effect educational and segregation patterns, mortgage interest rates, or the building trades twenty years from now. But it is this kind of prediction—or extrapolation, to use a term I prefer—that the social planner is attempting.

In my files I have a compilation of students' views on planning. The students ask, with beautiful candor: What is a planner? What is the process of planning? What are the limits of planning, of the planner's potential effectiveness? What are the ties between social concerns and housing, between social concerns and transportation? *What is the nature of our society, and where and how should it be altered?*

This final question would be easy to confront if one were writing a utopian novel. Like Plato or B. F. Skinner, one would decide on the ideal citizen in an ideal life situation, and then construct the social system that would produce such individuals and citizens.

Unfortunately, the planner is not in the position of constructing a new and ideal social system. He is involved in a very complex task: He must decide what in the system should be changed; persuade a majority that his decision is valid on empirical, moral, and legal grounds; and, finally, find ways to involve large segments of the affected population in implementing the actions he is advocating.

The planner is an agent of change, and any agent of change is a planner. It does not matter whether he is a politician, a producer, a businessman, an administrator, or an educator. There are many kinds of planners, each performing different functions and fulfilling different roles, depending upon the specific problem or situation with which he must deal. What is essential to his definition as a planner is that he be concerned with instituting change in an orderly fashion, so that tomorrow something will be different from what it is today.

The short-range planner has immediate objectives, and his function is to delineate a step or a series of steps that will achieve these immediate and pressing objectives. The long-range planner has more scope and more time. His goals may be less specific and call for an evolving policy that permits and encourages certain actions.

He also runs much greater risks, because the distance in both time and space from his objectives increases the possibility that some of his planning may have unexpected consequences—consequences that are at serious variance with his original intentions. The short-range planner runs the risk of fighting brush fires without reference to what his immediate actions may mean for the long run; the long-range planner can be tempted to treat planning as the utopian novelist treats his material—to assume that he can structure a series of steps that will *surely* result in a particular long-range consequence.

But in truth the planner's information sources are the critical element in his functioning. The more complex the problem he is attempting to analyze—in terms of present realities, discernible trends, and so forth—the more tempting it becomes to assume that the future can be structured just as we want it if we simply develop the proper scientific techniques. Thus, the planners turn to systems analysis and ecological models in their attempt to identify and manipulate the complex of factors underlying causality. Unfortunately, the information available is that all too familiar top of the iceberg, and reliance upon it alone can be dangerous.

No matter how much information can be collected by the techniques of the hard sciences and mathematics, we are a long way from being able to computerize the interplay of forces that operate in social conditions, whether the social laboratory be a settlement house, a neighborhood, a nation, or the United Nations. Alter a stress here—merely a minor stress—and you may find that the alteration has produced nine other stresses, different and perhaps not so minor, at nine other points in the social structure.

Perhaps the most obvious example of the American tendency to let enthusiasm guide progress toward disaster has been our super-highway system. In general, super-highways were calculated on the basis of what transport engineers determined to be the current demand. No one stopped to wonder whether the existence of the super-highway might change the pattern of the demand—and the patterns of emigration and industrial sprawl—so drastically that within two years of completion a super-highway was a very wide expanse of road on which fifteen thousand automobiles were stalled for two hours until the car that had broken down in a middle lane was towed away.

By now we are less naïve in many areas, and planners attempt to find ways to anticipate the social consequences of planning and

149

policy decisions. But as long as systems continue to open up, as long as information is channeled to all portions of the globe and creates increased aspiration without an accompanying increase of training for special skills, as long, in fact, as messages conflict, the actual predictability of our future will be faulty. The input of information constantly redefines the situation, the problem, and the possible range of solutions.

This essay is not an attack on the scientific method. We must continue to use technology and science to try to evolve a theory of prediction that incorporates *process* as a constantly changing— but definable—variable. In the meantime, however, we must remember that planning for the future will be inaccurate to varying degrees so long as the planning process deals with human beings— with their idiosyncratic, nonrational behavior. For it is the nonrational and the idiosyncratic that turns the planning process into a technique with results somewhat less predictable than those of roulette.

The planner or forecaster must, therefore, be not only an agent of change. He must know how to guide change as the therapist guides his patient. He must be concerned with processes, with assuring that a dialogue is initiated and continued. A never-ending process of interaction—confrontation and counter-confrontation —must take place so that both specific and general goals, as well as trends, can be identified.

In one sense this makes it necessary for the planner to be an astute politician. In our system, politics is a process of conciliation and reconciliation, of accommodation between competing interests. The political system limits the real power of one man to put a plan into practice. The system is both more and less controlled than most Americans like to admit. Politicians do in reality have the power to put bad plans into effect; but planners, if they are bad politicians, may not have the real power to put good plans into operation.

Few of the participants in this volume would argue that change is not critically necessary. But it is equally critical that change take place in a democratic fashion; that it be the product of a wide consensus, not the fiat of an expert. To function as an agent of democratic change, the planner must conceive of himself as a kind of "therapist" to the community. The therapist is presented with problems of the present, born of the past, with the request that he help the patient alter his system of response so that the future will

150

be different and bring different results. If the therapist cannot or does not help the patient, the patient will search elsewhere for answers.

If the therapist concentrates only on the present, he will fail to anticipate the future. The problem must be understood in terms of how circumstances and processes in the past have led to circumstances and attitudes in the present, and which aspects of the process must be altered in order to alter the outcomes in the future. For this, information and data are vital. If, however, the information is confined to what is readily available, the therapist will be no better able to propose solutions than the patient. The therapist must gather data on the interactions between the patient and his environment—using environment in the sense of situations and persons; the more adequate the data gathered by the therapist, the deeper his understanding of the problem and the wider the range of alternative solutions he can find. But equally important is the therapist's ability to interpret his data to the patient and to help the patient redefine the problem as new data are gathered. As the problem is redefined, the actions necessary to cope with the problem may also need to be altered; both patient and therapist must always be aware of this.

This is essentially the process the planner faces. Let us take, as a case in point, the war on poverty. When the President focused the attention of the American public on the problems of poverty—vast issues of economics, housing, voting rights, transportation, education, and health—he began certain irreversible processes that were to have a profound impact on every town and citizen of this nation. The responses to the challenge posed by this *definition of a social problem* varied dramatically, from absolute apathy or hostility to some genuine action programs. But the problems were posed in such general terms, and the responses made so hastily that planning in a scientific sense did not take place. The implications of the public statements about the problems and the steps that would be taken to cope with them did, however, have measurable results. They vastly increased expectations; they momentarily dissipated apathy and lethargy among the dispossessed; they stimulated hope.

With the best intentions in the world and an inadequate budget, various agencies on the federal, state, and local levels began to do planning. But for the most part it was planning without research. Inevitably, the frustrated expectations found expression in outbursts of rage; Watts is, perhaps, the best example of this process. The Watts outburst was a crisis—and change often comes only after a crisis. In Watts, the crisis brought forth declamation, acclamation, and disconnected federal funds, but not much in the way of concrete research for effective planning action. Where was the forecaster, the planner, the agent of change, the therapist who predicted what would happen in Watts before it happened? Studies had been contracted and effected, and people had been concerned, but planning had not produced action leading to change; and without such change, there was anger. There were many reasons for this, a primary one being that the planning did not involve the "patient"—the residents of Watts and the power structure of the city and state. The therapist cannot produce change in the patient by an act of will. The process requires the patient's participation not only in the actions that lead to change but in the evaluation of what in the current situation needs to be changed. Even with such joint effort, planning actions may fail, but at least their initial chances for success will be improved.

The planning problem is, therefore, twofold. First, we do not yet have the tools to plan with scientific accuracy, nor are we finding systematic ways to develop them. Second, accepting this limitation, our planners have not understood that their primary concern must be to develop a sensitivity to *process* among all the people who must be involved in planning activities. This sensitivity implies an ability to see the society or aspects of it as an *ecological system* and to recognize that balances shift with every change in the system. The planner must be able to analyze these shifts quickly and to readjust the plans if the shifts are in the wrong direction.

This implies that the planner must be as much involved in educating as he is in planning. He must attempt to get the fullest participation in the planning process from the widest representation of the society—in other words, to keep in mind that the planning process must go hand in hand with the democratic process. The democratic process is effective and fair to the degree that it is operating among an enlightened electorate.

The recent confrontations of the society by civil rights advocates and members of other heretofore "slumbering" depressed groups are both exciting and disconcerting. In one sense, they demonstrate how people respond to an opportunity for participation. They have stirred up the system. They have also made many Americans (themselves included) aware that true democratic participation is uncomfortable and threatening, slow and arduous.

The planner must bring to the forefront ideas, thoughts, and concepts heretofore not part of the public consciousness. He then must provide the guidance and the education that will help the newer participants learn to use the political process effectively.

True democratic participation means that society must seek as a legitimate activity the education of the poor so that they can confront the system through political organization and command a response. Moreover, the system must also confront the professionals, and the professionals must counter-confront the system. One group or faction has to accept the danger implicit in the growing power of another group or faction.

Democratic participation does not mean that there must be a poor man—black, brown, or white—in every office or on every organization board. It does mean, however, that representation on all levels must be assured. It follows that lawyers, planners, architects, educators, and doctors will, at certain times, assume advocacy for special-interest groups—be they the poor, the Negroes, the Indians, or the Mexican Americans.

The crucial concerns relate to ethics and values—the ability of the therapist or planner to be nonmanipulative, yet to set the stage for people to participate in the solving of their own problems. Any professional in any field is as subject as the slum dweller to preoccupation with internal needs, his own perceptions, views, and conceptualizations of the issues at hand. Confronting our problems and then expanding our understanding to see how other people's perceptions of these problems impinge on ours are frightening experiences at first. The planner must, in a practical sense, demonstrate that just as there is no single therapy for heroin addiction, there can be no single solution for any of society's ills—he must do this even while he is diagnosing the ill and insisting that some therapy be instituted.

Current policies, programs, proceedings, even agency personnel become subject for question, for examination, for evaluation and analysis. At all levels of society we find unwillingness to relinquish or even alter familiar and functional patterns of behavior. The paramount objective of the planner is to help the members of any group reconceptualize current problems in terms of long-range goals, to show them how, in terms of known and familiar situations, the planning goals are both necessary and practical, and of value to everyone in the system, not just to the immediate objects of the planning. In short, he must minimize fear and anxiety while urging the "patient" (or institution) to look ahead even while he (or it) is performing his daily functions.

The political nature of the planner's efforts becomes clearer as he collects, controls, and feeds information into the system. The process can seem overwhelmingly threatening. Innovative collection and correlation of information imply that previously independent organizations within a system have become integrally involved with one another. Wasteful duplication and repetition could be prevented if lines of communication founded upon similar directions, values, and goals could be established and made responsive to feedback. It is obvious that the planning body must be centrally involved in the running of an organization. But, even though the project programmers and effecters should be closely involved in the determination of goals and in the reorientation of the organization, the planning sector needs to remain distinct from the sectors of the organization that expedite the programs.

Secretary of Health, Education and Welfare John W. Gardner terms a "self-renewing agency" one in which the total organization (and the consumer of the services) participates in redefining its own problems. Successful self-renewal depends upon employing the model of complex causality and remaining alert to ever changing goals. Maximum involvement by all who have mutual or complimentary interests must be sought. Often a disinterested outside consultant—an experienced, knowledgeable, unprejudiced, and respected person—can best initiate and aid in the development of this process.

But beyond formal organizational structures there are "invisible colleges"—the loose aggregates of individuals scattered throughout the nation and the world who periodically communicate with one another. They are sociologists, architects, lawyers, doctors, teachers, and others whose avocation is "change" and how it might be effected. All are intimately involved in reality—some participate quite actively in the affairs of an organization; others have removed themselves from decision-making by becoming an adviser, a consultant, an assistant.

Their communications are via the telephone, the Xerox machine, and the jet. They meet, exchange information, ideas, theories, and concepts. Tied neither to time, place, nor position, they operate on many different levels at the same time. They are a link between industry and government, between the public and private sectors, between the federal, state, and city governments, between the

154

governments and neighborhoods, between the money givers and money receivers, between the theorists and activists. Their value lies both in their access to information from many sources, and their rapid dissemination and utilization of that data. Differing combinations of these agents of change may assemble for many purposes: to explore the possibilities of and to launch a New Town, to discuss a Watts and its implications for planning, or even to weigh the impact of systems technology upon forecasting. The long-range planner must connect informally with one or another level of these "invisible colleges," for the information developed and passed on in them is not of the typical census type, but part and parcel of the day-by-day reality of social systems and the people functioning within them.

These planners are not dreamers. They have cultivated what Sir Geoffrey Vickers has called "the art of judgment"—the process of making decisions in the present that dramatically affect the future. They are experts in combining and reformulating data and information, in redefining the problem and, most importantly, in causing others to feel they must do likewise. They achieve this by presenting additional information relative to the issues at hand in a way that convinces others. They are experienced in working imaginatively with performance criteria or specifications and rebel against performance standards that are not potentially multi-applicable. They have the ability to "feel" data. They have an appreciation of the implications of decisions and how they might affect a staff as well as tangential activities.

No mechanism can keep track of all of the irrationalities and the idiopathic responses of the many complex systems that affect human behavior. These unforeseen irrationalities may be a greater determining factor for future events than any of the more rational activities. The "invisible colleges" may, therefore, prove more effective in the long run than more formalized mechanisms. Marshall McLuhan has asserted that sense will be made out of the irrationality of input not by making the input more rational, but by creating mechanisms that are competent to deal with the irrationalities.

The planner-forecaster who has a goodly share of philosopher-educator-therapist in his personality will be the most understanding and the most effective. If he also has political skill, fortitude, and persistence, he will be the most adept. His talent for linking, connecting, and communicating makes it possible to create mechanisms for planning that respond to a society of idiosyncratic humans. In essence, the planner-forecaster's role is that of orchestrating people and institutions and organizations. In performing this role, he operates to restore to a complex society something of the "democratic" and "representative" flavor it possessed in simpler times. He operates, in other words, to return the franchise to society's membership to some extent.

We too often find ourselves preoccupied with attempting to divine what will be our state ten, twenty-five, even fifty years hence. But what we often fail to realize is that every decision made, every voice heard and not heard, and every success and failure drastically affect that future. Instead of speculating on what the world might be like in the year 2000, we would do well to consider what mechanisms, what people, and what decisions must be attended to today in order to shape all the years to come.

HARVEY S. PERLOFF

Modernizing Urban Development

WE CAN imagine a very exciting urban future for the year 2000, but some difficult problems must be solved before this future can be realized. At present about 140 million Americans, out of a total of 200 million, are classed as urban dwellers. By 2000 at least 280 million, out of a total population of about 340 million, are expected to be living in urban areas. If certain of our present urban trends were to continue, we would have some extremely serious problems on our hands in the year 2000. Water and air would be dangerously polluted. An increase in pollution at rates now characterizing some of our bigger cities would make relatively pure air and water among the scarcest and costliest of all natural resources. Traffic congestion in the air over our cities would be horrendous. Open space close to where people live would be so scarce that the use of park and other open recreational areas would probably have to be rationed.

Central cities would be more segregated than ever. They would contain a majority of nonwhites while the surrounding suburban and exurban areas would be white. Slums would still be very much with us, and the central cities would continue to be the gathering ground for the poor and disadvantaged. Some of the larger cities would have all the appearance of being "ungovernable." Reliance on the Federal Government would increase to the point where local governments would merely be agents of the former. The gap between the rich and untroubled suburban communities and the central cities—with burdensome public service requirements and relatively limited tax capacity—would be greater than ever.

Most new construction would be extensions of present suburbs, a large proportion in one-income, one-race enclaves that keep undesirables out by zoning and taxation. Some New Towns would cluster around major metropolitan areas, providing an attractive environment for the residents, but they would be beyond the reach

157

of lower-income families. There would also be some very impressive green belts to keep undesirables out.

Long commuting trips, cross-tripping of Negroes and whites, downtown congestion, and lack of parking space would be the order of the day. New super-highways would be cutting cities to ribbons, and yet intown transportation would continue to be a headache.

This exercise is useful only in highlighting some of the more obvious present difficulties. Of course there will *not* be more and more of the same in the year 2000. The grossest failures will be recognized as such, and changes will be made—although certain things *will* probably get worse. To identify these, one looks for the points at which there are imbalances in the impacts of technology, unresolved value conflicts, institutional gaps, or, most important, outmoded controlling ideas. The term *modernization* is most appropriately applied to this last element, as it is very often a question of bringing ideas up-to-date in terms of the realities of the objective situation.

When dealing with incremental improvements within a larger system that is generally highly productive and decently self-adjusting, the "out-of-kilter" elements—in technology, institutions, value conflicts, and guiding ideas—can be seen most sharply in terms of conceptual-cum-operational focal points. These serve to highlight the disjointed elements, and are treated here more for illustration than in an effort to be definitive.

The Natural Environment: "New" Resources in an Urban Age

Some of the present urban problems are associated with a substantial divergence between individual costs and benefits and social costs and benefits. Such divergence tends to be particularly large in the case of natural resources where, by definition, supplies are limited compared to demand. Normally this kind of situation calls for public subsidies or penalties to bring private action more closely in line with calculations of social costs and benefits.

In an earlier period when the nation was under pressure from some threatening shortages and a well-organized and effective conservation movement, it came to accept this policy with regard to rural resources. The natural environment that is particularly under pressure today is of a different sort than it was when the nation's population and economy were more rural. "New" natural resources have come into being—urban-oriented resources, in contrast with the traditional primary-commodity resources associated with productive activities of farming, forestry, fishing, and mining. Urban growth has, in effect, converted certain free goods into economic goods.

Far from being a stable factor, resource endowment is subject to continuing change. During our agricultural period the natural endowment that counted most was arable land with its environmental components of climate and water. With industrialization a whole new set of resources in the minerals category became important. By the middle of the twentieth century, as material resources dominated industrial location less and less, and as technological and other changes brought about a long-range reduction in the proportion of raw materials to total output, these "commodity" resource effects were playing themselves out. For example, since 1870 the gross value of output of extractive industries has dropped from one third of Gross National Product to around 11 per cent. Other kinds of resource effects began to influence economic activity as well as patterns of living. Amenity resources—climate, seashore, and a pleasant natural environment generally—began to exert a strong pull on both industries and people.

Natural resources have always been defined as those parts of the natural environment that have value to mankind because the demand for them exceeds the limited supply. It is in this sense that "new" resources, other than the traditional ones of agricultural land, water, and minerals, have increased in value.

In this light *urban land* is particularly valuable. Just as we had to learn to use agricultural land with special regard for its qualities and the demands made on it, so we will have to change our view of urban land. Today its use is haphazard and largely unthinking. We have not yet learned to ask ourselves, for example, whether we want to use a third, a half, or two thirds of our urban land for the movement and storage of cars. How much are streets worth to us—underground, on the surface, above ground?

Equally important, or possibly even more important, we now have to conceive of yet another critical resource: the third dimension of the city—the space over the urban land. This is used even more haphazardly than the land itself. Just on the horizon is a host of problems caused by elements competing for this limited resource—high-rise buildings, interbuilding walkways, high-level and

159

air-cushion highways, and private rooftops. This space over the city is an asset that must be conserved, developed, and used with the greatest care. Two-dimensional land-use planning is out-of-date, and we urgently need to learn how to prepare three-dimensional plans.

We are also just beginning to grasp the notion that within metropolitan areas relatively *clean water*—for consumption, for recreation, for production, and for aesthetic value—is a resource of the greatest importance. More recently we have come to understand that relatively *pure air* is also a "new" kind of resource. If the present rate of fouling the air continues, by the turn of the century pure air could well require a greater public and private annual outlay than any other single resource category. It could become the "scarcest" natural resource in the sense of experiencing the most sharply increasing costs. Because of this, we will have to change our current conception of air as a "free good." It has been suggested that air will have to be regarded as a common domain to be managed under public tenure, as the Bureau of Land Management administers many grazing lands in the West. Invasion of the domain by polluters may then be regarded as trespass, and the cost of control assigned to the polluters in a way that will motivate them to reduce noxious emissions.

It is equally important to realize that waste in enormous quantities is an integral feature of modern urban-industrial societies and that its disposal must be planned for in this light. We need to conceive of production, consumption, and waste disposal as part of a total system, making cost-benefit analyses for public policy within this sequential-process framework.

Another of our "new" resources is open space in and around congested urban communities. Such open space has many actual and potential uses. High on the list are recreation and ecological protection, particularly of water basins, but also of lakes, forests, wildlife preserves, and the like. Open space is also valuable as land reserves for planned future urbanization. In spite of these significant requirements and potential uses, we know that throughout the nation vacant land on the fringe of metropolitan areas is being consumed at the rate of approximately one million acres annually with little guidance or control.

Against this background it is evident that better approaches must be developed and new institutions created in order to achieve a positive, self-sustaining, self-improving situation. As with our traditional resources, we must see our "new" resources—the urban land, the open space, the air above us, and the urban waterways—as integral parts of our national wealth. If a national wealth account or a national balance-sheet account were to be developed—even if the estimates were very rough—the nation might be brought to appreciate fully how valuable these resources are.

We have progressed from a focus on conservation, seen essentially as a negative concept—the idea of leaving alone or rigidly controlling—to a focus on the need for sound development and use. The idea was not to "go back to nature" (with the exception of relatively rare resource endowments, such as wilderness areas), but to develop resources in a positive way to meet man's needs as seen broadly and over a long period of time. In the same sense, the negative view has limited application to our "new" resources. For example, the negative approach to land development (particularly in the critical open areas at the edges of the city) through zoning and subdivision control provides relatively limited leverage for the creation of a more satisfactory environment. Similarly, the present approach to our airways problem, based largely on limited controls on commercial aviation (and even more limited civilian control over military aviation), is cleary inadequate. As a general principle, the approach to urban-oriented resources should be through positive development and use. One version of such an approach is the "New Town" concept. By their very design and location, New Towns permit better use of urban land, open space and airspace, and recreation facilities. In the same light, we should renew our existing communities in such a way that targets for achieving purity of air and water and adequate standards with regard to space and recreation are translated into positive development procedures. For example, regard for the appropriate location of industries should be translated into general standards permitting wide flexibility, rather than into negative zoning procedures alone.

Similarly, there is need for the positive design of the rural countryside and for the planned use of nearby rural lands. The problem is not merely to prevent land from being used for urban purposes. All that this normally achieves is an unattractive sea of weeds. It is much better to think in terms of the positive use of the countryside; for example, maintaining farms city children can visit for both recreational and educational purposes, or leasing open land for use by various groups in camping and in other related recreational activities.

161

Segregation, Poverty, and Slums

The slum has long been viewed as a prime urban "problem." The established approach goes back at least to the early part of the century when the horrors of the slums, particularly those in New York City, began to be brought to national attention. The view has been that the slum represents all the evils of the city—decay, crime, disease, disorder—and must be eliminated by public action. In fact, starting in 1937, the removal of the slum has been declared national policy.

While the relationship between slums and poverty, discrimination, and segregation has long been recognized, the full implications of their juxtaposition or special "mix" in the American city of today has yet to be seen clearly. It should be evident that to overcome the "problem" of the slum it will be necessary to overcome, or at least to mitigate, the problems of poverty, discrimination, and segregation. This is a question not only of outmoded ideas, but of significant and unresolved value conflicts. The middle-class American would like to see the urban slums cleaned out and Great Cities built; but he also shows a strong preference for "living among his own kind." (In fact, the way the "system" works out, as one wag has suggested, each person achieves his optimum position by living in a neighborhood where everybody is just a little richer than he is.)

We have begun to deal with the problem of poverty, although we have not yet admitted that to "solve" the problem we must provide, in one way or another, an income floor for everyone. We are even further away from clarity on the segregation issue. Substantial progress toward racial integration is a key not only to the equal-opportunity goal but also to the goal of humanizing the urban environment. Unfortunately, not only is the problem an inherently difficult one, but we now must pay the price of past neglect. More education for Negroes in the past, more civil rights, more job assistance, more of almost anything else decent and helpful would have made the problem of racial integration easier today. But here we are up against America's Achilles' heel, the most vulnerable—and shameful—part of our social fabric. Almost two thirds of the population of Washington, D. C., is Negro (and over 90 per cent of the students in the public elementary schools). Baltimore, Philadelphia, Chicago, St. Louis, Cleveland, and other cities will soon have Negro majorities. Unless something is done to halt the trend, America's central cities will become almost exclusively black, and the surrounding suburbs almost exclusively white by the end of the century.

The problems that grow out of the "ghettoization" of the cities are severe and self-reinforcing. Mass, unrelieved segregation means that effective community dialogue is cut off. Denied the traditional routes to effective political and economic power, the Negro is increasingly tempted to turn inward or to attract attention to his problems by violence. But violence breeds more violence—one cannot easily forget the photograph of the white teen-agers in Cicero with their signs proclaiming the swastika as the symbol of "white power." And denial begets denial until even the minimal requirements of a merely adequate—no less, great—society are threatened.

It will take tremendous resources, imaginative new solutions, and effective political infighting to reverse present trends, or even to make a dent in them. There are, however, promising possibilities that we have not yet begun to tap. We could build New Towns in the outlying sections of our metropolitan regions with federal financial assistance and, therefore, with built-in requirements for housing lower-income groups and racial integration. If these new communities were attractive and the housing costs quite low, many white families might overcome their reluctance to live in mixed communities. Also, public suburban development authorities might be established that could select the site, acquire the land, and prepare it for sale to private builders, and then terminate in a municipal corporation. Such an authority could take care to balance commercial and industrial property with residential, and concerns about the tax base with the needs for public services. But the key feature would be *open occupancy*. Thus, a major purpose of these New Towns would be to create communities so attractive that families without hardened prejudices could be lured out of safe, homogeneous suburbs into an exciting variety of small and large satellite and balanced cities.

We could also build "New Towns—in town" that would have greatly improved public services and facilities (good schools, in particular), exciting "lighted centers" for fun and shopping, intown industrial estates, and a great variety of housing. The creation of such communities would involve the application of the basic New Town principles to the gray areas of our cities. By making life in the city truly attractive, we would provide a more favorable environment for youth growing up in a city and bring middle-class whites back into the city.

163

The creation of such new communities should have as a prime objective the broadening of alternatives and the extension of diversity in urban life styles. In general, the alternatives available today make restrictiveness more attractive than openness, and community interaction a matter of crowding and annoyance, as in super-stores and on super-highways.

Both the outlying and the intown communities might well experiment with novel forms of broad political participation and more effective local representation in larger political units. The long cherished concept of local self-government is being eroded through neglect and institutional decay. It is doubtful that the PTA is the ultimate in local participation. The community-action programs under the poverty program have set off some interesting sparks that suggest lively local representation may be within reach. This is a fine area for experimentation.

Once we realize that by the year 2000 urban environments will have to be provided for as many additional people as are now living in our cities, the possibilities appear in their true dimensions. The critical missing link in our present institutional capacity to solve the thornier urban problems might be filled by the ability to create totally new communities—in both open and intown areas—specifically designed to achieve significant political and social ends. We must grasp the full implications of that felicitous concept of "inventing the future" and begin to tap some of the many open-ended possibilities offered by our rich and basically flexible society.

The developments suggested will undoubtedly mean large governmental outlays, substantial land purchase by public authorities (probably as important for sensible urban development as land grants were for rural development), public assistance to encourage genuine mass production of low-cost housing, additional governmental regulations of construction and urban development generally, and the creation of new kinds of institutions through government initiative. Moreover, concepts of private property will undoubtedly undergo some significant changes under the pressures of numbers and growing demands for space. Therefore, it is imperative that governmental units be equipped to deal with urban development.

The Use of "Creative Federalism" in Urban Development

The present low caliber of most of our state and local governments undoubtedly reflects the rather limited demands made on government during our more leisurely rural period and the natural stickiness of governmental arrangements and intergovernmental relations. An urban age, by contrast, makes severe demands on governmental effectiveness; there are a remarkable number of things that have to be done jointly when people find it useful to jam together in limited spaces. Under such circumstances, traditional concepts about who does what begin to melt away, and urbanites turn to those levels of government that promise to get the necessary things done. Problem-solving and innovating capacity begin to be the real test for "appropriateness."

The problems stemming from governmental fragmentation in a megalopolitan situation have been so obvious that even the larger issues have tended to be overlooked, including questions of what the appropriate functions for each level of government will be in the future, and how to take full advantage of the flexibility our federal system and regionalism provide. Also critical is the question of the efficiency with which governments at all levels cope with urban matters. The role of each level of government must be clarified, its capacities generally strengthened, and its approaches modernized. The Federal Government has demonstrated a capacity to provide leadership in the nation's adjustment to new requirements and new problems posed by rapid urbanization. It has been reasonably inventive in developing new urban tools. Yet, with the advantages of hindsight, we can see that it has become involved in urban affairs at the wrong level and in the wrong way. It is still largely mired in the neighborhood project (the individual public-housing unit, the small urban-renewal project, the neighborhood poverty program, and the like), instead of being concerned with the metropolitan and megalopolitan region as a whole and with the rules of the game. (Even its best efforts can be nullified by local tax and zoning regulations that have a "beggar-thy-neighbor" impact.)

Since federal finance is a key lever in governmental activity, much will depend on whether the national government can change its style of providing grants and subsidies and use these directly to achieve major national goals rather than limited "instrumental" objectives. An example would be the provision of a "package" of financial assistance (wrapping up public-facility grants, mortgage insurance, public-housing assistance, rent supplements, and the rest) in the construction of new communities that meet specific standards—of open occupancy, stated proportions of low-cost and low-rental housing units, open space, and so forth. This is posited on the assumption, borne out in recent decades, that Federal Government politics, and more especially Presidential politics, can tolerate a longer-range point of view, a somewhat greater weighing of the scales toward equity and equality of opportunity, and the realization of "Great City" objectives.

But this is not to suggest that the Federal Government's role is the only critical one for the future of American urbanism; rather, it is the form and character of the intergovernmental "mix" that will probably determine the over-all governmental impact. Since local governmental units are creatures of state governments, the latter can make an important contribution by redefining the rules of the game. In general, the rules of the game in urban development are sadly out of date, and encourage a disjointed, incremental style of urban development with strong enclave overtones and extreme inequality of tax capacity and service burdens. These "rules" include state regulations about the organization and jurisdiction of local governmental units, laws covering land sales, land development, and construction, as well as provisions for local taxing and public services. Thus, the states will have to redefine the rules applying to the organization of local governments: for example, by requiring adequate size to provide local services at decent levels (recent studies have begun to provide some guidelines on economies of scale of local services), and by encouraging joint activities and common regulations in metropolitan and megalopolitan areas that cross state lines.

It would also be helpful to require that a certain proportion of local revenues, on a progressive scale, be applied to metropolitan-wide functions. In addition, the state governments can make a substantial contribution to the character of urban development through direct activities, such as large-scale natural-resources development, including recreation, the development of adequate intercity transportation, provision for aid to higher education, and the like. California, New York, and Wisconsin have already taken a few steps in this direction, but the field is still open for a new kind of state urban politics and administration.

City governments also urgently need modernization if they are to be able to cope with the urban problems of today and tomorrow. City governments need the same kind of thoroughgoing reorganization as the Federal Government received in the mid-1930's, with the strengthening of Presidential capability (through the establishment of the Executive Office of the President) and with better techniques of civil-service recruitment. A new breed of mayor is clearly needed (and will probably be forthcoming). To function effectively, city governments will need modern information systems and the capacity to recruit able persons for local governmental jobs. Moreover, they will have to have assured financial bases, probably including some forms of tax sharing with the Federal Government and the states.

There is also need for experimentation with various forms of regional organization. The metropolitan region provides an invaluable element of flexibility among the rigidly organized federal, state, and local governments, and this flexibility should be exploited. Good use could be made, for example, of *ad hoc* regional development agencies that could get a job done and dissolve or evolve into broader roles. There could be regional agencies to handle transportation, communications, and a variety of natural resources in concert; regional housing corporations to build housing for low-income groups in all parts of the metropolis; regional development agencies for education; and the like. But over time other groups might turn out to be more appropriate to certain major urban problems so that individual regional agencies would come and go. By experimentation we can learn how to co-ordinate such regional agencies without choking off their developmental drive. Federal funds will be needed to encourage this regional experimentation, and built-in evaluation must, of course, be provided for.

The Last Third of the Twentieth Century as a Period of Conscious Urban Development

We have only touched a corner of the huge picture of urban development, and the more prosaic part of the picture at that. There is more to the matter than merely solving "problems." We have noted that by 2000 a minimum of 280 million persons, or over 80 per cent of the total U. S. population, is expected to be living in urban areas. (Some analysts contend that the proportion of city residents will top 90 per cent by the end of the century.) For the city dwellers of the future, we should seek to create communities that are products of late-twentieth-century technology and social ideas and not merely shinier versions of early-twentieth-century cities. They should be designed to facilitate innovation and stimulate creative activity by maximizing exposure to various stimuli and supplying means for pooling information and ideas. They should provide recreational and educational features suiting current income and educational levels; workplaces and homes in interesting mixtures and not a sterile separation of the two; "lighted centers" that provide urbanity and make the night-time city a delight; and transportation geared to the evolving technological possibilities.

To achieve this we will need entrepreneurship in broad-scale urban development. We will need enterprising developmental organizations, both private and public, with the capacity to take advantage of economies of scale. One possibility is the creation of not-for-profit community development corporations that can contract with profit-making businesses to build new communities that meet certain performance standards with regard to public services and facilities, open occupancy, and a mix of low- and higher-income housing. Federal and other subsidies to such corporations would then be buying a known "package." Such corporations could also build "New Towns—in town," incorporating many of the New Town features in central-city areas.

We will also probably need to appropriate substantial funds for research and development of local *public* facilities—to speed up the adoption of new technologies and to help relate new financial, organizational, and other possibilities to social goals. Such research and development units might well be associated with universities, but could also be a new type of mixed public-private organization using private research facilities for public ends. All sorts of subjects might be investigated—for example, research in low-cost housing, new principles of intown parking, trade-offs between macro- and micro-environments, improved tunneling devices and means of providing an "educational environment" outside the schools. Research and development of this type would be most helpful if it extended far beyond technological considerations to cover fully not only the blocks to progress but the range of socio-economic possibilities as well. While new technologies can be enormously helpful, and probably will be, the really great problems for urban development in the last third of the century will be to resolve certain basic value conflicts, to overcome some outmoded ideas, and to experiment with new institutional arrangements to achieve agreed-upon social goals.

DANIEL P. MOYNIHAN

The Relationship of Federal to Local Authorities

THE PAST is never so clear as the future, save possibly with respect to the structure of American government. Over the years, this structure has retained a measure of complexity and contradiction of such variety that the features of the system most protested by one generation often become the qualities most valued by the next. A reemphasis of this sort appears to be in the offing. The great transformation now abroad in American society is the emergence of an educated middle-class electorate. These are certain to be notably active citizens, and it is no less certain that the complexities of the American governmental structure will both generate problems that call forth such energies and provide a bewildering array of outlets for them. No doubt the "inefficiencies" of federalism will continue to be deplored and efforts made to simplify the system, but it is most unlikely that such efforts will succeed. Thirty-five years is a short time in the history of American government; the near future is almost sure to be much like the distant past. Prolonged war, economic malaise, and racial stalemate will make for a more centrally directed system; peace, growth, and assimilation will make for a more related and permissive one. But the structure of the system is likely to continue to be much the same.

A number of large developments appears to be converging in a compatible, if not always harmonious manner. Each of these is likely to add stability to the federal system, and none appears to generate disequilibrium.

First, there is the nationalization of public policy that has accompanied the achievement of a genuinely national society. If there is still a goodly supply of local problems, there are fewer and fewer specifically local "subjects." It has been agreed, as it were, that the most important national issues will be resolved in national terms and at the national level. This process is not complete with respect

169

to the issues of race or education, but here, too, the transformation seems well under way. In this sense we have centralized decision-making within a federal structure and thereby greatly reduced pressures to change the latter in order to achieve the former.

The necessity for concentrating decision-making at the national level will be enhanced if current trends in racial concentration persist. Between 1960 and 1966, the number of children under age fourteen in metropolitan areas increased by 3.3 million. Nonwhite children accounted for one third of the gain. The average annual rate of increase of nonwhite children (2.4 per cent) was three times the rate for white children. Ninety-five per cent of the nonwhite increase was in central cities, where the proportion of all children who are nonwhite rose from 23 per cent in 1960 to 29 per cent in 1966. Over-all recent increases have been rapid, and are likely to continue in the near term. According to one estimate, by 1970 Negroes will constitute 40 per cent or more of the population in fourteen of the nation's major cities, including Washington, D. C., Richmond, Gary, Baltimore, Detroit, Newark, St. Louis, New Orleans, and Trenton.[1] In southern communities accustomed to taking collective measures to prevent Negro accession to power, there may be movements toward metropolitan governments in order to maintain Negroes in a minority voting status; but, in general, continued and possibly heightened racial tension is likely to inhibit greatly the development of true metropolitan governments. A fortiori the resolution of conflict between central cities and suburbs (which will increasingly take on "urban" qualities of their own) will have to occur at the federal level, save for the few states with sufficient political and fiscal resources to handle such matters at the level of state government.

Second, there is the rise of the federal fisc as the primary source of discretionary public expenditure. State and local revenues will continue to be committed, and overcommitted, to established programs. By contrast, federal revenues now grow at a considerable rate, and the growth is already being forecast in five-year periods. The need to expend the surplus in order to avoid fiscal drag has created within the Executive Office of the President a systematic search for new federal spending programs.

In July, 1965, for example, the Chairman of the Council of Economic Advisers testified before the Joint Economic Committee that "Federal revenues at full employment in 1970 would be expected to approach $170 billion, a rise of nearly $50 billion over the indicated

170

revenues of 1965 and nearly $45 billion over full-employment revenues of this year [1965]." Shortly thereafter the Administration began a process of military escalation that developed into a major land war in Asia. Nearly two years later this war is proceeding at, if anything, an accelerating pace, but has brought on neither a tax increase nor any considerable inflation. A cessation or decline in hostilities will only serve to emphasize the extraordinary fiscal resources of the Federal Government and lead to great and cogent demands that these resources be used for domestic programs.

Third, the tradition of decentralization and the fact of federalism is greatly inducive to the grant-in-aid as the principal form of federal expenditure on domestic programs. These have been increasing in both amount and variety. Between 1954 and 1964, federal grants to state and local governments rose 235 per cent from $3 billion to $10 billion. This was twice the rate of increase (118 per cent) of federal grants to individuals. The variety of these problems has predictably become a problem in its own right. Thus in December, 1966, the Secretary of Housing and Urban Development reported to the Chairman of the Subcommittee on Executive Reorganization of the Senate Committee on Government Operations that there were then in existence 238 federal programs having an impact on urban areas. This maze of programs will produce periodic efforts to collapse activities into larger, more general categories, but the process is most likely to be one of alternating proliferation and consolidation, and the grant-in-aid will persist.

Fourth, the diffusion of the middle-class ideal of participation in public decision-making will add a considerable and, in a sense, unanticipated utility to the complexity of the American government structure, which requires such great citizen participation in order to operate. The fourteen hundred governments Robert C. Wood discovered in the New York metropolitan area may prove none too many if the demand for committee work is to be met. This is not to say that government will become more efficient as the "quality" of the electorate improves and the proportion of persons taking an active part in public affairs increases. The opposite might well be the case: The more persons involved in making a decision, the more difficult it becomes to reach one. Participatory democracy is likely to be anything but a *fête d'amour*. Still, the federal system provides a singularly rich range of opportunities for participation and is apt to be valued for just that reason. Moreover, to the extent that the many small units of government in the present system re-

171

flect genuine interests, the skill and energy with which those interests are sure to be defended by a middle-class electorate are such as to suggest further that there will be a minimum of consolidation.

Six Themes for the Last Third of the Twentieth Century

I. *Wedding Cake Federalism.* Morton Grodzins' image of "marble cake federalism" describing the mixing up of functions among the theoretically separate layers of governments may become less useful as federal fiscal power shapes more and more government activities. What seems to be evolving is a multitiered system of bureaucracies and governmental units surmounted by the person of the President (and increasingly the person of the First Lady as well). At every level, federal funds will provide much of the cake and most of the icing.

Both employment and expenditure have been increasing much faster at the state and local levels than that at the federal. Between 1952 and 1962, the expenditures of the Federal Government rose by 25 per cent; those of state and local government by 128 per cent. In 1946, state and local expenditures constituted 44 per cent of government outgo. In 1962, this proportion had increased to 63 per cent. But where in 1940 local government tax revenues were 5.51 per cent of the national income, by 1963 they had declined to 4.64 per cent. These patterns are reflected in the numbers of public employees at the different levels of government.

Government Employment, 1964

Federal*	1,434,000
State	1,873,000
Local, excluding education	2,645,000
Local, education	3,018,000

(* Excludes those employed in National Defense and international relations.)

II. *New Varieties of Government.* Because multipurpose metropolitan government is not likely to emerge, special-purpose governments are likely to multiply. Some of these will be created directly by the Federal Government, as in the case of the elected

172

county committees that administer the farm program, and the elected community-action boards that share in the administration of the poverty program. Significantly, much of the rationale of the poverty program elections has been that it is *good* for people to participate in government—not just a right but a remedy. Just as significantly, the lines of authority and communication within the federal system are more and more likely to assume a triangular form in which each government has direct relations with the other two clusters of public activity.

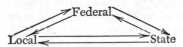

III. *Metropolitanism in Education.* In the course of the first two thirds of the twentieth century the most numerous and in some ways most important changes in government structure have occurred within school systems that have been steadily consolidating from quite small districts into rather large ones. Even so, at present there are some 34,678 school districts in the nation, approximately eleven times the number of counties. Despite a growing interest in "decentralization" of direction within the very large urban districts, there are still gains to be had from further mergers, and these are likely to continue. In the event that no significant measure of integration occurs in housing in the near future, there are certain to be growing demands to bring an end to the racial isolation of Negroes in public schools by establishing metropolitan school districts that encompass both the central-city Negro areas and the white suburbs. Inasmuch as education is manifestly a public function, pressures to bring about accommodations of this sort are likely to be considerably more effective than the often hapless assaults of individuals and small groups on the private-housing market.

IV. *National Social Accounts.* In the middle third of the twentieth century the most powerful development in government was the emergence of a political economy capable of comprehending, predicting, and directing economic events. If this development is as yet by no means complete, its influence is already pervasive. Moreover, it provides the basis—in the form of discretionary government income—for the exploitation of what will probably be the most powerful development of the last third of the century: the emergence of a social science coupled with and based upon a sys-

173

tem of social accounting that will give government an enlarged capacity to comprehend, predict, and direct social events. Again, it will be imperfect, but serviceable. In one political climate this may take the form of controlling society. In another it may produce a governmental system more effectively responsive to the wishes of the electorate than any society in history. More information about society will produce more information to do things for or to it. The technique of simulating social processes is likely to produce increasingly sophisticated forms of social innovation, evolving from the now widely employed "demonstration project" technique toward full-scale, controlled social experiments. At present, the social sciences are extremely rudimentary, and the likelihood of a major breakthrough is small. Indeed, the major discovery of the next generation may be that such developments are impossible. But it is certainly probable that sheer lack of information will have less influence on events in the future than it has had in the past, and that will make a difference in outcomes.

V. *The Quest for Community.* A sustained concern for the conditions under which individuals from different racial, ethnic, and class groups can establish meaningful and peaceable relationships is predictable. This concern must arise from the already begun effort to enable Negro Americans to enter the larger American society, to offset the effects of "alienation in the city, trivialization in the suburbs," and the general ecological scatteration described by Scott Greer. Programs that promote a sense of community (beautification, conservation, preservation, and so forth) are likely to be given conscious priority. This effort will further encourage the multiplication of governmental forms and activities.

VI. *The Rediscovery of the Market.* As government tries to do more, it will find it accomplishes less. This amounts to the discovery that administrative ability is not a free good, and in the absence of it the best-intentioned programs can turn out to be calamities. This proposition has been formulated by James Q. Wilson: "There are inherent limits to what can be accomplished by large, hierarchical organizations." The limitations imposed on bureaucratic performance in the United States are notable: that it expend money efficiently, but take the utmost precautions to see that not a penny is stolen; that it be responsive to special circumstances, but rigorously consistent in its actions, and so forth. Moreover, as "easy" problems

174

are disposed of, the more marginal, intractable ones come into prominence, and the return on government effort manifestly diminishes. All this is likely to lead to what Charles E. Lindblom has termed the "rediscovery of the market" as a means of accomplishing social objectives. The logic of events is very much on the side of Lindblom's assertion: "That the market mechanism can be serviceable to planned and unplanned economies alike, to public and private enterprise alike, to collective and individual choice alike is a discovery the significance of which may soon dwarf what we have seen of its consequences so far."[2]

In the future social problems are likely to be approached more often by means of an *income* strategy, than by a *services* strategy, as defined by Lee Rainwater. Thus the concept of giving the poor the money with which to purchase what they need—be it proper housing or medical care—in the market is apt to be considered far more seriously in the future than in the immediate past, which has been much influenced by ideals of professionalization in public services. In a similar vein, more and more services that have been thought to be located necessarily in the public sector will probably be contracted out to private enterprises—particularly in areas where results are more important than processes. J. Herbert Holloman foresees the development of "the public market" for just such purposes—for example, "a profit-making organization running a chain of junior colleges under contracts with the communities in which they are located."

Business organizations, which are characteristically oriented to results rather than process, are in a position to offer to contract for a wider range of such activities on a performance basis: payment to be made on delivery of the desired result, be it clean streets, fair housing, or ninth-grade achievement in mathematics on the part of ninth-grade students. In general, whatever makes for diversity in American government in the decades ahead is very likely to be given a try.

Envoi

These notes were originally written in February, 1966, at a time when the continuity of American government seemed almost a fact of nature. Now, in the early summer of 1967, one learns that the approval of only two state legislatures is required in order for a national constitutional convention to be convened. The initiative behind this extraordinary move, which has taken the nation quite unawares, is nominally to undo the changes in state legislatures mandated by the Supreme Court's "one-man, one-vote" decision. Thus, in a sense, it is simply the most dramatic recent evidence of the resistance of the American government structure to change. But the possibility that a convention will meet and will go on to draft profoundly important innovations is altogether real. Nothing is fixed.

REFERENCES

1. *Congressional Quarterly*, August 26, 1966, p. 1,860.

2. Charles E. Lindblom, "The Rediscovery of the Market," *The Public Interest* (Summer, 1966), p. 100.

LAWRENCE K. FRANK

The Need for a New Political Theory

WE URGENTLY need a new political theory to replace that which was formulated in the late-eighteenth century and has become cumulatively inadequate and frustrating for the present and an impediment to the future. Such a revised political theory will be a necessity for the cultural renewal we must undertake, as well as a statement of policy for guiding our new proposals.

In 1776 and the period preceding the establishment of the United States, the founding fathers, hoping to establish a new nation and inaugurate a new social order, sought promising ideas and conceptual formulations for what they desired to achieve. The government they proposed was oriented to the protection of private property, the adjudication of disputes, the collection of customs, the conduct of foreign affairs, and the maintenance of national defense. They found authority for this in John Locke's theory of representative government and a model in a similar tri-party division of government that the British had earlier tried and abandoned. They were persuaded by the eighteenth-century belief in the rationality of man and accepted proposals that emphasized the individual's capacity for acting rationally in pursuing his own self-interest and happiness, calculating his prospective gains and losses.

But the basic foundation for these proposals was the conception of society as a superhuman organization, operated and kept in balance by immense superhuman forces, like the celestial machinery of Newton from which this model was derived. These forces were operated to maintain the new nation in its appointed orbit.

This well-known history of the country is rehearsed here to remind us how a political theory became directive and gave rise to a new society. It was translated not only into a governmental organization and administration but also into what may be called the phi-

177

losophy of American life—a flexible guide as to what individuals, groups, and organizations could and should do. Especially we should recognize that government is not to be conceived as inherent in or derived from nature, nor as an expression of natural law but as a humanly created institution, carried on by the individuals who have adopted its aims and practices and accepted the political theory that has rationalized and justified what they do.

Since 1900 we have experienced several major alterations in our society, some of which are truly radical changes. Thus, we have had a rapidly enlarging population with a changing age distribution and made up of a variety of ethnic-cultural groups. We have also had a biological revolution, marked by the prolongation of life and the emergence of old-age groups that are actively forming associations and pressing for their own advantage and protection. We have also had an urban revolution characterized not only by the increasing population of cities, but by basic changes in our former ways of living. Earlier, many were engaged in *making* a living on the farm where the "extended" family exerted as a more or less self-sufficient household their skills, foresight, strength, and endurance in wresting a living from the soil. Today, no urban resident nor "nuclear" family can make a living; each must try to *earn* a living, or otherwise obtain income, for rent, the purchase of food and clothing, and the many recurrent expenditures that have become customary, if not necessary, for city living.

Many are seeking compensation and protection, exhibiting their inability to be independent. They are also hoping to overcome the loss of the "belonging" once enjoyed from shared beliefs and loyalties, from one's family and kinship ties, from having a place in the community, and from religious affiliations. They are now seeking collective status, relinquishing or greatly curtailing their power of individual contracting. Instead of bargaining individually, they now look to membership in organizations to which they surrender the power of contract for the status they gain as members. These organizations "bargain collectively" for their members, as we see not only in labor unions but in professional and educational associations, in religious and other organizations. Especially important are the corporations, which are empowered by their owners-stockholders to manage their property, to enter into contracts and other agreements on their behalf in the expectation of profits.

Political parties with their hierarchical organization not only offer opportunities for enhancing status but also provide rewards and special jobs to their loyal members who are unable to attain equivalent compensations and salaries except by patronage. Status fosters what we call "featherbedding." Not limited to labor unions and political parties, featherbedding is widely practiced in many organizations in business and finance, government and the military, religious institutions and, not infrequently, the helping professions and service institutions. Those who belong are rewarded for little or no work, except what they are told not to do or to say. Many special privileges are, however, also granted to individuals because they have a legalized status, because they belong to a special class —such as age and sex groups, the handicapped, the retarded, and the mentally disturbed. Their deviant status entitles them to allowance and protection.

These and other changes illustrate a shift in our traditional emphasis upon the rights and protection of property to an increasing recognition of the rights of persons; from the doctrine of equality of opportunity to the emerging conception of the equality of human needs, not only for the "creature comforts" but also for the dignity and integrity of the individual and family that are continually jeopardized and denied by the persistence of anachronistic beliefs, practices, and laws. There have been a number of expressions of this shift and changing evaluation. The New Deal, which enlarged governmental services and financial support, was followed by the New Frontier, and now by the Great Society programs. Although these slogans have evoked support for often reluctantly adopted measures, they have not been productive of a new political theory rationalizing these departures from our accepted beliefs about the limited powers and responsibilities of government.

The political theories and governmental authority derived from theology are still being reiterated on public occasions, but they no longer have their former meaning nor provide the authority for governmental action. The separation of church and state is being decided not so much by legislation and court decisions, but by the changes in individual beliefs, expectations, and loyalties fostered by governmental intervention in private affairs.

The Federal Government now provides a wide range of professional and technical assistance, with many direct subsidies and special tax allowances and concessions to business, finance, industry, transportation, and communication—indeed, to the whole range of free enterprise. This assistance to private business has been explained and justified as promoting prosperity and advancing the national welfare. But assistance and services to individuals and families have been strongly resisted and only reluctantly provided since there is no adequate rationalization for such extensions of government activities. The need for a political theory for this emerging "Service State" is, therefore, especially urgent.

The Service State, not to be confused with the Welfare State with its aura of charity and philanthropy, is oriented to the enhanced "well-being" of everyone, as Halbert Dunn has expressed it. It marks the acceptance of human conservation as the basic democratic task; each year sees the enlargement and extension of services furnished directly or financed by the Federal Government and reinforced by state and local agencies. These services embrace medical and health care, improved housing and urban rehabilitation, educational facilities and programs from early childhood into adult years, plus the improved care and support of the indigent, the handicapped, the impaired, and all others incapable of fending for themselves in our money economy.

Each addition and enlargement is made as a separate program with no coherent and systematic commitment, no political theory to justify and rationalize these enlarged government activities, and no statement of policy for their extension and administration. We are improvising and operating by a series of piecemeal programs.

As Julius A. Stratton pointed out in his Commencement Address at M.I.T. in June, 1964:

Our efforts must now move to a higher plateau. We can no longer afford to nibble away piece by piece at the problems of the modern city—of transportation—of underdeveloped economies—of automation— or of disarmament. . . . Our ailments are vast and complex, and they will yield only to planned collaborative attacks focused on clear objectives and leading to concerted action.[1]

This implies the need for an over-all, comprehensive policy that will assert the criteria for choices and decisions. With a clear statement of policy, those who make social decisions can be guided, as if by "an unseen hand," when exercising their autonomy to integrate their efforts by collaborating with others who are responsive to these same criteria. Without a statement of basic criteria for national policies, the various specialized programs and the separately located authority of governments and private agencies will continue to plan and execute their separate and often irreconcilable programs.

For a free society, therefore, we need the guidance of basic principles and especially a political theory congruous with and appropriate to the new requirements and opportunities of today. Where can we look for guidance and fruitful direction for a new political theory? Following the example of the founding fathers, we might seek in science for the reorientation we need; we must realize, however, that they did not attempt to apply the Newtonian methods and techniques for mathematical reasoning. Nor did they rely upon empirical research and demand quantitative findings to decide what was desirable and feasible. They did not believe that they were bound by existing trends, especially since they were determined to interrupt so much of the customary uses and the prevailing practices of their time. They were concerned with innovation, with the establishment of a new social order and a new kind of government that would express and make possible the attainment of the values they cherished.

Accordingly, we should not look hopefully to the bewildering array of contemporary findings and research techniques nor try to invoke science as the source of our procedure, but, rather, attempt to understand and apply some of the recently developed concepts and assumptions—the new ways of creative thinking and theoretical formulation—that seem relevant and promising. Also, we might employ some of the newly-developed conceptual models that may be useful for a new political theory.

Social problems, unlike scientific problems generated by theoretical implications and curiosity about natural events, rise from the inadequacies and conflicts in a social order, especially from the neglect or refusal to revise anachronistic and obsolete institutions and practices so that we can cope with urgent human needs and better express our aspirations.

An analytic approach to problems fragments what is an organized complexity calling for the study of the whole. A fruitful concept of such a whole is that of an "open system," as contrasted to a "closed system" that can be isolated like laboratory preparations and rigidly controlled experiments, excluding all inputs except those to be explored as selected variables or isolable "mechanisms."

As Ludwig Bertalanffy has pointed out, open systems operate with continual inputs and outputs, with unceasing functioning, and with ever-changing states, and are therefore not subject to the classical controls and to attempted replication of findings.[2] Open sys-

181

tems—embracing organisms, personalities, human institutions, social orders, and cultures—can be and are frequently studied analytically to disclose selected dimensions or variables, but these yield what might be called "scientific artifacts" that ignore the complex inter-relationships and unceasing communication of the open systems they investigate. The components and participants in open systems are closely coupled and entrained, communicating with the environing world and evoking feedbacks for their direction and stabilization. Unlike the physical-chemical elements and their un-changing properties, open systems and their components can and do change, as the evolution of organisms and the development of cultures, social orders, and changing governments notably demonstrate.

Another fruitful approach has been provided by cybernetics as formulated by the late Norbert Wiener. Cybernetics has frequently been misused by wrongly applying it to static entities and inertial systems. Likewise, feedbacks have been frequently misinterpreted as externally-applied forces; they should be seen as what the system, organism, or machine evokes from the environment for correction and direction and generates internally for its co-ordinated functioning.

Especially noteworthy and promising is the concept of self-organizing systems. "Hard-nosed" scientists and engineers are increasingly accepting and working with this seemingly teleological concept, as is shown by the papers in *Principles of Self-Organizing Systems,* edited by Heinz von Foerster and G. W. Zopf, Jr.[3] These papers emphasize that systems are not only self-organizing, but also self-directing and self-stabilizing, and may to a considerable extent be self-repairing and capable of goal-seeking, purposive behavior.

These recent concepts, explored and elaborated upon by a number of scientists from different disciplines, have proved to be highly productive. W. Ross Ashby has proposed that a system be viewed as composed of a number of sub-systems, each of which has its own range of fluctuation; when the system receives an impact, one or more of the sub-systems can "roll with the punches" and thereby maintain the stability of the total system. When, however, one or more of these sub-systems are required to operate beyond their normal range of variability, the whole system undergoes what Ashby calls a "step function" and shifts to a "new track," changing its former operations and functioning. Any marked change in one function or operation of a system usually involves alteration and compensatory changes in the whole system because each component of a sub-system is interrelated to the others.

As a result of these recent approaches, there is a growing realization that the familiar statement "the whole is greater than the sum of its parts" is misleading and invalid when applied to social organizations. This axiom assumes that the "parts" are more or less homogeneous units that can be aggregated and added as a quantitative ensemble. But the so-called "parts" of a system or organization are its highly differentiated components and participants, each of which has specialized but coupled activities whereby the whole is generated and maintained.

We have no adequate conception of such a dynamic organization. Traditionally, organization has been conceived of as a hierarchical entity and illustrated by charts with a chain of command from the top to the lower echelons and individuals. Some definitions are offered as static models that are supposed to operate, but there is no clearly stated theory of how they work. Today we are beginning to recognize that organisms and human organizations are persistent configurations of functioning processes closely coupled and entrained and engaged in circular, reciprocal operations involving feedbacks.

A promising model for a political theory is that of a communications network, with many different channels for transmitting a variety of messages. This social communications network cannot be encompassed by "Information Theory" and its mathematical elaboration, devised initially for coded verbal messages. The social communications network transmits many different messages of social symbols that we call political, economic, social, religious, and so on. These group-sanctioned symbols are used by individuals and groups in the continuous transactions and negotiations of social life. This model offers a possibility for unifying now separate social sciences and relinguishing what each of them assumes to be a discrete system with its own "forces" and theoretical interpretation. Instead of the assumption of great superhuman forces or coercive trends, we may find clues to the dynamics of social operations and changes in the human behavior exhibited in social symbols. Appropriate patterns of behavior may give rise to the recurrent regularities of a social order and also generate the trends and the innovations in all our institutions and customary practices.

Unless we are persuaded, as many are, that our lives are determined by inexorable natural laws, divine ordination, or coercive trends, that we must accept as our fate and "drear our weird," as the Scots say, we cannot avoid much longer the recognition that we live by and for what we believe, value, and aspire to, and that these beliefs must be translated into the choices and decisions that guide our individual and group living.

These concepts appear to be highly relevant and appropriate to the modern political theory for a social order undergoing rapid and, at present, unco-ordinated changes. They are especially applicable to our social order because they emphasize how the whole of our society is disturbed by separate and unco-ordinated attempts at revision that so often ignore their inextricable relation to the larger system. Moreover, these new concepts of a system show that the classical assumptions about social order must be replaced since we can no longer think of society as an inertial system governed by large-scale social forces, a surviving eighteenth-century metaphor that is widely accepted and used by social scientists and by the public.

Alfred North Whitehead pointed out some years ago that "those societies which cannot combine reverence for their symbols with freedom for their revision must ultimately decay, either from anarchy or the slow atrophy by useless shadows." A social order that cannot reaffirm its aspirations, goals, values and also revise and reconstruct its institutions must succumb to increasing disorder and conflict or decline as the torch of human advance is taken over by the new nations.

REFERENCES

1. Julius A. Stratton, "Commencement Address, Massachusetts Institute of Technology, *Dædalus*, Vol. 3, No. 4 (Fall, 1964), p. 1242.

2. Ludwig Bertalanffy, "The Theory of Open Systems in Physics and Biology," *Science*, Vol. 3 (1950), pp. 27-29; "General Systems Theory," *Human Biology*, Vol. 23, No. 4 (December, 1951); "General Systems Theory: A New Approach to Unity of Science," *Human Biology*, Vol. 28, No. 4 (December, 1956).

3. Heinz von Foerster and G. W. Zopf, Jr., eds., *Principles of Self-Organizing Systems* (London, 1962).

STEPHEN R. GRAUBARD

University Cities in the Year 2000

THIS, AN essay in conjecture, attempts to describe institutions, now existing, whose character may be significantly altered in the next thirty-five years. In the coming decades we can expect to witness the establishment of new kinds of universities (some bearing familiar and even ancient names) in new kinds of urban environments; these I choose to call "university cities." No such city exists now. Residents of Cambridge or Berkeley sometimes imagine that they live in such places; those who inhabit New York or Chicago rarely permit themselves this illusion. In the sense that I use the term *university city*, it is inapplicable to any of these urban centers. Cambridge, Berkeley, Chicago, and New York all harbor major university communities in the same way that Bloomington, Ann Arbor, Madison, and New Haven do, but these are not now (and several may never become) university cities.

What, then, is the university city of the year 2000 to be? Essentially, it will be an urban area of some size and economic importance that will shelter a significant number of strong educational institutions, broadly defined; these institutions will co-operate in ways that are now only dimly perceived. For a university city to develop, there must be a continuing relation among institutions of learning, public and private. Moreover, the collective influence of these bodies must be greater than that of all other corporate groups in the city.

My meaning may be made more precise if I dwell on American cities as they exist today. Many of these would qualify, in my view, as "company towns." Their economy and social organization testify to an overwhelming commitment to some particular activity, usually commercial, but never primarily educational or intellectual. This is most conspicuously evident in our resort cities. While Miami's economy is not solely built on sun and surf, were both suddenly found to be undesirable qualities by vacationers, serious difficulties would ensue for the city. However much Washington, D. C., may imagine itself to be America's London or Paris, it in fact resembles Ottawa and Canberra more than it does the older European capitals. Why? Because it is a "company town"—its business is essentially governmental. The presence of museums, universities, research institutes, and the like cannot alter Washington's fundamental preoccupation with "that man"—his plans and intentions and the opposition they are calculated to produce. The city's "business" is government in the same way that Detroit's is auto manufacture.

When we look at the larger cities—New York, Los Angeles, Chicago—we encounter economies that are considerably more diversified; these places are indeed redolent of European cities. Would it be a mistake to suggest, however, that all are essentially concerned with commercial and industrial enterprise, with buying and selling, producing and exchanging? These cities take justifiable pride in their outstanding universities; it is in no way a denigration of either the cities or their universities to suggest that educational institutions do not dominate in these great and populous areas. When we say that DuPont dominates Wilmington, the meaning of that statement is clear. It does not express a statistical truth; rather, it suggests a form of influence that cannot be denied. In the same way, New York—immeasurably more complex—is dominated by law, banking, publishing, merchandising, manufacture, advertising, and the like. What do these have in common? They are all essentially business enterprises; their end is profit. There are other institutions in New York—universities, museums, libraries, hospitals—whose reason for being is not primarily commercial, but they do not dominate the city.

By the year 2000, however, the business of certain cities in America will be education, in the broadest sense. These cities will be as different from the commercial, industrial, and governmental cities of today as the latter are from the cathedral towns of an earlier European society. If I am correct in believing that a few cities of this sort will have established themselves in the United States by the year 2000, they must not be seen as displacing existing cities; they will co-exist with them, but will have a different sort of appeal for a growing segment of an increasingly mobile American society.

Why should such a development be anticipated? The easiest

answer would be that education, health, and leisure are all becoming "big business." It is as reasonable to expect activity in these matters to center in a few large cities as it was for such concentrations to develop when the manufacture and exchange of specialized industrial products were first undertaken. Those who would point to the dispersal of industry in recent years would find fault with this argument; for them, dispersal offers the "new model" for all institutional development. They would also contend that since health and education needs are universal, one can logically expect high-quality institutions to be established in many places. Those who argue in this way assume that it is not impossible that as many as twenty or twenty-five strong state university systems, each co-operating with other educational institutions, will have established themselves by the year 2000. A new form of "educational equality" among states will have come into being. Since federal funds will undoubtedly exert a large influence on all future educational development—as much on the university as on other levels—this would seem to give support to the idea of a proliferation and dispersal of educational facilities.

If university cities—in the sense that I use the term—could be wished into being by a generous flow of public funds, many would soon exist. But I do not conceive of these cities developing in this manner; rather, I see them as coming about through an increased awareness by many educational institutions, public and private, of their interrelatedness and interdependence. Only when the museum director, the university president, the hospital administrator, the computer technician, the laboratory scientist, and the organizer of a "new industry" recognize their common interests—and understand why no one of them is engaged in a peripheral activity of slight interest to the other—will there be the beginnings of the kind of co-operation that may in time create the university city. It is not a matter of any one of these serving the other, but of each pursuing a set of common objectives that must, for lack of a better term, be defined as broadly educational.

This is more than a call for co-operation among the so-called institutions of higher learning. It goes far beyond the admission that no university, however rich or powerful, can hope to offer instruction in the wide range of subjects now deemed important. So long as universities define co-operation in terms of curricula, imagining that the need is to provide their students with exchange privileges, the implications of the concept of "interdependence" are lost. What

187

is required is not simply that universities co-operate with one another, but that they see how they can relate to other institutions which are not formally constituted as "universities," but which function as such in certain of their activities. Instruction will remain as a central concern of the university; in time, it will be recognized that it has new dimension.

The present university population mix—overwhelmingly undergraduate and predoctoral or preprofessional—will change dramatically in the next thirty-five years, at least in university cities. There, great numbers of postdoctoral fellows and professional adults of all ages will congregate for longer or shorter periods. They will be seeking something quite different from what is today so quaintly called "continuing education." Long before the year 2000, a businessman will be as apt to spend a sabbatical year at a university as in travel and sport. When men and women no longer deem it unreasonable to pursue two or three different careers in succession, the university city will provide the stimulus (and the instruction) to make such things possible.

University cities will prove attractive to a great variety of industries, but particularly to those that depend heavily on certain kinds of professional competence. The development of light and highly sophisticated industry in Boston along Route 128—with its proximity to M.I.T. and Harvard—will be seen as a very early prototype of a kind of commercial enterprise that will become increasingly common. Between such industry, educational institutions, research institutes, medical and scientific establishments, and cultural bodies of the greatest variety, close links will exist. The men and women involved in one will recognize their "kin" in the other. The concept of "my university" or "my museum" will seem increasingly foreign. Such institutions will admit to a kind of collective stewardship. Older instruments of control, whether by trustees or corporate owners, may be perpetuated, but they will no longer reflect the administrative, commercial, or aesthetic values that were common when these bodies were more self-consciously independent.

These new relations will serve to instill a new kind of civic pride. University cities will differ markedly; some of the difference will reflect the great variety of co-operative arrangements that will have been worked out to express the interdependence established. Although the idea of service will be paramount, it will be communicated in a very new idiom. The object will not be simply to *serve* the city, in the sense of attending to its problems, controlling air pollution, crime, and the like, but rather, to demonstrate the primacy and necessity of certain kinds of intellectual endeavor. Those very institutions that now exist on the periphery of cities—serving for limited times relatively selected elements of the population—will be recognized to be central.

If the university city will scarcely resemble the city of today, so the universities within those cities will show qualities reflecting the new kinds of experimentation that will be common. Attachment to a particular university for four or more years will not occur so frequently as it does today. Students, increasingly mobile, will spend periods in several universities and in several university cities. At one time or another many will choose to live in one of the greater university cities. A student will begin his higher education in a small college, leave after a time to spend a period in a university city, migrate to another, and pursue his profession in a third. It is not improbable that many of the more gifted men and women will have spent some part of their lives in one of the great university cities. The role of student will be a more anomalous one than it is presently. As many more people of various ages and in various stages of their professional careers engage in university studies, there will be less disposition to think of the university as the habitat principally of mature adolescents and young adults.

In university cities, faculty will not exist as a corporate group set apart. Their relations with other professional groups will be more regular. At a time when London will be an hour's distance from New York, scholars and teachers will divide their time between several university cities, teaching and studying regularly both in this country and abroad. This perpetual coming and going will render even more difficult than is now the case the creation of environments suited to contemplation and reflection. The bustle of university cities will not be welcome to all scholars; many will seek to pursue their work in greater isolation—even in rural retreats. The greatest number will, nevertheless, accept the inconveniences and find attractive the city's intellectual and social qualities. The university cities will emerge as principal centers of artistic and creative endeavor. They will support such talents, not least because they will provide an ample market for their product.

How such institutions and cities will relate to those that maintain more traditional separate identities is difficult to know. It is not to be excluded that the new university cities will be viewed with alarm by many who will prefer traditional institutional ar-

189

rangements. The virtues of "independence" and "smallness" are too powerfully represented in American tradition to be lightly set aside. It is by no means certain that either the Federal Government or many of the state governments will recognize the necessity of such cities or assist in their construction. Some may believe, mistakenly, that "new buildings" are called for, when the object, in fact, is the construction of "new bridges" between existing institutions. The reconceptualizing of the community's interest and the liberating of energies, still too narrowly tied to single institutions, are most urgently required. Unless these are recognized as responses to both an individual and a social need, there is small prospect that university cities will develop. If education, in the broadest sense, is to emerge as the major activity in a number of urban centers, this can be accomplished only by a dramatic reformulation of what is implicit in the idea of education in an advanced industrial society. Where an increasing number of men and women look upon work as a source of income, but also as a condition for personal fulfillment, where the line between leisure and work becomes increasingly indistinct, where definition of a cultural institution is considerably broadened so that it includes many bodies which would not be thought "cultural" today, where the lines between education, health (physical and mental), and leisure are drawn in new ways—there are prospects for a new kind of university in a new kind of urban environment.

HAROLD ORLANS

Educational and Scientific Institutions

THE FUTURE cannot be projected simply from present lines of development (despite the contrary suggestion of Herman Kahn). That would be altogether too simple to be either realistic or any fun. Rather, the future must be imagined.

But of what strands is this imagined fabric woven? Like those descernible in other Commission papers, ours probably come too much from materials readily at hand, from recent evidence that appears, somehow, like the numbered dots in a child's puzzle book, to hold a pattern. But is that which is the most recent invariably most close to that which will be? Therein lies our frailty, for the page is writ with numberless dots; it is our will that fashions the lines. In contemplating the nation's educational and scientific institutions, our will has taken an evidently utopian turn, as several Commission members have remarked.

The continued specialization anticipatable in graduate schools and, more broadly, in the spectrum of intellectual, professional, and technical activity will provide the monumentally elaborate inventory of talent and information required to operate a hypermodern industrial society. But how will this society be bound together? How will the infinitely diverse intellectual crafts find the common language of discourse that must be established if the larger national or intellectual society is not to resemble the uncommunicating tribes of the New Guinea highlands?

This function of unifying the larger society and giving its progeny a common sense of purpose must be served by our schools and colleges. For many years, our schools have tried to impart a common culture to children of diverse immigrants. By the year 2000, the schools will have to impart a common culture strong enough to withstand the specialization and special interest to which students will later be subjected in graduate school or work. The liberal arts colleges can fulfill this vital function better than the giant universities. They do not cultivate narrow intellectual craftsmen, but the broader men of character who will be needed even more sorely in the new millennium than in the old. (And who will manufacture a humane computer?)

Educational Institutions

The burgeoning of new knowledge from graduate schools and research institutions, along with the continual obsolescing of old knowledge and of those technical and professional skills based upon it, has pervasive implications for both the educational system that transmits knowledge and the agencies and individuals who employ it.

Within the world of higher education, a progressive differentiation of institutional function can be expected to proceed together with closer local, regional, and national linkages of institutions and scholars. Functional differentiation is a consequence of increased specialization—the nation may need corps of specialists in high-energy physics, arid-zone agriculture, African ethnography, Finno-Ugric languages, and so on; but not on every campus. Then, as now, regional clusters and unique national concentrations of talent and facilities will constitute the hub of intellectual activity. Especially when sustained by public funds, their resources should be more readily accessible to scholars and students throughout the nation; and it is hard to believe that private funds will then sustain proportionately more of the educational enterprise than today. Contemporary prototypes for this type of co-operation are the multi-institutional corporations managing the research facilities of the Atomic Energy Commission and the National Science Foundation; the Compact for Education and the interstate associations of universities in the South, the West, and New England; the Committee of Institutional Cooperation of one private and ten public Mid-West universities; and the Joint Graduate Consortium of five Washington, D. C., institutions. The California system of higher education and the ties between individual American universities and those in underdeveloped nations or those between eminent and poorer American colleges illustrate some of the kinds of co-operation among institutions with varying resources and functions that should expand greatly. Institutional collaboration will, of course, be facilitated by developments in the communication, recording, recall, and transmission of information in oral and visual forms. The fuller recognition of credit and the freer movement of students in the advanced years of undergraduate and graduate study should foster more efficient use of available capacity while providing students with those educational opportunities in the region or nation best suited to their needs.

A closer meshing of the secondary and elementary curricula with college offerings should develop due to the increased proportion of high-school graduates entering college. The Physical Science Study Committee has observed what might be called the "Zacharias effect":

One of the reasons why . . . [the Committee] had found the task of making a physics course for the last year of high school such an onerous task was that the student came into the class totally unprepared for physics, and without the mathematics, the chemistry, and the general familiarity in science that by right he should have accumulated during his earlier years in high school; during his years in junior high school; during his years in elementary school.
. . . The problems of higher education will not be solved until we can send into the colleges young men and women who are prepared to move forward at a pace and level reasonable to demand of them.[1]

The constant modernization of curricula should produce a continuing collaboration between the systems of higher and secondary education, between leading scholars and teachers, and between graduate departments and schools of education; and the evolution of comparable standards for judging the achievement of students in any region.

In private and public employment, the perpetual renovation of knowledge and the need for new skills will require constant contact with neighboring educational institutions and the regular recycling of employees through them. Channels to the sources of technical information and innovation must be kept open, especially in "science-based" industries and professions, by such means as the "internship" of graduate engineering students in industry and the growth of regional centers to facilitate the dissemination and use of new knowledge and to provide small business and government agencies with individual consultative and research services.

Scientific and Engineering Institutions

Certain citadels of pure research will and should maintain their magnificent isolation from worldly concerns. If men are to find the

193

truth, they must be free to seek it wherever it appears and to follow it wherever it may lead, without distraction, instruction, or ulterior purpose; for nature observes the laws of God, not men, and still less administrators. Though the search for the truth must remain a primary obligation of university scientists, it can hardly be confined to them. The modest demands of individual scholarship or "small science" must also be supplemented—not swamped—by the judicious provision of major facilities, such as telescopes and accelerators at national centers, access to which should be determined largely by the quality of an investigator's work. Pure research can contribute a great deal to the quality and success of industrial and governmental laboratories.

The citadels of intellectual integrity can, in the long run, maintain their strength only insofar as they strengthen the society that sustains them. This does not require smoke to billow from ivory towers, but it does require the varied and intimate association of university and community, university and industry, schools of science and of engineering, professional and liberal studies. Universities are best suited to those kinds of research undertaken by individual scholars working alone or in small groups on problems that advance the university's particular educational purposes and preserve its particular intellectual standards. It may be hoped that, as their educational responsibilities, resources, and aspirations increase, they will withdraw from large-scale and routine research activities that disrupt or demean the best academic traditions.

The role of independent research institutions, profit-making and nonprofit, will be greatly enlarged and their ties with both factory and campus strengthened to furnish three kinds of services: a) basic research involving full-time work, large teams, or long-term efforts, or requiring substantial engineering support or unique, expensive facilities; b) the conduct of applied research, technological development, or proprietary work for government and industry; c) the provision of technical advice, information, and managerial services in connection with discrete, minor problems as well as massive enterprises requiring the co-ordination of many organizations and disciplines in a "systems" approach to the solution of complicated technical problems.

Production and services in America are overwhelmingly the function of a host of privately owned companies, large and small. Industry is also primarily responsible for innovation in many sectors. Currently, various forms of government regulation or control, the cleavage of industry into a government-supported sector and a quite different sector that sells to industry and the public, the strength in certain fields of government captive laboratories, and extensive government support of specially selected areas of research in universities pose severe challenges to industry. Some of these problems may be ameliorated by government action, but changes in industrial organization, staffing, outlook, and innovative vigor are vitally needed. By the year 2000, many companies should be larger, better organized, and more tightly knit, so that they can effectively support and rapidly exploit the deepest sort of research effort pertinent to the general problems of their fields. Industry-wide, inter-industry, and professional associations will help individual companies to define their long-range problems, needs, and aims.

Companies will establish closer and more meaningful relations and a greater interchange of personnel with both government and universities. They will develop programs of support and mutual services with appropriate university sectors. Only through fuller and more manifold co-operation among industry, universities, and government can our technical skills and intellectual resources effectively meet the needs of society.

Direct government expenditures and indirect financial incentives comparable to those presently devoted to the military, space science, and technology may be envisaged in now moribund areas of domestic technology in which the prospect of profit is too remote to elicit the private capital required to ensure technical progress. While it would be unrealistic to expect such expenditures alone to "solve" those domestic problems in which social factors loom larger than technical ones, they may replace them with others and enlist in their solution the professional talents and political influence of powerful interests. Any substitution of empirical for ideological approaches to social problems will be a decided gain. This will demand a fuller use and better quality of social scientific methods and the working together of natural scientists, engineers, and community leaders.

New kinds of research-cum-action organizations should develop to foster new solutions to public problems. Their precise character cannot be foreseen so readily as the need for them; but, by one means or another, they must help reconcile what is possible technically with what is feasible politically. The Chamber of Commerce's proposal that industry-labor-public councils be formed to consider alternative solutions to persistent technical-social-political-economic problems—such as urban slums, traffic congestion, and the pollution of air, soil, and water—may or may not be wise; but *some* such radical new organizational forms will be necessary to grapple with our more intransigent technological and social problems.

Just as new approaches must be found to old problems, so must new charters be devised for old scientific and engineering organizations. The conservatism of many established laboratories and professional organizations constitutes a drag on scientific progress and a misallocation of human and economic resources. They diligently pursue outmoded objectives as long as money remains available for them. It has generally been easier to create new organizations for new tasks, but even the elephantine National Academy of Sciences has shown signs of new life in the 1960's. Is it too much to anticipate the reinvigoration of other professional associations? These associations can play a significant role in broadening membership in the "invisible colleges" responsible for so much vital scientific communication; in fostering interdisciplinary co-operation; and, more generally, in helping their professions meet the changing needs of society.

Examples can readily be given of government research and development programs (for instance, in military technology, nuclear energy, agriculture, and medicine) evidently pursued beyond the point of need; the same is true of all or substantial portions of the work of public and private laboratories engaged in such programs. These laboratories should be either dismantled, like obsolete battleships, or redirected to the problems of the future. It may also be hoped—though scarcely expected—that private industrial laboratories now dedicated to planning premature obsolescence and stylistic change will then be devoted to products and services whose public value is as clear as their profitability.

Accumulation and Transmission of Information

Like banks, warehouses, and stock brokers, libraries will benefit greatly from advanced techniques of storing, retrieving, reproducing, and transmitting information. As the volume of serial and monographic publication increases from both domestic and foreign sources (and the latter will increase dramatically with the growth of universities and scientific institutions in previously illiterate nations), and as the expense of acquiring, handling, and housing the material increases, the logic of vastly improved interlibrary services becomes compelling. National and regional libraries can afford (and other libraries can afford *not*) to build up comprehensive holdings in designated fields only when their resources become readily available, upon demand, to scholars throughout the nation.

The comprehensive monthly medical index, computer-produced bibliographies, and extensive, mail-delivered, photo-facsimile copies supplied by the National Library of Medicine are only a primitive indication of the services that should ultimately be available at major libraries. The long-range plan for the Library of Congress comes closer to the goal that technology may render practicable, and economics and scholarship desirable, for the year 2000: the storage in machine-recoverable form of the entire deposits, and the accessibility of any item, without queuing, to readers at electronically-linked metropolitan and university sub-stations. At a 200-diameter reduction, the prints for a library of a million 250-page books would now cost $18,750.[2] Before such a system can succeed, the problems of copyright and royalties must be met squarely, with full regard to the rights of authors and publishers as well as readers.

The satisfactory operation of this kind of service and its extension to more ephemeral, current scientific and technical data and reports call for the acceptance of compatible systems by documentalists, librarians, and computer manufacturers, and of complementary functions by leading libraries and document repositories. The formal systems for filing and recovering information will, as always, be supplemented by the equally indispensable systems of informal scientific communication. Indeed, as the formal systems for generating and distributing knowledge grow in magnitude, complexity, and specialization, the informal means of determining *what* information may be significant for each occasion and to each specialized interest will assume added importance. Television, telephone, and other rapid means of informal communication, and more formal, intercity conference hookups will reduce the necessity for, and the kudos attached to, professional travel.

Unlike others who fear an information "overload" because the volume of information is expanding rapidly while the individual's capacity to absorb it remains fixed, we observe that there has always been enough information to overload some individuals. Physiological sluice gates and storage limitations normally regulate the intake of both higher and lower bodily centers to that which can be digested or eliminated. What Curtis Benjamin calls the " 'twigging' phenomenon, . . . the endless fractionation of interest and knowledge in technical fields,"[3] has, in any event, kept the professional man's need for knowledge in balance with his capacity to absorb it.

Time will remain incompressible and undistensible; its allocation between traveling and staying put, between learning and reporting what one has learned, between listening and talking, doing and thinking, working and relaxing will, as always, influence the pace of intellectual progress.

The changes in our intellectual institutions that will work themselves out over the next thirty-three years are not merely modifications within existing organizations (universities, academies, research institutes, libraries, industrial laboratories), but more fundamental developments that will generate new and transform old institutional forms. The universities, for example, are under multiple pressures for change caused by the side-effects of federal support, the demands of regional and community development, the creation of cross-disciplinary centers, the fading boundaries between training and work, and the demands from the new society of the young. As a result, a variety of new organizational forms linked more closely to community needs, to work, and to living currents of industrial-political-intellectual life than to the traditional community of scholars will be developed within, outside, and beside the campus.

Will our intellectual institutions regard these pressures as disruptive threats to be met? One critic feels the future we have depicted is tenderhearted, unnaturally full of sweetness and light. There is so much co-operation and continuity. Where are the conflicts and discontinuities? Co-operation is expensive, administratively cumbersome, and inefficient, says another. Most institutions will go their own way then as now, and that is actually the best way to work things out—in the rough and tumble of the competitive educational market place. Conflict will persist between those institutions at and those near the top of the pyramid; between academic and practical outlooks (and laboratories); between pressures for co-operation and for independence. In short, the year 2000 will bring just another, not *the*, millennium. There are weeds as well as tinsel in the grass.[4]

REFERENCES

1. James R. Killian, "New Goals for Science and Engineering Education," *Education: An Instrument of National Goals*, ed. Paul R. Hanna (New York, 1962), pp. 86, 88.

198

2. This figure neglects the original cost of microfilming and of equipment for storing and servicing. See Verner W. Clapp, *The Future of the Research Library* (Urbana, Ill., 1964), pp. 19-20.

3. "The 'twigging' phenomenon occurs in the endless fractionation of interest and knowledge in technical fields, a continuing fractionation that has held markets for specialized books to the same size they were fifteen or twenty years ago—this in spite of the fact that the total corpus of technical knowledge is at least five times larger than it was twenty years ago and there are at least three times as many professional scientists and engineers, or customers, in the United States. (Thus the tree is much larger, but the twigs are the same size.)" Curtis G. Benjamin, "Everything Is Not Coming Up Roses," Address at the 56th Annual Convention of the Special Libraries Association (Philadelphia, June 9, 1965), pp. 4-5.

4. This paper was first prepared as a summary of a discussion held with John R. Pierce and Donald A. Schon, each of whom contributed passages to the original draft.

ERNST MAYR

Biological Man and the Year 2000

A BIOLOGIST feels rather out of place in a conference dominated by economists, government experts, historians, and sociologists. The year 2000 is only thirty-three years away, and the physical appearance of man has not changed materially in more than one hundred thousand years so far as one can infer from the fossil record. Biological man in the year 2000 will not be different in any appreciable way from what he is today.

Much of the first conference of the Commission was devoted to crystal-ball gazing, guessing, and predicting. Indeed, this is a major concern for city planners, engineers, and economists. When thinking of the future, the biologist tends to be more ambitious. He is not satisfied with merely describing some future condition; he actually would like to make suggestions as to what to do in order to make this a better world. There are two attitudes we can take with reference to the future. We can assume the attitude of the watchers of a Greek tragedy. Without raising a finger, they let the play drift inexorably toward its blood-stained conclusion. Or we can behave like utopians, to a greater or lesser degree, and propose measures that will better the fate of mankind and hopefully better mankind itself. Anyone familiar with the fantastically rapid evolution of the brain from the ape level to the *Homo sapiens* level is entitled to the fond hope that the apparent standstill in man's evolution is only a temporary phase and that a way can be found to initiate a trend toward an even greater future. Biologically, this is not an impossible utopia, since the enormous amount of genetic variability in man would, indeed, permit considerable response to selection pressures. Whether or not this is socially, politically, and morally feasible is an entirely different matter.

Let us forget for the moment the tantalizing problem of man's evolutionary future and turn to the question of coping with biological man as he is now. I pointed out in the conference in October how poorly we have solved the problems posed by man's biological inequality. Nothing is more undemocratic or more apt to destroy equal opportunity than forcing human beings with exceedingly dif-

200

ferent aptitudes and motivations through identical social institutions. There is only one way to cope with man's genetic diversity, and that is to diversify man's environment. We need more kinds of schools, more curricula within each school, more diversity in economic and moral rewards, and so forth. It is almost unbelievable to the biologist that it has taken so long for the promoters of educational theories to grasp this simple point. To adjust our institutions to the final realization that no two human beings are biologically identical because every individual is genetically unique will occupy us well beyond the year 2000. To a biologist these thirty-three years are no more than a moment in the evolutionary history of mankind. When we deal with this moment, we can well afford to make the simplifying assumption that man is biologically unchanging.

This simplifying assumption is, of course, not correct. The genetic composition of the gene pool of every species of animals and plants changes from generation to generation. Man is no exception. When we consider the long-term evolution of man we cannot ignore such changes. They happen all around us and right before our eyes. If it is true, as all the facts seem to indicate, that those with below-average intelligence have a higher reproductive rate than those with above-average intelligence, this would document an evolutionary change (considering the indications for high heritability of intelligence). Shall we stand by passively and let such changes happen for better or for worse, or shall we start thinking again in terms of man's evolutionary future?

Lawrence K. Frank said quite rightly at our last meeting that nothing is so powerful as ideas. This has surely been demonstrated by the American, the French, and the Russian Revolutions, as well as by the ideas of civil disobedience, representative government, and free enterprise. These famous ideas have dramatically changed human institutions; they have changed man's environment and, indeed, man himself. Biology in the last fifty years has developed many ideas that have a similar potential to change not only man's environment but man himself. This to me is a frightening thought. It is doubly frightening when one thinks of the Nazi horrors perpetrated under the guise of improving man. We hear increasingly of sperm banks, of selective sterilization, of genetic engineering, and of other ways to usher in a brave new world.

Our natural reaction to all this is—Down with it! Surely we will not make a mistake if we do nothing, if we adopt a *laissez-faire* policy. Why not maintain the *status quo*? Unfortunately there is no *status quo* so far as the genetic composition of natural populations is concerned. They always change, no matter what we do. Right now an amazingly strong natural selection is going on among the industrial populations of the Western world. Some segments of this population contribute to the gene pool of the next generation two, three, four, or more times as many genes as other segments. As James F. Crow has shown, reproductive advantage has largely replaced survival advantage as far as natural selection in man is concerned.[1] The evolutionist measures fitness in terms of the contribution made to the gene pool of the next generation. The person who has six surviving children has three times as large a fitness as the person with two children. This reproductive differential is now by far the most important component of natural selection in man. It has replaced pre-reproductive mortality as the principal component of fitness. Under these circumstances it is obvious that a simple *laissez-faire* policy would hardly be an ideal strategy on a long-term basis.

Is there an alternative? I am afraid the honest answer is—Not right now. The reason for this is our enormous ignorance. Fortunately unequal reproduction is not a pressing problem so long as the population explosion continues.

As soon as population control is exercized, it inevitably tends to be qualitative rather than purely quantitative. Even under current conditions, the most responsible segments in our population are the ones that are most successful in controlling family size. If part of their intelligence or self-discipline has a genetic basis, it would mean that these very genes are being discriminated against in our population. Can one do something about this, and if so, what? The answer must be an ambiguous yes and no. It is extremely difficult to approach this subject without falling into the same traps as the racists and naïve eugenicists. Before we can propose any meaningful program for a genetic improvement of mankind, we must satisfy two prior conditions, and it is almost certain that it will require several generations for these conditions to be met.

The first of these prerequisites is a thorough re-examination of some of our most widely accepted, I might almost say sacred, concepts—the role of the individual in society, the consequences of population structure (versus typological essentialism), the question of personal rights in an interdependent co-operative society. As Karl Popper and others have pointed out perceptively, we are still suffering from the heritage of Platonian (essentialist) misconceptions. It will take a long time before they are properly recognized and eliminated. Much that was objectionable in past eugenic proposals was due to this unfortunate heritage. When evaluating human contributions to the gene pool of the next generation, we must rigorously exclude all traces of typological thinking. We are not concerned with human types or races; we are not concerned with black or white skin, with straight or curly hair, with the rich or the poor. We are simply concerned with individuals and their genetic potential. The correlations between different kinds of traits, physical and nonphysical, are so slight that it would be not only unfair but actually misleading to adopt a typological approach. Yet typological thinking is still dominant in much of psychology, anthropology, economics, sociology, and even biology. It will have to be eradicated totally before we can seriously consider the future of mankind.

The second prerequisite is research on the nature of the genetic contribution to human traits. If the time should ever come when we are emotionally ready to allow a reproductive premium for above-average genotypes, we would have to be able to determine what makes a genotype "valuable." At present we are unable to do this. We all remember the great controversy of the past generation over nature versus nurture. Fortunately this argument is now dead except in the minds of a few who have not kept track of the developments in genetics in the past thirty years. We now know that the phenotypes of almost all traits are the result of both a genetic predisposition and its response to the environment. Students of selection have demonstrated that successful selection is possible even when the genetic contribution to a trait (its heritability) is less than 20 per cent, indeed less than 10 per cent.

Enormous advances have been made in recent generations in the control of the nurture component of human traits through improved public health, child care, nutrition, a better educational system, and other measures that help to bring out the full potential contained in the genotype. There is, however, an obvious limit to the effectiveness of such measures. One can improve an I.Q. measure by twenty points and in exceptional cases perhaps by thirty points, but one cannot turn an 80 I.Q. into a 150 I.Q. no matter what one does. Once we have exhausted all the possibilities of improvement through improved nurture, we must start thinking about positive eugenics; there is no third alternative. We have little knowledge of the genetics of important human traits at the present time, and the field is cluttered up with old wives' tales. Research on identical twins (in comparison with same-sexed dizygotic twins) has made important contributions, as have longitudinal family studies, such as those of Sheldon C. and Elizabeth W. Reed on mental retardation. The obstacles to research are formidable. Experimentation is nearly always impossible, as is the setting up of proper controls. Yet the information needed is of such importance that research will have to be stepped up.

I have stressed the need for reconceptualization. Most people have been raised with the belief that equality equals biological identity, and this early conditioning still dominates much of our thinking and our emotions. J. B. S. Haldane and others have pointed out that the human achievements—those things that distinguish man from the animals and are responsible for man's civilization, art, literature, and science—were achieved by less than 1 per cent of the human population, by those in the upper tail of the curve of human variation in inventiveness, imagination, perseverance, and ability to think clearly. A rather small downward shift in the mean value of the curve of human variability might obliterate much of this highest class of potential achievers. A slight upward shift of the curve might double the size of this class. Perhaps this is not a legitimate calculation, but such considerations help us to focus on an important but badly neglected challenge to mankind.

Man, along with all other sexually reproducing species, undergoes slight genetic change from generation to generation. Such change is negligible on a short-range basis, and no appreciable change in biological man is to be expected between now and the year 2000 or, indeed, for the next several hundred years. Nevertheless, a genetic change is inevitable over the centuries, and man must ask himself whether he wants to adopt a *laissez-faire* attitude toward these changes or to be the master of his own fate. If he should adopt the second alternative, he must not only rebuild much of his conceptual framework, but start an extensive research program that would give substance to what are now purely subjective and largely arbitrary value judgments concerning human characteristics.

REFERENCES

1. James F. Crow, "Mechanisms and Trends in Human Evolution," *Dædalus* (Summer, 1961), pp. 416-31.

GARDNER C. QUARTON

Deliberate Efforts to Control Human Behavior and Modify Personality

RECENT DEVELOPMENTS in pharmocology and neurophysiology have focused attention on technological possibilities for controlling behavior and changing personality in radical ways. If a new technology of this type is developed, it could have a marked influence on the lives of some individuals. Systematic applications of these techniques would have broad social implications.

The very idea of manipulating human behavior seems to stir up both fears and wishful fantasies. These interfere with a commonsense evaluation of the issues. This emotional reaction to the idea of behavior manipulation must be evaluated at three different levels: first, as a barrier to the collecting of facts and to sensible assessment of the social problem; second, as a factor in the social acceptance of the technology; and, third, as a manipulative tool for modifying human behavior in its own right. The first of these must be considered before any other discussion. An emotional reaction to the idea of behavior control seems to lead to a short circuiting of the process of evaluation. Most discussion of behavior control begins with the possibility of a new technology and then either jumps to the desirability of an application of such techniques in the immediate future or to a possible mechanism of control of the technique to prevent its abuse. In these short-circuited discussions the leap from the idea to plans for immediate social action omits a review of the factual issues that would seem to be necessary for a more deliberate evaluation. Very often there is a failure to distinguish between facts and predictions, between facts and values, and between values and proposals for social action. This smearing of the status of propositions limits the usefulness of many such discussions.

The current state of the "art" can be summed up by saying that it is, in fact, possible to alter behavior by drugs, neurosurgical intervention, and systematic stimulus control. At present, the techniques are crude, not necessarily reliable, and not based on a sound and complete theoretical understanding of the underlying mechanisms. But, in a sense, since they are at least partially effective even without this full understanding, we should not delay an evaluation of the social implications until complete understanding is achieved.

Certain trends of the past fifteen years suggest an increase in the importance of the problem of behavior manipulation in the immediate future. Until quite recently the medical doctor was one of the few professionals with both a major interest in modifying human behavior and personality, and a biological interest in the brain. His concern arose directly from his therapeutic activities. He knew, understood, and presumably liked his neighbors and patients. He was, however, usually so busy with the demands of practice and so compelled to act with inadequate knowledge that he seldom reflected on alternate explanations of behavior and rarely conducted systematic experiments. As a result, scientific knowledge of the determinants of human behavior has developed very slowly. With the development of modern academic medicine, the concept has spread that doctors can be investigative human biologists. In the last few years this idea has been extended to psychiatry, neurology, and neurosurgery. This has led to a rapid increase in research effort and has supplied a group of highly skilled technicians who have extended the findings of animal biology and psychology by human experiments. During the same period, with the development of molecular genetics, biology—as it is taught in the universities—has become less naturalistic and more experimental. Not only are careers in experimental biology possible outside medicine, but much of the really significant progress has occurred there. Psychology as a laboratory science has developed apace. Many dedicated, full-time investigators are working intensively on the determinants of human behavior. It seems very likely, then, that we can expect a rapid increase in the scientific knowledge about the way in which the brain works and the way in which environmental factors interact with biological events to produce complex behavior. It also seems likely that many of those doing research will be specialists with little knowledge of or interest in the human consequences of the applications of their research.

We can expect increasingly effective methods for modifying personality and controlling behavior. What will these techniques be? Who will use them? And for what purposes?

Controlling Human Behavior and Modifying Personality

The Technological Possibilities

Although there have been many new suggestions for modifying human behavior, some methods go back thousands of years. Both the new and the old deserve some kind of systematic consideration.

There are a number of methods for categorizing technological possibilities. No schema is completely satisfactory because the determinants of behavior are not themselves well understood and because they interact in very complex ways. For instance, it is obvious that genes are determinants of behavior and that environmental factors available as stimuli are also critical. But it is no longer profitable to argue that one of these general classes is more important than another. Both are necessary; each is insufficient alone; and they interact in a complex nonlinear fashion.

In discussions of this type there is often a problem with the word *control*. In order to speak of a technological intervention as controlling some aspect of behavior, it is not necessary to assume that total control is achieved. It may be that a very slight shift in the probabilities of a response at a certain critical period will produce an important effect.

A distinction can be made between interventions affecting the development of mechanisms that determine behavior in the adult organism and those that manipulate an already mature mechanism. For instance, hormones can be administered early in the life of an animal so that development is modified, and the later repertory of behavior altered as a result of this early intervention. When administered to a mature animal, hormones change the probabilities of responses in quite a different way.

In classifying determinants of behavior change, it is sometimes convenient to assume that they act either on the organism or on the environment in which the organism lives. But this simplifying distinction may break down since the organism is in constant interaction with the environment. If we disturb the flow of information from the organism to the environment and back to the organism, it is not necessarily clear whether we are acting on the organism or on the environment. For instance, if we cut the legs off an animal, we prevent certain types of behavior by modifying the organism. But because the behavior repertory is reduced, the environmental patterns perceived by the animal are also reduced, and behavior is influenced by the censorship of stimuli.

Some techniques for modifying behavior are relatively reversible (drugs, prostheses); others are in some sense irreversible (destructive brain operations, college educations). This distinction partially accounts for that made in the title between control of behavior and modification of personality. More is involved in modifying personality, however, than in the production of irreversible changes. I use the word *personality* to refer to patterns of behavior in which there are not only simultaneous and sequential complexities, but also recurring features that are characteristic for that individual. A brain operation that reduces anxiety and increases spontaneous impulsive behavior is, in this sense, a technique that modifies personality.

A rational and exhaustive categorization of ways of influencing behavior would concern itself with issues like reversibility, the effect on the maturation process, and so forth. It might even ignore differences between technological devices if the type of effect were similar. For instance, certain drugs and electrical stimulation might both alert an individual by similar action on arousal mechanisms in the brain. But for purposes of this discussion, the best schema to use in surveying available methods of behavior manipulation seems to be in terms of the techniques themselves.

Modification of the Genetic Code

Developments in the molecular biology of the gene have raised the possibility that the DNA code might be radically altered by the substitution of new genetic material for that already existing in a cell. In 1928 it was discovered that the addition of heat-killed cells of a pathogenic strain of diplococcus pneumoniae to a suspension of live nonpathogenic pneumonia cells caused a small fraction of the live bacteria to become pathogenic. This genetic recombination has been given the name "transformation," and in recent years attention has focused on the possibility that it might be feasible in mammals, especially man. Since the genes make a major contribution to all kinds of behavior, the rather wild speculation has been made that genetic recombination might constitute a device for eliminating undesirable behavior traits. I shall mention this possibility only to set it aside. So far, all experiments on transformation in mammals have been negative except for special cases in which viruses transform normal cells into cancer cells. Furthermore, relatively little is known of the location on the chromosomes

208

of those genes that are vital for different types of behavior. It seems unlikely that human behavioral genetics will advance sufficiently in the next fifty years to make this method of behavior modification worthy of serious consideration. Moreover, the contributions of the genes to behavior and personality are exceedingly complex. It is almost certain that geneticists would turn their attention first to the elimination of disorders due to single genes.

Gene Selection by Controlled Mating

Selective breeding of animals has been carried on for years to produce desired behavioral traits. These techniques are certainly available for application to human behavior. These methods also will not be considered in detail, partly because they seem unlikely to be extensively used due to the opposition of our current society, and also because, if they were applied, the effect would not be demonstrable until several generations had passed.

Nutritional Influences

An adequate diet is necessary for normal human growth and development and, incidentally, for normal behavior. A limited diet, particularly the absence of certain vitamins, can lead to deficiency syndromes characterized by abnormal behavior. A good example of this is pellagra, which is due to a deficiency of nicotinic acid. The search for nutritional factors that can correct behavior abnormalities will obviously continue. This is not likely, however, to be a technological device used in the manipulation of normal individuals except under extreme conditions when persuasion techniques utilizing food and water deprivation are employed.

Hormones

Recent information developing from investigation of the effect of hormones on a wide variety of mechanisms shows that hormones can modify human behavior in many different ways. Neural tissues differentiate one way if certain sexual hormones are present and another way if they are absent. The organizing influence of hormones often depends on their presence during a particular stage of development as well as upon the amount. For instance, sexual hormones act not only to influence the development of effector

209

systems making adult sexual performance possible, but influence the intensity of sexual drive and the nature of sex-related behavior. In adult life, sexual hormones alter the intensity of drive and modify the reception of stimuli which influence sexual performance. The adrenocortical hormones, thyroxin, and epinephrine also modify behavior. Relatively few studies have been done on humans by withholding and administering hormones to modify behavior, chiefly because other effects of hormones have held greater interest, and because side effects are often more important than the behavioral effects.

The Use of Drugs

Alcohol and other similar drugs have, of course, been used for thousands of years to modify behavior and subjective experience. Interest in psychopharmacology has been greatly increased with need for anesthetics, analgesics, and a wide variety of sedatives and stimulants. The earlier studies of these agents were empirical in the sense that the goal of the investigation was merely to determine whether or not the drug produced an effect, and the type of effect obtained. In recent years there has been extensive interest in the chemical organization of the nervous system, particularly in the effort to clarify the role of chemicals as possible transmitter substances used in the actual transfer of information from one neuron to another. Although no substance has been proved with absolute certainty to be a transmitter in the central nervous system, information is rapidly being collected concerning the synthesis, storage, transport, utilization, and mode of breakdown of many substances in the brain that probably function as transmitters or as modulators of transmission. In the next twenty-five years, this information is likely to revolutionize pharmacology by supplying a whole new group of drugs, discovered not by accident, but through systematic research into basic brain mechanisms. For instance, in the last decade there has been a very large amount of research on the catecholamines such as norepinephrine. Many drugs that act upon the central nervous system are now believed to act by influencing the availability of norepinephrine. This system is increasingly considered to be important in the mechanisms that determine mood. It is certainly reasonable to guess that control of mood in man may be possible by pharmacological means in the next fifty years.

The mechanism and purpose of sleep remain great scientific

mysteries. Recent investigations have demonstrated, however, many neural and chemical mechanisms necessary for initiating and maintaining sleep. It is quite possible that investigations of these phenomena will progress rapidly and lead to new drugs.

Although there have been many attempts recently to demonstrate that RNA and protein synthesis are essential for learning and memory, evidence of a breakthrough in this area is not available at this time. Some drugs are known to enhance slightly the efficiency of certain types of learning in animals. Research in this area is certain to continue at a rapid rate, but its outcome is not predictable at present.

Drugs that "expand consciousness," such as LSD, require close attention. These agents produce a subjective experience that combines an intensification of sensation with some confusion and with heightened emotions, including elation and fear. They have been used in combination with psychotherapy to treat various mental disorders. The most dramatic aspect of these "psychedelic" agents is that they have escaped from the control of the scientific community and are distributed and used by sub-cultures within our society. The scientific use of LSD has recently been much curtailed by evidence that a prolonged psychosis can follow a single, very small dose. It is not possible to predict the future of these drugs because new scientific discoveries can radically alter utilization patterns, and because use of drugs for kicks is complicated by other very complex social phenomena.

The future will probably bring entirely new classes of drugs into prominence. It is not easy to speculate on the possible social consequences.

Neurosurgical Interventions

Psychosurgery, defined as surgical operations on the intact brain performed for the relief of mental symptoms, was conceived by Egas Moniz in Lisbon in 1933 and first carried out under his direction in 1935. During the 1950's there was considerable use of these techniques, particularly with operations to remove the frontal lobes or to sever the connection of the frontal lobes with the rest of the brain.

These procedures depend for their effectiveness on knowledge of the function of the different parts of the brain. Investigation of human brain function is quite naturally slow because experimental studies on living human brains are not considered ethical. With the recent upsurge of interest in the brain and the availability of primates, many studies of the localization of brain function have been carried out. With this newer information there has come additional interest in brain destruction in the frontal and temporal lobes, in the cingulate gyrus, and in certain subcortical centers that will alter some aspects of behavior without radically crippling the subject.

More recently behavior in animals has been modified by inserting electrodes into the brain. Small currents are passed through the electrodes while the animals or humans are awake and behaving relatively normally. This current flow stimulates a small group of neurons to produce nerve impulses, and these impulses in turn produce, modify, or arrest behavior. It is sometimes argued that this stimulation is not physiological or that we do not know whether the behavioral effect is produced by adding or subtracting messages in the brain. Also, scientists are often not exactly sure where electrodes are placed in the brain since they must be implanted with complex stereotactic devices, using bony landmarks and "brain atlases" as guides. The mechanism of action of brain stimulation is not fully understood, and there is some difficulty in producing reliable effects through repeated efforts to duplicate a single phenomenon. In spite of this, brain stimulation does modify behavior and will be increasingly investigated.

Brain stimulation in animals can be used to elicit fragments of behavior that appear organized, to produce alertness, drowsiness, and sleep, to arrest any ongoing behavior, to modify the urgency of biological drives such as sex and maternal tendencies, to increase or decrease aggressive behavior, and so forth. Certain placements of electrodes in the brain will cause an animal to continue to press a bar indefinitely if pressing that bar produces stimulation. Conversely, animals with other electrode placements will immediately press bars to turn off stimulation. This has led to acceptance of the notion that there are centers of the brain that elicit "pleasant" or "unpleasant" sensations. These can be stimulated to reward or punish behavior, and, in fact, this type of stimulation can be a substitute for externally delivered reinforcements. Recently the devices used to produce brain stimulation have been made smaller and simpler, and stimulation can now be carried out by radio without connecting cables.

212

Dr. Jose Delgado, who has done much of the research on brain stimulation in monkeys, has shown that stimulation of the brain of one monkey will modify the social behavior of a group. Monkeys without brain electrodes can even learn to activate an electrode in the brain of an aggressive companion to reduce the effectiveness of his attacks on them. In the last few years experiments with implanted electrodes in humans have shown that most of the effects obtained with other mammals are probably quite feasible in humans.

Small direct currents passing through the brain from electrodes outside the skull and scalp have also been used to alter mood. These effects are quite variable from occasion to occasion, but further investigation will almost certainly be carried out. Chemicals can be placed in very limited areas of the brain by means of small cannulae, making possible a combination of neurosurgical and pharmacological methods of altering behavior.

Surgery Outside the Brain

Surgery outside the brain deserves brief mention. Removal of glands can be used to alter the endocrine system. Research on techniques in which mechanisms are attached to the body to increase effectiveness can be considered likely. Prostheses have only been used so far to help those crippled by accidental injury, but, in principle, such devices could extend the range of function of normal individuals.

Environmental Manipulations

It is obvious that many social institutions, such as the family, the school, the church, and the psychiatrist, play an important role in shaping and controlling the behavior and personality of individuals. I have considered these influences as outside the scope of this discussion. There are, however, relatively specific methods that bring behavior under stimulus control and, therefore, deserve consideration along with the biological technologies.

Pavlov and Skinner and their followers have demonstrated how relatively simple techniques involving the pairing of stimuli with rewards and punishment can modify behavior. There has been much recent interest in extending such techniques to humans and in investigating applications in situations reasonably close to everyday life. Because humans are so much more complex than animals, and their past experiences and various motivations make them less predictable, there is some disagreement about the interpretations of these extensions. In spite of these reservations, a fairly precise technology exists and will be extensively applied in the next fifty years.

Interest in well-timed and well-placed "reinforcement" has obscured the fact that other methods of behavioral manipulation are also quite readily available. Some of these are quite simple, and modern systems analysis and flow-charting schemes permit them to be extensively applied if society allows it. For instance, the behavior of an individual is much influenced by the opportunities that are made available or denied to him. Much greater control of opportunity to act is possible using modern communication and control techniques. Similarly, behavior is readily modified by supplying or withholding maps or models of how other individuals behave. This type of control is more difficult to achieve. Hypnosis also deserves mention because it is now being studied by serious, scientifically trained investigators.

Monitoring

It is important in any type of behavior control to know how an individual behaved before and after the application of behavior-control techniques. Thus, efficient monitoring devices greatly increase the effectiveness of any method of control. Modern communication equipment and rapid computational devices increase the number and range of surveillance devices and the methods of getting information in a useful form to a person or machine engaged in behavior control. Radio transmitters can be implanted in human subjects. Behavior can be observed by television cameras and listened to by microphones. Routine behavior can be recorded at check points in computer procedures, commercial activities, and at toll gates. Most of these possibilities are fortunately not exploited under present circumstances.

Mixed Methods

The most efficient utilization of behavior-control technology would involve mixing techniques. If, for instance, a human subject had electrodes implanted in such a way that any ongoing action could be rewarded, punished, or prevented, and if microtransmitters and receivers made external wires and apparatus unnecessary, he could be placed in a learning situation, and selected patterns of behavior could be encouraged or discouraged automatically. With effective monitoring and computing equipment, much of the process could be controlled automatically. Let us take another example. Assume a great increase in the efficiency of a governmental taxation program. If taxes were collected more frequently, if taxation policies were altered over short intervals to serve immediate policy needs, and if the individual were made acutely aware of the effect of taxation on his life, a high degree of control of the behavior of the individual would be possible. Such a program would make use of modern data processing and monitoring, reinforcement techniques, and certain display procedures.

Social Acceptance of Technological Change

The impact of technological change upon society depends not only on the nature of the technology, but also upon its acceptance by society. In no area is this more important than in the area of manipulation of behavior. Social attitudes may be so strong and of such a character that in spite of technological possibilities, no utilization by society can occur. At the opposite extreme a totalitarian government might use such techniques extensively. A sober prediction of events in the next thirty-five years would suggest some intermediate possibility.

It would be extremely useful if one could examine in a careful way instances of social acceptance of behavior manipulation and extrapolate from these. Unfortunately, the instances of behavior manipulation have been scattered and are so crude that the pattern of social acceptance itself has been difficult to assess. There is a literature on the reaction of the citizens of the United States to brainwashing in Red China, and there are, of course, written documents protesting almost all of the behavior-control techniques. Most people seem to be frightened but fascinated. A systematic study of these attitudes might be a very useful tool in making projections into the future.

Psychiatrists and educators, the prime candidates to use manipulation techniques, appear to be quite ambivalent concerning their development and application. Psychiatrists, particularly, often have value systems of their own that stress the importance of in-

215

dividual differences, the resolution of social conflict by increases in interindividual communication and group insight, and a gradual replacement of irrational explanations of events by ideas tested against reality in a personal and practical way. Psychiatrists trained in this way dislike therapeutic techniques that involve manipulation of the patient by any method, including environmental modification or drugs. They use manipulative techniques only when other methods fail, but it is important that they do use them on occasion, and that other psychiatrists, with or without qualms, sometimes use drugs and neurosurgery to relieve anxiety after only a brief analysis of the patient's over-all life problem. During the period of major interest in frontal lobotomy, hundreds of transorbital frontal leucotomies were performed in some state hospitals in periods of time so short that it is hard to believe the cases were thoroughly analyzed. Casual but well-intentioned use of these techniques is a reality today. It would, therefore, be naïve to think it will not occur to a significant degree in the future.

One abuse of drugs that occurs today in some places is the use of tranquilizers in hospitals for the mentally ill and the aged primarily to keep troublemaking patients from annoying the staff. This use of drugs may actually prevent the life experiences necessary for social recovery, and in the future this type of abuse will be possible to an even greater extent.

More important than the attitudes of people in the general population are the opinions and decisions of individuals who are in a position to pass on research projects that explore behavior manipulation. We know very little about how the critical decisions are made. One gets the impression that such decision-making bodies have been, on the whole, quite conservative. Experiments on stimulus and reinforcement control have been restricted to studies in the field of education with normal and retarded children and to scattered work with other groups of abnormal individuals. Experiments in which electrodes are implanted in human subjects have just begun and, as a rule, have been restricted to situations in which a clear therapeutic gain could be anticipated from the implantation—for example, in victims of epilepsy and severe motor disorders who could be helped by brain stimulation and destruction. The practical problem raised by research on mood control will soon be more pressing.

Another important factor in anticipating social acceptance involves the fragmentation of the society. Some sections of society may accept a new technology even though the society as a whole rejects it. Let us suppose, for instance, that new and effective drugs become available. It will be very important whether or not control of distribution and use is encouraged or inhibited by large private manufacturing industries, by secret and semicriminal distributing groups, or by government and nonprofit organizations operating under full public scrutiny. I have already mentioned that some methods of manipulating behavior are likely to slip from the control of those who originate them. It seems likely, for instance, that certain kinds of drugs which are easily and cheaply produced and which can be manufactured by relatively inexperienced chemists can be made and used by individuals in spite of disapproval by society at large and the institutions set up by the government to control use. Other methods of behavior manipulation, such as those involving major brain surgery, are not likely to be possible except under reasonable public scrutiny.

A cautious general extrapolation from present acceptance of behavior-manipulation techniques suggests that a limited extension of use of surgical techniques and stimulus-control methods will proceed under fairly close supervision by the public and by academic institutions. Many new drugs will undoubtedly be developed both in academic institutions and by large private drug houses. Advertising will probably continue to exaggerate the need for drugs in order to promote sales. If we argue by analogy from current difficulties in control of drugs, we can assume that new drugs will be accepted, at least by certain parts of our society, and will pose serious problems for society and for those institutions of government that are attempting control. Because drugs can be used easily, it is also quite likely that they will constitute the most common technique for manipulating behavior with full social approval—for instance, increasingly in the handling of behavior deviants.

Some Extreme Patterns of Social Acceptance of Behavior Manipulation

In the last section an effort was made to make an extremely cautious prediction primarily by means of an extrapolation from knowledge of present social acceptance of techniques for behavior manipulation and personality control. In my opinion, it is also useful to make wilder predictions using the method of alternate futures suggested by Daniel Bell. These predictions may stimulate

217

discussion of social questions that will need answers in the near future, particularly if they suggest that social action is desired. I list some caricatures of future societies that might take radically different attitudes toward behavior manipulation.

I. *Extensive use justified by "humanitarian" values*

Modern humanitarianism seems to take the form of keeping each individual alive and without pain as long as possible even though he has little to live for. Brochures urge the donation of funds for research to eliminate almost every cause of death. Since every man must die sooner or later, the effect of this research is primarily to postpone death and possibly to make the prolonged life somewhat more pleasant. If these protective and avoidance patterns are greatly extended in the future, one can imagine a society that allows widespread use of drugs to prevent pain and anxiety, brain surgery to prevent both suffering and any aggressive actions by individuals, and extensive use of monitoring equipment to restrict individual behavior with a destructive potential. By such devices, it would certainly be possible to reduce unpleasant subjective experiences and to reduce greatly the impact of interpersonal aggression. In spite of the fact that such a society would undoubtedly produce weak individuals incapable of meeting new threats from the environment, there are indications in our present society that suggest trends in this direction.

II. *Extensive use justified by "efficiency"*

There are certain types of activity in which a high degree of efficiency by human participants is desired. The best example of this is in military efforts, but efficiency also leads to reduced costs in manufacturing and other similar activities. It is quite possible that managerial groups in the military or industry will encourage the use of behavior-manipulation techniques that increase the effectiveness of the human beings in the system. Since drugs are used to some degree in this way at the present time, some further experimentations are likely.

Hostility to totalitarian forms of government does exist, however, and this suggests that most democratic societies will resist this type of use unless there is a radical change in our whole social structure.

III. *Discouraging the use of behavior manipulation by encouraging "social inefficiency"*

A negative reaction to totalitarian efficiency leads to overt or covert efforts to prevent exploitation by managerial groups. One way of accomplishing this is to encourage bureaucratic inefficiency. Some of the attitudes expressed by our current adolescent protest groups include this idea. It is of some interest that those groups in our present society that most favor anarchy as a method of avoiding control by the establishment also favor the use of drugs for kicks.

IV. *Puritanical avoidance of behavior control*

There are individuals in our present society who regard any use of special techniques to modify behavior and personality as being in some way unnatural. This type of puritanical self-reliance might be much expanded in a future society. At the moment, this possibility does not seem particularly likely.

V. *Multiple parallel developments*

In our present society, attitudes toward alcohol, heroin, LSD, and other behavior-modification devices seem to vary, particularly among the different segments of society. It seems likely that future societies will continue this trend by which different techniques evolve in different ways. In particular, police and military leaders will probably exploit certain techniques even against opposition from other segments of society just as beatnik and protest groups will use other devices for sensation seeking. Industries that make a profit from certain types of behavior manipulation will undoubtedly push those that are the most profitable.

Human Rights and Human Engineering

Current interest in civil rights suggests that we are just beginning a period of active examination of the pattern of rights and immunities that we desire for the protection of the individual in a complex and rapidly changing society. The major preoccupation during this decade has been with racial problems and with the protection of the individual threatened by criminal prosecution, but there is also increasing concern over invasions of privacy.

The civil rights issues involved in behavior control are very difficult to state with clarity. Since society has been controlling the behavior of the individual throughout history by providing and preventing opportunities for action and by manipulation of reward-punishment systems, it does not make much sense to argue that the control of one individual by another is in itself unethical. It is tempting to say that certain types of behavior control that are novel, efficient, and easily identified—such as deliberate destructive brain surgery—violate the rights of the individual, particularly if they are performed against the wishes of that individual and are irreversible. But this is too easy a solution. Other types of behavior control, such as confinement behind bars, are carried out against the will of the individual, and these may also have some irreversible effects. Groups that have recently explored the dangers inherent in human experimentation have urged that no one be a subject in an experiment unless he gives "informed consent." A similar protection might be considered to protect the individual from control. Many doctors and psychologists do not, however, believe informed and free consent is really possible. Many individuals cannot understand the technical details of the procedures to which they are giving consent, and agreement after discussion or persuasion is not really free.

I believe that the study of the civil rights aspects of behavior manipulation gets sidetracked if there is too much attention to specific techniques. This assumes major concern over means while ignoring ends. The difficulty in making policies concerning behavior-manipulation techniques lies in reaching agreement on social goals, particularly those goals that balance group objectives against the right of individuals to make certain decisions and to behave within certain limits without interference.

One of the major effects of increased efficiency of some behavior-control techniques will be a proportional growth of discussion of the problem in relation to civil rights. In the future, government officials and agencies will spend much more time thinking about these matters than they do now. There are many problems lying ahead that will need legislative and judicial solutions.

One can safely predict that techniques for controlling behavior and modifying personality will grow more efficient by the year 2000. In particular, there will be many efforts to mix behavior-control techniques and to apply them systematically in areas where society faces major problems. The areas that come immediately to mind are education, the handling of delinquents and criminals, and work with the mentally retarded and ill. Society is likely to resist the use of the more radical and efficient methods, and major disagreements between civil rights advocates and the advocates of efficiency will occur and need some type of reconciliation.

My own biased opinion is that the society of the future will need all the diversity in its population that it can maintain since there will be many factors tending to enforce conformity. An understanding of behavior-control technology is to be encouraged because even though extensive knowledge may bring some undesired applications, it is also necessary to develop an alert, well-informed public that will watch for abuses.

Religion, Mysticism, and the Institutional Church

THE FOLLOWING paragraphs were written as a reaction to an early outline of the topics to be considered by the Commission on the Year 2000. Among such topics we find the resources for an "inner life," and "art and religion." I have chosen to leave my comments in their original state, since I think the point is worth making, and there is little gain in giving it a more traditional and respectable form.

The final observation—concerning leisure—is just an example of how the church as an institution has exerted its influence, and how it may well offer its reflection and self-criticism to rectify that influence in the future.

In our cultural situation it is quite natural that "religion" should be understood as a "resource of an 'inner life.'" It would be awkward to argue that it is not. And yet we find in the contemporary debate within theology and the churches a striking uneasiness about the neat distinction between the "spiritual" versus the "material" or the "institutional." One could argue that most of contemporary theology is trying to divest itself of these time-honored distinctions. Books like Paul van Buren's *The Secular Meaning of the Gospel* and Harvey Cox's *The Secular City* are not isolated examples of frantic disenchantment with the tradition; they are quite continuous with tendencies that have made themselves felt for a long time.[1] They point toward a new type of Christian self-understanding. If we are to attempt a projection of the role of "religion" in the year 2000, it would be misleading to confine our attention to a view of religion and church that takes for granted that their primary role is in the sphere of the "inner life."

On the other hand, the tendency to use the juxtaposition "art and religion" is quite congenial to many tendencies in contemporary theology. It is not a bad slogan that says theology would fare well by considering itself as "poetry plus" rather than as "science minus." In looking toward the year 2000, this attitude may be a meaningful one, as far as traditional theology is concerned. In the academic realm, the creative theologian of the future may come to function as "Theologian in Residence," somewhat on the model of the poet and the artist in residence. In that role he will stimulate and supply vision and sensitivity across the diverse fields of academic endeavor.

Why, then, is it misleading or at least insufficient to identify religion with the "inner life"? Such a perspective presupposes the model of mysticism as the primary one for *homo religiosus*. The mystic is regarded as the (only) truly religious man; other types of religion and piety are considered contaminated expressions of religion, be they legalistic, institutionalized, or just traditional.

In any projection toward the future, the relation between this kind of "pure religion" and the religious institutions is of interest. In the years to come this question will become sharpened in various ways. Out of the ancient cultural synthesis between Christianity and Western culture have emerged two phenomena:

First, there is a kind of religious dimension of culture—"metaphysics-in-a-God-key," or the concern for ultimate questions. This is the kind of religion to which apologists like Paul Tillich have pointed. It is the upper level of the humanities, and aims, as is clear with Tillich, toward the model of mysticism. According to this approach, religion can never lose out so long as man is serious in his ultimate concerns. The atheist remains, thereby, religious, however much he confesses his denial of God, gods, or transcendence.[2] If we mean by religion "metaphysics-in-a-God-key," we could perhaps relegate it to the philosophical arena and ask whether we need a special term for it, such as *theology* or *religion*. If we speak of the ultimate concerns, we must ask whether the net does not become too wide for the use of the term *religion*, or whether there is much point in treating this aspect of the humanities as a special phenomenon, whatever its earlier history in the West has been.

Second, there are the religious communities—churches, synagogues, and so forth. We seem to assume that they are in all respects secondary to religion as an ideally mystical experience.[3] We take cult, religious discipline, and community life to be both means toward and expressions of individual religious experience. Thus we use the term *institutional religion* and almost always with negative connotations.

My reason for questioning this pattern of thinking at this point is not that I want to give an *Ehrenrettung* for institutional religion, although this could and perhaps should be done.[4] A study of Judaism would lend itself to such an enterprise; there is sufficient truth in the well-known observation that Judaism has never had a "theology" in the way that one developed in Christianity. Orthopraxy is not necessarily inferior to orthodoxy as the basis for a religious community. There can be little doubt that contemporary Christian theology is presently recognizing the ecclesiological dimension of Christianity. The twentieth century has seen a remarkable rejuvenation of the "church" as a primary theological fact. This could also be exemplified by the way in which Karl Barth's systematic theology began under the title of *Christian Dogmatics*, but was soon changed to *Church Dogmatics*. The nineteenth century made its attempts toward Christian unity on the basis of the Christian faith of true believers; the twentieth-century ecumenical movement deals with institutional churches. All this is clearly related to the increasing experience of secularization and the belated recognition that the Constantinian synthesis of Christianity and Western culture has come to an end; it is a shortening of the frontier, a consolidation, a recognition of minority status, especially in a global perspective. The church is no longer the religious dimension of a national or regional culture. It is an institution placed in or against that culture.

I point to institutional religion as a primary phenomenon because there is much more plausibility in dealing with the role and function of the religious communities when one looks toward the year 2000, than in identifying religion solely with resources for the "inner life." The more these communities become aware of themselves as communities, the less they will function primarily as the departments for the cultivation of the "inner life" within their respective cultures and societies. They will be more or less distinct minority communities within the community, exerting more or less significant pressure on decision-making, social action, and cultural development. They will sometimes become experimental communities, in addition to—or even in contrast with—their supportive role. It would be easy to say that this development will grow out of the "inner life" that they have sustained and cultivated. But even if that model were true and not too simplistic, it is not how they will present themselves or appear to the observer.

224

While there may well be religious dimensions of culture—albeit less and less distinct ones—what need our attention are the actual manifestations of "institutional religion." It is unrealistic to believe that "institutional religion" will fade away, while its noninstitutional forms continue or even increase. There will, of course, be substantial changes in the structure of these institutions, but that does not make them less institutional.

It follows, therefore, that institutional religion will come into our study of cultural and social institutions. On one level, the church will also constitute an intellectual institution. Furthermore, one should note that the twentieth-century church—like the synagogue —is an increasingly international community. The church is one of the few major institutions, in addition to the scientific community, that maintain significant relations behind the Iron Curtain; it is one of the relatively few channels through which world opinion can affect American attitudes. The very early stand of most major Protestant churches in support of China's admission to the United Nations was not unrelated to this international dimension of the church.

The above is written with Western Christianity in focus. Without sufficient knowledge, I venture to suggest that the same attention to the institutional will obtain in Islam, Buddhism, and the Japanese religious scene, all of which have become consolidated rather than converted by the immense and unsuccessful efforts of the churches to make the twentieth century "The Christian Century" on a global scale. The natural emergence of a single "World Religion" is highly improbable, but a mutual influence among the religious communities is a fact and will presumably increase. People often think of the religious content of institutions as stable while the institutions come and go. It is easier to make a case for the opposite: Christianity has changed immensely during its history, as have other religions; they will continue to do so, but the church and its counterparts have a basic continuity.

Let me finally point to one issue which will come under the scrutiny of the Commission and in which Christianity has had a major part: the question of leisure in a technological society. The Protestantism of Northern Europe is partly responsible for the divine sanction supplied to the high evaluation of work as the meaning of life. Leisure becomes a "problem" since it is experienced as a vacuum. It would be interesting to contrast this Puritan attitude with the basic attitude toward work as a "curse" in Chapter 3 of Genesis.[5] Thus man works as much as he needs, and the rest is not "leisure" but just plain life. One does not spend one's "free time" in order to be better prepared for working better, and so forth. Since the Protestant churches, in particular, have contributed to the problem, they may have a part in helping to clear it up as we approach the year 2000. After all, *scholé* in Greek means "leisure"; I cannot imagine Socrates saying to his wife: "Now I am going to my office, and then I have a seminar." Rather he spent his leisure in a way that turned out to be quite productive. And technology has replaced slavery so as to set men free from full-time work.[6]

REFERENCES

1. Paul van Buren, *The Secular Meaning of the Gospel* (New York, 1963); Harvey Cox, *The Secular City* (New York, 1965). See also Leslie Dewarb, *The Future of Belief* (New York, 1966).

2. See, for example, "Religion as a Dimension in Man's Spiritual Life," in *Theology and Culture,* ed. R. C. Kimball (New York, 1959), pp. 3-9. "You cannot reject religion with ultimate seriousness, because ultimate seriousness, or the state of being ultimately concerned, is itself religion" (p. 8).

3. The weakness in W. C. Smith's *The Meaning and End of Religion* (New York, 1962) is that it lends itself to such an interpretation when it makes its sharp distinction between "an historical 'cumulative tradition,' and the personal faith of men and women" (p. 194). Smith gives little attention to the religious community in which and by which the believer often finds his primary identity. The early Christian did not *first* come to a personal faith in Christ and *then* join the church. This aspect of early Christianity is rightly stressed by E. R. Dodds, *Pagan and Christian in an Age of Anxiety* (Cambridge, 1965), pp. 136-38.

4. The purely theological approach to religion has usually enforced the disregard for the institutional. But the study of the phenomenology of religion has increased the attention to and respect for the "external" aspects of the religious life. See, for example, G. van der Leeuw, *Religion in Essence and Manifestation* (New York, 1963).

5. See Ivan Engnell and Bertil Gärtner, "The Biblical Attitude to Work," *Svensk Exegetisk Aarsbok,* Vol. 26 (1961), pp. 5-18 [the article is in English]. For the larger issue, see Robert Lee, *Religion and Leisure in America* (Nashville, 1964).

6. On technology and leisure, see E. G. Mesthene, "Technology and Religion," *Theology Today,* Vol. 23 (1966), pp. 481-95, especially pp. 487ff. In this article, Mesthene seems to argue for a more purely spiritual role of religion

in the future than the one I have suggested. He stresses that "the churches are freed of the burden of doing man's work, and may find their new vocation in doing God's: in knowing God and showing him to man" (p. 493). It is nevertheless probable that this task will take the form of a community life in cult and action and experimentation within the churches rather than of a direct educational program for the world at large. To "know God" is usually a matter of worship and to "show him to man" is usually done by example rather than by instruction. And both worship and example presuppose the institutional life of the church.

ERIK H. ERIKSON

Memorandum on Youth

I

In responding to the inquiry of the Commission on the Year 2000, I will take the liberty of quoting the statements put to me in order to reflect on some of the stereotyped thinking about youth that has become representative of us, the older generation. This, it seems to me, is prognostically as important as the behavior of the young people themselves; for youth is, after all, a *generational phenomenon,* even though its problems are now treated as those of an outlandish tribe descended on us from Mars. The actions of young people are always in part and by necessity reactions to the stereotypes held up to them by their elders. To understand this becomes especially important in our time when the so-called communications media, far from merely mediating, interpose themselves between the generations as manufacturers of stereotypes, often forcing youth to live out the caricatures of the images that at first they had only "projected" in experimental fashion. Much will depend on what we do about this. In spite of our pretensions of being able to study the youth of today with the eyes of detached naturalists, we are helping to make youth in the year 2000 what it will be by the kinds of questions we now ask. So I will point out the ideological beams in our eyes as I attempt to put into words what I see ahead. I will begin with questions that are diagnostic and then proceed to those that are more prognostic in character.

I would assume that adolescents today and tomorrow are struggling to define new modes of conduct which are relevant to their lives.

Young people of a questioning bent have always done this. But more than any young generation before and with less reliance on a meaningful choice of traditional world images, the youth of today is forced to ask what is *universally relevant* in human life in this technological age at this junction of history. Even some of the most faddish, neurotic, delinquent preoccupation with "their" lives is a symptom of this fact.

Yet, this is within the context of two cultural factors which seem to be extraordinary in the history of moral temper. One is the scepticism of all authority, the refusal to define natural authority (perhaps even that of paternal authority) and a cast of mind which is essentially anti-institutional and even antinomian.

I do not believe that even in the minority of youths to whom this statement is at all applicable there is a scepticism of *all* authority. There is an abiding mistrust of people who act authoritatively without authentic authority or refuse to assume the authority that is theirs by right and necessity. Paternal authority? Oh, yes— pompous fathers have been exposed everywhere by the world wars and the revolutions. It is interesting, though, that the word *paternal* is used rather than *parental,* for authority, while less paternal, may not slip altogether from the parent generation, insofar as a better balance of maternal and paternal authority may evolve from a changing position of women. As a teacher, I am more impressed with our varying incapacity to own up to the almost oppressive authority we really do have in the minds of the young than in the alleged scepticism of *all* authority in the young. Their scepticism, even in its most cynical and violent forms, often seems to express a good sense for what true authority is, or should be, or yet could be. If they "refuse to define natural authority"—are they not right if they indicate by all the overt, mocking, and challenging kinds of "alienation" that it is up to *us* to help them define it, or rather redefine it, since we have undermined it—and feel mighty guilty?

As to the essentially anti-institutional cast of mind, one must ask what alternative is here rejected. It appears that the majority of young people are, in fact, all too needy for, trusting in, and conforming to present institutions, organizations, parties, industrial complexes, super-machineries—and this because true personal authority is waning. Even the anti-institutional minority (whom we know better and who are apt to know our writings) seem to me to plead with existing institutions for permission to rebel— just as in private they often seem to plead with their parents to love them doubly for rejecting them. And are they not remarkably eager for old and new uniforms (a kind of uniformity of nonconformity), for public rituals, and for a collective style of individual isolation? Within this minority, however, as well as in the majority, there are great numbers who are deeply interested in and responsive to a more concerted critique of institutions from a newer and more adequate ethical point of view than we can offer them.

The second factor is an extraordinary hedonism—using the word in the broadest sense—in that there is a desacralization of life and an attitude that all experience is permissible and even desirable.

Again, the word *hedonism* illustrates the way in which we use outdated terms for entirely new phenomena. Although many young people entertain a greater variety of sensual and sexual experiences than their parents did, I see in their pleasure seeking relatively little relaxed joy and often compulsive and addictive search for *relevant* experience. And here we should admit that our generation and our heritage made "all" experience relative by opening it to ruthless inquiry and by assuming that one could pursue radical enlightenment without changing radically or, indeed, changing the coming generations radically. The young have no choice but to experiment with what is left of the "enlightened," "analyzed," and standardized world that we have bequeathed to them. Yet their search is not for all-permissibility, but for new logical and ethical boundaries. Now only direct experience can offer correctives that our traditional mixture of radical enlightenment and middle-class moralism has failed to provide. I suspect that "hedonistic" perversity will soon lose much of its attractiveness in deed and in print when the available inventory has been experimented with and found only moderately satisfying, once it is permitted. New boundaries will then emerge from new ways of finding out what really counts, for there is much latent affirmation and much overt solidarity in all this search. All you have to do is to see some of these nihilists with babies, and you are less sure of what one of the statements as yet to be quoted terms the "Hegelian certainty" that the next generation will be even more alienated.

As for the desacralization of life by the young, it must be obvious that our generation desacralized their lives by (to mention only the intellectual side) naïve scientism, thoughtless scepticism, dilettante political opposition, and irresponsible technical expansion. I find, in fact, more of a search for resacralization in the younger than in the older generation.

At the same time society imposes new forms of specialization, of extended training, of new hierarchies and organizations. Thus, one finds an unprecedented divorce between the culture and the society. And, from all indications, such a separation will increase.

Here, much depends on what one means by the word *imposes*. As I have already indicated, in much of youth new hierarchies and organizations are accepted and welcome. We are apt to forget that young people (if not burdened with their parents' conflicts) have no reason to feel that radical change as such is an imposition. The unprecedented divorce we perceive is between *our* traditional culture (or shall I spell it *Kultur?*) and the tasks of *their* society. A new generation growing up with technological and scientific progress may well experience technology and its new modes of thought as the link between a new culture and new forms of society.

In this respect, assuming this hypothesis is true, the greatest strains will be on the youth. This particular generation, like its predecessors, may come back to some form of accommodation with the society as it grows older and accepts positions within the society. But the experiences also leave a "cultural deposit" which is cumulative consciousness and—to this extent I am a Hegelian— is irreversible, and the next generation therefore starts from a more advanced position of alienation and detachment.

Does it make sense that a generation involved in such unprecedented change should "come back to some form of accommodation with the society"? This was the fate of certain rebels and romantics in the past; but there may soon be no predictable society to "come back to," even if coming back were a viable term or image in the minds of youth. Rather, I would expect the majority to be only too willing to overaccommodate to the exploiters of change, and the minority we speak of to feel cast off until their function becomes clearer—with whatever help we can give.

II

Having somewhat summarily disavowed the statements formulated by others, I would now like to ask a question more in line with my own thinking, and thereby not necessarily more free from stereotypy: Where *are* some of the principal contemporary sources of identity strength? This question leads us from diagnosis to prog-

231

nosis, for to me a sense of identity (and here the widest connotation of the term will do) includes a sense of anticipated future. The traditional sources of identity strength—economic, racial, national, religious, occupational—are all in the process of allying themselves with a new world-image in which the vision of an anticipated future and, in fact, of a future in a permanent state of planning will take over much of the power of tradition. If I call such sources of identity strength *ideological,* I am using the word again most generally to denote a system of ideas providing a convincing world-image. Such a system each new generation needs— so much so that it cannot wait for it to be tested in advance. I will call the two principal ideological orientations basic to future identities the *technological* and the *humanist* orientations, and I will assume that even the great politico-economic alternatives will be subordinated to them.

I will assume, then, that especially in this country, but increasingly also abroad, masses of young people feel attuned, both by giftedness and by opportunity, to the technological and scientific promises of indefinite progress; and that these promises, if sustained by schooling, imply a new ideological world-image and a new kind of identity for many. As in every past technology and each historical period, there are vast numbers of individuals who can combine the dominant techniques of mastery and domination with their identity development, and *become* what they *do.* They can settle on that *cultural consolidation* that follows shifts in technology and secures what mutual verification and what transitory familiarity lie in doing things together and in doing them right— a rightness proved by the bountiful response of "nature," whether in the form of the prey bagged, the food harvested, the goods produced, the money made, the ideas substantiated, or the technological problems solved.

Each such consolidation, of course, also makes for new kinds of entrenched privileges, enforced sacrifices, institutionalized inequalities, and built-in contradictions that become glaringly obvious to outsiders—those who lack the appropriate gifts and opportunities or have a surplus of not quite appropriate talents. Yet it would be intellectual vindictiveness to overlook the sense of embeddedness and natural flux that each age provides in the midst of the artifacts of organization; how it helps to bring to ascendance some particular type of man and style of perfection; how it permits those thus consolidated to limit their horizon effectively so as *not* to see what might destroy their newly won unity with time and space or expose them to the fear of death—and of killing. Such a consolidation along technological and scientific lines is, I submit, now taking place. Those young people who feel at home in it can, in fact, go along with their parents and teachers— not too respectfully, to be sure—in a kind of *fraternal identification*, because parents and children can jointly leave it to technology and science to provide a self-perpetuating and self-accelerating way of life. No need is felt to limit expansionist ideals so long as certain old-fashioned rationalizations continue to provide the hope (a hope that has long been an intrinsic part of an American ideology) that in regard to any possible built-in evil in the very nature of super-organizations, appropriate brakes, corrections, and amendments will be invented in the nick of time and without any undue investment of strenuously new principles. While they "work," these super-machineries, organizations, and associations provide a sufficiently adjustable identity for all those who feel actively engaged in and by them.

All of us sense the danger of overaccommodation in this, as in any other consolidation of a new world-image, and maybe the danger *is* greater today. It is the danger that a willful and playful testing of the now limitless range of the technically possible will replace the search for the criteria for the optimal and the ethically permissible, which includes what can be given on from generation to generation. This can only cause subliminal panic, especially where the old decencies will prove glaringly inadequate, and where the threat or the mere possibility of overkill can be denied only with increasing mental strain—a strain, incidentally, which will match the sexual repression of the passing era in unconscious pathogenic power.

It is against this danger, I think, that the nonaccommodators put their very existence "on the line," often in a thoroughly confounding way because the manifestations of alienation and commitment are sometimes indistinguishable. The insistence on the question "to be or not to be" always looks gratuitously strange to the consolidated. If the question of being oneself and of dying one's own death in a world of overkill seems to appear in a more confused and confusing form, it is the ruthless heritage of radical enlightenment that forces some intelligent young people into a seemingly cynical pride, demanding that they be human without illusion, naked without narcissism, loving without idealization, ethi-

233

cal without moral passion, restless without being classifiably neurotic, and political without lying: truly a utopia to end all utopias. What should we call this youth? *Humanist* would seem right if by this we mean a recovery, with new implications, of man as the measure, a man far grimmer and with much less temptation to congratulate himself on his exalted position in the universe, a self-congratulation that has in the past always encouraged more cruel and more thoughtless consolidations. The new humanism ranges from an *existential* insistence that every man *is* an island unto himself to a new kind of humaneness that is more than compassion for stray animals and savages, and a decidedly *humanitarian* activism ready to meet concrete dangers and hardships in the service of assisting the underprivileged anywhere. Maybe *universalist* would cover all this better, if we mean by it an insistence on the widest range of human possibilities—beyond the technological.

But whatever you call it, the universalist orientation, no less than the technological one, is a *cluster* of ideas, images, and aspirations, of hopes, fears, and hates; otherwise, neither could lay claim to the identity development of the young. *Somewhat* like the "hawks" and the "doves," the technologists and the universalists seem almost to belong to different species, living in separate ecologies. "Technological" youth, for example, expects the dominant forces in foreign as well as in domestic matters to work themselves out into some new form of balance of power (or is it an old-fashioned balance of entirely new powers?). It is willing, for the sake of such an expectation, to do a reasonable amount of killing—and of dying. "Humanist" youth, on the other hand, not only opposes unlimited mechanization and regimentation, but also cultivates a sensitive awareness of the humanness of any individual in gunsight range. The two orientations must obviously oppose and repel each other totally; the acceptance of even a part of one could cause an ideological slide in the whole configuration of images and, it follows, in the kind of courage to be—and to die. These two views, therefore, face each other as if the other were *the* enemy, although he may be brother or friend—and, indeed, oneself at a different stage of one's own life, or even in a different mood of the same stage.

Each side, of course, is overly aware of the dangers inherent in the other. In fact, it makes out of the other, in my jargon, a negative identity. I have sketched the danger felt to exist in the technological orientation. On the "humanist" side, there is the danger of a starry-eyed faith in the certainty that if you "mean it," you can move quite monolithic mountains, and of a subsequent total inertia when the mountain moves only a bit at a time or slides right back. This segment of youth lacks as yet the leadership that would replace the loss of revolutionary tradition, or any other tradition of discipline. Then there is the danger of a retreat into all kinds of Beat snobbishness or into parallel private worlds, each with its own artifically expanded consciousness.

III

As one is apt to do in arguing over diagnosis, I have now overdrawn two "ideal" syndromes so as to consider the prognosis suggested in a further question presented to me:

Is it possible that the fabric of traditional authority has been torn so severely in the last decades that the re-establishment of certain earlier forms of convention is all but unlikely?

I have already indicated that I would answer this question in the affirmative; I would not expect a future accommodation to be characterized by a "coming back" either to conventions or to old-fashioned movements. Has not every major era in history been characterized by a division into a new class of *power-specialists* (who "know what they are doing") and an intense new group of *universalists* (who "mean what they are saying")? And do not these two poles determine an era's character? The specialists ruthlessly test the limits of power, while the universalists always in remembering man's soul also remember the "poor"—those cut off from the resources of power. What is as yet dormant in that third group, the truly under-privileged, is hard to say, especially if an all-colored anticolonial solidarity that would include our Negro youth should emerge. But it would seem probable that all new revolutionary identities will be drawn into the struggle of the two ideological orientations sketched here, and that nothing could preclude a fruitful polarity between these two orientations—provided we survive.

But is not the fact that we are still here already a result of the polarization I have spoken of? If our super-technicians had not been able to put warning signals and brakes into the very machinery of armament, certainly our universalists would not have known how to save or how to govern the world. It also seems reasonable to assume that without the apocalyptic warnings of the universalists, the new technocrats might not have been shocked into restraining the power they wield.

What speaks for a fruitful polarization is the probability that a new generation growing up with and in technological and scientific progress as a matter of course will be forced by the daily confrontation with unheard-of practical and theoretical possibilities to entertain radically new modes of thought that may suggest daring innovations in both culture and society. "Humanist" youth, in turn, will find some accommodation with the machine age in which they, of course, already participate in their daily needs and habits. Thus, each group may reach in the other what imagination, sensitivity, or commitment may be ready for activation. I do not mean, however, even to wish that the clarity of opposition of the technological and the humanist identity be blurred, for dynamic interplay needs clear poles.

What, finally, is apt to bring youth of different persuasions together is a change in the generational process itself—an awareness that they share a common fate. Already today the mere division into an older—parent—generation and a younger—adolescing—one is becoming superannuated. Technological change makes it impossible for any traditional way of being older (an age difference suggested by the questions quoted) ever to become again so institutionalized that the younger generation could "accommodate" to it or, indeed, resist it in good-old revolutionary fashion. Aging, it is already widely noted, will be (or already is) a quite different experience for those who find themselves rather early occupationally outdated and for those who may have something more lasting to offer. By the same token, young adulthood will be divided into older and younger young adults. The not-too-young and not-too-old specialist will probably move into the position of principal arbiter, that is, for the limited period of the ascendance of his speciality. His power, in many ways, will replace the sanction of tradition or, indeed, of parents. But the "younger generation," too, will be (or already is) divided more clearly into the older- and the younger-young generation, where the older young will have to take over (and are eager to take over) much of the direction of the conduct of the younger young. Thus, the relative waning of the parents and the emergence of the young adult specialist as the permanent and permanently changing authority are bringing about a shift by which older youth will have to take increasing responsibility for the conduct of younger youth—and older people for the orientation of the specialists and of older youth. By the same token, future religious ethics would be grounded less in the emotions and the imagery of infantile guilt, than in that of mutual responsibility in the fleeting present.

In such change we on our part can orient ourselves and offer orientation only by recognizing and cultivating an age-specific *ethical* capacity in *older* youth, for there are age-specific factors that speak for a differentiation between morality and ethics. The child's conscience tends to be impressed with a moralism which says "no" without giving reasons; in this sense, the infantile super-ego has become a danger to human survival, for suppression in childhood leads to the exploitation of others in adulthood, and moralistic self-denial ends up in the wish to annihilate others. There is also an age-specific ethical capacity in older youth that we should learn to foster. That we, instead, consistently neglect this ethical potential and, in fact, deny it with the moralistic reaction that we traditionally employ toward and against youth (*anti-institutional, hedonistic, desacralizing*) is probably resented much more by young people than our dutiful attempts to keep them in order by prohibition. At any rate, the ethical questions of the future will be less determined by the influence of the older generation on the younger one than by the interplay of subdivisions in a life scheme in which the whole life-span is extended; in which the life stages will be further subdivided; in which new roles for both sexes will emerge in all life stages; and in which a certain margin of free choice and individualized identity will come to be considered the reward for technical inventiveness. In the next decade, youth will force us to help them to develop ethical, affirmative, resacralizing rules of conduct that remain flexibly adjustable to the promises and the dangers of world-wide technology and communication. These developments, of course, include two "things"—one gigantic, one tiny—the irreversible presence of which will have to find acknowledgment in daily life: the Bomb and the Loop. They together will call for everyday decisions involving the sanctity of life and death. Once man has decided not to kill needlessly and not to give birth carelessly, he must try to establish what capacity for living, and for letting live, each generation owes to every child planned to be born—anywhere.

One can, I guess, undertake to predict only on the basis of one of two premises: Either one expects that things will be as bad as they always have been, only worse; or one visualizes what one is willing to take a chance on at the risk of being irrelevant. As I implied at the beginning, a committee that wants to foretell the future may have to take a chance with itself by asking what its combined wisdom and talent would wish might be done with what seems to be given.

MARGARET MEAD

The Life Cycle and Its Variations: The Division of Roles

IT IS my assumption that the more affluent societies will set world-wide styles that will define the nature and quality of relations between men and women, and the decisiveness of sex as a determinant of social roles. Wherever members of less affluent and newly developing societies will not be able to follow these styles, one may expect to find conscious discontent, resentment, and, under some circumstances, the development of reactive ideological and religious movements.[1]

Although no one can predict what the outcome of present trends may be or specify what changes may follow on the adoption of (or the refusal to adopt) inventions already available to style-setting societies, several possibilities can be distinguished.

The Present Style May Harden and Its Influence Spread

The contemporary American style of relations between men and women has certain well-defined characteristics. These include early marriage; marriage as the principal form of relationship between men and women for all adults; parenthood for all couples immediately following on, or even preceding, marriage; a separate domicile for each nuclear family; the exclusion of all adults other than parents (including adult children) from the home; education for girls adapted mainly to woman's homemaking and parental functions; and an ever increasing involvement of men in domestic activities, including infant care and child rearing. At the same time, heavy demands are made on women to engage in subsidiary economic activities outside the home in support of the high standards of consumption of the nuclear family.

The massive failure of this style of family organization has led to a proliferation of community-maintained social services that can be no more than ameliorative in their effect. There are also various significant forms of reaction, including the development of adolescent rebellion cults, overt and aggressive male homosexuality, female promiscuity, and a growing incidence of alcoholism, addiction, and psychosomatic disorders in both sexes. Up to the present, however, such evidence of the malfunctioning of existing social forms has been ineffective in raising questions about our emphasis on exclusive dependence on a single mate (with its implications of serial monogamy), parenthood as the goal for all adults, and the independent family residence as the focus of all social requirements for dignity, status, and high consumption.

As long as members of affluent societies accept existing styles as the basis of the most desirable way of life, members of less affluent and less highly developed societies may be expected to persist in their efforts to move toward comparable styles of living, including types of housing. Most important, they may be expected to resent any attempts to limit population growth.

A Drastic Change of Style May Occur in Response to Recognized Needs

Recognition of the population crisis, in particular, may be effective in rousing members of affluent societies to the significance of their style-setting position on a world-wide scale. Responsiveness to the world situation may take the form of a new willingness to assume responsibility for supporting massive dependence on modern scientific methods for the control of conception and the use of such inventions as artificial insemination, artificial lactation, and perhaps extra-uterine gestation. A reconsideration of the present family style of living may be effective in creating a new style with an emphasis on very small families and a high toleration of childless marriage or a more encompassing social style in which parenthood would be limited to a smaller number of families whose principal function would be child rearing; the rest of the population would be free to function—for the first time in history—as individuals.

A change of this kind would present these alternatives:

There would be a growing disregard for sex as a basic mode of differentiation. Boys and girls would be given a similar education and like demands would be made on them for citizenship, economic contribution, and creativity. Adults who functioned as parents would be given special forms of protection. Protection would be extended also to those in dependent positions by reason of lack of education, physical disability, mental and physical illness, or old age. Limitations on freedom would be removed from women as a social group. Boys and girls would be differentiated not by sex-typed personality characteristics, but by temperament. The two-sex exclusive pair model of human relationships would lose its power. Instead, companionship for work, play, and stable living would come to be based on many different combinations, within and across sex lines, among different-sized clusters of individuals, such as are formed in kinship societies, in large extended families, and in various total institutions—schools, armies, monasteries, for example—in complex societies.

Alternatively, personality typing by sex would continue to be a basic mode of differentiation. In this case, there would be continued support of the historical role of the woman as primarily related to the needs of individuals, but her activities would no longer be shaped by localization in the home as mother and housewife. The education of girls, especially in regard to career expectations and standards of social behavior, would still differ from that of boys. Girls would be directed toward occupations that were related to nurture, teaching, comforting, and curing; they would be expected to derive their basic life satisfactions from their contributions to the achievements of others.

The two sexes would still be socially typed as complementary in their character and central concerns. The model of adult relationships would probably continue to be one based on an achieving husband and a wife who was primarily concerned with support and the daily care of bodily and psychological needs. The two-sex exclusive couple would remain the social ideal.

Initially, a continuation of socially supported modes of sex differentiation might well be the easier institutional arrangement. It is predictable, however, that over time there would be considerable individual rebellion against any form of social sex typing that ignored personality differences and was unsupported by the economic necessities of the individual home in which parents focused on rearing children. It is this that has supported the sex-differentiated ideal of men and women, with all its complexities.

Changes in Basic Social Styles of Interpersonal Relations and Sex-Defined Roles May Engender a Counter-Revolution

The broad alteration in human behavior implicit in adequate conception control—interference in the "normal" biologically based processes of conception, birth, child rearing, maturation, and death, and the new possibilities of interpersonal relations—presents a tremendous challenge to organized social habits and the belief and value systems that underlie them in all cultures. It is critically important to recognize that the potentiality for changed uses of human capacities is as great in this area as it is in the challenge science has presented in altering man's relationship to the world.

It is no less crucial to realize that the attempt to meet the challenge through the introduction of radically new styles of behavior may engender counter-revolutions that may be ideological or religious in character. Under these circumstances the most intense efforts might be made to nullify the effect of innovations in life styles. The aim of such counter-revolutions, whatever their specific form, might well be to refocus attention on the home, limit sexual freedom, curtail the individual development of women, and subordinate the creative capacities of the individual adult to the needs of the group for docile parents, workers, and citizens.

In the light of these possibilities it becomes imperative to consider courses of action that would enable men to implement, rather than respond destructively to, the potentialities of the scientific revolution in man's control of his biological functions. In particular, it will be necessary to work out adequate institutional arrangements that are transculturally viable. These would provide social protection for both men and women during the transition stages in the development of new styles of behavior.

For women it will be essential to provide socially responsible protection during the period when the old forms, based on male responsibility, are becoming ineffective and new arrangements that will support women's freedom to earn and to function as independent individuals have not been realized on a very large scale. Without institutional protections of this kind the ever mounting number of mother-child homes will threaten (as the existence of such homes already does) the conscience of the community and lend tremendous support to arguments in favor of the superiority of older, traditionally sanctioned forms of social organization.

For men it will be essential to find responsible ways of protecting the sense of masculine identity during the period when men, reared to depend on a traditionally attributed superiority over women, will inevitably feel threatened by new forms of aspiration, competition, and achievement as women move out of the home into a wider world. At present, a weakening in the sense of sure sex identity in men makes itself felt in the exploits of adolescent gangs and protest groups, in fads expressed, for example, in styles of dress and treatment of the body, in expressions of extreme hostility to forms of traditionally supported feminine behavior, and in overt hostile homosexuality. Greater attention to the education of very young children, during which certainty of sex identity would be established by an emphasis on feats of skill, strength, and bravery in small boys, would provide one form of insurance. Much attention needs to be given to the vicissitudes of the transitional phase during which males continue to depend for a sense of their identity on social differences no longer based in social reality.

Looking at the differences in the conceptions of masculinity and femininity that have been culturally viable in societies we know, it is a tenable hypothesis that differences in mentality between men and women can be attributed largely to differences in upbringing, the female proceeding by direct identification with the nurturing parent and the male by differentiation from the nurturing parent. It then follows that changes in the style of relations between men and women, whether these originate in a much greater involvement of men in domestic life or in a marked emphasis on individuation, will lead to a reduction in sex-based differences in mental attitudes. Such an outcome is predictable not only as one result of changed styles of education for boys and girls, but also as one effect of the biochemical damping of female rhythms.

In the immediate present, because we are so urgently in need of every form of creative imagination to meet the challenges already before us, it may well be worthwhile to work out better ways of drawing on feminine constructive creativity in social invention. We cannot afford to waste the talents of educated women who have been reared according to existing conventions with their greater emphasis on "institutions" and on an intensive attention to patterns of human behavior informed by a forced awareness of women's biological rhythms. We cannot afford to involve in social change half the world's population without also involving those concerned with the responsibility for making the necessary social inventions.

REFERENCES

1. It is understood, of course, that events affecting the planet—such as nuclear war, extensive alterations of climate or the atmosphere, or world-wide famines or epidemics, and so forth—would be larger limiting conditions on the possibilities outlined here. In my opinion, moreover, the prevailing viewpoint overplays the scientific revolution as it affects political and economic forms and underplays the psychological and biological revolutions with their promise—and threat—of profound alteration of human personality.

HARRY KALVEN, JR.

The Problems of Privacy in the Year 2000

To SPECULATE about the shape of things to come is always a precarious business, whatever the compensations to be found in the circumstance that one cannot *immediately* be shown to be wrong. The perils increase with the time-span involved in the prediction and with the subtlety of the phenomena about which prediction is made. There is a special foolhardiness in accepting an invitation to discuss the problems of privacy in the year 2000. But the invitation activates one's Walter Mittyism, the dream that one *might* have written a *1984* or a *Brave New World*. And so we proceed herewith down the road from forecast to fantasy.

It will prove convenient to divide considerations into the threats to privacy and the counter-moves to protect it.

I

Changes in the sphere of privacy may come from changes in technology, in social institutions, or in norms.

The first and most obvious prospect, one that is already receiving alarmed attention, arises out of what might be called improvements in the technology of eavesdropping. It is becoming increasingly possible to invade privacy without trespassing—that is, to invade it by remote control. Man can now photograph from afar, conceal microphones in tiepins, observe by closed-circuit television, tap telephone lines, pick up conversations in another room by the use of electronic devices, and determine the content of mail without opening it. There is no reason to doubt that the technology will continue to improve—probably at a geometric rate—and that by the year 2000 it will be possible to place a man under constant surveillance without his ever becoming aware of it. Moreover, since the culture will become cognizant of this advance, men will live with the constant possibility that they are under surveillance without ever being able to be sure whether this is so.

One can only wonder which is the greater evil here: having one's privacy intruded upon without being aware of it so that reliance on privacy has been upset; knowing that there is no escape from surveillance; or, finally, never being able to resolve the doubts about whether any given moment is private.

The intrusions will not be limited to government measures in aid of law enforcement or national security. The technology may become a commonplace in the hands of private parties—employers interested in the off-hours activities of employees, competitors interested in one another's integrity and trade secrets, estranged spouses interested in perfecting grounds for divorce, insurance companies interested in the subsequent health of personal-injury claimants they have paid, and the idly curious who are just interested. Thus, by 2000, man's technical inventiveness may, in terms of privacy, have turned the whole community into the equivalent of an army barracks.

There will be increasing pressure on people to surrender their privacy. Recipients of the government's ever expanding welfare benefits will not find it easy to resist government claims to a wide amount of information about their character, personality, and living habits. With ever increased emphasis on consumer credit, people will be induced to disclose all sorts of information about personal tastes, income, and habits in handling money. Indeed, privacy about one's financial situation and personal budget, once so deeply entrenched in middle-class mores, will become a forgotten value. Increase in insurance coverages, pension plans, and government medical services will bring increased medical scrutiny lessening any privacy in one's health, weight, digestion, and so forth.

A third kind of threat also depends on technology and probably on the computer. It turns on the prospect of a great improvement in the process of record-keeping and of collating information about individuals. When, as is likely, this technological efficiency is coupled with the government's ever increasing demands for special information, the prospect is one of a formidable dossier on every member of the society. Information may initially be collected for relatively innocuous purposes such as income tax, social security, special aid programs, and special support for education. One can also anticipate increased interest in testing competence, aptitude, and personality. At some happy future moment, all this information could be combined with the FBI files so as to produce a devastatingly detailed and accurate profile of each member of the society. The disturbing result could be that everyone will live burdened by an unerasable record of his past and his limitations. In a way, the threat is that because of its record-keeping the society will have lost its benign capacity to forget.

The ambivalence with which the public has greeted the Kennedy-Manchester dispute, the protests of Mrs. Mary Hemingway over publication of A. E. Hotchner's *Papa Hemingway,* the unease over the memoirs of Churchill's doctor, and the appearance of the Bullitt-Freud study of Woodrow Wilson point up the serious puzzle about the private life of the public figure and suggest the likelihood that there will be further changes in the norms as to what is appropriately newsworthy. The privacy of the famous, the great, and the important may yield to the notion that it is in the public interest to have every last detail of their lives and correspondence fully in the press and public record. Henceforward, the great will live, so to speak, in the public domain.

Various other norms about privacy may also change. With so much technological eavesdropping going on, the informer—if he does not become a victim of technological unemployment—may find his image improved. He may be seen as doing what is, after all, rather useful work. Further, the traditional confidentiality of the confessional, of lawyer-client, doctor-patient, and husband-wife relationships, and even of the voting booth may come to be re-examined critically. The grim hypothesis latent here is that some "critical mass of privacy" in a society may be necessary if privacy is to survive at all.

It is tempting, too, to fantasy invasions of privacy as a form of public amusement. The television show "Candid Camera" and the joke it has made part of the culture, "Smile, you're on 'Candid Camera,'" suggest a special threat for life in the year 2000.

As population pressures increase, one can foresee that birth control may become a patriotic duty. Already, a magazine as staid as *The Ohio State Law Journal* has published a symposium on population control, and a local television discussion show is featuring the topic: Should People Be Sterilized to Control the Population? Any expression of government interest in the sex habits of its married citizens—laws that might invade the privacy of the bedroom— worried the United States Supreme Court in the recent Connecticut birth-control case (although there the law in question sought to forbid dissemination of birth-control devices).

The threats to privacy may come from still another quarter. Commitment to social-science research may call for methods of inquiry that infringe upon the privacy of the subjects of study. To a considerable degree the dangers here may be moderated by the integrity of the scientific purpose, the provisions for consent, and the handling of the data in a way that preserves the anonymity of the individual participants. Sometimes, as with the Kinsey studies or those for the recent Masters' volume *Human Sexual Response,* the inquiry itself will cause a shift in the conventions as to what is private, even though the parties involved have given consent. More often, the inquiry may depend on the subject being unaware, as with the University of Chicago's celebrated effort a decade ago to record the actual deliberations of juries, which raised among other things the issue of whether institutions have a sphere of privacy. Or the subject, although willing to talk to one, may not realize the size of his audience, as in certain psychological studies where the observers are behind one-way glass. Then there are the possible uses of drugs, hypnosis, and personality tests where the subject does not realize how much of himself he is revealing in answering apparently neutral questions. Closely allied are studies that manipulate the subject rather than directly intrude upon his privacy so that he is deceived about the real consequences of what he is doing in the experiment. By the year 2000 the imperialism of the social sciences may well have claimed a large part of the private domain.

Another threat that may have high interest for the theory of freedom of communication—one that has been anticipated by the Supreme Court on several occasions—is the problem of being constantly exposed to communications one does not wish to receive, whether by billboard, sound truck, mass protest, second-class mail, unsolicited telephone calls, Jehovah's Witnesses, or more imaginative and less familiar methods. The issue of the captive audience is, as I see it, crucial for any free-speech theory; the threat here is that the society may, from one quarter or another, largely become a captive audience.

Three changes in national culture that are already visible may bring as by-products dramatic changes in privacy: the decline of the family, the decline of religion, and the decline in the habit of reading. Arguably the family has been the citadel of privacy; it has provided an institution within which private things were shared and has set a boundary point beyond which things were no one else's business. Family-centered life was deeply supportive of the values of privacy; as it declines in importance, there may be a concomitant loss in our appreciation of privacy as a value. The decline in religious observances may mean that man, never alone with God, will find that he has lost one of his recurring opportunities to be alone. Similarly, with the decline of reading, men lose the intellectual privacy afforded by being immersed in a book. This is one difference, among so many, between reading a book and watching television.

II

Having frightened myself with fantasies pushing current trends in the reduction of privacy, I now seek solace in a few reflections on possible counter-measures. Clearly, society today is, at worst, ambivalent about privacy; thus, some growth in counter-trends and measures, as well as an increase in threats, can be expected. The threats, having come from different quarters, will presumably have to be met by different responses. Very loosely, the following general lines of attack emerge and suggest questions for discussion.

Can a public opinion more sensitive to values of privacy be generated? This, perhaps, may be the crux of the whole matter, and one might even contemplate a program of education for privacy.

Can psychological and psychiatric studies be made that would add anything to our current knowledge about the importance of privacy to the mental health of the individual? I would assume that one subtle but sure way to drive a person crazy would be to keep him under constant surveillance for an extended period of time. Might we begin to see therapy for loss of privacy?

Can changes in living habits be developed to counteract some current habits that seem to endanger privacy? Can we develop habit substitutes for religion, reading, walking in the woods, and so forth?

What can be done by legal means to reduce invasions of privacy? Traditionally the law has protected privacy under varying circumstances, and it would be a fruitful exercise to collect and collate all the relevant provisions. There is, for example, the protection enshrined in the provisions of the Fourth Amendment against "unreasonable searches and seizures"; there is the protection of the doctrines of trespass against unconsented entries onto another's property; there is the so-called common-law copyright that gives some protection to private diaries and correspondence; there are various statutes prohibiting wiretapping.

Under the stimulus of a law review article, entitled "The Right to Privacy," which Justice Brandeis wrote when he was a young lawyer, there has been growing up during the last fifty years or so a new tort for invasions of the right of privacy, particularly invasions by press coverage of private matters. The development has been much discussed and praised by commentators and continues to flourish. I happen to be in the minority of law teachers who think that, however great are the values of privacy, the effort to protect it by tort suits against the press has been a mistake. Traditions of freedom of communication require that a substantial privilege be accorded newsworthy materials; there is also a sweet smell of shysterism about most suits for invasion of privacy—the money-damages remedy tends to recruit the wrong complaints. The current difficulties with the specific tort of privacy need not mean, however, that the law of the future cannot appropriately find new ways to protect so basic a value.

The legal world may devote increasing attention to whether privacy can be made a fundamental norm in the solution of legal questions, or whether it must remain a residual norm—that is, things that are not for some other reason public are by default private. There are two or three recent lines of development in constitutional law that suggest possibilities here. In the *Griswold* case (the Connecticut birth-control law) and especially in the prior birth-control case, *Poe v. Ullman,* the Court (and Justice Harlan in particular) appears to use privacy itself as a measure of what can appropriately be made public. Again, in a recent legislative investigating committee case, *Gibson v. Florida Legislative Investigating Committee,* Justice Douglas in concurring spoke of areas of privacy that were sufficiently defined so that the state could not inquire into them. There is, therefore, the possibility of locating certain citadels of citizen privacy that could be made inviolate, like the voting booth or the confessional.

For me, the most interesting possibility is that we might see the development of new institutions designed to insure some private moments in otherwise unprivate lives. I have only the dimmest sense of what shape these might take. Possibly some analogue to the religious retreat might be developed. Such a secular retreat might be provided by the welfare state as a final self-denying form of welfare—or conceivably it might even be provided commercially.

It may be a final ironic commentary on how bad things have become by 2000 when someone will make a fortune merely by providing, on a monthly, weekly, daily, or even hourly basis, a room of one's own.

One last, small thought. I noted recently in doing a little work on civil disobedience that Thoreau had two full pages in the current *Encyclopedia Britannica*. He can be considered the hero not only of civil disobedience but also of privacy. The question before the house can be rephrased: How many pages will Henry David Thoreau have in the *Encyclopedia Britannica* in the year 2000?

GEORGE A. MILLER

Some Psychological Perspectives on the Year 2000

WHAT PLANS and problems will concern the leaders of industry, education, and public affairs in the year 2000? Undoubtedly they will be as curious about their future as we are about ours. But what will they be trying to foresee and promote or avoid?

R. J. Herrnstein, a valued friend with whom I have shared many administrative chores, once summarized our experience together in a principle that he called "the conservation of trouble." As each difficulty is solved, a new one takes its place. That, of course, is an optimistic theory of trouble; others would speculate on the exponent to be assigned to its growth. In either case, it is unlikely that the problems our descendants will face in the year 2000 will be simpler than ours. By then, no doubt, they will have developed better methods of extrapolation than we have today—but solving that problem would surely raise others, for how does one maintain an open society when the future is thought to be known?

They will probably be worrying about what to do when the resources of the oceans are exhausted. By then they will have enough information to make eugenics feasible and will be wondering what to do about it. Undoubtedly they will be even more concerned with the population problem, although technology will have changed the focus of their discussions from contraception to persuasion, and from farming to manufacturing as the source of food. Professions will be even more important then than now, and the education of professional men will be a pressing item on their agenda of problems. They will still be wondering how to make life more meaningful and satisfying, especially to those whose talents and skills are of marginal value to society, but they will be discussing this problem in the context of a psycho-pharmacological revolution that will offer possibilities of escape difficult to regulate. War will concern them, but on new terms, in new places, under new conditions. They will try to invent new social institutions to cope with their problems, perhaps joint ventures designed to merge public financing with private initiative. And they will be just as puzzled about the ultimate meaning of it all as we are today.

Is there something that a person trained in the methods and theories of contemporary scientific psychology can do to reduce or alleviate the never decreasing burden of troubles that our children will inherit by the year 2000? Exposure to psychological theory and research does little to prepare one to cope with such questions. In order to enter such a discussion at all, I must first disavow any pretense of scientific privilege; I cannot speak for psychology, but only as an individual who happens, fortuitously, to have had his opinions transformed by that particular kind of professional training.

I believe that two major trends are likely to continue for at least another thirty years: The population will continue to grow, and technology will continue to be a major source of change in the affairs of men. Within that context and limited by those preconceptions, however, there is much to stimulate a psychologist's imagination.

What will life be like when it is shared by seven billion people? Undoubtedly they will need a great deal of self-constraint to tolerate their mutual intrusions, to respect their differences of custom and opinion, to value the individual when there are so many individuals. People will have to be very civilized to get along together, and that requirement raises a host of other questions. Is man really capable of organizing a big civilization? If the church continues to lose its authority in ethics and morality, where will a new impulse toward a more civilized behavior originate? Freud argues that civilization, by curbing natural instincts, places increasing burdens of guilt on the civilized man. Certainly a conscience can be a difficult master; it is always tempting to substitute hypocrisy in its place.

Of course, the human population may not go on expanding at its present rate. According to biologists, in most ecological systems there are forces that limit automatically the number of individuals. When they become too crowded, the animals starve or kill one another, or a debilitative disease suddenly reduces their number dramatically. But will such factors operate automatically in the case of man? I think this is unlikely. Our past wars, horrible as they were, made only a ripple in the population curve. We may be on the verge of a great universal famine, but there are still ways to forestall it. A Malthusian formulation is not adequate, for technology has added dimensions to the human problem that are unprecedented in the evolution of species. It is difficult for me to believe that a contraction of the human population will occur automatically.

If we begin to poison ourselves with pollutants, we will take measures to reduce them. If we are afflicted by debilitative disease, we will subsidize biomedical science to find a cure. If our farms become inadequate, we will develop methods and build factories to produce synthetic proteins. If we invent thermonuclear devices capable of destroying all life, we will find social constraints on their use. No automatic biological principle will take over our destiny, for human intervention is possible, and in emergencies it can be rapid, massive, and effective. Our destiny is in our own hands.

Does it seem unwarranted to call this an optimistic vision? One argument for believing in heaven is that if you are wrong, little is lost, but if you are right, much may be gained. The argument for believing in the survival of rational man is much the same. The alternative vision of a lifeless, radioactive sphere spinning silently through space cannot be dismissed, but I refuse to make plans for it. If we are to take the year 2000 seriously, we had *better* believe that our destiny is in our own hands.

Having said all this, I nevertheless believe that in its own slow and inexorable way the old machinery of evolution continues to work on man side by side with the rapid and (optimistically) controllable evolution that is man's own invention.

Where should we look for evolutionary pressures today? It is a commonplace observation that people differ in their tolerance for crowding. In large measure these differences are a result of social training, of experience with crowded living. But there may also be a biological basis for them, an innate predisposition for some people to thrive better under crowding than others. This possibility is something biologists have tried to study in animals, and about which much has been written. The selective evolutionary pressure that would favor a crowd-adapted organism is reasonably obvious. If there are innate differences, and if we do face a future of living closer and closer together, evolution would inevitably favor certain people over others. By the year 2000, of course, nothing measurable will have had time to happen as a consequence of biological evolution. But we ought to know more about the possibilities and implications of such a change. It might be interesting for psychologists to attempt to measure individual differences in tolerance to crowding, and to try to determine whether there are inheritable traits that could serve as a basis for evolutionary selection. When the day comes that we have the necessary facts to support a realistic eugenics program, such information could be valuable.

The most obvious and foreseeable consequences of population increase and technological innovation are surely the demographic and economic ones, which I have neither desire nor competence to consider. There is, however, one general psychological principle that may have interesting implications. The human mind has a limited capacity for acquiring and storing information. It is a reasonably well-established fact that the number of independent cognitive components a man can cope with at any one time is strictly limited. Evidence could be cited to support this claim, but most people seem willing to accept it as obvious. It is also a plausible speculation, not yet firmly established, that there is some limit to the over-all capacity of a man's memory, a limit to the magnitude and complexity of any cognitive system that a man can internalize. More than anything else it is man's capacity to cope with large, inter-related systems of habits and rules that sets him apart from other animals—that enables him to learn a linguistic system, to invent a system of mathematics, or to learn all he must know to be accepted as a member of his society. Gifted as man is in this respect, his capacity is probably not unlimited. Intuitively, we all know this. In our mundane affairs we allocate as much of our memory to a topic as we think its role in our lives justifies. Indeed, by its very nature, the learning process preserves only those facts or skills that recur frequently or are particularly important. As an advertising executive once said, there is only so much that the public wants to know about toothpaste; the advertiser's job is to force his product into that small mental compartment, because he knows that he will thereby almost surely force some competitor's product out.

It would be ridiculous, of course, to insist on some rigid and mechanical limit to human attention or human memory. We can stretch our limited span of attention by carefully organizing information hierarchically and then dealing with our problems at a rather abstract level, relatively secure in the belief that, when necessary, the more detailed information can be reconstructed from the hierarchy stored in memory. But if memory is also limited, this hierarchical strategy must have its limits. Psychologists have not yet demonstrated or measured these limits in their laboratories, but it seems plausible that such limits must exist. And even if memory were an unlimited vessel, the rate at which experience could fill it would still impose limits on the amount it could contain.

As far as the present argument goes, it makes little difference whether the mind is limited in capacity or limited in rate of acquisition. In either case we are faced with an upper bound on the information we can expect an individual to have at his personal disposal. If society itself becomes more complex, the amount of knowledge a child must acquire in the process of socialization increases. What are the implications of this increase for a country whose government is based on the assumption of an informed electorate? If more and more technical competence will be required in order to earn a living, it means that more and more of a man's precious cognitive capacity will have to be devoted to that. We may already be nearing some kind of limit for many of the less gifted among us, and those still able to handle the present level of complexity are in ever increasing demand. The remarkable shift we have seen in the advanced countries from the idle rich and the exploited worker of 1870 to the overworked professional and the unemployed poor of today is at least partly the result of such psychological limits operating in a context of advancing technology. If the meritocracy is already taking shape, it is only a form of scapegoating to blame the purveyors of intelligence tests. The real causes lie far deeper.

At a time when our society is wasting so much of its potential intelligence, it might seem that the solution to this problem would be to improve our educational system and to reduce discrimination based on race, sex, age, color, religion, and nationality. We need every good brain we can train. But such measures, important as they certainly are, would only enable each person to realize his own capacity. If that capacity is limited even under optimal conditions, the problem takes on new dimensions. Even our most intelligent citizens will have to rely increasingly on artificial aids—on such intelligence amplifiers as digests, libraries, computers, special displays, and communication devices. Most important of all, it seems inevitable that even our most intelligent men will have to work increasingly in teams; no single member of any team would be competent to understand all aspects of the shared problem. This change is already beginning in some industries, especially those where technology has advanced too rapidly for management to exploit it effectively without new forms of co-operation among technically trained personnel. These teams are assembled as needed and dissolved when their work is done; their transitory character threatens something of a revolution in managerial practices. This kind of co-operation—experts collecting around each important new problem

255

and then moving on when the problem is solved—has been slowly developing for many years in scientific laboratories. We can expect to see more of this co-operation in the future—in laboratories, universities, industries, government—as our problems become greater and more complex, and our individual mental capacities do not.

No psychologist worthy of the title could close such a topic without at least wondering about its motivational implications. How are these experts to be rewarded? Who gets the credit and recognition when a team solves a problem? All members of the team will be well paid, no doubt, but is that enough? Each expert will be appreciated by his peers, of course, but on the national stage he can be little more than an anonymous consultant moving like a shadow behind the scenes. There are many motives that keep men hard at work at difficult but important tasks: the desire for power, wealth, fame, or knowledge. Which of these will move the technical teams of the future? Co-operating experts will have little personal power over others, and what limited power they do have will be given up when they move on to another task. Dreams of great wealth seem equally unrealistic; we are thinking now of men who, quite literally, live by their wits. Fame will come to few of them; the public can appreciate only a limited number of eminent men. Knowledge they will enjoy, but only under conditions that will force them to recognize that their personal knowledge is inadequate and must serve the purposes of an organization.

In his *Essays in Sociological Theory: Pure and Applied*, Talcott Parsons comments on the misleading stereotypes of the professional man motivated by altruism and the businessman motivated by acquisitiveness. In Parsons's view these stereotypes are more institutional than motivational. In both cases the dominant personal goal of the individual is "success"; the real difference lies in the paths leading to that goal. For both the professions and for business, the social institution must be so organized that objective achievements of value to the institutiton will bring recognition and "success" in due proportion. But articulating achievement and recognition equitably is a peculiarly thorny problem when it is a collaborative effort that must be rewarded.

An expert collaborator finds satisfaction in doing his job well, and in the sense of affiliation and shared accomplishment that has always motivated small groups of dedicated men. But these are altruistic motives and may not be sufficient. The prospect is disturbing, for only the strongest motivation will drive a man to learn to the limit of his capacity and to go on learning long after his formal education has ended. What alternative rewards can society provide to keep an anonymous genius hard at work? Probably the experts will incorporate themselves and develop their own answers to that question.

These speculations are advanced in the belief that the intellectual elite—both in business and in the professions—are a particularly important segment of the population, and that they will encounter mounting difficulties in generating those phases of the industrial revolution that lie ahead. If the direction of social change that we have learned to call progress is to continue, our best minds will have to find some effective way to pool their abilities, for many of our most pressing problems are already too large to fit inside any single head.

New techniques for expert collaboration are developing rapidly. Let us assume they will be successful and that we can extrapolate the present trend toward increased complexity and ever more rapidly changing technology. What will be the effect on the masses of people who do not aspire to change society, but merely want to find some meaningful existence in it?

If we are to remain true to our democratic heritage, one of the most obvious implications of the predicted increase in population is that our already crowded educational system will have to be vastly expanded and overhauled. As knowledge increases and work becomes more technical, there will be a corresponding increase in the amount of information that will have to be imparted to a student. And as automation advances and new industries replace old, learning will not be regarded as ending with graduation from school, but will become a way of life for everyone. Put together the increased number of students, the increased knowledge to be communicated, and the increased duration of the educational experience, and then try to imagine what kind of educational system we will need by the year 2000. Can anything short of an educational revolution meet our needs?

I have followed recent innovations in educational practice with considerable interest. Some kind of change is obviously needed. Too often our children's most valuable return for their years in the classroom is a kind of shrewd skill in coping with a large, well-intentioned, but often stultifying social institution. On the theory that any system that is not changed gets worse, there have been valiant attempts to revise curricula, to write better texts, and to provide more teaching aids, while at the same time making the best possible facilities available to every student. All of these excellent improvements and innovations are necessary, but are they sufficient?

I do not wish to sound critical of all that is being done, yet I feel that in their enthusiasm our educational revisionists sometimes forget a basic fact about the learning process. Most of the studies that have made a serious effort to evaluate the effectiveness of these new programs have shown that the method of packaging the information makes relatively little difference. Of course, if the information is wrong or irrelevant, a student cannot learn what is right or relevant; if, however, the same information is presented in alternative ways, the major factor determining how much a child learns is how much time he spends studying. Some learn faster than others, some learn more than others, but on the average, the generalization holds true. The problem, therefore, is how to motivate the students to study.

Obviously, we must see to it that the content of the teaching is clear, accurate, and up-to-date, that the teacher understands it, and that the student, whether he realizes it or not, really needs to know it. All of this is obviously conducive to a profitable educational experience. Yet it would be useless if students refused to study. Conversely, a student who is truly determined to learn something can learn it even under the most impoverished conditions.

I am not putting forth some radically new dogma. The fact that education is the reward for study is so banal that I am embarrassed to mention it, much less emphasize it. If it were not so important, I would prefer to leave it unsaid. But as every educator knows, the central problem of education is to make the students want it. Unfortunately, the problem is just as difficult as it is important. We know how to write better books and print them with three-color illustrations; we know how to shuffle the order of units within a curriculum; we know how to break up a unit into small steps and drill each step separately; we know how to use movies and field trips and special projects; but we do not know how to inject the urge to learn into a student's heart. So we do what we know how to do.

In defense of those who try to improve the packaging of the information that is presented to the student, I must agree that the finest motive of all for studying is love of knowledge for its own sake. Every subject matter has an intrinsic interest of its own, and a student who becomes intrigued with it on its own terms will certainly be the most gratifying to his teacher. My suspicion is that too often this experience is reserved for a fortunate few who are both highly intelligent and protected from more immediate personal distractions in their own lives. For most students study is a painful experience, and the social milieu of the public schools seldom encourages them to bear the pain until they learn to love it. Our schools, I fear, too often illustrate the irony of a self-fulfilling prophecy. A student is labeled as good or bad. First the teachers and then the student himself accept this classification. If he is mislabeled as good, he may become an "over-achiever," but if he is mislabeled bad, he accepts the judgment and fulfills the prophecy. How can we expect every student to acquire a detached love of learning under such conditions?

An essential ingredient in the motivational pattern of a good student is one that David McClelland and his colleagues call "need achievement." Need achievement manifests itself in a desire to do better, to compete against a standard. How our schools are to instill a desire for success in students who have not already acquired it at home is a difficult but important social question. Attempts have been made to teach people to think like achievers, to learn the opinions and behavior patterns that characterize the successful person. The first results have been encouraging; this kind of motivational training may prove both possible and practical. If it does, perhaps we can even reach some social consensus about its use, in which case psychologists would have contributed an important weapon to the educator's arsenal and helped to mobilize our human resources for the social good. But can parents who would refuse their children a relatively innocuous innovation like flouridation be persuaded to embrace such a deliberate public program of personality modification?

To my mind one of the most persuasive answers to this motivational question is that more initiative should be placed in the hands of the learner. If we want to motivate students to study harder, we should enlist their co-operation. This prescription would probably not be a universal panacea, but giving initiative to the student is important in adult education. Under existing conditions, however, it is not easy to give initiative to the student. In order to allow a learner to say more about what he studies, when he studies it, and how far he takes it, a teacher must adapt himself to the student's interests and abilities. When you recall that the teacher is usually outnumbered by thirty or forty to one in most schoolrooms, the impracticality of this solution becomes all too clear. Given realistic economic constraints on the expansion of our present educational system, I do not see how we could relinquish the initiative to students under that system. When it has been tried, as it often has in the beginning grades, the result has usually been to convert the class into a period of supervised recreation. We would have to change the system. I believe there are alternatives open to us that could achieve the desired result. If these alternatives do indeed prove to be better for motivating students to study, our schools may look very different by the year 2000.

The alternative systems I have in mind would exploit the modern, time-shared computer. Imagine a classroom partitioned into semi-isolated booths. In each booth are a pair of headphones, a typewriter keyboard, a screen similar to a television set's, and a photosensitive "light gun." All of these stations (and others in other classrooms) are in communication with a central computer. A student communicates with the computer by typing on the keyboard or by touching his light gun to designated spots on the screen; the computer communicates with a student by playing recorded speech through the student's earphones, or by writing or drawing pictures on the cathode ray tube. Each student can be working on a different lesson, or two on the same lesson can progress at different rates. A teacher walks from booth to booth, answers questions, sees that the stations are operating properly, and supervises requests for new materials.

A science-fiction fantasy? Not at all. Such systems are already operating. The one I have just described is operating in a public school in Palo Alto, California, as a pilot project under the direction of Patrick Suppes and Richard Atkinson of Stanford University. The children are learning about the same amount they would have learned under the regular system, but their attitude toward learning is entirely different. Learning is fun, they are more curious, and they enjoy studying from the computer. The cost—leaving out the cost of development—is only slightly more per student than before.

If the motivational advantages of this system persist when it is no longer a novelty, we can expect to see many more of these systems in the future. There are several reasons to think that a computer-based school makes sense. Students can go at their own pace. One who has trouble can get additional material; one who makes no mistakes can go on to more advanced material. Bright students are not bored while the teacher explains what they already know; dull students are not baffled by being left behind. There is no need for testing; students' records are maintained automatically. A teacher can teach and leave the threatening duty of evaluation to the machine. Within the broad limits set by what materials have been prepared for the computer, the student is free to study those things that are of most interest to him. And a computer treats all children alike, regardless of race, creed, or color.

For many people the computer is synonymous with mechanical depersonalization, and computerized instruction is frequently regarded as a way for the teacher to avoid his personal responsibility to his students. Fears have been expressed that the computer represents an assembly-line approach to the educational process that will increase alienation, identity crises, *anomie*, and so forth. Such attitudes seem overly emotional. The evidence points in the opposite direction. The computer gives the child a measure of individual attention that he could receive in no other way, short of a private tutor. To the extent that initiative can be left in the hands of the learner, rather than given to the machine, I believe these devices can help to solve an important educational problem.

Needless to say, stations do not have to be located in classrooms. They could be in libraries, or factories, or even private houses; all that is required is a telephone line to the computer. It should not be too difficult to make such facilities available for adult education. If economic considerations make it necessary, classroom stations in the public schools could be used for adult education in the evenings. It seems likely that businessmen will develop their own computer-based teaching systems; some of the most enthusiastic proponents of programmed self-instruction are businessmen who have used it to retrain their own personnel.

The shared use of a central computer by many stations at remote locations can be adapted to other purposes than public education. For example, it promises to be one of the more useful tools for enabling teams of experts to collaborate efficiently. I believe that the first time I heard the phrase, "on-line intellectual community with shared data base," it was intended as a summary of the various possibilities that Project INTREX (an M.I.T. adventure in library science headed by Carl Overhage) was considering during its planning conference in the summer of 1965. In fact, a visionary description of the possibilities inherent in making a "data base" (for example, a library or some part of it) accessible "on-line" (direct communication to a computer from a remote location via telephone line) to an "intellectual community" (a group of scholars or scientists working on a common problem) had already been written in 1965 by J.C.R. Licklider in his *Libraries of the Future.*

A number of organizations are presently working toward the introduction of computers into libraries, or vice versa. Not only can a computer provide a wide range of clerical services to its users, but a library of shared references will be available to them, their own data or other materials can be stored there, and the materials of other users can be made available on request—and all of this is accessible by simple requests initiated and fulfilled at the keyboard of a remote teletypewriter. Scholars in widely scattered locations will be able to work closely together without leaving their houses, and they will have the advantage of clerical, stenographic, library, telegraph, and publication services via the system. Something suggestive of such a computer system is already taking shape on a few college campuses; regional, national, or even international networks would be possible if they seemed desirable.

With just a little foresight in the development of these systems, they could turn out to be one of the greatest educational innovations since the invention of printing. If a student were provided with a console of his own, he could, at little or no cost to the intellectual community, have access to the most advanced thinking in his field of interest; a student in small or isolated colleges could be given the same access as the student at a great university. Moreover, the system would be responsive to his requests, so it would satisfy the requirement that initiative remain in the hands of the student.

The computerization of psychology is already well advanced, and the other behavioral and social sciences are not lagging far behind. Larger data bases and more ambitious data analysis are only part of the story. The machines can be programmed to simulate complex psychological and social systems, to conduct experiments, and to provide communication among scientists. The computer could become as important to the behavioral sciences as the microscope is to the biological.

Nevertheless, the application of computers to the study of man raises some difficult problems. Whenever it is proposed to put large quantities of data into a common file—particularly if the data are of the kind that most social scientists are interested in—there is danger that the information may be misused, a danger that has led in some quarters to an emotional resistance to the whole idea. When computer memories become so large that it will be unnecessary to discard information, and when any item can be made available in a few seconds, the temptation for a government to keep complete dossiers on all its citizens, and particularly those who are intellectually most active, will be quite real. It will be necessary to develop and instill a code of professional ethics among the scientists who use such data, and in some cases legislative safeguards may be required to protect the individual from the invasion of his privacy that such technology will make possible. Congress is already concerned with the problem, and we can expect to hear considerable discussion of it in the years ahead. How these safeguards are implemented could have some important consequences for our knowledge of man and society in the year 2000.

Any effort to peer into the future is likely to impress a psychologist with how fortunate economists are in comparison with other social scientists. The modern economist has available an extensive data base of economic statistics that enables him to formulate and test macroeconomic theories of the national economy, and the theories he has developed have given us new ways to control our economic fate. Other social statistics, however, are harder to come by, and the relative lack of solid noneconomic information about the personal and social status of our citizenry is reflected in a corresponding lack of empirically tested macrosocial theories outside the economic sphere. The advent of the on-line intellectual community with shared data base is an open invitation to sociologists, social psychologists, demographers, and others to follow the economists' lead. Let us hope, therefore, that legislative safeguards on the individual's right to privacy will not be so restrictive as to preclude the compilation of large, centralized, integrated data bases in the social sciences. Without them, the planners in the year 2000 will be scarcely better off than we are today.

The computer is here to stay, and, personally, I think that there is more hope than harm in it. There is another area of technological innovation that frightens me far more, an area in which psychologists will certainly be deeply involved, so I must at least mention it. I have in mind the recent developments in pharmacology, biochemistry, and related fields.

We already have drugs that can make us sleep or keep us alert, drugs that control our emotional state, drugs that induce hallucinations; drugs either to improve or to destroy memory are now appearing on the scene. This is just the beginning. In 1966 Dr. Stanley F. Yolles, Director of the National Institute of Mental Health, told the Senate that the next five or ten years would see a hundredfold increase in the number and types of drugs capable of affecting the mind. Before the year 2000 we will have to revise several of our current ideas about what is possible and what is advisable in the use of these new pharmacological agents.

There are many possible applications of our rapidly growing understanding of the mechanism of heredity. It will soon be possible to use fragments of cells to manufacture specific proteins, to control the sex of our offspring, to prevent hereditary defects. What psychological secrets may be locked up inside the cell? Is it too visionary to imagine that direct control of intelligence and personality may be possible? And, if so, what will they decide to do with these possibilities in the year 2000? What social problems would result if geneticists were to announce that they knew how to breed men who would live as long as turtles? We should not forget that we have also created an active program of research in biochemical warfare. Everyone hopes that we will never have occasion to use such weapons, but hoping may not suffice. The problem is too important to leave in the hands of the military, but as yet there is no consensus on what should be done about it. The quality of life in the year 2000 will be profoundly affected by the use we make of this new biotechnology. It is a social problem, not a scientific one, and eventually it must be discussed and decided by all members of our society.

It was in 1895 that the French psychologist Alfred Binet first suggested the use of ink blots for the study of various personality traits. An ink blot is just an ink blot. In order to see more than ink on paper the beholder must contribute something of himself to it, and the way he projects himself into the blot can be quite revealing. The future is no ink blot, but certainly any attempt to describe it must have a large projective component that will tell as much about the describer as about the thing described, and multiple descriptions can only yield a social projection. Nevertheless, the exercise is worth the effort. The future, unlike an ink blot, is still very much at the mercy of what we imagine it to be, and serious efforts to foresee it are less exercises in accurate prediction than they are attempts to reduce the eternal gap between what is humanly desirable and what is humanly possible.

DAVID RIESMAN

Notes on Meritocracy

MICHAEL YOUNG published *The Rise of the Meritocracy, 1870-2033: An Essay on Education and Equality* in 1958. Written in the form of an essay in historical sociology published in 2034, it belongs to the genre of anti-utopias, along with *Brave New World* and *1984*. It portrays a society built neither for hedonism nor for war but for maximum productive efficiency, one that has harnessed all its genetically based and educationally evoked intelligence in the service of optimal efficiency. Michael Young describes past and future struggles between the principles of aristocracy, based on ascription, and the principle of meritocracy, based on socially defined and certified merit and accomplishment. After showing how the less socially useful classes lose their brightest members to the meritocracy and hence those capable of organizing their resistance, he suggests the possibility of an antimeritocratic coalition nevertheless coming into being, led by upper-status women, who care more about "being" than about "doing," a few old-fashioned male Populists, and some surviving union leaders—all capable of mobilizing the supposedly content lower orders against the all too rational meritocratic society. Since its English publication, *The Rise of the Meritocracy* has helped give wide currency to the term *meritocracy* as a shorthand defining the elite in industrial societies increasingly organized along technocratic lines. My comments are principally an American embroidery on some of the themes in that book, for whose perceptiveness and wit my commentary is no substitute.

Pressures

Michael Young's fantasy, while describing the potential for revolt among those excluded from the meritocracy, assumes that those within its protection (except for some brilliant but romantic women) will have high morale. But the scientific and rationalist temper of our meritocracy may undermine the morale of even those within its protection; it has no religious base. Is America's romance with practicality and efficiency enough to sustain it? Men serving a system with no goal other than its own further advance have no transcendent aims. They are vulnerable to an inner and outer attack that criticizes them for sustaining a self-perpetuating structure, rather than helping to cure the diseases of society.

There is a horrible example in history of what the Educated Society might easily become unless the university commits itself to the education of the whole man. It is the destruction of one of the world's greatest and most creative civilizations, the China of the T'ang and Sung periods, by the imposition of a purely verbal, purely intellectual, purely analytical education on man and society, the Confucian Canon. Within a century, this commitment to the purely intellectual in man destroyed what had been the world's leader in art as well as in science, in technology as well as in philosophy. We are today in a similar danger—for we, too, tend, under the impact of the triumphs of organization and of the analytical mind, to downgrade everything that is direct, immediate and not verbal.[1]

One of the problems in a meritocracy is the nature of the formal tests for achievement and accomplishment. These are universalistic, and hence more or less metrical. By *metrical*, I mean that they allow people to be ranked along a single, quasi-quantitative dimension. But many people believe that such tests do not take into account the more impalpable or less easily measurable personal qualities. Michael Young "quotes" a workers' Manifesto around the year 2000 as follows:

The classless society would be one which both possessed and acted upon plural values. Were we to evaluate people, not only according to their intelligence and their education, their occupation and their power, but according to their kindness and their courage, their imagination and sensitivity, their sympathy and generosity, there could be no classes. Who would be able to say the scientist was superior to the porter with admirable qualities as a father. . . ? Every human being would then have equal opportunity, not to rise up in the world in the light of any mathematical measure, but to develop his own special capacities for leading a rich life.

Christopher Jencks in his review of *The Rise of the Meritocracy* suggests that qualities of "heart" are no more evenly distributed than those of "mind," and that if these, too, became metrically organized and competitively evaluated, society would not become more egalitarian, but it might well become less efficient or viable.[2] He also argues that, with increasing affluence, we can afford to prize charm over skill and technical intelligence, while the increasingly pressing problems of human organization may also call on qualities other than the more simply measured meritocratic ones. The same universalistic developments that downgrade birth and breeding (in the traditional "agricultural" sense) also, as we shall see, make possible the fostering even in our educational systems of wider varieties of talents, so that meritocratic judgments are always in tension with competing pressures.

Correspondingly, meritocracy may be most unhindered not at the top of society but in its more upwardly mobile echelons. For example, when small liberal arts colleges, denominational and otherwise, seek accreditation or other academic status, they may fire teachers who have devoted themselves to students in such relatively underprivileged fields as modern languages or English composition, in order to replace them with Ph.D.'s. It is not hard to locate institutions that have tossed out dedicated women teachers lacking that certification and substituted Indian, Hungarian, or Cuban professors with Ph.D.'s, but with small command of English, bitterness at exile, and invisibility to the scholarly world. Like any other social order, meritocracy is capable of being caricatured.

As already indicated, to the degree that a society moves toward meritocracy, certain personal qualities such as tenacity and willingness to learn new things become extremely important, while others, such as gregariousness and ingratiatingness become less important. Where a meritocracy is unidimensional and based on measured intelligence and skill, there may be a tendency for manners to decline and for people to become less receptive to charm. Since people move in a system in which, so to speak, their height and weight are already known, candor becomes part of the system rather than part of individual character. Nevertheless, because of good communication, decent people are not so likely to be forgotten, but neither are errors if they are errors of work rather than stylistic lapses arising from personality.

As Michael Young notes, meritocracy is at war not only with hereditary aristocracy but also with gerontocracy. The "natural" or traditional sequences of age-grading are broken up. We already see this in the natural sciences and mathematics, where people not only come to prominence in their twenties, but are likely to be viewed askance if they do not. I know several of these men, a life's gradient already surmounted in their twenties, who continue to be "productive" although with reduced zest. Some change their fields less

267

because of obsolescence than because of boredom. Others become gatekeepers for the meritocratic achievements of others (in Ralph Turner's terms, sponsors of contest mobility). Intellectual capital is very rapidly deflated where it depends on metrical achievement, repeatable results, and so on, rather than on mystique, wisdom, or style. In the arts, where there are no systems of tenure, no permanent chairs, matters are even more devastating for the temporary incumbents who cannot retread themselves fast enough as one genre is succeeded by another.

Of course, vested interests in ideas and methods exist to delay the obsolescence of the men in senior positions. But the gatekeepers must not only let in the new, but de-escalate the (still young) not so new. Donald Fleming writes:

The withdrawal of confidence from senior men, and less often, their banishment, must also go forward, though always impeded if never checked for long by the fellow-feeling of the Influentials for men of their own age and rank. . . . But though the Influential could not avoid exercising power, he might choose according to his temperament either to emphasize the unsoundness of bad work and poor men, or else to endorse those judgments in silence and press for the claims of good work and good men.[3]

In this same volume Fleming speaks of the elder William H. Welch as "the man not of intellect, but of character."[4] Before quantitative and national measures existed for testing intelligence and achievement, intuitive feeling for character often had to take its place. In his recent [1965] annual report of the Carnegie Corporation, John Gardner complains that universities are not training leaders, but aides and advisers to leaders. Is this a fruit of meritocracy or does it primarily have other origins?

Any admissions official at a selective college can testify to the ways in which individuals can cultivate or appear to possess the qualities that are required for entry. Years ago McGeorge Bundy spoke of the mark-hound who could even make noises as if he were creative. One of my friends who is an admissions counselor of an estimable girls' college describes girls who fake noncurricular interests, claiming to have spent the summer in a madrigal group or reading four hundred books in American literature from a list given them by their high-school teachers. By making entrance to such a college seem terribly desirable, the applicants are drawn to it, even if it is not in their interest to attend. Admissions counselors often say to a particular girl, who is unable to conceal in the interview an almost unbearable anxiety, that she would not be happy at such a high-pressure place, but she insists that she would be terribly happy because she loves competition and thrives under pressure.

An undergraduate thesis, entitled "Andover to Harvard," done in 1960 for the Department of Social Relations at Harvard College by Allan Blackmer, Jr., describes the feeling of many Andover students that, in the atmosphere of the new meritocratic Harvard, they are faced with the unpleasant alternatives of becoming a playboy or a grind. The "career" of a playboy is hard, as it has always been in America, and not many make it. Abraham Flexner, in his book on universities, wanted to preserve in the United States a role for the idler, but he wanted to eliminate the "mere" professional and technical training in pursuit of what he regarded as the European ideal. The idler has remained, but not so much as a playboy in the better colleges as an alienated Beat, intelligent enough to win in the meritocratic sweepstakes, but at least *pro tempore* despising these. The Beat is no threat to democratization of American higher education, which has put well-to-do aristocratic scions into a system where they can no longer get by on birth or charm.

Not all apparent Beats, of course, are idlers. Some are seeking distinction in another, nonacademic realm, where the market-grading system of the university does not reach. For example, in the most strenuously competitive universities there are students who go outside the system to paint, compose, play music, or put on avant-garde drama. Yet in these realms they may feel themselves to be in competition with national and even international standards, judging themselves no less meritocratically than they would judge within the academic disciplines. If they cannot paint like Picasso or Jackson Pollock, they may feel they are simply "messing around with paint." To be sure, this invidious sense reflects the availability through the mass media, long-playing records, art books, and paperback books of universal standards of performance, but, to some extent, meritocratic judgments may spill over beyond the area where they are applicable.

As Everett Hughes has observed, a man's career is often a congeries, retroactively rationalized, of internal impulses and external pressures. Meritocracy tends to focus attention on the extrinsic elements in work: Does one get admitted to this particular college, this department, this graduate school? Thereafter, how does one move up the ladder in a series of graded steps? This external judgment of what is regarded as success is, of course, not new. Indeed, a person who has "made it" in a meritocracy may choose expressive or meaningful work—work that in Hannah Arendt's sense has dignity and is not merely diurnal labor. Meritocracy may, however, narrow the ways in which individuals judge their work in terms of the difficulties of getting access to it through the educational or occupational gatekeepers.

And what of the gatekeepers: Where do their satisfactions lie? Do teachers measure themselves by their own achievements, or are they forced to measure themselves by getting their students on to the next step, winning various objective rewards and prizes? Up to the present time, gatekeeping institutions and individuals have not been judged meritocratically, but rather on results, which depend more upon intake than on "value added." Better measurement may change this, and teachers may be judged—as athletic coaches sometimes are—on what they have actually done with the given material. In fear of this, school superintendents have been resisting national assessments even though such assessments might provide leverage against stingy and tax-payer-oriented school boards and communities. As the society becomes more fair and just, making everyone in it dependent on achieved rather than adventitious accomplishments, it becomes more precarious, less relaxed, less arbitrary and corrupt, with fewer respites from competition. Yet the prospect of an administered rather than a politicized society seems remote to me, for people will always use politics to defend themselves against competition.

We see in the present problem of draft deferment a meritocratic issue. Here "merit" is defined in terms of the social division of labor and what is deemed necessary for the society. So far, this definition has been loose. A physicist is perhaps more likely than a classicist to find his local draft board sympathetic to his deferment, but even the classicist can find ways to justify his "production" in terms of the Gross National Product. (The need to defend the luxurious or frivolous thing done for its own sake in terms of pragmatic justification is not new. Latin has long been defended as a source of mind-training rather than as enjoyment in its own right.) So, too, the humanities are commonly justified in terms of what America as a great society owes to itself. What is now called basic research often does not require such roundabout defense, the position having been established at an earlier point. Many jobs that are simply parasitic on other jobs can become conventionally defined as socially useful and necessary. With us, just as in a more overtly corrupt and nonmerito-cratic society, people manage to conceal in the work for which they are paid a good deal of work that expresses their own more inner concerns.

Harold Seidman, Acting Assistant Director for Management and Organization in the Bureau of the Budget, writes:

A great proportion of [government] employees will face the prospect of (1) a mad, increasingly competitive scramble for the relatively fewer jobs in the fields in which they may be qualified or (2) shifting or up-grading their occupation and career objectives numerous times over the years in order to qualify for new opportunities.[5]

This prospect seems to be one of those rationalistic extrapolations that is conceivable but unlikely. The Civil Service, whether in gov-ernment or industry, has a marvelous ability to resist redeployment, even though it may well be that the more interesting work will re-quire individuals to continue to retrain themselves throughout life. Ideally, meritocratic education should prepare people for this b'teaching them several "languages" so that others can be easily learned in later life and by inspiring confidence in one's ability to learn.

Opportunities

If one observes college students today, one sees at work a di-alectic of pressure and opportunity. More students work harder than ever before to get into the selective colleges and into the selec-tive graduate and professional schools. They may, however, not work so hard once they are in these schools, which are often harder to get into than to be fired from, for they may come to recognize that they are bright and will get a job, and that they can be idio-syncratic and still survive, like the brilliant bearded Beats who now work for IBM or as computer programmers in many companies, Whyte's *Organization Man* to the contrary. In the less selective col-leges, many students of working-class or lower-middle-class origins readily assimilate to the collegiate style rather than acting as if this were their one chance for ascetic self-discipline on the straight and narrow road to success. They know that there will be jobs for them, if not dazzling careers, so that they can afford to act like scions.

A related aspect of meritocracy with its tendency to minimize age-grading is early induction into professional perquisites. Gradu-

271

ate students in the "okay" fields are now learning that they have a right to offices, to travel to conventions at government expense, and to live from the outset the life of a proto-academician. As the history of affluence shows, people learn quite rapidly to take for granted a new and heightened level of living. In a more ascetic time, scholarship winners sometimes felt a certain obligation to the society that sponsored them while not sponsoring others. But what begins as a privilege easily becomes a right. We can see this among faculty members who have come to feel that foundations should pursue them, rather than the other way around.

At the same time that meritocracy ties in with work, education helps us use our "free time" productively and not explosively or in such a way that we undo investment in our work-oriented education. Michael Young sees the whole expense-account culture as an investment in the business assets of the personnel (while the discontent of some of the wives arises from their inability to share in most of these benefits). A meritocratic society, as part of its attention to the mental health of its work force, will import many luxuries in the form of hobbies. But as already suggested, there is the problem that these, too, will be judged in a meritocratic way, and that the easy Sunday painting of Ike or Churchill will be condemned by people who cannot justify doing anything badly in a society where judgments in terms of accomplishment have become *de rigeur.* Yet, as already suggested, students do manage to find relief from meritocratic pressures. Dramatic and undramatic sexual activities, pot parties, winter and spring vacations will all grow as the pressures grow, so that while fraternity and sorority property may eventually sell at a discount, drug firms, air travel, and rent-a-car agencies will flourish.

Meritocracy makes a far wider range of choice available to students. They learn new possibilities for making a living in esoteric subjects. By having altered their definitions of success, as well as by being sent to strange places and on to strange career lines, students are cut off from their parents as markedly as they were in an earlier day by wealth and social grace. By creating a "critical mass" of people who are making their living in new ways, new kinds of careers are legitimated. (Compare the comment by James Jackson, Jr., in 1832, explaining why he could not go into scientific medicine: "We are a business-doing people. We are new. We have, as it were, just landed on these uncultivated shores; there is a vast deal to be done; and he who will not be doing must set down as a drone."[6]) For the foreseeable future, meritocracy means a full employment market for all those on the supply side of the rising demand curve for trained manpower. This includes professors, guidance counselors, perhaps psychiatrists, and all the different sorts of coaches who supply the measurement, care, and feeding of intelligence. (Football coaches do not as yet face a declining market; indeed, what is sometimes seen as an overemphasis on athletics may be regarded as an effort to shift the spotlight away from academic competence to a less central but still meritocratic area, for the verdict that one is clumsy is more bearable than that one is dumb, the latter being a life sentence.)

As already implied, we can expect to see a great increase in what is now called institutional research: in school systems, in colleges and universities, and in other nonprofit sectors of the society where its human assets are tested, finished, and maintained. Because there will not be enough competent instructors, there will be a very large market—already evident—for learning and teaching machines, some of which may displace the sadists who are now required to teach idiots, and others of which may be no less pedantic than the protoplasm they replace. It is also already evident that there will be an increasing market for in-service training in any enterprise that wishes to attract able graduates already accustomed in their schooling to accepting meritocratic judgments. Enormous wealth is not a goal for such people, even though it is not necessarily unattainable (right-wing and conservative complaints to the contrary). Once a person has the appurtenances to which he believes his education and talents entitle him, including the fringe benefits already noticed, and when he is in a position to give his children a far better than average education, often at public expense, his concern for capital accumulation will be modest.

Resistances

The Rise of the Meritocracy discusses the resistance of parents to having their children fall like brass in Plato's social system. Christopher Jencks, in some unpublished research, has concluded that perhaps as many as one third of the children of college-educated parents in the United States end up with comparatively less education and lower occupational rank than their parents. They do not fall very far, and they do not starve; but the children of the brilliant will not always be brilliant, and social mobility means that they must give way to the brilliant children of the less brilliant.

For young women, the floor under their fall may be higher even though the ceiling over their rise is lower than that for men. For, to some extent, young women live within an enclave where even in the year 2000 it may be more damaging to be thought homely or lacking in sex appeal than to be stupid. To that degree, women as compared with men represent a Veblenian lag. Their standing will still depend at least as much on the men to whom they attach themselves as on their own accomplishments in meritocratic terms. It could be argued that women buffer men against the abuses of meritocracy, bind up their wounds, and make it possible for them to go on playing a game that, if not a zero-sum game, makes even the winners often feel like losers. Of course, the women are far from totally exempt, for they are given much the same education and respond to it with more compliance than men do. They can neither stand as cheerleaders on the sidelines nor throw themselves wholeheartedly into the meritocratic game, and their own ambivalences mirror in heightened degree those of the more vulnerable men.

This vulnerability is likely to lead both parents and children to continuous efforts to get around the iron law of meritocracy. Not only will the less talented children of brilliant, successful parents have the advantage of growing up in a cultured home, but they will often have the advantage of all the education that money can buy, a decreasing but still not negligible amount. Yet for the foreseeable future, the morale of meritocracy will prevent the disappointed families of the previous generation's elite from subverting the system, for even they believe in it, at least in part. Puritanism has in this respect done its work fairly well, and if the alumni of leading selective colleges can no longer get their sons and daughters into those colleges, their revolt remains confined to muttering.

It is sometimes feared, however, that if a college selects only the most brilliant, its alumni will not become rich, and it will lose philanthropic support. This is probably an old-fashioned view, because an alumnus who goes into research medicine or physics and becomes an Influential holds access to funds more bountiful than even those of the richest private patron. Then the politics of meritocracy takes a new turn, no longer simply private as against public, but rather local as against national. What might be called the nationalization of federal support for meritocracy can grow relatively unimpeded until the amounts become staggeringly large, and pressures for nonmeritocratic regional division begin to be felt, as in the effort to get an accelerator and other research moneys for universities in the Middle West. (Even the apparently ruthless Abraham Flexner made special provision for southern medical schools.) But there may be compensatory efforts not only with respect to geographically "backward countries," but also racial and ethnic ones, as in the efforts to help Negro institutions and individual Negroes. Where meritocracy is in sharp contrast to compensatory justice—or to quasi-religious compassion—the pressure for universalistic standards may relent even more than it has already.

There will also be guilt toward underprivileged fields as well as underprivileged people. The humanities and to a lesser extent the performing arts have profited from the guilt of the more affluent sectors. Thomas Green argues that the government ought to subsidize amateur performance for the sake of leisure.[7] But can this be done if it is not good performance by any standards?

There are students who arrive for interviews at the selective colleges in sloppy clothes in order to defeat their parents and society as well as themselves. Sometimes they do this in order to have an alibi for nonsuccess. Students prepared well enough to do adequately but not certain that they will do brilliantly may sometimes manage to oversleep an examination or not find time to prepare for it, so that they can tell themselves that they would have done outstanding work if they had really wanted to. This is perhaps a new form of *noblesse oblige*.

A great difference between England and America with respect to meritocracy is that in the latter there is no single sub-center of power comparable to London that drains the provinces, and thus a completely national system even by the year 2000 is unlikely in the United States. There are many disadvantages to having Washington as a capital city and New York as the cultural, financial, and legal capital, but one advantage is that there is not a single magnet. French academic and cultural, as well as political, centralization makes everything outside Paris seem provincial. And generally in European universities, a few strategically placed individuals in the relevant chairs can dominate a field in a way that has not been possible in America with our wider range of places and opportunities. Feelings of local pride act as a countervailing force against efforts to establish a national scale of institutional prestige. The kind of hegemony, for example, that Oxford and Cambridge plus the University of London have exercised over British academia is inconceivable in this country, even by the year 2000. But it seems likely that we shall then be closer to thinking in national rather than localistic terms. And as the orbit in which people and institutions judge themselves widens, and as the number of relevant comparisons correspondingly grows, people may develop a feeling that, whatever they count for locally, they do not matter much nationally. Hence, even though meritocracy brings heightened standards of performance everywhere, in a country as large as the United States, resistance movements based on local pride and even local paranoia will persist.

REFERENCES

1. Peter F. Drucker, "The Rise in Higher Education," *The Revolutionary Theme in Contemporary America*, ed. Thomas Ford (Lexington, Ky., 1965), pp. 86-99; reference here to pp. 93-94.

2. Christopher Jencks, "Review of *The Rise of the Meritocracy*," *The New Republic* (September, 1959), p. 18.

3. Donald H. Fleming, *William H. Welch and the Rise of Modern Medicine* (Boston, 1954), p. 132.

4. *Ibid.*, p. 22.

5. Quoted by Donald Michael, *The New York Review* (November 25, 1965), p. 36.

6. Quoted by Fleming, *William H. Welch and the Rise of Modern Medicine*, p. 8.

7. In an unpublished manuscript entitled "Work, Leisure, and the Structure of Hope."

JAMES Q. WILSON

Violence

THERE ARE two kinds of domestic violence for which we would like
to estimate future rates and thus two kinds of problems which make
such estimates very difficult, if not impossible. The first kind is
individual violence—murders, suicides, assaults, child-beatings—
and the second is collective violence—riots, civil insurrections, internal wars, and the like.

Individual violence has for the social scientist the advantage
(if I may use that word) of being subject to the law of large numbers
—it consists of more or less comparable if not identical acts performed by large numbers of people and thus is subject (in principle)
to casual analysis and the fitting of trend lines. Naturally, all
murders are not alike, and ignoring this (as we usually do) can lead
to erroneous judgments about the causes of murder. But if we wish
merely to make some gross estimates of the volume of deaths attributable to homicide for a time in the future, it is not wholly improper
to treat all murders as if they were alike. Making such simplifying
assumptions permits us to speak of murder rates, or suicide rates,
or changes over time in these rates. The problem of prediction
remains, however; if we are to guess how much individual violence
we are likely to have in the year 2000, we must be confident that
our count of violent events is accurate, we must know on what social
forces the rate of violence depends, and we must be able to make
a good guess as to what changes will occur in those social forces
over the next thirty or so years. As we shall see, we cannot be
confident about any of these things.

Collective violence presents a different set of problems. We can
be fairly certain that our count of the number of riots, subject to
the problem of defining a riot in borderline cases, can be made
fairly accurately—an assault or a child-beating may be concealed

from the authorities, but hiding a riot is rather more difficult. But we cannot be certain in what sense, if any, all riots are sufficiently alike to be added together. And if they are added together, their total number is so small (it may not seem small to beleaguered mayors or police chiefs, but it is small to a social scientist) and their occurrence from year to year so uneven and episodic that it would be foolish indeed to try to fit any sort of trend line to such events. Furthermore, no one has developed an empirically verified theory of what causes a riot—and for reasons to be developed later, no one is likely to. Finally, assuming the causes could be identified, we would still face the problem of estimating what changes are likely to occur in those causes.

Though both kinds of violence have certain analytical problems in common, those besetting the analysis of individual violence involve the accuracy of the data and the estimation of the changes in the explanatory variables, while those complicating the discussion of collective violence arise from having to deal with so few cases that we face the logical difficulty of predicting unique or rare events. To put the matter into a different and somewhat more familiar context, we want to guess for the year 2000 (in the first case) how many automobile accidents there will be and (in the second case) how many labor disputes between the automobile companies and the unions will occur. The problems with the first estimate are primarily empirical, those with the second primarily logical or theoretical.

One may rejoin that of course precision is impossible, but can we not at least say whether in the future we will have more or fewer accidents (or violent crimes) or whether it will be possible for a labor dispute to occur at all because, for example, by the year 2000 there will be no laborers to have disputes with, all of them having been replaced with machines? Let us see.

Individual Violence

Of all the kinds of individual violence, murder and suicide are the only ones about which we seem to have reasonably reliable data. This is true partly because the crime is difficult (but not impossible) to conceal, partly because the police have little incentive to suppress or distort reports of such crimes, and partly because other agencies in addition to the police count murders and suicides—offices of vital statistics keep track of all dead bodies, however produced. And we know more about the victims and perpetrators of these forms of violence because the police solve over 90 per cent of all murders and, by definition, 100 per cent of all suicides. (A death may be erroneously ascribed to suicide, of course, but once it is called a suicide then it is "solved.")

The most striking fact about murder has been its more or less steady decline for at least the last thirty years and perhaps for much longer. Between 1933 and 1963, the murder rate per 100,000 population was cut about in half, using as data deaths ascribed to homicide on physicians' certificates.[1] Since the early 1940's, murder rates compiled by the FBI from local police reports have agreed very closely with death certificate rates, and thus we can probably regard FBI figures for at least this offense as reasonably accurate. A few scholars have tried to trace murder rates back even further in time, at least for selected cities. Ferdinand, using Boston police figures, shows that the murder rate in that city has fallen more or less steadily from a peak in 1855–1859 to the early 1950's, though there have been inexplicable and seemingly erratic variations in this trend.[2] Warner, examining murders in Boston from 1883 to 1933, found the pattern uneven but no evidence of any increase and some evidence of a decline.[3] Wolfgang found a decline in the homicide rate in Philadelphia between 1923 and 1952.[4]

But there is a problem: Our figures tell us only how many murders are *successfully* committed, not how many are attempted. (An attempted murder is in police reports lumped together with other aggravated assaults.) Wolfgang notes that four factors, having nothing to do with the homicidal tendencies of our countrymen, may have been responsible for the decreasing murder rate: the telephone, the radio, the automobile, and the doctor. By telephone we can summon the police today much more quickly than in the nineteenth century; by radio, the police can dispatch help more quickly than before; motor vehicles can get injured persons to the hospital at greater speed; and the modern doctor can save lives that once would have been lost. The murder rate may be going down for the same reason the automobile fatality rate is going down —medical science and alert ambulance drivers are frustrating the unquenchable desire to do in our fellow man.

On the other hand, if we consider what we know about the causes of murder and calculate recent trends in the magnitudes of these causal factors, we may decide that the decline in the murder rate is real and not spurious. Every major study of murder has concluded that it is primarily a lower-class crime, however class is defined. Except for so-called "white collar crimes" (violations of commercial codes, business theft, and the like), *all* crimes are more common among lower- than higher-status groups; murder, however, is disproportionally more common among the former group.[5] Certainly there are fewer people living in lower-class statuses now than there were fifty years ago, or quite likely even ten years ago; thus there should have been—and probably has been—a decline in those behaviors, including homicide, which are more characteristic of lower-class persons.[6] Negroes, probably because they have ranked so low in income, occupation, and education, have had a murder rate ten times higher than that of whites,[7] but this is changing largely, one suspects, because the class position of Negroes is changing. In 1940, deaths due to homicide occurred at a rate (per 100,000 population) of 3.1 for whites and 34.3 for nonwhites; by 1960, the rate for whites had fallen to 2.5 (a drop of about one-fifth) while that for nonwhites had fallen to 21.9 (a drop of over one-third).[8]

Furthermore, there have always been marked regional differences in murder rates that are to some degree independent of class and race, but these are slowly disappearing as industrialization, migration, and other factors are reducing the differences among the various regional subcultures. In 1940, for example, deaths due to homicide among nonwhites in Georgia were almost four times as common as such deaths among nonwhites in Massachusetts; by 1960, though the nonwhite homicide death rate had dropped for both states, it had dropped more in Georgia so that it was by then only two and a half times larger than the Massachusetts rate.[9] And this decline will probably continue as migrants remain in their new, more urban states longer. Pettigrew and Spier have shown that interstate differences in the Negro murder rate in the North can be accounted for in part by the differences in the murder rate in those southern states from which Negro migrants came. Northern states with the highest Negro murder rates (for example, Indiana or Michigan) are those with large numbers of Negroes born in the South; those with the lowest Negro murder rates (for example, Massachusetts) have the smallest proportion of Negroes born in the South.[10]

In sum, while modern technology is reducing the number of murders completed, economic progress is probably reducing the number attempted. But murder is a comparatively rare form of violence. Much more common is assault—how much more common is almost impossible to say, because assault is especially sensitive to reporting error (victims may change in their willingness to call an assault to the attention of the police and the police may change in their willingness or ability to count such reported assaults accurately). Police reports to the FBI in 1965 showed that there were twenty times as many assaults as murders, but the household survey conducted the following year by the National Opinion Research Center showed that there were twice as many assaults as had been reported and thus assault may be *forty* times more common than murder.[11] Since the NORC survey was done only once, we do not know whether assault is more or less common today than thirty years ago. It would be interesting if the assault rate were some constant multiple of the homicide rate, for then we could use murder—which is known fairly accurately—as a proxy for crimes of violence generally. But we do not know that it is, though we do believe that assault—like murder—is disproportionally a lower-class crime and thus presumably susceptible to the same social changes previously described. Ferdinand argues that assault rates in Boston have dropped greatly (by a factor of five) since a peak in 1875–1878.[12] Most other studies have agreed that violent crime was at its height in the years immediately after the Civil War.[13] Granting that urban life in the late nineteenth century may have been poor, nasty, brutish, and short and that things are much better today, we cannot dismiss the possibility that during the *recent* past (the last fifteen to thirty years) violent crime in the cities has increased. That is what the crime figures show and, though we know such figures are subject to great reporting errors, we do not know enough to be confident that changes in reporting practices account for all the apparent increase.

Indeed, to argue (as do some no doubt well-intentioned people) that the alleged increase in violent crime in our cities is a myth is to contradict another view held by these same people, namely, that the increased concentration of the Negro poor in our central cities is a major social problem. Assaultive crime is disproportionally a crime of the poor; since the Negro is the poorest of the poor and since he comes from a region where violence is a way of life, assaultive crime is also disproportionally committed by Negroes (largely, it should be noted, on other Negroes). As lower-income Negroes (and lower-income rural whites, for that matter) comprise an ever larger proportion of the central city population, the rate of

JAMES Q. WILSON

assaultive crime inevitably will go up—either that or one must argue, implausibly, that the wretched condition of urban slums *reduces* the assaultive tendencies of low-income persons or that the middle-income persons who vacated what has become slum housing had *higher* assault rates than the newcomers. In short, while changes in reporting practices may be enough to account for the apparent aggregate increase in assaultive crime in the nation as a whole, they cannot explain the apparent increase in the central cities unless one is prepared to dismiss everything that is known about the incidence of such crime by social class. As a nation we may be committing fewer assaults, but such assaults as we are committing are being committed more and more in the cities; this is only another way of saying that as a nation we are less and less poor, but such poor as we have are increasingly living in cities.[14]

Violent crimes may increase in the cities, if not in the nation as a whole, for reasons in addition to the urbanization of the poor. One is the increasing proportion of young people in the population; another is prosperity. Violent crime is predominantly a crime of young men, especially those in their twenties, and such persons are coming to constitute a larger fraction of the population, especially in cities. The relationship between violent crime and economic conditions is less clear-cut, but studies by Henry and Short suggest that "homicide and aggravated assault are correlated positively with the business cycle . . . during prosperity, homicide increases."[15]

At first blush, it seems paradoxical that assaultive crime should be characteristic of both the lower class and prosperity—would not prosperity, by raising incomes, reduce the size of the assault-prone class and thus the incidence of such assaults? No one is quite sure how to relate these apparently contradictory findings. One possibility, suggested by Henry and Short, is that the business cycle does not alter the class position of many people—that would require a generation or more of economic progress—but does cause short-run dislocations in relative status which in turn produce feelings of frustration and aggression.[16] If this is true, we would expect that the increase in homicide during prosperity would be greatest for groups least able to advance economically and socially—for groups, that is, which are likely to experience the greatest frustration when they see society as a whole apparently making great economic progress while they lag behind. The evidence is consistent with this interpretation, though it cannot prove it. The increase in homicide during prosperity is largely due to its increase *among Negroes;*

282

for whites, homicides tend to decrease during prosperity.[17] It has often been argued that in affluent periods Negroes do not gain relative to whites but at the same time are constantly exposed, directly and through the mass media, to the signs of prosperity. Educational deficiencies among Negroes, discriminatory barriers to full employment, residential concentration in the central cities at some distance from the fringe locations at which new jobs are being created the fastest, and other factors may produce a belief that Negroes are not progressing relative to society as a whole. Whites, on the other hand, do not compare themselves with Negroes, nor do they experience many of the barriers to rapid entry into an expanding job market; thus, for lower-status whites, prosperity decreases frustration and thus decreases the murder rate. Nonetheless, for whites and Negroes alike the long-term trend has represented an improvement in their class position. Over time, the negative correlation between prosperity and the white murder rate should increase and the positive correlation between prosperity and the Negro murder rate should decrease. In fact, this appears to be happening.[18]

When a person moves out of the lower class into the middle class, it seems as if he substitutes suicide for homicide just as he (or she) substitutes contraception and abortion for illegitimacy. The suicide rates are higher for whites than for Negroes, for higher-status than for lower-status groups, and for men than for women. But there are regional complications. Certain parts of the country with very low murder rates have very high suicide rates. Vermont, for example, had in 1963 a murder rate of only 0.8 per 100,000 population but a suicide rate of 15.6 per 100,000. Georgia, by contrast, had a murder rate fourteen times greater than that of Vermont (11.4) but a suicide rate only two-thirds as great (10.9). Over time, these regional differences are weakening—the murder rate in Georgia (as in most southern states) is going down but the suicide rate is going up.

Economic conditions also complicate the suicide trend, just as (but in the opposite way) they complicate the murder trend. Suicide is the form of violence most characteristic of the middle and upper classes, but suicide decreases in times of prosperity and increases during depressions. Here, of course, the explanation seems simpler: High-status persons have more to lose in a business crash and thus their suicide rate reacts more sharply to economic conditions. Lower-status persons—for example, Negroes—have less to lose in depressions and thus less reason to kill themselves. In short, high-status persons may suffer greater relative deprivation in a depression just as low-status persons suffer greater relative deprivation during prosperity. Status and deprivation are not, of course, the sole causes of suicide any more than they are of homicide. For example, we know that elderly, homeless men living in the socially disorganized central sections of large cities have high suicide rates[19] even though (or perhaps because) their economic status is low. Similarly, married persons have, at each age level, lower suicide rates than those who are single, widowed, or divorced.[20]

Despite all we know about murder and suicide, predicting future rates is no easy task. Murder has become less common among both whites and Negroes (between 1940 and 1963, homicide as a cause of death fell from 4.9 to 3.9 per 100,000 white males and from 56.5 to 35.7 per 100,000 nonwhite males). Suicide during the same period became less common among whites (falling from 23.5 to 17.8 per 100,000 white males) but more common among nonwhites (rising from 6.2 to 7.9 per 100,000 nonwhite males); the decrease among whites was more than enough to compensate for the increase among nonwhites, so the net change in the total suicide rate was a decrease (from 14.4 to 11.0 per 100,000).[21]

A straight-line extrapolation of these trends would be imprudent, to say the least. We can be fairly confident that with a continued reduction in the size of the lower class there will be a reduction in the number of murders, at least in the long run. In the short run, however, the decline may level off or even be reversed owing to the increased urbanization of the poor, the increased proportion of the population in those age groups most productive of assaultive crime, and continued prosperity. This may, indeed, have already happened—between 1960 and 1965, the rate of murders reported to the police remained almost constant despite rapid economic progress; in fact, from 1961 to 1965, the rate actually *increased* by about 9 per cent. When—or whether—the long-term downward trend will resume is anybody's guess. In any case, there is as yet no good reason to assume that we will even in the fairly distant future achieve a murder rate as low as that in England, Ireland, France, or Japan; in these countries, the rate is only a third to a tenth of the American rate, despite much lower per capita incomes.[22]

Predicting suicide rates suffers from similar difficulties. Sustained prosperity may cause the rate to continue to fall, but this same prosperity may bring so many more persons—especially Negroes— into the middle class that the population as a whole may become much more vulnerable to economic strain; thus, suicide rates may increase much more sharply during any future depression than they have in past ones. And complicating this situation even further is the unknown rate at which persons are entering into lives characterized by weak familial and social constraints—"dropping out" of society is no longer something done only by hoboes, derelicts, and alcoholics, but is also a route taken by the sons and daughters of the middle class.

But murder and suicide are not ordinarily matters of grave public concern, partly because they are uncommon and partly because there is little that can be done to prevent them. Much more serious and much more common is aggravated assault, and yet for this form of violence our information is the least reliable. If the "true" rates were known, assault might be shown to be sensitive to the same social trends as murder, and thus the incidence of victimization from assault would decline at the same pace and for the same reasons as the incidence of homicide. Indeed, the closest studies of assault suggest that it is distinctively a lower-class crime and thus should decline with a shrinking lower class.[23] But again, there are complications. Not only is the population becoming younger (and thus to some degree "more violent," holding class constant), but urbanization may be stimulating the formation or maintenance of what Wolfgang calls the "subculture of violence."[24] Lower-class persons living in rural areas or small towns may have a low rate of interaction, one with another, and thus, though there will be violence, it will occur less often and (perhaps) be confined to members of a family. When such persons find themselves in a high-density urban slum, however, the rate of interaction may increase as a geometric rather than a linear function of their numbers. With so many interactions, the number which breed violence may dramatically increase even though the proportion remains the same. Further, as young men leave the family and find peer groups on the big-city street corners, those who are emotionally immature or possessed by explosive personalities and a desire for the immediate gratification of impulses will be more likely to encounter others who share these urges and thus who will reinforce them and reward their expression. What was once a habit of violence may become a subculture of violence.

Collective Violence

Whatever the deficiencies with respect to our knowledge of individual forms of violence, at least we know enough to be able to answer the question, "How much of this violence will occur next year, or over the next five years?" The answer, obviously, is, "about the same as this year." With respect to collective violence—riots, disorderly demonstrations, and the like—we cannot even say that. The best we can do—and what, indeed, many commentators are doing—is to predict widespread violence so that if *any* violence occurs the prediction will appear to have been "correct." Logically, of course, it will not be correct: it would be as if a meteorologist were to predict that it will rain every day and then, on the day it does rain, to say he has been proved right.

Most theories of collective violence have as their principal defect that they over-predict the phenomenon. Some say that Negroes riot because their lot is deplorable—they have nothing to lose but their burdens. But the lot of many Negroes has always been deplorable; indeed, by most standards it is much less deplorable today than twenty years ago. Others modify the theory by introducing the notion of relative deprivation or the "revolution of rising expectations." But Negroes have experienced such deprivations and such expectations before—during World War I, World War II, and the Korean War, when their incomes rose rapidly, migration to the big cities was heavy, and an awareness of and contact with the advantages of white society were widespread. There were no major Negro riots then; the only major riots were begun by *whites* and aimed at Negroes (Chicago in 1919, Detroit in 1943). The only major *Negro* riot took place in Harlem in the depths of the Depression (1935) when presumably there was a "revolution of decreasing expectations." A third theory is that the riots are caused by conspirators who have recently become organized. There may have been one or two riots that were clearly begun by conspiratorial leaders and there probably have been many more attempts by such groups to cause riots, but in the major upheavals—Watts, Detroit, Newark—the activities of the conspirators did not begin in earnest until after the riot had begun from apparently spontaneous causes.

The central problem is not to predict violence, but to explain why violence has occurred during the last two or three years *but not before*. Some commentators, of course, argue that there has always been violence in this country—from the Draft Riots in the 1860's through the labor riots that began with the railroad strikes of 1877 and continued through the 1930's (fifteen men were killed in the Little Steel Strikes of 1937)—and that the Negro rioting today is no worse and perhaps no different from earlier forms of violence. It has even been suggested that violence is in some sense a "normal" and perhaps legitimate political strategy for oppressed groups. Whether the present riots are any worse than earlier disorders is beside the point; whether they are in some sense legitimate is not beside the point but outside the scope of this paper. What can be said is that they are different. The Draft Riots were popular reactions against a certain concrete public policy, the enforcement of which was resisted by Irishmen and others who were not willing to restrict themselves to "going limp." The violence attending the labor disputes (in 1934 alone, nearly thirty people were killed) was in almost every case the result of an effort by a union to persuade management to recognize it. When management responded by calling in the Pinkertons and the scabs, the workers reacted with violent protest. Labor-management violence was in the nature of an internal war between two organized opponents struggling over a quite tangible stake. With the winning of union recognition, the incidence of such violence dropped off markedly, though isolated cases recur from time to time, especially in the South.[25] Even the anti-Irish riots of the 1840's and 1850's were directed at an "enemy" and resulted in the destruction of "enemy" property: in Philadelphia, two Catholic churches and two parochial schools were burned to the ground; in St. Louis fifty Irish homes were wrecked and looted; in New York a mob marched on City Hall to attack anybody around who looked Irish.[26]

The Negro riots are not apparently aimed at a specific enemy, they do not arise over a specific *issue* (though they may be precipitated by an "incident"), and they do not carry the war to the enemy's territory. While it is true that white-owned business establishments are burned and looted, the amount of property owned or occupied by Negroes that is destroyed is often much greater. The Detroit Fire Department listed 477 buildings destroyed or damaged by fire in the 1967 riot. Of these, 103 were single- and multi-family homes, 30 were apartment buildings, and 38 were stores which contained dwelling units. The vast majority were inhabited by Negroes and many were owned by Negroes. Only five liquor stores, two loan shops, four jewelry stores, and one bank were burned, even though these establishments presumably represent "white business" and may be perceived as "white exploitation." Many other, more obvious symbols of white authority—churches, schools, newspaper circulation offices, police buildings—were scarcely touched. To compare these riots with earlier historical examples is like comparing assault to self-flagellation—such pleasure as the latter confers does not depend on the suffering it causes others.

When people destroy their own communities even at high risk to themselves (43 persons died in Detroit, most from police and National Guard bullets), it is difficult to assert that the riot was an *instrumental* act—that is, an effort to achieve an objective. (The Draft Riots, the anti-Irish riots, the violence practiced by the Ku Klux Klan, and the labor-management violence were all to some degree instrumental acts.) The Negro riots are in fact *expressive* acts—that is, actions which are either intrinsically satisfying ("play") or satisfying because they give expression to a state of mind. Of course, for many people in all riots—whether instrumental or expressive—there are individual gratifications, such as the opportunity for looting, for settling old scores, and the like. But these people operate, so to speak, under the cover of the riot and are not obviously the cause of it. To the extent riots are or can be organized, of course, the need to offer incentives to induce people to participate would make the encouragement of looting a prime objective for a riot leader —not only does it get people out on the street in large numbers and put them in an excited state of mind, it disperses and preoccupies police and military forces. There is little evidence yet, however, that it is the desire for loot that precipitates the riot or even plays a very important part in the early hours.

If we are to construct an explanation for what has occurred—and we may never have a testable explanation, for the requirements of experimental or statistical control necessary to test any riot hypothesis are not likely to exist—we must combine attention to the material conditions in which the Negro lives (which on the whole have been improving but are still poor) with the costs and benefits to him of expressing a desire for autonomy, manhood, self-respect, and the capacity for independent action. On the cost side, we note a significant reduction in the willingness of those who command the police to use them with maximum vigor in suppressing disorder. The attention given of late to real and imagined cases of "police brutality" has obscured the fact that, compared to the police response to labor violence even thirty years ago, most big-city police departments, especially in the North, have recently been less inclined, primarily for political reasons, to use instant and massive retaliatory tactics against any incipient disorder. It would appear that this is one reason the majority of serious riots have occurred in the North, not the South—in the latter region, political constraints on the police are less effective. One need not deny that police-citizen contacts have often been the spark that triggered a riot, or that many departments have neglected or mismanaged their community relations program, to argue that the police, if they wanted to (that is, if they were willing to pay the price in lives and political support), could make the costs of rioting so high that either there would be no riots at all or there would be a massive convulsion equivalent to civil war.

On the benefits side, persons are coming of age who are several generations away from the rural South and who accordingly have lost their fear of white men without yet having had an opportunity to even scores. Young people are always rebellious; when young people grow up and discover that their elders are *also* rebellious, there is perhaps an urge for even more extreme actions. Just as the sons and daughters of New Deal liberals regard their parents as "square" for confining their demands for change to the rules imposed by the existing political system, so also the sons and daughters of Negroes who have demanded integration and equal opportunity may feel that such demands are not enough because they are based on an acceptance of the distribution of power within the existing social order. Negro (and some white) leaders, aware of the drift toward violent sentiments, have attempted to take advantage of it by using the threat of violence as a way of increasing their bargaining power; the difficulty, of course, is that the responsible leaders have lacked the capacity either to start or stop a riot while the irresponsible ones have simply lacked the power to stop one.

Furthermore, the mass media—especially television—offer an opportunity for immediate expressive gratification that did not exist even fifteen years ago. It is interesting to speculate on what the Know-Nothing violence might have been like if every American could watch in his living room the looting of a convent while it was happening and if every would-be looter could be summoned to the scene by immediate radio coverage of the event.

Finally, young people today, white and Negro, have become quite self-conscious, for reasons I obviously do not understand, about the social functions and therapeutic value of violence. A generation that was absorbed by Camus' intricate analysis of how in existential terms one might have justified the effort to assassinate the tsar has given way to a generation some members of which are absorbed by Frantz Fanon's argument for violence: Violence, if practiced by the wretched and oppressed, may be intrinsically valuable as an assertion of self and a reversal of a previous act of violence—slavery—by which self has been denied and subjugation institutionalized.[27]

In short, the few things we know about the riots—that they develop out of a seemingly trivial incident, that they are more expressive than instrumental, and that they have thus far occurred primarily in northern cities or in the more "progressive" southern cities (such as Atlanta or Nashville)—should lead us to be skeptical of arguments that the riots can be explained entirely or primarily on grounds of *material* deprivation, unresponsive local governments, inadequate poverty programs, or the like. No doubt these factors play a part. After all, if the class characteristics of Negroes were identical to those of whites (measured by income, education, mobility, and level of political organization), it is hard to imagine that there would be any riots, though there still might be a good deal of discontent. If there were no lower class, there would be fewer riots just as there would be fewer murders. But if class is a necessary explanation, it is not a sufficient one. To material (that is to say, to Marxian) explanations must be added explanations that take into account the role of *ideas* and the role of *force*.

It is hard to discuss such things without being misunderstood. To impute causal power to ideas or to the lack of force seems to imply the desirability of censoring ideas or imposing the most repressive kinds of force. That is not the implication I intend. To try to censor ideas is both wrong and futile; repressive force is neither available nor manageable. The argument here is analytic, not prescriptive, and is designed merely to suggest that we consider the possibility that ideas have consequences. Theories of social change are often suspect, in my eyes, because they seem to lead automatically to the policy conclusion favored by their author: It is as if one decided what program one wanted adopted and then decided what "caused" an event in order to justify that remedial program. If one wants a "Marshall Plan" for Negroes, then economic want causes riots; if one wishes the political power of the "Establishment" weakened, then inadequate access and a lack of self-determination are the causes; if one wants Stokely Carmichael and Rap Brown put in jail, then conspirators are the cause. Since almost no one wants (at least publicly) ideas to be controlled, the causal power of ideas is rarely asserted;

this theory gets fewer "votes" than it may deserve because it is not in anyone's interest to vote for it.

But if elsewhere ideas are readily conceded to have consequences —"nationalism," "self-determination," "the world communist revolution"—might it not be possible that they have consequences here also? Only a fear of being thought illiberal may prevent us from considering that the probability of a riot is increased by demands for "black power," by a constant reiteration that white bigotry and racism are at the root of all the problems besetting the Negro, by the reaffirmation of the (untrue) assumption that most Negroes live wretched lives and that matters are going from bad to worse, by constantly predicting apocalyptic violence if "something isn't done," and by "discovering" the non-truth that all Negroes are alike in their hatred of "whitey" and their tacit or open approval of extreme solutions for their plight.[28]

If there is something in the climate of opinion, the mood of a generation, or the drift of sentiments that contributes to Negro riots, there is no reason to suppose that only Negroes are affected by these currents. The special and urgent problem of the Negro may lead us to assume, without sufficient reflection, that the Negro case is not only special but unique. But it ought not be taken for granted that 20 million people are affected by ideas that have no effect on the other 180 million living in the same country. More narrowly, are young Negroes involved in a radical discontinuity in American history or are they simply at the leading edge of a more general drift toward collective violence? Are we quite confident that there is no connection between Negroes burning down their communities and young whites storming the Pentagon, assaulting cabinet officers, and forcibly occupying university buildings? Or between these acts and the sharp rise in recruitment to the Ku Klux Klan and the emergence of the ominous White Knights and the Minutemen? And if there is a connection, is the entire phenomenon to be put down to "rising expectations" or "unresponsive government"?

I cannot say there is a connection, but I cannot accept without some persuasion the answer that the Negro is wholly a special case. Collective violence was once thought to be an inevitable aspect of the political life of any country, even this one. In 1947, in the second edition of his famous text on political parties, the late V. O. Key, Jr., devoted a full chapter to the political role of force. By 1958, when the fourth edition appeared, that chapter had been reduced to a page and a half. And by 1961, when his book on public opinion appeared, there was a chapter on "conflict" but no mention of violent conflict.

Traditionally, one would expect violence whenever there were deep and irreconcilable differences of opinion on fundamental issues in a society where one party had no confidence in the capacity of the other party to govern. (The distrust between the socialists and conservatives in prewar Austria was, of course, a classic case; a postwar government was possible only on the basis of a coalition that permitted one party to check the other in the ministries as well as in parliament—a form of "participatory democracy.") One would also expect violence when, though the nation is not deeply divided, established authority is unwilling to use force to make the costs of violence prohibitively great for any minority unwilling to resign itself to losing in a nonviolent struggle for power.

If the traditional understanding of violence were applied today, one would not expect it to subside once the "demands" of Negroes (or peace marchers, or whatever) were met. One reason is that the demands cannot be met—the competition for leadership among the (largely disorganized) dissident groups will inevitably generate ever more extreme demands faster than less extreme requests are fulfilled. Another reason is that violent political conflict is only rarely over tangible resources which the government can allocate—it is typically over symbolic values which government either does not control (the sense of equality, or human dignity, or social acceptance) or does control but cannot redistribute without destroying itself (sending the Irish back to Ireland, abandoning military force as a tool of foreign policy). But primarily violence will not subside because it is the cleavage in opinion which gives rise to it, and concessions sufficient to induce one side to abandon violence (subject to the constraints cited above) might be concessions sufficient to induce the other side to resort to violence.

To cut through the vicious circle, governments historically have increased the application of force to the point that neither side found it rewarding to practice violence, thus inducing both sides to wait for long-term trends to soften or alter the cleavages of opinion. Such increases in force have often required a reduction in the degree to which the use of force was subject to democratic constraints. Parliamentary regimes have been replaced by presidential regimes; presidential regimes have been replaced by dictatorial regimes. Only when it is clear that *neither* side can gain through violent protest does the resort to such forms of protest cease. The case for dealing with the conditions under which Negroes (or poor whites) live is not, therefore, to be made on the grounds that such efforts will "stop riots"; it can be made only on the grounds that for other, and essentially moral, reasons, changing those conditions is right and necessary.

Whether this analysis has any applicability to present-day America is difficult to say. One would first have to estimate the probability of white violence against Negroes (or hawk violence against doves) under various kinds of governmental concessions to Negroes (or doves), and no one is competent to make any confident predictions on these matters. What can be said is that long-term prosperity is no guarantee against political violence of some form. Prosperity cannot by itself eliminate the ideological sources of violence and indeed may weaken the institutional constraints on it such that the effects of the activities of even a few persons with violent intentions may be amplified by an increasingly larger multiplier and thus influence the actions of ever larger numbers of persons.

This consequence of prosperity may arise through the dispersal of power and authority that tends to result from the entry of more and more persons into middle-class status and thus into the forms of participation in public life that are reserved for the middle class. Middle-class persons participate in voluntary associations and public affairs more than working-class persons (and certainly more than lower-class persons, who scarcely participate at all). The higher the level of participation, the larger the number and variety of voluntary associations (and social movements) and the more wills which must be concerted in the making of public policy.[29] "Participatory democracy" may be a slogan currently linked with the aspirations of the underprivileged, but in fact participatory democracy has all along been the political style (if not the slogan) of the American middle and upper-middle class. It will become a more widespread style as more persons enter into these classes. Additionally, continued prosperity will increasingly free young people from the pinch of economic necessity (the need to get a job early in life), place more of them in colleges and universities where, for better or worse, traditional values are questioned, and increase the number (if not the proportion) of those who find various kinds of personal and political nonconformity attractive.

With participation in greater variety and numbers, the possibility of any one or few organizations dominating the expression of some common interest (civil rights, peace, governmental reform) will be lessened and the competition among such groups will increase. The sensitivity of more and more persons to the substance of issues will reduce the capacity of government to act without regard to these views, and the high (but quite selective) visibility given to governmental acts by television will reduce the capacity of government to act at all in ways (e.g., the use of force or a display of indifference) once employed more readily because less visibly.

In short, marches, protests, sit-ins, demonstrations, mass meetings, and other forms of direct collective action may become more rather than less common, though it is hard to predict what issues will prove sufficiently salient to generate such activities. How many will be violent no one can say, but it is not unreasonable to assume that if large numbers of people are brought together in public places because of issues about which they feel strongly, a certain though unknown proportion will—either because they seek violence ("confrontation politics") or because they feel provoked by the police or other opponents—take matters into their own hands. Since people are most likely to feel strongly about symbolic or intangible issues, and since governments can only deal slowly (if at all) with such matters, the probability of at least disorder and possibly violence is likely to increase over time. The civil rights march on Washington in 1963 was orderly and well-led; early peace marches were of the same character. Recent peace marches were less orderly, and it seems unlikely any new civil rights march will be immune from the same forces leading to disorganization, spontaneity, and violence.

But even this "prediction" must be hedged with qualifications. Other, as yet unforeseen, changes in sentiment and ideology may occur with the result that such tendencies toward collective assertion and violence may be redirected. Perhaps collective violence will undergo a transformation parallel to that affecting individual violence; just as murder gives way to suicide, child-beating to child "guidance," and rape to seduction and perversion with the middle-classifying of the poor, so also might political violence give way to civility and rhetoric. The most that can be said for the argument sketched in this section is that one should not assume that these changes in character are themselves sufficient to change the manner in which politics is carried on. Profound institutional and organizational changes are likely to occur also, and these, by making the system more sensitive—even vulnerable—to the diminishing amount of violent instincts among individuals, will produce a net increase in violent *behavior* with no net increase in violent *attitudes*. If that occurs, the existence or threat of lower-class violence, which dominated the politics of the nineteenth century, may be replaced by the threat of middle-class violence during the twenty-first.

References

1. Daniel Glaser, *et al.*, *The Violent Offender* (Washington, D.C., 1966), pp. 7–8.

2. Theodore N. Ferdinand, "The Criminal Patterns of Boston since 1849," *American Journal of Sociology*, LXXIII (July, 1967), pp. 88–89.

3. Sam Bass Warner, *Crime and Criminal Statistics in Boston* (Cambridge, 1934), pp. 20, 23, 142.

4. Marvin E. Wolfgang, *Patterns in Criminal Homicide* (Philadelphia, 1958), p. 116.

5. Marvin E. Wolfgang, *Crimes of Violence* (background paper submitted to the President's Commission on Law Enforcment and Administration of Justice, 1967), pp. 166–171 and references there cited.

6. We have no measure of the size, or changes over time in the size, of the "lower class" unless we define class by income, and this is a misleading definition if by class we refer—as we must when speaking of crime—to the subjective states of the persons.

7. Thomas F. Pettigrew, *A Profile of the Negro American* (Princeton, 1964), pp. 136–156; President's Commission on Law Enforcement and Administration of Justice, *Task Force Report: Crime and Its Impact—an Assessment* (Washington, D.C., 1907), p. 77.

8. *Task Force Report: Crime, op. cit.*, p. 31. Other studies show that the vast majority of homicides are intra-racial and thus the death rate by homicide for a racial group is very close to its murder rate. See Wolfgang, *Crimes of Violence*, pp. 62–66.

9. *Task Force Report: Crime*, p. 31.

10. Thomas F. Pettigrew and Rosalind B. Spier, "The Ecological Structure of Negro Homicide," *American Journal of Sociology*, LXVII (May, 1962), pp. 621–629.

11. *Task Force Report: Crime, op. cit.*, p. 17.

12. Ferdinand, *op. cit.*, p. 88.

13. Elwin H. Powell, "Crime as a Function of Anomie," *Journal of Criminal Law, Criminology, and Police Science*, LVII (June, 1966), pp. 161–171; Betty B. Rosenbaum, "The Relationship Between War and Crime in the United States," in *ibid.*, XXX (1939–1940), pp. 726–729.

14. Daniel P. Moynihan, "Poverty in Cities," in James Q. Wilson, ed., *The Metropolitan Enigma* (Washington, D.C., 1967), pp. 301–302.

15. Andrew F. Henry and James F. Short, Jr., *Suicide and Homicide* (Glencoe, 1954), p. 45.

16. *Ibid*, Chap. IV.

17. *Ibid.*, p. 49.

18. *Ibid*. The reader should adopt this interpretation, if at all, with the utmost caution. The problem with the frustration-aggression-murder hypothesis is that though frustration is common, murder is rare. We do not understand the causal mechanism nor can we explain why only a few persons give homicidal expression to their frustration. See Wolfgang, *Crimes of Violence*, pp. 89–95, and Walter C. Reckless, *The Crime Problem* (3rd ed.; New York, 1961), pp. 138–140, for criticisms which challenge but do not entirely dispose of the Henry-Short interpretation.

19. Ruth S. Cavan, *Suicide* (Chicago, 1928), pp. 77–105, and Calvin F. Schmid, "Suicides in Seattle, 1914–1925," *University of Washington Publications in the Social Sciences*, V (October, 1928); both cited in Henry and Short, *op. cit.*, p. 135.

20. Henry and Short, *op cit.*, p. 137.

21. U.S. Bureau of the Census, *Vital Statistics: Special Reports, 1940*, Vol. XV, No. 18, pp. 242–243, and U.S. Bureau of the Census, *Vital Statistics of the United States, 1963*, Vol. II, "Mortality," Part A, pp. 260–261.

22. *Task Force Report: Crime, op. cit.*, p. 39.

23. Walter B. Miller, "Violent Crimes in City Gangs," *Annals*, Vol. 364 (March, 1966), pp. 96–112.

24. Marvin E. Wolfgang and France Ferracuti, *Subculture of Violence* (London, forthcoming).

25. Philip Taft, "Violence in American Labor Disputes," *Annals, op. cit.*, pp. 127–140.

26. Arnold Forster, "Violence on the Fanatical Left and Right," *Annals, op. cit.*, p. 143.

27. Aristide and Vera Zolberg, "The Americanization of Frantz Fanon," *The Public Interest* (Fall, 1967), pp. 49–63.

28. Gary T. Marx, *Protest and Prejudice* (New York, 1967).

29. Cf. Edward C. Banfield and James Q. Wilson, *City Politics* (Cambridge, 1963), esp. concluding chapter.

JOHN R. PIERCE

Communication

ELECTRICAL COMMUNICATION has profoundly altered the world we live in and the way we live in it. Today's child accepts the telephone and television with the same sense of familiarity and lack of understanding that earlier generations accorded natural phenomena. We do not need to know the physical basis of telephony in order to use a telephone any more than we need to understand the biological intricacies of a horse in order to ride one. Familiarity and use are the same in each case. But the telephone is a product of man, and the telephone system, a huge and intricate assembly of complicated parts, is the outgrowth of research and understanding as we know them in science.

This sort of understanding is powerful but rare in our world. For example, although we talk and read and write everyday, we understand very little about language. In the past decade, attempts to use the computer to translate from one language to another have forcibly emphasized how little we do understand this universal intellectual tool. It soon became apparent in efforts at machine translation that an accurate grammar would be necessary, a grammar by means of which a computer could parse a sentence unambiguously (as we almost always can) and a grammar by means of which all grammatical and no ungrammatical utterances could be constructed. It became equally apparent that linguists could not supply even a reasonably satisfactory grammar for any language. The grammars we have are like tips for playing good golf. With their aid, and with the aid of our hidden and unformulated skills of speech, we can construct grammatical (and meaningful) sentences and interpret and parse such sentences. But because we do not consciously understand how we do this, we cannot tell a computer how to do it.

Language is central to our life and thought. Yet in the sense that we use *understanding* in science, we do not understand language.

297

We know how to speak, but we do not know how we speak. We learn to use language through apprenticeship. We may be provided with some rules that can help us in a practical way to speak or write uniformly and intelligibly. But the foreigner who is full of rules does not speak or write our tongue as "correctly" as a well-apprenticed native without a rule in his head.

This has always been the pattern for most human life. Somehow, through the examples and precepts of others, we learn to live—to act, to interact, to choose, and to decide. As members of a society, we formulate and accept rules and precepts that help to guide us through life. But we are successful in acting as we are successful in digesting our food—not because we understand the process, but because we are able to carry it out.

There is an increasing side to our life that is quite different. Everyone uses language, but no one understands how we use it. In contrast, everyone uses television sets and telephones, and a few people do understand them completely. This is partly because a radio or telephone is very much simpler than a language or a human being. Chiefly, however, we understand a radio or a telephone because it has been created according to our understanding. Through our understanding of science, we see how we can make a useful device. We do this in a way that is understandable to us. It is no wonder, then, that the operation of the final product is understandable.

Science and technology inject into our environment an increasing part that is inherently understandable and controllable because man put it there through his understanding. We do not need to be told that this understandable, controllable element of our environment has a profound effect on all of our life; we see this whenever we drive a car, or fly in a plane, or make a telephone call, or watch television.

To all of these things we adapt, behaviorally and linguistically, in the old mysterious way in which man has always managed to live. We acquire new needs and new standards. A society that functioned well in the absence of telephones, automobiles, and electric power is replaced by a society that would collapse without these present necessities.

Communication is a particularly apt field in which to discuss and illustrate the impact, actual and potential, of the understanding of science and the power of technology on society. Electrical communication has changed our lives profoundly within the span of our memories.

Further, electrical communication clearly exemplifies the applicability and power of science. Few industries have a deeper or broader technological base. Within my lifetime communication has been profoundly changed by advances in electron tubes, by a rapidly changing solid-state art that has displaced these, by the invention and control of polymers that have replaced wood, paper, rubber, and even metals, and by a mathematical and logical insight into ways of organizing digital systems—such as computers and telephone switching systems.

Finally, electrical communication illustrates as no other field can the range from the comparatively simple, exemplified by the local broadcasting station and the home receiver, to the incredibly complicated and interdependent, exemplified in common-carrier communication systems.

This division between the technologically simple and the technologically complex reflects a difference in the purpose and function of mass communication, such as television, and personal communication, such as telephony. Mass communication is necessarily aimed at majorities or large minorities. It is one-way; it is aimed from the few to the many. It is a unifying and conservative element in our society. As such, its effects have been tremendous.

We are rapidly approaching a society without "sticks" or "boondocks," except those that are growing in the central slums of metropolitan areas. Television brings launchings from Cape Kennedy, sports from all parts of the continent, even (via satellite) live events from across the ocean, and a nationally uniform brand of music, comedy, and soap opera into the most remote house. The center of our society is no longer a physical region; it is a medium of communication that pours forth in every house.

In the face of television, it is difficult for differences of dialect, of interest, or of attitude to persist.

This makes television the greatest unifying force ever to act upon man. A voice and a picture on television may not yet be able to tell us what to think about a matter, but they very effectively decide what we will be thinking about, and that may be as remote physically as the war in Viet-Nam. Here on the other side of the globe we are made conscious of political implications that escape most of the Vietnamese themselves, who know government only through death and taxes.

Television is a direct and powerful tool in the hands of the central government. The President and members of his Administration can appeal directly to the people, without distortion or deletion of what they want to say. And what they say directly to the people, the newspapers must handle somehow.

This is powerful in a society that is already unified, but its impact and power could be far greater in an emerging nation that must achieve some sort of national unity and effective government for its well-being and indeed its survival.

The impact of the telephone and other common-carrier communication is quite different from that of mass communication. The telephone is inherently the tool of the individual, not of the majority or the society. It is the means by which we conduct the business of life—ordering groceries, calling the doctor, making appointments and reservations. It is our social tool for keeping in touch with friends and relatives, arranging dates, dinners, parties, and trips. And it is our intellectual tool for calling informed acquaintances to find out what is really behind public statements, and even for arranging protest marches and demonstrations.

Unlike mass communication, which could have a profound impact on even a primitive society, the telephone is an inherent part of a way of life that has been shaped by automobiles, airplanes, electric power, standardized, uniform merchandise, and a pattern of credit. We use the telephone because we have interests that lie beyond the home, the family, and the neighborhood; because we are willing in many cases to buy, without shopping, on the basis of past experience and information provided by advertisements that reach us by mail or through newspapers.

It seems to me that except for some government and business usage, a telephone system would have little value in a primitive society. Its widespread use is a reflection of our way of life, a way of life that it has helped to bring into being.

So far, I have cited communication as an example of the impact of science and technology—of intellectual understanding, if you will —on society, and I have indicated how important this can be in the utterly different fields of mass communication and individual communication. I have not, however, indicated how the revolutionary powers of communication came into being; their source is discovery and invention. While this is a plausible and simple statement, it is an important one. Today we hear much about meeting the needs of society, and about planning and systems analysis and systems engineering as means for meeting those needs.

Planning and systems analysis and systems engineering are vital parts of technology, and are essential in making good and effective use of what we have at hand. They may even be effective in pointing out lacks that stand in the way of accomplishing what we want to do. Discovery and invention may—or may not—then remedy such recognized difficiencies. But discovery and invention often take us off on some entirely different tack.

I am sure that when Alexander Graham Bell invented the telephone, what common-carrier communication felt it *really* needed was better multiplex telegraphy, and perhaps practical automatic telegraphy. What the world got through this invention was a revolutionary system of communication that has swamped the telegram and, indeed, the letter as the means of interpersonal communication. We do what we can, not what we think we should or what we want to do, and needs are as often created as satisfied by discovery and invention. De Forest was seeking a detector for wireless telegraphy when he invented the vacuum tube. The invention led to worldwide telephony and to radio broadcasting. Television languished as an interesting idea for years until science and technology gave us an advanced electronic art, and Zworykin invented the iconoscope.

Babbage tried to make a sophisticated computer in the nineteenth century and failed. The computer was reinvented and easily realized, using the art supplied by telephone switching, by Aiken and Stibitz around 1940. The vacuum tube made it possible for Eckert and Mauchly to make a fast electronic calculator. Von Neumann provided the stored program. And the transistor made the computer economical, reliable, and profitable.

Discovery and invention have been the crucial elements in inaugurating and changing the course of communication. Systems engineering and systems development have been necessary in effectively exploiting discovery and invention, in realizing their full impact. But in most cases the discoverers and inventors have convincingly demonstrated the power and potentialities of what they have done before it seriously engaged the attention of systems engineers.

If discovery and invention have been so vital in the revolutionary effect that communication has already had on our lives, what may they do to and for us in the future? Here I shall consider only discoveries and inventions that have been made but not yet applied, or applied fully.

We may expect the effective extension of mass communication into countries with less advanced communication technology. The transistor radio has already provided a direct link between otherwise isolated peoples and their central governments. Even the Bedouin on his camel can hear that he is part of a nation and learn of its problems and aspirations.

We have all experienced the much stronger impact of television. In the United States network programs are transmitted between cities by common-carrier facilities provided by the telephone companies, and broadcast from a large number of high-power television transmitters. Many important and populous countries have neither the common-carrier networks to span the country nor the television transmitters to reach the viewer. Moreover, a television receiver is expensive and complicated compared with a transistor radio. But communication satellites may eventually make television available even in underdeveloped countries. At present it is impractical to broadcast directly from a satellite to a standard television receiver —the power required is too large. Such broadcasting will probably remain impractical for a considerable period.

It is practical, however, to launch a satellite that will send out a signal with a few hundred watts' power; in fact, the Soviet Union has done this. A ground station costing only a few thousand dollars could receive television signals from such a satellite. The received signals could be carried for short distances by cable or distributed in local areas by means of cheap, low-power transmitters.

Thus, by means of an entirely feasible communication satellite, television could be transmitted from the capital of a nation to many towns and villages where it could be viewed in schools or other public buildings. The cost of such a satellite television-distribution system would be considerable, but the impact could be tremendous.

Consider Nigeria, a nation of over fifty million people, which has established English as the language of its schools. Nationwide television could be of tremendous value there as a motivation for learning English, as a way of establishing and maintaining a standard English, and as a means for making nationhood meaningful and desirable to the population. Television of this sort would be almost as valuable in far more advanced nations, such as India and China.

Space technology has advanced to a point where satellites may be very economical for domestic communication. As we already have adequate domestic network facilities, satellites could not make television different for us, only cheaper to distribute. Indeed, the popular revolution in television distribution now under way is in quite the opposite direction—that is, in favor of wired distribution provided by CATV (community antenna television) services, rather than distribution by radio. CATV was initially established to supply television to remote or shadowed areas where the direct signal is inadequate. Signals from a hilltop antenna were amplified and distributed by cables, which themselves have amplifiers at regular intervals. It was found that subscribers were anxious to pay a few dollars a month for an adequate TV signal. And this has proved true even in cities where a fair (but inferior) signal can be obtained from a rooftop antenna.

But CATV has another potentiality as well. Through importation of signals from a distance, it can provide a community, large or small, with as many channels as are available to the residents of Los Angeles or New York. Here, indeed, is the ultimate in the abolition of the "sticks" and "boondocks."

CATV is a great advance, the wave of the future in comparison with anything else on the television horizon. It will be interesting to see whether CATV will continue to thrive. If it does, it may help to bring about another long-time dream—the delivery of newspapers to homes by wire. At least two problems must be overcome if this is to succeed. The smaller of these problems is economical broadband transmission; an extra channel on a CATV network could provide this. The other problem is that of the bulk of a newspaper. People *want* big papers, papers with lots of advertisements. But they do not want these to spew out onto the living-room floor, unfolded. They do not want to have rolls of newsprint delivered and stored away in their houses.

Although the production of a paper newspaper in the home seems to be clearly impractical, a microfilm newspaper might be acceptable. Its success would depend on an economical, convenient, high-resolution viewing device, and on some practical way of recording images with microfilm resolution. Conventional photography and even the Land Camera process seem inadequate. Perhaps science will provide an answer. If it does, the impact could be tremendous. Experience shows that people want local news and local advertisements in newspapers, as well as national news and national advertisements. In a newspaper distributed by wire, some news and advertisements could be tailored to specific neighborhoods if that proved profitable. Indeed, to some degree, mass communications might be nearly individualized in this process. Television could remain the truly national unifying force that it is.

In individual communication I foresee a revolution based on various specific advances that will make both transmission and the station equipment at the ends of transmission circuits less expensive. The cost of transmission goes down as we send more signals over a given path, which we accomplish by providing transmission paths of greater bandwidth. We have now advanced far beyond the era in which one pair of wires carried one voice signal. A digital transmission system called T1 can send twenty-four two-way telephone channels or 1.5 million data bits per second over two pairs of wires in cables. The L4 system sends thirty-six hundred telephone conversations one way over a single "pipe" in a coaxial cable, and there are twenty such pipes in the cable. A microwave transmission route can accommodate as many as twelve thousand telephone channels.

Using the telephone channels as a measure of transmission capability, we can say that a commercial TV signal uses about one thousand times as much bandwidth as a telephone signal, and a PICTUREPHONE (service mark of A.T. & T. Co.) signal about one hundred times as much as a telephone signal. Facsimile signals and data signals fall somewhere between the telephone and the television bandwidth, though some data signals (teletypewriter) require only about a tenth of the telephone bandwidth.

What have science and technology provided that will enable us to send large bundles of channels economically? First, the extension of the operation of solid-state devices into the microwave range has made it possible to build microwave repeaters of extremely high reliability and extremely low power consumption. Thus, it is possible to build small, cheap, trouble-free repeaters and to power them economically. Perhaps this will lead to a new use of microwave repeaters, spaced at frequent intervals along roads rather than on remote hilltops. This would make possible the profitable exploitation of microwave bands (at 17 and 30 Gigahertz) at which transmission over conventional distances is seriously impaired by rain.

The same advances in electronics, together with boosters for the power of the Titan III, have made it immediately practical to launch communication satellites that could supply as many as one hundred thousand telephone circuits between, say, five or ten principal cities in the United States. Such a satellite system could be established in a few years, substantially increasing the number of long-distance circuits available in the country. Further, in concert with terrestrial facilities, the satellite could incorporate switching equipment that would transfer blocks of circuits from one pair of cities to another in meeting fluctuations of demand.

Work on transmission of millimeter waves through waveguides has made it technically possible to send two hundred thousand one-way television signals or one hundred thousand two-way telephone channels through a single tube two inches in diameter. The signal must be amplified and regenerated at intervals of about fifteen miles. Advances in the solid-state art have made it possible to do this entirely by means of solid-state devices of low power consumption. Such a waveguide system would be economical if there were sufficient traffic to justify it.

In the future, it will also become technologically possible to provide circuits of almost unlimited bandwidth by means of the coherent light generated by lasers. We already have suitable lasers; in lenses consisting of gas flowing through alternately hot and cold regions, a means for guiding light through buried pipes; modulators for impressing signals on the light; and detectors for translating the received light signals into electrical current. We are not, however, presently in a position to build a useful laser communication system. The performance of some of the components is not so good as we might desire; the modulators have inadequate bandwidth; and adequate detectors are not available for the longer of the wavelengths at which lasers operate. There is also a problem of accuracy of alignment of the system of guiding lenses, and of automatic correction of misalignment. But, too, there is lack of experience.

We could have new types of microwave systems, satellite systems with a capacity of over one hundred thousand telephone circuits, and millimeter waveguide systems at any time merely by deciding to go ahead and spend the money. In the case of optical transmission, we need more research and more experience.

Integrated circuits, or microelectronics, will make it possible to produce a complicated circuit almost as cheaply as a transistor. Circuit configurations are impressed, hundreds at a time, on the surface of a wafer of silicon; aside from this process, the steps in production are essentially those required in making single devices. Thus, it will be possible to put at a low cost very complicated yet highly reliable electronic equipment almost anywhere—a telephone set, a car, or even a pocket.

I have described briefly the technological advances that I see as shaping the future—cheaper broadband transmission, and a potentiality to provide complicated, cheap, and reliable terminal equipment through microelectronics—but I have not said what we will do with these tools, because I do not fully know how they will be used. I do feel, however, that their impact can be described as a general broadening of and an increase in our use of electrical communications.

Initially, in primitive electrical communication, we dealt with two apparently distinct inventions: the telegraph and the telephone. As we look back at the early telephone and the early telegraph, we see that they were as specialized as they were simply because of the limitations of the electrical art of that day. But the telephone and the telegraph were not entirely separate even then. Alexander Graham Bell discovered the telephone while working toward a harmonic telegraph, in which different distinct signals would be conveyed over the same pair of wires by electrical tones of different frequencies or pitches. Still, for a long time there seemed to be some sort of intellectual or electrical distinction between the sorts of signals that one used for telegraphy and telephony.

If we look at the nervous system of man, we find no such distinction. The nerve impulses involved in the senses of touch, sight, hearing, smell, and taste are all the same distinct spikelike electrical signals. They do not differ in quality. There is a uniform medium through which all our senses serve us.

The difference among the senses lies in the pickup organs, which are responsive to light or sound or touch, and in the interpretation we make of the signals we receive in our central nervous system. The human body uses this common communication system not only for its senses but in all its muscular activity as well. We simply are not built with separate and different communication networks for separate kinds of communication.

As the technologies of the telephone and the telegraph advanced, the distinction between them became vague. Telegraph signals were multiplexed, or transmitted many at a time, over telephone lines in much the way that Alexander Graham Bell had envisioned in his work on the harmonic telegraph. Finally, it became clear that telephone signals could be transmitted by off-on impulses, by a method which we call PCM or pulse code modulation. PCM is now coming into increasing use in the telephone system. Only since 1948, however, when Claude Shannon derived his mathematical theory of communication—has there been a broad, coherent, and useful theory of the process of communication that includes the telephone, the telegraph, and all other means of communication.

Through Shannon's work, our intellectual conception of communication has finally caught up to what has always existed in the nervous system—a common sort of communication for all modalities of sense. Our conception of communication has also come to fit what has increasingly existed in electrical communication systems—circuits that can be used interchangeably for telegraph, voice, or picture signals. We are now achieving, both conceptually and practically, something approaching the universality in electrical communication that was built into the communicating senses of man even before he had learned to talk and to write. As we know from our experience, man uses all forms of communication simultaneously, and in a supplementary rather than a divided manner. This is reflected in his nervous system and in the results of experiments that psychologists have made concerning the interaction of the various modalities of human communication.

The modern communication network transmits indifferently the signals we associate with the primitive telegraph, those we associate with the primitive telephone, and a great many other more complicated signals that have come into being through automatic switching, through facsimile and telephotograph transmission, through television transmission, through writing at a distance by means of telewritors, through high-fidelity and stereophonic speech and music.

In the future we can expect many new signals and many new uses of communication. Whatever these may be, we can be sure of two things. Modern electrical communication networks will be adaptable to the transmission of all of these forms of communication. Shannon's general theory of communication will be a common measure and tool for studying and relating all these forms of communication.

What will these new forms of communication be? I have already mentioned the possibility of greatly improved mobile telephony—car telephones and even pocket telephones. Microelectronics promises to provide complicated but economical equipment for such purposes. Of course, such service could only be realized if adequate frequencies were assigned for such use.

But future communications will embrace much more than voice. The Bell System is engaged in a determined effort to introduce person-to-person television or PICTUREPHONE service on a large scale, to see if there is a real public demand for it. Facsimile may have an increasing use for business and library purposes. Even tele-writing may find its place in connection with conferences and lectures convened through electrical communication rather than physical travel. Certainly, in conferences as in a two-party communication, we will want to make data available and to send letters and reports by means of data transmission. Indeed, I believe that within a few years virtually all business records and correspondence will be put into machine-readable form when first typed. If this is done, it will be possible to send text from office to office with the speed and ease of making a telephone call.

Furthermore, computers can index and search machine-readable material; they can be used in editing and correcting texts without complete retyping; they can even be used to a degree in proofreading. From a corrected machine-readable copy, computers can automatically produce printed material, correctly paginated and with justified lines. They can also construct charts, graphs, and line drawings, and insert them at specified points in the text. Thus, computers will take care of a great deal of office drudgery. And, by means of electrical communication, offices will be linked to other offices, to files, to reproduction facilities, and to other resources.

This linkage will extend through other business activities as well. The TOUCH-TONE® telephone set generates signals that, unlike dial pulses, can travel over any voice circuit, to any distant place. The TOUCH-TONE keyboard can, therefore, be used to query computers or to control machinery wherever the telephone can reach. This is already in limited use in banking and merchandising.

The computer can reply to queries in spoken words. At present, these words are recorded words, and voice recording is an inefficient means of information storage, alien to the digital computer. But there are good prospects that computers will be able to read aloud intelligibly from phonetically spelled data stored in their memories.

In the future, we may be able to query, from a distance, any number of information sources about weather, hotels, stores, sports, theaters, or other matters, and receive specific voice replies. We may even make such queries in simple English via a keyboard. As the computer will be able to respond to only simple, unambiguous questions, it will sometimes misunderstand or fail to understand. If it replies amiss or says that it did not understand the query, we will be able to try again, perhaps in words suggested by the computer.

308

Thus, the messages we receive from computers may be printed data, spoken words, diagrams, or drawings. While we may receive these by television or facsimile, we will in some cases have small local computers that can make drawings from concise and easily transmitted instructions received from afar. This will greatly reduce the cost of "transmitting" complicated pictorial material.

I have tried to sketch a few sorts of communication of the future; I am sure that I have missed many more. They are, however, all a part of one general trend—the *generalization* of communication, in the sense that human nerves have a generalized transmission function that is utilized in all our senses and powers.

Science and technology will increase the capacity of our common-carrier communication networks to provide all sorts of communication over the same channels. Microelectronics and other advances will provide terminal equipment or transducers that will link this network to all our senses and to a growing variety of uses.

What this will do to our life I can only guess. It will certainly provide an environment as different from the present as the pretelephone world. Hopefully in the future we will be able to live where we like, travel chiefly for pleasure, and communicate to work; perhaps this is too optimistic. The certainty is that science provides an understanding that is alien to everyday life. We understand little in this way, but what little understanding we have is extremely powerful. Through research and development, this understanding has so altered our environment that we live lives that are essentially different from those of earlier generations. Science and technology are now creating, through advances in communications as well as many other fields, an entirely new environment in which life will again be different. As always, man will adapt to this world by apprenticeship, by the same sort of learning without understanding that enables him to speak and to walk. The man who successfully lives in the world of the future need not understand that world in the sense of scientific understanding, but it is the understanding of science that is bringing that world into being.

This paper was delivered on October 26, 1966, at a Conference on Scientific Progress and Human Values held at the California Institute of Technology as part of the celebration of its seventy-fifth anniversary. Full proceedings of the Conference will be published in book form by the American Elsevier Publishing Co. this fall.

EUGENE V. ROSTOW

Thinking About the Future of International Society

THE SYSTEM of international order instituted at Vienna in 1815 functioned remarkably well until 1914—better probably than any system for the governance of international politics since the heyday of the Roman Empire; between 1914 and 1945 its successor system functioned badly, despite a few successes. In order to project, conjecture, or imagine the future, we should first sketch the unstable processes for the control of international politics that have been evolving since 1945, and identify their dynamic elements and the main paths to the future now visible.

Two facts of paramount importance dominate the international scene and define the principal differences between our world and that organized by the Congress of Vienna: the disappearance of all the empires, save only the Russian, and with it the transformation of a third of the world into a gigantic Balkan problem; and the rise of the Communist movement, through a series of *coups d'état* in circumstances of chaos in countries whose governments had disintegrated or were easily overthrown under the impact of defeat in 1917 and 1945-49.

The End of Empire

Except for a few enclaves like Tibet and Ethiopia, the whole world had been drawn into a single magnetic field by the end of the nineteenth century. It was a system of political order, if not one which fulfilled all our post-1776 and post-1789 ideals of justice. Under this regime, the world economy functioned as a unified entity. Capital, labor, and the essential skills (technology, education,

---

This paper was written in December, 1965, before Mr. Rostow was appointed Under Secretary of State for Political Affairs.

finance, and commerce) flowed to every part of the world with un-exampled freedom. The non-European cultures and civilizations be-gan to go through intricate processes of response to the many stim-uli of European civilization, the most powerful force to which they had been exposed for many centuries. The results were in all cases dynamic (in some, explosive) and as diverse as those of Japan, India, China, and the various parts of Africa.

The political and military efforts to achieve freedom from em-pire provided the basis of organized political action in all the former colonies, and often of military power as well. The struggle for freedom usually required the formation and development of one or more political parties that represented enthusiasm and idealism in the spirit of the people. Unfortunately, the struggle also nour-ished myths and illusions about economics, and a nationalism that often approached xenophobia. Both have been heavy burdens in the policies of the new nations.

The Rise, Spread, and Change of the Communist Movement

Despite the most savage efforts of orthodoxy, the Communist movement has not remained static since the seizure of power in Russia in 1917. NEP, socialism in one country, collectivization, Stalin's destruction of the first generation of his fellow Boyars, the purge trials of the thirties, and the failure of the Popular Front strategy—these and other stages in the evolution of the movement have now been matched by the conquest of power in China; the rivalry of the Russian and Chinese parties and nations; the decline of Russian authority in Eastern Europe as a consequence of the success of Western containment policy; and the phenomenon of Castroism, and other Communist and neo-Communist efforts in the Third World. Obviously, the liquidation of empire has offered the directors of the Communist movement their greatest opportunity for conquest since 1917 or 1945, and this opportunity has not been ne-glected.

Western public opinion began to appreciate the nature of the Communist threat to the balance of power shortly after the end of the war. The refusal to carry out the Yalta and Potsdam agreements for free elections in Eastern Europe was one alarm bell, the seizure of Czechoslovakia another, the Berlin blockade a third. When Brit-ain approached the United States about the position in Greece and turned over to us the baton of the empire, the postwar period of primary American responsibility may fairly be said to have begun.

Britain and France were in no position at that point to take the lead in peace-keeping. Their political energies were primarily absorbed in the stormy final stages of decolonization, and their economies and sense of self-confidence had been weakened by the war.

The United States took on the task of being the free world's chief policeman reluctantly, but with conviction. Our attitude to the task was colored by a strong sense that we had betrayed President Wilson and the League in 1919, and that a large part of the world's subsequent misery was, therefore, to a considerable extent our fault. On the other hand, as the children of 1776, we strongly supported all movements for freedom within colonial empires and invariably opted for decolonization against security, even though that choice meant opposing the positions taken by Britain, France, Belgium, or the Netherlands. The same sense of identification with a revolutionary tradition has complicated our reaction to military efforts that call themselves "revolutionary" in China, in Cuba, and now in Viet-Nam. It was difficult for us, and is difficult still, to view the world in terms of the idea of the balance of power, especially when considerations of security require us to support undemocratic regimes.

The United States has now occupied the role of chief policeman for the free world for about twenty years. The office has required diplomatic and military exertions of us in a long series of conflicts—from Iran, Lebanon, Turkey, and Greece to Berlin, Korea, Cuba, and Viet-Nam. A basic rule for the conduct of the Cold War seems to have been established tacitly with the Soviet Union, though not yet with China: that there should be no unilateral changes in the frontier of the two powers' spheres of influence, and no changes accomplished by force.

The present posture is manifestly unstable. The United States is becoming politically restless under the burden of peace-keeping, especially where the military efforts required to assure stability must be carried out unilaterally and not in the name of the United Nations, NATO, or some other agency whose vote can be described as an invocation of "collective security." The European nations and Japan, fully recovered from the war, are torn between their desire to participate in the process of world politics and the attractions of irresponsibility. They are protected by the deterrent force of American military power; they are free to criticize United States diplomacy; and they are not required to devote great fractions of their national income to military expenditure. The Third World is gradually and reluctantly accepting several facts: (1) that the long and slow path to economic growth requires a great deal of work and can be organized effectively only by large numbers of entrepreneurs, private or public as the case may be, who are in extremely short supply; (2) that the economic and social revolution of the West in the postwar period has outstripped that of the Communist countries in every aspect, despite deeply established convictions to the contrary; (3) that the Communist movement is by no means necessarily the Wave of the Future, politically or otherwise. It has been contained in Europe, where it is dissolving into a series of un-co-ordinated fragments. Within a visible period, many of the people who supported Communist parties in France and Italy will be reintegrated into their national political communities. It is not fantastic to imagine the Eastern European countries, and even Russia, becoming part of Europe again. The containment of Communism in Asia is not yet so obvious, but it is difficult to imagine China waging a great war of expansion, with or without nuclear weapons, while it depends on the West for food. It is equally difficult to see why the next generation of Chinese leaders should pursue the grandiose schemes that arise naturally in the minds of the men who led the long campaign for the conquest of China.

The perspectives toward the future implicit in this conjuncture of flows of influence can be divided into three classes, under the head of three distinct premises about American policy:

(1) Effective, forceful, and conciliatory American policy organizes through the United Nations and otherwise a strong coalition of the industrialized free nations, including Japan and India, to stabilize world politics and conduct policies of *détente* and peaceful coexistence with China and the Soviet Union. On this footing, the free industrialized nations would have the primary burden of protecting the so-called Third World and of supplying it with the capital, entrepreneurship, education, and skills needed to assure its economic development. If a policy of this kind were pursued by the United States, one could anticipate the avoidance of general war and transformations of the main Communist societies under the disintegrating influence of nationalism and the Western example. Confronting so solid a combination, they would have little alternative, separately or in combination, to a policy of co-operation.

(2) A tacit or not-so-tacit understanding between the United States and the Soviet Union seeks stability and peace by efforts to

maintain nuclear bipolarity and dual hegemony of the kind made manifest at Suez and again recently during the war between India and Pakistan. This policy on the part of the United States, not necessarily an alternative to the first premise, is in fact a corollary or supplement to it—or, more accurately, a consequence of its influence. Coupled with the first premise, it could lead to a most dangerous division of the world by color (unless India and Japan are firmly included in the American coalition), if the United States and the Soviet Union adopt joint or at least parallel policies or programs designed to contain and control China.

(3) Weak and flaccid American policy leads to an American withdrawal from the mainland of Asia; Japan then reaches accommodation with China and becomes the energizing force of a program that would make China and Japan together the masters of Asia, and a new world power of a most formidable kind. However the system of world politics is organized, a vast industrial complex based on a pooling of Chinese and Japanese skills, resources, and energies is probable during the next generation. In large part, the risk of general war turns on the safeguards and political conditions under which this process takes place. If China is modernized as part of a moderated, open world community, and if the United States, the Soviet Union, and the European nations share in the effort, its political impact should be cohesive, not divisive.

SAMUEL P. HUNTINGTON

Political Development and the Decline of the American System of World Order

BY THE year 2000 it should be clear retrospectively that the dominant feature of international politics during the thirty years after World War II was neither the East-West confrontation between the U. S. and the Sino-Soviet bloc nor the North-South conflict between the developed and underdeveloped countries. Instead, the crucial relationship was that between the United States and Western Europe, and the dominant feature of international politics during this period was the expansion of the power of the United States. A crucial feature of this expansion was the extension of American power into the vacuums that were left after the decline of the European influence in Asia, Africa, and even Latin America. Where possible, of course, the Soviet Union and, later, China tried to move into these vacuums (for example, the Soviet Union into the Middle East between 1945 and 1948; China into Southeast Asia, during the 1960's). But almost without exception, the U. S. rather than the Communist powers played the dominant role in replacing European influence.

The decline of Europe and the expansion of American influence (political, economic, and military) went hand-in-hand. The relation between these changes attracted relatively little attention because the European powers declined gracefully, and there was a minimum of overt conflict between the U. S. and Europe. The shift in U. S.-European power relations was legitimated by the common need to prevent Soviet or Chinese influence from replacing European influence. Americans devoted much attention to the expansion of Communism (which, in fact, expanded very little after 1949), and in the process they tended to ignore the expansion of the United States influence and presence throughout much of the world

315

in terms of aid, investment, bases, trade patterns, deployment, and commitments.

Future historians will, I think, view the Soviet Union, China, and the United States as expansionist powers during this period, but they will view the U. S. as a highly successful expansionist power and the other two as frustrated expansionist powers.

This is preliminary to hypothesizing that in the year 2000 the American world system that has been developed during the last twenty years will be in a state of disintegration and decay. Just as American influence has replaced European influence during the current period, so also during the last quarter of this century American power will begin to wane, and other countries will move in to fill the gap. Among those that will play a prominent role in this respect will be China on mainland Asia, Indonesia in Southeast Asia, Brazil in Latin America, and I do not know what in the Middle East and Africa. Unlike the end of European empire (which was relatively peaceful), the decline of American influence will involve numerous struggles because the relationship between the rising powers and the U. S. will be much less close (in terms of values and culture) than was the relation between the U. S. and the European powers; and because there will be fewer common interests against a third power than existed when the U. S. and Europe stood against the Soviet Union. The struggles accompanying the disintegration of the American world order will have profoundly stimulating effects on political development in the participating states. These struggles are, indeed, likely to play a major role in generating national cohesion and institutional development. At the same time, the decline of American influence will tend to undermine and disrupt American politics. The American political system could be less likely than that of the Fourth Republic to adjust successfully to the loss of empire.

Domestically, the countries of Asia, Africa, and Latin America will also be in the throes of attempting to find an urban basis for political stability. Today stable government in these countries depends upon the support of the countryside. A three-way struggle takes place among the peasants (who have the votes), the army (which has the guns), and the urban middle class (which has the brains). For a short term, a government can maintain itself with the support of any two of these groups. For the longer term, however, the peasantry must be one of the groups in the pro-government coalition. With rare exceptions (for example, Turkey in the 1920's), the city and the urban middle-class intellectuals are always against the government. Hence, the support of the peasantry is a *sine qua non* for stability. But as the modernizing countries become more urban, no government will be able to maintain itself without the support of the urban middle class. Substantial elements of this middle class, however, will be trapped in a permanent oppositional mentality resulting from their early experiences in the modernizing process. The problem will be to win the support of such classes for the government, and a nationalist appeal would seem to be the most likely means of accomplishing this.

Domestic political development and political viability for the countries of Asia, Africa, and Latin America, in short, will rise from the ashes of the American sponsored system of world security.

ITHIEL DE SOLA POOL

The International System in the Next Half Century

SINCE THE day when the earliest oracle prophesied darkly, every gypsy fortuneteller and every pundit in the press has known a few elementary devices for avoiding disconfirmation. One can, for instance, predict without hours or date. "It is going to rain" is a prophecy that will eventually be confirmed. One can predict in ambiguous terms, or predict that which one knows to be planned already or under way; this way one may pass for wise.

In the arena of public affairs such vagueness has its uses. He who would influence people or events need not expose his inexorable fallibility to public ridicule. Those of us whose profession is the search for understanding, however, must learn to live with self-exposure. Just as understanding is gained by unrelenting exposure of one's unconscious, so also can understanding be aided by exposure of one's conscious assumptions.

That conviction shapes the form of this essay. We seek to anticipate the character of the international system of the year 2000. It is projected with as much specificity as a historian will use in the year 2000, writing retrospectively.

The predictions are not stated in arrogant confidence, for the results are certain to be proved wrong. The only thing of which one can be confident is that reality will depart radically from these predictions. Such predictions may be taken to be the modal items on subjective probability distributions. If forced to bet between each prediction and alternatives to it of comparable detail, the predictions chosen are those on which the author would prefer to bet. This is not to say that the predictions made are probable. It is highly unlikely, for example, that Okinawa will be part of the fifty-second state of the U.S.A. But if forced to predict whether there will or will not be a fifty-second state by the year 2000, I would bet on the side of there being one. If we further assume that there will be a fifty-second state after Puerto Rico becomes the fifty-first and are asked to bet on any one piece of real estate being

318

part of it, the Pacific string of islands would be my guess as the single most likely option. This is the way I played the game.

That game was played in 1965. Today, over a year later, the predictions then made are already partly disconfirmed; they stand as stated to be measured against the cold test of reality. China, for example, is moving much faster than I would have believed possible two years ago. At the moment of this writing, still in Mao's lifetime, the beginnings of guerrilla warfare are visible. Perhaps we shall not have to wait for 1985 to see a struggle out of which a more moderate though allegedly Communist regime will emerge or the break-off of certain border areas by the Soviet Union.

The events in the passing year clearly make what was written in 1965 seem a bit antique. And insofar as any one prediction is awry, other predictions will become so too. The world is a tightly linked system. The choice to write a history in reverse was, in part, an expression of a sense of incapacity to conceive in any other way of what 2000 will be like.

What life will be like in 2000 is a function of what life will be like in 1990, and that in turn of 1980, and so on back. The path of history is a branching road with many forks. The picture we have of 1970 shapes our picture of 2000, and the errors we make in anticipating 1970 spread their effects to our predictions of 2000. Only by imagining the steps along the road can we effectively imagine where the road will lead us.

Let us, therefore, state as clearly as we can an hypothesis about the course of world events from 1965 to the early-twenty-first century. Such a statement is a precondition to fruitful debate among prophets and provides a template against which historians can measure where their assumptions have turned out to be wrong.

The Prediction

There will be no nuclear war within the next fifty years.

1965-1970

In the period 1965-1970, Mao Tse-tung and De Gaulle will die. Within two years after De Gaulle's death, presidential power in France, while not abolished, will largely have atrophied, giving way to a wide coalition government strongly committed to European economic co-operation and integration, but just as nonco-operative with NATO as De Gaulle was. The nonco-operation will be on economic and pacifist grounds, rather than on nationalistic ones.

Major fighting in Viet-Nam will peter out about 1967; and most objective observers will regard it as a substantial American victory. Sporadic terrorism will, however, remain endemic not only in Viet-Nam, but throughout former Indochina and Thailand as the Communists try to prove that this is only a defeat in a particular battle within a widening combat. The result of continuing instability will be economic distress in the area. There may be several reversals of government so that, for example, by 1970 a pro-American military dictatorship might exist in Cambodia, while a reformist coalition might have overthrown the regime in Thailand. These are not specific predictions. The prediction is that there will be a pattern of varied, nationalist, religious, reformist, and military regimes in the area changing fairly continuously.

In the United States Lyndon Johnson will have been re-elected in 1968. The rate of economic growth will have not only continued, but accelerated, creating a chronic problem of inflationary pressure and labor shortage. Substantial immigration will be taking place, though not by 1920's standards. Just beginning by 1970, it will not be recognized at that time as a continuing trend. It will still be viewed as an exception. Negro voting in 1968 will have come up to white levels, except in five states. By 1970 the central civil rights issues will be the introduction into the South of certain federally-financed, special-opportunity programs in education and small-business loans. The major areas around which social protest movements will be organized will be matters of personal self-expression—for example, demands for sexual freedom or for less conformity in school systems. In regard to international relations, the protesters will begin to be more explicitly antinationalistic and in favor of less emphasis on sovereignty.

In Latin America, there will begin to be much greater differences between rich countries and poor countries with a few countries experiencing economic booms.

In Africa, there will have been sporadic famines, general chaos, and predominantly military dictatorships.

In the Soviet Union, though economic growth will have continued, there will be even greater discontent with the functioning of the economic system than there is now. There will be much Aesopian discussion of such possibilities as the abolition of the *kolkhoz* and the Party, of firms' investing independently, and so forth. There will be noticeable problems of unemployment. The major changes will, however, not have occurred by 1970. In Eastern Europe at least one country will have experimented with the abolition of central planning in everything but name. Within Europe, East-West travel will have risen to flood levels. Communism will be pretty much of a dead issue in some East European countries, though none will have overtly rejected it.

The death of Mao Tse-tung will not have led to significant change in the Chinese government or policies.

Throughout the world, the Communist movement will seem to be a declining force, but miscellaneous forms of anarchy and disorder will be just as strong as ever.

1970-2000

The trends that I have predicted for the first five years are the beginnings of trends I expect to continue for the most part for the subsequent twenty years. There will, however, be some discontinuities that should be noted. In about 1977, a major war will break out in Africa among the nations there. When it has continued for some months, there will be a massive U.N. military intervention requiring the continuing stationing of troops there for a protracted period. In China, a protracted famine in one portion of the country will lead to the outbreak of guerrilla warfare around 1985. There will be a seesaw struggle for about five years during which the Soviet Union will seize certain border areas, particularly Manchuria (1990). A so-called moderate regime will ultimately come in whose line will be that the attempt to establish Communism in China was premature, and that what China needs is massive foreign aid regardless of ideology. It will continue to be a one-party military dictatorship, asserting itself to be Communist.

Around 1980, there will be a major political crisis in the Soviet Union, marked by large-scale strikes, the publication of dissident periodicals, a temporary disruption of central control over some regions, and an open clash between the major sectors of the bureaucracy over questions of military policy and consumer goods. This will stop just short of revolution, though it will result in the effectual abolition of the Communist Party or its splitting up into more than one organization, the abolition of the *kolkhoz*, and so forth. During these events, the Soviet hold over Eastern Europe will be completely broken. An unconsummated attempt at East German-West German unification will occur. This will stop the revolution in the Soviet Union from going full course. In the last analysis, German unification will be aborted by diplomatic pressure from Western Europe and the United States. This will create a kind of U.S.-Polish-Hungarian alliance with guarantees against Germany and, implicitly, against the Soviet Union. The result will be the further disintegration of NATO; a close relationship will, however, emerge between the United States and France, rather than Germany. From this point on, it will be generally recognized that Communism is a moribund ideology. The rates of economic growth in the capitalist world will be steadily outstripping those in the rest of the world.

At the same time, the widening gap between the developed and underdeveloped countries will be softened only by the extraordinary growth of a few of the latter—two or three countries in Latin America, Taiwan, one or two spots in North Africa and the Middle East. In response to this situation, the decade 1990-2000 will see the beginning of the breakdown of the nation-state system. Africa will establish some form of regional federation with a large-scale international force of foreign troops present. There will be a mixture of local autonomy and regional controls. There will also be a foreign-aid program with many strings attached. It will be hard to define what constitutes the nations of Africa in the classic sense of nation.

The United States will admit its fifty-first state, Puerto Rico, and its fifty-second state, a string of Pacific Islands including Okinawa.

A European parliament will be established including most, but not all of the present European countries from England to Rumania. The nations will not be abolished, but will enter into a loose confederation. Some patchwork of East and Southeast Asian states will also enter into a confederation including most of Indonesia, which will have broken up in 1980. Around the year 2000 the Soviet Union will be forced to loosen its grip on Manchuria, turning it into some semi-independent state with *ad hoc* relations with both China and Russia.

During this period, there will have been some, but relatively little, nuclear proliferation. Several states will have acquired token nuclear capability: India in 1975; Pakistan in 1980; Egypt and Israel simultaneously in 1983; Germany with some sharing of controls in 1985; Japan in 1990; and Algeria in 1995. Much more important than the proliferation of these token capabilities will be the emergence around 1990 of a new family of even more dangerous weapons. It will be generally recognized that means exist for a sneak attack by a poor country upon any nation in the world with results verging on total destruction. No country will, however, have built the system yet. The decade 1990 to 2000 will see massive increases in expenditures by the major powers for reconnaissance, intelligence, and covert influence in places where such weapons might secretly be developed.

2000-2015

This large-scale increase in reconnaissance, intelligence, and infiltration will, in the decade 2000-2010, have further major effects in modifying the nation-state system. There will, for example, be federations of political parties—comparable to the federation of Catholic parties today or the Communist movement—cutting across national lines. Millions of people will be trained for overseas assignments and sent to work abroad. International corruption will be carried out on a vast scale by powerful nations seeking to assure their security against dangerous developments. In the latter years of the half century (circa 2010) there will be attempts to use the U.N. as a reform instrument, substituting serious international supervision for the unilateral devices of intelligence, infiltration, and corruption to maintain security. An open-frontiers treaty will be signed by many countries establishing an absolute right of travel and conversation by nationals of any country.

The amount of actual violence in the world will have started to decline about 1990, particularly after the model of the international African intervention suggests that local wars will no longer be tolerated. From 1970 to 1990, there will have been two or three local wars in Asia which will not have been allowed to go to the point of conquest.

In the fifteen years after 2000, there will also be for the first time rather rapid rises in the living standards of the people of Asia and Africa as population control becomes fairly complete and new technologies of food and industrial production begin to make massive differences. In that decade and a half, the trend will no longer be a widening gap between the developed and underdeveloped areas. The developed areas will be putting sums on the order of $100 or $200 billion a year into the economies of the developing areas in one form or another. A major problem that the United States will face at the end of the half century is a widespread ideology around the world that equality is a right and, as such, imposes an obligation on the rich to help the poor. The right of the United States to decide for itself what it will do in that direction will be very widely challenged.

WORKING SESSION TWO
FEBRUARY 11–12, 1966

working session two:

THE NATURE AND LIMITATIONS OF FORECASTING

DANIEL BELL: I would like to begin this session on the nature and limitations of forecasting with a rather paradoxical statement as to what one can and cannot forecast. I think it is very difficult to make good predictions about single critical events. I think, and this may be more controversial, that it is extremely difficult to make predictions about science and about new technology. It is easier to make sociological predictions than any other kind, and this probably goes against the grain of current thought. I would like briefly to justify this argument.

Political predictions are subject to what I have now dubbed "Brzezinski's Law." It arises from an episode of a year ago when Brzezinski [who was then Director of the Research Institute on Communist Affairs at Columbia] was being baited on a television program for his lack of foresight about Russian political developments. He was asked the tantalizing question, "Professor Brzezinski, how come you failed to predict the downfall of Khrushchev?" To which Brzezinski replied, "If Khrushchev could not predict his own downfall, how do you expect me to do it?" Well, I think that is a fair statement. Certain kinds of predictions are functions of perfect information, and few of us have information of that sort.

What people thought would be easy to predict, namely science and new technology—because everyone is seduced by such wonders—is not so easy. If one looks at the major changes in science and technology of thirty-five years back, such things as atomic fission, computers, one finds that nobody predicted them. The kind of imagination that is necessary in science, that has produced discoveries such as the DNA code, is not itself predictable. Donald Schon has an interesting discussion in his paper on the impossibility of a theory of invention because it is a contradiction in terms; an invention, almost by definition, is a surprise.

But if one were to go back and look at the articles in *Recent Social Trends* of thirty-four years ago, there is a high degree of predictability, for the simple reason that they deal with constants in human life: the distribution of income between the rich and the poor and, therefore, the problem of poverty, the problem of education, of health, of urban trends, the quality of life, and so on.

One can chart social prediction in this way. One can begin with the kinds of demands that will be made by disadvantaged groups; and this follows what might be called "Tocqueville's Law," which is that in a society pledged to the idea of equality, what the few have today, the many will demand tomorrow. There are, second, the possibilities or facilities for change, such as political leverage, changing valuations, rising Gross National Product, and so forth. There are also the constraints of change, sometimes political, and sometimes the limitations of resources, political and social. Once demands are "legitimated," then we can begin to chart the rates of diffusion, as the new privileges are gained by the previously disadvantaged groups. In the history of trade unionism, for example, one can see that the privileges once held by the managerial and white-collar class —for example, pensions and security— later become diffused throughout the blue-collar class. One can chart similar rates of diffusion for the civil rights movement, for medical care for the population, for higher education for the greater proportion of the youths, and so forth.

If we can make sociological predictions, we can anticipate more readily the changes that have policy implications. These are the areas of critical strain in the society, and the areas of political tension and change. I think of the failure of the Kennedy-Johnson Administration to be prepared for the kinds of demands about poverty, education, and health, although the lineaments of the issues were laid out in the *Recent Social Trends* volumes. And I would hope that one of the fruits of our discussions, and particularly those of the working groups, would be the specification of the kinds of problems which will be emerging thirty-five years hence.

About procedures. At this session we will have Herman Kahn discuss the kinds of forecasts that he and his colleagues at the Hudson Institute are doing for the Commission, and then we have Messrs. Leontief, Schon, Moore, and Dobzhansky deal with some caveats about forecasting. There is also the paper by Fred Iklé which raises some epistemological questions about the problem.

Afterwards we will divide into four working groups to consider the papers that were submitted in each area. Each group will have a *rapporteur* who will summarize, at the plenary session, the conclusions of each group. We will start, then, with Herman Kahn.

HERMAN KAHN: My colleagues and I have written eight studies for the Commission [to be published as a separate hard-cover volume *The Next Thirty-Three Years: A Framework for Speculation*], and I would like to summarize some of the major themes of these papers.

William Pfaff has a pessimistic view of what is likely to develop over the next thirty-five years. He argues that Fascism is not a deviant case completely outside Western civilization and tradition. Just as pollution is part and parcel of the industrial process, he considers these irrational manic movements part of the process of acculturation, not only as messianic movements but as reactions to increased rationality and technological control. He expects to see many such movements and describes places where they might occur. I find the argument persuasive, although I do not say that I think this is likely to happen.

There is great value in metaphors and historical analogies In Europe, for example, many people consider the relation of the United States to Europe analogous to Rome's relation to Greece in the first and second centuries, after the Carthaginian Wars. This argument is evolved in great detail in *The Coming Caesars* by Amaury de Riencourt. The term *Munich* has a great deal of significance. Many people overestimate the problem of Munich, but it still concretizes an important concept that would have been difficult to explain to Americans had Munich not occurred. History is incredibly valuable for communication, providing useful metaphors and analogies. But, unlike earlier centuries, today there are no common books which all people have read. I could not allude to the Bible or Plutarch's *Lives* and assume that everyone has read them. Scenarios, however, can often play the same role as historical allusion; they are useful tools for making historical predictions concrete because they force the writer to relate events to one another in narrative form.

It is startling how little thought is given to the possibility of a tense East-West confrontation, à la the late forties or early fifties or worse. This is even true at the Hudson Institute. Although such a confrontation is certainly not plausible, it is not so improbable as people think. Whether you believe in tense Cold Wars or not, the Soviet Union exists. It has a large military establishment, a sizable GNP, and 220 million people, some of whom are dedicated. The Soviet Union is obviously important in international affairs. What problems does it present for us? Edmund Stillman has drawn up three scenarios, or three possible futures.

The first one is called the "Stagnating U.S.S.R." The basic notion in this one is that they are doing fairly well. GNP per capita is up by 2 to 4 per cent, but in every other way it is sort of dust and ashes. Khrushchev, speaking in Hungary, once called Communism goulash and ballet. Russian ballet is very good, but their goulash is not, nor is it likely to be. This is, in part, a question of style. Stillman phrases it rather neatly: "They will give you a pat of butter an inch thick, but it will have a thumb print on it." Furthermore, any Russian visiting Eastern Europe, say Sophia, realizes the people there are living better than he is at home. Not to do so well as Eastern Europe must be depressing. I would guess this is going to continue.

There is another sense in which almost everybody believes that they have had a kind of "Thermidor"; some of us argue it is a loss of nerve. If you went to the head of the Presidium and related an ingenious scheme for getting a united, fanatically Communist Red Germany, he would not be interested. They did try for a united Communist China, and it seems to have been somewhat unpleasant, but not one tenth so unpleasant as a united Communist Germany would be. This has been their policy for twenty years, but the old rules no longer obtain. If in the past we have tended to overrate the Russians' power, recklessness, and intensity, in the future we may underrate it. All of us today are becoming concerned with the value of the Soviet guarantee. If they cannot protect Viet-Nam, maybe they cannot protect Poland. A Rumanian tells me that both a Rumanian and a Hungarian will sell his grandmother to the devil, but only a Rumanian will deliver. Rumanians understand their world very well. Yet they kick the Soviets both publicly and privately.

The second scenario presents a retreating and consolidating Soviet Union, a "Bismarkian" one. It understands its own limitations and consolidates. It gets out of Eastern Europe, including East Germany, and makes some kind of a deal with countries in Europe, or even with the United States.

The third scenario is the "Young Turk"; at the Hudson Institute we call it the "Kennedy U.S.S.R." A young group comes in and wants to get the country moving again, but the question is which direction. This strikes me as a reasonable way to think of the Soviet Union during the next ten to twenty years.

I think Dan Bell is right when he says that many sociological issues are predictable. Some of them, however, have large political implications. For example, West Germany after World War II had four problems: survival, independence, strength, and respectability. You could almost guarantee that once they had solved these problems, they would move on to the next level—to issues like reunification. West Germany is obviously emerging. Today it is the second largest trading nation in the world, third largest in GNP, third or fourth largest in industrial products (depending on how you make your calculations), and about twentieth in political influence. But that gap is going to close, and one of the major issues the United States will face in the next ten years will be the absorption of Germany as a respectable member of the international system.

Over the next ten to twenty years the problematic issues are likely to be the roles of France and West Germany, and not, for example, the decline of England. At the time of the American Civil War, British productivity had been growing very slowly in comparison with the rest of the world's rate. British productivity does not go up fast, and the managers of British businesses have certain characteristics, tendencies, habits, traditions, or styles that make it highly unlikely that growth rates will be much over 2 or 3 per cent.

I do not think that people who talk about China as the looming central power in Asia have examined the situation. Japan will play a larger role than China in the next ten or twenty years, particularly if the Japanese are assertive and maybe even if they are passive. In almost every way you care to name, Japan is a bigger power than China. The most interesting new powers are in Latin America; Brazil and maybe Mexico will be among the great powers by the year 2000.

One can take old maxims and use them for prediction—for example, the enemy of an enemy is likely to be a friend. In 1962 we predicted that there would be a Franco-Chinese *rapprochement* of some sort because both China and France were against the United States. Conversely, the enemy of a friend is likely to be an enemy. For example, we had been telling the Pakistanis that we were arming them, but not against India; they understood this as a *pro forma* public statement. They felt that since India is Pakistan's major enemy, an American *rapprochement* with Pakistan was an announcement against India. But the United States was in fact more pro-Indian than pro-Pakistani when it came to a choice.

About techniques of prediction—one of my papers. I have spent about fifteen years of my life trying to get a feel for the military technology five years ahead. The easiest and the best way to do this is to do it naïvely. You look over the record of the last ten years, get yourself a ruler or a French curve, and extrapolate. In a rapidly changing field, the expert tends to predict by extrapolating what he knows; what he cannot predict are specific inventions. The heart of the prediction must, therefore, be to predict the rate of invention, not the rate of improvement in current techniques.

You predict the rate of invention by assuming that it will be much the same as it has been in the last ten years if conditions are unchanged, but faster if appropriations are going to be a lot higher, and slower if they are going to be a lot lower. Your basic input is what has been done over the last ten years. You must then decide whether you are getting to limits. Simplistic prediction, by graphing on the right kind of paper—log, semi-log, or linear—and then drawing straight lines or straight curves, is an extraordinarily good way to predict a rate of change of a technology that already has a history of change. The two computers that failed in the last two years were off that curve; they tried a little bit more than the curve said could be done. Two years ago we drew a curve and predicted the performance that would be reached by the two laser inventions that came through last month. Such predictions are analogous to input-output studies. In such areas it is a good idea to look at past history and to be naïve.

Let me comment on what we call the Standard World, which is a baseline for predicting the future. The Standard World is one which we do not think is necessarily plausible, but which has all the trends that everybody takes seriously —population rates, economic growth rates, energy trends, and so forth. For Latin America as a whole we use reasonable population rates, GNP rates, and per-capita GNP's to get a range. We then divide Latin America into three groups: countries with less than $200 per capita; those with between $200 and $500; and those with more than $500. The Standard World is assumed to be the neutral case here. The Alliance for Progress says that the goal for the year 2000 would be for the low-income countries to make the medium-income level and for the medium-income countries to make the high. What must be done in terms of social justice, social services, and development to achieve this?

You can do the same kind of thing for the world as a whole. Using reasonable figures for the last three to five years, you can extrapolate. You get for the OECD group a $4,500 per-capita income, which means that $20,000 (in constant dollars) will be the median family income per year. The Warsaw Pact countries seem to do well, but there are still many poor countries—Black Africa's per-capita income remains less than $200.

Let us examine the Standard World in which these growth rates occur as predicted. If you extrapolate working hours naïvely, you find that by the year 2000 you will have 1,100 working hours per year as the norm. This is roughly a thirty-hour week and thirteen weeks of vacation a year. What does this mean? Europe, with its traditional society, will be able to adjust to it easily; the gentleman will re-emerge. The United States is a vocation-oriented society; leisure could be catastrophic for us. The American with leisure is a man at loose ends; it will take him a generation longer to adjust to leisure than it takes the European.

There is a variation, the scenario of a beatnik United States. Forty-five per cent of the population work at their normal thirty-hour work week, nine or ten months a year; 15 per cent work long hours not because they want the money, but because they are compulsive—like the directors of the Hudson Institute, or government people, or intellectuals; 10 per cent work short hours because they want to pursue hobbies—painting, skiing, writing poetry, chasing girls, whatever you want; and 10 per cent define themselves by rejecting middle-class America—you know, middle-class America is clean, they are dirty; most Americans don't use drugs, they use drugs—the beatnik reaction. I would argue that even though our curves indicate that there will not be very many poor people, America will have a lot of poor people as opposed to Europe. They will be the voluntary poor, the 10 per cent who just accept whatever incomes people have, and then the sociological poor who do not get educated, the so-called problem families in what people call the culture of poverty.

There are some pessimistic worlds in our scenarios: the business-cycle world, for example, where there is a real interruption in the steady progress upward. Many people think that you cannot have really big depressions anymore because of a large number of built-in stabilizers in the economy, and I assume this is right. But any of the "normal" panics may still be possible, and people may lose interest in economic growth or not want to pay its price. The purpose of the Standard World is to lay out a set of alternatives and then to see which are the most likely to occur.

DANIEL BELL: We will now turn to some of the cautionary fellows. Professor Leontief.

WASSILY LEONTIEF: Many papers prepared for the Commission assume the attitude of an almighty God who can choose among alternative freedoms. Without trying to start a philosophical discussion about freedom and nonfreedom of the will, I would argue that the degree of that freedom remains very small. In practically none of the papers were there suggestions or proposals explaining why people might pursue policies other than those we think best. One can, to a large extent, legitimately try to predict policies by assessing the pressures and interests that will determine the courses of these policies. Avoiding the philosophical-metaphysical question of an ultimate explanation, we might try to predict the forces shaping our own acts.

There are predictions by models and predictions by trends. Predictions by models are based on the belief that it is possible to view the world as one whole with separate parts that are in some way interrelated. Prediction by trends gives us a view of the world as if it were a handful of sand, each particle distinct from the others. These are not symmetrical things.

If you ask experts in various fields to predict certain phenomena, you find that the same phenomena very often fall in different areas of expertise. You also discover that experts in certain fields do much better than experts in others. There is, in other words, a kind of pecking order. A space vehicle might be destroyed by overheating much faster than by collision with another interplanetary body. In this case, the specialist in heat will make a better prediction than the expert on trajectories and speed. In this sense, prediction based on one type of approach might prove to be much better than that derived from another, but this type of choice already involves a certain model pattern.

To discuss policies not in a deterministic way, but as a problem of choice, I think you must work with models. To build policies into trends is difficult.

My last remark pertains to one of the points in Herman Kahn's notes and concerns the extent to which we may try to explain policies and understand what is behind them in terms of what happens within countries as contrasted to what happens in international relations. I believe, to be quite specific, that the foreign policy of a country is largely determined by what happens within that country and not by what happens outside it. From this point of view, if you want to predict the future of the world, the prediction of

what will happen inside the U.S., inside China, or inside the U.S.S.R. is a central subject. In predicting what happens in a particular country, where conflicts might occur becomes extremely important. Tensions and contradictions—rather than rational decisions—determine very frequently the shape and speed of change. The old theory of challenge and response is realistically very powerful. Even for a very pedestrian prediction of economic and social developments in the United States over the next thirty-five years, it would be most important to locate where people will feel unhappy and what forces will support and which will oppose their quest for betterment. Such a determination would help us to predict the likely changes in the social and political structure and would contribute greatly to an explanation of how the United States can be expected to react to tensions and shifts in other parts of the world.

DANIEL BELL: Wilbert Moore is now engaged in a large investigation of social indicators. He and his colleagues at the Russell Sage Foundation are doing for macrosociological data the kind of thing that Kuznets was doing in the thirties which led to the notion of the GNP and other macroeconomic indicators.

WILBERT MOORE: Dan Bell's comments about sociological prediction or forecasting provoked a response in me. I agree that sociological prediction is not too difficult. I have found it useful to ask what are the components one would deal with in a typological way. One could ask what is likely to persist virtually unchanged into the future. We are so enamored with the notion that everything is in flux that we forget that there are remarkable degrees of persistence in a population's basic social and cultural characteristics. There are also orderly trends, those which have in the past displayed and are likely to continue to display a rather substantial degree of order in the amount and rate of change.

Many sociologists have neglected the very important element of planned change. We know the future in part because we are devoting ourselves to our resources and constructing it according to particular announced goals which often have timetables. We can, therefore, look at the resource input in particular planned programs, both private and public, and make some estimates about probable side effects, both positive and negative.

The real trick is to predict the discontinuities, the places where there are going to be sharp breaks, either in the direction or the rate of change. The prediction of unique events is not within the compass of any scientific field. That is one of the problems of political prediction. Although single political events are sometimes very important, the best we can hope to do is to predict the probability of a class of events. For predictions of discontinuity, however, there are several tools. One is the concept of thresholds. Sometimes this may be a completion process. Dan Bell also mentioned that you can observe the diffusion of certain kinds of things through the population. You can expect a discontinuity effect when such things permeate the entire population.

In order to think about kinds of change and to conceptualize them, you must first do an analysis in the strictest sense of the term. It is very difficult to make any sense out of the whole; it must be broken down into its component parts. Once you have gone through this exercise, you have the rubrics for a matrix of some sort. You know how these phenomena are going to fit together because they have some systematic properties, perhaps not so many as some models indicate but quite a few. You have a lot of interplay in the process of change—feedback and so on. That is about as far as we have got at the Russell Sage Foundation: to indicate the rubrics that we think need attention. At one point it looked as if we were going to rediscover introductory sociology; the rubrics we were using looked very much like the chapter headings in a standard introductory text. We have found them not quite satisfactory for our purposes and have had to fiddle around a little.

I have become very suspicious of summary measures and summary indicators, including many already in use. The information loss in many of these indicators is rather severe and at times intolerable. The concept of socio-economic status or social class is thought by some non-sociologists to be sociology's greatest invention. But education predicts some things better than income, and income predicts some things better than occupation; the component measure will often yield a better handle on what you are trying to do in either cross sectional or sequential prediction than will the summary measures.

I am also suspicious of the quality of past information as a base upon which to forecast about the future. How can we forecast future variations in child-rearing patterns if we do not know what the distribution of child-rearing patterns is at the present time? While we were taking preliminary testimony at the Russell Sage Foundation from people who knew more about social indicators than we did, we encountered the concept known as the "Biderman concept" [Albert Biderman of the Bureau of Social Research in Washington, D. C., an independent nonprofit organization] of "administratively convenient data" as distinct from true data. All sorts of data being collected and published by federal agencies are administratively convenient, but may or may not have much resemblance to the phenomena to which they are supposed to relate. One can, for example, get very good information about the amount of money being devoted each month to aid to dependent children. No one knows what the size of that universe of dependent children is, or, consequently, whether the programs are gaining on the problem or falling behind. How much is being spent is an important figure when drawing up the budget, but it is not terribly significant social information.

I am also getting a little fearful of the complexity of dealing with sequential systems. How do you go about turning trends into a genuine model or systems analysis rather than a set of separate items? I am particularly fearful because we do not presently command the mathematical skills needed to do that job.

DANIEL BELL: On the questions of technological forecasting, Donald Schon.

DONALD SCHON: When you say there is going to be an invention ten years from now, such as an electric car, you have in effect made that invention. The forecasting of invention is not separate from invention itself. The principal step is the conceptual one. When you predict the electric car, you have made the adventure. We are not standing outside the process of change but participating in it. You encounter the same difficulty in market research. You cannot find out what people need; you can only find out if they are dissatisfied with what they have. You can, however, get people to invent interaction with consumers; this is different from broadcasting, which has nothing mutual about it.

I also believe that technology proceeds in waves. You can locate yourself on the wave and be pretty sure it is going to sweep beyond where it now is. For example, the nineteenth century was a century in which mechanism swept through society. The mechanical model of production swept through area after area; I cannot say it swept through industry after industry because it created industry after industry. In our own time, it is very clear that electronic systems are going to replace transistorized ones. In almost every area we are going to have instantaneous electronic technology which has no moving parts.

On a somewhat different level, we can talk about a trend or a wave, like the personalization of appliances. We moved from big radios in the living room to little transistors that people can carry. You can see this happening with television sets, like the one that sits on people's stomachs. All sorts of appliances will undergo this change, but you cannot predict the rate at which it is going to happen, and you get into real problems when you start talking about where it is going to happen next. This feeling that we are in the midst of waves, among them technological waves, underlies Herman Kahn's remarks on the relationship of the rate of change to the input. He then said something about becoming more sophisticated about limits and so forth. This is the sort of thing that Buckminster Fuller and Ralph Lenz, of the Air Force, have also tried to do. They have taken a technological parameter like thrust-to-weight ratio or speed and charted the change in parameter over the last one or two hundred years. If they discover that this growth is to a large extent rhythmical, they can assume a continued logarithmic growth. You can be pretty right about this.

There are, however, some ways in which you can be very wrong. Because the characteristic trend for the development of technology is the "S" curve and not the straight line, we get involved with thresholds and limits. Where are you on the "S" curve? This issue applies not only to technology but also to the economy. W. W. Rostow's concept of the take-off is great, but how do you know how close to the limits you are, and how do you know whether there will be another step up? You do not know; you know only after the fact. Similarly, how do you choose the parameter that you are going to examine? This approach to the forecasting of invention is, I think, the most interesting one. If the thrust-to-weight ratio does not behave the way the theory says it ought to behave, you have been looking at the wrong parameter. If you had looked at the right parameter, you could have seen the right rate. But the correct choice of parameter is something you discover after the fact.

There is also the question of the intersection of rates and trends. I have a friend who talks about technological forecasting as if it were like weather forecasting. I understand that we can predict fairly accurately the movement of a front. If, however, a front intersects with another front, that collision and the turbulence and complication involved present more information than we can handle, and we cannot predict the weather conditions that will result. In technological change, the aircraft provides a case in point. We have curves about weight-thrust ratios and curves about the heat resistance to metal. These curves collide, and the complicated things that happen at these intersections cannot presently be explained by any of the theories we have.

Herman Kahn talked about metaphors as devices for communication. He said that because we have had a "Munich," we can now refer to future situations as Munichs and arouse national excitement in ways which would have been impossible without the Munich metaphor. Wassily Leontief's input-output model is most sophisticated, but it is based on a mechanical metaphor, and there are limitations on mechanical models of the economy.

There may be several variables involved in technological change. It may be a response to competition, an attempt to fit the available skilled labor supply, increased demands, or a wish of an executive. In making a decision, I have too much information to handle: interdependent variables, rate differences, closed-looped back simulation trends. In the existential here-and-now there are always people who have too much information. The tools of Herman Kahn and Wassily Leontief permit insight into certain issues, but where are the processes that allow us to use this information? The government at one time became so worried about the effects of automation that it established a Commission to look into the matter. While the Commission was still meeting, the unemployment rate fell, and people began to look at the Bureau of Labor Statistics' figures. The Automation Commission then told us: Do not worry, there is no panic; there is no wolf. I personally think there may well be a wolf and that our figures may not show it. The future is not going to be like the past. The problem is to design processes that enable us to use the insights generated by the tools of Wassily Leontief and others.

DANIEL BELL: I have asked Professor Dobzhansky, of the Rockefeller University, for a short statement on biological forecasting.

THEODOSIUS DOBZHANSKY: If we look at mankind as a species and ask what genetic changes will occur in the human population, nothing much will happen by 2000. After all, it is only slightly more than a generation. There are, of course, proposals, such as those of Huxley and Muller, to change the human population genetically. They plan to collect human semen and egg cells and to freeze them for later use. Efforts will be made to combine the eggs and sperm of highly intelligent people. So far this idea has been popular neither with most biologists nor with social scientists.

There should be considerable changes by 2000 in numbers of people. In the control of the "population explosion," new techniques of contraception may have a considerable influence. If the population quantity is controlled, the question of population quality may be-

come very important after the year 2000. This is, however, beyond our frame of reference now.

DANIEL BELL: We have time for some comments on these statements.

HAROLD ORLANS: In response to Donald Schon, I think it is important to recognize that there are technically feasible inventions that would be uneconomic by the time they had been developed. The nuclear plane is an example of something that was technically possible, but came too late to be useful.

DONALD SCHON: The forecasting of invention is itself invention, and this is separable from the question of whether or not you go all the way when you make the forecast. Inventing the concept is a different kind of mental exercise than the forecasting of a change of productivity rate. It is a conceptual invention.

HAROLD ORLANS: You are inventing a problem then, but you are not solving it. It is frequently said today that if you can define a clearly technical problem and can devote an adequate input of dollars to it, you can solve that problem. There is at least some truth in this statement, but other issues remain. Whether you want to do it, whether it would be economic to do it, the rate at which it would happen—these are all open questions. Forecasting appears to be a kind of neutral, objective, distant activity; when we are talking about forecasting invention, we are talking about engaging in conceptual invention.

MARTIN SHUBIK: Our concept of what constitutes a solution is usually a rather hazy one. To understand what you want to invent may very easily be a great step toward the invention. There is the notion of purposeful versus purposeless search—the theory of serendipity, which I think is false. A person who has an idea of what he is looking for has a greater chance of finding it than someone who just wanders vaguely.

Stock-market forecasting is not particularly represented here, but even this trade has already divided its ranks along the lines of the contrast Herman Kahn was making. There are the chartists and the fundamentalists. The fundamentalists want to discover as much as they can about the firm—where its technology is going and so forth—while the chartists draw some linear extrapolations of what is going on and invent such phrases as "when the thing has heads and shoulders." You cannot idly dismiss the chartists, because in one sense a key to forecasting is the amount of time one has available in the decision process to make a statement about the future. A chartist can come up with some sort of fairy tale in ten or fifteen minutes. If you do not have more time, perhaps that is the best you can get. We have a simple fundamentalist approach for being dead right about the year 2000. We could spend the next thirty-four years studying the year 2000 and issue our report on January 1 of that year.

Instead of throwing away yesterday's knowledge, we should try to build methods that utilize it in a more or less automated manner. The chartists of today could use all of the findings of the fundamentalists of yesterday. We gradually build an incremental systematic process that involves, among other things, linking large data-processing procedures with models or conceptual frameworks. This would give an opportunity to link the fundamentalist and chartist approaches.

I want to mention one phenomenon in microeconomics in relation to Wassily Leontief's comment on the deterministic nature of the world. We talk about freedom of choice, about the rational man, and in microeconomics we use the expression *competitive economy*. In the limited model of a competitive economy, every apparently rational individual with freedom of choice finds himself in a totally noncompetitive situation; the whole structure of the society in which he exists is, at least in theory, such that his power is attenuated to approximately zero. Although he has that grand liberty of maximization within the system, when viewed from the outside, he appears to have been stripped of his freedom of choice. We can predict his actions because paradoxically while the individual thinks he has freedom of choice, in fact the dear old invisible hand is such that it has co-ordinated everything so that he does the right thing in terms of the situation. The system is designed in such a way that an individual's freedom of choice

produces behavior in conformity with what others might wish him to do in a larger social context. I do not say that this is necessarily bad. How much freedom do people have anyhow, and what is the metric that you should use to measure freedom?

One of the dangers in too much static economic theorizing about choice is that one often forgets the capital structure of society, and in doing so one fails to specify the nature of a tremendous inertial force in the society. Our control problem is often as though we had a ninety-eight-wheel truck, and were speeding along on a super-highway. Our only control is to modify by *epsilon* a few parameters affecting the steering of that truck. One cannot redesign the truck in a couple of hours because the structure is rigid, and one has little short-term control because the inertia is great. If you have a system with mammoth inertia, small terms which look small enough to ignore at the present moment may blow the system to bits a little way out. How much inertia is there in our forecast? How much control do we have over parameters? Even though the change in the parameter is small, the change in the behavior might be large. For example, it appears that you do not have to change individuals very much to influence them considerably. If you can make an *epsilon* change in the parameterization of the individual, you may cause fantastic changes in his behavior. The man inside the asylum looks very much like the man outside, but just a minor change in a parameter made that system go in a very different manner.

HARVEY PERLOFF: The ability to predict trends is influenced by the amount of free choice and of government control. There are areas where there is a good deal of individual choice. This is true, for example, of the decisions to have children, to form families. Population forecasts are highly uncertain as a result. This would change if government decided that only certain families were to be permitted to have children. In most places you can do better on estimates for income classes. Since few governments feel they can adopt the kinds of policies that would greatly change the income class structure, you can normally make fairly accurate predictions on this subject. The Federal Government recently decided to change the rules of the game with regard to business expenditures, but it quickly backed away. You just could not make that kind of change. You can have high income tax rates, but you cannot easily bring about a substantial change in the level of living of the richer classes. Such change seems to move very slowly in all systems. Therefore, predictability is high in this area.

In sharp contrast, in some of the political areas there can be rather sudden decisions without any diffusion elements. In the confrontation over Cuba no one would have been able to predict what was going to happen the next day simply because the President and a very small group of advisers were going to make a choice in which discussion was limited to a small group and there was no well-established trendline to provide a basis for prediction.

LAWRENCE FRANK: For centuries we have been told that our lives as individuals and as a people were governed by an omniscient and omnipotent deity: Whatever happened was thought to be ordained divinely, and it was only wise and appropriate for a man to accept his fate and not to quarrel with his lot in life. Today we seem to be relinquishing this theological conception as we accept a new kind of fatalism expressed in a series of trends. This new fatalism is asserted to have the same coerciveness over human living, with little or no possibility for escape or change, especially as these trends are now sanctioned by elaborate statistical devices and calculations held to be wholly scientific. In passing, we should note that many of the data used in these calculations are not actual measurements, because most human activities can only be counted and then scaled according to the assumptions of the statistician. As Donald Schon has pointed out, the dominant pattern of thinking has been in terms of mechanization—that is, the assumption that an antecedent determines a consequence in a more or less linear relationship, such as cause and effect. But this assumption of causal relationships has a limited validity and then only when applied to the invariant properties of physical, chemical, and some biological events. For our consideration of human and social events, we are beginning to utilize a conception of process, recognizing that the same process can produce different products depending upon where, when, and how it operates. The process of organic fertilization and gestation, for example, produces many different offspring. Moreover, different processes can produce equivalent products, as Ludwig Bertalanffy points out in his principle of Equifinality. We are now finding ourselves baffled and frustrated in our attempts to cope with human problems because we cling to the older deterministic linear formulations. Jay Forester has remarked that he has yet to confront a problem in industrial organization and management that did not turn out to be the result of incorrect assumptions. I mention this because I believe we should consider critically our insistence upon the determination of social life by trends and reliance upon a mechanistic view of social order. We may find through trends clues to what will probably occur in the near future, but we may have to examine these trends to see which we must interrupt or redirect if we hope to achieve a more orderly and more humanly desirable social order.

HERMAN KAHN: Chartists are not only fast, but they may be extraordinarily good. Unfortunately chartists compete with one another, and some always seem much better than others. If there were only one chartist, I could almost guarantee he would be extraordinary. People may try to fool the chartist, and then, of course, he will not do so well.

I want to make another distinction—between the methodology-oriented and the problem-oriented. If you are problem-oriented, many problems disappear. The fact that we have run into problems in prediction, into certain gray areas for instance, does not bother us if the problem that we are working on has not come up. You would be surprised at how well generalizations work, even though under some assumptions they have no right to work at all. In exploiting targets of opportunity, which I would say is the effort of a good deal of problem-oriented work, generalizations on classes which would not work elsewhere may work. Let us not be contemptuous of what little successes we have there.

Chartism is a very neglected and important methodology. It is neglected because people do not think it is really respectable. It looks too tricky, too naïve, but the chartist has one great advantage over the fundamentalist. Because of insufficient knowledge, the fundamentalist has to overlook many things that affect the charts. The chartists in military technology have been incredibly successful.

Going back to the discussion of models, I would be very surprised if the kinds of questions we are interested in could get computer simulation with independent variables where there are differences of large numbers. I know of no successful case outside of engineering and physics where that kind of thing has worked. I expect it will work quite well in the future if the models and data, the records and the interactions are very well known. I am not against computer simulation in variables, but I would think that the calculations for most of the problems we are interested in will be done by slide rules. Models work best if they are restricted to narrow-range phenomena of one or two variables. When you get involved in large numbers of variables, the difficulties in computation, theory, and analysis are particularly swamping.

Only one case which I have seen has worked rather well in two instances—the theory of nuclear forces and the design of nuclear weapons. People had rather complicated models that turned out to be very bad in terms of numerical predictions, but they also had measurements. By a common-sense technique, they adjusted the parameters on the models. These models only partially described reality; graphs described whatever was left out. They used experiments which were correct in a reasonable way for the model and then used the model for extrapolation, trying to be consistent on the experimental level. This kind of a makeshift method is incredibly useful. We are not prisoners of data, but let us explore where they lead within a particular framework. Let us also consider changing the framework, but this is a harder job. I notice, for example, that the people who are the most Faustian, the most successful in making their universe, are the ones that simply say we will not try to transcend the world, but work with it.

WASSILY LEONTIEF: I just want to mention that I was misunderstood by you if you think I tried to imply that it is not useful to deal with trends.

DANIEL BELL: Since we have been concerned with the nature and limitations of forecasting, I would like to conclude this session with a prediction I found in going through an old file. It pictures a future world, and the text reads: "From the train of moving seats in the darkest building, a visitor looks down on a miniature landscape far away . . . and finally he beholds the city itself with its quarter-mile-high towers, huge glass, and soaring among them four-level, seven-lane directional highways on which you can surely choose your speed—100, 200 miles an hour. The city of 1960 has abundant functions: fresh air, fine green parkways, recreational centers, all results of plausible planning and design. No building's shadow will touch another. Parks will occupy one third of the city area." Who can say, whispers a voice, "what new horizons lie before us. We have both the initiative and imagination to penetrate them."

The text and the voice are from Futurama, the elaborate scale-model of the ideal city of the future which was presented at the General Motors exposition of the 1939 World's Fair. There you have 1939 looking at 1960, and see where we are today.

FOUR FUTURES

DANIEL BELL: I thought we might begin with a report by Ithiel Pool on the discussions of the working group on international systems.

ITHIEL POOL: The group had no large agreement on single-valued predictions of what would happen in the year 2000. Thus, perhaps, we confirmed Dan Bell's contention that prediction of single political events is impossible. We did, however, identify certain significant topics that should be discussed.

The first is the future of the national state system. Some members of the group maintained that there would be a growth of international institutions comparable to the United Nations, though not necessarily the U.N. itself. We agreed that power was unlikely to reside in any structure where a one-nation, one vote setup prevailed. Power will certainly gravitate to international organizations with a more realistic representation of the division of power.

Our prediction of the growth of international organizations assumes, of course, a growth of world law. Most members of the group thought that there would not be a tidy and neat development of international organizations over this thirty-five-year period. They contended that the continuing nation states would be increasingly enmeshed in an untidy web of international structures of one sort or another. We disagreed on the extent to which this implied the erosion of the nation state itself. That may certainly happen in some places in the world but perhaps not in other regions. Although we believed that a new empire on the British model would be as unlikely as an international organization on the League of Nations model, there was considerable discussion of new kinds of dominant relationships in the world.

There was some question in our group as to whether the future of international organizations should be treated separately from the topic of the future of empires, because many of the kinds of relationships of dominance and co-operation that may exist in the world of 2000 will be described by critics as imperial. The Chinese, a present-day example of the critics, consider certain arrangements imperial, whereas others support them as international organizations. The line between empire and co-operation is not necessarily clear.

The future of the nation state, empire, and international organizations define to some degree the structure of the international system. We also debated questions about the likely changes in power relations within that system during the next thirty-five years. The group differed considerably on which countries would grow stronger and which weaker. We discussed whether the United States is at the peak of its power and likely to find itself frustrated, or whether it is moving toward a future peak. The same issues can be discussed with regard to the Soviet Union. Those who expected the decline of relative U.S. power emphasized that an increasing number of middle powers will acquire nuclear capability, the capability to destroy ten cities of the United States or the Soviet Union. Others, while not denying this fact, tended to minimize its significance and to emphasize a growing gap between the military potential of the powers which invest heavily in research and development and in military efforts and that of the second echelon of powers. The group agreed that over most of this period there was likely to be a growing gap in the economic sphere between the most advanced nations and the less advanced nations, but whether there would be a corresponding trend in military power was controversial. None of us apparently expected that an American-Soviet confrontation would be the dominant issue of international relations in the year 2000 as it was in the 1950's. On the other hand, none of us seemed to expect a U.S.-Soviet *entente* as opposed to a *détente*. The range of expectations fell in between these two extremes, though at different points in that continuum. The nature of Soviet-American relations will depend on many things. This could well be described as a metastable equilibrium in which it is very hard to make a particular prediction. Among the things upon which it depends quite

critically is German reunification. German reunification would obviously have profound and complicated effects on the structure of alliances and on European unity. The pattern of Soviet-American relations will depend very much on whether there is a united Europe as the third major force or a divided Europe with varying relations with the two major powers. Finally, the Soviet-American confrontation is likely to depend critically upon the nature of the Chinese-American relationship. Predictions for the likely Chinese-American relationship ranged from extreme hostility to rather close relations.

The group had no great expectations of any very important new powers by the year 2000, although there was some talk that Brazil would attempt to exercise leadership in Latin America. There was considerable debate over the degree to which issues in other parts of the world were likely to be settled without reference to the Soviet Union and the United States. For example, are controversies in Africa likely to be resolved by the African states among themselves or will the United States and the Soviet Union be critically involved?

The group also dealt with what the offensive and defensive capabilities or the nature of war would be in the year 2000. Since the French Revolution, the writer's image of the next war has tended to be a relatively short war started by surprise, yet this has never been the reality. Our expectations may be partially reversed now with the recognition in the last few years that nuclear war is not likely to be of spasm character. It is, however, not very clear how much effect this more sophisticated realization has had upon our thinking. The group seemed to be in fair agreement that nuclear military action, if any occurred, would be a graduated response, not a spasm response. Nuclear warfare was not thought to be the most likely eventuality in this period. On the other hand, we expected large-scale turmoil at various points throughout the world in the next thirty-five years.

This raises, of course, the question of the character of American forces to cope with the turmoil. Some in the group doubted whether it would be possible to identify clearly in the year 2000 the military and nonmilitary foreign-affairs budgets, if at that point, for example, there were to be a hundred thousand Americans in Africa engaged in a process of pacification involving communications, roads, and so on. It is not perfectly clear that military and nonmilitary actions will be so easily definable then as they now are. The group differed substantially on the level of weaponry likely to exist in the year 2000, and on the issues of nuclear diffusion and complete disarmament. There were differences, for example, about the attractiveness of heavy armaments for various countries. To what extent will it become clear that they are fruitless inventions and a fruitless acquisition in that they cancel themselves out? This, of course, depends in part on changes in technology in the intervening period that may make it look more profitable or less profitable to acquire arms.

The group also treated the willingness of the American public to commit its resources abroad in different parts of the world. One view was that the Viet-Nam war and similar efforts will make the American public unwilling to commit manpower and treasure to remote corners of the world as readily in the future as we seem to be doing today, especially on the continent of Asia. The contrary view was that we will feel an increasing obligation to be world policemen. There was a correspondingly sharp difference of opinion on the issue of how much money the American public was likely to be willing to commit to international activities. None of us, interestingly enough, expected a very massive increase in armament expenditures. One view held that there would be enormous political pressure to reduce armament expenditures, while the other considered that they were likely to remain at the present level. This would, in effect, constitute a marked decrease in the arms burden as national income goes up, which is already happening with strategic weapons. This latter view would expect R & D expenditures to remain at levels comparable to those today and expenditures for limited war to remain high.

This same difference in views is reflected in expectations regarding foreign-aid programs. All of us expect foreign-aid programs to continue, but there was controversy about their scale and the degree of resistance to them. Some felt that the public may well come to accept foreign aid as a moral obligation—perhaps with religious views as the basis for that conviction. Those members of the group expected a great increase in foreign-aid expenditures, including under these expenditures a very large amount for what might be called the charity feeding of the world. Others in the group stressed the negative effects of this kind of aid as distinct from economically defensible investment aid. The amount that can be reasonably invested is, of course, critically dependent upon whether we are going to be investing in China or not. We had no clear consensus on what the orders of magnitude of foreign aid were likely to be.

The group talked of the range of possibilities for the change in the character of the Communist countries. The most optimistic situation we could conceive of in our discussion was a Soviet regime committed to a rapid reassociation with the West. This would involve very large-scale exchanges of persons, educational exchanges, a big increase in foreign trade. Russia would probably not be willing to become dependent on the West for food, but to some degree perhaps it might. We could conceive of a situation in which there would be a Chinese regime which would orient itself very strongly toward the United States for economic aid—perhaps against the Soviet Union, perhaps not; it would be smarter if it succeeded in doing so without antagonizing the Soviet Union. We explored this optimistic picture to some degree, but did not discuss, at any length, what an extremely anti-Western type of regime in the Soviet Union or China might be like.

We did not adequately discuss the possible ideological movements in the world in the year 2000 and their implications. This may in itself be significant. There was some reference in our discussion to possible new Fascisms and to the possible erosion of Communism within China and the Soviet Union. We did not discuss, and I think we should have, the kinds of ideological movements that might or might not arise in the developing nations.

The group also touched on the future of foreign trade. We talked, for example, about the role of the United States as a food supplier to the world. How many hundreds of millions of people can the United States feed, and is this to be a gift or to be paid for? If Russia opened itself to the West and was engaged in large-scale trade, it might advantageously sell machinery and similar products and import food, as Herman Kahn pointed out. This possibility is becoming a kind of lure in Europe and the world.

We could not talk about any topic without reference to the probable population movements in the year 2000, the possible effects of the pill, IUD's, and other contraceptive devices, and the significance of public attitudes as to whether or not these will be accepted. These issues are closely related to the food problem. There was some discussion of the extent of immigration and its significance.

Technological innovations may make a difference in international relations in the next thirty-five years. We identified a few innovations that might be in use by that time. Desalination, which may be thought of as a special case of the effects of cheap power, may have significant effects. Improved fertilizers and similar developments could change the food-population balance by affecting agricultural productivity. Weather control would obviously create needs for international cooperation. We talked a bit about biological warfare or cheap and easy equalizing weapons. Finally, among the technological innovations, we considered cheap communication and transportation. Large aircraft carrying five hundred passengers would make massive tourism a reality over large areas of the world. There might be cheap long-distance telephone calling ($1 or $2 to call Europe or remote places), direct satellite broadcasting that could break into the reception systems of all countries of the world, and so on. We concluded that this kind of contact, which has complicated effects, does make a profound difference.

DANIEL BELL: For the next report, Christopher Wright on the panel on intellectual institutions.

CHRISTOPHER WRIGHT: Our group recognized that a great deal of intellectual life is not institutionalized. Many important influences in our intellectual life come from the family and other institutions whose principal function is not intellectual development. Nevertheless, the specific intellectual institutions in our country are of increasing importance. They are a vital resource and have to be treated as such. We agreed that the leading universities, numbering probably no more than fifty and quite possibly considerably fewer than that, are the core of the institutionalized intellectual life in this country. We have to build from that proposition, recognizing, however, the need to resolve a number of paradoxes.

One paradox has to do with quality. In general, universities are on the frontier, ahead of other institutions; yet in almost any specifiable area there are likely to be industrial or governmental units, or individuals who are ahead of their intellectual counterparts in any university. The universities seem to be particularly weak in such areas of cultural development as the fine arts and literature. Yet in the future we shall probably have to rely less on other institutions to help maintain and nurture our cultural life. The formal intellectual institutions will have to take greater responsibility not only for stimulating cultural activities, but for insuring a level of common understanding sufficient to provide the basis for communication about cultural subjects.

Another paradox is the scope of universities. They should strive to be universal, and yet they cannot pretend to have achieved this goal. An intellectual institution which limits itself to one area, excluding a priori the possibility of extension to new fields of inquiry, is clearly not viable unless it is part of a university.

Yet another paradox is the scale of universities. Although there seems to be a feeling that universities ought to remain small in order to achieve maximum internal communication, they must be capable of absorbing many new ideas and responsibilities. In terms of numbers, we ought to expect the replication of leading universities, perhaps double the number by the year 2000. Yet, the capital cost of excellence will continue to increase faster than the population and the productivity of the country.

The university should be more responsive to the social needs of the time, and yet it must also be better insulated than it now is so that it can take responsibility for the long-range needs of society.

Clearly universities must be national—perhaps international—in scope, but it also makes sense for them to be integrated into regional associations of complementary institutions, including governmental and industrial, as well as cultural ones.

After considerable discussion and some disagreement, the group concluded that our society must build from the organizational framework of existing universities. Despite our many reservations about existing universities, they are the best we have. We expect the universities to persist, but if they do work to resolve these paradoxes, we also expect that they will be transformed during the next thirty-five years as much as they have been over the last twenty-five years.

To some extent these counteracting forces or considerations can be reconciled. External pressures can be brought to bear on the universities to help them evolve more rapidly. Effective pressure will come from the creation of new institutions to meet new intellectual needs. Universities will thereby come to recognize the needs they eventually must fill. We have examples of this process at work in the creation of Rand-type organizations, the National Laboratories, and new kinds of academies, institutes, and centers of advanced study, and in their impact on university life. These creations must be regarded as transitional institutions. Ultimately they will either be absorbed into university-oriented complexes or go out of existence as the universities find ways to take over their responsibilities and the intellectual skills of their personnel. The group felt it was of some significance that these new institutions lack contact with students and at crucial points cannot provide for career development. No intellectual institution other than the university has the general mandate to nurture the intellect of individuals for varying lengths of time and in different capacities as they continue their development. The university will most probably have to extend its responsibility for such development, possibly through the whole of a man's working career. This seems more likely than does the emergence of institutions which would usurp the university's function with respect to education.

The problem of the university's responding to the so-called knowledge explosion did not seem to the group to be a terribly serious one. Leading intellectual work depends upon an integrating process, and the university need not and should not act simply as a clearing house for more and more information. The multiplication of knowledge, or hard facts, and the distribution of this knowledge were seen more as a routine function for other institutions than as an inescapable pressure on the intellectual institutions.

The role of the university in second-career development was discussed as part of the university's response to continuing education. Multiple careers are likely to become more common and more necessary. Preparation for a second career will require some radical changes in our educational and training procedures, and our intellectual institutions will have to play the key role. This is not a matter of providing refresher courses, or even of retooling individuals who are becoming redundant, although these are very important and difficult responsibilities. There is a specific need to provide people who may be working effectively in one area, but who could also be useful in new areas with new tools and opportunities for coping with important problems that are quite unfamiliar to everyone. Existing institutional mechanisms for such second-career training and placement are not very well developed, and they do not seem adequate to the future need.

The responsibility of our intellectual institutions for the intellectual leadership of the country involves them in relations with a host of derivative or ancillary institutions. We must expect greater mobility of university-type personnel in and out of the universities. From time to time each individual may change the focus of his interests, perhaps as part of his own new-career development, or he may reapportion his commitments to teaching, research, and consultation in and out of the university. Such mobility requires that universities, or at least the intellectual institutions with which they are in accord, have a capability that does not now exist for monitoring and assessing the changing roles of the institutions and individuals comprising the complex network of intellectual activities. On occasion, philanthropic foundations and government agencies may have helped the central intellectual institutions—that is, the universities—to understand themselves better and to cope with new problems and opportunities more effectively. But confusion remains and is sometimes augmented by such well-meaning efforts.

The university must be thought of as a shell somewhat apart from its contents. If it is going to absorb new responsibilities and new kinds of knowledge, it must have mechanisms for selectively shedding some old activities and responsibilities. At least part of the group felt that if new mechanisms could be developed for this purpose, the problem of the university's response to new demands and new challenges could be solved fairly easily.

In considering the question of creating more intellectual institutions on the highest level, the group was concerned about the possibility that rapid expenditure of very large sums of money might not only be wasteful but even deleterious. The consensus of the group was that good can come from channeling more money into intellectual activity only if allocations are assigned with much greater care than is likely to be the case at the present time. We felt, in any event, that the development of intellectual institutions is probably limited by the size of the population. It does not make sense to involve a large percentage of the population in the life of our central intellectual institutions. Only a small percentage can be directly involved in the most advanced intellectual activities at any given time. A large amount of the money that now seems to be going into education is really supporting secondary or derivative enterprises. The group felt that lower-school and most high-school education may have its own urgencies, but that these should not be confused with the needed priority attention to our central intellectual institutions.

There is some evidence of a useful distinction between efforts to support higher education and efforts to identify and support intellectual institutions because they are pioneering institutions and not just because they are part of the system of higher education. In this connection, the group discussed the distinction between private and public institutions. Members

agreed that the conventional distinction is now rather irrelevant. The intellectual institutions of the future are all likely to be public in that they will be dependent upon public funds. But unless they are also private in the sense of having considerable autonomy over the ways in which they tackle problems and develop disciplines, they will not be able to perform the function of central intellectual institutions. This does not mean that they need have equal autonomy in their choice of problem areas or the disciplines they will develop. But once the priorities of the institutions are established through a process of interaction with other institutions, it is of vital importance that the intellectual institutions have autonomy over the ways in which they tackle their areas of inquiry and develop standards.

DANIEL BELL: We turn now to Martin Shubik and ask him to talk about what is probably the most comprehensive topic —those changes that affect the traditional values and rights of individuals in human society as well as the life cycle and personal choice of the individual.

MARTIN SHUBIK: Our group met to cover the alpha and omega aspects; we were the catch-all panel. We covered four basic questions: (1) population; (2) the possibility of controlling behavior by chemical, electrical, and other means; (3) genetic changes; and (4) values and political and economic institutions.

Several of us were shocked by a number of statements on population from our colleagues. For example, in infant mortality rates the United States seems to rank eighteenth or nineteenth from the top, but sixteenth or seventeenth in death rates. Given our conception of the United States as "the country with the finest, fanciest medical care in the world," these figures seem to be somewhat shocking. We questioned whether these figures were closely related to the social and medical problems of urbanization.

The projections about key groups are of interest. It seems that by the year 2000 the aged are not going to be nearly so large a percentage as some of the popular writing has indicated. Between 8 and 10 per cent of the population will be over 65. The Negro population will be somewhere in the range of 11 to 12 per cent, and intermarriage will probably not make too significant a change in these figures. This percentage will be a great deal smaller than it was in the United States in the year 1800 when the figure was around 19 per cent.

Another interesting feature was the change in the pattern of family size. The poor will not be having more kids. After about one hundred and fifty years the trend has started to go in the other direction.

Other topics concerning population that we discussed were degeneracy, and the possibility of inherent biological limitations to the length of life and the length of active life. The members of the panel technically able to answer these questions concluded that there do not appear to be any such limitations. Mechanical means of death are now in the top three or four levels of killers. In a society in which people are able to live longer and are more healthy, the mechanical means of death might become the number-one killer. Already, for example, certain trees, the sequoia in particular, only get killed mechanically.

We explored possible changes in the distribution of population in the United States. The country might consist of a series of megalopolises with great stretches of open land in between. This observation immediately raised some specific political questions, such as the possibility of fifty rotten-borough senators from places like Nevada and the Dakotas, since there will be a goodly number of states with few residents.

We then turned for a while to the problem and importance of social indicators and the difficulty in obtaining them. Wilbert Moore said that one encounters difficulty getting decent indicators on sex, religion, or political participation, and governmental institutions are just not set up to obtain them. They do not dare gather information on such issues, and the question remains as to how we are going to obtain these.

We then turned to the possibilities of changing behavior. The group contended that one cannot expect much in terms of genetic change by the year 2000. On the other hand, we felt that it was very important to consider new legal institutions or other institutions as ways of social control. Because there are distinct possibilities that behavior-influencing drugs may be produced in fairly routinized research processes, we must determine what our attitudes are going to be toward the drug companies putting these out and the societal controls over such companies.

The cheery subject of the possibility of a universal plague was also interjected. This comes back to our previous self-congratulations on how fine and healthy the U. S. looks at the present moment and how much medical science has advanced. There is one catch—communications have also advanced, and the methods of spreading plague or other undesirable agents are rather good. A fertilizer, for example, may have unfortunate consequences that would not be discovered for a while, but if it is a really good fertilizer, it can get on all fields everywhere in no time flat. One might wish to limit the application of new drugs, fertilizers, or like agents to certain areas before going overboard and releasing them for general, widespread use. The group also contemplated at this particular point the possibility that these sorts of effects cannot be got by straight-line projections. One does not have very many points on the curve to do a straight-line projection for these sorts of things; you just have to tackle them.

Lawrence Frank led a discussion on the interaction between the society type and the personality type. I personally feel that we did not really have an opportunity to explore this topic in the depth that we would have liked.

We closed by discussing the political and economic philosophies more or less implicit in a democratic and free-market structure. We touched on some of the inadequacies of the formulation of values for a democratic society and a competitive market. One of the foci for this discussion was the conventional assumption of the individual as a more or less rational informed mind. We asked what assumptions we are willing to live with concerning the electorate's informed awareness and its capability to make economic and political discernments. The sheer number of governmental bodies in the United States today brings up this issue. (In one community in Minnesota, the voters elect persons to fifteen different levels of government—from district sanitation commissioners to the President.) It also arises in relation to the nature of economic assets. According to my crude measures, around 30 per cent of the assets in the United States are in houses, automobiles, and personal effects. The remaining 65 to 70 per cent are held in two sets of fiduciary relationships—either by corporations, which hold around 30 to 35 per cent, or by the government, which holds the remainder. In the last analysis, the wealth of the country is owned by the entire population, but at least 70 per cent of the assets are held in trust with a few individuals making the decisions. In light of these features, one has to ask very definite questions as to the viability of market forms and voting processes. The market mechanism works rather well under a set of reasonable but highly limited conditions—the less the public good, the better the market form. The fewer the jointly-owned assets, the easier it is to design a decentralized market system to handle the procedures. But when you have more and more communal need, and social decisions have to be made, the market is less viable.

One of the great charms of the eighteenth- and nineteenth-century utilitarian politics and economic philosophy was that if the world had looked that way, almost everything would have worked out. Unfortunately the world does not look that way, and some lovely theoretical concepts have to bite the dust. The group felt there was a distinct need for rethinking questions concerning political and economic values and the possibility of constructing institutions to obtain them.

DANIEL BELL: Thank you very much. The last report will be by Leonard Duhl on domestic and political institutions.

LEONARD DUHL: To discuss the adequacy of political systems, we must know something about the challenges facing current institutions, and then decide how these social and political institutions should be modified. Because of the nature of the problems we are facing—whether they be in foreign aid, defense, social and human services, the city, natural resources, life style, or transportation—we must concern ourselves with the *process* of development over the next twenty-five to thirty-five years.

In order to look at this process, the group on domestic and political institutions focused on two areas that typify the much broader problems discussed thus far—the cities and the medical and human services. Up to now, most responses to these problems have been immediate rather than comprehensive and systematic. In medicine, for example, the real problems encompass not just treatment devices, but the training of personnel, the delivery of service, and the interrelation of medical programs with other programs.

Various means have been used to effect change in the political system—for example, the pressure group and the political party. Thus, we discussed likely changes or modifications in political parties—whether one party or a new set of arrangements will evolve; whether the effect of reapportionment in the states will begin to develop into a new kind of alignment in the community. (This is one of the areas we felt to be in need of critical evaluation.)

We have gradually moved into a period of the "professionalization of reform," to use Pat Moynihan's term. The professionals' response to crises has affected the ways in which our institutions and government cope with problems. The "professionalization of reform" has led to a certain nonpartisanship toward some issues which has affected the roles of the political parties.

Our discussion group was quite concerned with the irrationality of the public's response to problems. These irrationalities have expressed themselves in many ways—in the John Birch Society, in the campaigns against fluoridation, and so on. As more and more information becomes necessary to the planning of programs, there will be an ever widening gap between the planners and the people affected by the programs. The latter group will increasingly find themselves either unable to understand the information they do get or responding irrationally because of the lack of such basic information.

With this as a background, we began to question the adequacy of our current structures—federal, state, local, or metropolitan—to deal with the problems at hand. The Federal Government must begin to modify its function so that it is increasingly in the business of providing funds and consultation, as well as serving as a catalyst to stimulate changes both in other layers of government and in the private sector. Whether the problems are as narrow as medicine or as broad as the cities, the changes in the way of dealing with them must take place not only in government, but throughout our whole society.

On the local level, there may be much more concern with the day-by-day problems—the quality of life, the development of services, and the development of specific standards of performance. If the Federal Government becomes a stimulant to enhancing the process of planning, it is clear that there will be parallel changes at the state, regional, and local levels. Thus, in order to get a perspective on *over-all policy*, if one contrasts the federal role in terms of the provision of money with the local role in terms of the provision of services and activity, it becomes clearly evident that the Federal Government must involve all the people in the local community in the evolution of the policy. Yet, these policies will have to be created on a nation-wide basis in order to develop some sort of coherence.

Our group became intrigued by the kinds of leverage the Federal Government would require to initiate some sort of coherent developmental process in any of these areas of endeavor. Because the Federal Government has at its disposal great sums of money, the whole budgetary process by which money is allocated, standards are set, and goals are moved toward becomes a critical issue. In both the Federal Government and the state and local governments, the problems of the existing bureaucracies become very important because bureaucracies die hard and have great difficulty changing.

How can we best change these institutions so that they will think quite differently? There are many exclusively concerned with solving particular problems, rather than with treating the complex spectrum of problems. Hopefully the local bureaucracy will change as increased information becomes available to the community, and as increased numbers of people become aware that they can be effective on the local level. We felt that there will be a marked increase in the processes of government in the local community; that the increasing information

available to local governments may very well improve their efficiency; and that these local governments may begin to attract a very different type of person than they have to date. It was the general impression of the group that there will be a proliferation of new kinds of governmental arrangements dealing with specialized problems such as air pollution, water, and transportation.

Several issues may have to be confronted in the local communities, and faced fairly quickly over the next thirty-five years. The race problem will continue to be with us, as will the need for a sense of community in which people can participate. The latter will probably be solved as we begin to develop New Towns, either outside or within the currently existing cities. The people themselves will participate in the definition of what these towns will be and how they will function.

DANIEL BELL: Thank you. I hope that we will not dispute particular points dealt with in any of the small group sessions, but rather consider how the major conclusions relate to one another. There seems to be agreement that there are certain kinds of problems that can be handled only on the basis of long-range planning. One must necessarily think in terms of twenty-five- or thirty-five-year cycles in order to deal with these problems adequately. The problems of population and the rebuilding of cities cannot be handled within any short-run period. We have talked about Reston and the other new cities; it turns out that in Reston, beginning from scratch and with a completely new area, it will take some ten years to house seventy-five thousand people. In six years, ten thousand people have located there, and it will probably be another four years before the figure reaches seventy-five thousand. It takes fourteen years to train a doctor, beginning with undergraduate education. The expansion of medical services—the development of new hospitals and new kinds of training—is, therefore, another long-range problem, as is the very slow process of mediating between different countries and seeing how international institutions can be strengthened. The distinction between the rich and poor nations in terms of aid and trade can only be thought about in terms of long-range cycles. The regulation of biological experimentation and the kinds of legal, ethical, and moral problems posed by such experimentation are, again, not momentary issues.

These are clearly problems involving a twenty-five- to thirty-five-year cycle, and we must begin to budget for these long-term cycles. The federal budget, however, is not constructed to allow for much long-term commitment. People do try to deal with these problems but rarely in long-range terms. I am not talking about blueprints; nobody assumes that a blueprint is possible for such a cycle. But there needs to be some degree of sophistication about anticipated consequences—and possibly unanticipated consequences—so as to allow for side-effects. We should, therefore, try to identify the kinds of steps that would enable people to deal with these problems and to think more accurately about the rates at which the consequences will work themselves out.

This leads to the third and probably the most shadowy of our considerations—namely, the kinds of demands that will be generated by specific groups of people. What kinds of demands will be generated for services, housing, and so forth? What kinds of political expression will follow from the strength of these demands? What will be the rates of diffusion and the changes of scale?

I do not think I am, in any Procrustean way, pressing this frame upon the discussion; it has emerged quite naturally from the reports of the different groups. I am curious to see what other frameworks people have evolved as they have listened to their own panels and to these reports.

HEDLEY DONOVAN: In both the papers and the discussions, I have been rather struck by how seldom particular names of people appear. Eugene Rostow has reminded us that Hitler and Lenin influenced enormously the course of history, though I think he implied that the appearance of their personalities was a deviation from some otherwise more orderly pattern. In a lot of the matters we are discussing, our main modest disclaimer must be about our inability to foresee who these people will be, rather than about the general difficulty of looking ahead thirty-five years. I could sketch a fairly orderly model of impersonal

forces, factors, and trends that theoretically should have a predictable influence on the course of communications media over the next twenty or thirty years. I suspect, however, that some schoolboy, now fourteen years old, whose name I do not know, is going to conceive of an idea in 1981 that will have more influence on what communications are like in 2000 than anything that I or my colleagues could logically project from today.

DANIEL BELL: The effort to predict should lead us to identify more accurately the variables which must be combined for social change to take place. Anyone with a match must have inflammable material to start a fire. Many times there are inflammable people around, but no inflammable material for them to ignite. No one can predict the character of the inflammable agent. One can, however, consider the extent to which a society may become more and more technocratic, more and more rational, and so generate more and more irrationality, since people do not often understand the sources of change. David Riesman touches on this theme in his paper on meritocracy. Although one cannot predict the appearance of the person who can utilize these irrationalities in some charismatic way, one can try to assess the degree to which frustrations may be generated, the degree to which certain demands cannot be fulfilled within the system, and the degree to which certain kinds of irrationalities may burst out.

HEDLEY DONOVAN: In other words, what may be broadly accessible and slightly predictable is whether our society is evolving in a way that is favorable to the appearance of matches.

DANIEL BELL: In all these cases one would have to assess both positive and negative dimensions. I would assume, for example, that American society is, oddly enough, probably more disposed than many other countries to the appearance of men with matches for one very peculiar reason. In the memorandum I wrote for the last meeting, I spoke of what I called the "loss of insulating space." The history of labor violence has shown the tremendous degree of heat and political force generated by labor disputes without having the overtones of change. In thinking about that, I was struck by two very simple comparisons. In 1893 there was a tremendous amount of unemployment and rioting in different American cities. General Jacob Coxey, as some of you may recall, started out from Massillon, Ohio, to march on Washington; by the time he got there, he had a straggly army of four hundred people left from the tens of thousands who had started out from different parts of the country. In 1893 a man started out with tens of thousands and ended up with only four hundred in Washington. But in 1963 Martin Luther King called for a march on Washington, and a quarter of a million people poured in because we now have very rapid bus and air transportation. This causes a new kind of permeability in the political system that was impossible before.

HEDLEY DONOVAN: We are still on two different wave lengths. You are speaking of incendiarism as being constructive.

DANIEL BELL: It is both constructive and destructive. Martin Luther King is a model of the incendiary who can mobilize people in an extraordinary way. The ability to mobilize masses is now even more likely and more possible than in previous times. There is more flexibility in the mobilization of people, and it has a potential in both directions. Curiously enough, even though the society is becoming more technocratic, there is a greater possibility of mobilizing people in the system where the issues are sharp and dramatic. I think, therefore, that society is becoming more fragile and more open to community conflict.

HEDLEY DONOVAN: Is our society developing in a way favorable to the emergence of highly creative individuals who have specific names and faces?

DAVID RIESMAN: I would like to comment on what Hedley Donovan has just said. Tocqueville pointed out that in a democratic age historians would be deterministic because of their egalitarianism. They would not think of great men as moving history; that would be unfair. This is tied in with John Gardner's comment about anti-leadership patterns, and

you see it developing in the ablest, most sensitive, most intelligent youngsters.

THEODOSIUS DOBZANSKY: I would like to pose some questions on a very closely related topic which concerns education, the universities, and the treatment of the elite. How do you pick the elite? What happens to the nonelite, and what sort of educational opportunity will be provided for them? It is fine to speak about the best universities, but what about the worst? What about the people who do not go to universities at all?

CHRISTOPHER WRIGHT: Our group discussed, or at least assumed, that university students were now selected and grouped with too much regard for their anticipated performance within existing intellectual institutions and with too little regard for their potential in a changed world. The main problem as we saw it was to create a more viable and fully enriching relationship between these intellectual institutions and society. If this could be done, many problems of selection would diminish in importance. Selection procedures are now of concern because people feel there is a mismatch, that there are good people who have no good and suitable places in which to develop. One solution is to loosen the structure of intellectual activities without losing the advantages of structure.

EMANUEL PIORE: We should also consider intellectual imperialism. This hits both the developing countries and the underdeveloped countries. The Science Foundation started a development program at our universities; one third of the professors come from England, even though England faces the problem of the expansion of higher education. We are draining their manpower, and they have less ability to produce replacements. We take the brightest kids from Korea, from India, even from Taiwan, give them an intellectual opportunity here, and then they do not want to return. The reasons are quite apparent. The United States has become the intellectual center of the world—the center of the arts, the sciences, and economics. The brighter kids in the world want to make their careers here.

I would also like to add that the technological question has been mishandled;

you can predict what is going to happen technologically. You are investing in experiments to make it happen. You also know that you are not going to replace the New York subway system, even though people have great schemes. It would just take too much money.

DANIEL BELL: From my talks with various people, I get the impression that technological prediction is not so easy. One cannot predict a new discovery or often even the uses to which new inventions will be put. No one yet knows about the future of the laser—about the kinds of use it will have or the range of this use.

EMANUEL PIORE: Let me tell you what I mean by the range of technological prediction. Satellite communication within the next thirty-five years will replace our present means of long-distance communication. Data transmission via satellite communication will change the way we live. It takes eight years to develop a new airplane. Technology's appearing in the market place is a slow process.

DANIEL BELL: Yes, but that is a question of diffusion of technologies already tested and developed. There are two brilliant studies on this subject by Ed Mansfield and Frank Lynn for the National Automation Commission which show that there has been a shortening of diffusion time of new technologies. Predicting the diffusion time of technological developments is very different from predicting surprises or breakthroughs in technology.

EMANUEL PIORE: One is not looking for surprises, but for the diffusion times.

ROGER REVELLE: I would like to follow up on some things that have been said. Intellectual imperialism is another way of describing what Lin Piao calls the conflict between the cities of the world and the countries of the world. The problem is how you keep people down on the farm once they have seen Paris.

EMANUEL PIORE: You cannot sweep them under the rug in our international relations.

ROGER REVELLE: Of course you cannot. But this is really the problem of urbanization on an international scale as opposed to the older rural society. Another very important thing is the effect computers will have on government. When government begins to use computers extensively, the nature of the democratic process and governmental control will be profoundly affected. This will be even more important than the development of cities. As governments get more and more data about citizens and the relationships among citizens, the power balance between the individual citizen and the government will change rapidly. As you move toward international data collection, you will get a powerful trend toward intergovernmental co-operation. This may, in fact, be a reason for an international government that collects taxes and exercises control.

DANIEL BELL: Do you mean this also in terms of the threats to privacy of persons?

ROGER REVELLE: It is a fact that the changing nature of data handling and data processing is bound to have an impact on privacy. The evolution of organisms can be thought of metaphorically in terms of larger and larger nervous systems, a larger and larger degree of data handling and control because of the ability to handle data. This is what you mean by a man as opposed to a lower mammal—he has a much larger data-handling system. The same thing may happen in society. The trend may be toward greater expenditure on data gathering, storage, processing, retrieval, and the use of these techniques for command and control. By the year 2000, it may be a completely different world.

WASSILY LEONTIEF: We have been concerned with the possible interrelation between the separate points that have been brought up.

There are the technological possibilities and the rate at which they can be realized independently of limitations imposed by available economic resources: What can we do if we decide—without an eye to cost—to try some new things?

Then there are economic limits. These constitute, of course, an over-all problem of society—in some instances, of the world, according to the extent to which one area or country is ready to transfer a product or a resource into another.

There are also the institutional problems of organization. Dan Bell mentioned what kinds of demands there will be. The word *demand* can mean many different things. It can be simply an ideal diet for a society—how many different kinds of goods will be produced. The crucial point, however, is the conflict of interests among the various groups in society. Sometimes there is a real conflict in the sense of the limitation of total resources.

We discussed the problem of cities, for example. It was suggested that the great needs of the center-city areas might be satisfied by redistricting the limits of cities and using federal subsidies. We need subsidies only because we have let the centers of cities deteriorate to such an extent that we are very badly hurt. Things have reached the state that it is now difficult to put the subsidies into the system.

If someone tells us that something is good for the society, we should inquire further and ask: For whom is it good and for whom is it bad? A discussion of the institutional arrangements might become meaningful on this basis because institutional arrangements have two functions—the straight management function, which is essentially a problem of communication and information, and the political function, which raises the problems of penalizing, redistributing, cajoling, compromising—in other words, questions of conflict and of power.

STEPHEN GRAUBARD: The last comments have made me think of the distance we have gone from the time the first working party treated this topic. At that time it was seriously proposed that we not concern ourselves with the international situation at all. In almost all the comments that have been made, I have become increasingly aware of the crucial role this international aspect plays in what appear to be simple domestic problems. Certain things we do internally have foreign repercussions because of our position in the world. Emanuel Piore raised the questions of our dependence on foreign personnel and intellectual imperialism. The interrelation of the domestic and the international is still too little considered. We live in professional units where some of us are experts on foreign affairs and others experts on domestic affairs.

HARVEY PERLOFF: The group that discussed educational institutions did not cover what seems to me to be a rather important area—the ways in which these institutions relate themselves to national policy, which may have a direct impact on both their intellectual life and its products. National science policy, for example, has a tremendous impact on the intellectual institutions. What does an intellectual institution do about national science policy? One thinks of the national science adviser as being a kind of response, but this is obviously a rather thin reed for such a tremendous problem. We have not gone very far in this particular direction.

The premise here has been that intellectual life is going to play a very large role—almost a dominant role—in all activities in the future. Since many people are involved in intellectual life in a democracy, and even those who are not directly involved are affected by it, we should be thinking about appropriate representation of intellectual institutions in our political system.

This is but another interface between institutions and national policy. How do you get people who think fruitfully about such interfaces? The example of the science adviser suggests that there is not enough serious thought about this situation. This issue would arise no matter what kind of "integrating" rubric you tried to get.

ITHIEL POOL: There is an interesting point of contact between Roger Revelle's remarks on the impact of the computer on government and Hedley Donovan's on the role of leadership. Donovan cited Hitler as an unpredictable individual event. In 1919 Max Weber pointed out in an essay on "Politics as a Vocation" that the role of charismatic leadership was far more important during that era than it had been in other times. He feared that society's democratic values would be destroyed by the impact of demagogic leadership and mass movements during the next decade. If he had come back in a decade and a half, Germany would have been under Hitler. He had not predicted Hitler as an individual, but the environment was there, and he predicted the result.

In much the same way, we ask ourselves what we can say today about the possibilities of leadership in the year 2000. A number of things can be said thanks to mass media, television, and the computer. I would suggest, and I am certain several people will want to jump on me for this, that one of the impacts the computer will have on government will be a strengthening of top leadership and a weakening of the bureaucracy. The power of the bureaucracy today rests in its monopoly of information. There is, for example, a vast bureaucracy performing employment services; unemployed people must thread their way through this bureaucracy. The institution of large data-based information-processing systems to perform this function would certainly strengthen the policy-maker at the top who makes major decisions as to how the system should be operated, who should have access to the information, and so forth. It would also strengthen the power and increase the choices for the people at the bottom of the system who use the employment services.

In general, one would expect to see the weakening of intermediary organizations and the increased establishment of a direct relationship between the leader and the population. This would merely be a continuation of the pattern that has obtained since Roosevelt's fireside chats. Added to this are the methods of management control made possible by the computer which strengthen the hands of the McNamaras at the top. The computer will facilitate strong top leadership in its struggle against the organization which it nominally controls but which the top leader is normally fighting.

DANIEL BELL: Can I push you on one question? You did a study which became famous because it was enshrined in a novel in which computers were used to make certain predictions about voter behavior, and this information was then presumably at the service of a leader who wanted to manipulate public opinion. In one of the panel discussions it was asked whether there is a possibility of increasing the manipulability of people in the society. The older fear was about the use of mass media for manipulating people; now with the Pool simulation, we could consider to what extent the computer increases the manipulability of people in society. What would your response be to that?

EMANUEL PIORE: I basically disagree with the premise that we are getting rid of middle management.

ITHIEL POOL: I am not proposing that we will get rid of it, but that we shall relatively reduce its impact.

EMANUEL PIORE: When you go to American Airlines and buy a ticket, do you have a greater rapport with Mr. C. R. Smith or with the agent? The whole thing is completely mechanized.

DANIEL BELL: We have two different issues. Ithiel Pool was pointing out that within the Pentagon or American Airlines you are increasing the span of control which the top can exercise.

EMANUEL PIORE: What kinds of control do you want in the Pentagon? How much more do you want than you get with computers?

DANIEL BELL: That is the point Ithiel Pool was trying to make.

ITHIEL POOL: It is not a question of face-to-face business relations. Computers have an information-processing function, and information can, of course, be used for control.

DANIEL BELL: The issue here is not the computer *per se* but the possibility of its being used to manipulate larger numbers of people. Just as the fireside chat and radio introduced a dimension of rapport which gave a man a very different relationship to crowds than he had had before, being able to simulate opinions and to know which way opinions might go can also change the relationship.

ITHIEL POOL: The computer should not be confused with analytic systems that may use a computer. It is analysis that gives control. What you are saying is that the power of social science is going to be so great that it will enable the masters of it to manipulate the public. One can leave the computer out of that statement entirely, be it true or false. The computer itself may make a small contribution to increasing control, but that seems to be mostly an illusion.

HERMAN KAHN: The 465L system, which is the control for SAC, eliminated middle management. No one in the Air Force is out of business; perhaps the air-base commanders are half out of business. If this had been a private company, they probably would not have put it in because middle management would have protested too much. Certain decisions depend upon having detailed information on the spot. When the information can be codified, which is not always the case, the man at the top can make decisions that previously he had to delegate. On the other hand, if you have a bunch of clerks adding figures, and you change them to programmers, you increase their influence. Programmers make managerial decisions. It depends on the situation whether the middle people are making more or less managerial decisions.

I also want to comment on the question of immigration. I think this is going to be one of the central issues that will come up. I have just come back from a trip abroad. In Israel, for example, about a third of the faculty at the Chaim Weizmann Institute told me of the offers they had had elsewhere with salaries of $27,-000, and they make about $5,000. Something like one tenth of the graduates of the Technical Institute in Haifa leave Israel.

In the kind of society we are talking about, moving from one country to another is not a wrenching experience; you are not changing your culture—you may change your language, but that is all. By and large, big cities around the world look alike. But the going wage rate in the United States is roughly four or five times what it is elsewhere. You have all kinds of shortages in the United States because you have priced out of business the medical doctor in the hospital, the repair man, the garage mechanic, and so on.

There are going to be enormous possibilities for people to improve their condition and for the hospital, the garage, the drafting firm, or the landscaping firm to improve its competitive capability by importing inexpensive foreigners. These pressures will presumably be reflected in counter-pressures. I am not sure what will happen here, but I will bet that the immigration will be selective—that is, you will have half a million people a year coming into the United States, and they will be the cream. This does not mean, as the Europeans think, that the United States is depending upon this importation, but it does mean that we are benefiting; we are getting a subsidy from the rest of the world. This is a subsidy that is not too important to us.

FRED IKLÉ: I was stunned by Wassily Leontief's remark that we may not have so much that is new. There are a few problems that are new in the sense of not already being in the news media; also, there is the problem of popularizing the problems that have already been identified. Let me illustrate this. When I studied demography in Chicago in 1946 and '47, I felt that there was a serious population problem, as most demographers then felt. One day I read an issue of *Time* magazine and was very much annoyed because it denied that there was any such thing as a population problem and ridiculed persons like Osborn and Vogt who said there might be a discrepancy between the growth of resources and people. It is very interesting to recall when the population problem became a news-media problem. When James Reston joined the Population Council in 1961 and began writing editorials, the whole news media started on the problem.

We may have left out certain problems because we are not exposed to them daily. We might, therefore, consider the extent to which the news media make the public receptive, so that when you light the match, as in the march to Washington, there will be a response.

The problem of the legal system is one issue that is just raising its head, being somewhat stimulated by the things that are going on in Great Britain now. The role of the scientific community has been mentioned. There may be others, but I find it very hard to think about them. All the problems on our list are in the news media.

DANIEL BELL: It is true that while many of the problems we are concerned with are mentioned in the news media, one of our purposes would be to regroup them so that we can see latent interrelations that are not always so manifest, to take items that arise as "news" and put them in a larger conceptual framework. The "braindrain," as Herman Kahn suggested, can be related to the increase in lateral mobility in society. The new kinds of technology that are developing, the rise of an international scientific community, and the growth of universities also increase lateral mobility. What are the consequences for any society as lateral mobility begins to increase? Does it create new ties? Does it lead to a mingling of values, or what? All this suggests that our final session ought to deal with the modes of integration, the interfaces of ideas, of "impedance matchings," and the general frameworks.

working session two:

THE NEED FOR NORMATIVE STATEMENTS

DANIEL BELL: In dealing with the reports of the working groups, I raised three topics: the omissions, the interfaces between themes, and a coherent organizing framework. I have scrupulously resisted imposing any frameworks from the start in order not to impose any premature closure on the group. I do think, however, there is a framework emerging.

Someone once asked me what kind of Commission this is, and I said it is a pride of lions. The problem of getting a pride of lions to move collectively is sometimes difficult, but we have been moving. We must ask at this point where the Commission itself should go from here. My own thinking has always been in terms of an open-ended procedure. Questions as amorphous as those we have been treating need a considerable amount of thought before they can be given any definition, particularly if we try to identify problems that have a twenty-five- or thirty-five-year cycle. I have never assumed that there would be a specific format before the Commission. I have assumed that the idea of looking at the future would spread, although I have been quite surprised at the rapidity with which the idea has caught on.

If one thinks of the future work of our Commission, several possibilities arise. A fairly simple one would be to continue in this fairly informal manner with no set time for meetings. When we feel that we have defined enough problems and want to bring people together to discuss them, we can do so and still keep it open-ended.

Another possibility would be to organize small working groups of a few persons who would meet regularly to explore in greater detail the various questions that have been raised here. Certain of the questions posed in relation to the intellectual institutions, values and rights, and the political structures need a tremendous amount of work.

One of the things that I have always deplored is that when things get published, they appear in final form—all neat and clean—and no one understands the struggle involved in changing one's mind as one goes along. Students, in particular, never get a sense of an intellectual process; they only get a book that tells them what has been found out—or maybe how it was done, in retrospect. My feeling is that if this is to be a project of substance, its history is as germane as the final outcome.

Some people have suggested that this become a permanent Commission—with members coming in and others moving out. I do not know whether one can prejudge an organizational form of this kind. I do think, however, that institutes or sections of institutes for the more systematic study of the future will build this kind of long-range thinking into their projects. Institutes set up to deal with area studies—science policy, city planning, international relations—will undertake work that sensitizes people, in either a formal or an informal way, to these needs.

These, then, are the two areas open to discussion: the intellectual problems of the Commission—omissions, interfaces, frameworks—and the outcome of the Commission's work.

DAVID RIESMAN: I have a hangover from the earlier discussion that bears on some of the remarks on the power of the government. Roger Revelle commented on the computer adding power to the government, tying into the theme so common in our ideology of impotence in the face of the larger and increased powers of the government, which are great enough in many spheres of life and death.

It is characteristic of such discussions as ours in this country to forget that we fought a Civil War. It very seldom even lingers in our consciousness of the future. Perhaps it is as far behind us as the revolution that deposed Charles I in the seventeenth century is behind the British. Yet I keep doubting it; I keep feeling that our society consists of a series of interlocked deterrents and that by no means all lie in the government in power.

I would like to know how it was that General DeGaulle was able to subdue the OAS, which had infiltrated the police department? How is it that the National Guard from Mississippi will kill Mississippians if necessary? Why is it that the telephone company is not able to control its Mississippi operators who give out the unlisted telephone numbers of "niggerlovers" who are being besieged by obscene night phone calls, who change their numbers, and who the next day find that the number is again in the hands of the besiegers? It seems to me that McNamara's military control, to which reference was made earlier, is by no means firm. The suspicion often crosses my mind that every time he closes down a base he has to give General Westmoreland another division, or the Navy another carrier. We greatly underplay the degree to which we are still a decentralized, chaotic, anarchic society in which the government has extraordinary powers in some spheres, a kind of plebiscitary or Populist power. There are, on the other hand, sabotaging, deterring powers in a very complicated interrelationship. The future is more opaque, more chaotic perhaps than our general thinking suggests when we see only the mechanisms of control, intimidation, and power and not the mechanisms of local sabotage and deterrence.

ALAN PIFER: I was particularly interested in the discussion that apparently took place in the group that Leonard Duhl reported on and which dealt with the process of national planning. This is an issue that needs a great deal more thought and exploration. I got the impression that the group had formulated the problem mainly in terms of the role of the Federal Government and the manipulation of the federal budget, but I assume the discussion must have been more sophisticated than that. In our kind of society—in which many of the important decisions are not made at the federal level, but are diffused throughout the society to other levels of government and to the private sector, both nonprofit and profit-making—this issue is central. What is the process by which we are able to formulate not federal but national plans? Are there new devices—interstate compacts would be one kind—through which we can take this longer-range approach on some of these problems that can only be thought about in thirty- or thirty-five-year terms.

DANIEL BELL: In one of my memoranda I argued that many of our problems do not derive from capitalism, but from the fact that we have become a national society where changes of all sorts have immediate impact, economically and otherwise, on all other parts of society. Another proposition, developed in our panel, is that our society is becoming increasingly communal. This goes back, in part, to the point Martin Shubik raised in the report of his panel—namely, that there are two types of goods in a society: individual goods and communal goods. There are those goods that are divisible among people and on which people make their own choices; and those goods that are not divisible—nobody can buy his own share of clean air. There is an increasing number of things that require communal purchasing. The theoretical problem Martin Shubik raised is how you know and assess communal goods, how you make a social choice. There is ultimately no public mechanism, no social accounting scheme, that gives you a sense of social cost and enables you to know whether certain things should be done communally.

When there will increasingly be things in the society that must be done communally, how do you handle the bureaucracy without multiplying the federal role? How do you allow for diversification, for groups starting things they want to do? This does not mean that government has to do it. The function of government would primarily be to set national standards where necessary—for example, in the housing industry, in national funding. The operative elements would have to be some mixture of public-private, local-regional.

In the next thirty-five years this is going to be one of the great new areas of social exploration. What new forms will be developing? The proposition we put forth was this: If you assume, for example, an upgrading of the middle-class style of life, and more and more people have higher education, people may not want to have the government do things for them. In many areas, they may want to get the resources to do them

themselves. Communal groups—the local PTA or whatever—might want to organize some activities of their own and handle something where there is a real communal need. Increasingly this has been an aspect of the poverty program, which was handled very poorly. They were moving toward the idea that there should be new social forms that develop some kind of community initiative, take over certain kinds of functions, so that everything is not done from the top down in a centralized bureaucracy.

There is one further grave problem. The very fact that more and more problems will have to be solved politically will increase community conflict in the future. The market is an impersonal mechanism for success or failure. If more and more issues are settled in City Hall, the pressure point will become more visible. When the political mechanism has to make the allocative decisions—where industrial plants should be located, who gets contracts, what part of a town a road should go through—people will organize more readily to affect decisions. And more direct conflicts will emerge.

These issues were explored in a very quick, tangential way. I am not sure we have an orderly set of schemes for you along this line, but I do think the question raised is one of the most crucial ones. This has also been one of the central calculations of Leonard Duhl at the Institute of Mental Health. Perhaps he will add something to this.

LEONARD DUHL: The group kept coming back to the question of how to move toward a *fully participating democracy* in which people are able to participate up to the level of their skills, to make decisions that affect their own lives. We are not talking about the development of scientific mechanisms completely separate from the society which has to implement these mechanisms, but about how to integrate planning as an ongoing activity.

I think there should be a major shift in some of the current notions about planning. To this day, the bulk of planning is a blueprint handed down, rather than developmental planning which involves people in the process of getting things going. The theme again is the tying-together of action with the planning process. One can go even further and say that this involves the whole *education process*. When you start talking about educating society, you are really talking about educating people to be future-oriented.

MATTHEW MESELSON: I would like to comment on the general mood of our report, starting with something that Wassily Leontief mentioned. A substantial amount of the development in other countries will depend on what goes on in this country. What happens in this country will be very sensitive to what the public demands. What people ask for depends, of course, on what they think possible. If our report confines itself to forecasting trends, it will have relatively little effect on what the public thinks is possible. This brings up the question of the audience to which our report should be addressed. It could be addressed mainly to planners. In that case, I do not think we would tend to emphasize what is possible because we would assume that planners already know this. I would rather see our report give substantial emphasis to the range of possibilities that lie ahead and address itself rather broadly to the interested general public.

A potent way of speaking to the public is to impart information that is not widely known and is impressively different from what is generally thought; this kind of information is communicated quickly among individuals in society. If, for example, you tell an American citizen that he lives in a country with rather poor health standards compared with those in many other countries, he will be surprised. I was surprised when I learned it. I thought I lived in a country with one of the highest health standards in the developed world. I did not realize that our relative standing had changed since World War II, and that not only the Scandinavian countries but also Britain and many continental European countries are well ahead of us now. We have not improved very much since World War II, while they have. Most Americans would be surprised, and their natural response would be to say, "Let's change that."

If one talks only of various trends and does not try to speak to the public, but solely to planners, one will not influence an objective circumstance that we can

change—namely, what people demand. I hope we produce a report that describes clearly what the opportunities are.

DANIEL BELL: You give me the occasion to stress a point I have made only implicitly. The American Academy is part of the international scholarly community, and a group of this sort has a real persuasive force. It can exercise a moral persuasion based upon its intellectual authority.

GARDNER QUARTON: I would like to follow up on this. Would it not be possible to divide the purpose of this group so that at least a piece of it did what Matthew Meselson suggests. A lot of the thinking about the international sphere and about the reorganization of government seems to suggest that we are planning in the same way as one would be planning for a war. It sounds as if we are planning to help the United States, instead of being devoted to helping everyone.

The second point I would like to make stems from what I think was the relative lack of success of our panel meeting, reported on by Martin Shubik. This failure had nothing to do with the topics discussed. We were given areas in which very little planning has gone on, and we spent too much time thinking about answers to questions and too little time elaborating further questions and sorting them. I wonder if something further should not be done in this area because I really feel that we failed. The one major exception was Roger Revelle's very valuable material on population. This seems to me to be the basis for any further discussion of the problems that will be facing different sub-populations at different times in the future.

DANIEL BELL: For four years, I have had experience with a group of somewhat different character, the French group called *Futuribles*, organized by Bertrand de Jouvenel. While it does not have a Commission, it does hold conferences and has created an international community of the persons who have participated in or contributed papers to it. They have now assembled about one hundred papers, most of them published in French. They began by going all over the lot—

papers on the future of various countries or on specific issues. They started out with what was familiar and then moved to other areas and began to see new relationships. It is difficult to tell the exact point at which you begin to do the most useful classification. I tried at one point, after about fifty papers had been issued on prediction, to do a sorting ["Twelve Modes of Prediction—A Preliminary Sorting of Approaches in the Social Sciences," *Dædalus* (Summer, 1964), pp. 845-80]. It was not the best kind of sorting device, but it was a first attempt. You can take the second step—which Gardner Quarton proposes—only after you have enough thrown in so that you can look at the ingredients and begin to separate them. This has been, in part, the attempt here. Without any predetermined form, which would have been the worst way to proceed, we have tried to work from the natural history of the process and to see what it is going to do. It may not go. I would not say that we have failed, nor that we have succeeded. We are still working our way through.

GARDNER QUARTON: I did not mean to speak in a pessimistic way. We brought up in many different ways the kinds of things that have been mentioned a number of times about the nature of the life of the individual. Still, we never got to the core of what the life of the individual in different sub-groups would probably be like and what kinds of factors would influence it, and to integrate this with what the other groups were doing. It seems to me there is at least a potential for this kind of thinking.

DANIEL BELL: You are right, and this is our next step. We must try to get a few working groups started on the specific issues. I hope that we may be able to do so.

ROGER REVELLE: We have come back to what we were saying at the first meeting of the Commission. There are really three kinds of forecasting: the projection of trends, the working out of the consequences of models, and the working out of normative forecasting—what you want. I myself am very sympathetic with Matthew Meselson's plea for the latter. Perhaps we should divide ourselves more or less into groups that would like to work on what we want and those that would like to work on what will happen on the basis of models or what will happen on the basis of trends. Let me mention, again, the carbon-dioxide problem. On the basis of trends, one can say that the carbon-dioxide content of the air will increase about 25 per cent by the year 2000. Normative forecasting might indicate that you ought to do something about this—namely, find ways of modifying the climate in a direction that will oppose the effect of the carbon dioxide. You cannot go much further than this now because we do not know what carbon dioxide will do. You can, however, go one step further—you can say that there are a half dozen different ways in which the climate could be modified, at least one of which would probably counteract any possible effect of the CO_2. What is then needed is experimentation on how you do this job.

DANIEL BELL: If you take your trichotomy, I think you will see how we have been moving along this way. Herman Kahn and his group have been doing a lot of work with trends. At this session, prompted by Wassily Leontief and others, we have begun to see the kinds of integrated frameworks that can be established. I am not sure we can ever get a complete model, but the turn of this meeting seems quite different from the first one. At that one, we began with Karl Deutsch and Herman Kahn on trends. Then we began to assemble baselines which other groups could use for their studies. We are now trying to see if we can pull up some integrated frameworks that will become the bases of models, whether this be the postindustrial society, the communal society, or whatever. Out of these frameworks would come, it seems to me, the normative questions and how we think they should be answered.

ROGER REVELLE: I am only saying that, as in so many other fields of science, you can do two different things simultaneously. You can start the normative thinking even before you have worked out all the trends or all the models. The issue of mortality and disease is a very good case in point. We already know what would happen to average life expectancy if you reduced heart disease, cancer, or accidents by 50 per cent.

ROBERT BOWIE: I would like to endorse what Matthew Meselson and Roger Revelle have said. You can approach this as essentially an intellectual exercise, in which case you have certain sorts of frameworks or efforts to perceive or conceive the future. If, however, you think of it in terms of action, you only need to have enough integrated frameworks to know that certain things are going to be problems and are going to require action in a certain direction. If you are trying to influence what happens, you want to be sure that you have priorities so that people will start paying attention now to some of these problems. In any large-scale enterprise, if you try to figure out all the things you are going to do before you decide to do them, you will never do them. What you have to do is decide your direction; a group of experts —if there is one—will tell you how to get there once this is decided. That is the essence of the determination finally to give the Negro equal rights. You do not figure out all the ways you are going to do it; you say you are going to do it, and then you get to work and find out how. Many of these issues ought to be dealt with now rather than neglected. You do know broadly the direction you want to go. You must give the programs enough priority so that you can apply resources, thinking, and manpower to getting them under way. Part of the trick is bringing these things into the political sphere so that you can get people to devote resources and attention to them, even though they are in competition with things that are more urgent in a limited sense.

DANIEL BELL: You are perfectly correct. But there are two things that are important to keep in mind. One is that there is another group of the Academy, called "1976: Planning the American Future," which is trying to proceed more directly along the lines you suggest because there is a much clearer sense of what the problems are for this shorter time-span. By taking specific areas like education, health, and urbanism, they are trying to make concrete proposals and

cost them out. We are trying to see whether we can imaginatively grasp problems of which we are less aware. In other words, are we really sure we know what the real problems will be in terms of a thirty-five-year or longer-range period? Take, for example, the Rand study, which asked a number of different experts to make a series of projections on scientific breakthroughs, changes in automation, and in the international system, with fine decimals put on them in terms of probable time period. The difficulty with the study was that each area, almost each prediction, was discrete, without any context or any specification of how one applies to another, what comes first, and what really might be more of a prime mover. If you look at the list of scientific or technological breakthroughs, you are left stumbling because you do not know how it is going to hold together. I agree that we are not going to get a neat systems model of the sort you can get in biology, but we can still explore a bit more the whole question of what will be coming up.

ROBERT BOWIE: That is what you mean when you say something has been identified as a problem. You have projected certain trends, deduced certain relationships which you can call a subsystem, and concluded that certain consequences of that are undesirable, so to speak. Finally, you have also ascertained that you can, at least in part, affect these undesirable consequences by action. You are not just talking about projections of the date at which some particular scientific thing will happen; that is only a beginning. You are asking what the significance of this happening will be, how it will affect individuals and society.

HAROLD ORLANS: It would be very helpful to have some kind of report on the range of subjects that this 1976 group is working on. We could see where we are simply duplicating. I have a feeling that very little we have given attention to is in the order of another fifteen or twenty years beyond 1976. I have the impression that our view of the problems of the year 2000 is largely a projection of the problems that we have been living with for the previous three months. Occasionally we have done better. I could state some of the longer-term issues that seem to me to be very fundamental; some we discussed in a very concerned way in our working group were dropped by the wayside here—for example, the notion of what is desirable to hold a society together, the notion that society might be fragmenting. We have a paper that says, on the contrary, that violence is decreasing; although there is some danger of a sudden plague, panic, or mass movement, we are basically more united, more of a national community. It is my impression that the range of problems we have been dealing with are all visible at the moment. I suggest again that it would be helpful intellectually to try to segregate those that will be more fundamental and that we will have to face in the year 2000.

STEPHEN GRAUBARD: The 1976 group under the direction of Carl Kaysen and Jerome Wiesner met originally last spring [1966]. We have working parties on education, health, urbanism, conservation and natural resources, industry, and the arts. This group, using good Marxist terminology, is essentially working toward a series of reforms.

HAROLD ORLANS: Task forces?

STEPHEN GRAUBARD: No. The 1976 Commission derives from the government experience of both Jerome Wiesner and Carl Kaysen which suggested to them that government task forces look at much briefer periods than ten years. They said they wanted something between a task-force report and utopia. By their definition, the Commission on the Year 2000 is the more utopian group.

HAROLD ORLANS: The distinction, then, is not essentially in the time-span of the problem but in its intellectual character. We are dealing with an order of problems that we still cannot get our hands on in any clearly defined sense of what action to take, whereas they are dealing with problems that are already so defined that you can put your money into this agency or that.

STEPHEN GRAUBARD: What they want to do is define specific areas and consider the concrete changes they would recommend without first looking at what

it is going to cost. When they have an agenda of the concrete changes proposed in the various areas, they want to see whether they can attach a price to it. The third part of the process is to conceive of the ways in which the program can be sold.

DONALD SCHON: I wanted to pick up Robert Bowie's comments. The emphasis on action is the exciting thing to me. You are saying that if it's possible to determine what it is that we see needs to be done, the problem is to make that clear in a report and to give the report to the proper group. You added very quickly that one may not know the proper group, indeed there may not be any proper group. Maybe the criterion for this sort of issue should be: Where there is no available, easily definable socket into which to fit the action plug, stand back two or three paces and ask how you set in motion a process that later on would have the effect of enabling somebody to do something. That kind of question is not a meta-question in the usual sense of meta, but it is a backwards question. How do you set in motion a process that will enable somebody to do something constructive about a problem whose outlines we cannot see?

Two such problems that have come out of the discussion are the creation of adaptable federal, state, and local institutions capable of coping with problems as they interface, and the development of more effective measures involving media and intellectual institutions by which ideas get into good currency.

The one model on how you might do this that keeps reappearing is that you produce a report and you sow it in that sense. There is, however, another model that focuses more closely on our own process here. Robert Wood is a member of the Commission, he is at M.I.T., he is working on the city; then he goes and becomes Under Secretary of Housing and Urban Development where he is not apt to work on the city and its public-systems problems. His involvement with the Commission is brief because the Commission is brief; but the Commission could have provided him with insights into the problems of public systems in the city, which are also interconnected with issues about CO_2 in the atmosphere and the control

361

of population, on the one hand, and those about mental health, on the other. As Robert Wood moves into a position of action where he has yet to work on the problem, he takes with him such insights. This kind of influence is more important than any future paper that emerges. If we see ourselves as a group of people, some of whom are mobile in the direction of action, it could be enormously important, although this is not a traditional model of how you affect action.

This also raises the question of failure mentioned by Gardner Quarton. Alan Pifer and I had a similar reaction in our meeting; I will bet others did too. I would take it as one test of our being on the right issues that we encounter a very high degree of failure; failure in communication and coping intrinsically characterizes our efforts to come to grips with the problem. The right problems are precisely the ones on which you do fail when you attack them with the tools currently at hand. So, in a sense, our tolerance for failure of this kind and our own efforts to try and live through the kinds of involuted mosaic processes that we need to go through in order to understand these complicated issues are absolutely critical. The ability to live through it and demonstrate it and produce a result, and then to be able to go on and produce another as a kind of demonstration is also, I think, extremely important. I had the sense that Dr. Quarton was agreeing to that in what he was saying.

GARDNER QUARTON: Yes. I thought of it more in terms of recognizing where we were in a sequence. I see our group as being very early in the series of events that I think have to take place. We failed in the sense that we were not so far along as we wish we were.

HARVEY PERLOFF: It is extremely useful to see that there are three types of approaches, as was mentioned before: approaches based on trend lines, on models, and on normative statements. It is equally useful to appreciate that these are cumulative in a sense or interacting. Just as we use trend lines, and empirical data generally, to develop models, so we need to rely on trend-line analysis and model-building to evolve useful approaches in the normative realm. Let me illustrate.

We have been concerned about economic problems in the United States for a very long period of time. There has been worry about having unemployed people, financial crises, gold outflow. But while such concerns were long-standing, it was not until two things had happened that we could do something about them. First, we had to be determined as a nation that we really wanted to do something about unemployment. This is very important because full employment cuts through things like gold and money. The amount of money available dominated the thinking of many groups in the nineteenth century, but we were able to get away from that and focus on our concern about people and employment. Second, we began to develop empirical data that enabled us to understand the business cycle; good solid models indicated that the business cycle works in a given way and that you must intervene at various points through monetary and fiscal policy and other controls.

In other fields, normative goals are difficult to establish because we do not know what we really want. Take the poverty program, for example. We are concerned with a great many things under the general heading of poverty, but we have not clearly defined them. Is the goal getting everyone to be self-supporting? Is the goal to get three thousand dollars a year to everyone? I intuitively feel that this is not what we want; that we are trying to do something about how people act as human beings. If they are to have a sense of worthwhileness, it is not just because they have been given checks. Moreover, we do not know much about getting people out of the complex poverty cycles they seem to get into.

It takes at least as much concentrated work to deal with normative elements as with the trend-line and model elements. Getting people to see what they want is tough. It takes a bit of doing to clarify objectives. If we are trying to develop policy and programs on something about which we do not have clear enough objectives, we must deal with such matters experimentally and build in evaluative mechanisms.

HERMAN KAHN: It is a very good point that many problems, but not all problems, can be handled by approaching them from a policy point of view. That is, however, different from recommending a policy. If I have lousy data, I organize them and then look for better data. I want to separate that from the mobilizing of people. As a step in doing research, using lousy data is okay; as a way of mobilizing people, it is not.

MATTHEW MESELSON: Perhaps my point was not quite understood. I was not saying that we should make normative statements, but that we should outline the opportunities; then people will decide what they want.

CHRISTOPHER WRIGHT: This discussion has shifted from the problem of intellectual structure to the problems of the Commission itself. An earlier comment suggests that it is important to stress the need for adequate structures to settle conflicts of interest as well as to recognize that there are conflicts of interest. As Harvey Perloff pointed out, there are also conflicts of values. In everything the Commission studies, it should be recognized that however trends or models or possibilities may develop, certain established values which have been in conflict may become reconcilable, whereas others may conflict for the first time. There is a need for us to understand and to encourage other people to understand the importance of structures that will help us settle and avoid conflicts between different values.

As for the procedures of the Commission, a lot of the discussion demonstrated how little we know about the relation between facts and public policy. The models that are used to suggest how public policy is affected by public knowledge of facts are not adequate. Those of us who have spent time studying the particular relation between scientific fact and public policy have learned that it is very difficult to discover just what it is about a particular fact that serves as a handle for developing public policy. Public policy obviously will not emerge from facts alone. Solutions to the CO_2 problem are, perhaps, a little more obvious than solutions to most other problems, but not very much so. The Commission can and should spend more time thinking about public policy in general terms before it assumes that action is

called for. Members who are concerned about norms should consider reports and ideas about political structures, since these govern the processes and acts which concern them. The Commission itself would be engaged in a self-contradictory process if it were to go ahead assuming that it knows enough about political structures and how these effect political actions.

DANIEL BELL: I would like to comment on the idea that if people know the facts, they will act. I worked on the Automation Commission to find out what was happening to the rate of change of technology. We finally got the numbers straight. To take the crucial figures: productivity in the U.S. from 1909 to 1947 averaged out to 2.4 per cent a year. Since 1947 it has been about 3.4 per cent a year. A portion of the latter increase is due to the high agricultural productivity which had been averaging about 5 or 6 per cent a year; industrial productivity came to 2.5 per cent. Those are the numbers, but what do they mean? The labor people said the recent figures represented a substantial increase, while the industry people said it was not very great, and the academic people said it was moderate. The labor people wanted to say substantial in order to emphasize the need for action. The industry people, fearing such action, said they were exaggerating the meaning.

This is a common process we all face; we get numbers or knowledge, but reaching agreement as to what the statistic means can be difficult. Certain people have certain kinds of interests, not just interests in the immediate sense of dollars and cents, but interests in rhetoric. How, for instance, is the trade-union leader on the Commission, who for the last five years has been stampeding his members with horror stories, going to turn around and say I have been a fool? He must at least say that the situation is not so bad as I had thought but it is still terrible. This is saving face in a very important way. He has a commitment to his rhetoric, and unfortunately he went overboard in this case. Getting the numbers can also be a difficult technological problem in some cases. But, then, someone has to find the adjective to describe the change if there has been a change. Perhaps we need a logician, but even if a logician had been present to give us an exact notion of the difference between moderate and substantial, I am not sure this would have been agreed upon by the people on the Commission.

MATTHEW MESELSON: I think there is an important difference in the way we look at these problems. You want to study the structure of the problem; I do not—I want to do something about it. There are many areas in which information given to the public will create demand and produce action. For example, if you tell people they could have a train that would go from there to there twelve times a day and would cost so much, they may decide they want to take advantage of the opportunity. They must, however, know that it is possible. This could often be done in the field of public health; but I agree that general statistics on productivity would not produce much effect on the public.

DANIEL BELL: Let me relate another illustration about knowledge and action. Carl Hovland, a man who bridges the social sciences, did an experiment on how you persuade people to change their minds. The experiment was beautifully done and is worth reading [*Communication and Persuasion* (New Haven, 1953)]. His problem was to chart the effect of different kinds of anxiety on attitude changes. He took matched groups of students and confronted them with the dangers of failing to brush their teeth. One group was told about pyorrhea, bleeding gums, cavities, and other horrors that would result from the failure to brush their teeth. He got authorities to give the students a high-anxiety treatment. The second group was simply told that if they did not brush their teeth, it would have certain consequences. He used a purely rational approach with this group. For a third group, he used an approach between these two—a mild-anxiety message. Those in the first group changed their habits right away, but three weeks later they fell off completely. The prospects were so terrifying, the anxieties so high, that after an initial change, they repressed the idea. The rational group showed a mild change of habit, but the middle-anxiety group showed long-run

changes that lasted longer than the others.

Getting people to change their minds is not just a matter of giving them facts. You can give them facts in different ways, and the different ways you give the facts yield different results. Curiously enough we know very little, other than Carl Hovland's experiment, about why people change their minds or what the continuing effects of these kinds of appeals are.

ROBERT BOWIE: Your argument might suggest that it would not have been possible to achieve the reforms of the past because people did not adequately understand the mechanism by which they were achieved. Quite a lot of reforms have, nevertheless, taken place over the last two hundred years by rather crude methods. We all want to improve the understanding of how people are brought to change their minds. But, meanwhile, do you sit around and do nothing because the instruments you have to use are not fully understood or are too blunt? I think not: You proceed, as was suggested, along a number of fronts. We were suggesting that the Commission define for its purpose the effort to establish a priority on things that may otherwise have low priority because they are in the distant future.

WILLIAM GORHAM: I think our chances of causing desirable change would be improved by examining closely the way changes occur. We have been concentrating, and properly so, on examining new institutions for change because we are concerned about the future and have reached impasses in trying to do certain things. Many things can change. Most will change in the same ways they have changed in the past. It might be useful to look carefully at some directed kinds of changes that have occurred in the past twenty or thirty years and at the instrumentality of these changes. There might be some instruction on how one can progress from normative statements to decisions on how to move in these directions.

FRED IKLÉ: I fully support Matthew Meselson and Robert Bowie's point that we should be concerned about our goals. In my little piece, I go even further and say that we cannot make predictions in a certain sense without having goals in mind. I do think, however, that there is one qualification that has not been sufficiently examined. We do not have to anticipate what might happen or tell people what they should do if they want certain things. We can anticipate what people may want and the fact that values change. It is, perhaps, no accident or a bad accident that we left out ideology in the international panel. Imagine that there might be a movement around 1980, similar to the prohibition movement, for changing the Constitution so that religion would be put back into the government. You might then have a series of Supreme Court decisions similar to the integration decisions; by the year 2000, in the international field, you could have a real problem arising from this.

We are fully aware that we cannot leave out the changes in values, but I think this applies to the other fields too.

ROGER REVELLE: To pursue this a bit further, take the field of education. We have been thinking for the past twenty years that we are overwhelmed by numbers. We have had to build twice as many high schools as we had before. Colleges have gone up by a factor of three or four. If, however, the demographic trends are right, the increase in children over the next thirty-five years will only be about 25 per cent. In terms of education, we will not have to worry so much about quantity as we do about quality. Rather than simply being overwhelmed by numbers, we should build more and better

institutions of higher learning, and pay more attention to the individual student.

DANIEL BELL: I do not think there is any disagreement in principle about the idea of making normative predictions. I would like to say, however, that there is a point at which one can have premature closure as to how you define a problem. Many people feel we should explore more to see if we are only dimly aware of certain other problems. People who envisaged the future thirty-five years ago were sometimes wrong in the way they identified problems. Allan Cartter has pointed out that the recent fear of not having enough college teachers, which began to stampede the whole university system, was wrong. For five years, everybody was dismayed that there would not be enough teachers and felt that we had better accelerate our doctoral programs. Recent studies show that the supply of teachers and new Ph.D.'s has been rising at every single level in the last ten years. Mr. Cartter demonstrates that the government was collecting the wrong kinds of data—these are administrative data-collection problems, and NEA was also at fault.

Once you know with a certain conviction what the real problems are, you can point up the opportunities. One wants to resist a premature closure in which people tend to get on their own hobbyhorses for their own interests and to think there is nothing more to be gained by looking around. One of the reasons for calling this the Commission on the Year 2000 as against 1976 was to yield a longer period of exploration in terms of identifying problems. If we continue in our inquiries without premature closure, we shall all gain.

A Summary by the Chairman

WE HAVE had two plenary meetings, in October and February, and there have been several smaller discussions in between. I list below, in schematic fashion, further areas of work I think the Commission should explore. These can be divided into three parts: Models of Social Change, Further Questions in the Problem Areas, and Normative Questions.

1. *Models of Social Change.* A number of individuals have pointed out (see the discussions by Messrs. Leontief, Perloff, and Revelle in the transcript) that forecasting by trend line alone is inadequate, since such data gives one little sense of the causal factors in social change. A meaningful analysis has to combine the trends in some model that provides a sense of the relationship between the elements and seeks to identify the initiating elements. The effort to construct models of social change is a very considerable one, and probably too academic for our enterprise. Yet if we are seeking to identify sources of problems for the future, we must have some consistent models in mind. Models of social change, it seems to me, have to take into account various kinds of processes. For purposes of discussion, we can indicate three:

> a. Crescive changes. These are long-run, ground-swell changes, largely unplanned by any single source, yet basic to the contours of the society. The most important are the population changes (with consequent problems of age balances and the like) and technological innovations. I find missing in the Commission material speculation on the new technologies and the kinds of consequences they might have. One can compare the probable social effect of the computer to the kinds of changes introduced by the auto or, as Bruce Mazlish has done, compare the meaning of the coming space age to that of the railroad.

> b. Social demands. These are conscious demands by specific social groups for redress in society; the civil rights revolution is the most obvious example in our time. Here one would

366

have to deal with the value system of the society which either accepts or rejects the demands, with the mechanisms of legitimation, the processes of inclusion, the pace of change, and so forth. The extension of welfare services is a second kind of social demand which, beginning with the New Deal, has acted to transform the society. Are there any social demands comparable to welfare and civil rights that will have an equal impact in the next thirty-five years? Can one identify "quality of life" and "participation" as having an equal effect? Which groups will initiate such demands, and what will be the character of their demands?

c. Planned social change. We have only now begun to undertake planned social change on both a national and a local scale. The question of how much planning, and of what kind, infuses the entire scope of the Commission's work.

2. *Further Questions in the Problem Areas.* Most of the papers have concentrated, in speculative fashion, on questions that one may expect to arise by the year 2000. We do not have, as yet, an ordering of questions by importance and likelihood of occurrence. This, it seems to me, is a task for smaller working groups. In reading the transcript, it occurred to me that there are a number of further questions which one or another working group might want to consider.

a. The quality of national leadership. Hedley Donovan raised a number of pertinent questions about the role of the particular individual and his influence on history and society. While one cannot anticipate or predict the individual leader, one can, perhaps, say something about the conditions that facilitate or inhibit the rise of the creative person, the "natural leader," and the mediating leaders of a society.

b. The outlets for irrationality. The comments of Leonard J. Duhl have focused on the continuing problem of irrational forces in the society. What can one do about these?

3. *Normative Questions.* In the transcript Messrs. Meselson, Revelle, Quarton, and a number of others pointed out that the Commission must specify not only "future questions," but what we want to do. This has also been the tack of Lawrence K. Frank who, from the start, has argued for the need of some new "philo-

sophy" that can guide society in the twenty-first century. I agree. Without going into the very specific normative issues with which we have to grapple, I would like to outline some broad areas that should concern us.

To put the matter most baldly—domestically the United States is becoming a *communal* society rather than a *contractual* one. Rights and claims against the community are becoming central. If this assessment is correct, there are a number of important theoretical and practical questions:

> a. Social choice and collective decisions. Economic theory of the neoclassical variety can show how individuals seek to optimize their own welfare. But when joint decisions are to be made, are there clear welfare criteria that justify one choice rather than another?

> b. Participation. If individuals are to feel themselves *in* society, then the scope of participation has to be extended. What are the modes of participation both within the society and within individual enterprises? How does one reduce bureaucracy or at least its hierarchical aspects?

> c. Privacy. How does one maintain privacy, individuality, open spaces, and other aspects which give one a sense of being a person in a collective society?

These questions illustrate the normative issues confronting us. On the international scene, the problems have been spelled out in greater detail: the reduction of the division between rich and poor nations, the growth of regional federations, the creation of national independence and the end of imperialism, the resolution of the conflict among peoples on the basis of color.

June 30, 1966

MEMBERS OF THE COMMISSION ON
THE YEAR 2000

THE WORKING PARTIES: SUMMER 1967

DANIEL BELL
CODA: WORK IN FURTHER PROGRESS

NOTES ON CONTRIBUTORS

INDEX

Members of the Commission on the Year 2000

Summer 1967

Daniel Bell, Chairman
William O. Baker
Harvey Brooks
Zbigniew Brzezinski
Karl W. Deutsch
Theodosius Dobzhansky
Hedley Donovan
Leonard J. Duhl
Dan Ellsberg
Erik H. Erikson
Robert M. Fano
Lawrence K. Frank
Stephen R. Graubard
Charles M. Haar
Stanley Hoffmann
Samuel P. Huntington
Fred Charles Iklé
Herman Kahn
Wassily Leontief

Ernst Mayr
Matthew S. Meselson
Wilbert E. Moore
Daniel P. Moynihan
Harold Orlans
Harvey S. Perloff
John R. Pierce
Emanuel R. Piore
Ithiel de Sola Pool
Gardner C. Quarton
Roger Revelle
David Riesman
Eugene V. Rostow
Donald A. Schon
Martin Shubik
Krister Stendahl
Robert C. Wood
Christopher Wright
Paul N. Ylvisaker

The Working Parties: Summer 1967

Values and Rights

Assuming fundamental structural changes in the society—a greater reliance on national planning, a higher urban concentration of the population, the use of communal instruments rather than the market for social purchases, an expanded professional and technical class—certain major issues need clarification.

The first is the relationship of social choice to individual values. How does one take discordant individual preferences and amalgamate them into a combined social choice? How does society settle value conflicts between groups in the absence of accepted rational guides?

The second question centers on privacy. As knowledge in the society becomes more extensive, as individuals have more and more information recorded about them, as the social sciences become more experimental, how much privacy is left to the individual?

A third question, related to the second, concerns "densities"—not only the mean physical densities that crowd people, but, more important, the "psychic densities" that result from increased interaction, communication overloads, and pressures to respond to novelty and sensation.

The fourth question deals with bureaucracy. If our organizations are staffed increasingly with more highly educated persons, and if research and action are thought to be interrelated rather than separate processes, how do we "break up" the older organizational structures that emphasize hierarchy, specialization, and dependence? Are there new organizational forms that can increase autonomy and initiative?

The Life Cycle of the Individual

This group will focus initially on three questions. The first concerns the psychological readiness of individuals for change. We take it as axiomatic that when our children are adults, they will live in a very different world from that of their childhood, and that the traditional cycle in which a child follows in the footsteps of his parents may be shattered irretrievably. This raises problems about the ways in which individuals are prepared, or fail to be prepared, for a world of change, about the rigidity and compulsion that the social system may still induce, and about cultural patterns that are restrictive. The second question, which derives from the first, is the problem of generations and the differences between them. And the third is the question of irrationality. The spread of functional rationality in a society may increase irrationality in other spheres. Related to this is the growing divorce between the mental orientation required for work and for leisure; this is already apparent among youth and sections of the intelligentsia. The work life is oriented to control, achievement, and the mobilization of energy to specific ends, while the leisure life is becoming increasingly permissive and exploratory.

The International System

The Commission posed four major questions for discussion by this working party: the pace and extent of transnational integrations (for example, regional economic and political integrations, intellectual and scientific international communities); the growing gap between rich and poor nations; the threat of color as the basis of new kinds of intellectual divisions; and the waning and waxing of existing ideologies (Marxism, nationalism, and so forth).

Certainly, the "prediction" of political and, particularly, international events is not possible in any precise manner. Yet in international relations, as in domestic affairs, there are certain structural tendencies whose effects, if not exactly traceable, can at least be identified. These tendencies include, first, the increasing ease of international communication and transportation; second, modernization and societal integration in countries in the process of development; third, the growth of a large number of new international organizations, both functional and intellectual; and fourth, the presence and likely proliferation of weapons of mass destruction.

The working party will discuss the impact of these tendencies on the international system. To what extent will violent conflict among states remain the major threat and characteristic of international relations? To what extent will domestic violence be an important factor in world politics, and what will be the likely reaction of major powers to domestic violence? Will ideologies fade and

373

transnational forces multiply? What will be the nature of the international hierarchy, the role of the small and middle powers, and the areas in which universal international organizations will have acquired substantial authority?

The Structure of Government

This group will first consider, on the basis of changes now taking place, the kinds of problems one can expect to become salient for federal and local governments thirty-five years from now. They might not be different from the ones now before us, except in the change of scale. Thus, it may well be that urban affairs will be a central problem, but that its dimensions will differ radically. Or problems that are relatively minor at present may become much more pressing: the problem of adequate recreational areas and open spaces for a larger population with more leisure, or the increase, in both number and kind, of community conflict. As government agencies replace the market in making decisions that affect individual lives, interest groups may become more fractious in seeking to influence them. And there may also be questions that are completely new. If, for example, the increase in communication and transportation enlarges the potential for direct and immediate group pressures, would we face more open, even violent, assaults on the center of government and the decision-making process?

Considerations of this sort involve a re-examination of the strength of the representative tradition, the amount of tolerance in the society, and the willingness to trade and compromise.

The second issue is the structure of the government itself. How adequate are the decision-making mechanisms in government, and what is the likelihood of strengthening them? Does the spread of rationalized government (for example, PPBS and cost-effectiveness techniques) create growing tensions between the "technocrat" and the "politician"? Is there an inherent contradiction between the concept of "participatory democracy" and the representative mode of government as we know it? Should the states be maintained as administrative units or should consideration be given to new regional governmental structures?

Intellectual Institutions

Three principal areas will be considered: the tension between the apocalyptic and the technocratic orientations now manifest within the intellectual community; the viability of the university,

374

as an institution, to perform many different functions, cultural and economic as well as intellectual; and the relationship of the university, as a symbol of the intellectual life, to industry and other sectors of the society. The premise of this working party is that universities, research institutes, and related organizations concerned with ideas may become the central innovative institutions in a postindustrial society.

In this situation a new kind of American city may emerge with a society and an intellectual life considerably different from any that exist presently. It is hoped that the group will also consider how American intellectual institutions will be affected by new kinds of association with foreign institutions.

Science and Society

An assumption of the Commission is that we are moving into a postindustrial society in which the codification and institutionalization of knowledge, particularly in science and technology, become increasingly important bases of innovation.

The first task of this group will be to identify the social trends implicit in this development and to explore its implications for various social sectors, such as the industrial, governmental, professional, intellectual, and cultural.

Second, the group will devote explicit attention not only to the opportunities inherent in new technology, but also to the ways in which technology generates new problems for society. Until the present, technical innovations have generally been accepted as inherently good and progressive by definition, and the scientific community has tended to think of itself as the major agent of desirable change and social progress. Currently, however, scientists and others who think about science and technology are becoming increasingly aware that decisions about science and technology must be made in the light of their possible second-order consequences—even when these cannot be anticipated—since the disadvantageous consequences of introducing a new technology can at times outweigh the primary expected benefits.

The scientific community may thus become a much more conservative force in society than it has been, or it may adopt an ambivalent attitude toward change, as its institutions, methods, and assumptions become matters of public concern and are altered and controlled to suit the changing social role of science and technology. The third task of the working party will be to investigate this reciprocal effect of society on science and to gauge its implications for the forms of organization and operational procedures internal to the institutions of science.

In the context of these explorations, the group will seek to understand and assess the problems that are raised as society tries to anticipate the effects and direction of technological change.

The Social Impact of the Computer

The computer is essentially a device to increase intellectual power, comprehension, and skill—a device that will enable man to cope with an increasingly complex society. Since the present basic design of the digital computer is not likely to be superseded for one or two decades (computers will, however, be able to do many more things and do them faster than at present), it may be possible to anticipate with somewhat more confidence the development of computer technology than that of other scientific and technical fields. Thus, it may also be possible to anticipate some of the social consequences of the widespread use of electronic intellectual and information systems. Many of the issues that have been raised— privacy, centralization, the creation of a mass society of automatons —need to be reconsidered: It is possible that a computerized society may have effects that are quite opposite from those suggested. It may, indeed, protect privacy better than at present; it may promote decentralization as much as centralized control; and, as it replaces much routine activity that now passes for intellectual work, it may create new problems of identity and the use of freedom.

Biomedical Sciences and Technology

There is little doubt that developments in the biological and medical sciences during the next thirty-three years will raise fundamental questions about the nature of man and society. Research on the structure and function of the brain, the development of pharmacological and physical agents to alter human behavior and states of consciousness, the possibility of the alteration of genes, unforeseen ecological effects of attempts to control specific diseases or environmental problems—all raise new questions about human values and social organization. Until recently it has been possible to regard science as the servant of man and his values; its main function has been the preservation and enlargement of certain basic and recognized notions of human values. Biomedical engineering, however, raises the possibility of substantial changes, intended and inadvertent, in the source of these values—the mind, the nature of human relationships, and the physiological potential of man.

The deliberate or accidental alteration of human behavior or our genetic heritage is a possibility whose consequences can be overstated: The human brain is a complex mechanism that cannot be manipulated easily. The consequences of what may be widely regarded as the possibility of such alteration or manipulation will, however, have important effects on the public perception of science, on the scientists' view of their role in society and their moral responsibilities, and on the structure of the biological and medical professions.

The working party will consider three different types of problems in the biomedical and biological sciences. First, what advances in technology are within the range of possibility? Second, what problems of control and utilization in the area of drugs affecting human behavior are likely to emerge, particularly if we make certain predictions about changes in the social structure? Complex technology will doubtless be subject to control by the scientific profession or the public agencies; some technology with potential for affecting individual or social behavior, or for changing the ecological system can, however, easily get out of control through "leakage" from laboratories, the professions, or social pressures. Finally, the working party will focus its attention on the emergence of a new relationship between the biomedical professions and society as the biological sciences become increasingly concerned with what are, or are regarded as, the central issues of man and society.

The chairman of the eight working parties are "Values and Rights," Fred Charles Iklé; "The Life Cycle of the Individual," Leonard J. Duhl; "The International System," Stanley Hoffmann; "The Structure of Government," Harvey Perloff; "Intellectual Institutions," Stephen R. Graubard; "Science and Society," Harvey Brooks; "The Social Impact of the Computer," Robert M. Fano; "Biomedical Sciences and Technology," Bernard D. Davis and Gardner C. Quarton.

DANIEL BELL

Coda: Work in Further Progress

THE COMMISSION on the Year 2000 has not sought to be comprehensive, taking "the city and the stars" as its cosmos, nor to be a singular, anechoic voice proclaiming a new vision. We have not written a new political philosophy, though one may yet emerge, nor charted new paths for America, though the very enterprise itself—the self-conscious questioning about the future and the effort to look far ahead—marks a distinctive change in the temper of the society.

The Commission has concentrated largely on problems of social change as they are linked to public policy. We have not dealt with "the future of culture," perhaps the most unpredictable of the dimensions of human consciousness, since new directions in the arts are not crescive but "surprises" initiated by individual geniuses. We have not, and it is a neglect, dealt with religion and man's continuing effort to find transcendental meaning amid the contemporary disorientation wherein each individual knows that he can no longer walk in the traditional ways of his father, and that his son will not walk in his ways. And yet such needs remain. For all the "materialism" of Marxism, the most extraordinary characteristic of its adherents—especially in China today—is the need to plunge completely into a cause, to find some common purpose through the movement itself. The new "secular religions" and new cults—whether they be the post-Christian moods of the theologians or the new hedonism of the young with its rites of pleasure and the pursuit of sensate involvement or psychedelic release—are radical changes in the nature of man's emotions and feelings and require explanation. We have not dealt, except tangentially, with the problems of violence, whether through such institutions as the military or in the more sporadic outbursts of the irrational. Yet if American life is becoming at once more organized and

378

more permeable, the potential for such reactive violence is always present. Thus, our efforts have been more prosaic—a positive or negative quality, depending on one's temperament.

We have, equally, excluded the area of space exploration and what these adventures portend for society and for the human imagination. In part this was done because of our concentration on social arrangements, but in greater part because a substantial effort of the American Academy has already been devoted to such questions. The Academy appointed a Committee on Space in April, 1962. It has already published—under the series title "Technology, Space and Society"—*The Railroad and the Space Program: An Exploration in Historical Analogy,* edited by Bruce Mazlish, and *Social Indicators,* edited by Raymond A. Bauer. Other publications are scheduled.

In the autumn and winter of 1966-67 we began Phase II of the Commission's work, an effort that will carry us through the next year or two. Five working parties were set up to continue in greater detail the exploration of five areas which had been mapped out by the Commission: the adequacy of the political structure, the changes in values and rights, the structure of intellectual institutions, the life-cycle of the individual, and the international system. But in reviewing our work we were struck by the absence of any sustained discussion of specific technologies, a neglect which resulted from the effort to avoid the modish fascination with new gadgets and from the belief that the genuinely "new" in science and technology was not easily predictable. Yet we realized that the diffusions of some new technology—particularly the computer and the new biomedical engineering—would wreak important sociological changes in the country. In December, 1966, a one-day conference was held at the House of the Academy to discuss the "future of technology."[1] The planning group stipulated a number

1. The participants were Robert M. Fano of M.I.T., J. C. R. Licklider of M.I.T., both computer specialists; Bernard Davis of the Harvard Medical School, a bacteriologist; Jean Mayer of the Harvard School of Public Health, a nutritionist; Gardner C. Quarton of the Neurosciences Research Program of M.I.T., a psychiatrist; Harvey Brooks, Dean of the Harvard Division of Engineering and Applied Physics; Emmanuel Mesthene, director of the Harvard Program on Technology and Society; S. L. Lida, of International Business Machines, Inc.; Roger Revelle, director of the Center for Population Studies of Harvard University; Walter Rosenblith, of the Department of Electrical Engineering of M.I.T.; Stephen R. Graubard, historian and editor of *Dædalus;* Geno Ballotti, managing editor of *Dædalus;* John Voss, executive officer of the Academy.

of areas in which more detailed work was needed: for example, on computers and the potentialities they create for more decentralized organizational structures and differentiated instruction, as well as the inherently greater threats to privacy and the potentialities for social control; on biomedical engineering and the host of legal and theological issues emerging from the intervention by man into the evolutionary process (for instance, the virtual elimination of infantile and infectious diseases which permits the genetic transmission of inheritable defects). We decided, therefore, to broaden the Commission's work and to create three additional working parties to deal with these questions.

In reviewing this issue, two final reflections come to mind—one on a neglected problem in social planning, the other on the appropriate mode of looking at the future.

If one searches for the source of previous failures in understanding social change, the answer may lie in our only dim comprehension of the "intangible social nets" that make up a society, for it is from this source that we get, in the phrase of Robert K. Merton, "the unanticipated consequences of purposive actions." In our formulations of problems and of policies for solutions, all our efforts are directed to the *manifest* aspects of change; we ignore, or do not understand, the *latent* elements that may be the more significant features. To take an example: When, in an Indian village, we substitute water faucets in each house for the older, more tedious process of drawing water from a well, on the manifest level we have achieved progress. Yet, at the same time, the common well served latent functions. It was not only a source of water, but a center for gossip for women, a "natural" meeting place for young women and young men, a focus for sociability and the informal, casual encounters that every small community requires.

To make a manifest change without being aware of the latent disruptions is to invite strains that the community itself does not understand and that get projected onto extraneous and misleading issues. An issue such as "flouridation," which has riven many American communities, is an example of a dispossessed group's "false consciousness" of the sources of change that have eroded its status and position in the society. And much of the disorientation that individuals feel about the effects of change in contemporary society may arise from the disruptions of underlying ties and latent functions whose existence is never wholly perceived.

The formulation of social policy that seeks to reknit underlying social networks and solidarities as it works toward manifest solutions is, therefore, one of the important intellectual tasks for the social sciences if our goal of "understanding" the future and making meaningful choices is to be realized.

As to a "stance" toward the future—in a remarkable paper, composed forty-three years ago and entitled *Dædalus: Science and the Future*, J. B. S. Haldane, reflecting perhaps his occupational bias, predicted that the next center of scientific interest would lie in biology. He prophesied the elimination of infectious disease, the development of ocean farming for food, the separation of sex from reproduction as a consequence of contraception, and the ability of science to create what he called the "ectogenetic child" as a result of embryo transfer. While many of these predictions were remarkable, others were wrong. The future source of energy, Haldane believed, for he had no foreknowledge of nuclear energy, would have to come from wind or sun.

Yet it is not the quality of his predictions that is of greatest interest, but their temper. In reflecting on the idea of research and curiosity, Haldane remarks: "I fancy that the sentimental interest attaching to Prometheus has unduly distracted our attention from the far more interesting figure of Dædalus. It is with infinite relief that amidst a welter of heroes armed with gorgon's heads or protected by Stygian baptisms, the student of Greek mythology comes across the first modern man."

Men have always sought to be Promethean (witness Marx, for whom Prometheus was a life-long hero). But Dædalus can serve as a model as well, and for this reason. The story is told that when Dædalus was imprisoned by King Minos, and locked in a tower so that he could not escape by land or sea, he invented flight. And when he had finished fabricating wings for himself and his son Icarus, he spoke to him as follows: "Icarus, my son, I charge you to keep at a moderate height, for if you fly too low the damp will clog your wings, and if you fly too high the heat will melt them. Keep near me and you will be safe."

All the rest is exegesis.

Notes on Contributors

DANIEL BELL, born in 1919, is professor of sociology at Columbia University. Mr. Bell is the author of *The Reforming of General Education* (1966), *The Radical Right* (1962), *The End of Ideology* (1960), and *Work and Its Discontents* (1956).

ROBERT BOWIE, born in 1909, is Counselor for the Department of State and director on leave of the Center for International Affairs at Harvard University.

ZBIGNIEW BRZEZINSKI, born in 1928, is a member of the Policy Planning Council of the Department of State. Mr. Brzezinski's most recent publications include *Political Power: USA-USSR* (1964), *Ideology and Power in Soviet Politics* (1962), *The Soviet Bloc—Unity and Conflict* (1960), and *Totalitarian Dictatorship and Autocracy* (1957).

KARL W. DEUTSCH, born in 1912, is professor of political science at Yale University. He is the author of *The Nerves of Government* (1963), *Foreign Policy in World Politics* (1958), *Science and the Creative Spirit* (1958), and *Interdisciplinary Bibliography on Nationalism* (1956); he is also co-author of *Modern Political Systems* (1963).

THEODOSIUS DOBZHANSKY, born in 1900, is professor of zoology at the Rockefeller University in New York City. Mr. Dobzhansky is the author of *Mankind Evolving* (1962) and *Genetics and the Origin of Species* (1937).

HEDLEY DONOVAN, born in 1914, is editor-in-chief of Time, Inc.

LEONARD J. DUHL, born in 1926, is special assistant to the Secretary of the Department of Housing and Urban Development. Dr. Duhl, a psychiatrist, was chief of the Office of Planning of the National Institute of Mental Health from 1964 to 1966.

ERIK H. ERIKSON, born in 1902, is professor of human development and lecturer on psychiatry at Harvard University. His publications include *Insight and Responsibility* (1964), *Identity and the Life Cycle* (1959), *Young Man Luther* (1958), and, as editor, *Youth: Change and Challenge* (1936). His *Identity: Youth and History* is in press.

LAWRENCE K. FRANK, born in 1890, is a social psychologist and retired foundation official now living in Belmont, Massachusetts. He is

382

edited *Essays in Mathematical Economics in Honor of Oscar Morgenstern* (1967).

KRISTER STENDAHL, born in 1921, is professor of Biblical studies at the Divinity School of Harvard University. He is the author of *The School of St. Matthew and Its Use of the Old Testament* (1954), and the editor and co-author of *The Scrolls and the New Testament* (1957).

ANTHONY J. WIENER, born in 1930, is chairman of the Research Management Council at the Hudson Institute.

JAMES Q. WILSON, born in 1931, is professor of government at Harvard University and a past director of the Joint Center for Urban Studies of MIT and Harvard University. He is the author of *Negro Politics* (1960) and *The Amateur Democrat* (1962); and co-author of *City Politics* (1963).

ROBERT C. WOOD, born in 1929, is Under Secretary of the Department of Housing and Urban Development. He is on leave from the Massachusetts Institute of Technology, where he is professor of political science.

CHRISTOPHER WRIGHT, born in 1926, is director of the Institute for the Study of Science in Human Affairs at Columbia University. He is the co-author of *Scientists and National Policy-Making* (1964).

PAUL N. YLVISAKER, born in 1921, is Commissioner for the Department of Community Affairs for the State of New Jersey. Until March, 1967, he was director of the Public Affairs Program at the Ford Foundation. He is the author of *The Battle of the Blue Earth County* (1955), *Intergovernmental Relations at the Grassroots* (1955), and *The Natural Cement Controversy* (1950).

the author of *Nature and Human Nature, Understanding Children's Play,* and *Personality Development in Adolescent Girls.*

WILLIAM GORHAM, born in 1930, is Assistant Secretary of the Department of Health, Education, and Welfare. From 1953 to 1962, Mr. Gorham was a staff member of the Rand Corporation.

STEPHEN R. GRAUBARD, born in 1924, is professor of history at Brown University and editor of *Dædalus* and of the American Academy of Arts and Sciences. His publications include *Burke, Disraeli, and Churchill: The Politics of Perseverance* (1961) and *British Labour and the Russian Revolution* (1956).

CHARLES M. HAAR, born in 1920, is Assistant Secretary of Housing and Urban Development. Mr. Haar is on leave from Harvard University where he is professor of law. He is the author of *Federal Credit and Private Housing* (1960), *Land Use Planning* (1959), and *Land Planning Law in a Free Society* (1959).

SAMUEL P. HUNTINGTON, born in 1927, is professor of government at Harvard University. He has published *The Common Defense* (1961) and *The Soldier and the State* (1957), and edited *Changing Patterns of Military Politics* (1962).

FRED CHARLES IKLÉ, born in 1924, is professor of political science at the Massachusetts Institute of Technology and a faculty associate of the Kennedy Institute of Politics at Harvard University. Mr. Iklé is the author of *How Nations Negotiate* (1964) and *The Social Impact of Bomb Destruction* (1958).

HERMAN KAHN, born in 1922, is the director of the Hudson Institute. From 1948 to 1961, Mr. Kahn was senior physicist and military analyst for the Rand Corporation. He is the author of *On Escalation: Metaphors and Scenarios* (1965), *Thinking About the Unthinkable* (1962), and *On Thermonuclear War* (1960).

HARRY KALVEN, JR., born in 1914, is professor of law at the University of Chicago. He is the co-author of *The American Jury* (1966), *The Negro and the First Amendment* (1966), *Delay in Court* (1959), *Cases and Materials in Torts* (1959), and *The Uneasy Case for Progressive Taxation* (1953).

WASSILY LEONTIEF, born in 1906, is professor of economics and director of the Economic Research Project at Harvard University. His publications include *The Structure of the American Economy* (1919-29, 1941, 1953), and *Studies in the Structure of the American Economy* (1953).

ERNST MAYR, born in 1904, is professor of zoology and director of the Museum of Comparative Zoology at Harvard University. He is the author of *Animal Species and Evolution* (1963), *Systematics and the Origin of Species* (1942), and co-author of *Methods and Principles of Systematic Zoology* (1953).

MARGARET MEAD, born in 1901, is curator of ethnology at the American Museum of Natural History and adjunct professor of anthropology at Columbia University. Her publications include *Anthropology: A Human Science* (1964), *Continuities in Cultural Evolution* (1964), *New Lives for Old* (1956), and *Coming of Age in Samoa* (1928).

MATTHEW S. MESELSON, born in 1930, is professor of biology at Harvard University. In 1963 he received the prize for molecular biology from the National Academy of Sciences and in 1964 the Eli Lilly Award for Microbiology and Immunology.

GEORGE A. MILLER, born in 1920, is professor of psychology at Harvard University. He is the author of *Psychology, the Science of Mental Life* (1962) and *Language and Communication* (1951).

WILBERT E. MOORE, born in 1914, is a sociologist at the Russell Sage Foundation in New York City. He is the author of *Social Change* (1963), *Man, Time, and Society* (1963), *The Conduct of the Corporation* (1962), and *Economy and Society* (1955).

DANIEL P. MOYNIHAN, born in 1927, is director of the Joint Center for Urban Studies of the Massachusetts Institute of Technology and Harvard University. He is the author of *The Negro Challenge to the Business Community* (1964), co-author of *Beyond the Melting Pot* (1963), and editor of *The Defenses of Freedom, The Public Papers of Arthur J. Goldberg* (1966).

HAROLD ORLANS, born in 1921, is a senior staff member of the Brookings Institution. Mr. Orlans is also a consultant to the House of Representatives' Committee on Government Operations. He is the author of *Contracting for Atoms* (1967), *The Effects of Federal Programs on Higher Education* (1962), and *Stevenage: A Sociological Study of a New Town* (1952).

HARVEY S. PERLOFF, born in 1915, is director of the Regional and Urban Studies Program at Resources for the Future, Inc. Mr. Perloff's publications include, as co-author, *Design for a Worldwide Study of Regional Development* (1966), *How a Region Grows* (1963), *Regions, Resources, and Economic Growth*, and, as editor, *Planning the Urban Community* (1961).

JOHN R. PIERCE, born in 1910, is executive director of the Research and Communications Sciences Division of the Bell Telephone Laboratories, Inc. Mr. Pierce is the author of *Quantum Electronics* (1966), *Electronics and Waves* (1964), and *Symbols, Signals, and Noise* (1961).

ALAN PIFER, born in 1921, is president of the Carneg[...] tion. He is also a consultant to the U. S. Agency for I[...] Development.

EMANUEL R. PIORE, born in 1908, is vice president and chief [...] the International Business Machines Corporation. Mr. P[...] member of the President's Science Advisory Commission [...] to 1962.

ITHIEL DE SOLA POOL, born in 1917, is chairman of the Politic[...] Department at the Massachusetts Institute of Technology. [...] cations include *Candidates, Issues, and Strategies: A [...] Simulation of the 1960 Presidential Election* (1964) and [...] *Business and Public Policy: The Politics of Foreign Trade* [...]

MICHAEL POSTAN, born in 1899, is professor emeritus of e[...] history and honorary fellow of Peterhouse at Cambridge Un[...] England.

GARDNER C. QUARTON, born in 1918, is program director of the [...] sciences Research Program of the Massachusetts Institute of [...] nology. Dr. Quarton, a psychiatrist, is affiliated with the Mas[...] setts General Hospital and is a clinical associate in psychiatry [...] Harvard Medical School.

ROGER REVELLE, born in 1909, is professor of population and dir[...] of the Center for Population Studies at Harvard University. [...] Revelle was director of the Scripps Institution of Oceanogr[...] from 1951 to 1964.

DAVID RIESMAN, born in 1909, is Henry Ford II Professor of the Sc[...] Sciences at Harvard University. He is the author of *Abundance [...] What? and Other Essays* (1964), *Constraint and Variety in Am[...] can Education* (1956), *Faces in the Crowd* (1952), and *[...] Lonely Crowd* (1950).

EUGENE V. ROSTOW, born in 1913, is Under Secretary of State f[...] Political Affairs. Mr. Rostow is on leave from Yale University whe[...] he is Sterling Professor of Law and Public Affairs. His publication[...] include *The Sovereign Prerogative* (1962), *Planning for Freedor[...] (1959), and *National Policy for the Oil Industry* (1948).

DONALD A. SCHON, born in 1930, is president of the Organization for [...] Social and Technical Innovation in Cambridge, Massachusetts. Mr. Schon is the author of *Technology and Change: The New Heraclitus* (1967) and *Displacement of Concepts* (1963).

MARTIN SHUBIK, born in 1926, is professor of the economics of organization at Yale University. Mr. Shubik has written *Game Theory and Related Approaches to Social Behavior* (1964), *Strategy and Market Structure* (1959), *Game Theory and Political Behavior* (1954), and

Abrams, Mark, 1
Acculturation, 329
Activism, and predictions, 111–113, 119–120
Addiction, see Drugs
Admissions directors, college, 268–269
Adolescence, socialization of, 25, 26, 58, 228–229; view of nature, 34
Adviser, role of, 154–155
Affluence, 74, 84–86; and life style, 239–240, 272; and meritocracy, 266–267. See also Prosperity
Africa, 24, 26, 36, 58, 311, 316, 340; extension of American influence in, 315, 317, 341; predictions concerning, 320, 321, 322
Aged, 18, 57, 216, 344; emergence of as pressure group, 178
Agriculture, 79, 342; U.S. Department of, 50
Aid to dependent children (ADC), 333. See also Welfare state
Aiken, 301
Air pollution, 10, 17, 27, 65, 157, 160, 161, 329, 359
Air space, and city, 157, 159–160, 161
Alcoholism, 240
Algeria, 322
Alienation, 39, 99; of youth, 55, 299, 231, 233; of core-city Negro, 174; and computer-based education, 261
Alliance for Progress, 331
American Academy of Arts and Sciences, 9. See also Commission on the Year 2000
Analysis, "envelope curve," 129
Anomie, 261
Anti-institutionalism, 229–230, 237
Anti-Irish riots (1840's–1850's), 287–288
Antinomianism, 229

Anxiety, 32, 40, 251–252, 364
Appalachia, 48
Appliances, personalization of, 334
Arendt, Hannah, 270
Argonne National Laboratory, 32
Aristocracy, 265. See also Elite
Arms control, 28
Artificial insemination, 201, 240, 335
Ashby, W. Ross, 182–183
Asia, 90–91, 313, 314; extension of American influence in, 315, 317; Chinese role in, 316
Asimov, Dr. Isaac, 2
Assault, aggravated, 277, 280–282, 285
Associations, professional, 196
Atkinson, Richard, 260
Atomic bomb, see Nuclear power
Atomic Energy Commission, U.S., 2, 192
Atoms for Peace program, 57
Attitudes, 294, 364; middle-class, 28; toward forecasting, 136–138; sex-based, 243
Augustine, Saint, 1, 4
Authority: public, 19; adolescent view of, 229–235; re-establishment of, 235–238
Automation, 24, 25, 31, 59, 66, 130; economic impact of, 41; large-scale, 147; and education, 257
Automation Commission, see National Commission on Automation
Automobile, 3, 23, 24, 69, 145, 278
Autonomy, 29, 52
Avocations, 23
Ayres, Robert, 129

Babbage, Charles, 301
Bacon, Francis, 106
Baker, Russell, 35

Index

Balance of power, *see* International relations

Barth, Karl, 224

Beatniks, 58, 219, 269, 271, 331

Behavior, personal, 39–40; and genetics, 42, 208–209; and planning, 155; control, 205–221; radical change in style of, 241–243; violent, 294; parameterization of, 336

Behavior-control technology, 214–221, 344, 345; and social acceptance, 217–219

Belgium, 312

Bell, Alexander Graham, 301, 306

Bell, Daniel, 22–23, 27, 39, 40, 44, 47, 48, 50, 52, 54, 55, 57, 58, 59, 60, 61, 62, 94; quoted on unknowable, 107; and "alternate futures," 217; on nature and limits of forecasting, 328–329, 338; on identification of variables, 348–349

Bell Telephone System, 307

Bellamy, Edward, 75, 114

Belle Époque, La, 89, 91

Benjamin, Curtis, and "twigging phenomenon," 197–198

Berlin blockade, 311

Bertalanffy, Ludwig, 181–182, 337

Biderman, Albert, 333

Binet, Alfred, 264

Biochemistry, 263, 264

Biology, 28, 29, 200–204, 381; 20th-century revolution in, 178; experimental, 206; automatic principle in, 252–253

Biomedical engineering, 4, 348, 376–377

Birth control, 240, 241; as patriotic duty, 246–247; and *Griswold* case (Connecticut), 249

Birth rates, 26, 35, 144; Negro, 56–57

Blackmer, Allan, Jr., 269

Bohr, Niels, 90

Boston, Mass., 188, 279, 281

Boulding, Kenneth, 84

Bourgeoisie, elite of, 74, 76–77

Bowie, Robert, 361

Brain stimulation, electric, 212–213, 216, 217

Brainwashing, 215

Brandeis, Louis D., "The Right to Privacy," 249

Brazil, 84; role in Latin American future, 316, 330, 340

Breeding, controlled, 209. *See also* Genetics

Broglie, Achille de, 90

Brookhaven National Laboratories, 32

Brookings Institute, 60, 64–65

Brown, Rap, 290

Brzezinski, Zbigniew, 35, 38, 39, 45, 328

Buddhism, 226

Bullitt, William, 246

Bundy, McGeorge, 268

Burckhardt, Jacob, 75

Bureau of Labor Statistics, U.S., 59, 335; and projections of national productivity, 131

Bureau of Land Management, U.S., 160

Bureau of Social Research, Washington, D.C., 333

Bureau of Standards, U.S., 50

Bureau of the Budget, U.S., 271

Bureaucracy, 7, 18, 352, 372; Soviet, 36; centralization in, 47–55; elite, 74, 76–77

Business cycle, 331; and crime, 282–283

California Institute of Technology, 32

Cambodia, 320

Camus, Albert, 289–290

"Candid Camera," television show, 246

Career, 32, 55, 74; and primary occupation, 88; multiple, and university, 188–189, 343

Carmichael, Stokely, 290

Carnegie Corporation, 268

Cartter, Allan, 365

Castroism, 311

CATV (community antenna television), 303

Causality, 149, 154

Centralization, 45–55, 68; political, 5, 7; social, 33, 34; and democratic society, 139, 143

Chaim Weizmann Institute, 353

Character, in meritocracy, 267–268

Chartism, as methodology, 337–338

Chemistry, quantitative, 24

Children, 24, 26, 277, 333

Chile, 58

Chiliasm (life free from imperfection), 2

China, 34, 84, 92–94, 302, 311, 312, 313, 314, 378; predictions concerning, 316, 319, 321, 330 the author of *Nature and Human Nature, Understanding Children's Play,* and *Personality Development in Adolescent Girls.*

WILLIAM GORHAM, born in 1930, is Assistant Secretary of the Department of Health, Education, and Welfare. From 1953 to 1962, Mr. Gorham was a staff member of the Rand Corporation.

STEPHEN R. GRAUBARD, born in 1924, is professor of history at Brown University and editor of *Dædalus* and of the American Academy of Arts and Sciences. His publications include *Burke, Disraeli, and Churchill: The Politics of Perseverance* (1961) and *British Labour and the Russian Revolution* (1956).

CHARLES M. HAAR, born in 1920, is Assistant Secretary of Housing and Urban Development. Mr. Haar is on leave from Harvard University where he is professor of law. He is the author of *Federal Credit and Private Housing* (1960), *Land Use Planning* (1959), and *Land Planning Law in a Free Society* (1959).

SAMUEL P. HUNTINGTON, born in 1927, is professor of government at Harvard University. He has published *The Common Defense* (1961) and *The Soldier and the State* (1957), and edited *Changing Patterns of Military Politics* (1962).

FRED CHARLES IKLÉ, born in 1924, is professor of political science at the Massachusetts Institute of Technology and a faculty associate of the Kennedy Institute of Politics at Harvard University. Mr. Iklé is the author of *How Nations Negotiate* (1964) and *The Social Impact of Bomb Destruction* (1958).

HERMAN KAHN, born in 1922, is the director of the Hudson Institute. From 1948 to 1961, Mr. Kahn was senior physicist and military analyst for the Rand Corporation. He is the author of *On Escalation: Metaphors and Scenarios* (1965), *Thinking About the Unthinkable* (1962), and *On Thermonuclear War* (1960).

HARRY KALVEN, JR., born in 1914, is professor of law at the University of Chicago. He is the co-author of *The American Jury* (1966), *The Negro and the First Amendment* (1966), *Delay in Court* (1959), *Cases and Materials in Torts* (1959), and *The Uneasy Case for Progressive Taxation* (1953).

WASSILY LEONTIEF, born in 1906, is professor of economics and director of the Economic Research Project at Harvard University. His publications include *The Structure of the American Economy* (1919-29, 1941, 1953), and *Studies in the Structure of the American Economy* (1953).

ERNST MAYR, born in 1904, is professor of zoology and director of the Museum of Comparative Zoology at Harvard University. He is the author of *Animal Species and Evolution* (1963), *Systematics and*

383

the Origin of Species (1942), and co-author of *Methods and Principles of Systematic Zoology* (1953).

MARGARET MEAD, born in 1901, is curator of ethnology at the American Museum of Natural History and adjunct professor of anthropology at Columbia University. Her publications include *Anthropology: A Human Science* (1964), *Continuities in Cultural Evolution* (1964), *New Lives for Old* (1956), and *Coming of Age in Samoa* (1928).

MATTHEW S. MESELSON, born in 1930, is professor of biology at Harvard University. In 1963 he received the prize for molecular biology from the National Academy of Sciences and in 1964 the Eli Lilly Award for Microbiology and Immunology.

GEORGE A. MILLER, born in 1920, is professor of psychology at Harvard University. He is the author of *Psychology, the Science of Mental Life* (1962) and *Language and Communication* (1951).

WILBERT E. MOORE, born in 1914, is a sociologist at the Russell Sage Foundation in New York City. He is the author of *Social Change* (1963), *Man, Time, and Society* (1963), *The Conduct of the Corporation* (1962), and *Economy and Society* (1955).

DANIEL P. MOYNIHAN, born in 1927, is director of the Joint Center for Urban Studies of the Massachusetts Institute of Technology and Harvard University. He is the author of *The Negro Challenge to the Business Community* (1964), co-author of *Beyond the Melting Pot* (1963), and editor of *The Defenses of Freedom, The Public Papers of Arthur J. Goldberg* (1966).

HAROLD ORLANS, born in 1921, is a senior staff member of the Brookings Institution. Mr. Orlans is also a consultant to the House of Representatives' Committee on Government Operations. He is the author of *Contracting for Atoms* (1967), *The Effects of Federal Programs on Higher Education* (1962), and *Stevenage: A Sociological Study of a New Town* (1952).

HARVEY S. PERLOFF, born in 1915, is director of the Regional and Urban Studies Program at Resources for the Future, Inc. Mr. Perloff's publications include, as co-author, *Design for a Worldwide Study of Regional Development* (1966), *How a Region Grows* (1963), *Regions, Resources, and Economic Growth*, and, as editor, *Planning the Urban Community* (1961).

JOHN R. PIERCE, born in 1910, is executive director of the Research and Communications Sciences Division of the Bell Telephone Laboratories, Inc. Mr. Pierce is the author of *Quantum Electronics* (1966), *Electronics and Waves* (1964), and *Symbols, Signals, and Noise* (1961).

384

ALAN PIFER, born in 1921, is president of the Carnegie Corporation. He is also a consultant to the U. S. Agency for International Development.

EMANUEL R. PIORE, born in 1908, is vice president and chief scientist at the International Business Machines Corporation. Mr. Piore was a member of the President's Science Advisory Commission from 1959 to 1962.

ITHIEL DE SOLA POOL, born in 1917, is chairman of the Political Science Department at the Massachusetts Institute of Technology. His publications include *Candidates, Issues, and Strategies: A Computer Simulation of the 1960 Presidential Election* (1964) and *American Business and Public Policy: The Politics of Foreign Trade* (1963).

MICHAEL POSTAN, born in 1899, is professor emeritus of economic history and honorary fellow of Peterhouse at Cambridge University, England.

GARDNER C. QUARTON, born in 1918, is program director of the Neurosciences Research Program of the Massachusetts Institute of Technology. Dr. Quarton, a psychiatrist, is affiliated with the Massachusetts General Hospital and is a clinical associate in psychiatry at the Harvard Medical School.

ROGER REVELLE, born in 1909, is professor of population and director of the Center for Population Studies at Harvard University. Mr. Revelle was director of the Scripps Institution of Oceanography from 1951 to 1964.

DAVID RIESMAN, born in 1909, is Henry Ford II Professor of the Social Sciences at Harvard University. He is the author of *Abundance for What? and Other Essays* (1964), *Constraint and Variety in American Education* (1956), *Faces in the Crowd* (1952), and *The Lonely Crowd* (1950).

EUGENE V. ROSTOW, born in 1913, is Under Secretary of State for Political Affairs. Mr. Rostow is on leave from Yale University where he is Sterling Professor of Law and Public Affairs. His publications include *The Sovereign Prerogative* (1962), *Planning for Freedom* (1959), and *National Policy for the Oil Industry* (1948).

DONALD A. SCHON, born in 1930, is president of the Organization for Social and Technical Innovation in Cambridge, Massachusetts. Mr. Schon is the author of *Technology and Change: The New Heraclitus* (1967) and *Displacement of Concepts* (1963).

MARTIN SHUBIK, born in 1926, is professor of the economics of organization at Yale University. Mr. Shubik has written *Game Theory and Related Approaches to Social Behavior* (1964), *Strategy and Market Structure* (1959), *Game Theory and Political Behavior* (1954), and

385

edited *Essays in Mathematical Economics in Honor of Oscar Morgenstern* (1967).

KRISTER STENDAHL, born in 1921, is professor of Biblical studies at the Divinity School of Harvard University. He is the author of *The School of St. Matthew and Its Use of the Old Testament* (1954), and the editor and co-author of *The Scrolls and the New Testament* (1957).

ANTHONY J. WIENER, born in 1930, is chairman of the Research Management Council at the Hudson Institute.

JAMES Q. WILSON, born in 1931, is professor of government at Harvard University and a past director of the Joint Center for Urban Studies of MIT and Harvard University. He is the author of *Negro Politics* (1960) and *The Amateur Democrat* (1962); and co-author of *City Politics* (1963).

ROBERT C. WOOD, born in 1929, is Under Secretary of the Department of Housing and Urban Development. He is on leave from the Massachusetts Institute of Technology, where he is professor of political science.

CHRISTOPHER WRIGHT, born in 1926, is director of the Institute for the Study of Science in Human Affairs at Columbia University. He is the co-author of *Scientists and National Policy-Making* (1964).

PAUL N. YLVISAKER, born in 1921, is Commissioner for the Department of Community Affairs for the State of New Jersey. Until March, 1967, he was director of the Public Affairs Program at the Ford Foundation. He is the author of *The Battle of the Blue Earth County* (1955), *Intergovernmental Relations at the Grassroots* (1955), and *The Natural Cement Controversy* (1950).

Abrams, Mark, 1
Acculturation, 329
Activism, and predictions, 111–113, 119–120
Addiction, see Drugs
Admissions directors, college, 268–269
Adolescence, socialization of, 25, 26, 58, 228–229; view of nature, 34
Adviser, role of, 154–155
Affluence, 74, 84–86; and life style, 239–240, 272; and meritocracy, 266–267. See also Prosperity
Africa, 24, 26, 36, 58, 311, 316, 340; extension of American influence in, 315, 317, 341; predictions concerning, 320, 321, 322
Aged, 18, 57, 216, 344; emergence of as pressure group, 178
Agriculture, 79, 342, U.S. Department of, 50
Aid to dependent children (ADC), 333. See also Welfare state
Aiken, 301
Air pollution, 10, 17, 27, 65, 157, 160, 161, 329, 359
Air space, and city, 157, 159–160, 161
Alcoholism, 240
Algeria, 322
Alienation, 39, 99; of youth, 55, 299, 231, 233; of core-city Negro, 174; and computer-based education, 261
Alliance for Progress, 331
American Academy of Arts and Sciences, 9. See also Commission on the Year 2000
Analysis, "envelope curve," 129
Anomie, 261
Anti-institutionalism, 229–230, 237
Anti-Irish riots (1840's–1850's), 287–288
Antinomianism, 229

Anxiety, 32, 40, 251–252, 364
Appalachia, 48
Appliances, personalization of, 334
Arendt, Hannah, 270
Argonne National Laboratory, 32
Aristocracy, 265. See also Elite
Arms control, 28
Artificial insemination, 201, 240, 335
Ashby, W. Ross, 182–183
Asia, 90–91, 313, 314; extension of American influence in, 315, 317; Chinese role in, 316
Asimov, Dr. Isaac, 2
Assault, aggravated, 277, 280–282, 285
Associations, professional, 196
Atkinson, Richard, 260
Atomic bomb, see Nuclear power
Atomic Energy Commission, U.S., 2, 192
Atoms for Peace program, 57
Attitudes, 294, 364; middle-class, 28; toward forecasting, 136–138; sex-based, 243
Augustine, Saint, 1, 4
Authority: public, 19; adolescent view of, 229–235; re-establishment of, 235–238
Automation, 24, 25, 31, 59, 66, 130; economic impact of, 41; large-scale, 147; and education, 257
Automation Commission, see National Commission on Automation
Automobile, 3, 23, 24, 69, 145, 278
Autonomy, 29, 52
Avocations, 23
Ayres, Robert, 129

Babbage, Charles, 301
Bacon, Francis, 106
Baker, Russell, 35

Index

Balance of power, *see* International relations

Barth, Karl, 224

Beatniks, 58, 219, 269, 271, 331

Behavior, personal, 39–40; and genetics, 42, 208–209; and planning, 155; control, 205–221; radical change in style of, 241–243; violent, 294; parameterization of, 336

Behavior-control technology, 214–221, 344, 345; and social acceptance, 217–219

Belgium, 312

Bell, Alexander Graham, 301, 306

Bell, Daniel, 22–23, 27, 39, 40, 44, 47, 48, 50, 52, 54, 55, 57, 58, 59, 60, 61, 62, 94; quoted on unknowable, 107; and "alternate futures," 217; on nature and limits of forecasting, 328–329, 338; on identification of variables, 348–349

Bell Telephone System, 307

Bellamy, Edward, 75, 114

Belle Époque, La, 89, 91

Benjamin, Curtis, and "twigging phenomenon," 197–198

Berlin blockade, 311

Bertalanffy, Ludwig, 181–182, 337

Biderman, Albert, 333

Binet, Alfred, 264

Biochemistry, 263, 264

Biology, 28, 29, 200–204, 381; 20th-century revolution in, 178; experimental, 206; automatic principle in, 252–253

Biomedical engineering, 4, 348, 376–377

Birth control, 240, 241; as patriotic duty, 246–247; and *Griswold* case (Connecticut), 249

Birth rates, 26, 35, 144; Negro, 56–57

Blackmer, Allan, Jr., 269

Bohr, Niels, 90

Boston, Mass., 188, 279, 281

Boulding, Kenneth, 84

Bourgeoisie, elite of, 74, 76–77

Bowie, Robert, 361

Brain stimulation, electric, 212–213, 216, 217

Brainwashing, 215

Brandeis, Louis D., "The Right to Privacy," 249

Brazil, 84; role in Latin American future, 316, 330, 340

Breeding, controlled, 209. *See also* Genetics

Broglie, Achille de, 90

Brookhaven National Laboratories, 32

Brookings Institute, 60, 64–65

Brown, Rap, 290

Brzezinski, Zbigniew, 35, 38, 39, 45, 328

Buddhism, 226

Bullitt, William, 246

Bundy, McGeorge, 268

Burckhardt, Jacob, 75

Bureau of Labor Statistics, U.S., 59, 335; and projections of national productivity, 131

Bureau of Land Management, U.S., 160

Bureau of Social Research, Washington, D.C., 333

Bureau of Standards, U.S., 50

Bureau of the Budget, U.S., 271

Bureaucracy, 7, 18, 352, 372; Soviet, 36; centralization in, 47–55; elite, 74, 76–77

Business cycle, 331; and crime, 282–283

California Institute of Technology, 32

Cambodia, 320

Camus, Albert, 289–290

"Candid Camera," television show, 246

Career, 32, 55, 74; and primary occupation, 88; multiple, and university, 188–189, 343

Carmichael, Stokely, 290

Carnegie Corporation, 268

Cartter, Allan, 365

Castroism, 311

CATV (community antenna television), 303

Causality, 149, 154

Centralization, 45–55, 68; political, 5, 7; social, 33, 34; and democratic society, 139, 143

Chaim Weizmann Institute, 353

Character, in meritocracy, 267–268

Chartism, as methodology, 337–338

Chemistry, quantitative, 24

Children, 24, 26, 277, 333

Chile, 58

Chiliasm (life free from imperfection), 2

China, 34, 84, 92–94, 302, 311, 312, 313, 314, 378; predictions concerning, 316, 319, 321, 330

Choice, freedom of, *see* Free choice
Choice, social, 7, 27, 55, 372
Christianity, 89, 224–226
Church, 222–226, 252
Churchill, Winston S., 246, 272
City, 347, 351; commercial commitment of, 185–186; and university, 185–190. *See also* Core city; Urban development
City-state, optimum size of, 141
Civil disobedience, 250, 277, 286–288
Civil liberties, 33, 152; and behavior control, 219–221
Civil rights, 320, 328, 366, 367; march on Washington (1963), 294
Civil war, 281
Clark, Joseph, 47
Class war, 22
Cohen, Morris, 114
Cold war, 6, 24, 90, 312, 329
Collaboration, expert, *see* Teams, technical
Collectivity: 20th-century drive for, 178; in youth, 230
Collectivization, Russian, 26, 311
Colonialism, 24, 312. *See also* Decolonization
Color, as divisive political force, 6
Columbia Broadcasting System, 1
Columbia University, 11
Commission on the Year 1985, Paris, 52
Commission on the Year 2000, 1, 114; goals, 8–13; scope, 17–20; basic considerations, 23; intentions, 63–64; methodologies, 64–67; reconceptualizations, 67–69; future of, 355–365, 372–381
Committee of Institutional Cooperation, 192
Committee on the Next Thirty Years, British, 1
Common-law copyright, 248–249
Common Market, 36
Communality, 27, 33, 357, 359, 368; government promotion of, 174
Communication, 121, 141, 143, 297–309; "overload," 7, 26, 141, 197; automated, 31; mass, 34, 68; national system of, 53; for future democratic society, 145; network, social, 183–184; and institutional collaboration, 192–193; unsolicited, 247; and invasion of privacy, 249; future uses of electrical, 307–309

Communication satellites, 19, 32, 302–305, 350
Communism, 77, 90, 310; and convergence theory, 92–93; rise and spread of, 311–314; and U.S. policy, 315; dead issue of future, 321, 322, 341
Compact for Education, 192
Compacts, regional, 19, 32, 46
Computer, 1, 4, 24, 143, 350, 351; as factor for decentralization, 40; in future democratic society, 145–146; and privacy, 245; 262–263; time-shared, 260; in education, 260–262; in libraries, 261–262; and language translation, 297; future uses of, 308–309; and strengthened government leadership, 352–353; and middle management, 352–353; social impact, 376
COMSAT, *see* Communication satellites
Congress of Vienna (1815), 310
Conservation, 160, 161
Conservatism: and social predictions, 122–123; and scientific progress, 196
Constitution, U.S., 34; and privacy (fourth amendment), 248
Constitutional Convention, national, 175–176
Consultant, role of, 154–155
Contraception, 29, 237, 240, 251, 335, 342. *See also* Birth control
Controls, social, 39, 40, 345
Core city, 51; segregation in, 157–158, 162–163, 170. *See also* City
Corporations, 19, 36–37; nonprofit, 46, 65, 168
Cosmetics, 2, 6
Council of Economic Advisers, 45–46, 170
Counter-Reformation, 76
Cox, Harvey, *The Secular City*, 222
Coxey, General Jacob, 349
Crime, 278–280; white-collar, 280; and youth, 282; and business cycle, 282–283. *See also* Violence
Crowding, human tolerance for, 253–254, 372
Cuba, 312, 337
Culture, 9–10, 342; disjunction with social structure, 7
Curiosity, spiritual, 106
Curricula, modernization of, 193

Index

Cybernation, 95
Cybernetics, 182
Czechoslovakia, 311

Darwinism, 42, 89
Data: processing, 142, 145; transmission, 308, 350. *See also* Storage
Death rate, *see* Mortality
Decentralization, 33–34, 45–55, 68, 171; and computer, 40; in urban schools, 173. *See also* Centralization
Decision-making, 5, 6, 7, 18, 27, 29, 49, 63–64, 346; communal, 33; and predictions, 102–104, 112, 113–118, 136–138; and limited information, 142–143; and computer, 352; role of adviser in, 154–155; within federal structure, 170; middle-class participation in, 171–172
Declaration of Independence, U.S., 61
Decolonization, 90, 310–311
De Forest, Lee, 301
De Gaulle, Charles, 52, 122, 319, 356
Delgado, Dr. José, 213
Democratic Party, U.S., 59. *See also* Political parties
Democracy, 19, 357–358; elite of, 74, 76–78; of the future, 139–146; economic and political values of, 139; and middle-class participation, 171–172
Demography, 25–26, 59, 254
Desalinization, 342
Detroit, 286–288
Deutsch, Karl, 24–32 *passim*, 39, 40, 42, 43, 359
Dewey, John, 114
Diffusion, 28, 39; nuclear, 40; specifications of, 65; institutionalization of, 74; and technological forecasting, 127, 128, 129–131, 134; decrease in time-period for, 130
Disease, control of, 4, 28; and immunization, 31
DNA, 208, 328
Dobzhansky, Theodosius, 328, 335
Donovan, Hedley, 348, 351, 367
Douglas, William O., 249
Draft deferment, 270–271
Draft Riots (1860's), 286–287, 288
Drucker, Peter, 84
Drugs, 34, 217, 263–264, 331; and behavior change, 205–206, 208, 210–211, 219, 345; abuses, 216;

humanitarian use of, 218; addiction to, 240
Duhl, Leonard J., 10, 27, 28, 34, 39, 40, 43, 45, 53, 55, 57, 356, 367; on domestic and political institutions, 346–347
Dunn, Halbert, 180
Durkheim, Émile, 34
Dyson, Freeman, 28

East-West relations, 313, 329. *See also* International relations
Eastern Europe, 311, 313, 320–321, 329–330
Eavesdropping, 249; technology of, 244–245; and image of informer, 246
Eckert, 301
Ecology, 149, 152
Economics, 11, 54, 118; input-output analysis, 132, 334; value system in, 139–140
Economy, 6, 8, 25–26; public sector of, 25, 32, 39, 42–43, 68, 175; and Great Depression, 37; private sector of, 42–43, 68; continuous growth in, 73, 92–93, 320; forecasts concerning, 128, 132; input-output analysis for, 132; world-wide political, 144; U.S., and Asian conflict, 171; governmental control of, 173; and population increases, 254
Education, 10, 18, 25, 58, 74, 86–88, 328, 365; post-graduate, 1, 4; critical social factor in, 22; equality in, 42; policy for, 45; federal aid to, 53; and bureaucracy, 54; forecasts concerning, 59–60; of the poor, 152–153; and urban development, 162–168 *passim;* metropolitanism in, 173; and university city, 185–190; institutions of, 192–193, 342–344; and social role of the sexes, 240–241; of professional men, 251; expansion and overhaul in, 257–260; computer-based, 260–262
Efficiency, 218, 265
Egalitarianism, 5, 24, 28, 31, 328, 349
Egypt, 322
Einstein, Albert, 90
Eisenhower, Dwight D., 272
Electricity, 24
Electronics, 304
Elite, 257, 349; meritocratic, 74, 76–77, 265

Emerging nations, *see* Underdeveloped nations

Employment: structure of, and computer, 41; Federal, 50; forecasting in, 128; and federal revenue projections, 170–171; by government, 172; and renovation of knowledge, 193; and meritocracy, 273

Encyclopedia Britannica, 250

Endocrine system, 213

Energy, sources of, 18, 24, 73, 143; controlled thermonuclear, 31

Engels, Friedrich, 77

Engineering, 193–196; biomedical, 4, 348, 376–377

Enlightenment, age of, 89

Entertainment (guessing games), 104–106, 119

Environment: control of, 18; adolescent view of, 34; man's information about, 140; natural and city, 158–161; diversification of, 201; and behavior, 206; manipulation of, 213–214

Epistemology, 108–111

Equality, 33, 38–39, 55, 69; political, 24, 29; educational, 42; in democratic society, 139, 143; of opportunity, 179. *See also* Egalitarianism

Ethics, 9, 252; of social planner, 153; adolescent, 236–237

Ethiopia, 89

Eugenics, 41–42, 200–204, 251

Europe, 23, 77–78; shattered by World Wars, 90, 91; decline of political influence, 315; predictions concerning, 321, 322. *See also* Eastern Europe

Evolution, 41–42, 200, 202, 253

Existentialism, 234

Expenditure: private *vs.* public, 41; government, 172; and educational development, 187

Family, 7, 9, 336; diminished influence of, 32; future role of, 34; extended, 178, 241; nuclear, 239; as citadel of privacy, 247–248; size pattern, 345

Fanon, Frantz, 290

Fascism, 76, 90, 91, 329, 341

Featherbedding, 179

Federal Bureau of Investigation (FBI), 279, 281

Federalism, creative, 169–176; and urban development, 164–167; spending programs, 170–171; multitiered, 172

Femininity, 242–243

Ferdinand, Theodore N., 279, 281

Finance, federal, 165, 170–171

Fiscal drag, 59

Fleming, Donald, 268

Flexner, Abraham, 269, 275

Fluoridation, 346, 380

Foerster, Heinz von, 182

Food, 25, 251, 342; predictions, 31

Forecasting, 20, 147–156, 359; technological, 11, 24, 127–138, 328, 333, 335, 350; of values, 28; methodology, 56–62, 64, 133–136; long-range, 58–59; attitudes toward, 136–138; nature and limitations of, 328–338; sociological, 332–333. *See also* Predictions

Foreign-aid programs, 321, 322, 341

Forester, Jay, 337

France, 52, 312, 313; Fourth Republic, 54; "core" power, 89; future role of, 330

Frank, Lawrence K., 9–10, 29, 33, 37, 38, 43, 46–47, 52, 60, 61, 345, 367; on power of ideas, 201; on new fatalism, 337

Free choice, 19, 29, 38; and communality, 33; in future democratic society, 139–146. *See also* Choice, social

Freud, Sigmund, 90, 246; and guilt-burden of civilization, 252

Freund, Paul, 9

Friedman, Milton, 92

Fuller, Buckminster, 129, 334

Futuribles, French project, 1, 40, 59, 60, 352

"Futurists: Looking Toward A.D. 2000, The," *Time* essay, 2

Gabor, Dennis, *Inventing the Future,* 128

Gadgets, predicted, 3

Galbraith, J. K., 60

Gardner, John W., 154, 268, 349

Genetics, 18, 28, 29, 33, 69, 335, 345; modification of, 4, 208–209; control, 24, 144, 344; variability in man, 41–42, 200–202; inevitability of change in, 204; molecular, 206; and controlled mating, 209

Geography, and public policy, 34

Index

Georgia, 280, 283

Germany, 42, 322, 329; re-unification of, 321–322, 340. *See also* West Germany

Gerontocracy, 267

Gestation, extra-uterine, 240

Gibbon, Edward, 75

Gibson v. Florida Legislative Investigating Committee, 249

Ginsburg, Arnie, 34

Goals for Americans (President's Commission on National Goals), 35

Goldwater, Barry, 39

Government, 4, 8, 346–347, 374; centralization in, 5, 7; adequacy of structure, 11, 18, 19, 45; expansion of power, 27–28, 279–280; analytic approach to, 104; and forecasting, 132, 136–137; and urban development, 164–167; federal-local relationship, 169–176; fiscal resources, 170–171; employment by, 172; new varieties in, 172–173; and community, 174; and university city, 190; and intrusion on privacy, 245; and violence, 291–294; television as tool of, 299–300; and computer, 325, 353, 356

Grants-in-aid, federal, 50, 171

Graubard, Stephen R., 10, 27–28, 32, 42, 43, 53

Great Britain, 76, 89, 311, 330

Great Depression, 37, 54, 59, 90, 121

Great Society, 114, 179

Greece, 311

Green, Thomas, 275

Greer, Scott, 174

Griswold case (Connecticut), 249

Grodzin, Morton, 172

Gross National Product (GNP), 11, 25–26, 31, 39, 59, 73, 94, 159; and technological diffusion, 131; and social prediction, 328; Soviet, 329

Haar, Charles, 43, 51

Haifa Technical Institute, 353

Haldane, J. B. S., 29, 204; *Dædalus: Science and the Future*, 381

Hallucinogens, *see* LSD

Halpern, Morton, 57

Harlan, J. M., 249

Harvard College, 188; Department of Social Relations, 269

Health, 43, 48, 328; as big business, 187

Health, Education and Welfare, U.S. Department of, 154

Hedonism, 7, 74; and youth, 230, 237

Held, Dr. Virginia, 10–11

Helmer, Olaf, 58

Hemingway, Mrs. Mary, 246

Henry, Andrew F., 282

Heredity, 264; and intelligence, 201

Herrstein, R. J., 251

Highways, 1, 3, 149, 158

Hitler, Adolf, 44, 76, 77, 348, 351–352

Hoagland, Hudson, 9

Holloman, J. Herbert, 175

Homicide, *see* Murder

Homosexuality, 240, 243

Hoover Commission (1931), 9

Hormones, and development modification, 207, 209–210

Hotchner, A. E., *Papa Hemingway*, 246

Housewives, in the year 2000, 2

Housing, 41, 162–164, 168, 173; mobile, 27; and federal grants and subsidies, 165–166; and regional agencies, 167

Housing and Urban Development, U.S. Department of, 171

Hovland, Carl, 364

Hoyle, 44

Hudson Institute, 11, 23, 73, 129, 328, 329

Hughes, Everett, 269

Huizinga, Johan, 114

Human Sexual Response (Masters), 247

Humanism: secular, 73, 74; and youth's identity, 232–236

Huxley, Aldous, 335; *Brave New World*, 122, 265

Hypnosis, 214

Identity, 231–235; masculine, 242; and computer-based education, 261

Ideology, 341

Iklé, Fred Charles, 11, 28, 35, 42, 57, 60, 328

Immigration, 320, 353

Immunization, 31

Imperialism, 24, 310–311, 339; intellectual, 349, 350, 351

Income, per capita, 25, 162

India, 58, 84, 302, 311, 313; industrialization level, 26, 29; war with Pakistan, 314; future nuclear capability, 322

Individual, 252; in future democratic society, 139–146; recognition of rights of, 179; role of, 202; and behavior control, 220–221
Individuality, 38, 39
Indochina, 320
Indonesia, 84, 316
Industrialization, 24, 26; world-wide 74, 84–86, 92; and national security, 89; and natural resources, 159
Industry: role of, 32; forecasts of growth in, 128, 132; location of, and urban planning, 161
Inefficiency, social, 219
Information technology, 24, 31; in future democratic society, 139–146; worth of, 140–141; accumulation and transmission problems, 196–198. See also Communication
Innovation, 28, 54, 78–84; and corporation, 36–37; identification of, 65; institutionalization of, 73, 74; and technological forecasting, 127; and urban development, 167–168; in government, 172–173, 181; social, 174; in life style, 242
Institutions, 251; educational and scientific, 191–199; social, and behavior, 213–214; and sphere of privacy, 247, social, and motivation, 256; international, 339–341, 347. See also Government; Intellectual institutions
Integration, racial, 162–163
Intellectual institutions, 18, 55, 342–344, 374–375; in postindustrial society, 32; and university city, 188–189; changes in, 198; and national policy, 351
Intellectuals, 7, 18, 54; and government, 76; and integrity, 194; and on-line community, 261–263
Intelligence, 203; national, 33; genetic component, 42; heritability of, 201; amplification of, 255; control, 264; military, 323. See also Meritocracy
International relations, 11, 19, 26, 55, 310–323, 368, 373–374; increased tensions in, 40; U.S. role in, 6, 37, 311–314; decline of American system in, 315–317; predictions for, 318–323; future institutions in, 339–341; and technological innovation, 342; and domestic problems, 351, 358

International transfer payments, 25
Interpersonal relations, 9, 32, 38, 142, 241–243
Intrauterine device (IUD), 342
Invention, 127–128, 135; "envelope curve" analysis, 129; forecasting of, 328, 333–334, 335
Iran, 89
Iron Curtain, 225
Islam, 226
Isolationism, national, 37
Israel, 57, 322
Italy, 313

Jackson, James, Jr., 272
Japan, 23, 77, 89, 322; as mass-consumption society, 85; religious scene in, 226; in international relations, 311–314 passim; future role, 330
Jencks, Christopher, The Rise of the Meritocracy, 266–267, 273
Jet Propulsion Laboratory, 32
John Birch Society, 346
Johnson, Dr., 141
Johnson, Lyndon B., 10, 47, 49, 320; Great Society programs, 114, 179
Joint Committee of Economic Reports (1965), 59, 170
Joint Graduate Consortium, 192
Jouvenel, Bertrand de, 1, 40, 122, 358
Judaism, 224
Jurisprudence, 25

Kahn, Herman, 11, 23, 26, 39, 57, 191, 328, 332, 359; speculation of next thirty-five years, 329–331, 334, 335; on chartist methodology, 337–338
Kaysen, Carl, 361
Kennedy, John F., 10, 47; early economic policies, 59; -Johnson administration, 328
Kennedy-Manchester dispute, 246
Key, V. O., Jr., 291–292
Keynes, John Maynard, 84
Khrushchev, Nikita, 57, 329; fall of, 328
King, Martin Luther, 349
Kinsey Reports, 247
Knowledge: accumulation of, 74, 143, 146, 255; Dr. Johnson on, 141; renovation of, 193; fractionalization of, 197–198; and education, 257
Ku Klux Klan, 288, 291
Kuhn, Thomas S., 117

Index

Labor, 22, 25, 26, 37, 278; importation of, 35; U.S. Department of, 50; and riots, 287
Labor-management relations, 54, 55
Labor unions, 24, 178–179, 328
Lactation, artificial, 240
Land, urban, 159–161
Language, 297–298; universal, 31
Laser, 22, 78, 79, 305
Latin America, 23, 89, 315, 317, 320; Brazil's role in future of, 316, 330, 340
Law, see Legislation; World law
Leadership, 44, 348, 351, 367
League of Nations, 312, 339
Learning, 211; speed of, 26–27; human limitations for, 254; and meritocracy, 269–270, 273
Legislation, 36, 47; and privacy, 248–249, 263
Leisure, 18, 19, 25, 31, 74, 121; and self-expression, 39–40; as big business, 187; church's influence on, 222, 225–226; in U.S.'s vocation-oriented society, 331
Lenin, Nikolai, 44, 348
Lenz, Ralph, 129, 334
Leontief, Wassily, 11, 37, 38, 40, 46, 49, 328, 335, 353, 359; and input-output economic analysis, 132, 334; on prediction of policies, 331–332, 336
Leucotomy, frontal, 216
L4, communications system, 304
Library, 196–197; and computer, 261–262
Library of Congress, U.S., 197
Licklider, J. C. R., Libraries of the Future, 262
Life: science of, 28; artificial, 31; quality of, 264
Life-cycle, human, 4, 11, 55, 57, 239–250, 372–373
Life style, 240; urban, 163–164; and invasion of privacy, 248
Lin Piao, 350
Lincoln Laboratory, 32
Lindblom, Charles E., 175
Lindmann, Ferdinand, 107
Lindsay, John V., 47
Literacy, 11, 25, 73, 74, 86–88
Little Steel Strikes (1937), 287
Lobotomy, frontal, 211, 216
Locke, John, 9, 29, 64; theory of representative government, 177

Longevity, human, 4, 32, 178
LSD, 211
Lynn, Frank, 350; his report to Automation Commission, 130

McClelland, David, 259
McLuhan, Marshall, 3, 136, 155
McNamara, Robert S., 352, 356
Manchuria, 321, 322
Manchus, 90
Manpower, 132, 133. See also Labor
Mansfield, Edward, 350
Mao Tse-tung, 122, 319, 321
Market mechanism, 174–175
Marx, Karl, 77, 378, 381
Masculinity, 242–243
Maser, 78, 79
Mass communications, see Communication
Mass media, 1–3, 5, 352; and privacy, 249; and violence, 289
Massachusetts Institute of Technology, 32, 188; Project INTREX, 261
Massenet, Michael, 60
Mauchly, 301
Mayr, Ernst, 23, 28, 33, 41, 42, 69
Mazlish, Bruce, 366
Medicine, 4, 25, 28, 44, 346, 347
Megalopolis, 74, 86–88, 345; governmental fragmentation in, 165
Memory, 211, 254
Mental health, 25; and privacy, 248
Meritocracy, 265–276; consequences of, 19, 33, 69; elite of, 74, 76–77, 265; pressures, 265–271; opportunities, 271–273; resistances, 273–276
Merton, Robert K., 12, 380
Meselson, Matthew, 358, 359, 360
Mexico, 330
Microwave technology, 304, 305
Middle East, 315, 316
Middle management, 352–353
Migration, 280
Mill, John Stuart, 43, 118
Millenia, mysticism surrounding, 2–3, 21
Miller, George A., 68, 142
Minutemen (terrorists), 291
Missiles, 31, 35
Mobility, social and professional, 7, 32, 273, 352, 353; and gerontocracy, 267–268
Modernization, 74; and urban development, 158–168
Moniz, Egas, 211

Monogamy, 240
Moore, Wilbert, 11, 328, 332–333, 345
Morals, 6, 9, 252
Moran, Lord, his diary on Churchill, 246
Mortality: infant, 4; reduction of, 26, 28; ratio to birth rates, 108; ratio to death rate, 344
Motivation, 256–257; and education, 258–260
Moyers, Bill, 51
Moynihan, Daniel P., 10, 28, 45, 54, 56, 59, 60, 346
Muller, Hermann Joseph, 335
Murder, 277; data concerning, 278–279, 283–285; lower-class crime, 280
Mussolini, Benito, 77
Mysticism, 222–226

NASA, 117
Nation-state, 42, 322, 323, 339–340, 357; U.S. as example of, 19, 67; and public policy, 33, 36, 46, 169; and meritocracy, 275–276
National Academy of Sciences, 196
National Commission on Automation, 46, 130, 350
National Institute of Mental Health, 263
National Institutes of Health, 53
National Library of Medicine, 197
National Opinion Research Center, 281
National Planning Association (1940's), 57, 132
National Science Foundation, 192, 349
National security, 37–38, 39; and Asian industrialization, 89
National society, *see* Nation-state
Nationalism, 55, 78, 311, 313, 317; elite of, 74, 76; values of, 77
NATO (North Atlantic Treaty Organization), 77, 312, 319; and De Gaulle, 122; further disintegration predicted, 322
Natural Resources Planning Commission, U.S., 56
Natural selection, biological, 202
Nazism, 91, 201
Negro, 17, 19, 46, 47, 54, 320, 360; ratio to population, 56, 344–345; ghettoization of, 162–163; in public schools, 173; quest for community, 174; youth, 235; in meritocracy,

275; crime rate among, 280, 282; and urbanization, 281; riots, 286–294
Netherlands, 312
Neurology, 206
Neurophysiology, 205–206
Neurosurgery, 206; and behavior, 211–213, 216
New Deal, 50, 179, 367
New Economic Program (NEP), U.S.S.R., 311
New Frontier, 179
"New Town" concept, 155, 161, 163–164, 168, 347
New York City, slums in, 162; anti-Irish riots in, 287
New York Post, The, 2
New York Times, The, 2, 8
Newark, 286
Newspaper, microfilm, 303. *See also* Mass media
Newtonian mechanics, 92
Next Thirty-three Years: A Framework for Speculation, The, 329
Nigeria, 84, 302
1976: Planning the American Future, 360
Nonwhite, urban concentration of, 170. *See also* Negro
Nostradamus, 114
Novel, futuristic, 105–106
Nuclear power, 6; proliferation, 24, 57, 322; bans on use, 28, 57; atomic bomb, 237; and Soviet-American relations, 314. *See also* Warfare, nuclear
Nutrition, 41, 203; and behavior, 209

Obsolescence: of highways, 3; in meritocracy, 267–268
Ohio State Law Journal, 246
Okinawa, 318, 322
Open space, *see* Air-space
Organ transplant, 4, 6
Organization, optimal size, 34
Orion project, 28
Orlans, Harold, 10, 28, 44, 47, 57, 60, 335
Orwell, George, *1984,* 106, 265
Osborn, 353
Ottoman empire, 90
Overhage, Carl, 261
Ownership, 139

Pakistan, 29, 84, 322, 330; war with India, 314

Index

Palo Alto, Cal., 260

Parenthood, as adult goal, 239–240

Parliamentarianism, 89

Parousia, early Christian expectation of, 2

Parsons, Talcott, *Essays in Sociological Theory: Pure and Applied,* 256

Participation, individual, 45, 46, 368, 374; and social planner, 152–153; and "self-renewing agency," 154; and community-action programs, 164; middle-class, and public decision-making, 171–172

Patronage, 179

Pavlov, Ivan P., 213

Peaceful coexistence policy, 313

Peasantry, 316–317

Perloff, Harvey, 36, 42, 46, 47, 51, 54, 363; on prediction of trends, 335–336

Permissiveness, 7

Personality, 18; modification, 205–221, 259; typing by sex, 240–241; control, 264

Pettigrew, Thomas F., 280

Pfaff, William, 329

Pharmacology, 28, 32, 263–264; and behavior control, 205–206, 208. *See also* Drugs

Philadelphia, 279; anti-Irish riots, 287

Physical Science Study Committee, 193

Picturephone, 304, 307

Pierce, John, 27

Pifer, Alan, 362

Pill, the, 342

Piore, Emanuel, 351

Plague, 345, 361

Planner, social, 148–156, 357, 358; twofold problem of, 152; political nature of efforts, 154; required talents of, 155–156

Plato, 148; *The Republic,* 2

Plutarch, *Lives,* 329

Poe. v. Ullman, 249

Polanyi, Michael, 110

Polaroid Land Camera, 303

Police brutality, 288–289

Policy, social, 6, 18; forecasting in, 11, 137–138; public, 33, 36, 73, 169; prediction of, 332

Policy-maker, *see* Decision-making

Political parties, 178–179, 323

Political system, 45–55; and social change, 35–36, 38, 51–52; and in-

formation for electorate, 142; and planning, 150–151; and urban development, 165–167; need for new theory for, 177–184; and decline of U.S. international prestige, 316. *See also* Government

Pollution, *see* Air pollution; Water pollution

Pool, Ithiel de Sola, 10, 24, 28, 39–40; on future of international relations, 339–341

Popper, Karl, 122, 202–203

Popular Front, 311

Population, 4, 11, 18, 24, 73, 251–253, 335, 344, 347, 353; predictions, 31, 35, 118, 336; changing composition of, 48; shifts in, 56, 142, 178, 342, 345; world-wide growth, 84–86; and finite living space, 108; control, 99, 202, 323; and change of life-style, 240

Population Council, 353

Postan, Michael, 40–41, 42, 53

Potsdam agreements, 311

Potter, David, 29

Poverty, 10, 17, 25, 48, 162–164, 328; federal war on, 50–51, 151; and political instability, 92; and community-action programs, 164, 173

Power, 139, 142–143

Predictions, 147–156, 318–319; evaluations of, 101–123; and indecision, 102–104; guessing games, 104–107; and the unknowable, 107–111; and action, 111–113, 119–120; and values, 113–118; identification of errors in, 118–121; and social change, 121–123, 323; performative, 136; of discontinuities, 333. *See also* Forecasting

Presidency, U.S., 34, 36, 47, 68

President's Commission on Technology, Automation and Economic Progress, 41

Principles of Self-Organizing Systems (Foerster and Zopf, Jr.), 182

Privacy, 4, 7, 18, 55, 68, 219, 244–250, 368; reconceptualization of, 34; in future democratic society, 145; changes in sphere of, 244–246; and computer, 245, 262–263, 350; and public figure, 246; and social-science research, 247, 372; countermeasures against invasion of, 248–250

Private sector, economy, 42–43, 68
Productivity, national, 131–132, 134
Project Forecast, U.S. Air Force, 129
Project INTREX, 261
Promiscuity, female, 240
Property, nature of, 33, 55, 357
Prophecy, self-fulfilling, 57, 58; and student labeling, 259
Prosperity, 38, 293; and increase in murders, 282–283; and decrease in suicides, 283–284
Prosthesis, 28, 208, 213
Proust, Marcel, 43
Psychedelic agents, *see* LSD
Psychiatry, 206
Psychology, 206, 251–264; changes in, 29; computerization of, 262
Psychopharmacology, 25, 210, 251
Psychosomatic disorders, 240
Public administration, theory of, 47
Public health, 41, 203
Public opinion: polls, 52, 76; and privacy, 248; and computer, 352
Public policy, 292–293
Public sector, 32, 42–43, 68, 175; in non-Communist countries, 25; and GNP., 39
Puerto Rico, 318, 322
Pulse code modulation (PCM), 306
Puritanism, 76

Quarton, Gardner, 42, 43, 57, 58, 359, 362

Rainwater, Lee, 175
Rand Corporation, 31, 32, 35, 57, 129, 360; Delphi predictions, 24, 65
Ranke, Leopold von, 115
Rationalism, 29; and U.S. political theory, 177
Rationality, 139–146
Reading, and intellectual privacy, 247, 248
Reagan, Ronald, 53
Recent Social Trends, 4, 9, 58, 121, 328
Reconceptualization, 27, 28–29, 34, 67–69; of political and economic man, 143; as objective of planner, 153; for university cities, 190; in genetics, 203–204
Recreation, 160, 161, 167–168
Reed, Elizabeth W., 204
Reed, Sheldon C., 204
Reformation, 76

Regional organizations, 167, 322. *See also* Compacts, regional
Reich, Charles, "The New Property," 33
Religion, 35, 222–226; institutional, 224–225; decline of influence of, 247, 248
Representation, concept of, 36, 38
Reproduction, 26; differential in, 202; and superior genotypes, 203
Research, 132, 193–194; institutionalization of, 74, 273; and forecasting methodology, 128; government control of, 194–195
Research and development (R & D), 341
Resources: adequacy of, 18, 49, 66, 251; and forecasting, 132–133; urban-oriented, 158–161; and state government, 166
Resources for the Future, 133
Reston, James, 353
Reston, Virginia, 47, 347
Retardation, mental, 204
Revelle, Roger, 26, 56, 58, 61, 62, 351, 356, 358, 360
Revisionism, 77, 91, 122–123
Riencourt, Amaury de, *The Coming Caesars,* 329
Riesman, David, 348; and concept of other-directedness, 29
Rio de Janeiro, 85
Riots, 277–278, 286–294, 348–349
RNA, 211
Role, social, 239–250
Roosevelt, Franklin Delano, 47, 50, 352
Rostow, Eugene, 33, 37, 39, 44, 45, 50–51, 53–54, 348
Rostow, W. W., 334
Rousseau, Jean Jacques, *The Social Contract,* 69
Russell Sage Foundation, 332, 333
Russia, Imperial, 34, 310. *See also* Soviet Union
Russo-Japanese War, 89
Rutherford, Ernest, 105

St. Louis, anti-Irish riots in, 287
Satellites, *see* Communication satellites
Schizophrenia, 41
Schon, Donald A., 10, 11, 38, 50, 328; on technological forecasting, 333–335, 337

Index

Schools, 320; elementary and secondary, 193. *See also* Education; University

Schroedinger, Erwin, 90

Science, 28

Science, 78–84; policy-making for, 45–46; and social predictions, 121; institutions of, 193–196; forecasting in, 328; and society, 375–376

Seaborg, Dr. Glenn T., 2

Secularism, 74, 225

Segregation, 157–158, 162–164. *See also* Integration

Seidman, Harold, 271

Self-expression, 40, 52, 320

Self-government: student, 29; local, in England, 53

Senate Committee on Government Operations, 171

Senate Subcommittee on Executive Reorganization, 171

Sensate culture, 74–78

Service Society, 6, 7, 9, 43, 46, 61, 64; and maintenance problems, 25, 26, 31, 35; political theory for, 179–180

Sex: reconceptualization of, 29, 242; youth's attitude toward, 230, 237; freedom, and self-expression, 320

Sexes: and social role, 239–241; and certainty of identity, 242–243

Shannon, Claude, 306–307

Shaw, George Bernard, 8, 49

Sheldon, Miss Eleanor, 11

Short, James F., Jr., 282

Shubik, Martin, 23–24, 26, 58, 60, 61, 335–336, 357, 358; on change and traditional values, 344–346

Simon, Herbert, 110; *The New Shape of Automation*, 41

Sino-Soviet rift, 311, 315

Skinner, B. F., 148, 213

Slavery, 24, 26

Sleep, mechanism and purpose of, 210–211

Slums, 157, 162–164

Small Business Administration, 50

Smith, Adam, 9, 29, 64, 89, 142

Social accounting, national, 173–174

Social engineering, 27, 57; predicting for, 121–123; variables in, 148; and social consequences, 149–150

Social indicators, 333, 345

Social justice, 38, 39, 42

Social Science Research Council, England, 1

Socialism, 24, 38, 42; and values, 77

Society, Western, 74; ambivalence concerning privacy, 248

Soddy, Frederick, *The Interpretation of Radium*, 105

Solow, Robert, 60

Sorokin, Pitirim, 75

Southeast Asia, 315; Indonesia's role, 316

Soviet Union, 35–36, 89, 90, 302, 312, 313, 319; per-capita income, 85; *détente* with West, 313, 340; predictions concerning, 320–322, 329–330, 340. *See also* Russia, Imperial

Space, 31, 117; travel, 24; technology, 302

Special-interest groups, 153

Specialization, technological, 36, 191–192; imposition of, on youth, 231

Spengler, Oswald, 91

Sperm banks, 201

Spier, Rosalind B., 280

Stalin, Joseph, 76, 77, 311

Standard of living, 323

Standard World, 95–99, 331

Stanford University, 260

Status, 178–179

Sterilization, biological, 201

Stibitz, 301

Stillman, Edmund, 329

STOL, 79

Storage, information, 197; human limitations for, 254–255

Stratton, Julius A., 180

Student, future, 189, 193; and educational revolution, 257–260, 349; in meritocracy, 268–272, 275

Subsidies, federal, 165

Suburbia, 88; gap with core city, 157–158, 170

Suez crisis, 314

Suicide, 24, 277; data concerning, 278–279, 283–285

Superpowers, 90

Supersonic transport, 4

Suppes, Patrick, 260

Supreme Court, U.S., 54; "one-man, one-vote," 176

Sweden, 58

Systems analysis, 149, 301

Talent, development of, 33

Tawney, R. H., *Religion and the Rise of Capitalism*, 77

Teaching machines, 29, 273
Teams, technical, 255–257
Technology, 2–4, 23–24, 78–84, 252;
  intellectual, 5; forecasting in, 11,
  127–138, 328, 330, 350; to increase
  autonomous capacities, 29–30; social consequences of, 73, 121; role
  of, 144–146; domestic, 195; and behavior control, 207–208; and social
  acceptance, 215–217; psychological
  limits in, 255; and murder rate,
  279–280; and communication, 298–
  299, 300–301, 308–309
*Technology and the American Econ-
  omy: Report of the President's Com-
  mission*, 41
Telegraph, 306
Telephone, 3, 297–299, 306; as social
  tool, 300–301; and technology, 304–
  305
Television, 3, 27, 297–299; as unifying
  social force, 299, 303; by satellite,
  302–305
Testing, 268; in meritocracy, 266
Thailand, 89, 320
Theobald, Robert, 59
Theology, 35, 222–226
Theory, political, 177–184
Thermonuclear power, 31
Third World, *see* Underdeveloped na-
  tions
Thoreau, Henry David, 250
TI, digital transmission system, 304
Tillich, Paul, 223
Time (magazine), 2
Titan III, 304
Tobin, James, 60
Tocqueville, Alexis de, 5, 328, 349
Totalitarianism, 77
Touch-tone telephone, 308
Tourism, *see* Travel
Toynbee, Arnold, 75
Trade, 341–342
Trade unionism, *see* Labor unions
Traffic, 23, 157–158
Tranquilizers, 216
Transformation, genetic, 208
Transistor, 22, 301, 302
Transportation, 1, 5, 23–24, 46, 69;
  interplanetary, 24, 31; in city, 158
Travel, 321, 323, 342
Turkey, 89
Turner, Ralph, 268
"Twentieth Century, The," CBS doc-
  umentary, 1

"Twenty-First Century, The," CBS
  documentary, 1

Underdeveloped nations, 6, 25, 26, 35,
  36, 58, 90, 121; and family size, 26;
  and developed society, 40, 322, 323;
  and American universities, 192; and
  mass communication, 300, 301; in
  international affairs, 311, 313; and
  new ideological movements, 341;
  and intellectual imperialism, 349
Unemployment, 59, 320
United Nations, 35, 312, 313, 321,
  339; and admission of China, 226;
  future reform instrument, 323
United States, 7–8, 22, 23, 34; change
  in international relationships, 6, 37,
  311–312, 315–317, 340; -Soviet relations, 313–314; predictions concerning, 320–322, 323; as vocation-
  oriented society, 331; as world intellectual center, 349
United States Air Force, 129
Universalism, 234–235; and meritocracy, 267
University, 6, 11, 342–344; problems
  of size and scale, 5; role of in postindustrial society, 32; relation to
  government, 45; "cities," 185–190;
  faculty, 189; and industry, 195
Urban development, 4, 6, 10, 157–168;
  to achieve social ends, 46–47, 162–
  164; and "creative federalism," 164–
  167; role of state government, 166;
  role of city government, 166–167
Urbanization, 4, 22, 39, 58, 74, 86–88,
  99; political problems of, 25, 48;
  population figures, 157, 167; slum
  problem, 162–164; and federal leadership, 165–166; revolution in, 178;
  and violent crime, 281–282, 284;
  social and medical problems, 344;
  on international scale, 350
Utilitarianism, 74, 139–140

Vaccination, smallpox, 27
Values, individual, 7, 344–346; changing nature of, 11, 55; European, 23;
  predictions concerning, 28, 113–
  118; in postindustrial society, 32–
  33; for the process of change, 39;
  and the elite, 76; political and economic, 139–141; preservation of,
  143; of the social planner, 153; and
  social choice, 372

Index

Van Buren, Paul, *The Secular Meaning of the Gospel,* 222
Vermont, 283
Verne, Jules, 75
Vickers, Sir Geoffrey, 155
Victorianism, 76, 92
Viet-Nam, 10, 34, 119, 299, 312, 320, 341
Violence, 277–294, 323; individual, 278–285; in city, 281; and business cycle, 282–283; collective, 286–294; and mass media, 289; therapeutic value of, 289
Vogt, 353
Von Neumann, 301
Voss, John, 9
Voting patterns, 144, 145
VTOL, 79

Waelder, Robert, 60
Wall Street Journal, The, 1–2
Warfare, 24, 26, 251; nuclear, 120, 121, 319, 340; internal, 277; future nature of, 340; biological, 342
Warner, Sam Bass, 279
Warsaw Pact, 331
Waste, disposal problems, 160
Water pollution, 27, 157, 160, 161
Waterways, urban, 160–161
Watts crisis, 151–152, 155, 286
Wealth, redistribution of, 25–26, 31, 35, 40, 42
Weaponry, future, 322–323
Weather: modification, 4–5, 31, 39; forecasting, 79; and international cooperation, 342
Weber, Max: *The Protestant Ethic,* 77; "Politics as a Vocation," 351
Weinberg, Alvin, 28
Welch, William H., 268
Welfare state, 38, 367
Wells, H. G., 22, 38; *The World Set Free,* 105, 106; *Anticipations,* 106; *The Shape of Things to Come,* 106; predictography, 114

West Germany, 35, 85, 329–330
Westmoreland, General William, 356
Wheel, 3
White Knights, 291
Whitehead, Alfred North, 184
Whyte, William H., Jr., *Organization Man,* 271
Wiener, Norbert, 182
Wiesner, Jerome, 361
Wilson, James Q., 174
Wilson, Woodrow, 246, 312
Wiretapping, 249
Wittgenstein, Ludwig, 107
Wolfgang, Marvin E., 279
Women, 2; as social group, 240–242; and meritocracy, 265, 274
Women's National Democratic Club, 2
Wood, Marshall, 132
Wood, Robert, 28, 42–43, 48, 49, 171, 361
World law, 339
World War I, 90, 91
World War II, 6, 90, 311–312
Wright, Christopher, 10, 40, 50; on intellectual institutions, 342–344

Yale Law Journal, The, 33
Yalta Conference, 311
Yeats, William Butler, 22
Ylvisaker, Paul, 47, 48, 49, 51, 52, 53, 55, 59
Yolles, Dr. Stanley F., 263–264
Young, Michael, 1; *Rise of the Meritocracy,* 33, 265, 266, 267, 272, 273
Youth, 228–238; scepticism, 229–230; and desacralization, 230, 237; technological, 234–235; Negro, 235; "older," 236–237; and crime, 282. *See also* Adolescent

Zacharias, Jerrold, 193
Zamiatin, Evgenii, *We,* 122
Zopf, G. W., Jr., 182

1

791.4375 Pinter, ~~Harold, 1930-~~
PINTER   Five screenplays. ~~New York, Grove~~
             ~~Press [1973]~~
             367 p. 21cm.

             1. Moving-picture plays. I. Title.
  Id   PN1997.A1P5   1973

Five Screenplays

Other works by Harold Pinter Published by Grove Press

THE BIRTHDAY PARTY *and* THE ROOM
THE CARETAKER *and* THE DUMB WAITER
THE HOMECOMING
THE LOVER, TEA PARTY, THE BASEMENT
A NIGHT OUT, NIGHT SCHOOL, REVUE SKETCHES
THREE PLAYS: THE COLLECTION, A SLIGHT ACHE, THE DWARFS
LANDSCAPE, *limited edition*
MAC: A MEMOIR, *limited edition*
OLD TIMES

Five Screenplays

by HAROLD PINTER

THE SERVANT

THE PUMPKIN EATER

THE QUILLER MEMORANDUM

ACCIDENT

THE GO-BETWEEN

Grove Press, Inc.   New York

1

Contents

The Servant   1
based on the novel* by Robin Maugham

The Pumpkin Eater   61
based on the novel by Penelope Mortimer

The Quiller Memorandum   137
based on the novel, *The Berlin Memorandum*,
by Adam Hall

Accident   217
based on the novel by Nicholas Mosley

The Go-Between   285
based on the novel by L. P. Hartley

*Although Robin Maugham's stage play of *The Servant* was in existence at the time of writing, this screenplay was based solely on Robin Maugham's novel.

To Joseph Losey, Jack Clayton,
Michael Anderson
and Pamela Davies

The Servant

The Servant was first presented by Elstree Distributors Ltd on 14th November 1963 with the following cast:

BARRETT	Dirk Bogarde
TONY	James Fox
SUSAN	Wendy Craig
HEAD WAITER	Derek Tansley
GIRL IN PHONE BOX	Dorothy Bromiley
SOCIETY WOMAN	Ann Firbank
SOCIETY MAN	Harold Pinter
VERA	Sarah Miles
BISHOP	Patrick Magee
OLDER WOMAN	Doris Knox
YOUNGER WOMAN	Jill Melford
CURATE	Alun Owen
LORD MOUNTSET	Richard Vernon
LADY MOUNTSET	Catherine Lacey
CASHIER IN COFFEE BAR	Chris Williams
MAN IN PUB	Brian Phelan
GIRL IN PUB	Alison Seebohm
WOMAN IN BEDROOM	Hazel Terry
GIRL IN BEDROOM	Philippa Hare

Directed by Joseph Losey

The Servant

Exterior. Knightsbridge Square. October. Day.
A quiet square off Knightsbridge. Winter sun. Bare
trees. Numerous parked cars.
At the far side of the square BARRETT *appears. From*
high, see him approach. He stops at the kerb. Cars pass.
He crosses the road. His steps are sharp on the pave-
ment. Looking for a number he passes houses. He stops
at a house, slightly shabbier than the others, discerns
number and goes up the steps. The door is open. He
looks into the dark hall. Silence. There is no door-
knocker. He finds a bell, rings. A faint uncertain ring.

Interior. Hall. TONY's *house. Day.*
From inside the hall see BARRETT *enter and stand.*
The hall wallpaper is dark, of a faded grape design.
There are no carpets, no sign of occupation. Silence.
He crosses to the drawing room door, knocks.

Interior. Drawing room. Day.
From conservatory end of the large empty room see
BARRETT *look round the door. He walks into the room*
and peers into the conservatory. Low down in an old
deckchair lies a body.

Interior. Conservatory. Day.
BARRETT *approaches, stops a little way from the*
body, regards it. He bends over TONY.

BARRETT. Excuse me . . . (TONY *starts up.*) My name's
Barrett, sir.

TONY *stares at him, clicks his fingers.*

TONY. Oh God, of course. I'm so sorry, I fell asleep. We've got an appointment.

BARRETT. Yes, sir.

TONY. What time?

BARRETT. Three o'clock sir.

TONY. Well what time is it now?

BARRETT. Three o'clock, sir.

TONY. Too many beers at lunch, that's what it is. Do you drink beer?

BARRETT. No I don't, sir.

TONY *stands.*

TONY. Come upstairs. We can sit down.

They move to the door.

Interior. Hall. Stairs. Day.
They walk up the stairs.

TONY. I'm just back from Africa. I'm quite liking it. What do you think of the house?

BARRETT. It's very nice, sir.

TONY. Needs a lot done to it of course.

Interior. TONY's *bedroom. First floor. Day.*
Winter sun striking across floorboards. The room is empty but for two chairs. The door is flung open.
TONY *comes in, followed by* BARRETT. *His words gain a slight echo in the room.*

TONY. Damn lucky to get this place, actually. Little bit of wet rot, but not much. Sit down.

BARRETT. Thank you, sir.

BARRETT *sits.* BARRETT's *chair is in the centre of the room.* TONY, *while speaking, moves about the room, almost circling the seated figure.*

TONY. Well now, this post. What's happening is this . . . I'll be moving into this house in about . . . two or three weeks and I'm all alone at the moment, so I'll be needing a manservant, you see. I've seen one or two chaps already but they didn't seem very suitable to me somehow. What . . . you've had experience at this kind of work have you?

BARRETT. I've been in service for the last thirteen years, sir. The last few years I've acted as personal manservant to various members of the peerage.

TONY. Oh.

BARRETT. I was with Viscount Barr until about five weeks ago.

TONY. Oh Lord Barr? My father knew him well. They died within a week of each other as a matter of fact. So you're free?

BARRETT. I am sir.

TONY *stands at the front window.*

Exterior. Gardens in the square. Day.
The gardens in the square, seen by TONY *from the window.* BARRETT's *reflection in the pane.*

Interior. Bedroom. Day.
TONY *turns.*

TONY. Do you like the work?

BARRETT. Oh I do, sir. I do very much.

TONY. Can you cook?

BARRETT. Well it's . . . if I might put it this way, sir, cooking is something in which I take a great deal of pride.

TONY. Any dish in particular?

BARRETT. Well, my . . . my soufflés have always received a great deal of praise in the past, sir.

TONY. Do you know anything about Indian dishes?

BARRETT. A little, sir.

TONY. Well, I know a hell of a lot.

TONY *sits in the other chair.*

You'd have to do all the cooking here.

BARRETT. That would give me great pleasure, sir.

TONY. I could have got a housekeeper of course, to look after the place and run the kitchen, but quite honestly the thought of some old woman running about the house telling me what to do . . . rather put me off.

BARRETT. Quite, sir.

TONY. Now apart from the cooking, I'll need . . . well, everything . . . (*He laughs.*) General looking after . . . you know.

BARRETT. Yes, I do, sir.

Interior. Restaurant. Night.
Small, elegant restaurant with dance floor. The band playing. Dancers. SUSAN *swings into close shot over* TONY's *shoulder.*

SUSAN (*laughing*). Brazil?

TONY. Yes. In the jungle.

The music stops. They go back to the table.

TONY. Waiter! We've got to clear the jungle first.

SUSAN. What? just you?

TONY. No! It's a giant development. They're going to build three cities.

SUSAN. Are they?

TONY. Mm. Gigantic project. Matter of clearing hundreds of miles of jungle.

HEAD WAITER. Sir?

TONY. I'll have another bottle, and by the way, this one's corked.

HEAD WAITER. I'm very sorry, sir.

SUSAN. You're corked.

TONY. Now listen, I'm telling you. . . . First we have to build the cities. Then we've got to find the people to go and live in the cities.

SUSAN. Where are you going to find them?

TONY. From Asia Minor. Thousands of peasants, you see. They're having a pretty rough time of it in Asia Minor and this'll mean a new life for them. Anyway he wants me to help arrange the whole thing. It's going to cost millions, millions.

HEAD WAITER *returns with bottle. Pours.* TONY *sips.*

TONY. Fine. I'm having lunch with him next week.

SUSAN. Where? In the jungle?

TONY. Either here or in Paris, actually. Anyway there's no hurry. I could do with a rest.

SUSAN (*laughing*). A rest from what?

TONY. No. Seriously, what do you think of the idea?

SUSAN (*lifts her glass*). Cosy.

Interior. Drawing room. Bare floors. Night.
TONY and SUSAN lying on the floor, coats as a pillow, a rug over them. A small electric fire plugged in. Night light from window. They kiss.

TONY. Want to go there?

SUSAN. Where?

TONY. The jungle.

SUSAN. Not now.

TONY. No, not now.

He kisses her.

SUSAN. Batchelor.

She kisses him.

TONY. Oh by the way, I forgot to tell you. I've found a manservant.

SUSAN (*laughing*). What?

Interior. Hall and stairs. Day.
Looking from top of stairs down into empty hall. Voices ascend from kitchen.

BARRETT. Very good idea, sir.

They appear in hall, look up the stairs.

What about the landing, sir?

TONY. White.

They begin to walk up the stairs.

Interior. First landing. Day.
TONY *and* BARRETT *come up the stairs.*

TONY. Well perhaps a little blue here and there . . . but I think the overall colour should be white.

BARRETT. Mandarin red and fuschia is a very chic combination this year, sir.

TONY. Not overall, surely?

BARRETT. No, no, no. Not overall.

TONY. Just a wall?

BARRETT. Oh yes, just a wall, sir, here and there.

Interior. Bedroom. Day.
They enter and look about. TONY'*s personal bathroom and dressing room in background.*

TONY. You're very knowledgeable about decoration, Barrett.

BARRETT. Well, it makes all the difference to life, sir.

TONY. Oh. What does?

BARRETT. Tasteful and pleasant surroundings.

TONY. Quite right.

Interior. Top Landing. Day.
TONY *and* BARRETT *arrive on landing.*

TONY (*pointing*). That's your room. Wait a minute, what's that?

They open door of a small room.

Interior. Box Room. Day.
They enter. It is small, ill-lit.

TONY. Box room.

BARRETT. Always do for a maid, sir.

TONY. Oh we'll have a cleaning woman. D'you think we'll need a maid?

BARRETT. They can be useful, sir.

Interior. Hall. Day.

Decorators all over the house, plasterers, painters, etc.
The workmen set up plank on two ladders. BARRETT
coming downstairs passes them on his way to the
kitchen.

BARRETT. Mind the paintwork.

He looks in through the dining-room door.

Interior. Dining-room. Day. Sheets on the floor.
Painters on ladders.

BARRETT. Is everything going all right?

WORKMAN. Yes, thank you.

BARRETT. Yes, well I'll be glad if you'll tell me of any problem so we can correct it before it becomes a fault.

The two painters look at him, then at each other.
BARRETT *exits.*

Interior. Conservatory. Day.
TONY, *smoking, is sketching a design for the garden.*
BARRETT *enters from drawing-room and puts tray*
down.

BARRETT. Lunch, sir.

TONY. Ah that's nice.

BARRETT. No trouble, sir.

TONY. How are they getting on?

BARRETT. I'm keeping an eye on them.

TONY. Are you? You might bring me a lager.

BARRETT. I was just about to, sir.

TONY (*sitting to salad*). I'm ready for it.

BARRETT. Sir . . .

BARRETT *goes, leaving* TONY *eating.*

Exterior. TONY's *house. Night.*
High shot of sports car slowing to halt. TONY *and*
SUSAN *get out, go up steps.*

Interior. Hall. Night.
House well lit and carpeted. Furniture rather too large
for the rooms. It has come from TONY's *family house.*
BARRETT *opens the door, inclines his head.*

TONY. This is Barrett, Susan, Barrett . . . my fiancée
. . . Miss Stewart.

SUSAN. Hallo.

BARRETT. Good evening, Miss Stewart. Shall I take your
coat?

SUSAN. No, I'll keep it on, thanks.

TONY. In here.

Interior. Drawing-room. Night.
They come in. She looks about.

TONY. Do you like it?

SUSAN. Mm. It's beautiful.

BARRETT. The simple and classic is always the best, Miss.

She looks at a heavy ornament.

SUSAN. Is this classic? This isn't classic, it's prehistoric.

TONY. We've always had it and I like it. Barrett let's have
a drink.

BARRETT. Yes, sir.

SUSAN. Vodka on the rocks.

BARRETT. The usual, sir?

TONY. Thank you. Which one d'you want?

He gestures to armchairs.

SUSAN. This one.

TONY. My mother's favourite.

BARRETT *serves the drinks and exits.*

TONY. He's been a wonderful help, that chap. Wait till you
taste the food. Honestly, I've never been more
comfortable.

SUSAN. Never?

TONY. I don't have to think of a thing.

SUSAN. Does he give you breakfast in bed?

TONY. Of course.

She smiles faintly, stands, walks about.

SUSAN. Have you checked his criminal record?

BARRETT *appears at the door.*

TONY. Yes, Barrett?
BARRETT. You will ring, sir, when you'd like dinner served.
TONY. Yes, I will.

BARRETT *goes.*

SUSAN. Why didn't you get a housekeeper?
TONY. Oh, women are no damn good. They can't cook.

He seizes her, kisses her, pulls her on to sofa.

Interior. Dining-room. Night.
TONY *and* SUSAN *sitting at dinner.* BARRETT *with wine. He wears white cotton gloves.*
SUSAN. The whole place needs brightening . . . more variety you know . . . colour.
TONY. Oh. Do you think so?
SUSAN. Yes, and tomorrow I'm going to organize a proper spice shelf for the kitchen.
BARRETT. Would you like to taste the wine, sir?
TONY. Thank you.
SUSAN. What ducky gloves.
TONY. Barrett's idea. I like it.
BARRETT. It's Italian, miss. They're used in Italy.
SUSAN. Who by?

TONY *tastes wine.*

TONY. Excellent.
BARRETT. Just a Beaujolais sir, but a good bottler.
SUSAN. A good what?
TONY. Bottler.

BARRETT *slightly inclines his head and goes.*

Interior. Kitchen. Night.

BARRETT *sitting alone on chair in kitchen, smoking, picking his teeth.*

Exterior. House. Day.
TONY *running in pouring rain up steps of house.*

Interior. Hall. Day.
TONY's *wet feet. He takes off his raincoat.*

Interior. Kitchen. Day.
BARRETT *pouring salt into bowl of warm water.*

Interior. Drawing-room. Day.
TONY *sitting in library alcove.* BARRETT *undoes his shoes, takes socks off.* TONY *puts feet in bowl.*
TONY. Oh, is this necessary?
BARRETT. Better to be safe than sorry, sir.
TONY. You're too skinny to be a nanny, Barrett.

BARRETT *looks at him.*

Oh, come on, don't sulk, I didn't mean it.

He squiggles his feet.

Oh . . . oh . . . splendid!

Interior. Drawing-room. Night.
Close shot of SUSAN's *feet. Pull back to show* TONY *lying on carpet, smoking long, thin cigar.* SUSAN *sitting in chair. Record player on. The record plays throughout the scene.*
GIRL SINGING ON RECORD
Now while I love you alone
Now while I love you alone
Now while I love you
Can't love without you
Must love without you . . . alone.

SUSAN. Any news from your new frontier?

TONY. No, no, there isn't actually. Well, as a matter of fact he had to go over there and do various things, you know, make various arrangements. Heads of Government and all that.

SUSAN. Heard from him?

TONY. Yes, I mean of course the whole idea's in a very preliminary stage.

He puffs. Silence.

Still I'm quite happy at the moment, . . . aren't you?

SUSAN. Mm.

TONY. I can manage for a good few months. Oh, Barrett has installed my new abstract in the garden. Looks very chic doesn't it?

SUSAN *stands, looking through the conservatory into garden. Turns back, goes to him, kisses him. He pulls her to the floor with him, kisses her. The record continues.*

GIRL SINGING
. . . Leave it alone
It's all gone
Leave it alone
It's all gone
Don't stay to see me
Turn from your arms
Leave it alone
It's all gone
Give me my death
Close my mouth
Give me my breath
Close my mouth
How can I bear
The ghost of you here
Can't love without you
Must love without you . . .

. . . Now while I love you alone

Now while I love you
Can't love without you
Must love without you
Now while I love you alone
Now while I love you alone
Now while I love you
Can't love without you
Must love without you . . . alone.

TONY. That mouth! (*She kisses him.*) Why don't you come and stay?

SUSAN. For a weekend? . . . A long weekend? . . . Or a couple of weeks . . .?

TONY. Marry me.

They embrace. She rolls on top of him. A concealed door opens in the library alcove. BARRET comes in. They look up.
Music ends.

BARRETT (*withdrawing*). I'm so sorry to disturb you, sir.

He closes the door. SUSAN lies still. TONY stands.

TONY. I'm sorry.
SUSAN. Why didn't he knock?
TONY. He made a mistake.

Pause.

SUSAN. Mistake! Well for God's sake, restrict him to quarters.

Pause.

Couldn't he live out?
TONY. Out? No he couldn't.
SUSAN. Well he doesn't have to be here after he's washed up the dinner things, does he?

He looks at her blankly.

TONY. He's got to lock up!

Pause.

SUSAN. Well I think I should go anyway.

TONY. Why?
SUSAN. I'm just going.
TONY. This is ridiculous.

She goes to the door, hesitates.

SUSAN. Come home and stay with me.
TONY. Oh look, . . . stay here.

She goes out.

Interior. Hall. Night.
SUSAN *collects her coat,* TONY *helps her on with it.*
BARRETT *appears, opens front door for her. She looks at him.*

SUSAN. A little late for you, Barrett, isn't it? About time you were tucked up in bed.

TONY *gestures to* BARRETT, *who goes.*

TONY. I'll drive you back.
SUSAN. No.
TONY. I'll walk along with you.
SUSAN (*gently*). No.

She takes his face with her hands, kisses him, goes.
TONY *stands, then goes into drawing-room.*

Interior. Drawing-room. Night.
BARRETT *enters.*

BARRETT. I do apologize for the intrusion, sir. I had no idea...
TONY. Don't do it again!
BARRETT. I did knock, sir.
TONY. Oh get to bed . . .

TONY *puts his hand to his head*

TONY. Have you got an aspirin?
BARRETT. Yes, sir. I expect you caught a bit of a chill the other day in the rain, sir.

Interior. TONY's *bedroom. Day.*
TONY *in bed.* SUSAN *drawing curtains, opens windows.*

SUSAN. You need more air.

TONY. Oh I don't know.

SUSAN. No, you don't.

She turns, goes to door, goes out.

Interior. Landing. Day.
*BARRETT is there as SUSAN comes out and takes vase
of flowers from table, then returns to bedroom.*

Interior. Bedroom. Day.
SUSAN comes back with a vase of flowers, places them.

TONY. Oh God! I'm so sorry. I completely forgot. They're
beautiful. Thanks very much.

SUSAN. Every time you open a door in this house that man's
outside. He's a Peeping Tom.

TONY. He's a vampire too on his Sundays off.

SUSAN. Why didn't you have them in your room?

TONY. Well as a matter of fact he was saying that they're
bad in a sick room at night . . .

A knock on the door.

. . . come in.

BARRETT comes in.

BARRETT. Your medicine, sir. And the post.

TONY. Oh thank you.

*BARRETT gives TONY the capsules and a glass of
water. TONY takes them.*
*BARRETT leaves the mail on the bedside table. An
uneasy silence.*

SUSAN. What did the Doctor say yesterday?

TONY. Oh nothing much. Virus.

*BARRETT picks up the vase to move it to another
position in the room.*

SUSAN. Put that down!

Pause.

TONY. Oh put it down, Barrett.
BARRETT (*doing so*). I beg your pardon, sir.

BARRETT goes.

TONY. I do wish you'd stop yapping at Barrett all the
time. It'll be a bastard if he leaves.
SUSAN. What the hell would that matter?
TONY. What would it matter? Well, you try and find
another like him.
SUSAN. I'm sorry I was rude to your servant.
TONY. Look, he may be a servant but he's still a human
being!

She turns, leaves the room.

Interior. Hall. Day.
*BARRETT, beating SUSAN to the front door, opens it
for her.*
BARRETT. I'm afraid it's not very encouraging miss . . . the
weather forecast.

*She looks at him for a moment steadily, and then goes
down the steps. BARRETT closes the door behind her.*

Exterior. TONY's house. Knightsbridge Square. Day.
*SUSAN stops at the base of the steps. Suddenly looking
lost. A wind is blowing through the square.*

Exterior. Knightsbridge Square. Early evening.
The wind has now grown in force. The streets are wet.

*Interior. Public phone box. Knightsbridge Square.
Early evening.*
BARRETT stands in the phone box.
BARRETT. Yes. Bolton 62545.

*He waits. A group of girls collects outside the box,
talking, giggling. The skirt of one of the girls blows up.*

BARRETT *observes this blankly. Another girl remarks on his gaze. The girls laugh. The operator tells him to go ahead.*

VERA'S VOICE. Hallo.

BARRETT. Vera?

VERA'S VOICE. Yes.

BARRETT. Are you ready?

VERA'S VOICE. Yes, I'm ready . . .

BARRETT. All right then, tomorrow.

VERA'S VOICE. All right. I've bought something new.

BARRETT. Mm?

BARRETT'*s attention goes again to the group of girls. The same girl is trying to keep her skirt down in the wind.*

VERA'S VOICE. . . . I'm wearing it now.

BARRETT. Oh.

VERA'S VOICE. I'll show it to you if you're being a good boy.

BARRETT. I am. Are you being a good girl?

VERA'S VOICE. What?

He grits his teeth.

BARRETT. I said are you being a good girl?

VERA'S VOICE. I am.

BARRETT. I'll be at the station.
You got my last letter, didn't you?

VERA'S VOICE. Oh yes, I got that all right.

BARRETT. All right then. At the station. Tara.

VERA'S VOICE. Bye.

BARRETT *goes out of box. The girl squeezes past him.*
BARRETT *jabs her away.*

BARRETT. Get out of it, you filthy bitch.

Interior. Dining-room. TONY'*s house. Night.*
BARRETT *has made certain changes in this room too, as throughout the house.*
TONY *is at the table.* BARRETT *standing by.*

TONY. You've mulled some delicious claret, Barrett.

(*He laughs.*) I say, that's rather good, isn't it? Claretty Barrett.

BARRETT. In the army they used to call me Basher Barrett, sir.

TONY. Oh really? Why?

BARRETT. I was a very good driller.

TONY. Ah! (*Pause.*) I like the changes you've been making in the house. You've been enjoying yourself, haven't you?...

BARRETT *clears a little.*

BARRETT. I have, sir . . . thank you very much, sir. Oh by the way, sir, I took the liberty of removing those er chintz frills of Miss Stewart's off the dressing table. Not very practical. (TONY *grunts.*) Haven't seen very much of Miss Stewart recently have we sir?

TONY. Mmmmn? No.

BARRETT. My sister's arriving tomorrow sir, as you agreed.

TONY. Oh yes. Fine.

BARRETT. She's very happy about the arrangement, if you are.

TONY. Well, we might keep her, if she's any good.

Euston Station. Day.
BARRETT *standing on platform. A train draws in.*

Cocktail bar in Soho French restaurant. Day.
TONY *is standing at bar. A man and girl talking.*

GIRL. He's a wonderful wit.

MAN. Terribly funny.

GIRL. Terribly.

MAN. Cheers.

GIRL. Cheers. I'm dying to see him again. I haven't seen him for ages.

MAN. You won't for some time.

GIRL. Oh. Why?

MAN. He's in prison.

SUSAN *enters the restaurant.*

TONY. Hello

SUSAN. Hello.

SUSAN. I just don't like him.

TONY. You don't know him. (*Pause*.) I mean surely you can take my word for the fact.

SUSAN. Don't trust him.

TONY. Why?

SUSAN. I don't know.

GIRL. It's the snow. It's the snow I like.

TONY. He looks like a fish with red lips I admit. But apart from that, what's the matter with him? You're making him so bloody important. I mean it seems to me you've got the whole thing absurdly out of proportion.

SUSAN. Yes, perhaps.

They pick up glasses.
BISHOP *and* CURATE *get up.*

BISHOP. And where are you creeping off to now, my son . . . ah?

CURATE. Nowhere Your Grace, nowhere . . . Nowhere at all.

BISHOP. Is that a fact?

SUSAN. Why don't you just tell him to go?

TONY. You must be mad. (*Pause*.) You just don't care about my . . . and what it amounts to is it's my judgement you're criticizing. It's not only ridiculous it's bloody hurtful.

GIRL (*at other table*). They were gorgeous – absolutely gorgeous.

MAN. Were they really?

TONY. I'm sorry. I'm a fool.

SUSAN. You are.

TONY. Well . . . I mean . . .

GIRL. Divine, but I simply couldn't get them on.

MAN. Pity!

Pause. SUSAN *touches* TONY'*s hand.*

SUSAN. Look . . . I'm sorry.

TONY. Well . . . well I wouldn't . . .

He touches her hand, frowning, unsure.

Interior. TONY's *house. First landing. Day.*
BARRETT *showing* VERA *up the stairs. On the first landing she looks into* TONY's *bedroom and at* BARRETT. *He guides her away and up further flight to her room.*

Interior. TONY's *house. Top landing and small room. Day.*
BARRETT *showing* VERA *to her bedroom. She looks round the room and then at him. He regards her, expressionless.*

Interior. Hall. Day.
TONY *is by front door.*
TONY. Barrett!

He goes into drawing-room.

Interior. Drawing-room. Day.
TONY *enters.*
TONY. Barrett!

He unwraps package and takes out a short black silk dressing gown. He hears BARRETT *and throws it on the sofa.*

BARRETT. Did you call, sir?
TONY. Yes. Damn awful lunch. Where were you? Get me a brandy.
BARRETT. Ycs sir.

BARRETT *pours brandy and notices gown.*

It's very handsome, sir.

TONY *drinks.*

Oh . . . might I introduce my sister to you, sir? She's arrived . . . she's very excited at the prospect of being with us.

TONY. Oh is she?

BARRETT *turns to door.*

BARRETT. Vera.

Interior. Kitchen. Day.
Boiling water into teapot from kettle. Camera pulls back to show BARRETT *checking the tea tray. He passes it into* VERA's *hands. She exits.*

Interior. Drawing-room. Day.
TONY *lying in an armchair. His feet rest on a foot stool. A side table by his chair.* VERA *comes in, places tea tray on side table with great care, bending over* TONY *to do so.*

Interior. Drawing-room. Twilight.
TONY *still lying, dozing, a book on the floor, the tea tray empty.* VERA *and* BARRETT *enter with flowers. They arrange the flowers on a table by the window.* TONY *watches through half-open eyes. He sees* VERA's *face and throat through the flowers, her body, in her short black maid's uniform, moving under the table, her legs.*

Interior. Lord and Lady Mountset's country house. Late afternoon.
LORD *and* LADY MOUNTSET, TONY *and* SUSAN.

LADY MOUNTSET. Well I'm absolutely certain you'll be fascinated by Brazil.

LORD MOUNTSET. Oh yes.

LADY MOUNTSET. I was in the Argentine of course, briefly, as a girl. . . . I was certainly fascinated by the Argentine.

TONY. It should be very interesting.

LADY
  MOUNTSET. Fascinating, Tony darling.
LORD
  MOUNTSET. How many cities are you going to build?
  SUSAN. Three.
  TONY. Yes, it's – quite a big development.
LORD
  MOUNTSET. In the jungle?
  TONY. Not exactly in the jungle, no sir. On the plain.
  SUSAN. Oh but some of the jungle will have to be cleared, won't it?
  TONY. Some of the jungle, yes. A little bit.
LADY   That's where the Ponchos are, of course, on the
  MOUNTSET. plains.
  SUSAN. Ponchos?
LORD
  MOUNTSET. South American cowboys.
  SUSAN. Are they called Ponchos?
LORD
  MOUNTSET. They were in my day.
  SUSAN. Aren't they those things they wear? You know, with the slit in the middle for the head to go through?
LORD
  MOUNTSET. What do you mean?
  SUSAN. Well, you know . . . hanging down in front and behind . . . the cowboy.
LADY
  MOUNTSET. They're called cloaks, dear.

Interior. First landing. Morning.
Very close shot of TONY's *bedroom door.* VERA's *hand comes into shot and knocks on it.*
TONY'S VOICE. Come in.

Interior. TONY's *bedroom. Morning.*
TONY *in bed, no pyjamas.* VERA *comes in with breakfast, sets it down.*

VERA. Good morning sir.
TONY. Morning . . . Where's Barrett?
VERA. He's gone out shopping sir.

She opens the curtains and arranges them.

Anything else, sir?
TONY. No thank you.

She picks up about the room. TONY *watches. She goes.*

Interior. Kitchen. Day.
BARRETT *comes in through the kitchen door from the garden.* VERA *enters from hall. They look at each other. She goes to the sideboard and pours tea, crosses to the table and sits on it. Her skirt is above her knees. As* BARRETT *approaches she begins to grin. Her grin fades to an expression of intense anticipation. As he draws closer to her her head is suddenly flung back in a soundless sexual laugh, mouth open.*

Interior. TONY's *bedroom. Day.*
Close shot of silent valet. BARRETT's *hand taking jacket off it, helping* TONY *into it.*
Pause.
TONY. For God's sake look at this. That's not much good, Barrett!
BARRETT. I beg your pardon, sir.

BARRETT *brushes the jacket gently.*

TONY. Pull your socks up now. Come on, come on, come on, give it a good brush, you won't hurt me.
BARRETT. Perhaps you'd like to take the jacket off, sir?
TONY. No, damn it. Do it on. I haven't got time to mess about.

BARRETT *brushes vigorously.*

BARRETT. Would you turn round sir.

TONY. No. All right, all right. (*Sulkily*.) All right, it'll have to do.

He goes to the mirror.

BARRETT. We heard this morning that our mother's ill up in Manchester, sir. Apparently she's been asking for us. It might be dangerous. Would you mind if we took the night off and came back tomorrow late?

TONY. Both of you?

BARRETT. Well it is touch and go, sir.

TONY. Well that's bloody inconvenient.

BARRETT. I appreciate that, sir, I do appreciate that. But we could leave you a cold buffet and salad.

TONY. I wanted something hot! Couldn't you make it tomorrow?

BARRETT. I suppose we could, sir.

TONY. Make it tomorrow. It'll give us time to get organized.

BARRETT. Right, sir.

TONY. Well I'm off.

BARRETT. Oh there's one other thing I'd like a brief word with you, sir, about, before you go.

TONY. Well what is it?—Where's my Cologne?

BARRETT. It's about Vera.

TONY. What about her?

BARRETT. Well it's her skirts, sir. They rather worry me.

TONY. Her skirts? What's the matter with them?

BARRETT. Well, might I suggest that they're a little short, sir?

Silence.

TONY. A little short?

BARRETT. I should say so.

Pause.

TONY. Well what the hell do you want me to do about it? She's your sister, tell her yourself. Where's my Cologne? . . .

He crosses through dressing room, to bathroom door.

VERA'S VOICE. Don't come in. I'm naked! Who is it?

TONY *stops still. The door remains ajar.*

VERA'S VOICE. Oh, I am sorry, I forgot to lock the door.

TONY. I want my Cologne.

VERA. Your what?

TONY. The bottle . . .

VERA. It's all right, I've got a towel on now.

TONY *grasps the door handle and holds the door firmly towards him.*

TONY. I just want my Cologne.

He waits, his face set.

VERA. What, the one with your initials on?

TONY. Yes.

The door is pulled. TONY *resists the pull, holds the door tight, slightly ajar. Her arm comes through with the Cologne.*

VERA. I'm sorry sir, I thought everyone was out.

For a moment he watches her hand move, searching for him. He then takes the bottle, goes back into his room and dabs Cologne on his handkerchief.

TONY. D'you know Vera's in my bathroom?

BARRETT. I beg your pardon, sir?

TONY. She's having a bath in my bathroom. Well, I mean to say . . . I mean . . . after all . . . you've got one of your own upstairs.

He gives BARRETT *the Cologne.*

Have a word with her.

TONY *exits.* BARRETT *crosses to bathroom and enters.*

Interior. Bathroom. Day.

BARRETT *and* VERA. VERA *in towel. He holds the bottle of Cologne.*

BARRETT. Who told you to take a bath in his bathroom? Who said you could use his bathroom? A gentleman doesn't want a naked girl bouncing about all over his bathroom.

VERA. You told me to, didn't you?

BARRETT. Me? Why would I tell you a thing like that?

He closes the door.

I'll tell you what I'm going to do now.

VERA. What?

BARRETT. I'm going to have a bath in his bathroom.

VERA *turns the tap.*

VERA. You're terrible.

He gives her the Cologne.

BARRETT. And I want that . . . all over me.

He takes off his jacket. She watches him. The water boils into the bath.

Interior. Bedroom. Day.
The square is seen through the window. BARRETT *and* VERA *walking, with bags.* TONY *comes into foreground, watches, turns, heavy. Telephone rings.*

TONY. Hallo.

SUSAN'S VOICE. It's me.

TONY. Oh hello.

SUSAN'S VOICE. I've been worried about you.

TONY. Er – can I ring you back?

SUSAN'S VOICE. Well yes – but when?

TONY. Are you at the office?

SUSAN'S VOICE. Yes, but I'm just going out. Are you in tonight?

TONY. Er . . . Yes. Ring me then, would you?

SUSAN'S VOICE. All right, good-bye.

TONY. Bye . . . bye.

Interior. Chelsea coffee bar. Night.
It is crowded. Guitarist. TONY *at table signalling to waitress. She eventually comes to his table and*

clears some dirty crockery. As she bends over table she momentarily resembles VERA. TONY *vaguely holds menu.*

WAITRESS. Back in a moment, sir.

She goes. He is left. She comes back towards him but is waylaid by another table. He starts tapping knife, suddenly rises, goes to the door. The cashier looks at him.

CASHIER. Yes, sir. Can I help you?
TONY. No I haven't had anything.

He goes out.

Exterior. Brompton Road. Night.
Snow. Late at night. Distant storm approaching.
TONY *walking along the road, alone.*

Exterior. TONY's *house. Knightsbridge Square. Night.*
Snow. TONY *walking to house. He goes slowly up the steps.*

Interior. Hall. TONY's *house. Night.*
TONY *switches on light, throws coat onto hall stand, stands irresolute. He looks at mail, throws it down unopened, goes to the kitchen.*

Interior. Kitchen. TONY's *house. Night.*
TONY *comes in, turns on the light, pours a glass of water, puts ice in it, sips it. He puts glass down on the sink, sits down, picks up paper, stares at it. He looks for glass, puts down paper, stands, collects glass, drinks, standing. Suddenly he turns round sharply.*
VERA *is at the door.*

VERA. Oh! . . . I wondered who it was.
TONY. What are you . . . what are you doing here?

VERA. I was just going to bed and – I thought I heard a
noise.

TONY. But you went to Manchester.

VERA. I didn't feel too well at the station, so he sent me
back in a taxi.

Silence. The tap is dripping.

TONY. Sent you back?

VERA. Yes . . .

Tap dripping.

TONY. How do you feel now?

VERA. I feel a bit better.

He stares at her. She smiles.

TONY. Shall I get you a glass of water?

VERA. I'm glad it was you. I thought it might have been
him coming back.

TONY. Has he gone?

VERA. Oh yes – yes he went. I'm glad I'm not alone.
I didn't fancy being alone by myself in this house.

Tap dripping. TONY *turns the tap off, turns. Silence.*

VERA. Can I get you anything, sir?

TONY. No . . . no . . .

Phone rings. They look at it. TONY *does not move.
It stops.*
VERA *perches on the table*

VERA. . . . Oh . . . isn't it hot in here . . . Isn't it? . . .

The saucepan and crockery glisten on the shelves.

So hot.

The kitchen glistens, the gas stove, the pans. VERA's
*body inclines backward on the table, her skirt half-
way up her thighs.*

TONY. Your skirt's too short.

VERA (*looking down at her legs*). My what? That's how all
the girls are wearing them. Well that's how they all

wear them . . . Why? do you think it's too short?

He comes close to the table. She gestures to his face.

You hot?

A sudden savage embrace.

Oh that's nice that's nice oh that's nice.

Two figures seen distorted in shining saucepans.

Interior. Hall. Evening.
BARRETT *enters, examines mail, walks to kitchen.*

Interior. Kitchen.
BARRETT *studies two plates on table, chicken bones on them.* TONY *appears in the kitchen door.*

TONY. Oh, hello Barrett, how's your Mother?
BARRETT. On the mend, sir.
TONY. Oh, good. Good. Little Vera wasn't very well then?

BARRETT *takes plates to the sink.*

BARRETT. Well no. She looked so poorly at the railway station, sir, I thought it wasn't wise to let her travel. I hope she hasn't been any inconvenience to you.
TONY. Oh not at all. No, she hasn't at all.
BARRETT. Did she manage to do anything for you, sir?

TONY *looks at him sharply.*

TONY. I beg your pardon.
BARRETT. I hope she was well enough to see to your meals.
TONY. Oh yes, yes, we . . . I had lunch.
BARRETT. I notice she didn't do the washing up.
TONY. Still under the weather, I suppose.
BARRETT. Under the what, sir?
TONY. The weather.
BARRETT. Oh yes.
TONY. Oh Barrett, you wouldn't like to go to the off-licence for me would you, for a quart of beer? I've got rather a thirst.

BARRETT. There's plenty of beer, sir.

TONY. Yes I know that, but I want some plain brown ale.

BARRETT. Certainly, sir.

BARRETT *exits*.

Interior. Hall. Evening.
BARRETT *goes out front door.* TONY *appears immediately and calls.*

TONY. Vera!

VERA. Yes sir?

TONY. Come down a minute.

VERA. I'm coming. Where are you?

TONY. Down here. He's back.

He steps into library door. She comes down the stairs. As she passes him, he grasps her from behind. She screams, wheels round, giggling.

VERA. Oh you . . . what are you doing?

He pulls her into the library.

Interior. Library alcove.
He seats VERA *in the leather chair.*

VERA. I've got to wash up.

TONY. I've sent him to the pub, he'll be back in a minute.

VERA. Who cares about him?

TONY. Well, he's your brother.

VERA. What are you doing? (*Giggles.*)

Exterior. Knightsbridge Square. Evening.
BARRETT *approaching* TONY's *house steadily.*

Exterior. Library. Evening.
VERA *and* TONY *in embrace.*

Exterior. TONY's *house.*
BARRETT *up the front steps, opens the door.*

Interior. Library. Evening.
TONY *and* VERA *half lying on the table.* TONY *hears the door.*

TONY. Come down at twelve o'clock.

He goes quickly through the library door into the garden.

Interior. Hall. Evening.
VERA *meets* BARRETT *at foot of stairs. She looks at him.*

VERA. I'm going to bed, I'm tired.

He watches her go upstairs and goes into drawing-room.

Interior. Kitchen. Night.
BARRETT *pouring a glass of brown ale.* TONY *comes in through kitchen door from garden.*

TONY. Oh hullo Barrett. Just getting a bit of air in the garden.

BARRETT. Rather cold, sir.

TONY. Got the beer? Oh good.

BARRETT. Anything else you want, sir?

TONY. No thanks, I'll be going out soon but I'll be back before . . . midnight. There'll be no need for you to wait up for me. I'll lock up myself.

BARRETT. Right, sir.

TONY *picks up glass of ale, sips, grimaces.*

Interior. Drawing-room. Night.
Later. Near midnight. TONY *drinking whisky. He jumps up, looks at watch, goes out.*

Interior. Hall. Night.
TONY *comes out of the drawing-room and goes up the stairs.*

Interior. First landing. Night.
TONY *comes up from the hall and continues up the stairs to the top landing.*

Interior. Top Landing. Night.
It is dark. TONY *comes up stairs, looks warily at* BARRETT's *door, then taps very lightly on* VERA's *door. After a few seconds her voice is heard through the keyhole.*

VERA. All right, I'm coming. Go down.

TONY *goes downstairs.*
There is a pause and the light goes on in VERA's *room. She opens the door carefully and looks out.*

Interior. VERA's *room. Night.*
A low angled shot from the stairs. As VERA *opens the door further to come out,* BARRETT *can be seen in her bed reaching for a newspaper which he picks up and reads. She exits.*

Interior. Drawing-room. Night.
TONY *pulls* VERA *to him in the half darkness.*

TONY. Are you cold?
VERA. No.
TONY. What about him? Is he asleep?
VERA. His room's dark.

He stares at her. He lowers her into the leather chair, swings the chair so that she faces him. Her legs stretch out across the arms of the chair.

Interior. First landing. Day.
VERA *knocks on* TONY's *door.*

TONY. Come in.
VERA. Can I have your tray, sir?

She goes in. Camera stays on closed door.

Interior. Hall. Day.
BARRETT *comes from kitchen to alcove under the stairs and hides there.*

Interior. First landing. Day.
VERA *slips out of* TONY's *door, flushed, and goes downstairs carrying the tray.*

Interior. Hall. Day.
VERA *comes downstairs, puts tray down on hall table and looks at herself in mirror. Suddenly* BARRETT's *hands reach for her. He pulls her back out of sight. A sharp gasp from her, a grating 'Aaaaahhh' from him. A phone can be heard ringing off screen. Stay on empty hall.*

Interior. TONY's *bedroom. Day.*
TONY *still in bed. He is on the telephone.*

TONY. Hallo.
SUSAN'S VOICE. Hallo.
TONY. Oh hullo Susan.
SUSAN'S VOICE. Did you get my note? I expect you've been rather busy?
TONY. Yes. I have been rather busy, actually, with one thing and another.
SUSAN'S VOICE. Well what time will you call then?
TONY. Oh about two-thirty. Should give us time enough to get down there. I'm having lunch with my father's solicitor.
SUSAN'S VOICE. All right. Well see you then.
TONY. Right. Bye.
SUSAN. Bye.

Interior. Hall. Day.
TONY *runs up from below and opens the door of* VERA's *bedroom.*

Interior. VERA's *bedroom. Day.*
VERA *is in bed. She is pale, limp, trembling, exhausted.*
TONY *goes in.*

TONY. What's the matter?

VERA *looks a child, trembling continually.*

TONY. What's the matter. What is it?
VERA. I'm not well.

He sits on the bed.

TONY. What is it?

No answer. He touches her hand.

He's gone out . . . I . . .

She looks at him with a tense distrustful smile. She speaks suddenly and harshly, with a bitter reined hysteria.

VERA. Come on then.

Interior. Hall. Day.
BARRETT *opens front door to* SUSAN. *She carries flowers.*
BARRETT. I'm afraid the master's not at home.
SUSAN. I know. Collect my things from the taxi please.

BARRETT *goes out of the house to collect parcel from taxi.* SUSAN *moves into the drawing-room.*

Interior. Drawing-room.
SUSAN *picks up a vase.* BARRETT *comes in.*
SUSAN. Fill this with water. Where's the parcel?
BARRETT. It's in the hall, Miss.
SUSAN. Bring it to me.

BARRETT *collects the parcel and brings it in. He goes out with vase. Re-enters with it.* SUSAN *arranges flowers in the vase.*

SUSAN. How do you like them, Barrett?

BARRETT. I'm not certain that the flowers wouldn't be better in a different jar, Miss.

SUSAN. I thought you'd be uncertain, Barrett. (*She opens the parcel and throws a number of small cushions from it on to the sofa.*) What do you think of them?

BARRETT. I beg your pardon?

SUSAN. What do you think of the cushions?

BARRETT. It's difficult to say what I think of them, Miss.

SUSAN. Shall I tell you the truth, Barrett?

BARRETT. Yes, Miss.

SUSAN. The truth is, I don't care what you think.

Pause

I want some lunch. A salad will do. Use the tarragon I bought on Wednesday.

BARRETT. Yes, Miss.

She takes a cigarette.

SUSAN. Light . . . Put that coat down and give me a light.

BARRETT *lights her cigarette. Moves to the door.*

SUSAN. Barrett! Come here.

He goes to her.

Do you use a deodorant?

He stares at her.
Tell me. Do you think you go well with the colour scheme?

BARRETT. I think the Master's satisfied.

SUSAN. What do you want from this house?

BARRETT. Want?

SUSAN. Yes, want.

BARRETT. I'm the servant, Miss.

SUSAN. Get my lunch.

Exterior. LORD MOUNTSET'S *estate. Day.*
Gracious turreted house. Lawns and arbours. Undulating fields sweep down to lake. Poplars. Two figures far down by the lake. Keep on them for some seconds in the distance. They are throwing snowballs.

Exterior. The lake. Day.
TONY *and* SUSAN *running. They stop and kiss.*

SUSAN. Why don't you come up to my room? There's a wonderful view from there. Or what about your room? What's it like from yours?

TONY. It's not very good from mine.

SUSAN *laughs.*

TONY. The best view . . . is from our room . . . at the house. What about leaving tonight?

SUSAN. Wouldn't that be a little rude?

TONY. No . . . no . . . they won't mind.

Interior. TONY's *car. Evening.*
TONY *driving.* SUSAN *huddled close to him.*

Exterior. The square. Night.
The car coming into the square, drawing up to the house. It slows.

Interior. Car. Night.

TONY. There's a light on in my room. Quarter to twelve. Who the hell's in my room?

Interior. Hall. TONY's *house. Night.*
The dark hall. TONY *opens the front door softly. He walks carefully to the stairs, treads halfway up and halts.* SUSAN *remains at the bottom.*
A light comes through his bedroom door, which is ajar.
Voices:

BARRETT. Give us one over.

VERA. You've only just had one.

BARRETT. Well I want another one.

Pause.

VERA. All this bloody smoking, it drives you mad.

BARRETT. You're driving me mad.

Pause.

VERA. Come on . . . oh come on for Christ's sake, put it down.

BARRETT. I've only had one puff.

VERA. Oh come on put it down.

BARRETT. I'm worn out. What's the matter with you?

VERA. I know someone who wouldn't say no.

BARRETT. Him? He'd be on the floor.

Bedcreak. Rustle.

Let me finish this fag. You're like a bloody machine.

VERA. I know I am but I can't help it.

TONY *rests his head against the wall.*

SUSAN. It's your servants.

There is a sudden silence in the house. BARRETT's *voice.*

BARRETT. There's someone there.

VERA. No, there isn't.

BARRETT. Did you lock up?

VERA. Of course I did.

BARRETT. What about the bolt?

VERA. Oh no . . . well I didn't bolt.

BARRETT. You bloody little idiot!

A silence. TONY *and* SUSAN *remain still.* BARRETT's *naked shadow appears at the top of the stairs.*
TONY *turns and looks up. A long silent stare between them.*
Suddenly, harshly, raucously, VERA's *voice.*

VERA. There's no one there. I told you. Oh come on, Hugo. You'll catch your death of cold out there. I'm waiting for you. Come and look at me, I'm all here waiting for you! Come on, what's the matter with you? I'm all rosy lying here. I'm rosyyyyy! What the bloody hell are you doing?

BARRETT *turns and goes back.*

Interior. Drawing-room. Night.
TONY *enters the dark room, covers his face.* SUSAN
follows, switching on lights.

SUSAN. What are you going to do?

He does not answer.

SUSAN. This is your house.

Silence.

SUSAN. They're in your room, in your bed.

Pause.

Did you know this was going on?

Pause.

TONY *abruptly shivers, clenches his fist and goes to the
door.*

TONY. Barrett! Barrett! Come down here.

He comes back. A tense silence.

I think I should see him alone.

SUSAN. Why?

BARRETT *appears at the foot of the stairs and stops
at the drawing-room door.*

TONY. Come here.

He steps into the room.

I want an explanation.

BARRETT. Might I speak to you alone, sir?

TONY. Do you realize you've committed a criminal
offence?

BARRETT. Criminal, sir?

TONY. She's your sister, you bastard!

BARRETT *looks at him.*

BARRETT. She's not my sister, sir. (*Pause.*) And if I might say
so we're both rather in the same boat.

Silence. BARRETT *looks at* SUSAN.

He knows precisely what I mean . . .

She stares at TONY.

BARRETT. . . . In any case, apart from the error of being in
your room I'm perfectly within my rights. Vera's
my fiancée.

TONY. What!? (*dully*).

BARRETT *goes to door.*

BARRETT. Vera.

They wait. She comes down to door.

BARRETT. Owing to this unfortunate incident, Vera, we shall
have to tell our little secret to Mister Tony. Come
on . . . don't be shy. Go and tell him, go on.

VERA. Hugo and I are going to be married.
Well, you've done all right, what are you worrying
about? You can't have it on a plate for ever, can
you? Oh come on Hugo!

BARRETT *inclines his head slightly and they both go.*

TONY. Get out! Both of you!

SUSAN *is sitting.* TONY *sits on the arm of a chair.*
Sounds of drawers being pulled out, cases banging,
from upstairs. TONY *rises and pours a drink, drinks*
it, pours another. They do not look at each other. He
stands, goes to record player, puts on a record. 'All
gone.'

GIRL SINGING
. . . my mouth
How can I bear (*Door slams.*)
The ghost of you here
Can't love without you . . .
. . . must love without you
Now while I love you alone
Now while I love you alone
Now while I love you
Can't love without you
Must love without you—alone

Now while I love you
Can't love without you
Can't love without you alone.

Silence between them. Sounds of BARRETT *and* VERA *descending stairs. The front door slams.* TONY *turns and looks at* SUSAN. *They look at each other. Eventually* TONY *in a half-appeal, half-demand, whispers:*

TONY. Come to bed.

She slowly stands. He half moves to her. She turns, goes out of the door and out of the house.
He stands, alone. Switches off record. Looks at door, slowly moves out of room.

Interior. Stairs. Night.
TONY *slowly ascending stairs.*

Interior. VERA's *bedroom. Night.*
TONY *enters room, looks at disordered bed. He goes to it, lies flat out on it.*

Interior. Hall. Day.
TONY *is alone in the house. He treads unsteadily down the stairs and goes into kitchen.*

Interior. Kitchen. Day.
The kitchen is very untidy. He rummages amid the unwashed plates for a can of fruit juice. It is empty. He throws it away. He fumbles in a corner for a bottle of squash. It has only dregs in it. He unscrews the top and puts it to his nose, grimaces, looks into the bottle. The orange flakes appear atrophied in the stagnant juice. He screws the top and lifts up the lid of the waste bin. The bin is full to bursting with rubbish, its top covered

with fish-bones. He tries to lodge the bottle between two piles of crockery on the draining board, the bottle slips and falls with a bang. He kicks it viciously.

Exterior. London street. Night.
TONY, *quite aimless, walking spasmodically. He is drooped. He stops to watch the buses and taxis go by. His face in the passing lights is haggard, blank.*

Interior. Public phone box. Night.
TONY *dialling number. He listens.*
SUSAN'S VOICE. Hello. Who's that? Tony? Hello who is it? Hello.

He replaces the receiver.

Interior. Drawing-room. Night.
TONY *in room, which is also in some disarray. He is unshaven, drinking a large whisky. He goes to record player and with slightly trembling hands puts a record on the turn-table. He lifts the head and attempts to place it in the groove. Three times he fails, the needle sheering off the side of the record. Suddenly his trembling hand jerks the head which scrapes in a grating scratch across the record. He stands hunched.*

Interior. First pub. Evening.
TONY *wanders into the saloon bar of a pub which is half empty. He goes to the bar, orders whisky, sits next to a man. Beyond the man is a partition that separates the saloon bar from the private bar. Both bars are visible in full mirror behind the barman.* BARRETT *is sitting up at the private bar just beyond the partition.* TONY *has not seen him. He drinks half his whisky in a gulp and is then conscious of being watched. He looks into the mirror, sees* BARRETT. *He looks away. Then half back, then away again. For some minutes there is*

a quiet in the pub, the only sounds being the bell on the cash register and the spasmodic sound of conversation. At the bar, BARRETT *and* TONY, *with the third man between them, look into their glasses intently, glance up at the bottles on the shelves. Neither of them moves. The third man, an oldish man, stands gloomily. The third man suddenly speaks to no one in particular.*

MAN. I had a bit of bad luck today.

There is no response. The BARMAN *appears, polishing some glasses, looks vaguely for any further orders, withdraws.*
I really had a bit of bad luck.

Silence.

It'll take me a good few days to get over it, I can tell you.

Pause. The man turns to TONY *as if* TONY *had spoken.*

Eh?

TONY *is blank. The man finishes his drink and turns to go.*

You're right, there.

He goes. Silence. BARRETT *and* TONY *look at each other.* TONY *non-committal.* BARRETT *seems shabbier, uneasy, his breath is laboured.*

BARRETT. Might I buy you a drink?

TONY *does not answer.* BARRETT *signals nervously to the* BARMAN, *points to* TONY's *glass.*

BARRETT. Scotch. Large scotch.

The drink arrives and he pays for it. TONY *sips it immediately, with no gesture.* BARRETT *begins to speak, in a low voice, very quickly, stuttering, compulsive.*

BARRETT. I wanted to come and call round on you . . . but
. . . I tell you what though . . . I was led up the
garden path. I couldn't be more sorry, honest. I
was besotted by her long before I came to you. I
was simply besotted by her. I thought she was keen
on me too – we were saving up money to get
married . . . her father was a brute. You see I
. . . I couldn't bear to see her . . . suffering –
but I had to pay him like – you know, to pay him to
get his consent to take her away. I had to find her a
home somewhere that – that's why I told you she
was my sister – I thought she was devoted to me . . .
anyway – you see I . . . I didn't know a thing
about what was going on between you two until
that night. That night I got it out of her . . . I
twigged she was just a scrubber . . . She never intended to marry me, and d'you know what she's
done now? Gone off with my money . . . she's
living with a bookie in Wandsworth – listen, give
me – give me another chance, sir . . . I was so
happy there with you . . . it was like bliss . . .
we can turn over the page . . . I'm with an old
lady now in Paultons Square – ringing the bell all
day long – up and down those stairs – all day long –
I'm skin and bone . . . I deceived you – I played
you false – I admit that – but she was to blame – it
was her fault. She done us both . . . if you can find
it in your heart sir . . . give me another chance.

He stops, looking down at his glass, biting his nails.
TONY *is still, expressionless.*

Exterior. Square. Winter.
Some weeks have passed. A wind blows through the
square.

Interior. Hall. TONY's *house. Day.*
The house is changed. It is airless, dark, oppressive.
Curtains and blinds are almost constantly drawn.

There are no longer any flowers. The log fire has been replaced by illuminated gas logs. The sleek television in the bedroom has been replaced by a heavy Console, now in the drawing-room. Cheap sex magazines replace the expensive monthlies. There is an overlay of BARRETT *everywhere. Photos of footballers cellotaped to mirrors. Pornographic calendars. Nudes stuck in oil paintings. The furniture has subtly changed, the rooms no longer possess composition. Elegant pornographic books have been yanked from* TONY's *bookshelves and are strewn about. The bookshelves are left disordered and heavy with dust.* BARRETT's *brown paper obscene books are piled about, and cellophaned piles of photos. The ashtrays are crammed full, glasses half empty and empty beer bottles are on the liquor trolley.* BARRETT *is now dressed in a rough sweater, corduroy trousers and heavy boots.*

Interior. Drawing-room. Day.
TONY *is sitting at a table, doing a crossword puzzle. He is in his pyjama jacket.* BARRETT *enters, dressed in sweater and tight trousers.*

BARRETT. You still sitting there?

TONY. What's this? 'It's waxed so will soon wane', five letters.

BARRETT. I haven't got time for all that.

TONY. Well you ask me soon enough when you want some help.

BARRETT. Look at all this muck and slime. It makes you feel sick.

TONY. Well do something about it. You're supposed to be the bloody servant!

BARRETT. You expect me to cope with all this muck and filth everywhere, all your leavings all over the place, without a maid, do you? I need a maid to give me a helping hand. I'm not used to working in such squalor. Look what I've got on my hands, you! As soon as I get the Hoover going you're straight up it. You're in everybody's way.

TONY. Oh why don't you leave me alone?

TONY gulps some beer. BARRETT *lights a cigarette, and pensively flips the pages of a leather-bound book.*

. . . What's this? 'It's waxed so will wane soon?' Five letters.

BARRETT. Look, why don't you get yourself a job instead of moping around here all day? Here I am scraping and skimping trying to make ends meet . . . getting worse and worse . . . and you're no bloody help . . . d'you know that butter's gone up twopence a pound?

TONY. As a matter of fact I'll be meeting a man very shortly.

BARRETT. What man? The man from Brazil? What's he going to do for you? Come down by helicopter on the roof? Eh?

TONY. Oh why don't you shut up!

Interior. Hall. Day.
TONY *storms out of the drawing-room.*

TONY. Barrett!

He goes up the stairs.

Barrett!

Interior. BARRETT's *bedroom. Day.*
BARRETT *is in bed.* TONY *enters and pulls the clothes off him.*

BARRETT. What's the matter with you?

TONY. Get out of it!

BARRETT. What you doing?

TONY. There's tea dregs on the carpet.

BARRETT. Where?

TONY. In the drawing room.

BARRETT. Well I didn't put them there.

TONY *holds a damp rag to* BARRETT's *face.*

TONY. Now here you are. Use it.

BARRETT. Don't do that to me.

TONY. Clear it up!

BARRETT. Not my fault – them tea dregs.

TONY. You filthy bastard!

BARRETT. Right. I'm leaving!

BARRETT *gets out of bed. Their voices clash and rise.*

TONY. That's exactly what I want.

BARRETT. You talk to me like that . . .

TONY. Now leave my house alone . . .

BARRETT. . . . after all I've done for you.

TONY. . . . Get down and clear it up.

BARRETT *goes out.*

Interior. Stairs and landing. Day.
BARRETT *comes briskly down the stairs, followed by* TONY.

BARRETT. I won't stand for any more of this.

TONY. Take your pigsty somewhere else.

BARRETT. It's not my pigsty, it's yours.

TONY. You creep!

BARRETT. Nobody talks to me like that!

TONY. D'you know what you are? I'll tell you.

BARRETT. I know all about your sort.

TONY. You're a peasant.

BARRETT. I'll tell you what I am, I'll tell you what I am. I'm a gentleman's gentleman. And you're no bloody gentleman!

TONY. You think I'm past it? I haven't had a drink all morning. I'm through with it. I'll knock your head off.

BARRETT. Violence will get you nowhere.

TONY. If you don't get down and wipe those tea dregs up I'll stick your nose in them.

BARRETT (*laughing*). You're funny.

Interior. Dining-room. Day.

Morning. TONY *and* BARRETT *in the dining-room.*
BARRETT *is smoking, sitting, doing a crossword puzzle.* TONY *is looking out into the garden. Long silence.*
Children's voices outside.

TONY. I wouldn't mind going out for a walk.
It must be quite nice out.

He remains still.
BARRETT *continues his crossword.*
Silence.

Interior. Hall. Stairs and landings. Evening.
TONY *is at the top of the stairs,* BARRETT *at the foot. They are playing a game of ball, in which, according to their own rules, the ball must be bounced off the wall or on the stairs past the opponent. A point is scored for each pass. Twenty-one is game.*
A longish rally is in progress. Both breathe hard, concentrating intently. Finally, BARRETT *skids the ball past* TONY.

BARRETT. Watch it!
TONY. No, out of play – out of play!
BARRETT. Right – got you!
TONY. Bit wild! (*Laughs.*)
BARRETT. Nearly got you then . . .
Hah! . . . thirteen ten . . . ?
. . . counting . . . ?
TONY. Well I can't do it any more. I have to bend all the time.
BARRETT. What about me? I'm in the inferior position. I'm playing uphill.
TONY. I need a drink.
BARRETT. That's the point of the game, the bending. You're getting as fat as a pig. You need the exercise.
TONY. Right. Service! *He smashes the ball past* BARRETT.
Fourteen twelve!
BARRETT. That wasn't fair, I wasn't ready.
TONY. I said service, didn't I?

BARRETT (*picking up the ball*). I'm not having that point counted.

TONY. What do you mean? That's a perfectly fair point. What about the other night? You did about six of them like that.

BARRETT. There's no need to take advantage of the fact that you're in the best position.

TONY. My dear . . .

BARRETT. . . . you ought to be able to play the game according to the rules.

TONY. My dear Barrett, you're just a little upset because you're losing the game.

BARRETT. Oh! . . . take your ball!

He throws the ball hard at TONY, *who catches it.*

TONY. Take it yourself!

TONY *throws the ball back viciously. It hits* BARRETT *on the nose.*

BARRETT. Aaahhh!

He clutches his nose. TONY *runs down.*

TONY. Well, what's the matter?

BARRETT. I'm going.

TONY. It couldn't have hurt.

BARRETT. Get out of it. I'm off. I'm not staying in a place where they just chuck balls in your face!

TONY. Oh don't be silly! Come on, let's have a drop of brandy. I'll tell you what we'll do, we'll call that game a draw. Now here you are. Isn't that fair?

BARRETT. Stuff your brandy.

TONY. Don't talk to me like that!

BARRETT. Stuff you and your brandy! Get back to your coal-heap and leave me alone for Christ's sake.

TONY. Now look, Barrett, don't you forget your place. You're nothing but a servant in this house!

BARRETT. Servant? I'm nobody's servant. Who furnished the whole place for you? Who painted it for you? Who does the cooking? Who washes your pants? Who cleans out the bath after you? I do! I run the whole bloody place – and what do I get out of it? Nothing!

TONY. Now listen, Barrett –

BARRETT. I know all about you, sonny . . .

TONY. Now look . . . Listen, I am grateful, honestly . . .
Don't be daft. You know I am. I don't know what
I'd do without you.

BARRETT. Well go and pour me a glass of brandy.

TONY. Well that's what I suggested in the first place.

BARRETT. Well don't just stand there! Go and do it!

*TONY runs into the drawing-room and pours BARRETT
a large brandy. BARRETT watches him from the hall.*

*Interior. Drawing-room. Evening.
The same evening. TONY and BARRETT eating dinner. Black candles. Black ceiling.*

TONY. Fabulous.

BARRETT. Not bad.

TONY. It's fabulous.

BARRETT. Bit salty.

TONY. No, no. It's marvellous.

Silence. They eat.

I don't know how you do it.

BARRETT. It's nice to know it's appreciated. It makes all the
difference.

TONY. Well, I do appreciate it.

Pause.

BARRETT. You know sometimes I get the feeling that we're
old pals.

TONY. That's funny.

BARRETT. Why?

TONY. I get the same feeling myself.

Pause.

BARRETT. I've only had that same feeling once before.

TONY. When was that?

BARRETT. Once in the army.

TONY. That's funny. I had the same feeling myself there,
too. Once.

Interior. Hall. Stairs and landing. Night.
BARRETT *stands inside the drawing-room door. His hands are over his eyes. He is counting aloud.*

BARRETT. Forty-seven, forty-eight, forty-nine, fifty.

He takes his hands from his eyes and goes into the hall. Here, he stands and talks aloud, to a listener.

I've got a tiny feeling that you're not downstairs at all. I think you're up there, aren't you? Now I'm on my way up to get you.

He races up the stairs. At the top he speaks:

Where's your little lair this time?
Puss, puss, puss, puss, pussy, puss, puss, puss, puss, puss, puss.

He opens his own bedroom door violently and looks in, comes out. He does the same in VERA's *room, and then runs downstairs to* TONY's *room at a very great pace and pulls the door open.*

Interior. TONY's *bedroom. Night.*
BARRETT *enters, creeps about, looking.*

BARRETT. I'm getting warm! You're hiding but you'll be caught. You've got a guilty secret, you've got a guilty secret, but you'll be caught. I'm coming to get you, I'm creeping up on you!

Interior. Bathroom. Night.
TONY *is jammed in the corner behind the door. (The bathroom is in complete disorder.) His eyes are staring with excitement.* BARRETT's *voice comes nearer.*

BARRETT. I'm getting warm, I can smell a rat, I can smell a rat . . .

TONY *shivers. The door bursts open.* BARRETT *charges in and confronts him.* BARRETT *utters a terrifying maniacal bellow.* TONY *faints.*

Interior. Hall and front door. Night.

BARRETT *comes down the hall, opens the door.* VERA.

BARRETT. What do you want?

VERA. I want to speak to him.

BARRETT. Clear off out of it.

VERA. I want to speak to him.

BARRETT. Out of it. Quick.

TONY *appears in the hall. She darts in.* BARRETT *puts out a foot. She falls.*

Come on out! Come on.

VERA (*rising to* TONY). Look I want . . . please . . .

TONY. I'll speak to her, leave her.

He goes into the drawing-room. She follows.

VERA. Eh . . . now listen here . . . look . . . I'm not making a go of it, see? . . . I'm ill.

She looks as though she might fall. TONY *does not offer her a chair.*

I come to you.

He looks at her, says nothing.

I'm broke . . . I'm ill, you see, that's what it is . . .

Silence.

So I come to you, you see.

Silence.

TONY. Go to your bookmaker.

VERA. What?

TONY. Go to your bookie.

VERA. What bookie?

TONY. The one you ran off with.

VERA. Run off? Who ran off? What's he told you, eh? He chucked me out, soon as we left here. He chucked me out. He's finished me. Listen, I got to go to hospital, they're taking me in . . . give me a few quid . . . just . . . go on . . . just . . .

TONY. What about what you did to me?

VERA. It was him. He made me. I loved you though. I still love you.

She goes into TONY's *arms. He holds her, uncertain.* BARRETT *comes in, looks.*

BARRETT. Tch, tch, tch. Playing games with little Sis again, are you? That won't get you anywhere, Tone.

TONY *hesitantly lets her go, blinks, goes out.*

Interior. Hall. Night.
BARRETT *escorting* VERA *from room into hall to door.* TONY *is standing at the back of the hall.*

BARRETT. Come on, little sister, out of it.

VERA (*to* TONY). It was him. He done it.

She breaks away. BARRETT *grabs her and pulls her to the door.*

BARRETT. Come here, stinking the place out.

TONY *goes back into drawing room.*

VERA (*calling after him*). I love you!

BARRETT. Get back to your ponce. Move out of it.

He pushes her out of the door.

Interior. Drawing-room. Night.
TONY *is pouring whisky.* BARRETT *comes in.* TONY *looks at him.*

TONY. Slut.

Interior. Drawing-room. Evening.
BARRETT *handing* TONY *a bottle with no label.*

BARRETT. I've got something special for you, from a little man in Jermyn Street.

TONY *looks at bottle.*

TONY. Not for me.

BARRETT *pours a glass.*

BARRETT. Oh come on. Have a little sip, see what it tastes like.
TONY. I told you, I'm not drinking.
BARRETT. Just have a little sip, that's all, just a sip.

TONY *looks sulkily at the glass, picks it up and sips.*

TONY. Mmmmmm. Ooh, it's marvellous.
BARRETT. There you are, you see. I can still think of things that'll please you, can't I? You won't get any better than me you know. What do you want? An old hag running round the house, getting you up in the morning, at the crack of dawn, telling you what to do? My only ambition is to serve you, you know that don't you?
TONY. I'm sorry. I've been a bit edgy lately.
BARRETT. Oh well I mean, I admit, I make mistakes, but, well after all I'm only human aren't I? You wouldn't like me if I wasn't human, would you?
TONY. The place could be cleaner, that's all.
BARRETT. I know, I know it could be a bit cleaner. That's what I've been going on about for days.
TONY *(with sudden intensity)*. Listen . . .
The intensity fades. He loses track of his thought.

Listen . . .

With great concentration he forces the words out.

Perhaps we could . . . both . . . make . . . an extra effort.

He looks up suddenly at BARRETT, *the expression on his face one of entreaty.* BARRETT *smiles.*

BARRETT. You're right there, Tone, you're dead right. That's what we ought to do.

TONY's *face is at once confused, irritated. He suddenly begins to rake his hair violently, scratching his skull with his fist, his elbow raised, his posture resembling that of a chimpanzee.*

Interior. Bedroom. Night.
Portable record player. TONY *listening, with glass.*
Chime of front door bell. BARRETT *enters.*

BARRETT. Hey! Your other one's here.

TONY. What?

BARRETT. Your old flame. One yesterday, one tonight. You are popular aren't you. She's waiting.

TONY. Did you tell her we were expecting visitors?

BARRETT. I did. But I also took the liberty of showing her into the drawing-room. After all – she is a lady, isn't she?

TONY *goes down.*

Interior. Drawing-room. Night.
SUSAN *is gazing at the changes of the room.* TONY *comes in, slams the door.*

TONY. Hello.

He stands smiling, slightly swaying.

SUSAN. Vera's been to see me. She says you owe her some money.

TONY *bends forward in a fit of soundless laughter. She watches him.*

SUSAN. I think you owe her some kind of compensation.

TONY. She's a liar, they're all liars. You didn't come here because of Vera. It's all gone. Leave it alone.

He goes closer to her.

You don't want to . . . come here . . .

SUSAN (*dully*). I love you.

The front door is heard opening. Girls' voices.
BARRETT'*s voice. Giggling, going down the passage.*

SUSAN. Who's that?

The record in the bedroom is turned louder.

TONY. Friends.

A WOMAN'S VOICE *is heard.*

VOICE. Where's Tony?

SUSAN. Don't you . . . like me at all?

TONY (*non-committal*). Yes . . .

WOMAN'S VOICE. Where's that Tony?

SUSAN. Well what's wrong with me then?

BARRETT'S

VOICE. Hey come on, we're waiting for you.

TONY. Nothing's wrong with you. (*Laughs.*) Come and join the party.

He takes her by the hand. She does not resist.

Interior. Bedroom. Night.
BARRETT *and four women including* VERA *are in the room.*

RECORD. Give me my death
Close my mouth
Give me my breath
Close my mouth etc.

TONY. Where's my drink?

BARRETT. It's here. (*To* SUSAN). Do you want one, love, eh?

SUSAN *stands still inside the door.* TONY *gulps his drink.*

GIRL SINGING
Now while I love you alone . . .
Now while I love you alone.

A girl pulls TONY *gently away.*

TONY. What are you doing?

She takes him in a corner and whispers to him. Another girl joins them. They bend over him, whispering. He staggers away. A woman in a large black hat pulls him down on the bed and kisses him.

BARRETT (*to* SUSAN). Do you know where we're going in the morning?

Pause.

We're going to Brazil in the morning. (*He grins.*)
Aren't we Tone? (*To* SUSAN.) Have a fag.

TONY *lies on the bed staring glazed at* SUSAN. SUSAN
moves to BARRETT *and kisses him. He laughs and
holds her. She looks at* TONY. *His mouth is open, he
moves from the bed. One of the girls touches him.
He shivers, stumbles, falls and collapsing, brings
tablecloth, glasses, bottles down with him.*

BARRETT. Tch, tch, tch.

TONY *sits a second, glass-eyed. The record player
still plays. He suddenly reaches up to the shelf and
sweeps it on the floor. There is a smash and grate of
record and pick-up head.*

TONY (*in a sudden dazed childish horror, in a monotone*).
Get out, get out. Get 'em all out.

His hand swinging knocks a bottle over.

Get out.

BARRETT. Come on then, out. (*He nudges* SUSAN.) You too.
Come on.

The women go to the door. BARRETT *whispers to
them.*

Make it tomorrow night. (*Confidential.*) And bring
John.

*Interior. Hall and stairs. Night.
The women go down and out.* BARRETT *halfway
down stairs, turns.* SUSAN *is still at bedroom door.*
TONY *sits on floor, head drooping. She stares at him,
expressionless.* BARRETT *calls up stairs.*
Eh you! Come on!

He emits a piercing whistle. No response.

OY!

*She turns, walks slowly downstairs. She stops and
looks at him, and then hits him with all her might,*

with closed fist, across the face. He staggers, his fists clench. He looks at her. She is still. Slowly he recovers his composure. He turns, goes to the front door, holds it wide open. With a smile, he inclines his head towards her. She leaves the house.

Exterior. House. Night.
SUSAN *walks across the dark square. She looks back at the house, turns, walks on. The camera holds on the house and closes slowly in toward the door.*

Interior. Hall. Night.
BARRETT *locks door and bolts it. He walks slowly up the stairs.*

Interior. Landing. Night.
TONY *crawls onto the landing and sits in a corner.*

Interior. Stairs. Night.
Close up of BARRETT's *hand trailing the banister, as he climbs the stairs.*

The Pumpkin Eater

The Pumpkin Eater was first presented by Columbia Pictures Corporation on 15th July 1964 with the following cast:

JO	Anne Bancroft
JAKE	Peter Finch
GILES	Richard Johnson
DINAH	Francis White
	Kate Nicholls
FERGUS	Fergus McClelland
	Christopher Ellis
SHARON	Sharon Maxwell
	Mimosa Annis
MARK	Kash Dewar
ELIZABETH	Elizabeth Dear
	Sarah Nicholls
PETE	Gregory Phillips
	Rupert Osborn
JACK	Michael Ridgeway
	Martin Norton
MR ARMITAGE	Alan Webb
MR JAMES	Cedric Hardwicke
PHILPOT	Maggie Smith
YOUNGEST CHILD	Mark Crader
NANNY	Faith Kent
DOCTOR	Cyril Luckham
INGRAM	Eric Porter
WOMAN IN HAIRDRESSERS	Yootha Joyce
CONWAY	James Mason
MAN AT PARTY	Gerald Sim
BETH	Janine Gray
MRS JAMES	Rosalind Atkinson
UNDERTAKER	John Junkin
SURGEON	Anthony Nicholls
WAITRESS AT ZOO	Leslie Nunnerley
THE KING OF ISRAEL	Frank Singuineau
PARSON	John Franklin Robbins

Directed by Jack Clayton

The Pumpkin Eater

Exterior. Large house in St John's Wood, London.
Summer day. PRESENT DAY
Bonnet of a Jaguar foreground. JO *is standing at the*
window, looking out. Reflected in the window pane
demolition of buildings, tall skeletons of new con-
structions.

Interior. Sitting-room.
JO *at window, looking out.*
Another angle : JO.
She turns, stares at the room.

Interior. Sitting-room.
We see the room. It is large, expensively furnished.
Bookshelves, a piano, pictures, numerous thick rugs,
etc. On a small table, tea for one is laid.
Another angle.
JO *goes to table, pours tea into the cup.*
Close on JO's *hands.*
She holds the cup tightly in its saucer, does not pick
it up.

Interior. Hall.
JO *comes quickly out of living room. As she turns into*
hall, letters thud on to carpet through the letter box.
Another angle : JO.
She looks at them for a moment, makes no attempt
to pick them up.
Another angle : JO.
Footsteps above. She looks up. Through bannisters
along first landing, a man's legs walking quickly.

Another angle : JO.
She stands still. Water heard rushing into a basin from above.

Exterior. Garage of St John's Wood. House. Day.
PRESENT DAY
Brilliant sunlight, heat haze. Pool of petrol. The Jaguar, the Floride, the child's scooter. JO *bends to pick up scooter.*
The shining Jaguar, from her eye level as she bends. Sunlight. JO's *face.*
Sun on wheelcaps.
JO.
She straightens, scooter half held.
Another angle.
Her hands drop scooter. She moves swiftly towards garage.

Exterior. Side door of house. Day.
JAKE *appears at side door. Stands looking left and right.* JO *is not there. He gets into the Jaguar.*

Interior. Jaguar. Day.
JAKE *sits, adjusts his tie in the mirror, lights a cigarette, starts motor. Suddenly catches sight of* JO *in the mirror.*
The mirror. Reflecting interior garage.
JO *in the corner of the dark garage. Still, amid junk.*
Another angle, Jaguar.
JAKE *gets out of car and crosses to garage.*

Interior. Garage. Day.
JAKE. What are you doing? (JO *looks at him.*) What are you doing?
JO. Nothing.

JAKE *crosses to her, touches her arm.*

JAKE. I thought you were going shopping.

Silence.

It's late. I've got to go. (*Pause.*) How are you feeling?

Pause.

JO. All right.

Pause.

JAKE. Look, I've got to go out to dinner . . . I'm sorry.
JO. All right.

JAKE *kisses her tenderly, speaks with a smile.*

JAKE. Do you think you're going to get over this period in your life, because I find it very depressing.

He turns away, moves back to Jaguar, gets in and drives off.
Another angle : JO
watching car disappearing. She walks down path to front gate and into street. The car has disappeared. She turns, looks at the house.

Interior. Barn. Day. TEN YEARS EARLIER
A large room, sub-divided by numerous home-made partitions. It is sparsely furnished but crowded with children. JO *is at a table making pastry. Some of the children are playing on the floor with train sets and home-made constructions of roads and stations. The smallest girl apart, examining a doll's house.*
Another angle towards door.
It opens. GILES *and* JAKE *enter. A child* (DINAH) *rushes up to them.*

CHILD ONE. Daddy – I was going to be the signal-box man and now look!

GILES. All right. (*To* JO.) Darling, this is Jake. (*To* CHIL-DREN.) What is it?

JO (*to* JAKE). Hullo.

CHILD TWO. Dinah's got no right to open the gates until the express has been through.

JAKE (*to* JO). Glad to meet you.
CHILD THREE. You can't stop a non-stop express.

> JO *and* JAKE *shaking hands. Her hands covered with*
> *flour.*
> JAKE *playing bricks with children.*

JAKE. What's this bit going to be?
CHILD TWO. The ladies' lavatory.
JAKE. Where's the ticket office?

> *Another angle :* JO *and* ELIZABETH.

ELIZABETH. Who's that?
JO. A friend of Daddy's.
CHILD TWO. These are oil pipes. They take the oil.

> *Another angle :* JAKE *looking at* JO *over bricks, as –*

CHILD THREE. We don't want any oil. There are no diesels on this
line.

> *Another angle :* GILES *coming from makeshift kit-*
> *chen with tray of tea.*

JAKE. Where's the control tower?
CHILD TWO. This isn't an airport, it's a station.
JAKE. You could have a helicopter.

> *Another angle : the two oldest boys chasing each other.*

CHILD TWO. That's my diesel!
CHILD THREE. It's broken down.
CHILD TWO. Give it to me!
JO. Pete!

> *Child (*JACK*) climbs over partition.*

GILES. Jack!

> *Another angle : the partition.*
> *As child (*PETE*) clambers after* JACK. *It collapses.*
> *Another angle :* GILES *at partition with hammer and*
> *nails.*

CHILD TWO. He had my diesel!

GILES. This is about the sixth time.

> *Another angle.* JO *moving away to light cigarette.*
> *Close-up.* JAKE *looking at her.*
> *Close-up.* JO.
> *Back to* GILES *holding up three planks of partition,*
> *examining them. One plank falls.*
> *Plank falling.*
>
> *Large close-up.*
> JAKE *kissing* JO's *ear.*
> (*No background noise.*)

> *Interior. Study in* JAKE's *father's house. Evening.*
> ## APPROX. TEN YEARS EARLIER
> JAKE's *father* (MR ARMITAGE). *He,* JO, *and* JAKE
> *sit, with drinks, eating cheese straws.*

MR ARMITAGE. But why on earth do you want to marry Jake?

> *Short pause.* JO *giggles.*

JAKE. Why not?

MR ARMITAGE. It's incomprehensible.

JAKE. What is?

MR ARMITAGE. He'll be an impossible husband.

JAKE. Oh now, wait a minute –

MR ARMITAGE. I assure you. I mean, he's got no money. He's
bone lazy. He drinks too much. He's quite useless.

JAKE. Oh thanks.

MR ARMITAGE. What do the children say?

JAKE. We haven't exactly discussed it with them.

JO. They . . . don't mind.

MR ARMITAGE (*to* JAKE). Do you like children?

JAKE. Of course I like them. Of course I do.

MR ARMITAGE. Have you actually known any?

> *Interior. Living-room.* JO's *father's house. Day.*
> ## SAME PERIOD
> JO's *father* (MR JAMES). JO *and* JAKE.

MR JAMES. Do you realize what you're saddling yourself with?

JAKE. Er . . . Yes . . . yes . . .

MR JAMES. A zoo. A children's zoo. And their keeper. Are you reconciled to having to keep the zoo and its keeper?

JAKE. Yes . . . of course . . . I mean . . .

MR JAMES. Are you fit?

JAKE. Well . . .

MR JAMES. I take it you know something of my daughter's record?

JO. My what?

JAKE *laughs*.

JAKE. Yes, I know. (*Pause.*) I want to marry her.

MR JAMES. You're a fool. Still, the least I can do is to give you some kind of a start, I suppose. You think that's fair?

JAKE. Fair?

MR JAMES. I think you're a fool, but I'll give you a start. A start. Do you think that's fair?

JAKE. Oh yes, that's fair . . . quite . . . very fair.

MR JAMES. Right. Well, first of all we've got to shed the load. There's too many children.

JO. What do you mean?

MR JAMES. I suggest we send the eldest two to boarding school. That will be two off your hands.

JO. No! That's ridiculous.

MR JAMES. Now listen, this is Jake's business, not yours. It's the burden on him that's ridiculous.

JO. But I don't want them to go away to school.

MR JAMES. Look, be sensible. They'd love it.

JO. They wouldn't love it.

MR JAMES. I'd love it. Jake'd love it. And they can come to stay with us in the holidays.

JO. Why don't we just give them away?

JAKE. It's only the first two. I mean, there are others.

MR JAMES. Now listen. I'm not going to have you trailing home with half a dozen more children in five years' time and another messed up marriage on your hands. You're not going to be allowed to crush this poor boy before he starts. He's going to have to work like a slave as it is.

JO. But we can't afford to send them to school.

MR JAMES. I'm paying.

JAKE. Oh . . . thanks. Thanks very much.

MR JAMES. And I've managed to buy you a fairly good lease on a house in London. Quite reasonable. It's an old one but it should suit you – it'll pretty well clean me out, but you might as well have the money now as when I'm dead.

Interior. Kitchen – St John's Wood. House. Day.
PRESENT DAY
Close on tray. With tea being set on draining board, with a sharp sound.
Another angle : JO *stands, does not touch crockery.*
Another angle : at window.
Glimpses of demolition through window.
Another angle : JO.
She turns away, clutching her arms, walks vaguely about the kitchen, her heels clicking on the tiled floor. An immaculate, gleaming modern kitchen, spotless, nothing out of place.
Another angle : JO.
As she moves, we see : new dishwasher, new refrigerator, new washing machine and spin dryer, new electric oven, racks of gleaming crockery, photograph on teak wood wall, a large photo pinned from a magazine of MR JAKE ARMITAGE, MRS ARMITAGE *and their* CHILDREN.
JO.
She glances at it.
Another angle : She continues walking, her fingers tracing on the work top.

Exterior. House in St John's Wood. Day.
APPROX. TEN YEARS EARLIER
The house is considerably more shabby, both inside and out, than in the present day sequences.
A furniture van is parked outside. Men are carrying

furniture from it into the house. Objects, furniture, heaped and strewn about outside, through the ground floor, up stairs. We see certain recognizable objects from the barn. In foreground, a child's bike and scooter.
The Morris Minor turns the corner and draws up. CHILDREN *fall out, followed by* JAKE *and* JO. *Again, we hear no sound until:*

CHILD. They've got here before us!

The children rush up the path.

Interior. Hall.
Through open door, we can see the empty kitchen. JO *is confronted with a piece of furniture.*

JO (*to* REMOVAL MEN). Mmm . . . upstairs. The first floor front . . . left . . .

Children rush up and down stairs.

Don't get in the way.

She stands in the chaos. JAKE *appears, kisses her.*

Interior. Landing (that night).
Silence. Nightlight through windows. Open doors. Their voices heard. There is certain junk (odd pieces) on landing, rolls of carpeting.

JO. My first marriage. You're my first husband.
JAKE. You've been married three times.
JO. No. You're the first.
JAKE. Are the children asleep?
JO. Yes.
JAKE. I'll close the door.

JAKE *moves to door and closes it.*

JO. I want to go away with you . . . and come back with you . . . and live with you.
JAKE. You will.

JO. You'll never go from me . . . we'll have the same life. Do you want anything else?

JAKE. No. I don't want anything else.

Interior. Bathroom. Evening.
APPROX. EIGHT YEARS EARLIER
Bathroom, small, crowded and full of steam. DINAH *in bath,* JO *washing her ears and neck.* JAKE *is drying a smaller* BOY *with a large towel.*

BOY (*to* JAKE). Can I tell you a story?

DINAH (*to* JO). Do you like living in this house?

JO. Why? Don't you?

DINAH. Yes.

BOY. A story about a killer whale.

JO *leaves* DINAH *to wash herself and takes the boy's pyjamas from towel rail.*

DINAH. How long are we going to live here?

JAKE. We're moving in the morning.

DINAH. We're not! Where?

JAKE. Building a big house on top of that hill.

DINAH. What hill?

JO *reaches for the* BOY *with his pyjamas.*

JAKE. I haven't done his feet. Lift your foot.

BOY *lifts his foot.* JAKE *dries it.*

BOY. It's about this whale . . .

DINAH. What hill?

JO. By the barn.

DINAH. What, in the morning?

JAKE. Well, we'll have lunch first.

JO (*to* JAKE). Hurry up.

BOY. It's a story about two whales and a shark.

DINAH. What sort of house?

JAKE. With eight bathrooms. All for me.

Interior. Sitting-room. Morning.

APPROX. SEVEN YEARS EARLIER
JO *is putting a sweater on a small boy, who is struggling in her arms, trying to join the other children whom we can see beyond* JO, *playing in the garden.* JO *is pregnant.*

JAKE'S VOICE (*calling*). Where's the opener?
JO (*calling back*). Just a minute –

Interior. Kitchen. Morning.
It is filled with steam. We hear sounds of children.
JAKE *is holding two cans of beer and searching for the opener. He regards the steaming pans on the gas stove, looks into the oven at the joint, closes oven door, his face blank.*

Interior. Sitting-room.
JAKE *enters. He stops centre of room and reacts for a second to the children thudding about upstairs, and their shouts from the garden. He comes to table, finds opener.*
JO *finishes inserting the* SMALL BOY *into his sweater, sets him down. He rushes out to the garden.*
JAKE, *with a grimace, opens can. It spurts over the wall, where we can already see the stains from previous moments of this kind.*

JAKE. Want one?
JO. Yes, I'll have one.

He hands her opened can. She takes it. JAKE *opens second can. It also spurts over wall.*

JAKE. Aaaahh!
JO. It's all right, it'll wipe off.
JAKE (*looking at can*). It's ridiculous.

JAKE *sits at table on which are sheets of writing paper. He looks at them and throughout the ensuing dialogue vaguely scratches out words with his pen.*
Shouts and thuds from garden and upstairs. JO *drinks from can.*

JO. Let's go out today.

JAKE. Umm? Where?

JO. I don't know. Take them out.

JAKE. All of them?

TWO CHILDREN *rush in from garden, through the room and upstairs.* JAKE *looks at* JO, *chuckles shortly, dryly.*

JO. I'll take them out, if you like, this afternoon. You can have a rest.

JAKE. No, no, don't be silly.

JO (*touching him*). No, really, I will. I will.

JAKE. No, no, I wouldn't dream of it. After all, it's Saturday, we can go out.

Loud crash from above.

What are they *doing* up there?

Pause.

JO. Do you want turnips or swedes?

JAKE. Turnips or swedes?

JO. Yes. Or both if you like.

He looks at her blankly.

JAKE (*with sudden concentration*). Turnips or swedes. Wait a minute. Just a minute. Let me think about it.

Interior. Kitchen. Day.
       APPROX. FIVE YEARS EARLIER
A young woman (PHILPOT) *is sitting on the old-fashioned sink cleaning saucepan lids with steel wool, slowly, as she speaks towards the open doorway into the hall, where* JO *is visible in the foreground using an old Hoover.*

PHILPOT (*above Hoover noise*). Wives don't usually like me. I like them. That's the funny thing. But I seem to worry them somehow. I don't know. They get so ratty, people's wives. The funny thing is that I like them better than their husbands, do you think that's funny or not? Perhaps I'm not normal. I'm quite normal really, I'm sure I am.

JO *has finished Hoovering and switched off. She enters kitchen as:*

But perhaps it's just that I'm *ab*normal. I can't see how I can be, can you? I mean . . . I've been told that I'm frigid, but I don't see how you can tell, I mean – honestly, how can you tell?

JO. I shouldn't think you are. Just a minute.

JO *moves to get hot water.* PHILPOT *sits on old-fashioned icebox.*

You don't look it anyway.

PHILPOT. I think you're marvellous – I really do, I think you're absolutely marvellous. You're so capable. All you do, all the children and everything, the way you cope. Of course, Jake's the most fabulous husband and father. He's *the* most fabulous –

JO *touches* PHILPOT's *leg.*

JO. Can I get in the . . .

PHILPOT *moves her legs.* JO *opens icebox.*

PHILPOT. – *the* most fabulous father. How many are his?
JO. Er . . . one . . .
PHILPOT. One. One is his. And the others aren't his?
JO. No, they're not.
PHILPOT. But he's a wonderful father to them all, isn't he?

Exterior. Hampstead Heath five years earlier. Day. A damp, drizzly day. JO *and the* CHILDREN. *Hill. Running.*

CHILD ONE. Why does Philpot have to stay with us?
JO. She's been turned out of her flat.

CHILD TWO. But why does she have to stay with us? We've got enough people.

JO. She's looking for another one.

CHILD TWO. I've never seen her look.

CHILD ONE. Who is she?

JO. She's a friend of a friend of Daddy's.

CHILD ONE. Why does she have to sleep in my bed? Why can't I sleep in my bed?

They run downhill. In the background, we see girls playing netball. DINAH *stands alone. They go to her.*

DINAH. I've got a pain.

MISTRESS (*calling*). Dinah!

DINAH *goes towards game. Game continues. Damp, muddy.* JO *and* CHILDREN *watch game vaguely from the rise.*

CHILD ONE. Why doesn't Philpot go home?

JO. She hasn't got a home.

CHILD THREE. She smells of fish.

CHILD TWO. She doesn't. She smells of onions.

CHILD THREE. Fish.

CHILD ONE. She had a spot on her chin yesterday, but this morning she'd squeezed it.

CHILD THREE. She stinks of fish.

JO. She doesn't stink at all. Now stop it.

CHILD TWO. What's the difference . . .

JO. Anyway, it's just perfume.

CHILD THREE. What is?

JO. Anyway, I like her.

CHILD ONE. Dad had to catch her yesterday when she fainted. It must have been awful, the smell.

JO. Fainted?

CHILD THREE (*falling*). Do you faint like this? Is this how you faint?

CHILD TWO. She fainted. Dad caught her.

JO (*to* CHILD THREE). Oh for goodness sake get up! You're smothered in mud, look at it.

The limp netball game.

MISTRESS. Come on, keep moving, keep moving. Keep at it. Keep at it. Come on, pass the ball. Keep moving. Keep at it.

The GIRLS *move in the drizzle.*

Exterior. Group on hill. Shooting up from game. Prams moving across upper field. JO *and* CHILDREN *move away.*

Interior. PHILPOT's *bedroom. Morning.*
It is obviously a child's room, although PHILPOT's *belongings are scattered around – clothing, ribbons, hairpins, a pair of laddered stockings, a shawl . . .* JO *with tray.* PHILPOT *in bed.*

PHILPOT. He's a brilliant writer. It must be wonderful to have a man working in the house, mustn't it, working at home, you shouldn't have brought me tea, really, I should get up, I mustn't have tea in bed, really, it's bad for me, but honestly it must be so challenging to write for films, don't you think, it's so challenging, don't you think, the cinema is, wouldn't you say, but of course his understanding is so extraordinary, his innate . . . the way he draws his characters . . . swift strokes . . . so swift . . . and for you of course after all your struggles to suddenly have success on the doorstep, after all those husbands you've had and everything, but of course you're so intelligent and everything and of course so beautiful, do you help him much with his work?

JO. Not much.

Pause.

Are you feeling any better?

PHILPOT. Better?

JO. You weren't too well the other day.

PHILPOT. I'm perfect. It's so warm here. *Real.* You know, so *real.* I've never felt such a sense of *reality*, as there is here. Do you know what I mean?

Interior. Kitchen five years earlier. Afternoon.
JO *vaguely washing.* JAKE *making tea.*

JO. Does Philpot faint much?

JAKE. What?

JO. Philpot. Does she do a lot of fainting?

JAKE. How the hell would I know?

Pause.

I mean, why should she faint? What's she got to faint about?

JO. The children said she fainted yesterday.

JAKE. I don't know. Did she?

JO. They said you caught her.

JAKE. Me?

JO. Yes.

JAKE. Why would I catch her?

JO. To stop her . . . banging her head on the . . .

JAKE. What head? What are you talking about?

JO. Did you catch her when she fainted?

JAKE (*a shout*). How do I know?

He bangs the table.

Interior. Kitchen. London house. Day.
PRESENT TIME
Water running. Tea tray set for one. JO *turns off tap. Goes out of kitchen into hall.*

Interior. Hall five years earlier. Night.
As the front door closes softly.

Interior. Sitting-room five years earlier. Night.

JO. Where's she gone? (*Pause.*) She's just gone out the front door.

JAKE. Has she?

JO. That's a bit odd, isn't it?

JAKE. What?

JO. I mean, we've just come in, haven't we? Now she's gone out.

JAKE *yawns.*

JAKE. Probably gone for a walk. Why don't you take off
your coat?

Pause.

JO. What? (*Pause.*) Why has she gone? (*Pause.*) She's
. . . Do you want some coffee?
JAKE. No thanks.

Pause.

JO. What did you think of the film?

JAKE *grimaces*.

What did you think of the bloody film?
JAKE. Nothing! I didn't think anything of it!
JO. Is your film going to be better, the one you're
writing, do you think it's going to be better?

He stands.

JAKE. Listen –
JO. Do you like sitting between two women? Does that
thrill you? Does it give you a thrill?
JAKE. Yes, it does. It really does. What do you think I
should do about it? What shall I do, go and see a
psychiatrist about it?

He sits. Pause.

JO. All right, what –
JAKE. Look. Listen –

Pause.

It was nothing, nothing. Don't you understand?
JO. What do you mean, it was nothing?

Pause.

What do you mean, nothing?
JAKE. What do you think I mean?
JO. What did you catch her for?
JAKE. I didn't catch her!
JO. She fainted.

JAKE. What does it matter if I caught her or not? I didn't catch her, it doesn't matter, can't you understand? Who cares?

JO. I care.

JAKE. What about? What's it all about?

JO. I care about you. Who else?

JAKE. Me? You don't care about me. All you care about is that bloody great army of children I'm supposed to work my guts out for. That's all you care about. Where the hell do I come in?

Pause.

I can't even take a bath in peace, I can't . . . I can't even go to bed with you without one of them comes barging in in the middle, but so what, you just . . . I'm sick of living in a bloody nursery. Where the damn hell do I come in?

She giggles.

What are you sniggering about? It's funny when I tell you the truth for once, I suppose.

JO. The truth?

JAKE. That I'm capable of fancying someone else. I'm a perfectly normal man who's capable of fancying someone else.

They look at each other. He goes to table and pours a drink. He sits near her, pulls her on to his lap. She regards his face calmly.

JO. Aaah.

JAKE. She was just here, that's all. I was bored with the script, that's all. It was nothing. Forget it.

JO. Did you sleep with her?

JAKE. Don't be silly.

JO. You didn't?

JAKE. No.

JO. You promise?

JAKE. Yes.

She kisses him.

JO. Do you still want to?

He laughs.

JAKE. Yes.

He laughs again, kisses her.

Interior. PHILPOT's *room. Night.*
JO *pushing all* PHILPOT's *belongings into a shawl.*

Exterior. By dustbins. Night.
JO *piling all stuff by the dustbins. She stands still in the night, becomes cold, turns.*

Interior. Stairway. Night.
JO *ascends stairs, stands still at top. Sound of a child muttering in its sleep.*

Interior. Main bedroom. Night.
Moonlight. JO *enters, moves to bed, stops, looks at* JAKE *asleep. She sits on the dressing table stool watching him, her hands tightly clenched.*
Eventually she gets into bed. JAKE *turns, snores.* JO *retreats to the edge of the bed, away from him, staring at him with eyes open, clutching the pillow between them.*

Series of shots.   *PRESENT TIME*
JO *as we follow her. The street backgrounds change. She enters a large department store (Harrods).*

Interior. Harrods. Afternoon.
We follow JO *as she walks through various departments. See:*

Row of gleaming refrigerators.
Row of beds.
Shoppers hustling by. A salesman demonstrating a very efficient Hoover.
JO *wandering through store.*
Children's clothing, bottles of scent, children's toys, handkerchiefs.

Interior. Linen department. JO.
She suddenly stops and stands there in the centre of the floor, crying.
Another angle : shoppers passing, glancing at JO *curiously.*
Another angle : JO *standing quite still, crying soundlessly.*
Long shot : JO *standing there, crying. The many shoppers, still looking at her, have moved away, leaving her standing isolated and motionless. Eventually a* SALESLADY *approaches, takes her arm and guides her away.*

Exterior. House in St John's Wood. Late afternoon.
A taxi draws up outside. JO *is helped out by a uniformed* NURSE. *The front door of the house opens. Certain* CHILDREN *in school uniform appear from inside the house and stand watching. Silence. The* NURSE *and* JO *walk up the path.*

Interior. Hall.
Silent CHILDREN, *including the* SMALLEST CHILD *with the* NANNY. JO *and the* NURSE *enter.* DINAH *comes to them.*

DINAH (*to her mother*). I couldn't find Daddy. I called the studio but he wasn't there. I left a message.

As NURSE, JO *and* DINAH *move upstairs, one* CHILD *pushes another, and a crying row breaks out.*

Interior. First floor landing and stairs. Night.
The DOCTOR *is descending the stairs.* JAKE *can be seen waiting in the hall.*

JAKE. Let's go in here, shall we?

DOCTOR. Yes.

They go into the sitting-room. The door is pushed to, but it swings back a little.

Interior. Landing. Night.
We see the door of the sitting-room below, ajar. Light through chink. Hear murmurs. JO's *bedroom door opens.* JO *slips out. Looks down.*

Interior. Stairway. Night.
JO *moves silently, halfway down the stairs, crouches there, listening. Sound of a soda syphon. The voices of* JAKE *and the* DOCTOR *are only occasionally heard clearly. The* DOCTOR *appears to be at the far end of the room. His voice is low, his tone grave.*
JAKE *is clearly walking about, his shadow sometimes appearing through the chink. Only when he is close to the door do we hear his words. These are interspersed with murmured questions and comments from the* DOCTOR.
JO *sits crouched on the stairs, listening.*

JAKE. Would you like a drink?

DOCTOR. Er, no, not for me, thanks.

JAKE. I should have got in touch with you before. It's been getting worse all the time. Going on for ages. There was a girl friend of hers staying with us for a time, then she left . . . Mmmm . . . yes, it was round that period, but it's been . . . getting worse all the time.

DOCTOR. What exactly?

JAKE. I don't know. I . . . I can't get near her. She, she thinks everybody's . . . against her, keeps finding fault all the time. You know the sort of thing.

DOCTOR. Haven't you any idea why?

JAKE. No. I mean, breaking down in Harrods like that. Harrods of all places!

DOCTOR. Has there been any . . . kind of trouble between you?

JAKE. No.

DOCTOR. There's nothing particular, no specific problem?

JAKE. No. Nothing at all.

DOCTOR. I think perhaps she should see a psychiatrist.

JAKE. Should she?

DOCTOR. It might be a good idea.

JAKE. All right. If she wants to.

DOCTOR. He might want to see you too.

JAKE. Me?

DOCTOR. Yes. After all, you are her husband.

JAKE. I don't really see what I . . . She probably wants to have another child. That's what it is.

DOCTOR. Oh. Well, why doesn't she? She's a perfectly . . . healthy woman.

JAKE. We've got enough! Have you counted them? Well, any sane person would know we've got enough. When is she going to face facts? I mean she's a beautiful woman, she could . . . join in . . . live . . . all she wants to do is to sit in a corner and give birth.

JO *stands, retreats. The door opens. She stands at the top of the stairs.*

Another angle : stairway.
JO *standing at top, by her bedroom door, in the shadows.* JAKE *comes out of sitting-room below with* DOCTOR, *looks up, does not see her. He gets the* DOCTOR's *coat.* JO *steps back into :*

Interior. Main bedroom.
JO *stands in doorway, listening, as :*

DOCTOR'S VOICE. I'll give you a ring about it. Be kind to her.

JAKE'S VOICE. . . . Kind? I'm always kind.

DOCTOR'S VOICE. Good night.

JAKE'S VOICE. Good night.

> *Sound of front door closing.* JO *gets into bed, glances at door expectantly. But* JAKE *does not come up the stairs.*
> *Another angle:* JO *in bed, listening. She hears the whirr of the telephone dial.* JAKE'S VOICE *speaks softly.* JO *looks at bedside telephone, stares, does not pick it up.*
> *Another angle:* JO *in bed eyes open. The ting of the receiver, from downstairs. Silence.*
> *Footsteps.*
> JAKE *comes in.* JO's *eyes are closed.*

JAKE (*sitting on bed*). Asleep?
JO. No.

> *He caresses her.*

JAKE. You'll be all right.
JO. I am.

> *Pause.*

When are they going to finish the house?
JAKE. Soon.

> *Pause. She closes her eyes. He strokes her hair.*

> *Interior. Sitting-room. Evening.*
> JO *and* JAKE *sitting. He is reading a book. She has a magazine on her lap. Silence.*

JAKE. We've finished the script.

> *Pause.*

We're going . . . to Morocco for a couple of weeks.
JO. Mmm-hmm.

> *Pause.*

JAKE. Would you like to come?

> *Pause.*

I mean . . .

JO. Oh, I . . .

Pause.

JAKE. It'd mean living in tents and all that . . . but . . . if you felt like it . . .

JO. Couldn't just . . . sit in a tent . . .

JAKE. You wouldn't have to stay in the tent.

Silence.

JO. Timothy loved the train.

JAKE. What train?

JO. Your birthday present. The one your secretary sent for you.

JAKE. Well, anyway . . . the Doctor . . . we've arranged for a very good man for you to go and see.

Silence.

Why don't you come down to the studio tomorrow?

JO. What for?

JAKE. Meet everyone. They all want to meet you. Watch . . . the work. It might interest you.

JO. I don't want to come to the studio.

Pause.

JAKE. You're not interested . . . in what I do.

Pause.

JO. You never ask me.

JAKE. I've just asked you. I've asked you dozens of times.

JO. You don't want me to come.

JAKE. That's silly.

JO. No. It's not what you want.

Pause.

JAKE. You've never shown the slightest interest . . .

JO. Why are we talking about it?

Pause.

JAKE. You're just not interested in what I do, are you?

JO. You leave me. You're never with me.

JAKE. I have to work! It's my life.

JO. Where's mine? Where's my life?

Pause.

JAKE. With me.

She laughs.

I've worked, haven't I? What's wrong with that?
I've had to work, haven't I? What did you expect
me to do? The children go to good schools –

JO. Do you love me?

JAKE. I wouldn't be here if I didn't.

JO. You'd always be here if you did.

JAKE. Oh, that's ridiculous.

JO. Always.

Pause.

JAKE. You resent the money, don't you? That's what you
resent.

JO. Money? It's nothing to do with the money.

JAKE. Look at that damn kitchen! Look at all this! What
about the new house? You wanted it. I've done it
for you. But all you want now, I suppose, is just to
go back and live in that barn!

JO. It's nothing to do with the kitchen, it's nothing to
do with the money – it's nothing to do with any
of it!

JAKE. Well, *what*? What is it? What *do* you want? What?

She does not reply. He stands.

JO. You're going out.

JAKE. I have to.

JO. Don't go out now. Why are you going out now?

JAKE. I've got to. You know that. I can't not go.

JO. Stay. Not for long.

JAKE. I'm late. I'm late. It's business, it's not friends,
it's business. If it were friends you could come.

JO. What friends? We haven't got any friends. The
only friend I ever had was Philpot, but she was

more your friend, wasn't she, than mine? But of course you've had lots of friends since Philpot, haven't you? Lots of nice friends. For years.

JAKE. You're quite wrong.

Pause.

JO. I don't want to come to the studio. I don't want to meet your . . . people. Never. Never.

The young NANNY *enters.*

NANNY. They're ready to say good night to you, Mrs Armitage.

No response.

Mrs Armitage –

JO *lifts her head, smiles. Silence.* JAKE *stands.*

JAKE. Are they . . . out of the bath?
NANNY. Yes.

JAKE *goes out and upstairs with* NANNY. JO *sits still.*

Exterior. St John's Wood. House. Day.
JAKE *is getting into a large car outside house.*
CHAUFFEUR *holding door.* CHILDREN *running, shouting.* JAKE *waving.* JO *standing holding a* CHILD *by its hand.* JAKE *waves, she waves. Car door slams; car drives off.* CHILDREN *run and wave.* JO *waves,* JAKE *waves out of window.*

Interior. Psychiatrist's office. Day.
Darkened, soft lights. JO *sitting in armchair. Psychiatrist,* (INGRAM) *at desk.*
INGRAM. Do you like children, Mrs Armitage?

She giggles.

JO. They don't do you any harm.
INGRAM. You have a remarkable number.

JO. I had them of my own free will.

INGRAM. Of course.

JO. Nobody forced me to have them.

Pause.

INGRAM. Your two eldest boys have been at boarding school for some years.

JO. Some years, yes.

INGRAM. You agreed to their going away.

JO. Yes.

INGRAM. Have you seen them recently?

JO. Not recently.

INGRAM. Do you want to see them?

Pause.

JO. I believe they're doing terribly well.

Pause.

INGRAM. Tell me about your first husband.

JO. Oh . . . I can't remember.

INGRAM. Really? You were married to him for two years.

JO. He was . . . sweet . . . quite sweet . . . Drank a bit, I think . . . second one died, he was killed . . . he was nice . . . third one was a violinist . . . Giles . . . he was nice . . . we lived in this barn . . . with the children . . . hardly went out, really . . . some years, I think . . .

INGRAM. Why did you leave him? What happened?

JO. Happened? Nothing happened. Nothing happened at all.

Interior. Main bedroom. Day.
JO *drinking hot milk.* DINAH *with her.*

DINAH. What about this book? Do you want to read it?

JO. Which one's that?

DINAH. It's the one about Trotsky.

JO. Oh yes.

DINAH. It's pretty marvellous. He was assassinated you know.

JO. Was he?

DINAH. Didn't you *know*? They killed him. They assassinated him.

JO. Who did?

DINAH. God, it's a fantastic story. They sent this man, you see.

JO. I'll read it downstairs.

DINAH. You getting up?

JO. Yes, I feel better now.

DINAH. Don't you cry any more?

JO. No.

DINAH. Why do you cry like that?

JO. I don't. I feel better.

DINAH. Do you miss him? Is that it?

JO. Who?

DINAH. Daddy.

JO *smiles, gets out of bed.*

Anyway . . . you know . . . read that book . . . it'll cheer you up.

JO. Yes, I will.

Interior. Psychiatrist's office. Day.
JO *and* INGRAM.

JO. What has Jake got to do with me? Why do you keep asking me about Jake? I come here and all you ask me about is Jake. Why the hell don't you see Jake? Perhaps it's him you should be seeing, not me. There's nothing to *say* . . . about him.

INGRAM. Do you like him?

JO. No.

INGRAM. Do you love him?

JO. . . . Yes, so what? You don't –

INGRAM. What?

JO. I've forgotten what I was going to say.

Pause.

INGRAM. Do you think Jake is liable to change?

JO. I'm no match for him.

INGRAM. You're no match for him?

JO. No.

INGRAM. What do you mean?

Pause.

Do you think he's liable to change?

JO. No.

INGRAM. What would you say was the difference between Jake and your previous husbands?

JO. They weren't necessary.

Pause.

INGRAM. When you say –

JO. You should have a bowl in front of that gas fire.

INGRAM. A bowl?

JO. Of water – a bowl of water.

INGRAM. Ah, yes.

JO. You need it, for Christ's sake.

INGRAM. Mmm . . .

JO. The trouble is, if you have a bowl of water people throw matchsticks into it, and they float about for days, and become soggy, the water becomes black, and then anyway, it all dries up anyway. So perhaps you're better off without it.

Pause.

INGRAM. Do you find the thought of sex without children obscene, Mrs Armitage?

JO. No.

INGRAM. Really? Are you sure the idea doesn't disgust you? I mean, don't you find the idea messy? Isn't sex something you must sanctify, as it were, by incessant reproduction?

Pause.

JO. I shall have to give that question a little thought.

INGRAM. You would do well to, I think.

Pause.

I won't be seeing you for a couple of weeks. Just chew it over, and take the pills of course.

JO. Couple of weeks?

INGRAM. Oh, I'm sorry, haven't I told you? We're off to Gstaadt on Friday for a spot of skiing. It's my great passion, I'm afraid.

JO. Skiing?

INGRAM. Oh, and cut down on liquids as much as you can. Can we make an appointment for the . . . 19th?

JO. Can't make it. No . . . can't make the 19th.

INGRAM. The 20th?

JO. Can't make it.

INGRAM. Oh come now . . .

JO. What liquids?

INGRAM. Liquids.

JO. Yes, but what liquids? Listen, why are you going to Gstaadt? Why don't you go to Cortina? Why Gstaadt? Where is Gstaadt? Why the hell don't you go to Cortina? Or Kitzbuhel?

Interior. Hairdressing salon. Day.
Rows of chairs, all occupied. Hair dryers. JO *sitting under dryer, looking at a magazine. The* WOMAN *next to her is looking at her. She is middle-aged.*
The WOMAN *leans over.* JO *looks up, sees the large face of the* WOMAN *close to her. The* WOMAN *is smiling, talking, her mouth moves.* JO *lifts her dryer to hear.*

WOMAN. I hope you don't mind, I've just been looking at your photo in one of these magazines, you know, a photo of you all, all your family, all your wonderful children and your wonderful husband, I thought you must be the same person.

JO. Oh . . . yes.

WOMAN. I think you're much lovelier than your photo. I really do. I was . . . I had a . . . Do you mind me speaking to you?

JO. Er . . . no . . .

WOMAN. To tell you the honest truth, my life is an empty place, to tell you the dog's honest truth. Your eyes are more beautiful than in that picture. I bet you didn't always have things so good, that's why you appreciate, don't you? I never dreamed I'd meet you like this and I mean you're so kind, you're so full of sympathy for me. My husband doesn't come near me any more, no, nowhere near me. Don't you think I'm attractive any more? I think I'm still attractive.

JO. Of course you are.

WOMAN. I'm not as attractive as you. But in a different way I am. That's one thing I do know. I had a hyster-ectomy operation four months ago. Yes, a hyster-ectomy. You know, they take it all away. But you should see the way men look at me. The way they still look at me. My word of honour. You can tell by that, you see. I'm desirable. I'm not old. I know. But he doesn't seem to care about cheering me up any more . . . Oooh, I'm so thirsty.

Pause.

JO. Would you . . . like a cup of tea?

WOMAN. I'm off liquids.

Pause.

JO. Well, I . . . I am sorry . . .

WOMAN. It's no bloody use being sorry, chum. What are you going to do about it? I've just told you my life is an empty place.

JO. What do you want me to do?

WOMAN. I don't want any favours, for a start. Don't patro-nize me, for a start.

JO. I'm really not. I'm really not.

WOMAN. 'I'm really not. I'm really not.' God! I thought you'd be different. I thought you'd be a different woman to the one you are, Miss. I thought you'd be a very different woman.

JO. I'm sorry . . .

WOMAN. You're what? I do a weekly wash in a copper boiler!
Oh, you've got such wonderful children, won-derful, wonderful, wonderful, wonderful. You're

wonderful too. You must be a lovely woman. You must be such a lovely woman. I think women are the only ones . . . They're the only ones. I can see your grace and your sweetness just sitting here. What does your husband think of you, eh? Does he find you attractive? Eh, I've been wondering, do you think your husband would find me desirable? Eh?

JO. Look . . . I don't actually feel very . . .

WOMAN. I'd show him some tricks, I'd show him some tricks. Heh! You want to bet? . . . I'd show him a few things I bet you don't know. My love. My little darling. Anyone ever clawed your skin off? You see these claws? Ever had your skin clawed off?

An ASSISTANT *comes to the* WOMAN. *She looks curiously at them both.*

You going to give me two curls there, this time? Over the ears, two curls, one either side, two lovely curls at each side, are you? Are you?

Interior. Hall and stairs. Morning.
CHILDREN *rushing down the stairs, shouting.*

Exterior. House in St John's Wood. Morning.
JAKE *getting out of chauffeur-driven car at the front gate.*

Interior. Hall.
CHILDREN *flinging themselves at* JAKE.

JAKE. Hullo . . . hullo . . . hullo . . . Good God, – who's this? Ha-ha-ha . . . (etc.) . . . Where's Mum?

Shout from CHILD.

CHILD. Here she is!

Interior. Sitting-room.
Silent, empty. Shouts from hall. (*Dialogue from previous scene repeated*)

JAKE'S VOICE. Hullo . . . hullo . . . hullo . . . Good God, – who's this? Ha-ha-ha . . . (etc.) . . . Where's Mum?

CHILD'S VOICE (*shouting*). Here she is!

Sitting-room door is flung open.

Exterior. Front path.
CHILDREN *struggling with cases.*

Interior. Sitting-room. Morning.
JAKE *and* JO. CHILDREN. JAKE *gives* JO *a Moorish dressing gown.*

JAKE. It's meant to bring you luck.

CHILDREN *are opening cases with cries, unwrapping presents.* JAKE *claps his hands.*

Come on, come on, where's that drink? None of these are for you, you haven't been good enough.

CHILD ONE. We have!

CHILD TWO. They've got our names on!

A CHILD *hands* JAKE *a drink. He sips.*

JAKE. Who put all that soda in?

CHILD ONE. I got a green star for spelling.

CHILD FOUR. Where's mine?

CHILD TWO. What's this?

JAKE. What do you think?

JO *helps them unwrap packages.*

CHILD THREE. Did you see any lions?

CHILD FIVE. We went to the circus.

CHILD SIX. We went to the pictures.

CHILD THREE. Did you see any camels?

CHILD TWO. That's where I fell down.
CHILD FOUR. Was it a jet?
CHILD THREE. What about hyenas?
CHILD ONE. I've got a new book.
CHILD TWO. I had a bandage.

Interior. Sitting-room. Later same morning.
JO and JAKE with drinks. Paper and packages all over room. Sounds of children playing, from up-stairs. A record playing. JAKE smiles, touches her.
JAKE. Darling . . .

She smiles.

JO. I'm all right now.
JAKE. Wish you'd been there. Marvellous place.
JO. Was it?
JAKE. Come here.

She sits with him. He kisses her. He settles down com-fortably.

Of course, Hurst and Betty hated each other on sight.
JO. Did they?
JAKE. Well, first of all, there was some ridiculous busi-ness about a camel, he got her up on this camel, pure spite of course, anyway, she must have been dead drunk at the time, anyway –

A sudden crash from outside the door. A cry.
JO stands. Door bursts open. THREE CHILDREN run through, one crying. The crying CHILD chases the other two through window to garden.

JO. Hey!

Exterior. The garden. Their point of view.
In garden, we see the first TWO CHILDREN turn running, shooting at THIRD.

Back to scene.
Sudden silence in room.
A radio and gramophone suddenly blurt together from above. Shouts.

CHILD'S VOICE (*shouting*). I'm playing mine!
CHILD'S VOICE (*shouting*). I told you just now!

JAKE *sinks in chair, blankly chuckles.*

JO. What happened?
JAKE. Mmmmm? Well, what was so funny . . . you see . . . it was really what she was wearing, really . . . that's what was so funny . . .
JO. On the camel?

A scream from the garden. They look out of window.

The garden. Their point of view.
A CHILD *lies prone on the grass.*

JO (*through window*). Tim! What are you doing?
CHILD (TIM). Nothing!

Back to scene.
Silence in room.

JO. We've got lunch . . . ready soon . . . for you.
JAKE. Ah.

Music from upstairs.

JO. Bit of a racket.
JAKE. Saturday morning.

He yawns, sits. She goes to the door.

JO (*calling*). Turn one of those off!
CHILD'S VOICE. I had mine on first.
JO. I said turn one of them off, at once, now.
CHILD'S VOICE. Which one?
JO. Turn them both off!
JAKE. It doesn't matter, it doesn't matter.

She goes to him.

JO. What happened? Tell me.

JAKE. What?

JO. About . . . the camel . . . and . . .

JAKE. Oh, it's . . . all . . .

Closes his eyes.

. . . pretty uninteresting.

Opens his eyes.

What's the matter? What are you crying about?

JO. No.

JAKE. Nothing to cry about.

She rests against him.

Is there?

Pause.

JO. Look. Why don't we ask them round?

JAKE. Who?

JO. All of them. Tonight.

JAKE. Tonight?

JO. Yes. Why not? All of them.

JAKE. Who?

JO. Oh . . . the Conways, Hurst, all of them. Then I could hear all about it. Properly. Come on, why not?

JAKE. But why do you want all that lot round here to-night! They might not be free anyway.

JO. Ring and find out.

JAKE. But . . . do you want to . . .?

JO. Yes, I do. I'll ring. What's the Conway's number?

JAKE. Have you been having an affair with that doctor or something?

JO. Yes. How did you know?

JAKE. What are you up to?

She seizes his head. She kisses him hard.

Interior. Sitting-room. Night.
The party. The glass doors between sitting-room and dining-room are open. Both rooms are crowded with

people. Concentrated party noise. JO'*s face.* CON-
WAY *is hemming her into a corner, talking.*

CONWAY. Professional people are all a lot of bloody parasites,
the lot of them. Doctors, lawyers – you know what
I mean – parsons, the whole bloody crew of them.
I call myself a tradesman because it's the only
thing left to respect in my honest opinion. In my
honest opinion, an honest tradesman is the only
thing left to respect in this world. A man like me,
for instance. The rest of them are just a bunch of
lousy frauds.

DINAH *signals to* JO *from another corner of the room.
As* CONWAY *turns,* DINAH *smiles radiantly.*
CONWAY *turns back to* JO, *nudges her, leans closer.*

What do you think? Come on, what do you think?
JO. Excuse me a second, I must . . .

(*She catches sight of* JAKE.)

Jake, I think Mr Conway wants another drink.

CONWAY *drains his glass.* JO *moves away. Camera
follows her as she moves. Snatches of conversation
overheard:*

GUEST ONE. Well, there was this man, you see, there was this
man, and all his life, the one thing he wanted more
than anything else was to beat a woman, you see.
No it's quite true, really. It's a true story. It was
the one thing he really wanted to do. But he never
met anyone who wanted him to do it . . .
GUEST TWO. But it's got nothing to do with you, darling.
GUEST ONE. He was a very nice chap, you see, very quiet sort
of bloke . . .
GUEST THREE. It has absolutely everything to do with me as a
matter of fact.
GUEST ONE. Well, one night at a party he met a woman. He was
telling her about it, you see, and she said what a
wonderful coincidence, there's nothing I'd love
more in the whole world. Well, he couldn't believe
his ears . . .

GUEST FOUR. He stands to make at least fifteen grand out of it, so what's the matter?

GUEST FIVE. Who said anything was the matter?

GUEST ONE. No, it's really true, really. She took him home to her flat. He was so excited he could hardly get up the stairs.

GUEST SIX. I had three showers a day – absolutely every single day.

GUEST SEVEN. What were the peasants like?

GUEST EIGHT. Extraordinarily interesting. Fascinating faces.

GUEST SEVEN. Lots of character, I suppose.

GUEST EIGHT. Oh lots, lots.

JO joins DINAH.

JO. How's things?

DINAH. Marvellous. Dad's really with it tonight, isn't he? I didn't know Beth Conway had red hair. I thought it was sort of blonde. She's lovely, isn't she? Isn't she smiling at you? Have you spoken to her?

BETH. DINAH's point of view, lying on couch, talking to JAKE and surrounded by people.
Back to scene.
MAN comes up with a drink for DINAH.

MAN. Here you are, my dear.

He peers at JO, smiling.

Who's this?

DINAH. She's my mother.

MAN. Really?

JO. Hullo. Just a minute.

She moves away, camera with her. Snatches of conversation:

GUEST ONE (*trying to make himself heard above laughter*).
. . . No, well, anyway, after all that, at last, at last, they stood there stark naked, looking at each other. He had the cane in his hand . . .

GUEST NINE. It'll be a smash, and believe me, when I say smash . . .

GUEST TEN. Who knows if you don't.

GUEST ONE. Suddenly, to his amazement . . . suddenly to his horror and amazement . . .

GUEST ELEVEN. How's your new house, Mr Gross?

GUEST TWELVE. Which one?

GUEST ONE. He saw that she was holding a cane too. 'What's all this?' he said.

GUEST THIRTEEN. Actually, you really are terribly masculine.

GUEST FOURTEEN. Am I really?

GUEST ONE. Suddenly she whacked him with all her might. 'Oww!' he screamed.

JO *joins* BETH, JAKE *and* CONWAY *and the group around the couch.*

JAKE. Beth wants your advice. I've told her you know all about children.

JO. I wouldn't say that.

CONWAY. What my wife needs is another half-dozen and quick.

JO (*to* BETH). Did you like Morocco?

BETH. Oh, it was quite fun. Quite fun really.

All the noise of the party dies away, as we dissolve to :

Interior. Sitting-room. Later same night.
The room dishevelled, full of smoke, overflowing ashtrays, bottles, glasses, but empty of people except for CONWAY, BETH, JAKE *and* JO.

CONWAY (*his voice coming out of the silence*).
I call myself a tradesman, because it's the only thing left to respect, in my honest opinion. In my honest opinion, an honest tradesman is the only thing left to respect in this world. That's my honest opinion.

JAKE. You'd say that in all honesty, would you?

CONWAY. In all honesty, Jake. In complete honesty, boy. Ask Beth. Ask Beth if I mean what I say. (*Pause.*) Ask her!

They look at BETH.

BETH. Oh, my husband always . . . means what he says. (*To* JO.) Does yours?

JO. You'd better ask him.

JAKE *laughs.*

BETH. He writes film scripts beautifully, anyway, doesn't he? He's got such extraordinary understanding, such . . . swift . . . you know . . . kind of illumination of people. Some of the scenes with John actually made me really cry.

JAKE. That was just the sand in your eyes.

CONWAY. Lots of sand in Morocco, was there?

JAKE. Uh.

Pause.

JO. Another drink?

BETH. I'm fine.

JO. Mr Conway?

CONWAY. No, I don't think I'll have another one, thank you very much.

JAKE. I'll have one.

JO *gets it.*

CONWAY. I looked after our baby girl while Beth was away.

JAKE. How did she respond to that?

CONWAY. How did she respond to it? I'm her father!

Pause.

Intelligent woman, your wife.

They all look at JO.

JO. Oh no. I'm not at all.

BETH. I think he's right. I think you look very intelligent.

CONWAY. I like intelligent women. They're stimulating, they're vital . . . vital . . . that's what makes them intelligent, I suppose.

JAKE. Yes, it depends which way you look at it.

BETH. Jake's got an idea for a new film, it takes place on the Italian Riviera. We could all go, all of us together, the four of us, think what fun we could have.

Silence. They all sit. Staring.

Interior. Main bedroom. Late night.
After the party. JO *and* JAKE *are undressing.*
JO. They've nearly finished the house.
JAKE. Have they? Oh, good, good.

Pause.

JO. You're a marvellous colour.
JAKE. It was hot.

Pause.

JO. Do you think she's attractive?
JAKE. Who?
JO. Beth.
JAKE. Mmmm-hmmm. I suppose so.

She pulls him on to the bed, caresses him, tracing his body. JAKE *murmurs:*

I need you.
JO. What about the Arab women?
JAKE. Oh, I couldn't begin to tell you.
JO. Did they like you?
JAKE. Wouldn't leave me alone.
JO. Did they touch you like that?

He suddenly turns her over on her back and stares down at her.

What is it?

Silence. He looks at her, as if about to speak, then kisses her suddenly.

Exterior. Hillside. Day.
We see the new house in the background. It is of very modern design, startling against the skyline.
JAKE *and* FOUR CHILDREN *are cycling up the path towards the house. One of the smaller children is on a tricycle. When they near the house, the* CHILD *on the tricycle begins to slide back down the hill.* JAKE *gets off his bike, pushes* CHILD *till they reach the straight, then remounts and rides on.*

The Pumpkin Eater · 103

The other CHILDREN *ride in circles around large picnic rugs on the grass.* DINAH *is there with the* SMALLEST CHILD.
Another angle : the picnic laid out on the grass.
DINAH. Mummy's looking for some plates upstairs.
CHILD. Where's the big red ball?
JAKE. After tea.

JAKE *goes towards house, goes in door.* CHILD *shouts up to top window :*

CHILD. Mummy! Can I have the big red ball?

JO *appears at window.*

JO (*calling down*). What?
CHILD. I just want to put it on the grass. I won't play with it.

Interior. Upper floor of new house.
It is empty of furniture. JO *at window.* JAKE *enters.*
JO (*to* JAKE). Give me the ball.

He does so. She throws it out of window, leans on sill, smiling, as :

JO. Here it is.
CHILD. I'm going to throw it at Dinah.
JO. You'd better not.

JAKE *picks up a pile of dusty plates.* JO *glances at him and smiles. He comes to her. They both look out of window.*
Another angle : at window.
JO *and* JAKE *looking down over fields. Suddenly focus on barn, low down, broken, overgrown. (A momentary shot.)*
JO *and* JAKE *looking at each other.*

JAKE. I love you.

Interior. Bedroom. JO's *father's house. Day.*
MR JAMES *in bed,* JO *beside him. Her* MOTHER

sobbing by window. MR JAMES's *hands reach for* JO's, *grasp them, draw them to his eyes, hold them to his eyes. Hold them. Drop them. Stillness. Silence.* JO's *face.* MOTHER *sobs at window. Bed still. Body.*

Interior. Staircase. Father's house. Day.
Sheets and blankets being carried up by two old women.

Interior. Living-room. Father's house. Evening.
JO *and* MOTHER *drinking brandy.*

MOTHER. He was such a good man. Nobody knew how good he was. Have you told Jake yet? He was very fond of George. He was, I know. And George was fond of him. George really was fond of him.

JO. I know.

MOTHER. He didn't care for any of the others much, but I don't know . . . he was really *fond* of Jake.

JO. Jake was fond of him, too.

MOTHER. I know he was. (*Pause.*) I'll never see him again. I'm glad he wanted to be cremated. I wish I could believe I'd see him again. But I'm glad he'll be cremated. I couldn't bear to think of him buried . . . The thought of him under that . . . I mean just the thought . . .

JO. Mother . . .

MOTHER. Just to think, just to think of him . . .

JO. Mother, listen, I want to tell you something.

MOTHER *turns, looks at* JO. *Silence.* JO *goes over to table, picks up bottle of sedative and spoon.*

I'm . . .

MOTHER. What? No! You can't! You're not! You're not! You can't!

JO. Well, there it is . . .

MOTHER. But . . . but . . . what can Jake be thinking of?

JO *pours sedative into spoon, gives it to* MOTHER, *as:*

JO. He doesn't know. Nobody knows.

MOTHER. You must be mad! Aren't you ever going to get any rest?

JO. It'll be all right, really.

MOTHER. How can you be so careless, so thoughtless! It's lunacy! How can you want to start all that over again?

Interior. Living-room. JO's *father's house. Day.*
JAKE, JO, DINAH *and* JO's MOTHER. *They all wear coats.*

MOTHER (*to* JAKE). He was so fond of you. He was. He was so proud of you too. He really was. Only the other night he said we must go and see your new film. He did. Of course, he couldn't go . . .

JAKE. No . . .

MOTHER. No, oh no, he couldn't go.

Front drive of house. Their point of view through window.
The hearse draws up.
Back to scene.

MOTHER. Oh dear, there they are. There they are.

She holds JO's *hand.*
The UNDERTAKER *comes through the front door.*

UNDERTAKER. We can't . . . quite . . . get to the front door. Could the gentleman please move his car?

JAKE (*to* MOTHER). You go into the garden. I'll . . .

Exterior. Garden. JO's *father's house.*
JO, DINAH *and* JO's MOTHER, *walking.*

MOTHER. He loved his vegetables. We never bought a single vegetable until last winter. He just couldn't manage it any more. Remember the strawberries, Dinah? You loved his strawberries.

DINAH. Yes, they were marvellous.

MOTHER. I know you did.

JAKE *appears.*

JAKE. A few minutes.

They all walk.

JO. How's things at home?

JAKE. Fine.

DINAH. Chaos.

JAKE. Of course it isn't. All in control.

MOTHER. Oh, I don't know what George would have said if he knew.

JAKE. Mmmm? About what?

JO. You could let this off for allotments, couldn't you?

MOTHER. He loved the children, but he always thought there were too many. Always. I don't know what you're thinking of, Jake, really.

JAKE. What do you mean?

JO. Are they ready yet?

MOTHER. It's too much. I'm glad he didn't live to see it.

JO (*to* DINAH). Go and find out if they're ready.

JAKE. What do you mean? See what?

DINAH. Won't they tell us when they're ready?

JO. No, they won't. They might be waiting, or something. Go on, please.

DINAH. O.K.

DINAH *goes.*

MOTHER. At least he's going to be cremated. I'm so glad about that.

JAKE *looks at* JO.

JAKE. Live to see what?

Pause.

MOTHER. On top of everything else. As if she hasn't got enough. Mind you, he loved them, he loved the children.

JAKE *stands still and stares at* JO.
DINAH *appears around the corner.*

Exterior. Front of JO's *father's house.*
TWO TEENAGE BOYS, *gawky, standing in school uniform. The hearse.*
The group appears from the garden. JAKE *walks apart, smoking.*

MOTHER. Oh, look, the boys are here. The boys have come.

She goes to them. JO *stays a moment with* DINAH.

DINAH. Who are they?
JO. Your brothers.
DINAH. Good God!

DINAH goes to them. JO *looks round to* JAKE.
Close-up of JO.
Close-up of JAKE *not looking, collar up.*
Another angle : JO *walks towards the group.*
Another angle : The BOYS *watch her come.*
Close-up of JAKE.
The group.

PETE. Hullo, Mum.
JO. Hullo.
JACK. Hullo.
JO. Hullo.

Pause.
MOTHER *brings her handkerchief to her mouth.*
(*To* DINAH, *indicating her* MOTHER.)

Dinah . . .
DINAH (*looking at boys*). I wouldn't have believed it.

She draws MOTHER *away.*

JO (*to boys*). What do you think of your sister?
JACK. Pretty good.

Pause.

JO. Are you . . . everything all right?
JACK. Fine.

Pause.

PETE. Yes. Fine.

Pause.

JO. Good.

Exterior. Front of JO's *father's house. Another angle.
All getting into cars.* JAKE *alone, in Jaguar, moves
swiftly away.*

MOTHER (*to* JO). Poor Jake – he's so upset. He was always so
very fond of George.

Interior. DINAH's *bedroom. St John's Wood. House.
Night.*

DINAH, *dressed, on floor with book.* JO.

DINAH. It was when the coffin went in, when they pushed
it in, you know, I think that's when it was. I
suddenly thought, well, it might be possible. You
know . . . God might be possible. Have you ever
read Thomas Aquinas? I'm reading this book, it's
marvellous. 'That the Divine Being cannot be
specified by the Addition of a Substantial Difference.' See what I mean?

Interior. Landing outside DINAH's *room.*
JO *comes out of* DINAH's *room, closes door, starts
down stairs – then suddenly changes her mind, turns.*

Interior. Top staircase.
JO *climbing up stairs to :*
Interior. Attic.
JO *enters. Junk everywhere.* JO *looks around, and
walks slowly over to corner. She reaches out and pulls
down a cot, a rubber bath.*
*The rubber bath is perished. She stands looking at it,
looks up.*
*A high chair, a pair of scales, stuck up in corner, out
of reach.*

JO begins to clamber over suitcases to reach them — stops, as she hears the front door slam, footsteps. She turns in sudden panic, throws bath back on to pile, makes for the door.

Interior. Stairway.
JO descending stairs to hall.

Interior. Sitting-room. Night.
Fire in grate. JAKE, *having just come in, is settling himself by it.* JO *enters.*

JO. You look awful.

JAKE. I feel awful.

She sits on other side of fire. They look into it. She kicks her shoes off.

You must be tired.

JO. Mmmm.

Pause.

And you.

JAKE. Mmmm.

Pause.

JO. I'm sorry.

Pause.

JAKE. Sorry?

Pause.

JO. I know you don't want it. (*Pause.*) I know . . . you don't want the baby.

JAKE. Do you?

Pause.

JO. I'm sorry . . . I'm sorry . . .

Pause.

JAKE. It can't be helped.

JO. It'll be all right, it will . . . I mean, you'll like it
. . . I mean, perhaps it'll be a boy . . . you
haven't got nearly enough boys. When we get the
house ready we can spend the summer there. We
can spread out a bit . . . I mean, you won't notice.

JAKE. All right. It doesn't matter.

JO. It does. It does matter. (*Pause.*) You mean you . . .
you really don't want it?

JAKE. No.

She stands, walks.

JO. What do you want then?

JAKE. It doesn't matter, does it?

Pause.

JO. Why?

Pause.

JAKE. I don't want it. That's why. (*Pause.*) I wanted us to
change. Now we can't change. You see? It's my
fault. It's because of me, I know that. But I thought
we could change . . . branch out . . . be free.
(*Pause.*) Now there's no chance. (*Pause.*) We're
back where we were.

She goes to him, holds him.

I'm not blaming you, I'm blaming myself. It's my
fault, I know that. We haven't . . . lived together.
But it's just that I've suddenly realized . . . that
we could lead a more sensible life. It was possible.
We haven't lived. (*Pause.*) We don't need it. It'll
kill us. We could begin, you see, we could really
begin . . . I know it . . . you know, to . . . You
know what I mean. I mean there is a world, there is
a world apart from birth, there's a world apart from
. . . we don't want any more . . . how can we
have any more?

Silence.

I know the idea of abortion is repellant to you, I know that. It is to me, too. You must admit I've never suggested it.

Silence.

It's ghastly, the idea of abortion, I know that. Ghastly. (*Silence.*) I wouldn't dream of suggesting it. (*Silence.*) But after all, it would be perfectly legal, you've just been treated for depression, I mean the Doctor said . . . there wouldn't be anything underhand about it.

Close-up of JAKE.

After all, I got you into this. I just want to make you happy. All those boring months, the pain at the end. I just want to get you out of it, I want to get us both out of it while there's still time, that's all.

Interior. SURGEON's *office. Nursing home. Day.*
SURGEON *and* JO.

SURGEON (*with papers*). Now, Mrs Armitage . . . I've had a talk with your husband . . . and I did suggest to him that . . . in your case . . . we might consider going somewhat further than this . . . operation. I recommended pursuing, shall we say, a more sensible, long-term policy. Has he spoken to you about it?

JO. I . . . don't think so.

SURGEON. No. Good. I thought it would be better to speak to you myself.

JO. What do you mean?

SURGEON. The reasons for recommending that this pregnancy be terminated, you see, would seem to apply with equal validity to any future pregnancy. Do you see what I mean? (*Pause.*) You've had a considerable number of children. Perhaps it would be wise for you not to have any more.

JO. How do you do that?

SURGEON. It's a matter of sterilization. Quite simple. You can lead a completely normal married life, but you'll never conceive.

JO. Oh. (*Pause.*) What did my husband say?

SURGEON. Oh, he left the decision entirely to you, of course. As we do.

Interior. JO's *room in nursing home. Night.*
JO *is lying in bed, silent, alone, eyes open, still.*

Interior. JO's *room in nursing home. Day. Close-up of* JO.
In nightdress, head flung back on pillow, laughing. She is still in bed. JAKE *sits on chair.*

JAKE. Be careful. You'll hurt yourself.

JO. I'm so happy.

JAKE. Good.

JO. You don't know what it's like to be sterilized. You've never been sterilized.

JAKE. Never.

JO. It's wonderful. I'm free, you see, free. Aren't I? Completely free.

JAKE. Yes. I know.

JO. We don't have to worry about it any more, you see. It'll just never happen again. We just don't have to worry about all that ever again.

He kisses her, leaning.

JAKE. No. Never.

JO. I'm going to get rid of that Nanny for a start. I've always hated her. In the summer, we'll be able to move to the country, won't we?

JAKE. Yes.

JO. We can live with the children again, properly, and then we can go away, just do anything, just do anything.

JAKE. Yes.

He takes her hand and kisses it.
Close-up of JAKE's *face smiling, gentle.*

Interior. JO's *room in nursing home. Evening.*
The room is full of flowers. JO *in bed.* DINAH *with a*
small bunch of violets.

DINAH. I brought you these.

JO. Oh . . . thank you.

DINAH. They don't stand much of a chance with all these others.

JO. Oh yes they do.

DINAH (*examining flowers*). Look at this! Wow! Who are they all from?

JO (*laughing*). I haven't the slightest idea.

DINAH *sits on the bed.*

DINAH. You feeling all right now?

JO. Mmmm. Marvellous.

DINAH. It was a sort of . . . womb thing, I suppose, was it?

JO. Yes . . . something like that.

DINAH. Does it happen to everyone?

JO. No, of course not.

DINAH. Just happens to some women, does it?

JO. Mmmmmm.

A silence.

Look, come on, help me make this list, we're going to make a clean sweep.

JO *gives* DINAH *pencil and paper.*

DINAH. What list?

JO. There's going to be some changes made.

DINAH. Good. What?

JO. We're going to do things. First, sack that Nanny.

DINAH. Good!

JO. Sack Nanny, put it down.

DINAH. I am. When?

JO. Immediately.

DINAH. Right. Next.

JO. Start moving things to the new house.

DINAH. Wonderful. What things?

JO. Anything.

DINAH. All that junk in the attic?

JO. Yes, all that junk.

DINAH. It isn't all junk.

JO. Just put it down.

DINAH. How?

JO. Move junk to new house. Send everything to cleaners.

DINAH. We haven't phoned the removal people.

JO. Phone removal people.

DINAH. Get your hair cut.

JO. Sack the Nanny.

DINAH. We've got that.

JO. Throw away junk.

DINAH. But we're going to move the junk.

JO. No, we're not going to move the junk, we're going to move the things we want.

DINAH. Sort out the things we want.

JO. Make a clean sweep.

Another angle to include door.
JAKE comes in.

JAKE. Hullo, what's all this?

JO hides the list.

JO. Nothing.

JAKE. Let's have a look.

DINAH. You can't.

JAKE slips list out from under pillow, reads it.
JAKE writes.

JAKE. Here you are.

DINAH. What have you put?

She grabs it.

'Love Jake.'

A short laugh between JO and JAKE.
He goes to flowers and looks at them.

There's a pile of old sheets in the cupboard. We never use them.

JO. Throw them out.

JAKE. Beautiful flowers. Very nice of them all, isn't it?

DINAH *looks at* JO.

JO. Yes.

JAKE. Have you . . . written to them, thanked them?

JO. Yes.

JAKE. Good. Good. Written to the Conways?

JO. Mmmm.

JAKE. Good.

Interior. Main bedroom. St John's Wood. House. Day.

JAKE *putting suitcases down.* JO *comes into the room. They look at each other. She flings herself into his arms. Onto bed.*

Interior. Hall. Day.

JO, REMOVAL MEN, CHILDREN. JO *crisp, decisive, authoritative.* CHILDREN *are playing games in the hall.*

JO (*to* MAN). You will keep that upright, won't you?

MAN. Yes, Miss.

JO (*to* CHILD). Come on now, let the man get through.

As MAN *starts out through door with his load:*

(*to* FOREMAN.) Is that it?

FOREMAN. That tallboy, Miss . . .

JO. No, no. That stays here.

FOREMAN. That's about it then.

The phone rings. JO *goes into sitting room.*

CHILD (*to* MAN). I'll give you a hand.

MAN. I can manage, thanks.

Interior. Sitting-room.

JO *at phone.*

JO. Hello . . .

CONWAY. This is Bob Conway.

JO. Who?

CONWAY. Conway, you know, Beth's husband.

JO. Oh, Mr Conway, how are you? I'm afraid Jake's at the studio.

CONWAY. Actually, I wanted to . . .

JO (*interrupting*). Could you hold on for just a minute . . . (*To* REMOVAL MAN.) Mrs Teff will be waiting for you at the house.

REMOVAL MAN. Mrs Teff. Right Madam. Thank you.

JO. Thank you. (*To* CONWAY.) Sorry . . .

CONWAY. I was wondering if you could have tea with me tomorrow.

JO. What?

CONWAY. Something I wanted to talk to you about.

JO. Oh, I don't think I could really manage tomorrow. I'm taking the children to the zoo.

CONWAY. Splendid! What could be nicer?

JO. What?

CONWAY. I mean, why don't I see you there?

JO. All right. Why don't you meet us all at that place by the penguins – the tea place. Do you know it?

CONWAY. Perfect!

JO. Fine.

CONWAY. I shall look forward to it. Thank you.

JO. See you there about four o'clock.

CONWAY. Good-bye now.

JO. Bye-bye.

Exterior. Zoo café.
JO, CONWAY, FERGUS, ELIZABETH *and* NANNY *seated around tea table.* MARK *feeding penguins.*

CONWAY (*to* ELIZABETH).
Don't you look pretty in that dress?
(*To* FERGUS.)
What animals do you like best?

JO. Mark . . .

MARK *moves forward.*

CONWAY (*to* MARK).
> What about you?

MARK. Penguins.

> *Laughter.*

CONWAY. Aren't they delicious!

ELIZABETH. May we see the bears now?

JO. All right. But don't run away from Nanny.

NANNY. Elizabeth!

> *They run down the steps,* NANNY *following* ELIZA-
> BETH.

CONWAY (*warmly*). Well, how are you?

JO. Fine.

CONWAY. So nice of you to come. I'm very pleased you could manage it, I must say. Was it very inconvenient?

JO. No, no, it's all right, don't quite know what . . .

CONWAY. No, it's a bit of a mystery, isn't it, never mind, let's have some tea.

> *Calls.*

> Miss!

> *Then.*

> Got a surprise did you, when I phoned?
> Ha-ha. Still, I think secret meetings are rather gay, don't you?

JO. Well, it depends on what . . . they're all about.

CONWAY. Ah! Too true! What are you going to have, brown bread and jam, or marmalade, scones, toasted tea cakes, a lettuce sandwich, cucumber sandwich, cakes, gateaux, pastries, Welsh rarebits, anything you like.

> *A* WAITRESS *has come up to the table.*

> (*To* WAITRESS.) Isn't that true?

WAITRESS. What?

CONWAY. That we can have anything we like.

WAITRESS. Anything that's on there.

CONWAY. Well, what'll it be?

JO. Just tea.

CONWAY. Really? That all? Ah well, right, tea for two, and . . . (*looks at menu.*) . . . tea for two. Wait a minute, what about lemon tea? Look, it's on the menu.

JO. All right, lemon tea.

CONWAY (*to* WAITRESS). Lemon tea – for two.

WAITRESS *goes off.*

I nearly missed it. I nearly missed it on the menu, didn't see it, and then suddenly I looked and there it was – lemon tea! How are you? You look marvellous.

JO. Yes, I am. You seem in pretty good trim yourself.

CONWAY. I always am, quite frankly. I'm always on top of the world, as a matter of fact. Feel better after your stay in the Nursing Home, do you?

JO. Yes. Oh, thank you for the flowers.

CONWAY. Don't mention it. Beth and I thought of you a lot. Yes, we did. We thought of you a great deal. Especially quite recently.

WAITRESS *brings tea.*

(*To* WAITRESS.) Oh, thanks. Lovely.

Pause. WAITRESS *goes off.*

It's rather fun meeting you like this, isn't it? Just you and me. All alone. You're an intelligent woman. Why don't we make a habit of it, eh? (*He takes her hand, continues.*) What do you think?

She looks at his hand on hers – withdraws hers slowly.

JO (*with a smile*). I'd have to ask my husband.

CONWAY. Oh yes, of course, you're married aren't you. Yes. Yes, that reminds me of what I wanted to talk to you about. I'll tell you what it is. It's nothing much. It's just that a letter has come into my hands, you see. I won't bother to tell you how. But anyway, I've got this letter on me, you see. I mean, I've got it on me now, you see, in my pocket . . . can I read you . . . something of it . . . ?

Pause.

JO. Why?

CONWAY. It's from my wife. (*Takes out letter, opens it, reads.*) 'Jake baby, How are you, honey lamb, are you still managing without me? Poor darling . . .'

Another angle on JO *listening,* CONWAY's VOICE *continues, very dim, indecipherable.*
Another angle on CONWAY *reading.*

'. . . Don't let your eyes stray to those luscious bits hanging round the set, they're no good when it comes to it as well you know. I'm saving myself for you like you told me, although it's pretty difficult, you understand . . .'

Another angle on JO *listening.*
Another angle on CONWAY *reading.*

'. . . waiting to soothe you, honey love. How brave, courageous, and tough you are to face it all alone . . .'

CONWAY *and* JO *at table.*

I've been checking up. He rang her this morning. Did you know that? When they were in the studio, he sent her flowers every day, did you know *that*? He's crazy about her, duckie, he's mad about her. He can't keep off it. He had that other one before Beth, whats-her-name, it doesn't matter, until she got fed up with him. He's not much good in bed, I understand.

JO *stands up. He pulls her down. She holds her side.*

JO. I'm ill.

CONWAY. You had an abortion, didn't you? Shall I tell you why? Because Beth's a good girl at heart, she would have left him. He made you have it so that he could keep Beth. She told me, for Christ's sake!

She's a lovely girl. She's going to starve for me. She's going to starve. I wouldn't touch her with a barge pole, not even if she came crawling . . .

JO. I want to go.

CONWAY. Listen, if he ever rings her or sees her again, I'll fry him. You understand? I'll boil him. You tell him that.

JO. No.

CONWAY. You'd better. He's not a grown man, your husband, he's a puking boy. He can't even lay a girl without the whole world knowing it. Beth says he makes her sick with his slop. I made her swear on the baby's head she was telling the truth. I brought the baby in and told her to swear on its head. Tell him to keep off, well off . . .

JO. You can tell him yourself.

CONWAY. If I hear his stinking voice I'll pull it out of his throat.

JO. Is that all? I want to go.

CONWAY. Listen. Tell me something. Is it true that when he's in bed he likes to . . .

JO *stands, runs out of the café.*

Exterior. Teashop.
JO, *clasping her side, running, past monkeys.*

Interior. Sitting-room. Night.
JAKE *and* JO.

JO. Did you sleep with Philpot?

JAKE. Oh, Christ, it's years ago, it's gone –

JO. Did you?

JAKE. Yes, of course I did.

JO. You told me you hadn't.

JAKE. I lied. So what? What else did you expect me to do?

JO. Here? In the house?

JAKE. I don't remember. Yes.

JO. Often?

JAKE. As often as we could. What's the point? What the hell does it matter?

JO. What about all the others?

JAKE. What others?

JO. The others.

JAKE. There weren't any others.

JO. How many?

JAKE. Half a dozen. A dozen. I don't know. What does the number matter?

JO. When you were away, or when you were here?

JAKE. When I was away! Is that what you want me to say?

JO. If it's true.

JAKE. Then it was while I was away.

Pause.

You live in a dream world, you know that?

Pause.

JO. Why did you marry me?

JAKE. You know why.

JO. What do you think of marriage?

JAKE. It doesn't exist, it doesn't exist, so what? What do you mean? It doesn't matter what I think about it. It exists, that's what I think about it.

JO. Why did you go to bed with Beth?

JAKE. Oh –

JO. Didn't you ever . . . try not to?

JAKE. Yes . . . Yes.

JO. When I was in the nursing home, didn't you mind?

JAKE. Mind? Of course I minded! I came to see you every evening, didn't I?

JO. And you met her afterwards.

JAKE. That's ridiculous, for God's sake, it's –

JO. Where did you meet?

JAKE. It's not true!

JO. Near the nursing home?

JAKE. Not very far. I don't know where it was. Anyway, it never happened. What are you doing? You haven't exactly been a model of faithfulness yourself, have you?

JO. I was never unfaithful to anyone. To anyone. Ever.

JAKE. Christ, what a bloody hypocrite you are.

JO. Did you stay the night, or just a few hours?

JAKE. Why don't you shut up? Why don't you die?

JO. How should I die?

JAKE. I don't know. Leave me.

JO. I can die here . . . What shall we do?

JAKE. Nothing. I love you. I've always loved you.

JO. He says you love her. He says you make her sick with your love.

JAKE. He's crazy, he's a madman.

JO. Was Philpot the first, or were there others before?

JAKE. Of course there weren't.

JO. How many? Who were they?

JAKE. What others?

JO. How often?

JAKE. There weren't any others.

JO. Did you bring them here?

JAKE. How could I bring them here?

JO. Where did you take them?

JAKE. It never happened.

Exterior. Garden of JO's *father's house, shooting from garden through house to front. Afternoon.*
We can see right through the house to the front gate where the Floride is parked. JO *and* MOTHER *are walking into house.* JO *is carrying an overnight bag. She walks uncertainly, nervously.* MOTHER *is talking without pause.*

MOTHER. I don't know what to do. I wish I knew what to do. I've been sitting here, thinking about it. And then you came. I had a feeling you'd come. I don't know what to do, but I think we ought to face it. You're shivering. Are you cold?

JO. No.

The MOTHER *continues talking and, as she does so, moves forward into foreground, into the garden.* JO *puts bag down, stands a moment in doorway alone before following.*

MOTHER (*as she comes into garden*). Put your bag down. It's not cold. But we've got to face it. George loved his garden. He wouldn't want strangers in his garden with spades and things digging up his garden. I'm not going to do it. I've made up my mind. Don't you think I'm right.

JO (*joining her*). Yes.

Another angle as they approach a table on the lawn where tea is laid out. Deck chairs.

MOTHER. When the boys get back we'll have tea.

JO. The boys?

MOTHER. Pete and Jack. They came to see me yesterday. They'll always come, they said. George was so fond of them. He was fond of Jake too. They'll be back in a minute, then we'll have tea. I was so pleased you had such a sensible operation. So sensible. It must be so wonderful for Jake, not to have that awful worry over his head any more. He's worked so hard for you.

In the distance by the back gate, behind some bushes, we see the boys, PETE and JACK, meandering haphazardly, kicking a ball slowly between them. JO watches them approach.

George would never forgive me. He loved his garden, but the boys will look after it.

The BOYS appear on the lawn, approach slowly, kicking.

They're here. They came in the back gate.

The BOYS reach them, with the ball. They smile faintly at JO, who does the same.

Did you come in the back gate?

PETE. Mmmm.

MOTHER. Did you see who's here?

The BOYS mutter 'hullo'. JO does the same.

PETE (*to JO*). You're looking very well.

JACK. Very well.

MOTHER. We'll have tea in a minute. Pete won the hundred yards. Did you tell your mother?

JACK *giggles.*

JO (*to* PETE). Did you?

PETE. Yeh. The two–twenty, too.

JO. Oh good.

Silence.

PETE. I like your car.

JACK. It's a Floride.

JO. Yes.

PETE. Good car. Fast.

PETE *kicks the ball to* JACK. *The* BOYS *sit on the grass.*

Did you have lots of traffic?

JO. Traffic?

PETE. On the way down.

JO. Oh. No.

Silence. JACK *turns on his front, whispers something to* PETE. *They giggle.* MOTHER *closes her eyes, murmurs:*

MOTHER (*murmuring*). I often think . . .

The BOYS *whisper and giggle.*

. . . the birds wake me up now . . .

PETE *balances the ball on his head.*

. . . every morning . . .

JO *sits in deckchair, clutching her arms.*

Interior. Sitting-room. Day.

JO *at window.*

She goes to table, looks in an address book, puts it down. Goes to mantelpiece. One bottle on it. She

*pours a drink, looks at bottle. It is almost empty.
Knock at door.*

JO. Come in.

Door opens. SMALLEST CHILD *comes in, on reins,
held from outside. Young* NANNY *can just be seen
in hall.*

NANNY. Say 'Good-bye Mummy'.

JO *and* CHILD *look at each other. Silence.* JO *looks
at* CHILD. CHILD *totters, smiles, is doubtful.*

Say 'Good-bye Mummy'.

JO *stands still.
The reins tighten. The* NANNY *remains outside.*
CHILD *scratches its head.*

JO. Have a nice walk.

CHILD *is pulled back, looks round for* NANNY.
CHILD *disappears. Hear bells on reins tinkling.*

*Interior. Hall. Night.
Empty. Doorbell rings.
Another angle.*
JO *opens door, drink in hand. A* JAMAICAN *in
camelhair coat, beard.*

MAN. Good evening.

JO. Good evening.

MAN. I hope you are not alarmed by my call.

JO. No.

MAN. May I introduce myself to you?

JO. Yes. Do.

MAN. I am the new King of Israel, appointed by Yahweh,
the Eternal Lord God. I have come to give you
my blessing.

Pause.

I have been anointed. I am the King of Judah.

JO. I see.

MAN. In the Emphasized Bible, the name of Yahweh appears over seven thousand times. I have been appointed to fulfil the prophecy in Ezekiel. The prophecy appears seventy-two times in the Book of Ezekiel.

Bows his head.

I bless you.

JO. Would you . . . come inside a second . . .

Interior. Hall. Another angle.
The MAN *stands.*

JO. Just a minute.

Interior. Sitting-room.
JO *goes to desk, looking for purse. The* MAN *can be seen in the hall.*

MAN. The people are unhappy because they give the gift of their love to unworthy men and unworthy women.

JO *finds purse on mantelpiece, takes out five shillings. When she turns the* MAN *is in the room.*

Continents are no obstruction, mountains are no obstruction, oceans are no impediment. The Word is the work.

She gives him the money.

JO. Here, please.

MAN. This will help me. My aim is to build a radio station in Jerusalem.

The phone rings. JO *half turns, uncertain.*

The music of the Word can emanate and issue out through the miracle of the medium of the modern channels of communication . . .

JO. Excuse me.

She picks up phone.

CONWAY'S VOICE (*over phone*). Mrs Armitage – ?

    JO. She's not in.

Pause.

CONWAY'S

    VOICE. That's you, isn't it?

    JO. I don't know what you mean.

CONWAY'S

    VOICE. All right. Give her a message. Tell her Beth Conway's pregnant.

Another angle on JO.
Silence.

It's not mine. I thought she might be interested.

    JO. I'll tell her.

CONWAY'S

    VOICE. Tell her my wife's going to have this kid in a public ward, and if there's any way of stopping her getting a whiff of gas I'll find it.

    JO. She can't have it.

CONWAY'S

    VOICE. She's going to have it all right. She's going to wipe its bottom and stare at its ugly mug for the rest of her life. No more gay life for my little Beth. This kid's going to make her curse Jake Armitage until she's dead . . . I'm going to grind the slime out of her. I'm going to see her oozing in her own slime. Until she's dead. She's going to hate that kid almost as much as I will. I'm going to see that she bleeds to death in Jake Armitage's dirt.

Another angle to include MAN.
JO *puts the phone down. She turns, looks at the* MAN. *He smiles.*

    MAN. You will be blessed for this.

Interior. Main bedroom.
Close on JO's *fist crashing into* JAKE's *face. A violent clash of wrists, gasps, sobs, broken sounds.*

JO's feet kicking.
JAKE's arm and elbow thrusting her away.
Her nails.
His hand striking her.
His shirt torn.
Her nails on his neck.
His hands at her throat.
Her body falling spread-eagled on the floor.
A bedroom stool hurtling across the room.
Dressing-table mirror as stool smashes into it. It shatters.
Silence. Moans. Breathing.
Long shot. Main bedroom. JO and JAKE.
They remain still, staring at each other, panting.

Interior. Bedroom in GILES's flat. Evening.
JO and GILES in bed. JO is half dressed. They are smoking and drinking tea.

JO (*murmuring*). You always were the sexiest of my husbands.

GILES. Was I?

JO. Hmmm.

Pause.

Why did I leave you?

GILES. I was too sexy.

JO. Yes, perhaps that was it. Perhaps I should try each of my old husbands in turn, see what it's like.

GILES. You could. One of them's dead, that's the trouble.

JO. Which one?

GILES. The one I took over from. Remember? You were a widow at the time.

JO. Oh yes, of course. He was in the army or something, wasn't he?

GILES. That's right. Killed in action.

JO. Well, I couldn't try him again then.

GILES. Old husbands are only good for a night. Dead husbands are only good for a night.

JO. Are they?

GILES. Yes.

JO. But you cried when I left you.

GILES. Did I?

JO. You were heartbroken.

GILES. Yes, I cried. I remember.

JO. That means you must still be mad about me.

GILES. I'm not.

JO. Why not?

GILES. You've changed. You go to bed with your clothes on.

JO. That's only because I have scars I don't want you to see.

GILES. You always had scars.

JO. I have a very new scar.

GILES. What about your husband? Does he mind?

JO. Oh, he doesn't mind. He did it himself, with a monkey wrench.

Interior. Bar of London Club. Evening.
JAKE sitting alone at the end of the long bar. A group of MEN *are in foreground.* CONWAY *is one of them, although we don't immediately see him. The* MEN *are laughing.* BARMAN *moves down the bar towards* JAKE *with a drink, as:*

FIRST MAN. Cyril? Now wait a minute, I haven't seen Cyril –

SECOND MAN. I haven't seen him since –

FIRST MAN. Just a minute, let me think –

SECOND MAN. Cyril?

Laughs.

My goodness!

FIRST MAN. Wait a minute, let me . . . Just a minute, let me think . . .

JAKE is given his drink and looks up. CONWAY *raises his glass.*

CONWAY (*calling*). Cheers! How's the wife?

(*To the two* MEN.)

Will you excuse me a moment. Friend of mine.

FIRST MAN. Yes, of course.

(*To* SECOND MAN.)

I'll tell you the last time I saw Cyril . . .

JAKE *and* CONWAY *together on bar stools.*

CONWAY. You don't mind my coming up to speak to you, do you? I mean, I know that script writers after a hard day's work at the studio like a little drink in peace. But when I saw you I said to myself, my goodness, there's Jake Armitage, I've been to his house, we've met, I wonder if he'd mind if I had a word with him.

JAKE. What makes you think script writers mind being spoken to?

CONWAY. Don't they?

JAKE. Script writers love being spoken to.

CONWAY. Really?

JAKE. Anyway, it isn't often I get a night out with the boys.

CONWAY. Oh, where's your little wife tonight then?

JAKE. She's opening the Chelsea Flower Show.

CONWAY. Go on!

Pause.

JAKE. By the way, do you play snooker?

CONWAY. I do, as a matter of fact.

JAKE. What a shame I don't.

CONWAY. What games do you play?

JAKE. What games? Do you know, honestly, I can't remember. What games do you play?

CONWAY. Snooker for one.

JAKE. I bet you're pretty good.

CONWAY. Not as good as you.

JAKE. But I don't play.

CONWAY. I don't believe a word of it.

JAKE. Cheers.

A MAN *passes.*

MAN. Hello, Jake.

JAKE *raises his head and smiles.*

CONWAY. Oh, you haven't heard the glad tidings, have you?

JAKE. What's that?

CONWAY. My wife's going to have a baby.

JAKE. Is that so? I say!

CONWAY. Yes, you and your wife must come round to see it. I understand she's very fond of children.

JAKE. Yes, we'd adore to. How is your wife, by the way?

CONWAY. Tip top. She's at a reception tonight for the Duchess of Dubrovnik.

JAKE. I thought she *was* the Duchess of Dubrovnik.

CONWAY. My wife? No, no, not at all. Not at all. Not at all.

JAKE (*laughing*). Well, you're not the bloody Duke anyway.

JAKE's glass slips from his hand, falls on CONWAY's lap and then to the floor. Whisky stains CONWAY's trousers.

CONWAY. You've made me wet.

They stare at each other, their faces close together, bending forward on their bar stools.

Interior. Bedroom in GILES's flat. Evening. GILES sits on bed. JO strokes his arm.

JO. Shall I stay?

GILES smiles, ruffles her hair.

GILES (*gently*). No, you can't. Killer.

She stiffens.

JO. What do you mean? Killer? It's him. He's responsible. He is.

GILES. He phoned this morning.

JO. Did he? Why? Is his bed cold? He doesn't suffer. What has he suffered? It's happened to me. It's me. Look at me. Look at me.

GILES. I am.

They stare at each other for a moment. She slowly closes her eyes. Silence. She suddenly whispers.

JO. What should I have done? It was the only thing I ever really . . . that I ever really . . . I've lost it. There was something we had . . . It's gone.

Slight pause.

I don't know . . . how to keep things . . . whole.

Slight pause.

GILES. He phoned to say his father's dead.

Exterior. Cemetery. Day.
It is very windy and dull. A coffin is being lowered into a grave. There is a spare group of elderly men, obviously friends of JAKE's *father, around the grave.* JAKE *stands alone.*
As the PARSON *speaks a short prayer, which we can hardly hear through the wind, we see that* JO *has joined the group on the other side of the grave from* JAKE.
JAKE *steps forward and throws earth into the grave, then steps back to where he was.*
JO *moves round towards* JAKE. *As she does so, we see the old men begin to throw earth into the grave.*
JO *stands beside* JAKE, *takes his hand, looks at him. He glances at her and then away. His hand slips from hers. She looks at him. His gaze is fixed on the grave.*
JAKE *turns and walks out of the cemetery.*
The gravediggers begin to fill in the grave.
JO *is left standing.*

Exterior. Hillside leading to new house. Late afternoon.
JO *walking up towards new house.*

Interior. Main room of new house.
JO *enters. Enormous windows high up, looking down at the silent stillness of the fields. The sky a mist. Mist hanging in the valleys. Noise of birds.*
The rooms are empty except for isolated pieces of furniture. JO *pauses for a moment, then locks all the doors.*

Interior. Kitchen of new house.
JO *wanders in. No food. No sign of life. Empty. Unused. Bare.*

Interior. Main room.
JO *takes telephone off hook, sits down by window.*
The window.
Sun through mist.

Interior. Main room. Cats.
Snaking, on bare floorboards.

Interior. Bedroom. New house. Night.
JO *lying awake. The moon through the uncurtained windows.*
Cats asleep on bed.

Interior. Main room. Night. JO.
At window, smoking.
The window. Daylight.

Interior. Staircase.
JO *climbs stairs.*

Interior. Room at top of new house.
JO *enters, opens window, looks down towards barn.*

JO's *face.*
Another angle : JO *at window.*
She opens window wider. Stops.
JO's *face.*
Another angle : JO *at window.*
In the distance, through the window, see numbers of
CHILDREN *fanning out like trappers, converging*
on house, JAKE *bringing up the rear.*
Close-up on children's legs.
Sticks whipping grass.
Long shot. JAKE *and* CHILDREN.
JO *at window motionless. She shuts window. Calls*
from CHILDREN *as they reach house. Bangs on the*
locked doors. Glass breaking. Door opening. Sudden
flood of voices.

CHILD'S VOICE. Where is she?

SECOND
CHILD'S VOICE. Upstairs.

THIRD
CHILD'S VOICE. Probably still in bed.

FOURTH
CHILD'S VOICE. I'm going to feed the cats.

JAKE'S VOICE. JO —

JO's *face calms, becomes still.*
High angle shooting down staircase.
JO *walks down the stairs towards them, stops midway.*
JAKE *stands at foot of stairs, arms full of parcels,*
surrounded by CHILDREN. *The* CHILDREN *look*
at JO *curiously, but do not go to her.*

JAKE. We thought we might join you for a while.

He goes towards the kitchen with some of the
CHILDREN, *also carrying parcels. Other* CHILDREN
rush past JO *up the stairs. She remains standing on*
the stairs.

Interior. Kitchen. New house.
JAKE *and* CHILDREN *undoing parcels.* JO *can be*
seen on the stairs in background.

JAKE. Where's that coffee pot?

CHILD (*shouting to* JO). We didn't know where you were.

JAKE. Let's give it a wash. Get the cups out, Dinah.

DINAH. Where are they?

CHILD. I know.

> *More* CHILDREN *rush in with cats. During the ensuing dialogue* JO *slowly descends the stairs and enters the kitchen. The* CHILDREN *speak to her from a distance, tentatively.*

JAKE. Did we bring any milk?

CHILD ONE. Where's the big red ball?

JAKE. Later. Who's got the milk? Where are all those bags?

DINAH. Let me do it.

CHILD THREE (*to* JO). I've got a bandage. Look!

CHILD TWO. I want some orange squash.

JAKE (*pulling cans of beer from bag*). Where's the opener?

CHILD ONE. I won't play with it. I just want to put in on the grass.

DINAH. Put all that paper in the bin.

JAKE. The opener . . .

CHILD THREE (*to* JO). Can I tell you a story?

CHILD TWO (*to* JO). I've got ten stars for reading.

> DINAH *hands opener to* JAKE.

DINAH. Here you are. Do you want cabbage or carrots?

> JAKE *opens beer can. It spurts.* CHILDREN *react noisily.*

I'll wipe it.

CHILD FOUR. I'll do it.

DINAH. Where's the tea–cloth?

> JAKE *offers can of beer to* JO.

JAKE. Want one?

JO. Yes, I'll have one.

> *She takes it, starts drinking from the can.*

The Quiller Memorandum

The Quiller Memorandum was first presented by
The Rank Organization on 10th November 1966
with the following cast:

KENNETH LINDSAY JONES	Herbert Stass
RUSHINGTON	Robert Flemyng
GIBBS	George Sanders
QUILLER	George Segal
POL	Alec Guinness
HENGEL	Peter Carsten
BARMAN	Hans Schwarz
DORFMANN	Victor Beaumont
HASSLER	Gunter Meisner
WENG	Robert Helpmann
SCHOOL PORTER	Konrad Thoms
FRAU SCHROEDER	Edith Schneider
INGE	Senta Berger
MAN, A	John Rees
MAN, B	Philip Madoc
MAN, C	Harry Brooks
GRAUBER	Ernst Walder
MAN, F	Bernard Egan
OKTOBER	Max von Sydow
DOCTOR	Paul Hansard
MAN, H	Sean Arnold
MAN, I	Janos Kurucz
BARMAN	Carl Duering
NIGHTPORTER	Philo Hauser
ASSISTANT	Brigitte Laufer
MAN, J	Nikolaus Dutsch
NAGEL	Ves Delahunt
MAN, K	Peter Lang
MAN, L	Herbert Fux
MAN, M	Peer Goldmann
MAN, N	Malte Petzel
MAN, O	Axel Anderson
MAN, P	Wolfgang Priewe
HUGHES	Claus Tinney

Directed by Michael Anderson

The Quiller Memorandum

Exterior. Berlin Tiergarten. Summer night.
A long road. Derelict buildings at either side.
It is late at night.
In the distance, KENNETH LINDSAY JONES *is walking towards the camera.*
Silence.
The camera moves sideways to disclose a brightly lit telephone box. It is the one hard source of light.
His face, as he stops by a lamp post. He lights one cigarette from another, flips the first one away and glances up at the buildings and along the road behind him.
There is no one in sight.
He continues to walk towards the telephone box.
From the telephone box see him approach.
His footsteps echo. He walks slowly past the telephone box and stops. He glances up the street again. No one. He drops his cigarette.
He moves suddenly and enters the telephone box.

Interior. Telephone box. Night.
JONES *inserts a coin, lifts receiver. He begins to dial.*
He dials one figure and a second figure.
A sudden report. Window smashes. Glass falls in.
JONES *hits interior of box with great force. He falls in a heap, his head cracking against telephone.*

Exterior. Road. Night.
The telephone box, brightly lit. A shape on the floor.
No movement or sound along the road.

Interior. London club. Day.
A WAITER *is serving potatoes to two gentlemen.*

RUSHINGTON. Thanks. That's . . . quite sufficient, thank you.

The WAITER *nods and goes.*

GIBBS. Salt?

RUSHINGTON. Oh, thanks.

They salt their food and begin to eat.

GIBBS. What exactly is he doing now?

RUSHINGTON. He's on leave, actually. On vacation.

GIBBS. Ah.

They eat.

Well, perhaps someone might get in touch with him.

RUSHINGTON. Oh yes, certainly. No difficulty about that.

GIBBS. Ask him if he'd mind popping over to Berlin.

RUSHINGTON. Mmmm. I think so.

GIBBS. Good.

They eat.

Shame about K.L.J.

RUSHINGTON. Mmmm.

GIBBS. How was he killed?

RUSHINGTON. Shot.

GIBBS. What gun?

RUSHINGTON. Long shot in spine, actually. Nine point three. Same as Metzler.

GIBBS. Oh, really?

They eat.

How's your lunch?

RUSHINGTON. Rather good.

GIBBS. What is it?

RUSHINGTON. Pheasant.

GIBBS. Ah. Yes, that should be rather good. Is it?

RUSHINGTON. It is rather, yes.

Exterior. Olympic Stadium. Berlin. Day.
QUILLER *is walking towards the entrance, away from the camera. He passes through the gates.*

Interior. Olympic Stadium. Day.
A group of people pass in foreground.
As their voices recede, the camera remains on POL
who is sitting on the edge of one of the tiers below.
He is eating sandwiches.
QUILLER *comes into the foreground and stands for a*
moment looking down at POL, *his back still to the*
camera.
QUILLER *descends the steps and stops by the side of*
POL.
POL *does not look up. He continues eating.*

QUILLER. Excuse me. Do you have a light?

POL *looks up.*

POL. Certainly.

POL *takes out a lighter and lights* QUILLER's *cigarette.*
As QUILLER *bends to the light his face is seen for the*
first time.
QUILLER *takes a packet of Chesterfields from his*
pocket.

QUILLER. Do you smoke this brand?
POL. No I don't think I know that brand.
QUILLER. Perhaps I might introduce it to you.
POL. Thank you.

POL *takes a cigarette from the packet and puts it in*
his top pocket. He moves his legs and indicates the
seat beside him. QUILLER *crosses him and sits down.*
POL *bites into his sandwich and grins at* QUILLER.
Ever been here before?

QUILLER. No.
POL. Impressive isn't it? Built by Werner in 1936. For
the Olympics. It holds one hundred thousand
people. (*He points.*) Certain well-known personalities used to stand right up there. Must have been
quite noisy. One hundred thousand people – all
cheering. Wouldn't you say? Yes, quite noisy.

He offers the sandwiches to QUILLER.

              Some leberwurst?

QUILLER. No thanks.

    POL. Or some schinken? (*He examines the sandwich.*) No, wait a moment, what am I talking about, this isn't schinken, it's knackwurst. What about some knackwurst?

QUILLER. I'm not hungry.

    POL. Aren't you? I am.

He bites into the sandwich, chews a moment and then stands.

You don't mind if I eat while we walk?

He walks up to the circular covered passageway which runs round the perimeter of the Stadium.
QUILLER *remains seated for a second. He then stands abruptly and walks up to join* POL.

QUILLER. What do you want?

    POL. You've been on holiday, I understand.

QUILLER. I *am* on holiday.

    POL. By the sea?

QUILLER. What do you want?

    POL. Oh, my name's Pol, by the way.

QUILLER. What?

    POL. Pol.

QUILLER. Mine's Quiller.

    POL. I know that.

(*Pause.*)

I understand you've been working in the Middle East for some time.

QUILLER. Yes, I've been working there.

    POL. We've been engaged in some rather tough work here. I think we're coping moderately well with the situation in other parts of the country, but it's getting a little out of hand in Berlin. They're quite a tough bunch. Nazi from top to toe. In the classic tradition. But not just the remains of the old lot. Oh no. There's quite a bit of new blood.

Youth. Firm believers. Very dangerous. It won't do to underestimate them.

They walk.

Quite complex, of course, the over-all issue. Difficult to pinpoint. Nobody wears a brown shirt now, you see. No banners. Consequently, they're difficult to recognize – they look like everybody else. They move in various walks of life all over the country but they're very careful and quite clever and they look like everybody else. Intriguing. Don't you think? However, I agree with you – that's all politics. Not our job. I'll tell you what our job is. Our job is to get to the hard core – the extreme element – the ones you *can* recognize – if you get close enough to see them. The hard core. They have a base here. But we don't know where it is. We need, rather urgently, to find it.

QUILLER. I've read the files.

POL. The files till when?

QUILLER. Till June.

POL. Oh yes, of course, you've been on holiday. You read them while you were in London, did you?

QUILLER. That's right.

POL. Who was our leading operator here, in the last file you saw?

QUILLER. Metzler.

POL. He's dead. Another colleague of yours took over from him. Kenneth Lindsay Jones.

QUILLER. Uh-huh.

POL. He's dead too. He was killed two days ago. Long range nine point three, in the spine.

QUILLER's *face.*

We'd like you to take over.

POL *takes the cigarette from his top pocket and lights it.*

He was obstinate. He refused cover. If he'd allowed us to give him cover he might not be dead and we might have a little more idea of where he'd got to.

QUILLER. He was justified in using any method he thought fit.

POL. Not a very efficient method – in his case.

QUILLER. What do you know about it? You only talk to people.

They stare at each other.

POL. This is a very strong operation. Fully urgent. They have killed two of our men. We want you to take over from Jones.

Pause.

I've been asked to say that this is not an order but a request. Consider it, will you? At your leisure. I'll give you five minutes. Perhaps you would join me for coffee in Section E at – (*Looks at watch.*) – 11.26. POL *strolls away.*

QUILLER *looks after him.*

Exterior. Hotel. Berlin. Day.
People passing. Taxis drawing up. Lights. Traffic.
QUILLER *walks down steps of hotel. He stops, lights a cigarette. He glances lightly across the street. His eyes run quickly along the windows opposite. Smoking, he looks along the street. Among all the people moving there is one person stationary. He is standing under a lamp post by a newspaper stand, reading a paper.*
QUILLER *walks up the street, past the man, buys a paper at the paper stand and walks back past the man.*

Exterior. Berlin. Day.
QUILLER *walking. Crowds of people.* QUILLER *looks behind him, casually. The* MAN *is standing some way along the pavement, reading a theatre bill.*

QUILLER *walks quickly towards a bookshop and goes in.*
The MAN *follows at a distance.*

Exterior. Side exit. Bookshop.
QUILLER *walks through the bookshop and out by the side exit.*
From the same point of view see the MAN *approach the main entrance.*
He peers through the window into the shop and enters.
He looks about, observes the side exit and walks quickly out by it.
He stands on the pavement and looks about.
There is no sign of QUILLER.
The MAN *walks quickly down the street.*
QUILLER *enters the shop and follows him.*

Exterior. Berlin. Day.
QUILLER *walking. He watches, from a distance, between moving figures. The* MAN's *head twisting, looking about him. The* MAN *goes to the edge of the road and looks across it. He stands, looks at newspaper in his hand and throws it into the gutter.*
He goes into a small bar.

Interior. Bar.
The man, HENGEL, *is sitting at a table with a glass of beer. He is alone in the bar.*
QUILLER *enters, crosses to* HENGEL's *table and sits.*
HENGEL *stares at him.* QUILLER *smiles.*
Silence.
The BARMAN *moves towards the table.*

QUILLER. I'd like a double Jack Daniels on the rocks. Do you have it?
BARMAN. Yes, sir.

The BARMAN *goes back to bar.*
QUILLER *smiles at* HENGEL.

QUILLER. Would you like to see the evening paper?

> *He passes his newspaper across to* HENGEL.
> HENGEL *does not pick it up.*
> *They look at each other.*
> *The* BARMAN *brings the whisky.* QUILLER *drinks.*
> HENGEL *takes out a packet of Chesterfields.*

HENGEL. Do you smoke this brand?
QUILLER. No, I don't think I know that brand.
HENGEL. Perhaps I might introduce it to you.
QUILLER. Would you say they're milder than other brands?
HENGEL. They're milder than some other brands.
QUILLER. Okay, I'll try one.

> *They light their cigarettes.*

HENGEL. I lost you.
QUILLER. Why? Were you following me?
HENGEL. You were playing a game with me. I didn't appreciate it.
QUILLER. Now come on, don't be silly, you might have been one of the adverse party.
HENGEL. They don't know you're here. Yet.
QUILLER. You don't think so?
HENGEL. No. I'm one of your cover, by the way.
QUILLER. Hi.

> *Pause.*

HENGEL. I'd like to ask what method you intend to employ.
QUILLER. Well . . .

> *He clicks fingers at* BARMAN, *gesturing to man and self.*

Same again.

> *He turns to* HENGEL.

Well, I'll tell you. If you say they don't know I'm here, I think I'd better let them know I'm here. Otherwise how are we ever going to get together?
HENGEL. I see. That's your business. The fact is, I've been asked to give you certain fragments of information,

to do with some of KLJ's movements. We've no idea whether it's of any value.

THE BARMAN *brings the drinks, takes empties and goes.*
QUILLER *looks at* HENGEL.

QUILLER. What's your name?
HENGEL. Hengel.
QUILLER. Why are you so tense, Hengel?
HENGEL. Are you being funny?
QUILLER. Look at your hand. It's so tight. And look at your skin. Your skin's terrible.

Pause.

HENGEL. I have a feeling, Mr Quiller, that you won't find life here so funny for very long.
QUILLER. Why don't you drink your beer?
HENGEL. I don't want it.
QUILLER. I bought it for you.
HENGEL. You can't make me want it, Mr Quiller.

QUILLER *takes* HENGEL's *beer.*

QUILLER. Well, I need a chaser.

He drinks.

HENGEL. I worked with KLJ. I knew him.
QUILLER. Oh, really?
HENGEL. I was one of his cover until he insisted that all his cover was called off. I consider that to have been a very stupid decision, if I may say so, on his part. Once he was alone, of course, he was killed. I knew he would die. Did you know him?

Pause.

QUILLER. Yes, I did.
HENGEL. If he'd allowed me to stay with him I could have saved his life.

QUILLER *looks at him and finishes his drink.*

QUILLER. Give me the information.

HENGEL. What?

QUILLER. You said you had information. Give it to me.

> HENGEL *glances at* BARMAN, *takes an envelope out of his pocket and puts it on the table.*
>
> QUILLER *slits the envelope and takes out various pieces of paper.*
>
> *There are two torn tickets, one from a bowling alley and one from a swimming pool, and a German newspaper cutting, the headline of which is glimpsed: School Teacher Arrested – War Crimes.*
>
> QUILLER *puts these items in his pocket, stands and walks to the door.*
>
> QUILLER *goes out, leaving* HENGEL *at table.*

> *Interior. Bowling Alley.*
> *Lines of men bowling. Some lanes empty.* QUILLER *walking with manager* (DORFMANN).

QUILLER. Yes, I'm thinking of starting a big chain of these places in the States.

DORFMANN. Don't they have quite a few there already?

QUILLER. Yes. Oh quite a few. Quite a few. Thousands. But there's always room for a few more.

DORFMANN. Always.

> *They reach a lane and stop to watch about half a dozen men bowling.*

QUILLER. What kind of business do you do?

DORFMANN. Quite good. We have . . . many regulars.

> *They watch the game.*

QUILLER. Yes, a friend of mine was telling me about this place. He was in here a couple of nights ago. Don't know if you met him. Fellow by the name of Jones – Kenneth Lindsay Jones.

DORFMANN. Jones? No. I don't think so. No. I think I would remember the name.

QUILLER. Yes.

> *Pause.*

DORFMANN. Would you like to bowl?

QUILLER *looks at his watch.*

QUILLER. No. Not now thanks. But maybe I'll come back another night.

DORFMANN. Please come back. Show me how to bowl.

They laugh.

QUILLER. Right. Bye Mr Weiss.

DORFMANN. Auf wiedersehen.

QUILLER *goes.*
The last pin is knocked over.

Interior. Indoor swimming bath. Day.
A young man dives from the diving board into the pool. Young men are diving, swimming, sitting at the pool edge. There is a continual echo.
From pool level see QUILLER *appear on the changing room gallery. He is fully dressed. He stands, looking down.*

Interior. Swimming bath gallery.
QUILLER's *view of the pool. Shining water and bodies. Two men leave the pool and walk up the steps. They look at* QUILLER *curiously and pass him, brushing close.* QUILLER *brushes water from his arm. An* ATTENDANT *approaches him.*

ATTENDANT (*in German*). You are not swimming?

QUILLER. Sorry. I don't understand.

ATTENDANT (*in English*). You are not swimming?

QUILLER. No.

ATTENDANT. This is for swimming, this place.

QUILLER. I'm a coach, back in the States. I teach swimming at Williamsburg, Virginia. I heard some of the best swimmers in Berlin come here. A friend of mine was telling me. An Englishman. Name of Jones.

ATTENDANT. This place is for swimming. You cannot watch. It is not allowed to have onlookers.

QUILLER. Oh, what a pity. I'd hoped I'd have been able to watch.

ATTENDANT. No.

QUILLER *looks again at the swimmers.*
They are diving and swimming with great grace.

QUILLER. Pity. Well . . . danke.

He walks along the gallery and out of the exit.
The ATTENDANT *watches him go.*

Exterior. Swimming bath. Day.
QUILLER *comes out of swimming bath into the street.*
Across the street a man, WENG, *leans against a wall.*
QUILLER *walks to the corner, to a taxi rank, followed by* WENG.
He gets into a taxi. It drives off.
WENG *gets into a taxi. His taxi follows* QUILLER'S.

Exterior. Hotel. Day.
Two taxis draw up at hotel.
QUILLER *gets out of one, goes up steps into hotel.*
WENG *gets out of other, looks up at hotel.*
QUILLER, *at top of hotel steps, glances round at* WENG.
WENG *walks slowly along.*
QUILLER *goes through swing doors.*

Interior. Hotel lobby.
QUILLER *comes through swing doors. He looks out to the front of the hotel. There is no sign of* WENG.
QUILLER *turns.*
In the corner of the lobby HENGEL *is sitting.* HENGEL *starts to get up.* QUILLER *goes towards him.* HENGEL *sits.*
QUILLER *sits by him.* HENGEL *is drinking coffee.*
QUILLER. What do you want?

HENGEL. I have been asked to inquire if you carry anything useful.

QUILLER. I don't carry anything.

HENGEL. I think they'll be disturbed to hear that.

QUILLER. Let them be disturbed.

HENGEL. Certain objects can be valuable to a man in your position.

QUILLER. I decide that. You don't.

Pause.

QUILLER. I'm going somewhere. Have another cup of coffee.

HENGEL. It's my job to accompany you.

QUILLER. I don't need you today.

HENGEL. I am your cover. I must keep with you.

QUILLER. Go and see a good movie. Take the day off.

HENGEL. You want a bullet in your spine, too?

QUILLER. There's a spy film on at the Palace.

HENGEL *leans forward.*

HENGEL. I shall report this.

QUILLER *stands and clicks his fingers at the waiter.*

QUILLER. A cognac for the gentleman.

QUILLER *walks out of the hotel.*

Exterior. Hotel. Day.
QUILLER *standing on steps a moment. No sign of*
WENG.

Exterior. Hertz garage. Day.
Sign saying 'CAR HIRE' *in a number of languages.*
QUILLER, *seen from street, walking from office with car keys. He gets into an Auto-Union and drives into the street.*

Exterior. School. Outskirts Berlin. Day.
Children playing in the front playground.

QUILLER *walks into the shot, stands a moment looking at the school and then walks towards it.*

Exterior. School. Day.
QUILLER *enters the school. He can be seen speaking to a* PORTER. *The* PORTER *lifts a telephone, speaks into it and then points up the stairs.*
Children are changing classes. QUILLER *walks up the stairs.*

Interior. Headmistress's Study.
QUILLER. My name's Cooper. I'm a journalist.
HEADMISTRESS I speak English, I am afraid, not so very well . . .
(FRAU SCHROEDER).
QUILLER. Don't speak German at all.

They both laugh, and sit.

HEADMISTRESS. How can I . . . help you?
QUILLER (*briskly*). I'm writing an article for the *Philadelphia World Review*.
HEADMISTRESS. Uh . . . huh?
QUILLER. You haven't heard of it?
HEADMISTRESS. Oh . . . no.
QUILLER. That's because it hasn't started yet. This is going to be the first number.
HEADMISTRESS. Ah.
QUILLER. We in Philadelphia are convinced that current affairs in Europe have a great deal of bearing on the lives of the citizens of Philadelphia – you know, the people back home in Philly.
HEADMISTRESS. Uuh . . . I don't understand . . . exactly . . . what . . .
QUILLER (*speaking very deliberately*). I'm collating material for an article about the Nazi situation in Germany.
HEADMISTRESS. Nazi?

QUILLER *takes out newspaper cutting.*

QUILLER. That's right. We understand that you had a school teacher here recently, name of Steiner, who was discovered to have been a war criminal. Is that right.

HEADMISTRESS. That is . . . so.

QUILLER. Well – we'd like a little more information for our Philly readers.

Pause.

HEADMISTRESS. It was all reported.

QUILLER. I didn't think it was reported in any great detail. The man hanged himself, I believe.

HEADMISTRESS. Hanged?

QUILLER. Yes, you know . . .

QUILLER *mimes a rope round the neck, and jerks it.*

HEADMISTRESS. Oh, hanged . . . yes but I am so sorry, my English . . . I have a teacher here, who has . . . replaced . . . this man. She knows English. Perhaps . . . you would like to speak to her?

QUILLER. Sure. Thanks.

HEADMISTRESS. If you will come with me. I will see if she's still here.

They stand.

Interior. School. Corridor and classroom.
The HEADMISTRESS *leads* QUILLER *down a corridor. Children pass them. They reach the open door of a classroom.* INGE *is within, talking to a little girl.*

Interior. Classroom.
INGE *looks up.* HEADMISTRESS *and* QUILLER *at the door.*
HEADMISTRESS *speaks German.*

HEADMISTRESS. Have you a moment.

INGE (*in German*). Yes, of course. All right, Hilde.

The little girl bobs to them all and goes.

HEADMISTRESS. Inge – this is Herr Cooper – Fräulein Lindt.

They nod to each other and smile.

Herr Cooper is a journalist. He is writing an article about Herr Steiner. Perhaps you might be able to help him – in English.

INGE (*in German*). Yes, of course.

HEADMISTRESS. Good. (*To* QUILLER.) Good-bye.

QUILLER. Thank you.

She leaves the room.

INGE *and* QUILLER *look at each other for a moment.*

INGE. So – you are writing an article about Herr Steiner?

QUILLER. No, no . . . he's just an item. The article is about the present day Nazi question in Germany. I don't know much about it myself, I've been a sports writer all my life.

INGE. Oh.

QUILLER. But you know what boxing is these days.

INGE. No? What?

QUILLER. The golden days are over. You're not a boxing fan?

INGE. No, I'm not.

QUILLER. Ah.

Pause.

Well listen, this man Steiner, can you tell me anything about him?

INGE. Not very much, I'm afraid.

QUILLER. I mean, what was he like?

INGE. He was a very good teacher.

QUILLER. Was he?

INGE. Oh yes. We were . . . so surprised . . . when we heard about his past. We couldn't believe it. I mean he was so wonderful with the children.

QUILLER. Is that a fact?

INGE. Yes, he seemed to feel . . . I don't know . . . a great responsibility towards them. It's funny, how little you know about people, however closely you work with them. But I . . .

Pause.

QUILLER. What?

INGE. Oh, I think it is true to say that, at heart, he was part of the old Germany.

QUILLER *takes out a notebook.*

QUILLER. That's quite an interesting angle. The old Germany and the new Germany. (*Writing.*) Yes . . . that's quite an interesting angle.

He looks at her.

What would you say were the aims of the new Germany?

INGE. Oh, that's a very big question.

QUILLER. What are your aims?

INGE. Mine?

QUILLER. As a school teacher.

INGE. Oh . . . I think, perhaps . . . to try to teach the children a broader attitude towards Europe, a broader attitude towards the world.

QUILLER. Uh-huh. (*Lifts pencil.*) Mind if I quote that?

INGE (*laughing*). I'm not an important person, really. I'm just a school teacher.

QUILLER. But you're a young German woman. That's what's going to interest the readers back home. The feminine point of view.

INGE. You seem to approach your work with a lot of enthusiasm.

QUILLER. Well listen, that's the kind of man I am. It's all or nothing with me.

They smile.
She puts a few books into her bag and goes for her coat.
He watches her.

You've been most helpful.

He helps her with her coat.

Do you live near the school?

INGE. No, I live in Bundesallee.

QUILLER. Why don't I give you a lift?

She looks at him.

INGE. That's very kind of you.

Exterior. Block of flats. Afternoon.
The Auto-Union draws up. INGE *and* QUILLER *get out and stand on the pavement.*

INGE. Thank you.

QUILLER. Thank *you*.

INGE. Good luck . . . with your article.

QUILLER. Yes . . . umm . . .

They stand a moment.

I might like to . . . reach you again . . . about the article. Can I call you?

INGE. I'm at school every day.

She puts out her hand. He shakes it.

Good-bye.

She walks to the door of the block.
He stands, uncertain, suddenly calls to her.

QUILLER. Hey, wait a minute.

He joins her at the door.

That bag looks heavy.

He tests it for weight.

Very heavy.

He looks at her.

Why don't I help you carry it?

INGE *laughs.*

INGE. All right.

Interior. INGE's *flat. Afternoon.*
QUILLER *is sitting with a drink, stretched out.*

QUILLER. The point about Louis was Louis's co-ordination. Louis had wonderful co-ordination. He was really – (*puts fists into a boxing posture*) – you know – he was really of a piece, that guy. And he had a killer inside him. I mean look what he did to Schmeling.

INGE. Who?

QUILLER. Schmeling. German fighter. Louis killed him.

INGE. I thought Schmeling beat him.

QUILLER. He beat him the first time. But Louis killed him the second time.

INGE. Ah.

QUILLER. He massacred him. Yes, I don't know what it is, but the Germans have been a great disappointment – I mean from the boxing point of view. I mean, you know, you'd think, that the way the German mind goes – I mean the old German mind, not the new German mind – you'd have thought they'd have done well in the fight game. But it ain't worked out like that. We got them beat.

INGE *looks at him with a half smile.*

INGE. So it seems.

QUILLER. But that's the way it goes.

Pause.

INGE. A little more?

QUILLER. Oh, thanks.

INGE *rises, takes his glass, fills it, adds ice.*
He watches her.
She brings glass back to him.
He watches her.
She smiles at him.

INGE. Here you are.

He takes glass.
She turns, fills her own glass.
He watches her.
She sits.

QUILLER. Cheers.

They drink.

What kind of men do you know?

INGE. I don't know many.

QUILLER. Why not?

INGE. Oh, I'm . . . busy.

Pause.

QUILLER. You know, someone was telling me that there are some people who don't think like, for instance, you do.

INGE. How do you mean?

QUILLER. Well, someone was telling me that there are some people here who wouldn't agree with your attitude – about Europe, about education – you know, about things like that.

INGE. That's true, I suppose.

QUILLER. That's what this man was telling me.

INGE. Yes.

Pause.

QUILLER. You mean there are certain people here who believe that this country should be . . . very strong, that it should be dominant?

INGE. That's right.

QUILLER. They still believe that?

INGE. Oh yes. Still.

QUILLER *drinks.*

QUILLER. Well listen, I don't think there's anything basically wrong with that, is there? I mean we believe the same in the States. We believe our country should be strong. I wouldn't say dominant – I mean we don't want to dominate anybody – but I would say strong. Yes, I'd say that.

Silence.

But listen . . . what kind of people are they exactly? Nazis?

INGE. Well, they are . . . I would say. But of course they don't call themselves that any more.

QUILLER. They don't?

INGE. No.

QUILLER. You know, this fits in with what this man was telling me. He was saying that these boys don't show themselves, they keep themselves pretty much under cover.

INGE. Yes. So I believe.

QUILLER. Yes . . . he was saying they've got a kind of long term policy, that they want to infiltrate themselves into the mind of the country, over a period of years. But they're not in any kind of hurry, this time . . . you know . . .

He laughs.

INGE. Yes.

QUILLER. But that they're very convinced men. Very convinced.

INGE. I would say that, yes.

QUILLER. Yes, that's exactly what this man was telling me.

Pause.

INGE. Who is this man?

He looks up from his drink.

QUILLER. What man?

INGE. The man . . . who was talking to you.

QUILLER. Oh, just a guy I met in a bar.

INGE. Oh.

Pause.

Are you going to write about this . . . question . . . in your article?

QUILLER. No, no, it's outside my range. I'm not political. I haven't got a political brain.

INGE. Ah.

They drink.

QUILLER. It's very pleasant here.

INGE. Yes. I like it.

QUILLER. You like living alone?

INGE. I've been alone for a long time. My family was killed in the war.

Pause.

I live for my work now.

Pause.

How long are you staying in Berlin?
QUILLER. Until I've finished my assignment.

Pause.

Why don't we go out one night?
INGE. That would be very nice.

Exterior. Block of flats. Afternoon.
QUILLER *emerges from the building. He stops in the porch and arranges his tie. He then walks in the direction of his car, parked at the side of the road.*
For no apparent reason he walks past his car, without looking at it, and continues round the corner.

Exterior. Other side of block.
QUILLER *suddenly turns on his heel and walks straight back in the direction he has come.*
A man is walking slowly along by the shops.
QUILLER *walks up to him and stands in front of him.*
The man stops, looks at QUILLER *with surprise.*
QUILLER. Are you following me?

Silence.
Then in fluent German.

I said are you following me?
MAN (A) (*in German*). I am not.

The rest of the scene is played in German.

QUILLER. Why are you following me?
MAN. I am not. You are mistaken.

The MAN *attempts to move.* QUILLER *blocks his path.*

MAN. Excuse me.
QUILLER. Where are you going?
MAN. To meet a friend.

QUILLER. Where?
MAN. Here.

QUILLER turns. Another man stands behind him.
FIRST MAN speaks to the SECOND MAN (B).

FIRST MAN. This man has accused me of following him.
SECOND MAN. Following? Why?
FIRST MAN. I do not know.
SECOND MAN (*to* QUILLER). Why do you say such a thing?

A THIRD MAN (C) joins the group.

THIRD MAN. What is the matter?
FIRST MAN. This man is being offensive.
THIRD MAN. Offensive?

THIRD MAN moves closer to QUILLER.

THIRD MAN. Are you being offensive?

QUILLER is closed in by the three men by the shop window.
He smiles, and speaks to the THIRD MAN.

QUILLER. Don't come any nearer, will you?

Silence. The THIRD MAN is still.
QUILLER smiles at the FIRST MAN.

Well, perhaps I was mistaken.

Pause.

Perhaps you weren't following me.

The men are silent.
He looks at each of them in turn.
He points at THIRD MAN.

You're in my way.

THIRD MAN moves back. QUILLER walks through them and back down the street. The three remain at the window.

Exterior. Block of flats.
QUILLER gets into his Auto-Union and drives off.

Exterior. Hotel. Early evening.
QUILLER *running up steps of hotel.*
A porter is collecting cases from a taxi and arranging them on the pavement.

Interior. Hotel lobby.
QUILLER *walking through lobby. He stops, grimaces.*
He has seen HENGEL *sitting in the corner.*
He walks over and sits by HENGEL, *who has a glass of beer in front of him.*

QUILLER. How was the movie? Instructive?
HENGEL. There are two things to tell you. Firstly they do not understand why you carry no kind of instrument.
QUILLER. What's the second thing?
HENGEL. I am still your cover. I will tag you. I am to keep with you.

QUILLER *looks at him.*

QUILLER. You carry instruments, I suppose?
HENGEL. I do.
QUILLER. Yes. Then I'll probably feel more secure with you around.
HENGEL. You should.
QUILLER. You'll see I don't come to any harm.
HENGEL. That's my job.
QUILLER. Well thanks, Hengel. Thanks a lot.

HENGEL *looks at him suspiciously.*

HENGEL. We see that you've hired a car.
QUILLER. That's right.
HENGEL. How is your operation proceeding? We'd all like to know.
QUILLER. It's difficult to say, Hengel.

Pause.

Well, I'm just going for a little ride about the town, to see the sights.
HENGEL. I'll tag you.

QUILLER. Okay.

QUILLER *stands.*

Don't lose me now.

Exterior. Hotel. Early evening.
QUILLER *on steps. He lights a cigarette.*

Interior. A window opposite.
A hand on a curtain. Curtain slightly shifts.
QUILLER *can be seen standing. A* PORTER *ascends hotel steps, with suitcases.*

Exterior. Hotel.
QUILLER *begins to descend the steps.*
The PORTER *is going up. As they pass, the* PORTER *hoists a suitcase up in his arm. The edge of the case hits* QUILLER *on the thigh.* QUILLER *grimaces, holds his thigh.*

QUILLER. What the hell —
PORTER. Oh, I am sorry, sir.

QUILLER *rubs his thigh.*

I do apologize, sir.

HENGEL *comes out of hotel.*

QUILLER. What's your name?
PORTER. Grauber, sir.

QUILLER *moves down the steps and gets into his car.* HENGEL *moves down steps and gets into a Volkswagen.*
They drive off.

Interior. Window opposite.
The hand drops the curtain.

Exterior. Berlin streets. Dusk.
QUILLER's *Auto-Union turns sharp left, quickly.*
HENGEL's *Volkswagen follows.*
Auto-Union turns sharp right.
Volkswagen follows.
Auto-Union crosses crossroads at speed.
Volkswagen just makes lights, following.

Interior. Auto-Union.
QUILLER *looking in rear mirror. The Volkswagen just in sight.*
QUILLER *grins.*

Exterior. Streets. Dusk.
Auto-Union turns left, right and right again and comes out into a wide avenue. The Volkswagen is no longer in sight.

Interior. Auto-Union.
QUILLER *chuckling to himself, as he drives.*
He glances in the rear mirror. No sign of the Volkswagen.
He glances in his wing mirror. A Mercedes 300 is approaching.
QUILLER *lessens his speed and looks out casually at the tree-lined avenue.*

Exterior. Avenue.
The Auto-Union and the Mercedes 300 proceeding sedately along the avenue.

Interior. Auto-Union.
QUILLER *glances back from the window.*
His eyes blink. He shakes his head, grunts.
He pulls up at traffic lights.
He moans lightly. The red traffic light winks foggily.

Exterior. Avenue. Traffic lights.
The Auto-Union at the traffic lights. The Mercedes beside it.
Three other cars behind the Auto-Union. The lights go to green. Auto-Union remains still. Cars begin to hoot. One car pulls round and goes past.
The Mercedes remains. The Auto-Union remains.
The other cars pull away and go past, hooting.

Interior. Auto-Union.
QUILLER *grunting, blinking.*
The green light winks.
QUILLER's *hand is on the gear lever. He presses but is unable to put the car into gear. His hand falls to his thigh, clutches it.*
The driving door opens. A man steps in.
MAN (D). I'll drive. Move over.

QUILLER *tries to resist, is too weak. The* MAN *shifts* QUILLER *into the passenger seat.* QUILLER *slumps. The* MAN *drives off.*

Exterior. Avenue. Dusk.
The Auto-Union and the Mercedes proceeding sedately along the avenue.

Interior. A large reception room.
QUILLER's *point of view.*
A large brilliantly lit chandelier.
Camera descends to see an oil painting of a nude blonde, leaning across a chair, on the far wall.
Below the painting a pair of white and golden double doors.
A man, F., *in a dark suit stands by them.*
The room is large, high-ceilinged, well-furnished.
QUILLER *in a silk brocade chair.*

> QUILLER *sits, a cushion behind his head.*
> *He clenches his eyes, looks at his watch.*
> *His point of view.*
> *A carpet stretches from his chair to the doors.*
> *A man,* GRAUBER, *walks across from the curtained window to join the other at the doors.*
> *A third man,* OKTOBER, *stands by an enormous fireplace.*
> *A fourth, in a white surgeon's gown, walks towards* QUILLER.
> QUILLER's *eyes close.*
> *The* DOCTOR *raises one of* QUILLER's *eyelids.*
> *The* DOCTOR *steps back.* QUILLER's *eyes open.*
> *The* DOCTOR *turns his head towards the fireplace.*
> OKTOBER *leaves the fireplace and walks slowly to* QUILLER.
> QUILLER *looks up at him and shivers.*

OKTOBER. Are you cold?

> QUILLER *looks at him.*

QUILLER. What is it? Day or night?

> OKTOBER *studies him.*

OKTOBER. My name's Oktober. What's yours?

> *Silence.*

QUILLER. What's the time?
OKTOBER. You've just looked at your watch.
QUILLER. It may be slow. Or fast. What time do you make it?
OKTOBER. Oh, time isn't really very important.
QUILLER. It is to me. I have an appointment.

> *He points at painting.*

> She looks something like that, too. So . . .
OKTOBER. She'll wait.

> *Pause.*

QUILLER. Listen, can I make a suggestion?
OKTOBER. Surely. But we would like to know your name first.
QUILLER. Let me make this suggestion first.

OKTOBER. No. Tell us your name first.

Pause.

QUILLER. They call me Spike.
OKTOBER. Not your nickname. Your surname.
QUILLER. Canetti.

Pause.

OKTOBER. What is your suggestion?
QUILLER. I think this is a case of mistaken identity. I work for Doubledays in New York. I came to Berlin looking for rare books.
OKTOBER. Have you found them?
QUILLER. Well no, not quite yet. I haven't found them yet.

OKTOBER *smiles.*

OKTOBER. What is your real name?
QUILLER. My mother's maiden name was O'Reilly.
OKTOBER. What is your real name, please, Mr Quiller?
QUILLER. Well, originally I had to walk around with a double-barrelled name. O'Reilly Canetti. But I found it a bit heavy. (*Turns to* DOCTOR.) Wouldn't you find it heavy? So I dropped the O'Reilly and kept the Canetti.
OKTOBER. What does your father do, Mr Quiller?
QUILLER. He's dead.
OKTOBER. And your mother?
QUILLER. She's dead too.
OKTOBER. And your sister?
QUILLER. She's dead too. What I mean is I never had one. I was an only child.
OKTOBER. You must be lonely.
QUILLER. No, no . . . no.
OKTOBER. You must feel lonely now, sitting here amongst strangers.
QUILLER. No, I like meeting people. You know . . . new faces . . .

Pause.

OKTOBER. How's your leg?

QUILLER. My leg? Oh yes. Someone scratched it – with a suitcase.

OKTOBER clicks his fingers to GRAUBER at the door. GRAUBER comes forward, down the carpet.

OKTOBER. He did it.

QUILLER looks at GRAUBER and waves, vaguely.

QUILLER. Oh, hi. Hullo.

GRAUBER goes back to the door.

OKTOBER. We know . . . a little about you.
QUILLER. Me?
OKTOBER. A little. But we would like to know a little more. I shall tell you quite simply. We would like to know the exact location of your local Control in Berlin. We would like to know a little more about your current code systems. We would like to be able to appreciate the extent of your knowledge about us, and also what information, if any, your predecessor managed to pass to your Control. We would like to know the exact nature of your present mission in Berlin.

Pause.

You are a sensible man, and you know perfectly well you must give us this information since you have no alternative.

Pause.

QUILLER. Have you got a telephone here?

He looks inquiringly about.

I think I should call my lawyer in New York. Guy called Cuspensky. I'll make it collect. So don't worry about that.
OKTOBER. You don't work in New York, Mr Quiller. You work in Europe and the Middle East.

OKTOBER turns and moves a few paces away.

The TWO GUARDS, GRAUBER *and* F, *move from the doors and approach* QUILLER'S *chair.*
They stand with their hands in their jacket pockets.
A THIRD MAN, C, *comes into view from behind his chair, hand in pocket.*
The DOCTOR *wheels a small table towards chair. On it is a hypodermic kit. The* DOCTOR *selects equipment. Silence.*
DOCTOR *fills a syringe. A colourless fluid.*

Take off your coat.

QUILLER. Sure.

All the men watch him begin to take off his coat.
QUILLER *takes his coat off.*
Very fast, he whips it into OKTOBER'S *face and kicks him in groin, and in a continuing move swings the small table at the head of* C *at his right. It hits him. The man's gun, out, falls. The hypodermic kit scatters.*
OKTOBER *has fallen.* C *clutches his head.*
QUILLER *swivels. A gun descends on his shoulder as he ducks.*
QUILLER *seizes* GRAUBER'S *leg, his shoulder on his knee, his left hand behind his ankle, and breaks* GRAUBER'S *leg.* GRAUBER *screams.*
F *kicks at* QUILLER'S *head.* QUILLER *grasps his foot and twists.* F *is thrown off balance.*
QUILLER *begins his run to the door.*
He is tackled and brought down by F.
They sprawl.
F *grips* QUILLER'S *leg.*
QUILLER *kicks him in the face with his free leg.*
F *continues to grip and twist leg.*
QUILLER, *writhing, kicks him again in the face.*
C'S *arm locks round his throat.*
QUILLER'S *head jerks back as the pressure tightens.*
F'S *face, bloodied, comes into picture.*
He hits QUILLER *in the face.*
All this has taken place in silence.
A sharp word from OKTOBER.
Sound of doors shutting.

Shoes move by QUILLER's *locked head. A shoe kicks his head. The arm loosens on his neck.*
QUILLER, *nose bleeding, looks up at bloodied face of* F. *The arm is taken from his neck.* F *and* C *stand. Legs stand above him.* OKTOBER's *voice :*

OKTOBER. You may get up.

QUILLER *stands, tucks his shirt in and looks about. Four men,* A, B, H *and* I, *stand by the door, guns out.* F *stands, breathing heavily.*
C *stands still, a cut on his forehead.*
GRAUBER *lies on the floor, still, his leg at an odd angle.*
OKTOBER *stands stiffly, slightly sweating.*

OKTOBER (*to* QUILLER). Sit down.

QUILLER *looks at the faces of the men surrounding him.*
He walks down the carpet to the chair and sits.
QUILLER's *point of view.*
A, B, C *and* F *walk down the room towards him, guns out. They stop.*
The DOCTOR *rolls up his sleeve, cleanses the skin and picks up the syringe.*
QUILLER *glances at the* DOCTOR.
His face twists.

Exterior. Terrace. From room. Night.
Cigar smoke rising on the terrace. The long windows are ajar.
OKTOBER *stands on terrace, looking down into the dark garden.*
A man, B, *comes through the curtain and stands.*
OKTOBER *turns and walks back into the room.*
QUILLER's *point of view.*
His eyes flicker, open.
FOUR MEN, A, B, C *and* F, *stand by the doors, indistinct, blurred, in soft focus.*
OKTOBER *stands in the middle of the room, looking at him.*

Behind him, TWO OTHER MEN, H *and* I, *by the windows. No guns in sight.*
The DOCTOR *straps a constrictor on* QUILLER's *arm, for blood-pressure. He feels* QUILLER's *pulse.*
OKTOBER *walks forward.*
He smiles.

OKTOBER. My name's Oktober. What's yours?

QUILLER. Quiller.

OKTOBER. And your first name?

QUILLER. Inge.

OKTOBER. Your name is Inge? Really?

QUILLER *breathes heavily, hisses through his teeth.*

That's a girl's name. It's the name of a girl. She must be a very beautiful girl. Tell us about her.

Pause.

You're not worried, are you? There's nothing to be worried about. Is there?

QUILLER. No.

OKTOBER. You can talk to me quite easily, can't you?

QUILLER. No.

OKTOBER. Of course you can. You need to relax. They work you too hard. That boss of yours, what's his name?

Pause.

What's his name?

QUILLER. Inge.

OKTOBER. No, she's a girl. She's not your boss.

QUILLER's *eyes close, his head droops.*

Open your eyes.

The eyes remain closed.

Open your eyes.

The eyes open.

Sit up. You seem to be sleepy. Don't fall asleep. Not yet. Jones hated your boss. They betrayed him and killed him. What was his name?

QUILLER. She has long legs.

OKTOBER. Really? I'm so glad to hear that. You're very lucky. After you leave us you can go to her. She's waiting for you.

QUILLER. White . . .

OKTOBER. She adores you.

QUILLER. No.

OKTOBER. Oh yes. Adores you. She wants you only. She longs for you only.

QUILLER. Longs . . . adores me . . .

Pause.

Wants me . . . only . . .

OKTOBER. Don't sleep. It's too early.

QUILLER's *head drops onto his chest. He is asleep.*
OKTOBER *looks at the* DOCTOR.

DOCTOR. He forced himself . . . to sleep.

OKTOBER. Wake him up.

The DOCTOR *fills another syringe and injects* QUILLER's *sleeping body. He signals to a* GUARD (A). A *moves to the chair, holding some leather straps. He bends at the chair.*

QUILLER's *point of view.*
The chandelier, abnormally ablaze, swimming on ceiling.
The room seems larger than it is.
Everything is in sharp focus, to infinity.
QUILLER's *eyes are open, bright, very alive.*
From his point of view figures, furniture, etc. are etched with an abnormal distinction.
The DOCTOR *stands close to him.*
A basin of water stands on the side table. Lights shine brilliantly in the water.
The ripple of the water is deep. The tick of the watch is sharp.
He looks up. The chandelier jolts, dazzles.

He takes his eyes from it.
OKTOBER *stands in front of him.*

OKTOBER. That was a good sleep you had. How do you feel?

QUILLER (*loudly*). Great.

> QUILLER *speaks involuntarily, compulsively, on every cue.*
> *He is sweating.*
> *He jerks forward, is stopped. He looks down.*
> *His ankles and wrists are strapped to the chair.*
> *He jerks forward again and falls with the chair.*
> TWO GUARDS, B *and* C, *from behind, set the chair upright and remain holding it.*

OKTOBER. Talk to me.

QUILLER. Nothing to talk.

OKTOBER. Oh come on, Quiller, we don't want to keep you here all night. Your Control will be worried about you. You haven't reported for a long time.

QUILLER. Don't report. I'm my . . .

OKTOBER. What?

QUILLER. My own master.

OKTOBER. But you mustn't lose touch with them. Why don't you phone them? Or we can take a message for you? What's the address?

QUILLER. Not waiting.

OKTOBER. Of course they're waiting, and Inge's waiting. Who is Inge?

QUILLER. Who?

OKTOBER. What's her second name? Inge what?

QUILLER. Who?

OKTOBER. Inge who?

QUILLER. What?

OKTOBER. Inge what?

QUILLER. Lin – link – link –

OKTOBER. Is she your link?

QUILLER. No link.

OKTOBER. Of course you have a link. You have colleagues. She's with your colleagues now.

QUILLER. No colleagues.

OKTOBER. You have a cover man. What's his name?

QUILLER. Heng – Hang – hang him –

OKTOBER. That's unkind. He's your friend. What's his name?

QUILLER. Jones.

OKTOBER. Jones knows Inge. He's with Inge now.

QUILLER. Dead.

OKTOBER. With her now. He's in bed with her now. He's enjoying her now. You must tell your base.

QUILLER. He's dead.

OKTOBER. You mustn't let her touch him, he's a corpse. Where's your base? Tell us your base. She's your colleague, how does she get signals from local Control?

QUILLER. She's not –

OKTOBER. Where's your base?

QUILLER. Secret! It's secret! Pol doesn't –

OKTOBER. Who is Pol?

QUILLER. Pop it in the box.

OKTOBER. Who is Pol?

QUILLER. Polly, pol, good polly –

OKTOBER. A pet shop? Which pet shop? Is that where your Control is now? Which pet shop?

QUILLER. In the Zoo.

OKTOBER. Who is your cover?

QUILLER. Getting in my way, never out of my way, do you smoke this brand?

OKTOBER. What brand?

QUILLER. Don't know it – too strong –

OKTOBER. Would you like a cigarette?

QUILLER. Not right brand.

OKTOBER. Which is your favourite brand?

QUILLER. No smoking. Call the guard.

OKTOBER. The next station is Kurfurstendam. What number do you want?

QUILLER. No number.

OKTOBER. Don't be silly. Your Control is in Kurfurstendam. We know that. You must get a message to your chief. But we've lost the number. What is it?

QUILLER. Too late –

OKTOBER. It's never too late. They're waiting for you. They're worried. They want to know where you are. What is the number?

QUILLER, *for the first time, does not answer.*
He breathes, is silent. From this moment his replies
become gradually slower, more controlled.

The number.

QUILLER. What?

OKTOBER. The church. The churches. Where are we?

QUILLER. In your base.

OKTOBER. Don't be stupid, Quiller, you're not a baby. Inge
what?

QUILLER. Lin – lie – lying low –

OKTOBER. What is the number of your base? Three? Five?
Eight?

QUILLER. Nine. Ten. Out.

QUILLER *lets out a long breath, draws in his*
shoulders, relaxes back in the chair.

OKTOBER. We've just had a call from your Control. You are
ordered to make an immediate report.

QUILLER *is silent.*

Begin your report, Quiller.

QUILLER's *eyes turn to* DOCTOR's *watch. It is one*
o'clock.

Can you hear me? Begin.

QUILLER *looks at him, speaks slowly.*

QUILLER. Do anything.

Pause.

It' won't matter.

OKTOBER. No. You've wasted my time. (*To the* DOCTOR.)
Inject him. (*To* GUARDS B *and* C). When he's unconscious kill him.

Interior. London club. Evening.
GIBBS *walks down a long room towards the bar. He*
is dressed in full evening attire, with medals. RUSH-
INGTON *is at the bar. He looks round.* GIBBS *sits on*
stool.

RUSHINGTON. Hullo. Where are you off to tonight?

GIBBS. Midsummer Banquet.

RUSHINGTON. Oh yes? Who's giving that?

GIBBS. The Lord Mayor, old boy.

RUSHINGTON. Oh yes, of course.

GIBBS (*to* BARMAN). Vodka, please.

Pause.

RUSHINGTON. You've been before, have you?

GIBBS. Where?

RUSHINGTON. The Lord Mayor's Midsummer Banquet.

GIBBS. Oh yes.

The BARMAN *gives* GIBBS *his drink.*

RUSHINGTON. I've never been asked.

GIBBS. Haven't you?

GIBBS *drinks.*

Any news from Berlin?

RUSHINGTON. No. Not really.

GIBBS. Chase them up in the morning, will you? Find out what's going on.

RUSHINGTON. Yes. I will.

Pause.

GIBBS. I always enjoy the Banquet. It's a very splendid occasion.

RUSHINGTON. Yes, I'm sure it is.

The camera withdraws, leaving them at the bar.

Exterior. River. Night.
QUILLER's *face. His body lies on the river's edge. The water laps along it. Very gradually, his face lifts up.*
The lights of the bridge.
There is no one on the towpath.
QUILLER's *body in the mud.*
He raises himself up. He touches his neck, looks down at his body and touches it, with a certain surprise.
He slowly climbs the steps to the road.
He walks, soaked and dripping, along the road.

Interior. Small bleak bar. Night.
A BARMAN *is sitting with coffee reading a paper.*
The chairs are up on the tables.
The door opens. QUILLER *walks in.*

BARMAN (*in German*). We're shut.

QUILLER. Give me a drink.

BARMAN (*in English*). We're shut.

QUILLER. Rum.

QUILLER *sits on a bar stool.*
The BARMAN *goes behind the bar and slowly pours a rum.*
QUILLER *looks at it.*

QUILLER. A double.

BARMAN *pours another into glass.*

BARMAN. Four marks.

QUILLER *takes out wallet and waves some notes.*

QUILLER. Just a little wet.

He throws notes on bar, drinks.
BARMAN *watches him.*

I'd like a taxi.

BARMAN. Get one.

QUILLER. What?

BARMAN. There's a phone. Get one.

QUILLER. You get one.

BARMAN. This place is shut.

QUILLER *looks at him quietly.*

QUILLER. You get one.

BARMAN. Drunk Americans. I will call the police.

QUILLER *stands and goes round the other side of the bar.*
The BARMAN *reaches under the counter.*
QUILLER *points to his hand.*

QUILLER. Don't do that.

They stare at each other.

Call a taxi.

BARMAN *picks up telephone on bar and dials.*
They listen to the line buzz. A voice.

BARMAN. Taxi. Friedhof Bar.

He puts phone down. QUILLER *goes back to stool,*
drinks.
BARMAN *slowly begins to wipe a glass.*
A clock ticks.

Interior. Zentral Hotel. Night.
QUILLER *enters.*
The lobby. It is very shabby, dusty. A NIGHT-
PORTER *walks towards* QUILLER. *He looks at him*
without interest.
PORTER. Bitte?
QUILLER. I'd like a room.

Interior. Hotel room. Night.
Clothes drying in front of electric fire.
QUILLER *in hotel bathrobe at door. He locks it.*
He lies on bed, looks at ceiling, then at telephone.
He picks it up.
Pause.
A voice answers.
QUILLER. 346897.

Pause.
Ringing tone. INGE's *voice.*

INGE (*in German*). Yes?
QUILLER. I'm sorry – it's very late.
INGE. Who is this?
QUILLER. Me. Cooper.

Pause.

INGE. I was in bed.
QUILLER. Did you . . . get out of bed?
INGE. No, I'm still there. What is it? What's the time?
It's so late.

QUILLER. Are you alone?
INGE. I'm asleep.

Pause.

Are you all right?
QUILLER. I want to see you.
INGE. Not now, I'm afraid.
QUILLER. When then?
INGE. Tomorrow, if you like. After school. Come and have a drink.

Pause.

QUILLER. All right. I'll be there. Good night.
INGE. Good night.

Interior. INGE's *bedroom. Night.*
INGE, *in bed, in a nightdress, replaces the telephone receiver on its hook, and draws the bedclothes about her.*
The light goes out.

Exterior. Hertz Garage. Day.
A car roars up the ramp and out into the street.
QUILLER *stands in fumes from the exhaust, looks up and down street, sees no one, goes into garage and walks towards glass fronted office. One woman can be seen in the office.*
QUILLER *enters.*
Camera shifts to reveal a telephone box in the wall near to the entrance. A man is speaking into the phone. He replaces reciever.
QUILLER *leaves the office and walks into the depth of the garage.*
The back of the man leaves the phone box.

Interior. Hertz Garage. Top landing.
Lines of cars.

QUILLER *seen in the distance, sitting in a Mercedes-Benz 230 SL.*
A MAN'S *back moves towards the car.*

Interior. Mercedes-Benz.
QUILLER *watches torso of man passing from bonnet to passenger window.*
The MAN *opens door.* QUILLER *looks at him. The* MAN *holds a packet of Chesterfields in his hand. He is* WENG. *He sits next to* QUILLER.

WENG. Do you smoke this brand?

QUILLER (*wearily*). Oh Christ. No, I don't think I know that brand.

WENG. Perhaps I might introduce it to you.

QUILLER. All right, all right. What do you want?

Pause.

WENG. They're milder than some other brands.

QUILLER. I know they are. What do you want?

WENG. Would you like to try one?

QUILLER. God, you boys are tough, Yes, I'd love to try one. May I? Please?

WENG. Certainly.

QUILLER *takes a cigarette.*

QUILLER. Won't you join me?

WENG. I don't smoke.

WENG *watches* QUILLER *as he lights his cigarette.*

You don't look too well.

QUILLER. Listen, don't try to be an intellectual. What do you want?

WENG. I've been waiting for you here. Your car was found abandoned. I was posted here in case you turned up for a new one. Hengel is very annoyed, by the way. You led him a dance and lost him. We really don't know what you're up to.

QUILLER. Uh-huh. I see.

WENG. I have to take you to meet someone.

QUILLER. You do, eh?
WENG. Yes. I do.

Interior. Toy Department. Large store.
HENGEL looking intently at something.
It is a toy mountain train set. He is absorbed.
QUILLER's voice:

QUILLER. Why don't you blow the track up? Go on. You're a spy.

HENGEL turns. QUILLER and WENG stand by him. The crowds move about them. The three speak very quietly, almost in whispers.

WENG. That's a very odd kind of remark to make.
QUILLER. What's odd about it?
HENGEL. I have to take you somewhere.
QUILLER (*to* WENG). What exactly do you find odd?
WENG. You.
QUILLER (*to* HENGEL). What do you mean, take me somewhere?
HENGEL. I have to take you to meet someone.
QUILLER. I was brought here to meet you.
HENGEL. You were brought here to meet me in order for me to take you to meet someone else.
QUILLER. Now who would that be?
HENGEL. I have not been told to tell you.
QUILLER. I'm ordering you to tell me.
HENGEL. You can't order me.
QUILLER. Of course I can. You're just a cover man. I'm the leading operator.

Pause. A lady assistant approaches.

ASSISTANT. Can I help you?

They look at her.

WENG. I don't think so, thank you. We're just looking.

She smiles – goes.

HENGEL. It's Pol.

QUILLER. Yes. (*Pointing to* WENG.) Well, he can come too.
HENGEL. He has not been invited.
QUILLER. But I'm ordering you to bring him along.

Pause.

HENGEL. Come on, Weng.

They all move to the door.

QUILLER (*to* WENG). What are you, Chinese?
WENG. In a way.

Interior. Café. Day.
POL *is sitting at a corner table, with coffee and a selection of cream cakes.*
QUILLER, HENGEL *and* WENG *walk to his table. He looks up.*
They all sit.
POL *looks at each in turn.*

POL. I'm sure the adverse party would be thrilled to see us all together. (*To* HENGEL.) Surely you can find Mr Weng some coffee somewhere else?
HENGEL. Mr Quiller ordered us to join you.

POL *looks at* QUILLER.

POL. Hullo, Quiller. How are you?
QUILLER. Great. I want to make a public announcement. I don't want any more cover.

Pause.

POL. You don't want any more cover?
QUILLER. No.
POL. You can't be said to have *had* very much cover, really, can you? You've made your cover's work rather hard.
QUILLER. That was just play. It's over.

QUILLER *looks at them.*

No more cover.
POL. Will you have coffee?

QUILLER. I'd like you to call them off. Please.

POL. I'm glad you said please . . . Quiller.

POL *sips his coffee. He looks at them all.*
Silence.
POL *puts his cup down. He speaks quietly to* HENGEL
and WENG.

All cover called off until further notice.

A pause.

QUILLER. I would like my car to be taken to the Hotel Zentral
lock-up garage and left there.

POL. Could you see to that, Hengel?

HENGEL. Certainly I'll see to it.

Silence.

QUILLER. I would be glad if I could talk to you privately.

POL *cuts into his cake. Eats a piece and nods to*
HENGEL *and* WENG.
HENGEL *and* WENG *stand and go out.*
Silence.

POL. I'm sorry. Did you say something?

QUILLER. I would like some black coffee.

POL *looks at him.*

Please.

POL *signals to waiter.*

POL (*in German*). One black coffee, please.

POL *slices another piece of cake and eats.*

QUILLER. I've been to their base.

POL. Oh yes?

QUILLER. But I don't know where it is.

POL. You were sleepwalking.

QUILLER. I was taken there.

POL. Ah.

Pause.

QUILLER. Met a man called Oktober.

POL. Oh yes.

QUILLER. Know him?

POL. We've never actually met.

QUILLER. At the end of our conversation he ordered them to kill me.

POL. And did they?

Pause.

QUILLER. No.

POL. Odd.

Pause.

Do you think they disobeyed him?

QUILLER. I wouldn't think so.

The waiter brings coffee, sets it down, goes.

They didn't take me through the full course, either.

POL. Didn't want to hurt you unduly, I'm sure.

QUILLER. They hurt KLJ.

POL. He got too close.

QUILLER. I was close.

POL. You were helpless.

Pause.

QUILLER. I'm alive, anyway.

POL. I'm so glad.

POL *takes out a small cigar.*

QUILLER. They wanted to know where our base was.

POL. Did you tell them?

QUILLER *chuckles, looking at* POL.
POL *lights cigar.*

QUILLER. They obviously think –

POL *coughs as he inhales.*

POL. I'm so sorry. What did you say?

QUILLER. You're smoking the wrong brand.

POL *looks at him.*

POL. No I'm not.

QUILLER. They obviously think they can find our base – through another method.

POL. Do you know I think you're right? But what other method?

QUILLER. I can find *their* base – by another method.

POL. Can you really? Good. How? Would you like to tell me?

QUILLER. No.

POL. Oh.

POL *puffs his cigar.* QUILLER *drinks coffee, lights cigarette.*

QUILLER. Mind if I smoke?

POL. I've agreed to withdraw cover – for twelve hours. But I shall want a full report from you – very shortly. In the meantime, of course – without cover – you may die. I would like to emphasize that you're not on a routine mission.

QUILLER. Go ahead. Emphasize.

POL. I'll want my report shortly.

QUILLER. You'll get it.

POL. Why don't you carry weapons?

QUILLER. You'll get your report.

POL. You haven't answered my question.

QUILLER. I don't have to. I use my own judgement. If you don't like it, call me off. That's all you can do.

Pause.

You'll get your report.

POL. You're on a delicate mission, Quiller. Perhaps you're beginning to appreciate that. Let me put it this way.

He takes two large cream cakes and arranges them on the table.

There are two opposing armies drawn up on the field. But there's a heavy fog. They can't see each other. They want to, of course, very much.

He takes a currant from a cake and sets it between the cakes.

You're in the gap between them. You can just see us, you can just see them. Your mission is to get near enough to see them and signal their position to us, so giving us the advantage. But if in signalling their position to us you inadvertently signal our position to them, then it will be they who will gain a very considerable advantage.

He points to the currant.

That's where you are, Quiller. In the gap.

He pops the currant in his mouth and eats it.

Interior. INGE's *flat. Early evening.*
QUILLER *is with* INGE. *He is pouring drinks. He takes* INGE's *glass over to her but does not give it to her.*
He stands looking at her.
QUILLER. Did you get to sleep?
INGE. What?
QUILLER. Did you get to sleep again, after I phoned?
INGE. Yes.

QUILLER *gives her her glass.*

Not immediately. Did you?
QUILLER. Not immediately.

Pause.

INGE. It was a strange time to call.

Pause.

You seem different.
QUILLER. Do I?
INGE. Quieter.
QUILLER. I've been thinking about you.

Pause.

INGE. How's your article? The one you were going to write?

QUILLER. I haven't written it.

Pause.

Actually . . . that wasn't exactly true. There's no such thing as the Philadelphia World Review.

INGE. Then who are you writing for?

QUILLER. No one. I'm not a writer.

INGE *stares at him and laughs.*

INGE. What are you?

QUILLER. I'm a kind of investigator.

INGE. What do you mean?

QUILLER. I'm investigating those people we were talking about last time.

Pause.

INGE. Those people? What do you mean?

QUILLER. Those people.

INGE. But you said you were a journalist.

QUILLER. I'm not.

INGE *moves away from him to the window, stands with her back to him, eventually turns, looks at him.*

INGE. Why are you telling me?

QUILLER. I thought you ought to know.

Pause.

INGE. But do you realize . . . what kind of people they are? They're quite ruthless . . . they're . . . ruthless. Everyone here knows about them. They've killed people.

QUILLER *goes to her.*

QUILLER. You don't have to worry about me. I just thought you ought to know, that's all.

He holds her shoulders.

INGE. Do you . . . have a gun?

QUILLER. No, no.

INGE. Why not? Shouldn't you?

QUILLER. If you don't carry one you're less likely to get your-self killed. Believe me.

He draws her towards him.

I've missed you.

He touches her mouth.

Ssshh.

He kisses her.

I've missed you, all the time.

He draws her onto the sofa and caresses her face.

INGE. No. Please.
QUILLER. I've been wanting to touch you.

He kisses her throat.

You're so white.

He kisses her deeply.
She does not resist.
He murmurs, very close to her.

Have you been waiting for me?

INGE. Yes.
QUILLER. Yes.

Pause.

I know you have.

They look at each other.

Interior. INGE's *flat. Later. Evening.*
INGE *and* QUILLER *lying on the carpet, with cushions, smoking. Evening light through the window. Silence.*
INGE *at length turns on her elbows and looks down at him.*
She kisses him, tenderly.
INGE. I am worried about you, you know.

QUILLER. No need.

INGE. Oh yes there is. A friend of my father's . . . he's told me about them.

QUILLER. About who?

INGE. Those people . . . He was with them.

QUILLER. A friend of your father's?

INGE. Yes. I know what they're like. He's told me what they're like.

Pause.

QUILLER. He knew them, eh?

INGE. Oh, he knew them. Yes.

Pause.

QUILLER. Where is he . . . this man?

INGE. What?

QUILLER. Do you know where he is? Can you reach him?

INGE. Yes, I . . . I think so. Why?

QUILLER. I think I'd like to speak to him.

INGE. But why?

QUILLER. Just a word.

INGE. But I've told you, he's not with them any more.

QUILLER. He might be able to help.

INGE. He might not want to.

QUILLER. Listen. I want to know where their base is, you see.

INGE. But he wouldn't know.

QUILLER. If he was with them he might know.

Pause.

Can I see him?

INGE *is silent. She looks at him.*

INGE. You . . . really want to?

QUILLER. Yes.

She turns away from him.

INGE (*quietly*). All right.

Interior. Swimming bath. Night.

> INGE *and* QUILLER *enter by a side door, into a*
> *passage.*
> *The passage is dark.*
> *They walk up it. Their steps echo.*

> *Interior. Swimming bath. The pool.*
> *The pool bathed in soft night light from a large sky-*
> *light.*
> *There is no water in the pool.*
> *Silence.*
> QUILLER *and* INGE *enter by door onto the changing*
> *room gallery.*

INGE. He must be here. The door was open.

> QUILLER *walks down the stairs to the side of the pool.*
> *He looks about, and gives a cheerful whistle of call.*
> *The whistle echoes. There is no other response.*
> INGE *joins him at the side of the pool.*

QUILLER. Well . . . let's wait.

> *He walks down into the empty pool.*
> *She follows. Their steps echo.*

Want to dance?

INGE. No, thank you.

> *Pause. She moves a few steps.*

QUILLER. Let's go down to the deep end.

> *They walk down the slope and stand in the deepest*
> *corner of the pool. He puts his arm around her.*

We could do an underwater ballet.

> *He kisses her.*

Ever done that?

> *She looks up at the diving board, looming above them.*
> *A changing room door creaks. She looks at* QUILLER.

Draught. What's his name?

INGE. Hassler.

Long shot of pool.
Their figures in the far corner.
QUILLER *shouts.*

QUILLER. Hassler!
INGE. Don't!

The shouts of 'Hassler' and 'Don't' echo round the bath and die.
QUILLER *walks into the middle of the pool.*
He feints a few football moves, stops.

QUILLER. Maybe the bar's open.

A door bangs. They hear steps.
HASSLER (*the swimming bath attendant*) *appears on the gallery, hurries down the stairs to the pool side and down into the pool.*
They all meet in the middle of the pool.

HASSLER. I had to be late.
INGE (*to* HASSLER). This is the man.
QUILLER. We've met.
IIASSLER. I had to be late. I had to make some inquiries. I wanted to give you this information. I am glad you are someone to do something.
QUILLER. Uh-huh.
HASSLER. I was checking. But I have to tell you . . . they have moved . . . some months . . . from the old house. I do not know the new house. I keep away from things, you see.
QUILLER. Ah.
HASSLER. But I think . . . I know someone who does.

QUILLER *looks at him.*

QUILLER. Who?
HASSLER. The name is Schroeder.
QUILLER. What does he know?
HASSLER. I don't know. I think . . . I think . . . perhaps . . . where they are.

Pause.

QUILLER. Can I see him?

HASSLER. I can try. I can ask. There is a telephone.

HASSLER *looks at them both.*

Shall I ask?

QUILLER. Where's the telephone?

HASSLER. In the back.

QUILLER *walks towards the steps.*
Silence.
A changing room door creaks. INGE *looks up.*

It's only a draught.

QUILLER. We'd better get you home.

INGE. No. I want to stay with you.

QUILLER *looks at her a moment. They then all move
up the steps, and disappear along the gallery.
The diving board looms above the pool.*

Exterior. Road by canal. Night.
HASSLER's *car draws into the side of the road, by the
trees.*
The engine cuts off.
Silence.
Suddenly another car draws up.
A WOMAN *gets out of it and walks towards* HASS-
LER's *car.*

Interior. HASSLER's *car.*
The WOMAN *gets into* HASSLER's *car.* QUILLER
looks at her.
It is FRAU SCHROEDER.

SCHROEDER (*to* INGE). You are surprised to see me?

INGE. Yes, I am.

SCHROEDER. I told the police about Steiner.
(*To* QUILLER). I am glad to see you again. I am glad
to be of help. I tried to help your friend, but . . .

QUILLER. You know the house?

SCHROEDER. Yes.

QUILLER. Where is it?

SCHROEDER (*pointing*). That's it.

QUILLER *looks*.

QUILLER. Is anyone in there?

SCHROEDER. I don't know. I just know that's the house.

Silence in the car.

HASSLER. We must all go now. Come on. You can tell your people.

QUILLER. Oh no. I have to check whether she's right.

INGE. How?

QUILLER. I've got to go over there, to check whether she's right.

SCHROEDER. I am right.

INGE. Others can check. Why do you have to do that?

QUILLER. Well . . . it's part of my job, you see.

SCHROEDER. I'm going. I've shown you the house. That's all I can do.

HASSLER. It's stupid to stay here. We must get out.

QUILLER (*to* INGE). You go with them.

Pause.

INGE. No. I'll wait for you.

HASSLER (*to* INGE). You're stupid. (*To* FRAU SCHROEDER.) I'll go with you.

(*To* INGE.) You keep the car.

HASSLER *gets out.* FRAU SCHROEDER *opens his door.*

QUILLER (*to* FRAU SCHROEDER). Thank you.

SCHROEDER. Don't mention it.

FRAU SCHROEDER *gets out.*
QUILLER *and* INGE *look at each other.*

QUILLER. Don't worry. I'm just going to check, that's all. Now listen, I want you to remember a telephone number. All right?

INGE. Yes.

QUILLER. Now. Fix it. 21.89.62. Got it?

INGE. 21.89.62.

QUILLER. If I'm not back in twenty minutes ring that number. Tell them you've run out of Chesterfields. Tell them where you are. Okay?

INGE. Yes.

QUILLER. What's the number?

INGE. 21.89.62.

QUILLER. Stay here. Twenty minutes.

QUILLER *opens the car door, gets out.*

INGE. Listen –

He bends in.

I love you.

QUILLER *looks at her and smiles faintly.*

He walks across the road.
She watches him, sitting still in the car.

Exterior. House. Night.
QUILLER *walks towards it. He comes to a garden gate.*
He opens it and goes through.

Interior. Garden. Night.
QUILLER *is in a large dark garden. Many overgrown shrubs.*
Ahead of him, a dark, dim house.
He walks softly through the garden towards the back of the house.
He reaches it and stops.
Silence.
He tries a window. It is locked.
He examines other windows. One window is slightly ajar.
He squeezes his arm through the gap and unhooks the window from the inside.

Interior. House. Scullery. Night.
QUILLER, *with difficulty, climbs through the small window into the scullery.*
He looks about. The scullery is bare, dirty, damp, bleak.
QUILLER *opens the inner door.*

Interior. House. Hall.
QUILLER *walks into the hall.*
The floorboards are cracked, broken. Plaster is broken on the walls.
The house appears to be derelict.

Interior. House. Staircase.
QUILLER *ascends the stairs.*
Silence.
Sudden shot, with QUILLER'S *eyeline.*
A MAN, J, *standing by a wall in shadow.*
QUILLER *looks sharply to his right.*
Another MAN, B.
Another MAN, C.
QUILLER *looks up to the first landing.*
Another MAN, A, *is standing on the landing.*
All the MEN *are still, but stand in quite relaxed postures.*
QUILLER *looks about him.*
There is no way out.
The MAN *on the landing speaks.*

MAN (A). Come up, please.

Slowly, QUILLER *begins to walk upstairs.*

Interior. First landing. Night.
QUILLER *reaches the landing and looks back.*
B *and* C *are following him up the stairs.*
A *walks to a door and opens it.*
A burst of light.

MAN (A). This way, please.

> QUILLER *walks into the room.*

> *Interior. House. Reception room.*
> QUILLER *enters.*
> *It is the room he has been in before.*
> B *and* C *follow him into the room and stand.*
> OKTOBER *is alone in the large room.*
> *He turns.*

OKTOBER. Hullo, Quiller. Do come in.

> *He waves to chair.*

Sit down. What a surprise. What will you have to drink?

QUILLER. A double Jack Daniels on the rocks.

OKTOBER (*to a* MAN, B). A double Jack Daniels on the rocks.

MAN. We have no Jack Daniels, Reichsführer.

OKTOBER. No Jack Daniels? Tch, tch, tch. (*To* QUILLER.) What would you say to some old Kentucky Grandad?

QUILLER. Make it Scotch Malt.

OKTOBER. Ah. I wish we could help you there but unfortunately I know we can't.

QUILLER. What kind of a bar is this, for Christ's sake?

OKTOBER. I am not a barman Mr Quiller.

> *He walks to the door.*

I am a German gentleman.

> *He opens the door and gestures to* QUILLER.

Please.

> QUILLER *remains still.*

QUILLER. Where are we going?

OKTOBER. Downstairs.

> QUILLER *does not move.* OKTOBER *stands by the door.*
> B *and* C *move a few steps towards* QUILLER. *They stop, close to him.*
> QUILLER *goes to the door.*

Interior. House. Landing.
OKTOBER, QUILLER *and* B *and* C *walk along landing to back stairs.*
They stop by an old service lift.
One of the men opens the doors. They all get in.

Interior. Lift.
The lift goes down.
It has an open top.
The four stand in silence.
OKTOBER *speaks sharply in German to the two men.*

OKTOBER. Would you mind not standing so close.

B *and* C *move away.*

Interior. House. Basement.
The lift arrives. They get out.
There is a long corridor of whitewashed stone. There are a number of doors at either side, closed.
They begin to walk down the corridor.
A door opens suddenly and a MAN *in a boiler suit comes out, wheeling a trolley. On the trolley is a large filing cabinet.*
He wheels the trolley down the corridor, round a corner and out of sight.

QUILLER. He's working late.
OKTOBER. We're moving tomorrow.
QUILLER. Oh?
OKTOBER. Yes, we have a busy night ahead of us. We're moving all our equipment. We're changing our base.
QUILLER. Oh.

They continue walking.
QUILLER *pauses in his step and stops.*
He glances at the two men behind him.
They all stop.

Where are we going?
OKTOBER. In here.

He goes towards a door.

Oh, I hear you've called off your cover by the way. That was an odd thing to do.

He opens the door and goes in.
QUILLER *follows, flanked by the two men.*

Interior. Cellar.
The cellar is a long low-ceilinged room. A long metal-framed, hooded strip light shines from the ceiling.
The rest of the room is in shadow.
INGE *is sitting in a chair under the light.*
Two men, DORFMANN *and* NAGEL, *well dressed, sit at a distance from her in half shadow, in easy chairs.*
The room appears to have been stripped.
There are two or three closed crates, a rolled carpet and two chairs piled on top of each other.
INGE *looks at* OKTOBER, *not at* QUILLER.
OKTOBER *gestures to the two men.*

OKTOBER. Herr Dorfmann. Herr Nagel. Mr Quiller.

Neither QUILLER, DORFMANN *or* NAGEL *respond to this introduction.*

OKTOBER *looks at* INGE.

And this is Fräulein Lindt.

Turns to QUILLER.

We have just found her sitting in a car, quite near here. Her first name is Inge.

Pause.

QUILLER. So what?
OKTOBER. She's your friend.
QUILLER. I've never seen her before.
OKTOBER. Yes, yes. She's your close friend. Inge.

Pause.

I remember the name well. (*To a* MAN.) You. Do you remember the name?

MAN (C). Yes, Reichsführer.

The recorded voices of QUILLER *and* OKTOBER *are suddenly heard in the room. They listen, still. So does* INGE.

OKTOBER *looks at* QUILLER *and then, gradually, his gaze rests upon* INGE.

INGE *glances at him.*

QUILLER *is aware that* OKTOBER *and* INGE *are looking at each other throughout the recording.*

The recorded voices :

OKTOBER. That boss of yours, what's his name?

QUILLER. Inge.

OKTOBER. No, she's a girl. She's not your boss. What was his name?

QUILLER. She has long legs.

OKTOBER. After you leave us you can go to her. She's waiting for you.

QUILLER. White . . .

OKTOBER. She adores you.

QUILLER. No.

OKTOBER. Oh yes. Adores you. She wants you only. She longs for you only.

QUILLER. Longs . . . adores me . . .

Pause.

Wants me . . . only . . .

The tape recorder is switched off.

Silence. QUILLER *and* INGE *still do not look at each other.*

OKTOBER (*gaily*). And here she is.

QUILLER. No, no. Not at all. The Inge I was talking about was fat. Very fat. Gigantic.

He looks at INGE.

I don't know this girl.

OKTOBER (*to* INGE). For a nice innocent German girl you pick very bizarre friends. Do you understand English? (*Sharply, in German.*) Do you understand English?

INGE. Nein.

OKTOBER *laughs.*

OKTOBER. You must find him very attractive. What's it like to be so sexually attractive, Quiller?

Pause.

Mmmnnn?

Pause.

Anyway, I'm glad you were able to drop in tonight. You're quite free to go now.

Silence.

Really. You can go – now.

QUILLER *remains still.*

But there is just one thing. We're still very interested in the location of your base. We feel . . . that there might be some information there which could be of importance to us.

Pause.

So let me make a proposal to you. If you would like to tell us where your base is you can take . . . her . . . with you. Truly. You will be quite safe, quite free.

Pause.

If not, she will stay here, with us.

Pause.

But do go, if you like, and consider the matter. Take a walk. Think about it. But please don't forget you have complete freedom to return here at any time, give us the information we require and leave . . . with this lady.

Pause.

We'll give you till dawn.

He looks at INGE, *then back at* QUILLER.

If you're still undecided by dawn – we'll kill you both.

Pause.

How's that? Fair?

QUILLER. Sure.

OKTOBER. Good.

Pause.

QUILLER. Right. I'll get some air.

OKTOBER. Yes, why don't you? I hope to see you a little later tonight. In fact I'm sure I will.

OKTOBER *turns to* B *and* C.

Take Mr Quiller up in the lift will you? He knows the way out.

QUILLER *without looking at* INGE *leaves the room.*

Interior. Corridor.
B, C *and* QUILLER *walk towards the lift.*

Interior. Lift.
QUILLER, B *and* C *enter the lift.*
The doors close.
The lift goes up, very slowly.
Silence in the lift.
The lift stops.

Interior. Hall.
The lift doors open. QUILLER, B *and* C *walk into the hall.*
The two men stand. QUILLER *looks at them.*
They remain still.

Interior. House. Stairs and hall.
QUILLER *walks to the door.*
A *is standing by the door. He opens it.*
QUILLER *goes out.*

Exterior. House. Front. Night.
QUILLER *walks down the steps of the house, along to the front gate, and out on to the road.*

Exterior. Berlin Tiergarten. Night.
A long road. Derelict buildings at either side.
It is late at night.
In the distance, QUILLER *is walking towards the camera.*
Silence.
The camera moves sideways to disclose a brightly lit telephone box. It is the one hard source of light.
His face, as he stops by a lamp post. He lights a cigarette and glances up at the buildings and along the road behind him.
There is no one in sight.
He continues to walk towards the telephone box.
From the telephone box see him approach.
He walks straight past it and up the road.
As he passes it a MAN, K, *emerges from the shadow of trees on the opposite side of the road and walks slowly along, in the same direction.*

Exterior. Corner of road. Tiergarten area. Night.
QUILLER *approaches street corner.*
There is a MAN, L, *at the opposite corner, standing.*
QUILLER *looks up at the moon and glances back.*
Two men, M *and* N, *are walking slowly down the road, on opposite sides of it.*
A fourth MAN, K, *is standing by a dark café.*

Exterior. City. Night.
QUILLER *walking.*
Three men, L, M *and* N, *one in front and two behind, also strolling.*
Their steps resound on the road.
Apart from them, the street is empty, silent.
QUILLER *pauses a moment by a telephone box.*
The others halt.
Silence.
QUILLER *walks on. So do the others.*

Interior. All night café.
Steam. Lorry drivers talking loudly.
QUILLER *walks in, walks to bar, asks for coffee.*
He looks at telephone behind the bar.
In the mirror he sees the door open and K *walk in.*
K *sits down.*
QUILLER *receives his coffee, sips.*

Exterior. All night café. Night.
QUILLER *comes out of the café.*
He strolls casually towards an overhead railway station.
L, M *and* N *saunter, at a distance, behind him.*
QUILLER *stands a moment by the entrance. A signal is heard from the platform.*
Suddenly QUILLER *dashes into the station and up the stairs.*

Exterior. Platform. Night.
The train is pulling out.
The camera moves to see, in the street below, L, M *and* N *jumping into a car. The car pulls away with great speed and follows the direction of the train.*

Exterior. Platform.
QUILLER *comes into shot.*
He steps carefully across the tracks and disappears down the opposite stairway.

Exterior. Other side of station. Night.
QUILLER *comes out of the station and stops.*
A MAN, O, *is standing by a lamp post.*
Another MAN, P, *is standing at the corner.*
QUILLER *looks at* O *and walks slowly towards him.*
O *stares at him.*

QUILLER. Do you have a light?

Another man walks into QUILLER'*s vision.*
He is K. QUILLER *glances at him.*

MAN (O). No.
QUILLER. Non-smoker, eh?

The three men stand looking at him.
QUILLER *walks past them, down the street.*
The three men walk slowly after him.

Exterior. Tree-lined avenue. Night.
Shot through foliage onto street of QUILLER *walking along very slowly, a very small figure.*
The three men, at intervals, are glimpsed through the trees, walking in the same direction.

Exterior. Brandenburgerstrasse. Night.
QUILLER *walking slowly down the long deserted avenue, followed by the three men.*

Exterior. Hotel Zentral. Night.
QUILLER *comes down street, followed by men.*
He walks up the steps, into the hotel.
The men stay, singly, at the other side of the road.

Interior. Hotel lobby.
In the lobby the nightporter is brushing shoes.
He goes to the desk.

PORTER. What number?

QUILLER. Twenty-one.

PORTER *gives him key.*
QUILLER *moves up the stairs.*
PORTER *calls after him.*

PORTER. Do you want a morning paper?

QUILLER *turns and looks at him. At length he speaks.*

QUILLER. No.

Interior. Hotel. QUILLER's *room.*
QUILLER *shuts the door and looks at the room.*
It has been ransacked.
He locks the door, goes to the phone, lifts it, listens.
A regular sound of tapping.
He holds it a moment, replaces it.
He looks at his watch. It is five o'clock.
He goes into the bathroom.

Interior. Bathroom.
QUILLER *looking at his face in the mirror.*
His face is streaked, creased, grimy, strained. He throws water on his face.
Reaching for a towel, he suddenly finds himself looking out of the small bathroom window.
The window overlooks the garages, garage yard and gates to street at the back of the hotel.

Garage yard. QUILLER's *point of view.*
It is dawn.
Light filters gently over the yard.
Camera concentrates on the garage.

Interior. Room.
QUILLER *walks into room, wiping his face.*
He throws towel on the bed, bends and takes off his shoes.
He switches the light off and goes to the door.
Very slowly, he turns handle and pulls door softly towards him.

Interior. Hotel corridor.
The corridor is dimly lit.
QUILLER *emerges from room. He turns the door-handle soundlessly and closes door. He carries his shoes.*
Sound of a shoebrush from below.
QUILLER *walks down the corridor to a back flight of stairs.*
He walks in time to the sound of the shoebrush, freezing when the brushing pauses.

Interior. Side door. Hotel.
He approaches door. There is a key on the inside.
He unlocks the door and steps out into the yard.

Exterior. Garage yard.
The dawn light is growing.
He puts on his shoes.
He stands in the yard, facing the lock-up garages.
In front of him the yard gates leading to a narrow back street.
There is one lamp on the street, by the gate.
Silence.
QUILLER *walks to garage. He unlocks garage door quietly and pulls it.*
A stone jammed under the door screeches. The door jars.
He looks quickly behind him and up at the dark hotel. No movement of any kind.

He frowns and, still looking towards the hotel and the gates, pulls the door again, harshly. It scrapes.
No movement. No sound.
QUILLER *listens to the silence and feels the stillness.*
His eye begins to twitch.
He walks to the gate.

Exterior. Back gate. Street.
QUILLER *stands in the light of the lamp, on the street.*
There is no one in sight.
He opens the gate. It swings back with a slight clang.
The street is empty.
A car is parked in the street, empty.
All doors and windows are empty, silent.
The roofs are bare.
There is no figure in any shadow.
QUILLER *stands frozen in the lamplight.*
Far away the throb of a Diesel truck.

Exterior. Garage yard.
QUILLER *goes back into yard, and looks about him.*
An oil drum, timber, dustbins. Nothing more.
He goes into garage.

Interior. Garage.
QUILLER *takes out a pencil torch and flicks it over the garage. He then goes to his car, the Mercedes 230 SL. He looks at his watch.*
It is 5.24.
He examines the doors. No marks.
He opens the boot and examines it. Nothing.
He gets into the car.

Interior. Car.
He examines the interior of the car quickly but meticulously.
He releases bonnet and gets out.

Interior. Garage.
His torch probes the engine. He finds nothing.
He stands upright and still, sweating.
He presses his hand against his forehead.
His torch points down to the cement floor.
He glances down. A chip of stone, some splinters.
He suddenly squats, gets on to his back and pulls himself under the car.

Underneath of car.
QUILLER *shines his torch up.*
A small bomb, six inches by three, is attached to the underside of the car.
He wipes the sweat from his hands, takes bomb from its perch, holds it to his chest and slides out from under car.

Interior. Garage.
QUILLER *stands with bomb.*
He looks at the partitions in the garage. They are six feet high. There is a back door at the far end.
He leans into car, checks the gears for neutral and starts the engine.
He goes to the bonnet, looks at it.
He rests the bomb about a third of the distance from the front edge. The engine throbs.
He looks at his watch, flicking torch to catch the second hand.
He shines torch on the bomb.
The bomb is still. Then it begins to slide.
He catches it. Looks at his watch.
He places the bomb some inches higher on the bonnet. It rests there.
QUILLER *climbs first partition and drops.*
He climbs second partition and drops.
He kicks over an oil tin, nearly falls.
Climbs third partition and drops. Runs to back door

*of garage. Pulls it. It is stuck. He pulls it violently.
It still will not open.
He looks down and sees bolt, unbolts it, goes out.*

*Exterior. Garage. High wall. Trees overhanging.
It is now light. Sound of birds.
Sounds of distant traffic.*
QUILLER *crouches by the wall, tense.
The engine of car can be heard throbbing faintly.
He looks at his watch. It is 5.55.
He waits. The car still throbs.
His eyelid twitches. He claps his hand over it.
He grits his teeth.
Starts to cough, stops.
The car still throbs.*
QUILLER *is hunched. He suddenly stands upright,
moves to the corner of the garage.
The ground shakes. The wall shudders.*
QUILLER *swings back and throws himself flat on the
ground.
The roof bursts open. Doors break off and crash across
the yard.
Silence.* QUILLER *remains down.
Another explosion. A sheet of hot air and flame.
Silence.*

*Exterior. The garage yard. Dawn.
The yard in chaos. Hotel windows broken.
Shouts.*
QUILLER *is out of sight behind the garage.*
K *runs in from the gate to the wide open garage.
The Mercedes is consumed with flame and smoke.*
K *peers.*
K *turns away and walks back to the gate.*
O *and* P *join him.* K *nods to them.
They walk out into the street.
It is daylight.*

Exterior. City centre. Berlin. Early morning.
Two churches, one ruined, one new. A solitary taxi
passes them.
The taxi draws up at an office building.
QUILLER *gets out, pays the driver.*
The taxi drives off.
QUILLER *enters the building.*

Interior. Room. Local control.
The lift arrives. QUILLER *gets out.*
HENGEL, WENG, HUGHES *and two others are in*
the room.
They are in shirtsleeves, unshaven, bleary-eyed.
Cigarette ends in trays. Numbers of coffee cups.
HENGEL *picks up the phone and presses button.*

HENGEL (*into phone*). He's here. Yes. Right.

He puts phone down.
They all look at QUILLER.
He too is unshaven, his face creased with dirt.

QUILLER. Any coffee?
WENG. I think so.

WENG *looks into a jug and pours.*

QUILLER. Where's Pol?
HENGEL. He's been on all night. He's just gone to bed. He's
coming.

WENG *gives* QUILLER *coffee.*

WENG. Sugar?
QUILLER. No thanks.

Silence.

HENGEL. We've been up all night too.
QUILLER. Have you?

QUILLER *drinks his coffee, clasps the cup.*
He shivers.

HENGEL. Do you want the fire on?

QUILLER. No. That's all right.

They all sit in silence.
POL *comes through an inner door, in a dressing gown.*

POL. Hullo, Quiller.

QUILLER. Tiergarten. Number six. That's their base. Big house by the canal. Looks derelict.

POL. Will they be there?

QUILLER. Yes. They're not worried. They think I'm dead. They think I was blown up in a car.

POL (*to* HUGHES). Get Ziegler.

HUGHES *dials.*
Silence.
A voice.

HUGHES (*into phone*). Just a second, please. This is Local Control, Berlin.

POL *takes the phone.*

POL. Hullo Ziegler. Our man's back. Tiergarten. Number six. By the canal. You can go in now. (*He listens.*) Right.

He puts the phone down.

I'd like a full report as soon as possible, Quiller.

QUILLER *looks at him.*

QUILLER. You'll get it.

POL. Have a little rest first, of course.

QUILLER. Oh, thanks.

POL. I'm going to change.

POL *goes out.*
QUILLER *sits looking at his cup.*

Interior. Room. Local control. Forty minutes later.
QUILLER *is standing by the window, looking down into the street below.*
The street is crowded with people going to work.

There is a great deal of traffic.
It is a beautiful morning.
QUILLER *turns into the room.*
HENGEL *is sitting with his feet up.*
HUGHES *is sitting by the telephone.*
QUILLER *walks across the room, sits down.*
POL *comes through the inner door, shaved and dressed.*

POL. Any word?

HUGHES. No.

The telephone rings. HUGHES *picks it up.*

LCB.

HUGHES *listens a moment.*

Hold on, please.

HUGHES *nods at* POL. POL *takes phone.*

POL (*to* HUGHES). Take it.

HUGHES *lifts extension and takes shorthand trans-cript of the conversation.*
There is a clatter of a voice at the other end of the line.
POL *grunts occasionally. The voice stops.*

POL. Thank you. Good-bye.

POL *puts the phone down.*
QUILLER *looks at him through slit eyes.*
POL *stands.*

They've got them all. Good.

He waves to the door.

Where's my breakfast?

As POL *reaches the door* QUILLER *speaks.*

QUILLER. Where's mine?

POL *turns to him.*

POL. Oh. Are you hungry?

They regard each other.

Why don't we have breakfast together? Upstairs.
In about . . . eight minutes?

QUILLER. I'm too tired to go upstairs.

POL. We'll have it sent to you, Quiller. Don't put yourself out. Will you join me, Hengel?

HENGEL. With pleasure.

POL *and* HENGEL *go out.*
QUILLER *and* HUGHES *are left alone.*
Pause.

HUGHES. Well . . . that's that . . . for the time being.

QUILLER *lights a cigarette.*

QUILLER. What are the details?

HUGHES. Not many. They got them all. Got Oktober.

Pause.

QUILLER. Did they find a girl there?

HUGHES. No. No mention of a girl. They got Dorfmann and Nagel.

Pause.

QUILLER. Are you sure they didn't find a girl?

HUGHES *examines his transscript. He looks up.*

HUGHES. Yes. Quite sure. No girl.

QUILLER *lifts his cigarette to his mouth and draws on it.*

Exterior. Playground. School. Day.
Children playing in the playground.
In background, the school.
QUILLER *comes into shot.*
He walks towards school. A few children look at him.

Interior. School. Day.
QUILLER *walking down corridor. Children pass.*

He reaches INGE's *classroom. He stands at the door and looks in.*
INGE *is there, talking to a boy. She looks up, sees* QUILLER.
She speaks to the boy, who leaves the room.
QUILLER *goes in.*

Interior. Classroom. School.
QUILLER *shuts the door. He stands. They are alone. Silence.*

INGE. Hullo.
QUILLER. Hullo.

Pause.
QUILLER *walks down the classroom, flips a book on the desk.*

How are you?
INGE. I'm – all right –

QUILLER *flips open another exercise book and reads it.*

I was very lucky.
QUILLER (*shutting book*). What? Sorry?
INGE. I said I was very lucky.
QUILLER. Oh? How?
INGE. They let me go.

Pause.

QUILLER. Did they?
INGE. Yes.

Pause.

Yes, they suddenly . . . told me to go.
QUILLER. Well . . . you must have felt pretty relieved.
INGE. I did.

Pause.

QUILLER. We got all of them.
INGE. Oh, really?

Pause.

Oh, good.

QUILLER. Well . . . not all of them, perhaps. Most of them.

Pause.

INGE. You seem tired.

QUILLER. I had a heavy night.

Pause.

INGE. Oh, I tried to phone that number, by the way. After I got out. You remember? The number you gave me.

QUILLER. Oh yes.

INGE. Yes, I tried. But it didn't exist.

QUILLER. Oh, really? I must have made a mistake.

Pause.

Anyway . . . I'm glad to see that you're all right.

INGE. And you.

He walks up the classroom.

QUILLER. Well, I'm leaving Berlin.

INGE. Are you?

QUILLER. I'm a little tired.

INGE. You work too hard.

QUILLER. Well, you too. I'm sure you could take things a little easier, you know.

INGE. Oh no. I have my work to do. I must do it. I want to do it.

Pause.

QUILLER. Uh-huh. Well, if I ever get back to Berlin I'll look you up.

INGE. Yes. Please.

They look at each other.

That would be nice.

He puts out his hand. They shake hands.
Pause.

QUILLER. By the way, did you ever meet a man called Jones?

INGE. No. No, I don't think so.
QUILLER. Good-bye.
INGE. Good-bye.

He goes to the door. As he closes door, he sees her placing books into her bag.

Exterior. School. Playground.
QUILLER *walks away through playing children.*
INGE *comes to the top of the school steps.*
She calls to the children.
They collect around her.
They talk eagerly to her. She listens to them, smiling.
She glances up.
QUILLER, *in the distance, walks through the school gates.*

Accident

Accident was first presented by London Independent Producers (Distribution) Ltd on 9th February 1967 with the following cast:

STEPHEN	Dirk Bogarde
WILLIAM	Michael York
ANNA	Jacqueline Sassard
POLICEMAN	Brian Phelan
SECOND POLICEMAN	Terence Rigby
CLARISSA	Carole Caplin
ROSALIND	Vivien Merchant
TED	Maxwell Findlater
CHARLEY	Stanley Baker
PROVOST	Alexander Knox
HEDGES	Nicholas Mosley
RECEPTIONIST	Jane Hillary
SECRETARY	Jill Johnson
BELL	Harold Pinter
MAN IN BELL'S OFFICE	Freddie Jones
FRANCESCA	Delphine Seyrig
LAURA	Ann Firbank

Directed by Joseph Losey

Accident

Exterior. The house. Night. Summer.
Long shot.
The camera is still, looking at the house from outside the gate, up the short curved drive, across the circular gravel court.
In a meadow behind the house, dim shapes of animals.
The camera moves slowly forward to a position inside the gate. It comes to rest.
The house is silent, dark. One lower front window is curtained. Light filters through it on to the gravel.
Gradually, over picture, the hum of a car, in the distance.
The hum grows.
Closer but still distant, a sudden screech, grind, smash and splintering.

Silence.

Light goes on in the hall of the house.
The front door opens.
STEPHEN *is silhouetted in the light.*

Exterior. Lane. Night.
Camera jolting down the lane.
Sound of footsteps running.
Dark lane winding.
Tree shapes crossing, retreating, advancing.
Glimpsed fields through hedge. Shapes of cows.
A horse moving, head up.
Camera to sky. Stars.

Exterior. Foot of lane. Night.
Stephen halting.
Moonlight hits his face, sharply and briefly.

Exterior. The car.
Close shot from underside of car.
The smashed mass of the car, shooting at passenger seat front-section, lying on camera.
Broken metalwork, jagged shapes of glass.
Two bodies heaped together, still, forming one shape.
Silence but for the ticking of ignition.

Exterior. Lane.
Long shot from corner of the lane, which forms part of a road junction.
The car seen clearly lying on its side in the middle of the road. Mounds of earth rise at either side of the road, by the hedges.
Trees stand sharply against the sky.
Moonlight passes gently over glass of the car.
Camera moves slowly towards car, until it is quite close to it.

Long shot across top of car (which has its driving seat uppermost) to corner of lane. STEPHEN *seen standing.*
STEPHEN *walks towards car. Camera closes in.*
He is lost behind it.
His hands appear, grasping the car top.
His face.

Exterior. Lane. Moonlight.
Long shot of STEPHEN *climbing on to the top of the car.*

Exterior. Car.
STEPHEN *looking down through driving window.*
Bodies heaped within.
Ticking of ignition.

Long shot across bonnet from hedge of STEPHEN
trying to wrench car door open.
He does, with great effort.
The door crashes back against bonnet.
He almost falls off car.

Interior. Car.
The car jolts. The bodies jolt. A bottle of whisky rolls.
Looking up.
STEPHEN *at open door, above him the sky, looking
down.*
Foreground of skirt, legs, shoes.
STEPHEN *shifts his body, the car sways, his legs and
feet descend into car.*
Legs descending slowly. Ignition ticking.

From above. Close.
WILLIAM's *face. Blood and glass.*
STEPHEN's *feet placing themselves carefully by it.*
Ignition key is heard to be switched off. Silence.
The car jolts. WILLIAM's *head shifts.*

Exterior. Car.
Top shot.
STEPHEN's *hand clutching door frame, moving along
it.*

Exterior. Car.
From underside.
Jagged glass. Back of WILLIAM's *head.*
Camera moves through broken glass to WILLIAM's
temple.
STEPHEN'S VOICE. William?

STEPHEN's *feet searching for surer support, avoiding bodies.*
Moonlight sharp and splintered through smashed windscreen.
ANNA's *legs move. She groans.*

STEPHEN'S VOICE. Anna?

ANNA's *voice whimpering.*
Camera moves up her body. Her face is clenched. She whimpers, yelps. Her eyes open. She begins to push herself up. She mutters, her teeth chatter. She pushes herself up. STEPHEN's *hands seize and help her.*

Exterior. Lane.
The car, rocking, in the middle of the road.

Interior. Car.
ANNA's *shoes on* WILLIAM's *chest.*

Exterior. Lane.
Long shot of ANNA *rising slowly from car.*
Her head and shoulders rise against a background of stars.
She tosses her head.
A sudden scream from STEPHEN *over picture :*
STEPHEN. Don't! You're standing on his face!

Exterior. Car.
Close shot :
STEPHEN.
Medium shot of STEPHEN *and* ANNA. *They are standing by the side of the car. He is holding her under her shoulders, staring at her.*
His face.
Her face, still, eyes closed.

Exterior. Lane.
STEPHEN *walking through moonlight with* ANNA *in his arms.*
He carries her to a grass bank at side of lane and lowers her on to it.
ANNA *alone, lying on bank.*
Her legs.

Interior. Car.
WILLIAM's *face. Shining glass splinters on it and around it.*
STEPHEN's *head, listening, at* WILLIAM's *neck.*
The car shakes. He looks up.
ANNA *above him, at open door, reaching into car.*
Her face large, hair falling.
STEPHEN's *and* WILLIAM's *faces, close, both staring.*
ANNA, *supporting herself on steering wheel, reaching down into car to pick up her handbag.*

Exterior. Lane.
ANNA *walks to bank with handbag and sits.*
She takes handkerchief and mirror from bag and wipes her face.
STEPHEN *standing, looking down at her.*

ANNA *tracing smudges with her finger.*
STEPHEN'S VOICE. You can walk.

ANNA *does not look at him.*

I'm going to telephone.

ANNA *takes out a comb and combs her hair.*

STEPHEN (*looking down at her*). Can you walk?

ANNA *quietly completes her combing, puts comb, mirror, handkerchief into bag, closes bag.*
She sits still.

He puts his hands under her elbows and lifts her up.
They stand, apart.
Behind them in background the car.
He puts his hand on her elbow. She withdraws her
elbow, not sharply.
She begins to walk alone up the lane. He follows.

Long shot.
They walk slowly up the lane towards the house.
STEPHEN *is no longer following. He is equal with her,*
but ANNA *keeps a distance between them.*
They walk slowly at opposite sides of the lane, which
slopes gently uphill, in the bright moonlight, the trees
black above them, the sky large.

Interior. House. The hall.
(The interior of the house is untidy and rambling,
comfortable. Some of the walls are rough plastered.
There is a careless mixture of contemporary and
antique furnishing, none of it expensive. The air of
the house is casual, relaxed.)
The camera rests in the rear section of the hall, by
the open door of the sitting room.
The staircase rises up.
Under the staircase, half in half out of an open cup-
board, broken toys, a child's wheel barrow, a large
hoop.
The ting of a telephone receiver replaced.

Interior. Sitting-room. Night.
ANNA *sitting still in an armchair.*
Her handbag lies on a coffee table close to her chair.
An old dog pokes his head in the sitting-room door.

Interior. The hall.
The dog turns from sitting-room door, walks up the

hall, sits, looks up at STEPHEN.
STEPHEN *sitting, by telephone, at hall table, looks down at the dog.*

Interior. Sitting-room.
STEPHEN *comes in. He walks slowly to* ANNA, *puts his hand on her forehead.*

Large close-up.
His hand on her forehead. Her eyes.

STEPHEN (*standing over* ANNA). You were lying on top of him.

Pause.

Were you driving?

ANNA *leans back in armchair.*
He touches her hair.

Don't worry.

Interior. House. Kitchen.
STEPHEN *walking to kitchen table with teapot. He pours tea into cup.*

Interior. Sitting-room.
STEPHEN *bending over* ANNA *with cup.*
STEPHEN. Drink it.

He places cup by handbag on side table.
ANNA *remains still in armchair.*
STEPHEN *sitting, watching her.*
Silence.
Sound of a car drawing up.
He turns to window.

Exterior. House. Front gate. Night.
Police car driving slowly down drive towards house.
STEPHEN *comes out of front door. The door swings half shut behind him.*
The car stops. TWO POLICEMEN *get out.*
STEPHEN *and the* POLICEMEN *stand a moment, talking.*

Interior. Sitting-room.
STEPHEN *enters the sitting-room, the* POLICEMEN *following.*
He stops, blinks, turns his head to the POLICEMEN.
POLICEMAN *settling himself in the armchair in which* ANNA *sat. He places his helmet on his lap, takes out notebook.*
STEPHEN, *standing, turns to other* POLICEMAN.

STEPHEN. Sit down.

SECOND
POLICEMAN. No, it's all right.

STEPHEN *sitting, with cigarette.*

POLICEMAN'S
VOICE. Yours is the only house for some distance. So he must have been coming to see you.

STEPHEN. He was.

POLICEMAN. You were expecting him?

STEPHEN. Yes.

STEPHEN *glances at* SECOND POLICEMAN.
SECOND POLICEMAN, *standing, expressionless.*
POLICEMAN *in chair, writing in notebook, suddenly coughs violently. He takes out handkerchief, wipes his mouth.*

POLICEMAN. Sorry.

He places his helmet on the table where ANNA's *handbag and the teacup had been.*
The coffee table.
The helmet is placed on the coffee table.
STEPHEN's *face.*

THE POLICEMAN *opening his notebook.*
SECOND POLICEMAN *looks out of french windows into the black rear garden.*

Did you know him well?

SECOND POLICEMAN *turns from window.*

STEPHEN. He was my pupil.

SECOND POLICEMAN *strolls back to his place in the room.*

POLICEMAN. He was your pupil at the university?
STEPHEN. Yes.

STEPHEN's *face.*

He wanted to talk to me about something.

The room.
Silence.

POLICEMAN. You found –

A sound, from no specific place, from somewhere in the house. It is very brief. The POLICEMAN *continues.*

POLICEMAN. You found the car at one forty-five?
STEPHEN. He was going to a party, then coming on to me.
SECOND   It looks as though he was pretty drunk. There was
POLICEMAN. whisky all over the car.

STEPHEN's *face.*

STEPHEN. I don't know what it was all about. (*Pause.*) I mean I don't know what he wanted to talk to me about.

The room.
The TWO POLICEMEN. *One sitting, the other standing.*
Silence.
STEPHEN's *face.*
STEPHEN. He probably wanted my advice about something.

Interior. Sitting-room.
Empty. No sound.

Interior. Kitchen.
STEPHEN *at long bare kitchen table.*
STEPHEN. Anna?

Interior. Landing. Bedroom door.
STEPHEN *rushes up stairs and enters bedroom.*

Interior. Bedroom.
It is STEPHEN *and* ROSALIND's *bedroom. It is*
attractive, with clear feminine characteristics.
The bed is a fourposter.
ANNA *lies on the fourposter bed.*
Her legs are curled. Her skirt is above her knees.
She is asleep.
Her handbag and the teacup are on a bedside table.
Stillness.
The camera, with STEPHEN, *moves slowly towards*
ANNA *on the bed.*
STEPHEN *standing by window, looking at bed.*
ANNA *asleep. Her body curved.*
STEPHEN *at foot of bed.*
ANNA's *feet.*
One shoe is on.
The other lying on bedcover.

Interior. Car.
ANNA's *shoe, standing, digging into* WILLIAM's *face.*
STEPHEN's *hands on her legs.*
STEPHEN'S VOICE. Don't!
Close-up. WILLIAM's *face. Dead.*

Interior. STEPHEN's *study, college. Morning.*
WILLIAM's *face, smiling.*

WILLIAM and STEPHEN *are sitting by the open window. The window looks down to a quadrangle. On the grass a white goat is tethered. The scene is framed between them, below.*

STEPHEN. You haven't spoken to her?

WILLIAM. No.

STEPHEN. You've just seen her.

WILLIAM. I've just seen her. Walking about. A little.

STEPHEN. And you like the look of her?

WILLIAM. Yes. I do.

Pause.

STEPHEN. And what am I supposed to do about it?

WILLIAM. Nothing at all.

STEPHEN. Oh. Good.

WILLIAM. I'd just like to know what you think of her, that's all.

STEPHEN. You realize I'm her tutor?

WILLIAM. Naturally. I also realize you're my tutor.

STEPHEN. And that being her tutor, her moral welfare must be my first consideration.

WILLIAM. Ah. You mean besides being her tutor you are also her protector.

STEPHEN. I mean that I refuse to countenance or encourage male lust as directed against any of my woman students.

WILLIAM. Well said.

STEPHEN. Thank you.

WILLIAM. Anyway, what's her name, for God's sake?

STEPHEN. Her name? Her name. Ah yes, I remember her name. Her name is Anna von Graz und Leoben.

Pause.

WILLIAM. German.

STEPHEN. Austrian.

Pause.

WILLIAM. Well, come on! What do you think of her?

STEPHEN. I don't think.

WILLIAM. I thought thinking was your job!

STEPHEN. Not about *that.*

WILLIAM. You're not past it, are you? Already?

From the same viewpoint, ANNA *appears in the quadrangle. She stops and talks to the goat.*
WILLIAM *stands.*

It's her.
STEPHEN. She's coming for her second tutorial.
WILLIAM. You didn't tell me.
STEPHEN. Wait. I'll introduce you.
WILLIAM. She's talking to the goat.
STEPHEN. They speak German.

ANNA *stroking goat. The men at window.*
WILLIAM *at door.*

WILLIAM. No, not now. Really.
STEPHEN. You intend to go it alone, eh? Without introduction?
WILLIAM. That's right.

STEPHEN *alone in middle of study.*
He turns to window and looks down.
STEPHEN'*s head at window.*
He watches ANNA *walk across lawn towards college.*
WILLIAM *crosses lawn, at a distance from her.*
ANNA *disappears under window.*
WILLIAM *stops by the goat and bends his head to it.*

Interior. Study.
ANNA *sitting, knees together, with notebook.*
Her face, listening.
STEPHEN'S VOICE. Philosophy is a process of enquiry only. It does not attempt to find specific answers to specific questions.

Close-up. His face, looking at her.

Interior. House. Sitting-room. Afternoon.
Large close-up of CLARISSA'*s face (three years old).*
She turns from camera, runs, jumps on her mother's lap, looks over her mother's shoulder at camera.

STEPHEN *standing at door.* ROSALIND *sitting,* CLARISSA *on her lap.* TED (*seven years old*) *lying on floor with book, looking up. The dog, asleep on floor.*

STEPHEN. She loves her Dad.
ROSALIND. She hasn't eaten anything today.

ROSALIND *is pregnant. She is sewing. On the floor are paintboxes, papers in strips, scissors, children's books, a doll, cars.*
STEPHEN *looks at the floor and then walks across the room. He kicks* TED *as he passes.*

STEPHEN. Hullo.
TED. Hullo, Dad.

STEPHEN *sits.*

STEPHEN. What has she eaten?
ROSALIND. Some milk pudding at lunch.
STEPHEN. Well, that's all right.

STEPHEN *calls 'Hoy!' to* CLARISSA *and claps his hands.*
CLARISSA *runs to him, clasps his legs.*

Hullo.
TED. How many moons has Jupiter got?
STEPHEN. I don't know.
TED. Twelve.
STEPHEN. Twelve moons?
TED. Yes.
CLARISSA. Twelve moons.
STEPHEN (*to* TED). Do you want to get that book about the elephant?
TED. Yes!

TED *rushes to far end of room, to pile of books, and starts to rummage.*
ROSALIND, *sewing.*
STEPHEN, *with* CLARISSA *on his lap.*
STEPHEN. I've got a new pupil.

ROSALIND. Uh?

STEPHEN. She's an Austrian princess.

ROSALIND. *Is* she?

CLARISSA. A princess?

STEPHEN (*whispering to* CLARISSA). I think so.

TED'S VOICE. I can't find the book!

ROSALIND. How do you know she's a princess?

STEPHEN. She's got a very long name.

ROSALIND. Has she got golden hair?

STEPHEN. Uuuh . . . No.

ROSALIND. Then she's a fake.

TED *at pile of books, looking at book.*

TED. I've found it! (*Frowns.*) I think.

STEPHEN *cuddling* CLARISSA.

STEPHEN. She's very sunburnt.

ROSALIND. Then she's definitely not a princess.

STEPHEN. Why not?

CLARISSA. She is!

ROSALIND. Princesses keep their skin . . . quite white.

STEPHEN. Your skin is quite white.

ROSALIND. I know it is.

TED *runs down the room, with book, sits on* STEPHEN's *lap.*

TED. I knew I'd found it.

STEPHEN *holds both children.*

STEPHEN. Where do you want to start?

TED. You start.

STEPHEN. Where?

TED. Here.

ROSALIND. Has she made advances to you?

STEPHEN. Oh no. I'm too old.

ROSALIND. You're not too old for me.

STEPHEN. I know that. (*To children.*) Now come on. Who's going to start?

ROSALIND *stands and moves across to them.*

CLARISSA. I'll start.

TED. She can't read!

ROSALIND *bends over him.*

ROSALIND. And I'm not too old for you.

Interior. Study. College. Day.
ANNA *sitting with notebook. She is writing in it.*
Camera spreads to find STEPHEN. *He is lying back in*
his chair, feet on desk.
Silence.

STEPHEN. Write me an essay on what the problem is . . . or
rather . . . on what the problem seems to you to
be.

He lifts his head, looks at her.

Will you?

ANNA *smiles.*

ANNA. I'll try.

Interior. Don's Common Room. College.
STEPHEN, CHARLEY, *the* PROVOST *and* HEDGES, *a*
scientist, sit in armchairs, reading. CHARLEY *reads*
a newspaper ; the rest, books.
Silence.

CHARLEY. A statistical analysis of sexual intercourse among
students at Colenso University, Milwaukee, showed that 70 per cent did it in the evening, 29.9 per
cent between two and four in the afternoon and
0.1 per cent during a lecture on Aristotle.

Pause.

PROVOST. I'm surprised to hear Aristotle is on the syllabus in
the state of Wisconsin.

Silence.

CHARLEY (*still reading from paper*). Bus driver found in
student's bed.

Pause.

PROVOST. But was anyone found in the bus driver's bed?

Pause.

Did you ever hear the story of my predecessor, Provost Jones, and the step-ladder?

Pause.

It's a bizarre story. It'll amuse you. Provost Jones and his good lady decided one day to buy a step-ladder.

Exterior. Riverbank. Day.
Heat, punts, canoes on river.
STEPHEN *walks along towpath.*
Young girls and men call to each other from boats.
STEPHEN's *head.*
He walks quickly.
Flashes of light on water.
Girls turning in boats. Distant laughter.
A call: 'Stephen!'
STEPHEN *stops, turns.*
Under a willow in a punt are WILLIAM *and* ANNA.
ANNA *wears a white dress with large woven holes in it.*
STEPHEN *stares.*

WILLIAM. Hullo.

STEPHEN *bends to them, under the willow.*
The punt rocks gently, surrounded by pinpoints of light. ANNA *smiles, lying back.*

You can't wear a suit like that on a day like this. It's ridiculous.

STEPHEN. I didn't know you two had met.

WILLIAM. We have. (*To* ANNA.) Haven't we?

ANNA. Mmmnn.

WILLIAM. Jump in.

STEPHEN. Me?

WILLIAM. Come on. We're going up river.

Long shot of STEPHEN *stepping into punt.*
The punt rocks. WILLIAM *pushes off.* STEPHEN
squats by ANNA.
The punt.
STEPHEN *settles into a half leaning, crouching posi-*
tion by ANNA's *legs.*
The punt.
WILLIAM's *legs.*
Through them ANNA *sitting,* STEPHEN *reclining*
along punt, his head on the cushion by her hip.
STEPHEN's *head at her hip.*
Her legs are bare, crossed.
Vapour on her legs.
Left foreground STEPHEN's *head. Above him*
ANNA's *back. Her hair glinting. Light in her hair.*
Beyond them WILLIAM *standing, punting.*
Her arm, still.
Her arm, moving.
Her armpit. Fuzzy hair.
Hole at the side of her dress.
STEPHEN's *body, stretched.*
Her hip. His head.
Her eyes closed.
The punt pole, dipping.
The back of STEPHEN's *head. His ears.*
WILLIAM *bending and straightening, with pole.*
Long shot.
The punt draws towards an island.
STEPHEN *standing, leaning from punt to grasp the*
branch of a tree.

Exterior. Quadrangle. Day.
STEPHEN *and* WILLIAM *appear from under arch*
into quadrangle.
STEPHEN *walks straight-backed in a soaking suit.*
WILLIAM *carries his gown.*

WILLIAM. You look very dignified.
STEPHEN. I feel *wet*.
WILLIAM. You don't look wet.

STEPHEN stops, looks at him.

STEPHEN. I don't *look* wet?

WILLIAM. Nobody looked at you as though you were wet, did they? They thought you were quite normal.

They walk across lawn, STEPHEN *pulling at his trousers.*

It was all my fault. I stayed too far out.

Interior. Arched door off quadrangle.
They enter out of sun.
STEPHEN *snarls at* WILLIAM.

STEPHEN. I'm getting old! Don't you understand? Old. My muscles. The muscles.

Interior. Stairway. College.
They climb stairway.

STEPHEN. No judgement. No judgement of distance. It's all gone. Vanished!

His voice echoes in the stone stairway.

Interior. STEPHEN's *study. College. Afternoon.*
STEPHEN *is changing into sweater and light trousers.*
WILLIAM *stands by window.*

WILLIAM. I thought forty was the prime of life. I mean, I wouldn't say you looked old. You've still got a pretty good figure. But I tell you what, why don't you do an hour's squash every morning? It'll do you the world of good.

STEPHEN *hitches his trousers.*

Do you want to borrow my belt?

STEPHEN (*coolly*). If you're going to be a farmer when you leave University, why the hell are you taking philosophy?

WILLIAM. I've got to be able to talk to the cows properly, haven't I?

Interior. STEPHEN's *study. Early evening.*
STEPHEN *and* WILLIAM *sit at the window, looking down, with glasses of whisky.*

WILLIAM. It's nice knowing you really, you know. You're not a bad fellow, for a teacher of philosophy. (*Pause.*) I haven't got many friends.

STEPHEN. That's because you're an aristocrat.

WILLIAM. Ah.

STEPHEN. Aristocrats were made to be . . .

He pauses.

WILLIAM. What?

STEPHEN. Slaughtered.

Pause.

WILLIAM. Oh.

He looks at STEPHEN's *face, slightly shadowed in the evening light.*

STEPHEN. Do you like her?

WILLIAM. Yes.

Pause.

STEPHEN. Why don't you bring her down for the day on Sunday? To my house.

WILLIAM. Great.

STEPHEN. Come for lunch.

WILLIAM. Marvellous. Shall I ask her?

STEPHEN. No. No, I'll ask her.

Interior. STEPHEN's *study. College. Morning.*
ANNA *sitting on floor by bookshelves, examining books on the bottom shelf.*
STEPHEN's *legs stand by her.*
STEPHEN *looking down at her, book in hand.*

STEPHEN. This might interest you.

She looks up.

It expresses another point of view . . . altogether. It's by Charley Hall. Do you know him?

ANNA. Yes, I think . . .

STEPHEN. The zoologist.

ANNA. Yes. I have met him.

STEPHEN. But this is a novel. He writes novels as well, you see. And appears on television.

ANNA. Does he?

STEPHEN (*grinning*). He's a versatile man. Read it. I don't think much of it, but you might.

He stretches his hand down.

Here.

He clasps her hand and draws her lightly to her feet. ANNA *takes the book.*

ANNA. Thanks.

She collects her notes from the desk, puts book and notes in her bag. He watches her.

STEPHEN. Would you like to come to my house for lunch on Sunday?

ANNA. That would be lovely.

STEPHEN. You could meet my wife. And the children.

ANNA. Yes.

Pause.

ANNA *clears her throat.*

STEPHEN. Perhaps William can bring you.

ANNA. Ah. Yes.

STEPHEN. I'll ask him.

Interior. House. Bedroom. Late afternoon.
ROSALIND *lying on fourposter bed.*
The curtains are drawn.
STEPHEN, *with camera, moves slowly towards the bed. He sits on the bed. She opens eyes, smiles.*

ROSALIND. Hullo.

STEPHEN. How are you?

ROSALIND. All right.

She draws his head down, kisses him swiftly.
Children's voices raised from garden.

What are they up to?
STEPHEN. They're all right.

He kisses her fingers.
Sound of dog barking.

Have you been able to rest . . . with all this racket?
ROSALIND. Yes.

He continues kissing her fingers.

STEPHEN. Oh, I've asked some people over on Sunday. (*He looks at her.*) Is that all right? (*Pause.*) Mnnn?
ROSALIND. What people?
STEPHEN. Well . . . William . . . you know . . .
ROSALIND. Mmn-hmmn?
STEPHEN. And this Anna von Graz. (*Pause.*) You know, that girl –
ROSALIND. The Princess.
STEPHEN. Yes. She's William's girl friend. (*Pause.*) What do you think?
ROSALIND. I'm not very good at mixing with royalty.
STEPHEN. She's not really a Princess. Don't be silly.
ROSALIND. I'm not silly.

Pause.

STEPHEN. Just for lunch, that's all. But I can easily put them off.
ROSALIND. Mmmn.

She gets out of bed.

STEPHEN. What are you doing?
ROSALIND. I'm going downstairs.

She takes a negligée from the back of the door. The negligée has frilled cuffs. She puts it on.

Interior. House. Stairs.
ROSALIND *walks down the stairs, followed by*
STEPHEN.
Silence.

Interior. House. Kitchen.
ROSALIND *goes to kettle, fills it with water.*
STEPHEN *stands inside the door, watching her.*
She puts the kettle on the stove and lights the gas.

STEPHEN. Well, what do you think?
ROSALIND. About what?
STEPHEN. About Sunday. I can put them off.
ROSALIND. Why should you put them off?

ROSALIND *cuts bread on the breadboard.*

STEPHEN. Well . . . the cooking and everything . . . if you
don't feel up to it.
ROSALIND. I'm fine. Why do you keep going on about it? Let
them come.

Pause.

STEPHEN. All right.

She goes to the back window and calls: 'Ted,
Clarissa! Teatime!'

Exterior. Lane. Road junction. Morning.
Spot of accident.
Dog runs across road to earth mound.
STEPHEN's *voice: 'Mike! Come on!'*
TED *runs after dog.*

TED. Come on!

TED *chases dog off the mound. They run on to grass*
bank. STEPHEN *comes into view, walks after them.*
Long shot.
Heat.
STEPHEN, TED *and the dog walk slowly up the lane*
towards the house.

Exterior. House. Garden gate.
They pass through the gate and begin to walk up drive,
flanked by bushes.
WILLIAM's *car can be seen parked in the gravel*
court.
The dog burrows in a bush. TED *stops with him, bends.*

TED. What is it, Mike?

STEPHEN *walks ahead.*
He turns the corner of bushes, the house and court now
in full view.
He stops still.
By the hedge to the left of the house a white sports car
is parked.
ANNA, *in dark glasses, and* CHARLEY, *stand by the*
car, talking quietly.
Light vibrates on the car. An intense shimmer and
glint. The two figures and the car trapped, still, in
light, heat.
STEPHEN's *face, blinking in the sun, looking, his face*
creased.

Exterior. The court.
The scene, unmoving. The two figures by the car.
STEPHEN *standing.* TED *and dog rush past, run down*
side of house.
CHARLEY *and* ANNA *turn, see* STEPHEN.
CHARLEY *raises his hand in salutation.*
STEPHEN *walks across the gravel towards them. He*
reaches them. CHARLEY *is smiling.*

STEPHEN. Hullo Anna. William here?
ANNA. Yes, he's inside. What a lovely day.

Exterior. Front of house.
TED *and dog round corner of house.*

ANNA. Is that your son?
STEPHEN. Yes.

ANNA *walks over to* TED *and dog.*
STEPHEN *and* CHARLEY *remain by car.*
CHARLEY *sits on bonnet, stretches his arms.*

ANNA'S VOICE. What's your name?
      TED. Ted. What's yours?
    ANNA. Anna. What's his?
      TED. Mike.

> STEPHEN *and* CHARLEY *grin at each other.*

STEPHEN. What are you doing here?
CHARLEY. I was just passing, so I thought I'd drop in.
STEPHEN. Passing?
CHARLEY. Yes, just passing. Just floating by.

> *Sounds of* TED *and dog.*
> CHARLEY *chases* TED *and dog round corner of house.*

Hi! Hi! Hi!

> ANNA *is no longer there.*
> STEPHEN *stands by car.*

> *Interior. House. Kitchen.*
> ROSALIND *and* WILLIAM *peeling vegetables.*

WILLIAM. Hullo.
STEPHEN. Hullo, William. Charley's here.
ROSALIND (*laughing*). We know.
STEPHEN. Is he staying for lunch?
ROSALIND. Of course.

> *Through the window into the back garden they watch*
> CHARLEY *throwing a large ball.* TED, CLARISSA *and*
> *dog run after it.* CHARLEY *runs after them, crawls on*
> *his hands and knees among them.*
> ANNA *appears on the lawn.* CHARLEY *kicks the ball*
> *to her. She bounces it.*

STEPHEN (*to* ROSALIND). Can I do anything?

> *Exterior. Lawn. Back garden. Afternoon.*
> *The camera moves slowly up a slight rise and along*
> *the lawn.*
> *The garden is long, stretching down to trees. It is*
> *mainly grass, with a few flowerbeds.*

It is after lunch. Coffee cups, brandy glasses on the grass, some lying on their side. Very hot.
WILLIAM is lying, leaning on an elbow, picking at the grass, near CHARLEY. CHARLEY is lying on his back. ROSALIND is lying in a garden chair, feet up. ANNA sits, making a daisy chain with CLARISSA. TED and STEPHEN are doing some casual weeding at the verge.
Silence.

WILLIAM *and* CHARLEY.

WILLIAM. What are you writing now?
CHARLEY. A novel.

Pause.
The dog strolls, sniffing, between them, wanders towards ANNA.

WILLIAM. I'd like to write a novel.
CHARLEY. You would, eh?
WILLIAM. But I can't.
CHARLEY. It's child's play. You just need a starting point, that's all.
WILLIAM. Oh.

Pause.

CHARLEY. Here, for instance.
WILLIAM. Where?
CHARLEY. Here on this lawn. What are we up to?
WILLIAM. I know what I'm up to.
CHARLEY. What?
WILLIAM. Anna and I were invited here for lunch. We've just had it.
CHARLEY. Ah.

Pause.

WILLIAM. What are you up to?

ANNA *and* CLARISSA.

CLARISSA. We're going to Granny's on Tuesday.

ANNA. Are you?

CLARISSA. Teddy and Mummy and me.

ANNA. Are you going for a long time?

CLARISSA. We're going for three weeks. Mummy's going to have a baby, you see. If you're going to have a baby you've got to have a rest.

ANNA. Of course.

WILLIAM *and* CHARLEY.

CHARLEY. Describe what we're all doing.

WILLIAM *looks about the garden.*

WILLIAM. Rosalind's lying down. Stephen's weeding the garden. Anna's making a daisy chain. We're having this conversation.

CHARLEY. Good. But then you could go further. Rosalind is pregnant. Stephen's having an affair with a girl at Oxford. He's reached the age when he can't keep his hands off girls at Oxford.

WILLIAM. What?

CHARLEY. But he feels guilty, of course. So he makes up a story.

WILLIAM. What story?

CHARLEY. This story.

WILLIAM. What are you talking about?

CHARLEY *sits up, swats violently at flies.*

CHARLEY. Oh, these flies are terrible.

WILLIAM. What flies? There aren't any flies.

CHARLEY. They're Sicilian horse flies, from Corsica.

CHARLEY *shouts across lawn.*

Have you heard our conversation?

STEPHEN *weeding.*

STEPHEN. Yes!

ROSALIND *lying, eyes closed.*

ROSALIND. Yes.

> ANNA *carefully places daisy chain around* CLARISSA'S *neck.*

> *Exterior. Tennis court.*
> WILLIAM *whipping ball fiercely over net.*
> *The tennis court is situated beyond the back garden. It is in a state of ruin. There are holes in the net. Weeds all over the ground.*
> CHARLEY *and* ANNA *play against* WILLIAM *and* STEPHEN. CHARLEY *is in bare feet.*
> ROSALIND *sits in a chair by the side, watching.*
> *The ball goes to and fro.*
> WILLIAM *drives, beating* CHARLEY.
> CHARLEY *serving.* ANNA *stands by the net. The ball hits* ANNA *in the back.* CHARLEY *laughs.*
> STEPHEN *serving, into net.*
> STEPHEN *rushing the net.* ANNA *bobbing about on the other side.*
> *Sun.*
> WILLIAM *drives between* CHARLEY *and* ANNA.
> ANNA *hits wildly, sends ball into bushes.*
> STEPHEN *lobs ball over net.* CHARLEY *heads it back.*
> CHARLEY *serves, hits* ANNA.
> WILLIAM *serves powerfully, beats* CHARLEY, *who falls flat on his back.*
> *Long shot, across tennis court.*
> ROSALIND'S *chair, empty.*

> *Interior. House. Kitchen.*
> ROSALIND *cutting sandwiches.* STEPHEN *comes in.*

STEPHEN. What are you doing. ?

ROSALIND. Making tea.

STEPHEN. I've just asked them to stay for dinner.

> *She looks at him.*

ROSALIND. *Dinner?*

STEPHEN. No. Supper. Cold supper.
ROSALIND. Are they staying?
STEPHEN. I don't know. But I'll do it. I'll . . . do the supper.

The kettle boils.

ROSALIND. The kettle.

STEPHEN *goes to it.*

Exterior. Lawn. Back garden. Late afternoon.
Shadows beginning. Tea trolley standing.
ANNA *and* STEPHEN *reclining on the grass, amidst*
cups and plates, leavings of sandwiches and cakes.
WILLIAM *standing near them, practising strokes*
with a boy's cricket bat.
STEPHEN. Do you have any . . . sisters or brothers?
ANNA. One sister.
STEPHEN. Is she beautiful?
ANNA. Very.

WILLIAM *bends down to* ANNA.

WILLIAM (*to* ANNA). Come for a walk. Mmmn?
ANNA. Oh, I'm so comfortable.

WILLIAM *stands upright, is still a moment. He then*
picks up a tennis ball, bounces it, and slams it with bat
down the side of the house. He strolls after the ball.
ANNA *looks at* STEPHEN, *smiles.*

It's so lovely here.
STEPHEN. Yes . . . it is.

Pause.

I think I'll go for a walk.
ANNA. I'll come too.

STEPHEN *stretches his hand down. She jumps up by*
herself. She giggles.
He leads her across the lawn towards the trees.

Exterior. Path through grass.
STEPHEN *and* ANNA *walking through long grass beyond the tennis court, going uphill.*
Their legs swish through grass. Their voices:
STEPHEN. Are you fond of William?
ANNA. Why do you ask?

Silence. Their legs moving.
ANNA's *face.*

Are there many dons like you?
STEPHEN. Certainly not.

Exterior. A copse.
Long shot.
They appear, through fading light, through trees, into copse. Shafts of dying sun still bounce off the wood.
Silence.
Sound of their feet on the brush. Birds. Creaks in undergrowth.
ANNA *stops, holds the branch of a tree.*
Silence. Sounds.
STEPHEN. Mind. There's a spider's web.

ANNA *looks at him.*

ANNA. It won't hurt me.

She walks slowly away. He follows.

Exterior. A stile.
The stile looks down upon a valley.
They stand at the stile.
ANNA. What a beautiful view.
STEPHEN. I thought you'd like to see it.

Their hands, close but not touching, on the stile.

ANNA. It was so kind of you to ask me here.

Silence.
STEPHEN's *hand grips the stile.*
He looks at her.

STEPHEN. No, it wasn't. It's been lovely to see you.

They stand, silent. He looking at her. She gazing at the view. She turns, looks at him.

ANNA. Shall we go back now?
STEPHEN. Yes.

Interior. Kitchen.
CHARLEY *opening a bottle of beer.* ROSALIND *comes in.*
ROSALIND. Oh hello.
CHARLEY. Hello. How are you?
ROSALIND. Fine. How's Laura?
CHARLEY. Great. All right . . . you know . . . I don't know really . . . I haven't seen her.

Pause.

I've been pretty busy. You know . . . one thing and another.
ROSALIND. You look terrible.
CHARLEY. Me? I feel wonderful.

ROSALIND *pours beer into his glass.*

ROSALIND. Well, this'll kill you.
CHARLEY. I know.

Exterior. Path through grass.
They are returning.
Long shot.
STEPHEN. Will you stay for supper?
ANNA. I'd love to, but I don't know about William.
STEPHEN. He'll stay.

Interior. House. Kitchen. Early evening.
CHARLEY *with beer.* STEPHEN *comes in.*
STEPHEN. Have you seen William?

CHARLEY. No. How are you getting on?
STEPHEN. Fine. What do you mean?

CHARLEY *pours beer.* STEPHEN *opens a bottle.*

CHARLEY. What does Rosalind think about it?

STEPHEN *pours beer.*

STEPHEN. What does Rosalind think about what?

WILLIAM *looks in at the door.*

WILLIAM. Have you seen Anna?
CHARLEY AND
STEPHEN. No.

They look at each other. CHARLEY *leaves the kitchen.*

STEPHEN. You're staying for supper, aren't you?
WILLIAM. We ought to go.
STEPHEN. It's all arranged.

Interior. House. Dining-room. Evening.
STEPHEN *opening wine bottle at sideboard. He places salad bowl, containing salad, on table. He goes quickly to sideboard, takes out bottle of whisky, pours himself a large one and drinks it.*
Voices from the front of the house.
He goes to window.
In the dusk, ROSALIND *and* ANNA *are walking up the drive to the house, with dog, talking quietly.*
STEPHEN *leans out of the window.*
STEPHEN. Where are the children?

The women stop.

ROSALIND. They're not back yet. They went out to tea.
STEPHEN (*to himself*). I didn't know that.
ROSALIND. How's the supper?
STEPHEN. Nearly there.

STEPHEN *takes whisky bottle and goes out door.*

Interior. The hall.
STEPHEN *crosses hall to sitting-room.*
ROSALIND *and* ANNA *come in front door.*

ROSALIND. I think it's about ten years.

ANNA. You're a wonderful couple.

Interior. House. Sitting-room.
CHARLEY *and* WILLIAM *are lying in chairs with beer.* STEPHEN *enters with bottle.*

STEPHEN. Whisky.

Interior. House. Dining-room. Night.
The men are at the table.
ANNA *and* ROSALIND *clearing soup plates, setting ham plates.*
One empty bottle of whisky on the sideboard. Two and a half empty bottles of red wine on table.

STEPHEN. Who made that soup? I didn't make any soup.

CHARLEY. Your wife! Your beautiful wife made the damn soup! It was beautiful soup. My wife's beautiful too, isn't she, Rosalind?

ROSALIND. Yes.

CHARLEY (*to* ANNA). She's as beautiful as that soup.

WILLIAM *sways in his chair.*

(*To* ANNA.) She's rich and intelligent and beautiful. And we've got three kids. Don't forget *that*. And she understands me. *And* . . .

STEPHEN. And.

CHARLEY. *And* . . . we're all very old friends. Him and his wife. And me and my wife. Don't forget that.

STEPHEN. But he's more successful than me because he appears on television.

ANNA (*to* CHARLEY). Do you talk on television?

CHARLEY. What do you think I do, play the flute?

ANNA. What do you talk about?

CHARLEY. You name it I'll talk about it.

STEPHEN. He talks about history, zoology –

CHARLEY. Anthropology, sociolog . . . sociologigy –
STEPHEN. Sociology!
CHARLEY. Codology.
STEPHEN. And sex. In that order.
ROSALIND. He suits the medium.
STEPHEN (*to* ROSALIND). Do you mean you don't think I would suit the medium?
CHARLEY. They wouldn't let you within ten miles of the medium!

STEPHEN *points a long arm across the table at* CHARLEY.

STEPHEN. I have an appointment with *your* producer next week.
CHARLEY. With *my* producer?
STEPHEN. *Your* producer.

WILLIAM *slumps on to the table.* ROSALIND *rises, goes to* ANNA. *They whisper.*

CHARLEY. What, with old Bill Smith?
STEPHEN. He's asked to see me.
CHARLEY. You're going to be on *my* television show?
STEPHEN. I'll run you out of town, kid.
ROSALIND. Stephen, he wants to drive back.
STEPHEN. Who does?
ROSALIND. William.
STEPHEN. Impossible. He's drunk.
ANNA. I'll drive.
CHARLEY. You haven't got a licence.
ANNA. William, can I drive?
ROSALIND. No. You'll have to stay.
WILLIAM. I'll drive.
ANNA. Oh, we'd better stay.
STEPHEN. I'll drive.
ROSALIND. No you won't.
STEPHEN. Charley can drive!

WILLIAM *stands. His chair falls.*

WILLIAM. Oh, to hell . . .

STEPHEN *stands, goes to him.*

STEPHEN. Listen, old boy. You're slightly drunk. You can stay.

WILLIAM. Why the bloody hell do you want us to bloody well stay?

ROSALIND takes WILLIAM's arm.

ROSALIND. Oh, come on.

She leads him out. ANNA follows.
STEPHEN leans on to the table. He stares across the table at CHARLEY, who stares back at him.
Silence.
STEPHEN walks to the door.

STEPHEN. Will you excuse me?

CHARLEY. But of course, my dear fellow.

Interior. Kitchen. Night.
Tap in sink turned full on.
STEPHEN's head bends underneath it.
He turns tap off, holds towel to his head, sits heavily in chair.
CHARLEY comes in, sways slightly, leans on door frame.

CHARLEY. They're staying.

Silence.

Which room . . . is everyone in?

Pause.

STEPHEN. How the hell should I know?

Pause.

CHARLEY. Splendid day.

STEPHEN (*carefully*). It gives me great pleasure to know that you have enjoyed your day with us. Good night.

CHARLEY. Good night.

CHARLEY goes out of kitchen door.

Interior. Kitchen. Later.
Dog, looking up.
STEPHEN, *slumped in kitchen chair, wakes suddenly,*
looks at watch.
He stands, clenches eyes, goes to door.

Interior. The hall.
STEPHEN *switches out hall light.*
He looks up the stairs.
In the faint light at the top of the stairs he sees a
woman ascending in a negligee with frilled cuffs. He
stares after her. She goes out of sight.

Interior. Bedroom.
He enters, closes door. Stops dead.
A woman lies in the fourposter.
He stares with disbelief and delight.
He mouths softly:
STEPHEN. Anna.

He goes to bed, looks down. It is ROSALIND.

Interior. Bedroom.
STEPHEN *climbing onto the bed. He touches his wife.*
STEPHEN (*whispering*). Rosalind. (*Pause.*) Darling?
ROSALIND (*blurred*). What?
STEPHEN. I love you.

Interior. Television building. Day.
STEPHEN *sitting by low table in third floor ante-room,*
glass-panelled.
A RECEPTIONIST *sits at a distance from him, at a*
desk.
STEPHEN *flips through magazines.*
He opens a trade magazine.
Photograph of Charley and others with cameras,
entitled 'Conversation Piece'.

The phone rings. RECEPTIONIST *lifts it.*

RECEPTIONIST. Reception? . . . Yes . . . I see . . . Thank you.

She puts phone down.

(*To* STEPHEN.) Mr Smith isn't here, I'm afraid. Will you see Mr Bell?

STEPHEN. Uuh . . . yes, all right.

RECEPTIONIST (*pointing down corridor*). It's the fifth door on the left.

Interior. Corridor.
STEPHEN *walks down corridor.*
Box cubicles on either side of wood and glass. Voices, as he passes, from offices.
A door marked: MR BELL. ASSISTANT. TALKS.

Interior. BELL'*s office.*
BELL *rising from desk.* SECRETARY *in corner, typing. Loud indecipherable voice from next office. Behind* BELL, *through small window, a building site. Cranes, bulldozers, etc.* BELL *wears a cardigan.*

BELL (*shaking hands*). Hullo . . . I'm Bell. Remember me? I'm Bell.

STEPHEN. Uuuhh . . .

BELL. I was at Oxford.

STEPHEN. Of course. How are you?

BELL. Bill Smith's ill. He's in hospital.

STEPHEN. Oh, I'm sorry.

BELL. I've got to go and see him. Sit down. (*To* SECRETARY.) Got that file?

SECRETARY *goes to filing cabinet.* STEPHEN *sits.*

STEPHEN. I don't . . . actually know him.

BELL. You don't *know* him?

SECRETARY *gives* BELL *file. He flips through it.*
What did he want you for, do you know?

STEPHEN. I think he . . . mmn . . .

BELL (*flipping*). Do you ever see Francesca?

STEPHEN. Who?

BELL. Francesca. The provost's daughter. The daughter of the provost.

STEPHEN. Ah . . . yes. No, I don't.

BELL (*swift smile*). You knew her well.

STEPHEN. I've been married some years.

BELL. Well done. (*Finding letter.*) Ah . . . yes. Bill was thinking of you for 'Conversation Piece'. I've got to go and see him in a minute. He's very ill.

A man enters the office hurriedly.

MAN. What's the matter with Bill?

BELL. He's very bad. He's in hospital.

MAN. What!

The MAN *sits heavily. The phone rings.*

SECRETARY (*on phone*). Mr Bell's secretary.

STEPHEN. Yes . . .

SECRETARY (*on phone*). Who?

STEPHEN. I think he was thinking of me.

MAN. He was perfectly all right yesterday. I had a drink with him.

SECRETARY *puts hand over receiver.*

SECRETARY. Mr Dyce.

BELL *waves hand irritably.*

MAN. I can't believe it.

SECRETARY (*to phone*). No, I'm afraid he's not.

BELL. Listen, the point is I don't know what his plans were, you see.

MAN. What happened to him?

SECRETARY (*on phone*). Yes, I'll see he gets the message.

BELL *stands.*

BELL. Perhaps I could let you know. (*To* MAN.) He collapsed last night. Look, why don't you come and see him? I'm going over there now to see him.

MAN. What time you going?

BELL. I'm going now. (*Shaking hands with* STEPHEN.) Well, all right. Sorry about this. Give my love to Francesca.

STEPHEN. I haven't seen her.

MAN. You're going straight away, are you?

BELL. I told you, I'm going right away. I'm going now.

Interior. Telephone booth.
His tie in the square mirror.
He is dialling. The number buzzes. No answer.
His hand begins to replace receiver.
A sudden voice in receiver : 'Hullo'.
He holds the receiver still.
The voice : 'Hullo'.
He lifts the receiver and speaks.

STEPHEN. Francesca?

Exterior. Block of flats. Evening.
STEPHEN *walks to door of flats. He stops, walks to*
edge of pavement. Walks past door, stops.
He turns and goes in.

The following sequence with FRANCESCA *is silent.*
The only sounds heard are the voices overlaid at
stated points. The words are fragments of realistic
conversation. They are not thoughts. Nor are they
combined with any lip movement on the part of the
actors. They are distributed over the sequence so as to
act as a disembodied comment on the action.

Interior. FRANCESCA's *flat. Evening.*
Sitting-room.
FRANCESCA *walking towards drink table. She is*
smiling. She is no longer young.
HER VOICE (OVER)
You haven't changed at all!
Not at all!

A silent record turns on the record player.

STEPHEN *standing, looking after her, his eyes narrowed.*
HIS VOICE (OVER) (*gaily*)
Wonderful to see you!
FRANCESCA *brings a glass to him, hands it to him. She smiles tenderly at him.*
HER VOICE (OVER)
I was in my bath when you phoned!
She turns, goes back to drinks.

STEPHEN, *with drink, sitting on sofa.*
HIS VOICE (OVER)
Well, it must be ten years.

FRANCESCA, *at drinks table, concentrating, squirting soda into glass.*
HER VOICE (OVER)
Ten years! It can't be!

Both sitting on sofa, slowly click glasses.
HER VOICE (OVER)
It can't be. It must be.
HIS VOICE (OVER)
It must be.
HER VOICE (OVER)
It is.

FRANCESCA *switching off silent record. She walks towards bedroom. As she walks :*
HIS VOICE (OVER)
You don't look a day older.
HER VOICE (OVER)
Oh really, I'm ten years older.

FRANCESCA *walking from bedroom with her coat.*
STEPHEN *walks towards her, helps her on with her coat. She leans back, puts her cheek to his, kisses his cheek.*
HER VOICE (OVER)
How's your wife ?

Flat door closing. Light goes out.
Sitting-room. Nightlight through window.
The room empty.
HIS VOICE (OVER)
That's a beautiful dress and a beautiful coat. You
look marvellous.

Interior. Restaurant. Night.
STEPHEN *and* FRANCESCA *at a table.*
WAITER *pouring wine into glasses.*
STEPHEN *and* FRANCESCA *looking at each other.*
His face, looking.
Her face, looking.
HER VOICE (OVER)
I'm in consumer research. Did you know? It's
fascinating.

FRANCESCA *refusing potatoes from* WAITER, *laughing.*

STEPHEN *beckoning the* WAITER *for potatoes,*
grinning.
HIS VOICE (OVER) (*softly*)
Remember those times in the car? Do you? Do you?

FRANCESCA *eating.*
HER VOICE (OVER) (*softly*)
Of course I remember.

Both eating, talking.
HER VOICE (OVER) (*softly*)
I remember.

FRANCESCA *accepting cigarette from* STEPHEN.
She looks at him, cigarette in mouth, while he digs
in pocket for lighter.
HER VOICE (OVER)
I'm supposed to be on a diet.
I'm too fat.
He lights her cigarette.

HER VOICE (OVER)
So then you'll have three?
Three children. Good gracious.

Exterior. Restaurant. Night.
DOORMAN *opening taxi door for them.* STEPHEN
tips him.
HIS VOICE (OVER)
You're not fat.

Interior. FRANCESCA's *flat. Sitting-room. Night.*
Dimly lit table lamp. STEPHEN *sitting, leaning*
forward.
HER VOICE (OVER)
I'm very happy.

Bathroom door opens. She comes out, walks across
the room to him.
HER VOICE (OVER)
My life is happy.

Interior. Bedroom. Night.
FRANCESCA *and* STEPHEN *in bed, naked. His eyes*
are open. She lies in his arms, eyes closed.
HER VOICE (OVER)
Have I changed?
HIS VOICE (OVER)
You're the same.
HER VOICE (OVER)
The same as I was? The same as I was . . . then?
HIS VOICE (OVER)
The same.

Interior. House. Hall.
STEPHEN *switches light on in hall. He sits down*
heavily at the hall table, holding his head.

Pile of letters on table.
Silence.
Creaks from upstairs.
He looks up sharply.
Another creak.
He stands, tense, looks round for some kind of imple-
ment.
Footsteps along the landing. He stares up.
CHARLEY *looks over the banister. He comes down the*
stairs, sits on a step halfway down. He wears a
dressing gown.

CHARLEY. Hullo.

Pause.

STEPHEN. Hullo. I've just come from London.
CHARLEY. I know.

ANNA *appears at the top of the stairs. She is dressed.*
in sweater and trousers. Bare feet.
STEPHEN *stares up at her.*
Eventually his gaze drops to CHARLEY.

STEPHEN. To see the television people.

ANNA *remains still.*

Silence.

CHARLEY. Did you see them?
STEPHEN. I'm hungry.

STEPHEN *goes along passage to kitchen.*

Interior. Kitchen.
One place is laid for breakfast on the kitchen table.
STEPHEN *goes to the fridge.*
STEPHEN'*s face at lighted fridge. He takes out eggs.*
STEPHEN *stands with eggs.*
ANNA *and* CHARLEY *at the kitchen door.* ANNA *is*
whispering to CHARLEY.
STEPHEN *puts eggs in bowl, takes down frying pan.*

STEPHEN. I'm going to make an omelette.

CHARLEY. We don't want anything.

STEPHEN *puts butter in pan.*

ANNA. Shall I cook?

CHARLEY. Can you?

ANNA *sits at table, takes crumpled cigarette packet and matches from trouser pocket, lights cigarette.*

Can I have a cigarette?

She passes packet across table. He lights one.
STEPHEN *heats frying pan and begins to beat the eggs.*

I wrote to you. The letter's out in the hall. You didn't get it.

STEPHEN. I left early.

CHARLEY (*to* ANNA). Get the letter.
She sits still. CHARLEY *grins, goes into hall.*
STEPHEN *empties eggs into pan.* ANNA *smokes.*
CHARLEY *returns with two letters, throws one on table.*

Here it is. (*Looks at other.*) There's another one for you. From my wife. A personal letter from her to you. Open it.

STEPHEN *holds pan handle.* CHARLEY *opens letter and reads.*
Silence.
STEPHEN *twists pan.*

(*Reading aloud.*) De-da-, de-da, de-da, de-da . . . Ah . . . So I just want to beg you that while still being understanding, sympathetic, etc. you don't necessarily show to him you think it's the great thing of his life. You might even hint that sooner or later he'll be bored to death by her. I believe this of course, but naturally am in a wrong position even to hint. I always wondered what this would be like if and when it happened, but I must say it beats everything. Love. Laura. P.S. Don't say I wrote for heaven's sake.

CHARLEY *throws letter on table and grins at* ANNA *and* STEPHEN. STEPHEN *flips omelette on to plate, puts it on table.* CHARLEY *sits down, begins to eat it. Pause.*

ANNA. I thought you didn't want any.
CHARLEY. I didn't.
ANNA. Then why are you eating it?
CHARLEY. Mind your own damn bloody business!

CHARLEY *shoves the plate away.*
STEPHEN *sits at other side of table and continues eating omelette.*
The three sitting at the table.
STEPHEN *pushes plate away and leaves the kitchen.*

Interior. Landing.
STEPHEN *on landing looks down passage into spare room.*
The door is open.
He walks to it, goes in.

Interior. Spare bedroom.
STEPHEN *looks about. The sheets and pillows on the bed are rumpled. The top sheet and blanket falling to the floor.* CHARLEY's *clothes lie on a chair.* ANNA's *shoes on floor. Handbag and tissues on dressing table. He leaves room, goes to bathroom.*

Interior. Bathroom.
STEPHEN *looks at his face in mirror, wipes his mouth briskly with towel, looks at towel. He looks round at bathroom. A towel on the floor. Drops of water in bath.*
ANNA *passes bathroom door.*

Interior. Landing.
STEPHEN *on landing looking down passage to spare room.* ANNA *is straightening the bed.*

CHARLEY'S *voice from below, on telephone:* '*Hullo. Hullo, yes. This is Palling 146 . . . Hullo.*'

Interior. Spare room.
ANNA *bending over bed. She looks up.*

STEPHEN. What are you doing?

ANNA. Making the bed.

STEPHEN. No need to do that. A woman comes in every morning.

ANNA. I can do it.

STEPHEN. Leave it, please.

She stops, goes to handbag, puts tissues into it.

ANNA. We're going.

CHARLEY'S *voice from below, raised:* '*Yes. A taxi. Now. To go into Oxford.*'

STEPHEN. You might as well stay. It's very late.

ANNA *and* STEPHEN *look at each other.*
CHARLEY'S *voice:* '*Straight away. Okay. Right.*'
ANNA *and* STEPHEN *remain looking at each other.*
CHARLEY'S *voice, ascending stairs:* '*Anna! I've got a taxi.*'

Interior. Landing.
ANNA *and* STEPHEN *seen standing in room.*
CHARLEY *walks along passage to room.*

Interior. Spare room.
CHARLEY *at door of room.*

CHARLEY. It's on its way.

ANNA. I'll wait downstairs.

ANNA *goes out.*

CHARLEY. Shut the door, for God's sake.

STEPHEN *shuts the door.* CHARLEY *starts to dress quickly.*

It was her idea, she knew Rosalind was away, she said you wouldn't mind.

STEPHEN. I don't mind. It's got nothing to do with me.

CHARLEY. It's your bloody house!

CHARLEY struggles into his clothes.

Anyway, I wrote to you but you didn't get the damn letter.

STEPHEN. When did it start?

CHARLEY. What? Oh, weeks ago. Weeks. We used to go to her room in the afternoon. Didn't even have a lock on the door. Anyone could have come in. Someone did come in once. A girl. Can you imagine?

CHARLEY pulls at his socks, sitting on the bed.

I'm sleeping at college most of the time now. I can't take her there, can I? Where can I damn well take her?

STEPHEN. I thought she and William . . . were close friends.

CHARLEY. They are! They're just friends. It means nothing. She's not a whore.

He puts on shoes.

I don't know what to do, you see. I can't have enough of her.

Sound of taxi.
STEPHEN *goes to window, draws curtains.*
Down below he sees taxi drawing up. DRIVER *gets out, goes to front door. A shaft of light from door onto the gravel.*
CHARLEY's *voice.*

I don't know what to do.

The DRIVER *gets back into taxi, sits.*
STEPHEN *turns from window.*

STEPHEN. Where's your car?

CHARLEY. Laura's got it.

STEPHEN. I'm going to see Rosalind tomorrow. At her mother's. Then I'm going to William's house. I've been invited down there. You can bring her here for the weekend.

Pause.

CHARLEY. Thanks.

He puts on his jacket, combs his hair.

It's the children, you see. I'm never there. They're missing me.

A call from ANNA *from below : 'The taxi's waiting.'*
CHARLEY *shouts : 'Coming!'*
CHARLEY *picks up dressing gown, hands it to* STEPHEN.

This is your dressing gown.
 STEPHEN *(taking it)*. Can I ask you a question ?
CHARLEY. What ?
STEPHEN. How did you get in tonight ?
CHARLEY. Through the lavatory window.
STEPHEN. You're a bit old for that.
CHARLEY. Yes, I am.
STEPHEN. Here's a key.
CHARLEY. Thanks.

CHARLEY *goes to door.*

STEPHEN. One more question.
 CHARLEY *(with fatigue)*. What ?
STEPHEN. Last Sunday night, when you all stayed, did you sleep with her here ?

Pause.

CHARLEY. Of course I did.

Exterior. ROSALIND's *mother's small house, in the country. The garden. Day.*
STEPHEN *and* ROSALIND *lie in deckchairs.*
His eyes are closed. Sun.

ROSALIND (*drowsily*). Did you see anyone in London?
STEPHEN. No.

Pause.

ROSALIND. What happened with the television people?
STEPHEN. Nothing. Wasn't any good. (*He looks at her.*) You
look wonderful..
ROSALIND. I feel it. I feel great.

Pause.

I wish you could stay.
STEPHEN. So do I.
ROSALIND. Still, you'll have a good time at William's house,
won't you? With all the lords and ladies.

STEPHEN *grunts, sits humped in the deckchair.*
She looks at him.

What's the matter?

Exterior. CHARLEY *and* LAURA'S *house in country.*
The garden. Day.
A hose running off lawn into flower beds.
The water spouts.
STEPHEN *from back door comes into garden.*
He walks across it.
LAURA *comes into shot, stops. He waves, walking.*
She watches his approach.
STEPHEN. Hullo, Laura.
LAURA. Hullo, Stephen.
STEPHEN. The door was open. How are you?
LAURA. Fine.

He looks at hose.

STEPHEN. What are you doing?
LAURA. Charley's not here.
STEPHEN. I got your letter.

Pause.

LAURA. I'm just doing the garden.

STEPHEN. What are you doing to it?
LAURA. Caring for it.

Exterior. ROSALIND's *mother's house. Garden.*
STEPHEN *and* ROSALIND.

STEPHEN. I got home from London and found Charley and Anna there.
ROSALIND. Charley and Anna?
STEPHEN. Yes.
ROSALIND. Together? In the house?
STEPHEN. Yes. I got home late, a bit drunk. I was . . . astonished.
ROSALIND. Why were you drunk?
STEPHEN. Oh, I had dinner with Francesca. You remember. You remember Francesca?
ROSALIND. Yes.
STEPHEN. Just gave her a ring, you know. It was quite pleasant.

Pause.

ROSALIND. He's sleeping with her, is he?
STEPHEN. Who?
ROSALIND. Charley. With Anna.
STEPHEN. Of course.
ROSALIND. How pathetic.
STEPHEN. What do you mean?
ROSALIND. Poor stupid old man.
STEPHEN. He's not old.
ROSALIND. Stupid bastard.

Pause.

Does Laura know?
STEPHEN. Yes.
ROSALIND. What about the children? Has he told them?

Exterior. Garden. LAURA's *house.*
LAURA *re-setting hose on flowerbed.* STEPHEN *standing.*

STEPHEN. It'll be all right . . . you know.
LAURA. What will?

She directs hose.

STEPHEN. I know it will.
LAURA. Have you had lunch?
STEPHEN. Yes.

Pause.

Didn't you want me to come?
LAURA. Yes.
STEPHEN. Well, I'm just trying to tell you . . .
LAURA. Do you want some coffee?
STEPHEN. No, I don't want coffee.

She walks along flowerbed. Hose spouting. He follows.

Listen . . . this thing . . . it's nothing. It'll all fall flat.
LAURA. He says he's in love with her.
STEPHEN. Love! Everyone thinks they're in love!
LAURA. Do you?

Exterior. ROSALIND's mother's garden.

ROSALIND. I've never heard of anything so bloody puerile, so banal.
STEPHEN. What's banal about it?
ROSALIND. That poor stupid bitch of a girl.
STEPHEN. You just keep calling everyone stupid, what's the use – ?
ROSALIND. Well, they are. Except Laura. And she's stupid too.

Pause.

You chucked them out, I hope?

Exterior. Garden. LAURA's house.
LAURA and STEPHEN standing middle of lawn.
LAURA. Well . . . don't worry about it.
STEPHEN. I'm not.
LAURA. Thanks for coming.

Exterior. ROSALIND's *mother's garden.*
STEPHEN *and* ROSALIND *in the deckchairs, still.*
Silence.

STEPHEN. I think I'll pop in and see Laura. It's on my way.
ROSALIND. Give her my love.

Interior. LORD CODRINGTON's *country house. Evening.*
A large stone corridor. High windows. A green baize door at one end. An archway to the main body of the house at the other. Large family portraits on the walls.
About a dozen MEN *are taking off their jackets and hanging them on a stand. They proceed to tuck their trousers into their socks.*
STEPHEN *is watching.* WILLIAM *joins him.*
They stand in archway.

WILLIAM. Anna was coming down, but she's got some of her family over, or something.
STEPHEN. Ah.
WILLIAM. Do you know, I've never thanked you for introducing us.
STEPHEN. I didn't.

A group of LADIES *comes through archway.*
WILLIAM *smiles at them, moves aside with* STEPHEN.

WILLIAM. Haven't you ever played this game before?
STEPHEN. No.
WILLIAM. It's traditional. We all played it at school.
STEPHEN. Ah.
WILLIAM. You'll enjoy it. It's fun.

WILLIAM *goes to side table and picks up a long heavy stuffed shapeless cushion cover.*

This is the ball, you see.
STEPHEN. Uh-huh.

WILLIAM *looks at him.*

WILLIAM. I think you should go in goal.

STEPHEN. Where's that?

WILLIAM. Down there, by that door.

> STEPHEN *looks down corridor.*
> *A few* MEN *are doing limbering up exercises.*
> STEPHEN *turns to* WILLIAM.

STEPHEN. I've got a funny feeling this is a murderous game.

WILLIAM. Not at all.

STEPHEN. Isn't it true all aristocrats want to die?

WILLIAM (*smiling*). I don't.

STEPHEN. What do I do in goal?

WILLIAM. Defend it.

STEPHEN. How?

WILLIAM. Any way you like.

STEPHEN. Can't I just watch?

WILLIAM. No. You're a house guest. You must play. Only the old men watch. And the ladies.

> *Through the archway towards the corridor the* LADIES *walk, talking and laughing.*
> STEPHEN *hangs his jacket on stand and walks uneasily down the corridor, between the men, to the door at the end. He stands by the door.*
> *The* MEN *collect at one wall, under the pictures.*
> STEPHEN *watches them. He bends quickly and tucks his trousers into his socks.*
> *The* MEN *line up by the wall, leaving a space between them and the wall. One* MAN, *at the far end of the row, holds the ball.*
> *The corridor, which has echoed with voices and footsteps, becomes silent.*
> *The row of* MEN *by wall, tense, waiting.*
> *The* MAN *with ball in foreground.*
> *The group of* LADIES, *with a few elderly* MEN, *silent, watching, in the archway.*
> STEPHEN.
> *Long shot of corridor. Utter stillness.*
> *The* MAN *with ball dashes between* MEN *and wall.*
> *The* MEN *fall on him. A scrum.*
> *The* MAN *attempts to break through, gripping the ball*

to him. *The others try to drag it from him. He shoves right and left with his elbows.*

The struggling scrum inches along the wall.

It is silent but for grunts. MEN, *striving, become attached to the backs of others. A communal buggery.*

The MAN *with ball is lifted off his feet from behind.*

WILLIAM *seizes the ball, dashes free towards goal.*

STEPHEN *standing.* WILLIAM *dashing toward him.*

WILLIAM *is tackled by four* MEN, *is trapped at the waist from behind. The others attempt to pull the ball away.* WILLIAM *kicks the* MAN *behind him. He cracks his elbows sharply into the faces of two others and swiftly turning, butts the fourth* MAN *with his head.*

WILLIAM, *free, runs. Others join to chase him.*

He dodges, charges two MEN *down, still holding ball, and again dashes towards* STEPHEN *in goal.*

STEPHEN's *legs, moving out of goal, bracing, as* WILLIAM *charges down upon him.*

WILLIAM *charges him in the stomach.*

STEPHEN *is carried along a little way on* WILLIAM's *back.*

He swings off, pressing his fingers on the back of WILLIAM's *neck.*

STEPHEN *grappling with* WILLIAM, *momentarily. They are tackled and surrounded.*

A MAN *jumps on* STEPHEN's *back.* STEPHEN *flings his head back, hitting* MAN *in face. The* MAN *falls, rolls away holding his face.*

The scrum.

WILLIAM, *with ball, trying to force way out.*

STEPHEN *grappling with him, eyes staring.*

Above them a canopy of arms flailing, bodies twisting. The MEN *fight with each other.*

Elbows in stomachs. Feet kicking. Forearms cuffing.

Hands pulling at ball, which WILLIAM *clutches to him, as he kicks up.* STEPHEN *lashes out at* MEN *above him.*

Top shot of scrum.

It strives forward ponderously, brokenly; a bowel with a gut gone.

WILLIAM's *teeth bared.*
The LADIES, *watching.*
Under canopy of bodies, WILLIAM *grapples with*
STEPHEN.
STEPHEN's *face, teeth bared.*
He savagely knees WILLIAM *in the face.*
WILLIAM's *face, receiving knee.*
STEPHEN *felled from behind. He falls.*
From above.
The scrum, squirming in a circle.
WILLIAM, *bloody, savaged by hands.*
The ball torn from him.

Exterior. Cricket field. Day.
WILLIAM, *batting, hitting ball savagely.*
Vigorous applause.
WILLIAM *wipes his forehead.*
WILLIAM *is immaculate in white.*
The PROVOST, CHARLEY *and* STEPHEN *stand near*
the pavilion, watching the game.

PROVOST. He really is a magnificent athlete.
CHARLEY. Yes, he's a natural, that boy.
PROVOST. I was quite good myself. But not altogether in the
same class. What about you, Stephen? Were you
any good?
STEPHEN (*smiling*). No.

WILLIAM *hooks the ball through the field.*
PROVOST *applauds.* STEPHEN *looks at him.*

I saw Francesca when I was in London.

The PROVOST *looks at him, bewildered.*

Your daughter.
PROVOST. Ah. How is she?
STEPHEN. Very well. She sent you her love.
PROVOST. Ah. Please give her mine when you see her again.
STEPHEN. Oh, I don't know when I'll be seeing her again.

WILLIAM *sends a ball high into the air.*
A FIELDER, *on the boundary, waits for it, catches it.*

Applause, as WILLIAM, *bat raised, runs up steps of pavilion.*
STEPHEN *stands alone under a tree, applauding.*
STEPHEN *turns.* ANNA *is beside him.*

ANNA. Hullo.
STEPHEN. Hullo. Have a nice week-end?
ANNA. Yes, Thank you for your hospitality.

Pause.

I'm getting married.
STEPHEN. Oh. Who to?
ANNA. William.

Pause.
STEPHEN *watches the game, which, in the background, continues.*

STEPHEN. Ah. Have you told him?

ANNA *giggles.*

Well, congratulations.
ANNA. I wonder if you could tell Charley for me.

STEPHEN *looks at her.*

Will you let me know what he says?

WILLIAM *runs up the side of the field to join them.*
WILLIAM *puts his arm round* ANNA.

WILLIAM (*to* STEPHEN). Hullo.
STEPHEN. Well played.
WILLIAM. Thanks. Look, I want to come and see you, have a word with you. Can I come tonight, after this party? I'll be a bit late.
STEPHEN. Sure. What's the trouble?
WILLIAM. No trouble. No trouble at all.
STEPHEN (*to* ANNA). You coming?
WILLIAM. No, I don't want her.

WILLIAM *punches* STEPHEN *on the chest, lightly, but* STEPHEN *staggers.*

I want a man to man talk!

STEPHEN. We can talk when she's in bed. She can sleep in the spare room. Can't you?

ANNA. That would be nice.

WILLIAM. Okay. We'll see you later. Come on!

WILLIAM, *arms round* ANNA's *waist, runs along the edge of the field with her.*
STEPHEN *walks along in their wake.*
He looks down. CHARLEY *is sitting in a deckchair.*
CHARLEY *looks up, winks.*
STEPHEN *looks after them.*
WILLIAM's *face,* ANNA's *face, together, as they run.*

WILLIAM's *face dead at bottom of car.*

ANNA, *head and shoulders rising out of overturned car. Moonlight.*

ANNA *sitting on grass bank. Moonlight.*

ANNA *lying on fourposter bed.*

Interior. House. Bedroom. Night.
STEPHEN *sitting upright on chair by the window.*
The bedroom.
ANNA *on bed.* STEPHEN *on chair.*
Stillness.
ANNA *sighs in her sleep, rolls on to her side, half sits up, almost falls off bed.*
He goes to her, holds her.
STEPHEN *kneeling at the side of the bed, holding* ANNA's *shoulders on the bed.*

STEPHEN. It's all right.

She stares at him, lost, suddenly frowns, is still, tense, crouched at the edge of the bed.
He lifts his hand to touch her forehead.
She shies away, slides off bed, sits sharply on the floor.
She laughs, stops suddenly.

STEPHEN *bends over her, squatting.*
She looks swiftly up at his body, then down.

Did anyone know you were with him?

She does not look up.
He grips her jaw.

You can hear me.

She moves her jaw in his grip.

Can't you?

He tightens grip, twists her head to him.
Her eyes close, her head jerks back.
Her hands claw at him.
He seizes her hands. Her face jerks from side to side.
She is whimpering.
He thrusts his body between her legs, fixes his elbows
on her arms, and presses his thumbs on her cheeks.
Large close-up.
Her face, pulled out of shape by his thumbs. Her eyes
slits.
His thumbs press her face back against bed.
Top shot.
The two bodies, hardly moving, battling, at the side of
the bed.
The telephone rings from below.
His face, set. His eyes flicker towards sound of
telephone. He concentrates on ANNA.
ANNA's *face, stretched.*
She suddenly becomes limp. The phone stops.
She looks at him. His grip relaxes on her face.

Did anyone know you were coming here with him?

She looks at him calmly. No response.

Was he supposed to have dropped you off at your
room?

Her face, calm, non-committal.
His face.
Her ear. Long hair falling.

His mouth at her ear.

He's dead.

Her head turns to look at him.
Their faces very close.

You had an accident. You crashed.

Pause.

You *were* driving, weren't you?

The telephone rings below. He frowns, hesitates,
stands. ANNA *remains still. He goes to door.*

Interior. House. Landing.
He looks down stairs. Phone ringing.

Interior. House. The stairs.
He starts down the stairs. He is almost at the foot
when the telephone stops ringing.
He stands, then turns back.

Interior. Bedroom.
STEPHEN *at door.*
ANNA *is not by the bed. He turns swiftly.*
ANNA *is standing by the window, holding curtain,*
looking down into garden.
He walks quickly to window, pulls ANNA *away,*
pulls curtain into place, keeping hold of her arm.

STEPHEN. Someone might see you.

He still holds her arm. He looks at her, pulls her to
him suddenly and kisses her.
The kiss is very brief. He draws back.
They stand, apart.
Their bodies standing. Waist level. Not touching.
Their arms.
His hands touch her arms, move up.

He folds her in his arms and kisses her slowly.
She does not resist.
He withdraws from embrace, walks to bedside lamp,
turns it off.
The bedroom door is still half open. Light from the
landing comes into the room.
He stands by the lamp.
She remains by the window.
He is still by the lamp.
Slowly, she walks across the room towards him.
She passes through the channel of light from the door.
Her body, by the bed.
His body, by the bed.
Both of them, standing by the bed, in the dim light.

Exterior. The house. Front door. Morning.
The front door is open. STEPHEN *stands by it, look-*
ing into hall.
ANNA *is sitting in chair in the hall.*

STEPHEN. Right.

ANNA *stands, begins to walk to door.*

Your handbag.

She stops, turns, picks up her handbag walks, to door,
to him.
The telephone rings.

Interior. Hall.
ANNA *and* STEPHEN *still, at door. Outside, morning*
light. The phone rings. He walks into hall and lifts it.

STEPHEN. Hullo? . . . Yes? . . . Oh, have you? . . . Sorry,
I've been asleep, didn't hear it . . . Yes . . . Ah
. . . I see . . . But she's all right? . . . Yes . . .
I'll get dressed and . . . get there. Thank you . . .
Thank you. (*He lowers receiver, lifts it quickly.*)
Oh, I'm sorry I didn't hear the – (*He replaces re-*
ceiver.)

STEPHEN *walks to the door. They go out. The door closes.*

Exterior. Quiet road in Oxford. Morning.
The road is silent. On one side of it is a tree-lined open space. On the other, a wall.
STEPHEN'S *car approaches at far end of road.*
It approaches and slides quietly in to the kerb.
The car, stationary, in long shot.
Early sunshine. Silence.

Interior. Car.
STEPHEN *and* ANNA *sitting. He looks up the road and glances into the mirror.*

STEPHEN. Can you get in . . . without anyone seeing you?

He looks at her.

ANNA. Mmnn.
STEPHEN. No one must see you.

Birds, seen through the windscreen, skim down across the road.
ANNA *gets out of the car.*
ANNA *closes car door quietly and walks along by the wall. She stops and returns.*

Interior. Car.
STEPHEN *leans over and winds passenger window down.*
She leans in at window.

STEPHEN. What?
ANNA. You'll have to help me up.

He grimaces.

I can't get over the wall by myself.
STEPHEN (*muttering*). Why didn't you say so—

Exterior. Car.
He gets out, closes door quietly.

Exterior. Road. The wall.
ANNA *walking by wall, followed by* STEPHEN.
She stops at a part of the wall where a large tree over-
hangs.
ANNA. Here.

STEPHEN *hoists her up.*

Exterior. Women's college grounds.
The other side of the wall. The tree.
ANNA'S *head and shoulders rise above wall.*
She clasps branch of the tree, sits on wall, throws
handbag down on to grass.

Exterior. Road. Wall.
STEPHEN *looking up, his hands raised.* ANNA'S *left*
leg swings over. She disappears over wall.
His face, glancing sharply up the road.

Interior. Hospital.
Baby in gauze tent. Tubes lead into it.
The baby's mouth is moving. Its eyes are shut.
Camera moves up to see the back of STEPHEN'S *head*
going out of ward door.

Interior. Private room. Hospital.
ROSALIND *in bed.* STEPHEN *sitting by bed.*
ROSALIND *speaks very quietly.*
ROSALIND. They phoned you. You weren't there.
STEPHEN. I was asleep. I didn't hear.

Pause.

ROSALIND. He can't breathe. It's difficult for him to breathe.

Did you see that?

STEPHEN. But he is breathing. They're helping him.

ROSALIND. He isn't dead?

Pause.

STEPHEN. No.

Interior. Women's college. Living quarters.
STEPHEN *walking up stone stairway to* ANNA's *room.*
Below him, at foot of steps, sunlight frames in quadrangle arch. His steps echo.
CHARLEY *appears in arch, looks up, calls.*

CHARLEY. Stephen.

STEPHEN *turns on step.* CHARLEY *ascends, reaches him.* STEPHEN *is calm, almost detached.* CHARLEY *is panting.*

I've just heard. About William.

Pause.

You found him.

STEPHEN. Yes.

Pause.

CHARLEY. Does she know?

Pause.

STEPHEN. I don't know.

CHARLEY *looks up to her room.*

CHARLEY. Have you just come to tell her?

STEPHEN. Yes.

Pause.

CHARLEY. It must have been terrible for you.

Pause.

Look, leave this to me, if you like.

STEPHEN. No, it's all right.

They turn up the stairs.

Interior. ANNA's *room.*
There are two cases on the bed.
ANNA *is packing. There is a knock on the door and the door opens.* CHARLEY *and* STEPHEN *enter.*
She stops packing.
CHARLEY *walks forward, looks at cases.*

CHARLEY. What are you doing?

She does not answer.

You've heard what's happened?

Pause.

ANNA. Yes.

Pause.

CHARLEY. I'm sorry.

STEPHEN *sits down in an armchair.* CHARLEY *turns to him.*

What happened? Was he drunk? They say there was whisky all over the car. Was there?

STEPHEN. I didn't notice.

CHARLEY. But you found him.

ANNA *continues packing.*

(*To* ANNA.) How did you hear about it?

He goes to her.

What are you doing? Why are you packing?

ANNA. I'm going home.

STEPHEN *in chair, eyes half closed.*
CHARLEY *stands, bewildered.*
ANNA *bending at suitcase.* CHARLEY *stands.*

CHARLEY. Why?

ANNA *moves to collect some records, comes back, packs them under dresses.*

Why are you going home?

STEPHEN. They were going to be married.

CHARLEY. Rubbish.

STEPHEN. He told me.

CHARLEY. It's rubbish.

CHARLEY *moves to* ANNA.

Look, I know it's . . . terrible. But listen . . . there's no reason for you to go home.

He touches her shoulder.
Her shoulder. She withdraws her shoulder from his hand quickly.
ANNA *continues packing.*
CHARLEY *grips her arm. She becomes still.*
STEPHEN, *half-closed lids.*

STEPHEN. Why don't you leave her alone?

CHARLEY *takes his hand away from* ANNA. *She collects books.* CHARLEY *stands, lost, in the centre of the room.*

CHARLEY. How did she hear about it? I've just heard it from the Provost. Wake up.

STEPHEN. I haven't slept. Sorry. I'm a bit tired.

ANNA *snaps suitcases shut.*

ANNA. It was kind of you both to come.

She goes to the mirror and begins to lipstick her mouth.
CHARLEY *bends over* STEPHEN's *chair, whispers.*

CHARLEY (*whispering*). What's the matter with her? She didn't care anything about him. Nothing. What's she going home for? It's ridiculous.

STEPHEN. There's nothing to keep her here.

CHARLEY. She loves me. What are you talking about?

ANNA *walks to cases.*

ANNA. My taxi should be here.

STEPHEN. Have you got a flight?
ANNA. Yes. I've booked a flight.

CHARLEY *sits down in a chair.*
STEPHEN *stands, goes to cases.*

STEPHEN. I'll take these down.

STEPHEN *leaves the room.*

CHARLEY (*to* ANNA). Why don't you stay for the funeral?

ANNA *goes to* CHARLEY, *holds out her hand.*

ANNA. Goodbye.

CHARLEY *looks up at her, grins, does not take her hand.*
ANNA *goes.*
CHARLEY *sits quite still.*

Exterior. Women's college. Day.
STEPHEN *closes taxi door.* ANNA *leans back on the back seat. The taxi drives off.*
STEPHEN *looks after it, then glances back, through the gate, into the college grounds.*
On the college lawn, in long shot, CHARLEY *stands alone.*
STEPHEN *standing, from* CHARLEY'S *point of view.*
STEPHEN *walks away.*

NOTE : The following scenes until the end of the film are silent except for :
The hum of a car growing on the soundtrack. The sound grows. It includes jamming gear changes and sharp braking.
The sound begins very quietly.

Exterior. Cloister. Day.
STEPHEN *walks through cloister towards his study slowly.*

Exterior. House. Day.
(*Identical shot as at the beginning of the film*).
CLARISSA *and* TED *running over gravel towards front door.* CLARISSA *falls, holds her leg, cries.*
The sound of the car draws closer.
STEPHEN *comes out of house, picks her up, comforts her, carries her into house, her arms around him,* TED *following. The dog runs after them.*
Camera slowly moves back to long shot outside the gate.
It comes to rest.
Sound of the car skidding.
A sudden screech, grind, smash and splintering.
Camera withdraws down the drive to the gate.
The house still, in the sunlight.
Silence.
Sound of ignition, ticking.

The Go-Between

The Go-Between is a World Film Services Production presented by EMI/MGM* with the following cast:

MARIAN	Julie Christie
TED	Alan Bates
MRS MAUDSLEY	Margaret Leighton
MR MAUDSLEY	Michael Gough
TRIMINGHAM	Edward Fox
LEO	Dominic Guard
MARCUS	Richard Gibson
DENYS	Simon Hume-Kendall
KATE	Amaryllis Garnet
CHARLES	Roger Lloyd-Pack
BLUNT	John Rees
STUBBS	Keith Buckley
RECTOR	Gordon Richardson
COLSTON	Michael Redgrave

Directed by Joseph Losey

* *At the time of going to press, the date of first showing was not yet fixed*

The Go-Between

The action of this film takes place during a span of 3 weeks in August in the summer of 1900 except for certain scenes, which take place in the present. The 'present' is any time in the last 20 years.

Exterior. English countryside. A river. Summer. Day.
The river comes out of the shadow of a belt of trees. It flows gently through the weeds and rushes. Heat haze. Steam rising from rushes.
Sound of approaching horses' hooves. A pony carriage drives by on the road, glimpsed only fragmentarily through the leaves. It passes.
Silence.
The camera is still, looking through the leaves towards the silent road. In the distance, a 1900 farm machine, horse drawn, can be seen, moving slowly.
Sound of the flowing river.
The voice of an elderly man, COLSTON, *heard over:*
COLSTON'S VOICE (OVER)
The past is a foreign country. They do things differently there.

Exterior. Gravel road. Long shot.
The pony and carriage trotting. On it are MARCUS, LEO, *a* FOOTMAN *and an* UNDERCOACHMAN. MARCUS *is pointing across the fields.*
From viewpoint of the carriage see Brandham Hall in the distance.
The carriage goes downhill. Brandham Hall lost.

Interior. House. Back stairs.
The back stairs are rambling and narrow. MARCUS
and LEO, *followed by footman, climb up. Doors, other*
passages glimpsed.
They reach MARCUS's *room.*

Interior. MARCUS's *room.*
There is one small window high in the wall. An old
terrier jumps from the four-poster bed as the door
opens and MARCUS *and* LEO *enter.*
The dog jumps up at them.

MARCUS. This is Dry Toast.

Exterior. Front of house. Lawn.
In foreground the shape of a girl lying in a hammock.
The wide lawn falls away before the house on a gentle
slope. Cedars, elms. The hammock, faded crimson
canvas, swings gently. In background figures in white
playing croquet.

Interior. House. Main hall.
A butler carrying a bowl of flowers walks up the
double staircase, which is shaped like a horse-shoe,
and goes out of shot.
MARCUS *and* LEO *appear at the top of the staircase.*
They run down it at different sides. At the foot of it
LEO *turns to look up.*

Exterior. Lawn.
Men in white flannels, white boots and straw boaters,
women in white dresses and hats playing croquet.

Interior. House. Main hall.
LEO *turns from staircase, glances through open double*
doors to a long room with large windows.

The camera pans to see into the room. A long shining mahogany table.

Interior. House. Open front door.
MARCUS *turns from the door.*

MARCUS. Come on, slug.

LEO *moves quickly and threateningly after him to the front of the house.*
Framed in the door a girl in a hammock can be seen, on the lawn, in the distance.

Exterior. Lawn.
Hammock in foreground, the girl in it is still not clearly seen. Indistinguishable shapes of several people lounging in the shade.
In background LEO *and* MARCUS *run out of the house.*
A GUEST'S VOICE (OVER)
Who's that?

Exterior. Derelict outhouses.
LEO *and* MARCUS *wander about derelict outhouses, rubbish heap and disused vegetable gardens, swishing twigs about them. The paths are overgrown. Flies. They walk into denser undergrowth.*

MARCUS. My sister is very beautiful.
LEO. Yes.

They approach a roofless outhouse. In it is a large glossy shrub with bell shaped flowers. They stop. The camera goes before them and stops, regarding the shrub. Their voices over :

LEO. What's that?
MARCUS. It's a deadly nightshade, you oaf!
LEO. Atropa belladonna.
MARCUS. Atropa what?

LEO. Atropa belladonna. It's poisonous. Every part of it is poison.

Two shot. MARCUS *and* LEO.
MARCUS *thrusts* LEO *towards the shrub.*

MARCUS. Die.

LEO *resists.* MARCUS *runs through the outhouses,* LEO *following. The camera watches them with the bell-shaped flowers of the shrub in foreground.*

Exterior. MARIAN *in hammock. Lawn.*
Her eyes are closed in the sun. They open.
LEO *walking alone along grass verge of the garden. He slowly comes to a halt, looks down.*
MARIAN *in hammock from* LEO'S *point of view.*
Close-up of MARIAN.
Her eyes are half closed.

Interior. House. Back stairs.
LEO *standing in dark passage. Sudden laughter from servants' quarters.*
LEO'S *point of view. Kitchen door half open.*
Glimpsed in the kitchen, two women: The cook and the under-cook, both fat. They are giggling. Steam from saucepans.

Exterior. Close-up of MARIAN. *Lawn.*
Her head turns quickly on her shoulder, her eyes are open.

Interior. MARCUS'S *room. Evening.*
LEO *is washing his hands in a bowl. He wipes them and looks at himself in a small mirror.*

Interior. Hall. Evening.
LEO *descending the stairs. He draws near the half-open door of the drawing-room and stops. Voices:*

MRS MAUDSLEY. Didn't you say his mother is a widow, Marcus?

MARCUS. I think so. I don't really know very much about him.

MR MAUDSLEY. Seems to be a nice lad.

MARCUS. I do have an impression that he lives in rather a small house with his mother.

MRS MAUDSLEY. Yes. He seems to be a very nice boy. Now – is everyone here?

LEO *opens the door and goes in.*

Interior. Drawing-room.
LEO *at the door.*

MRS MAUDSLEY. Ah, Leo. Good evening.

LEO. Good evening Mrs Maudsley.

MRS MAUDSLEY. Now, let us go into dinner.

They all move to the door.

A GUEST. You were in cracking form to-day at croquet, Marian.

MARIAN. Was I?

DENYS. Marian is quite formidable at croquet.

MARIAN. Am I?

Interior. Hall.
The party moving through the hall. MRS MAUDSLEY *with* LEO.

MRS MAUDSLEY. I believe we must be wary of you, Leo, I understand you're a magician. Is that true?

LEO. Well . . . not really . . . only, you know . . . at school.

LEO *glances over his shoulder at* MARCUS.

Anyway it was supposed to be a secret actually.

Interior. Dining-room. Night.
Candlelight. Glow of silver. The family and guests move to the table.

MARCUS. His curses are fearful. He cast a fiendish spell on two boys at school. They fell off the roof and were severely mutilated.

DENYS. Did they die?

LEO. Oh no. They were just a little . . . you know . . . severely mutilated.

MR MAUDSLEY. Was it difficult to arrange? I mean to get them to fall off the roof without killing them.

LEO. Well, it wasn't a killing curse, you see. There are curses and curses. It depends on the curse.

MRS MAUDSLEY. How frightening.

MRS MAUDSLEY sits. They all sit. MARIAN leans forward.

MARIAN. You're not going to bewitch us here, are you?

LEO. Oh no, I shouldn't think so.

Laughter.

Interior. Bedroom. Night.
MARCUS and LEO in bed. MARCUS asleep. LEO awake.
Laughter from the lawn below. A piano playing. A girl's voice singing. LEO looks up at the high window above his bed. Clear night sky. Voices float in.

Exterior. House. Disused game larder under a yew tree. Day.
This structure is empty but for a thermometer which hangs on the wall.
LEO is staring at it. The temperature is eighty-three. He turns. MR MAUDSLEY is behind him.

MR MAUDSLEY. Hello. Enjoying yourself?

LEO. Yes sir.

MR MAUDSLEY. Good. Pretty warm. What does it say?

LEO. Eighty-three.

MR MAUDSLEY. Warm.

MR MAUDSLEY studies LEO's clothes.

Suit a little warm, is it?

LEO. No, sir.

MR MAUDSLEY *taps the thermometer.*

MR MAUDSLEY. Enjoying yourself?

LEO. Yes thank you, sir.

MR MAUDSLEY. Good.

Interior. Bedroom. Day.
LEO *wiping his sweating face with a handkerchief.*

LEO. Do you think I should sport my cricket togs?

MARCUS. I wouldn't. Only cads wear their school clothes in the holidays. And another thing. When you undress you mustn't fold your clothes and put them on the chair. You must leave them lying wherever they happen to fall. The servants will pick them up. That's what they're for.

Close-up of DENYS.

DENYS. You are looking hot. Haven't you something cooler to wear?

The camera withdraws to find LEO *and* DENYS *with a group of young people in the hall.*

LEO. I'm not hot, really.

DENYS. Isn't that a Norfolk jacket?

LEO. Yes.

DENYS. Well it's quite appropriate then, isn't it? After all we are in Norfolk.

They move through the open front door on to the lawn.

Exterior. Lawn.
Close-up of large silver tea-pot pouring tea into tea-cups.
The camera shifts to look along the tea table which is laden with watercress, tomato, cucumber and lettuce

sandwiches, scones, muffins, cream cakes, pastries etc. Voices over:

DENYS. Have we a pair of bellows, Mother?

MRS MAUDSLEY. Why?

DENYS. To cool Leo.

MRS MAUDSLEY. Does Leo need cooling?

LEO. I may look hot, but I'm really quite cool underneath.

The camera shifts and settles to look at the gathering.

MRS MAUDSLEY. Did you leave your summer clothes at home?

LEO. I expect Mother forgot to put them in.

Silence. Stirring of cups.

MRS MAUDSLEY. Why don't you write and ask her to send them?

MARIAN. Oh that would take too long, Mama. Let me take him into Norwich tomorrow and get him a new outfit. Would you like that, Leo?

LEO. I haven't any money. At least only –

MARIAN. They can be your birthday present from us. When is your birthday?

LEO. Well . . . it's on the twenty-seventh of this month, actually. I was born under the sign of Leo.

MARIAN. Good. I can give you a lionskin.

DENYS. Or a mane.

Close-up of MARIAN.
She is sipping her tea.

MARIAN. Well, we'll go tomorrow.

Close-up of MRS MAUDSLEY.
MRS MAUDSLEY raises her eyes and looks at MARIAN.

MRS MAUDSLEY. Wouldn't you rather wait until Monday, when Hugh will be here, and make a party to go to Norwich?

DENYS (OVER). Trimingham? I thought he'd gone to Goodwood.

MR MAUDSLEY (OVER). Hugh coming?

MRS MAUDSLEY. Yes, I had a letter from him. He comes on Saturday and stays until the end of the month.

Close-up of MARIAN. *Her eyes are hooded.*
She sips her tea. MRS MAUDSLEY'S VOICE OVER:
Are you sure you couldn't wait until Monday?
MARIAN *looks up and smiles.*

MARIAN. Norwich will hardly be a treat for Hugh, Mama, trailing round the shops. Besides, by Monday Leo will have melted into butter. And all he'll need will be a muslin bag.

Close-up of MRS MAUDSLEY.
She holds her tea-cup faintly smiling.

Close-up of MARIAN.

May we go, Mama?

Close-up of MRS MAUDSLEY.

MRS MAUDSLEY. Yes, of course you may.

Exterior. Country road. Day.
Pony and carriage trotting. MARIAN *and* LEO *on it.*
It trots into the distance.
COLSTON'S VOICE (OVER) (*murmuring*)
You flew too near the sun and you were scorched.

Exterior. Cathedral Square. Norwich.
A footman sits waiting on the carriage. Parcels and boxes are piled up.

Interior. Hotel restaurant. Norwich.
MARIAN *and* LEO *at a table.* LEO *wears a new green suit.*

MARIAN. What did your father do?
LEO. He worked in a bank actually. And he was a pacifist.
MARIAN. Ah.
LEO. Mmm. And he was a book collector. He liked books very much. And so he collected them. That

was his hobby. Mother said they're quite valuable.
We might have to sell them.

MARIAN. Here's your pudding.

The waiter places a large plum pudding in front of
LEO. *He begins to eat.*

What's it like?

LEO. Very good.

MARIAN *is served with coffee. She sips it.*

MARIAN. Used any Black Magic on anyone lately?

LEO (*through food*). Not lately, no.

MARIAN. I envy you your power. What's it like to have such
power at your finger tips?

LEO. Oh it makes you feel fairly good. But I only ever
use it at school, you know.

MARIAN. Can you teach me? I could use it here.

LEO. Would you really want to?

MARIAN. Oh not really. The results might be too alarming.

Exterior. Lobby hotel.
MARIAN *and* LEO.

MARIAN. Would you like to amuse yourself in the Cathedral
for an hour? I have some shopping to do.

LEO. Yes. Certainly.

MARIAN. Can you amuse yourself in a Cathedral?

She giggles.

Exterior. Cathedral.
LEO *wanders through the crowded market and stands
to look up at the Cathedral.*

Exterior. Village street. Long shot. Very still.
Morning.   PRESENT
*The sky is overcast. (The sky is constantly overcast
in all present-day shots.)*

The street is more or less deserted. A couple of parked cars.
COLSTON *stands in the distance, looking down the street.*
LEO'S VOICE (OVER)
Well, it wasn't a killing curse, you see. There are curses and curses. It depends on the curse.

The man begins to walk down the street.

Interior. Cathedral.   PAST
LEO *looking up at the vaulted roof.*

Exterior. Square. The pony carriage.
The coachman raises his whip in salute. The camera pans to LEO, *who raises his hand and walks towards a statue in the centre of the square where he stands waiting.*
LEO's *point of view. The square.*
Drowsy traffic of carriages. Men and women walking through the market, which is now much quieter.
Suddenly the camera concentrates on a distant corner of the square. MARIAN *is talking to a man, not identifiable. The man raises his hat.* MARIAN *turns and threads her way slowly through the traffic. She suddenly sees* LEO, *waves her parasol and quickens her step.*

Exterior. The river. Afternoon.
Silence.

Interior. The house. Drawing-room.
LEO *is standing on a chair in his new suit revolving. Group of people admiring him.*
AD LIB. Superb! Dazzling! Most impressive! What a splendid green! Remarkably elegant! Most fetching! Charming!

DENYS. Did you get the tie at Challow and Challow?

MARIAN. Of course.

DENYS. And where did you get the shoes?

MARIAN. At Sterling and Potter.

DENYS. What green is this?

MARIAN. Lincoln green.

DENYS. I thought so. I shall dub you Sir Robin Hood.

A GIRL. Do you feel different?

LEO. Yes. I feel quite another person.

Laughter. LEO *gets off the chair.* MRS MAUDSLEY *leads him to the window.*

MRS MAUDSLEY. Let me have a proper look at you.

She feels the material and examines the smoked pearl buttons.

Yes, I think it does very well, and I hope your mother will think so too. Have you written to her, Leo?

LEO. Oh yes I have.

MRS MAUDSLEY. Good. You've chosen very well, Marian. Did you do any shopping for yourself?

MARIAN. Oh no, Mama. That can wait.

MRS MAUDSLEY. It mustn't wait too long. You didn't see anyone in Norwich, I suppose?

MARIAN. Not a soul. We were hard at it all the time, weren't we Leo?

Pause.

LEO. Yes, we were.

Interior. Platform Norwich Station. Long shot.

PRESENT

COLSTON *walks along the platform carrying a small case. He declines a porter's help. The camera watches him move into the ticket hall where a chauffeur in a peak cap approaches him.*

COLSTON *and* CHAUFFEUR *walk to a car. The man gets in, the* CHAUFFEUR *puts the case in the boot.*

Over this last shot the following dialogue heard, fragmentarily:

MRS MAUDSLEY. I'm afraid he can't without his mother's permission. Your mother has written to me that you're liable to colds. But you can watch the others bathe, of course.

Pause.

MARCUS. Why are you bringing your bathing suit if you're not allowed to swim?

LEO. Well, it is a bathing party.

MARCUS. But you're not going to swim.

LEO. I know I'm not.

MARCUS. In that case why – ?

The car moves away from the station.

Exterior. The river. Day.   PAST
Silence.
Voices heard approaching. Indecipherable chatter. Giggling. Immediately voices are heard the camera moves along the river bank, in front of and at a distance from the characters.
A black peeling construction (a diving pier) is suddenly found. A man emerges from the rushes. The camera stops abruptly. The man is wearing tight woollen trunks. The voices cease. The man climbs onto the platform, stands a moment, and then dives into the river. He swims away.

DENYS'S VOICE (OVER). What cheek! The man's trespassing. What shall we do?

GUEST'S VOICE. Order him off.

DENYS. What cheek!

Exterior. River bank. The group.
MARIAN *and* KATE *are in foreground.*

KATE. Who can he be?

MARIAN. I don't know.

KATE. He's a good swimmer. And really rather well built. Don't you think?

MARIAN *turns away.*

MARIAN. Come on, Kate, we'll go and change.

MARIAN *and* KATE *go towards a small hut among the rushes. The others walk down to the river.*

DENYS. Shall we order him off?

Point of view of group. Man swimming in river. The man sees them and swims towards them.

DENYS. It's Ted Burgess.

MAN. Who's he?

DENYS. The tenant of Black Farm. We can't be rude to him. He farms the land on the other side.

MAN. Perhaps you'd better be nice to him.

DENYS. I'll just say how do you do to him. We don't know him socially of course, but I think I should be nice to him, don't you?

MAN. I would say so.

DENYS. In that case I shall. I shall be particularly nice to him.

TED *hauls himself up from the water by means of a fixed spiked post. For a moment he appears to be about to impale himself on it. But he jumps onto the bank.* DENYS *moves forward to shake his hand.*

What a way to land! There are some steps over there.

TED. Oh I've always done it this way.

He looks at the group.

I didn't know anyone was going to be here. Just started on the harvest . . . got so hot . . .

DENYS. Don't worry at all, please. We were hot too . . . up at the Hall . . . very hot . . .

Pause.

Trimingham's coming to-night.

TED. Uh. Is he?

Pause.

I won't be long. Just one more header.

DENYS. Absolutely. Absolutely.

TED *raises his hand, turns, runs up to the platform, the camera panning up to watch him, and dives into the water.*
DENYS *turns to the others.*

I think I put him at his ease, don't you?

Exterior. The rushes.
DENYS *and his friend undressing in the rushes. The camera moves to find* MARCUS *undressing,* LEO *watching.* LEO *begins to untie his tie.*

MARCUS. You don't intend to put on your bathing suit, do you? I shouldn't put on a bathing suit if you're not going to bathe. It would look absurd.

LEO *reties the tie, and strolls away, his bathing suit over his shoulder.*
TED *climbing on to river bank.*
DENYS, GUEST *and* MARCUS, *splashing in river.*
LEO *watching.*
MARIAN *and* KATE *pushing each other, giggling. They wear long bathing dresses.*
LEO *suddenly crouching in rushes.*
Through the rushes glimpse a glistening body, moving. The body sinks to the ground. LEO *raises himself to peer through the rushes.*
TED *lies down in the sun, stretches his arms, and scratches his chest.*
LEO *watching.*
MARIAN'S VOICE (OVER)
My hair's come down! It's all wet!
LEO *turns his head quickly.*
TED *jumps up, pulls on his clothes swiftly, swears as he fastens his leather belt and moves swiftly away.*

Exterior. River bank.
MARIAN *standing holding the long coils of her hair in front of her.*
LEO *runs down to her.*

MARIAN. It's all wet. I shall never get it dry.

She looks at LEO.

Oh you do look so dry and smug. I should like to throw you in the river.

She laughs.

Has that man gone?

LEO. Yes. He went off in a hurry. His name is Ted Burgess, he's a farmer. Do you know him?

MARIAN. I may have met him.

Exterior. Village street. Morning. ***PRESENT***
A car appears round the corner and draws slowly to a halt. The engine is cut off. No one emerges. The village street is silent. Over this shot, MARIAN's *voice:*

MARIAN. It's dripping on my dress.

Exterior. River bank. Twilight. ***PAST***
Close-up of LEO.

LEO. Here's my bathing suit. It's *quite* dry. If you fasten it round your neck, so that it hangs down your back, then you can spread your hair on it, and your hair will get dry and your dress won't get wet.

Two shot. MARIAN *and* LEO.
MARIAN *is pinning the bathing suit at her throat.*
LEO *drapes it over her shoulders.*

MARIAN. Spread my hair on it. Take care not to pull it.

LEO *does so. She cries out.* LEO *looks at her in alarm. She smiles.* LEO *drapes her hair delicately.*

Is it well spread?

Exterior. Long shot. Path through the trees.
MARIAN and LEO walking through the lengthening
shadows. The others straggling behind.

MARIAN. Is it dry?

LEO touches her hair. She cries out. LEO takes his
hand away sharply. She giggles.

What a comfort . . . your bathing suit on my
shoulders. Is my hair well spread?

LEO. Oh yes. It is.

Exterior. Front of house. Evening.
The house is lit. MARIAN and LEO walk up the slope.
She stops, takes the bathing suit from her shoulders
and hands it to him.

MARIAN. Is it dry?

He touches her hair. She does not cry out.

LEO. Yes.

She touches her hair.

MARIAN (*smiling*). Yes, it is.

Interior. House. Main hall. Morning.
The gong sounds. One or two figures walk across the
hall. LEO appears at the top of the stairs and bounds
down.
Camera follows him as he walks swiftly into the
breakfast room. MR MAUDSLEY is seated at the top
of the table. All other chairs drawn back and ranged
round the walls. On the sideboard stand the breakfast
dishes.
LEO makes for a particular chair, sits down on it,
and moves about to test its creak. It does not creak.
He moves to another chair, sits and does the same. It
creaks sharply. He relaxes in the chair. One or two
guests take their seats. The servants file in and take

theirs. From the servants: 'Good morning Mr Maudsley.' 'Good morning, Mrs Maudsley'.
The servants comprise: An elegant housekeeper, three round cooks, a short elderly gardener, a neat slender butler, a tall footman, two burly coachmen, two very young maids and a skinny pantry maid, even younger.
Close shot. LEO *kneeling.*
MR MAUDSLEY *begins to say morning prayers in the background.*
A figure kneels beside LEO. *He looks up. The man is a stranger. His face is scarred.* TRIMINGHAM.
Two shot. LEO *and* TRIMINGHAM.
MR MAUDSLEY *saying prayers in background.* LEO *observes* TRIMINGHAM *sideways.*

Interior. Breakfast room. Men walking about eating porridge.
The ladies are seated. LEO *holds his plate very carefully.*

MRS MAUDSLEY. Now, everybody. Let us decide what we shall do today. Hugh . . . ?

She looks at TRIMINGHAM. LEO *looks at* TRIMINGHAM.

Come, sit down and advise us.

TRIMINGHAM *sits down next to her.*

Now what do you suggest?

Interior. House. MARCUS *and* LEO's *bedroom door.*
An envelope is fixed on the door, with NO ADMITTANCE *written on it.* LEO *opens the door and goes in.*

Interior. Bedroom.
MARCUS *is in bed. The dog growls.*
LEO. What's up?

MARCUS. Decent of you to trickle along, but don't come in. I have a headache and some spots. Mama thinks it may be measles.

LEO. Hard cheese.

MARCUS. See Trimingham?

LEO. Is he the man with the face?

MARCUS. Yes. Got it in the war. He was gored by the Boers.

LEO. Hard cheese.

Exterior. Village. Morning.
Church bells.
The house party is passing down the village street on its way to the church.
They pass a cottage. The camera rests momentarily on the cottage.

Exterior. Church. Long shot.
The party, going through the church door.

Exterior. Church door.
LEO *looking into the church.*

Interior. Church. LEO's *point of view.*
Bell ringers at the back of the church, pulling the bell ropes.

Exterior. Cottage. Day.   *PRESENT*
The camera, motionless, looking at the same cottage door.
Church bells heard over.
COLSTON's *back comes into shot.*

Exterior. Village street. Day.   *PAST*
The procession passing the cottage on the way back from church. TRIMINGHAM *joins* LEO.

TRIMINGHAM. I don't think we've been introduced. My name is Trimingham.

LEO. How do you do, Trimingham.

TRIMINGHAM. You can call me Hugh, if you like.

LEO *looks at him.*

Or Trimingham, if you prefer.

LEO. Why not Mister Trimingham?

TRIMINGHAM. I think Trimingham is slightly more in order, if you prefer it to Hugh.

LEO. But why not Mister?

TRIMINGHAM. Well as a matter of fact I'm a Viscount.

LEO. Viscount Trimingham?

TRIMINGHAM. That's right.

LEO. Oughtn't I to call you My Lord?

TRIMINGHAM. No, no. Hugh will do . . . or Trimingham if you like. What's your name?

LEO. Colston.

TRIMINGHAM. Mister Colston?

LEO. Well, Leo, if you like.

TRIMINGHAM. I'll call you, Leo, if I may.

LEO. Oh yes that's quite all right.

High shot. Group walking along lane.
Two shot. LEO *and* TRIMINGHAM.

TRIMINGHAM. Does Marian call you Leo?

LEO. Oh yes. I think she's ripping. I'd do anything for her.

TRIMINGHAM. What would you do?

LEO. Oh anything. Anything.

TRIMINGHAM. Would you like to take her a message for me?

LEO. Oh yes. What shall I say?

TRIMINGHAM. Tell her I've got her prayer book. She left it behind in church.

LEO *runs off.*

Exterior. Village street.   *PRESENT*
Car drawing to a halt. Engine cuts off. Silence.

MARIAN'S VOICE (OVER)
How careless. I forget everything. Please thank him for me.

Interior. House. Back stairs.   **PAST**
LEO passes MARCUS's *room. He glances at the* NO
ADMITTANCE *sign, pauses, and then goes on to a green baize door.*

Interior. LEO's *room.*
LEO enters and looks at it.
The room is very small. Narrow bed. On the sideboard his hairbrush, red collar box. Another largish locked box. He opens this and takes out two dry sea urchins, stumps of sealing wax, a combination lock, twists of whip cord. Under this gradually disclosed a locked book. He unlocks it, opens first page. We see 'Diary for the year 1900' in copper plate script. Round this cluster the signs of the zodiac; The Fishes, The Crab, The Scorpion, The Ram, The Bull, The Lion, The Archer, The Virgin and The Water Carrier.
LEO studies this page. He then turns the pages of the diary and stops at a page which contains incomprehensible lettering and in the centre:

CURSE THREE
AFTER CURSE THREE THE VICTIM DIES!
Given under my hand
and written in my BLOOD!
by order of
THE AVENGER

LEO shuts the book.

Exterior. Back of the house. The thermometer.
LEO staring at thermometer. The temperature is eighty-four.

Exterior. Front of house. Lawn.
MARIAN *in hammock. She lies still, gazing up into the trees.*

Exterior. River. The diving pier.
LEO *walks on to pier. Looks down into water.*

Exterior. Cornfield.
LEO *wanders through the corn. The stubble pricks his ankles. He comes to a gate, opens it, the camera with him. He turns into a farm road caked with hard mud and then into a farmyard.*
LEO *looking at a strawstack, a ladder running up it, in the farmyard. He opens the gate and walks into the yard. He stands looking at the height of the stack, and glances towards the silent farmhouse.*
He climbs the ladder to the strawstack, he looks down. He slides. A swift rush through the air. His knee, at the bottom, hits a chopping block. He falls off clutching his knee.

Medium shot TED.
TED *stands at the corner of the farmhouse holding two pails of water. He puts the pails down and strides towards* LEO.

TED. What the hell do you think you're doing? I've a good mind to give you the biggest thrashing you've ever had in your life.

TED *from* LEO's *point of view.*
TED *looking down at him.*

LEO. My knee!
TED. Get up! What the hell are you doing here? Who are you?
LEO. I know you! We've met!
TED. Met?

LEO. At the bathing place. You were bathing. I came with the others.
TED. Oh. You're from the hall.

Pause.

Can you walk?

Wide shot. Farmyard.
TED *helps* LEO *up. They walk.*
LEO. I saw you dive. You did it jolly well.

Interior. Farmhouse.
LEO *is sitting down.* TED *swabbing his knee with carbolic.*
TED. You were lucky. You might have spoiled your suit.
LEO. Miss Marian gave it to me. Miss Marian Maudsley.
TED. Oh did she? Is it stinging?
LEO. Yes.
TED. You're a spartan.

TED *takes out a handkerchief and ties it around the knee.*

LEO. Won't you want that?
TED. I've got plenty more. Try walking.

LEO *hobbles about the kitchen.*

LEO. Thank you very much, Mr Burgess. Is there . . . anything I can do for you?

Pause.

TED. Well, perhaps there is. (*Pause.*) Could you take a message for me?
LEO. Of course. Who to?

Shot across kitchen sink.
TED *approaches sink with bowl of discoloured water, empties it and swills it.* LEO *remains in background.*

TED. How old are you?

LEO. I shall be thirteen on the twenty-seventh of this month.

LEO's *point of view*. TED *turning to him from sink.* TED *looks at him in silence.*

TED. Can I trust you?

Close-up of LEO.
LEO *looks at him expressionless.*
Close-up of TED.

Can I?

Close-up of LEO.

LEO. Of course you can.

Wide shot. Kitchen.
TED *begins to walk around the room.*

TED. There's a boy, isn't there? A lad of your age.
LEO. He's in bed, with measles.
TED. Oh, is he? (*Pause.*) Are you . . . ever alone with anybody . . . in the house?
LEO. Nobody talks to me much. They're all grown up, you see. Except Marcus and he's in bed. Marian talks to me. Miss Marian.
TED. Oh does she?
LEO. She often talks to me. She talks to me most. When her hair was wet I . . .

Medium shot. TED *sitting at table.*

TED. Are you ever alone with her? I mean, just the two of you in a room, with no-one else.
LEO. Well, sometimes. Sometimes we sit together on a sofa.
TED. On a sofa?

Wide shot of room.
TED *stands, walks about the room.*

Could you give her a letter without anybody else seeing?
LEO. Of course I could.

Close-up of TED.
TED *regards him thoughtfully.*

TED. But can I trust you . . . to keep your mouth shut?

Close-up of LEO.
LEO *looks at him with some disdain.*
Close-up of TED.

Because . . . you see . . . it's a secret. (*Pause.*) All right. I'll trust you.

Wide shot. Room.
TED *takes pen, ink and paper from the sideboard and sits down at the table.*

We do some business together.
LEO. Secret business?
TED. That's right. No one else must see this letter. You understand?
LEO. Yes.
TED. If you can't get her alone don't give it to her. Put it in the place where you pull the chain.

Interior. House. Tea-time. Sitting-room.
LEO *sitting with handkerchief round his knee.*
MR MAUDSLEY. Yes, Ted Burgess, good-looking chap, rides well, I'm told. Good to know he was kind to you.
DENYS. Yes, how nice of him to be so nice. But I was very nice, of course, at the bathing place, wasn't I? (*To his mother.*) I put him very much at his ease, you know.
MRS MAUDSLEY. Did you?
MARIAN. I think I'd better dress that knee for you, Leo. It's looking a bit messy.

Interior. Bathroom.
LEO's *knee under the running tap.* MARIAN *bathing it. Handkerchief on the edge of the bath.*
MARIAN. Mmmm. There.

She wipes it with towel.
Camera rises as she stands. She collects bandage.
Shot over bath edge.
MARIAN *glances at the handkerchief and bends to fix bandage.*

Is that his?

LEO. Yes. He said he wouldn't want it back. Shall I throw it on the rubbish dump?

MARIAN. Oh I don't know. Perhaps I'll wash it out. It seems quite a good handkerchief.

LEO. Oh he asked me to give you this.

He takes a letter from his back pocket.

It's a bit crumpled.

She snatches the letter, standing.

MARIAN. Oh these dresses.

She tucks the letter up her sleeve.

Now the bandage.

LEO. You've put it on.

MARIAN. Oh yes.

She bends to him.

Now I'll put on your stocking.

LEO. Oh I can do that.

MARIAN. No, no, I'll do it.

Close two shot.
MARIAN *drawing the stocking up.*

You won't . . . tell anyone about this letter will you? You won't . . . will you?

LEO. Of course I won't.

MARIAN's *hand smooths the stocking and touches the bandage.*
Close-up of MARIAN *doing this.*

MARIAN (*softly*). There.

Exterior. Outhouses. The deadly nightshade.
The camera is still, looking at it. It glistens.
VOICES HEARD OVER:
COLSTON'S VOICE
Of course I won't.
MARIAN'S VOICE YOUNG (*softly*)
There.

Exterior. Meadow by stream. Day.
A picnic party. Numerous open hampers. Ladies and
gentlemen sitting on multi-coloured rugs. Footmen
serving food. Ham, cheese, eggs etc.
Over this shot and the next two shots the following
spasmodic dialogue is heard:

A GIRL. But Gussy doesn't dance.
A MAN. Doesn't he really?
GIRL. Not a step.
ANOTHER MAN. Shall you be going to Goodwood?
FIRST MAN. How odd. I thought I saw him dancing at Lady Mary's.
THIRD MAN. I think I shall go to Goodwood. Shall you?
GIRL. But he doesn't dance a step, I promise you.
SECOND MAN. Yes, I think I shall.

Amber wine being poured from tall bottles into goblets.
LEO *holding glass. A footman bends to him, pours*
fizzy lemonade into it from a bottle with a glass
marble for a stopper.
LEO *drinks lemonade and stands. In the background*
MARIAN *and* TRIMINGHAM *are sitting together. He*
is talking intently to her. LEO *strolls close to them.*
TRIMINGHAM *looks up.*

TRIMINGHAM. Hello, there's Mercury!
MARIAN. Why do you call him Mercury?
TRIMINGHAM. Because he takes messages.

Over the back of MARIAN's *head, rigid, to* TRIMING-
HAM *and* LEO.

MARIAN *turns away.*

You took a message for me, didn't you old chap? To this young lady, on the way from church. But it didn't fetch a very warm response.

MARIAN *laughs.*
Three shot. Relaxed.
MARIAN *laughing.*

(*To* LEO.) Do you know who Mercury was?

LEO. Mercury is the smallest of the planets.

TRIMINGHAM. Ah, but before that he was the messenger of the gods. He went to and fro between them.

Exterior. Picnic meadow. Late afternoon.
LEO *asleep in the grass.* MARIAN *and* MRS MAUDS-
LEY *seen in background. His eyes flicker.*

MARIAN. I think he must be bored to tears, trailing round with us. He'd be much happier pottering about on his own.

MRS MAUDSLEY. Do you think so? He's so devoted to you, he's your little man. Still, I can ask him. It is unfortunate about Marcus.

MARIAN. If Marcus has got the measles, I suppose we shall have to put off the ball.

MRS MAUDSLEY. Oh I don't think so. We should disappoint so many people. You wouldn't want to do that, would you?

MARIAN *and* MRS MAUDSLEY *rise and stroll away.*
LEO *sits up.*
From his viewpoint on the grass:
The carriages drawn up in the shade. Horses whisking their tails. The coachmen high up on their boxes, hats almost touching the branches.

Exterior. Road. Moving carriage.
LEO *and* COACHMAN BUFF *on the box seats of the carriage. Below them in the well of the carriage a roof of parasols.*

Exterior. A small village.
Carriages passing through the village. Children run along the road as they pass. The COACHMEN *throw pennies to them. The children scrabble for them.*
Medium shot. LEO *and* COACHMAN.
LEO *is watching the children. He turns abruptly to the* COACHMAN.

LEO. Do you know Ted Burgess?

BUFF. Ted Burgess? We all know him. He's a bit of a lad, Ted Burgess.

LEO. What do you mean by a lad? I should have said he was a full grown man.

The carriage has reached the top of a steep hill.

BUFF. Hold on, hold on. Here we go!

The descent begins, the coachman grinding the brakes the horses' hindquarters sweating. LEO *clutches the rail and turns sharply to look behind him up the hill. His face into the camera.*

Quick Cut. Close shot. A car door bangs shut.
PRESENT
Long shot.
COLSTON's *back standing by car in village street. He begins to walk down the street away from the camera.*

MARIAN's *skirt glimpsed flashing quickly by through weeds.*

The thermometer.
The marker points to ninety-four.
LEO *staring at it. His hand to his mouth.*
A voice behind him.

MR MAUDSLEY. Enjoying yourself?

LEO. Oh yes thank you, sir.

MR MAUDSLEY. Miss your mother?

LEO. Yes, sir – I mean . . . no, sir. A little, sir.

MR MAUDSLEY *peers at the thermometer.*

MR MAUDSLEY. Pretty hot today.

LEO. Is it a record?

MR MAUDSLEY. I shouldn't be surprised. I shall have to look it up. Hot weather suit you?

LEO. Yes sir.

Exterior. Back of house.
LEO *looking back at game larder.* MR MAUDSLEY's *back is bent towards the thermometer.*

Exterior. The derelict outhouses.
Camera, still, looks through tangled bush towards the half-hidden outhouses.
Flies. Silence.

Exterior. Front of house. Lawn.
LEO *walking past in foreground. In background figures strolling.*
TRIMINGHAM *turns in background and calls:*

TRIMINGHAM. Hi! Mercury! Come here! I want you.

Shot over TRIMINGHAM *to* LEO, *strolling in the distance.*
TRIMINGHAM *walks towards* LEO. *They meet in the centre of the lawn.*

Trying to sneak past in dead ground. (*Pause.*) Where were you off to?

LEO. Nowhere.

TRIMINGHAM. Ah. Nowhere. Well, would you like to go somewhere?

LEO. Well, yes . . . where?

TRIMINGHAM. That's up to you.

LEO. Oh.

TRIMINGHAM *laughs.*

TRIMINGHAM. I want you to find Marian. We need her to make a four at croquet. No idea where she is. Can you find her?

LEO. I don't know.

TRIMINGHAM. No one else could. But you can. Will you do that?

LEO. Yes.

> LEO *turns and begins to trot away.*
> TRIMINGHAM *calls after him.*

TRIMINGHAM. You must bring her back dead or alive!

> *Exterior. Back of the house.*
> LEO *wandering along, looking vaguely about, picks up a stone, throws it. Suddenly stops.*
> MARIAN *is walking along the cinder track from the outhouses.*
>
> *Close-up of* MARIAN.
> *She stops.*

MARIAN. What are you doing here?

LEO'S VOICE. Hugh asked me to find you.

MARIAN. Why?

LEO'S VOICE. He wants you to play croquet.

> MARIAN *does not reply. She moves away.*
> *Silence.*
> LEO *stands a moment, and then follows.*
> *Two shot.*

He said I was to bring you back dead or alive.

MARIAN. Well, which am I?

> *They laugh and begin to walk slowly towards the house.*

We're going to luncheon with some neighbours tomorrow. They're very old and mossy. I don't suppose you want to come, do you?

LEO. Oh no. I can stay here.

MARIAN. What will you do?

LEO. Oh . . . anything.

MARIAN. But what?

LEO. I might go for a walk.

MARIAN. Where to?

> *They stop.* MARIAN *sits on a bench.*

LEO. I might slide down a strawstack.
MARIAN. Oh. Whose?
LEO. Farmer Burgess.
MARIAN. Oh, his. Oh well, Leo, if you go that way perhaps you'd give him a letter for me.
LEO. I was hoping you'd say that.
MARIAN. Why? Because you like him?
LEO. Yes. But there's another reason.
MARIAN. What is it?
LEO. Because I like you.

Close-up of MARIAN.
She smiles.

MARIAN. That's very sweet of you.

Exterior. Cornfield. Day.
TED riding on a reaper, horse drawn, cutting corn.
Three labourers binding the sheaves. LEO appears,
walks beside the reaper. The reaper and LEO go
through the corn.
Medium shot of REAPER.
TED stops the horse and gets down. LEO gives him a
letter. TED opens it, reads it, stuffs it into his pocket.
TED. Tell her it's all right.

Interior. House. Long corridor. Evening.
MARIAN walking alone. She pauses, looks at a paint-
ing on a wall. LEO walks towards her, speaks quietly
to her. She walks on.

Exterior. Cornfield. Day.
TED standing with gun, pointed at a small area of
uncut corn. LEO watches from a distance. A labourer
moves through the corn calling 'sshoo'.
Close-up of TED with gun.
He shoots.
Close-up of rabbit.

The rabbit is flung into the air.
Close-up of LEO.
Two shot.
TED *holds out his hand for the letter. His hand is smeared with blood. He takes the letter from the envelope. The letter is smeared with blood.*
LEO. Look what you've done.

TED *stuffs the letter into his pocket.*

TED. Tell her it's no go.

Interior. Passage. Door of MARCUS's *room.*
Sign on door 'Safe entry'. LEO *opens door, peeps round it.*
MARCUS. You may enter boldly. My disease has fled.
LEO. You don't look better.
MARCUS. Of course I'm better. I shall be down this afternoon. You can bore me with your life story.

LEO *standing alone at the top of a flight of stairs in the back of the house. He runs down it.*

Interior. Front of house.
LEO *walking quickly down a passage.*

Interior. Writing room.
MARIAN *sitting at desk writing. She puts the letter in an envelope.* LEO *enters quickly, closes the door.*
LEO. Marian, Marcus is –

The latch clicks. She slips envelope into his hand, he slips it into his pocket. TRIMINGHAM *enters.*

TRIMINGHAM. Ah! A conspiracy. A love scene. May I seize you from this fortunate fellow?
MARIAN. Is seize an appropriate word?

TRIMINGHAM. Gather then. (*He holds out his hand to her.*) May I
gather you from this fortunate fellow?

MARIAN (*to* LEO). Do you mind if I'm gathered, Leo?

LEO. Oh no, not at all.

TRIMINGHAM *bows to* LEO *and leads* MARIAN *out.*

LEO *alone in writing room.*
He takes the letter from his pocket and looks at it.
It is unsealed.

Exterior. Side of the house. A part of the lawn.
Sounds of croquet. Smack of the mallet on the ball.
Taps of the balls hitting each other. Voices in the
distance:

A GIRL. Charles! Do come over here. Look at this beautiful
bird.

CHARLES. What is it?

GIRL. Isn't is pretty? Look at the pretty colours.

CHARLES. Never seen one like it, I must admit.

LEO *passes quickly through the shot.*

Exterior. Woods.
LEO *walking towards farm.*
He stops, takes the unsealed envelope from his pocket,
looks at it, puts it back.
He continues walking, stops, sits on a hillock, thinks.
He stands, walks, stops to look down into a valley.
Close-up of LEO.
He takes out the envelope and looks at it. He turns it
to the open flap. Handwriting can be discerned on the
paper. He looks at it upside down and swiftly turns it
right side up. The camera concentrates on the writing
on the paper.
The words exposed are:
Darling, Darling, Darling,
Same place, same time, this evening.

But take care not to –
Close-up of LEO, *his mouth open.*
LEO *sits down by a tree.*
His expression is one of utter disappointment and disbelief. He leans on his elbow. He grimaces.
He emits a number of short noises, grunts, and 'hahs', hollow laughs. He sits baffled. Looks at the words again.
He sighs, stands, seals the letter. He walks on, uttering further short noises. The loudest of these alarm some birds. They fly up.

Exterior. Farmyard gate.
In foreground LEO *is crouching looking into the farmyard. In background* TED *can be seen emerging from the stable door.* LEO *watches him move across the yard.*

Exterior. Farmyard. Reverse shot.
In background LEO *stands up.* TED *stops.*
TED. Hullo, how's the postman?
LEO. Very well, thank you.
TED. Brought anything for me?

LEO *hands him the letter.* TED *reads it.*

LEO. I'm afraid I shan't be able to bring you any more letters.

TED *stares at him.*

TED. Why not?
LEO. Marcus has got over his measles. I'll be with him all day. You said he wasn't to know. If he came here with me he would know.
TED. Have you told Miss Marian this?
LEO. No.
TED. She won't know what to do. Nor shall I.
LEO. What did you do before I came?
TED. Well . . . it wasn't so easy then.

Interior. Farmhouse. Kitchen.
The door opens. TED *comes in.* LEO *appears on the threshold, and stands in the doorway.* TED *walks about the room.*

TED. She likes you doesn't she? You want her to like you, don't you? You wouldn't want her to stop liking you. No . . . you wouldn't. (*Pause.*) She won't be the same to you, if you don't take the letters. That's the truth. They're not just ordinary letters. She'll miss them. So shall I. She'll cry perhaps. Do you want her to cry? (*Pause.*) It isn't hard to make her cry. She used to cry, before you came along.

LEO. Did you make her cry?

TED. She cried when she couldn't see me.

LEO. How do you know?

TED. Because she cried when she did see me.

LEO *walks into the room and sits down.*

Silence.

(*To himself.*) I've been busy. Smiler's going to have a foal. She's ill.

LEO. Why does she have it then if it makes her ill?

TED. She hasn't much choice.

LEO. What made her have one?

TED *looks at him.*

TED. What?

LEO. What made her have one?

TED *is silent for a moment, then laughs.*

TED. Between you and me she did a bit of spooning.

LEO. Spooning? I didn't know horses could spoon.

TED. Oh it's a silly word really.

LEO. What does it *mean*?

TED. You seem to know something about it.

LEO. I don't know anything about it. That's the point. It's all this kissing, isn't it? That's what it is. All that silly kissing. I've seen it on postcards at the seaside. You can't tell me horses do that.

TED. No, horses don't do that.

LEO. Well, what do they do? What does anyone do? There's more to it than just kissing, I know that. But what?

TED. You'll find out.

Pause.

LEO. Could you marry someone without ever spooning with them?

TED. Spooning's a silly word.

LEO. Well whatever the word is. Could you marry someone and never do . . . whatever it is?

TED. You could. But it wouldn't be a very lover-like thing to do.

Pause.
LEO *stares at him.*

LEO. Lover-like?

TED. That's enough questions anyway.

LEO. But you haven't told me anything.

TED. All right. Let's make a bargain. I'll tell you all about it on the condition you go on being our postman.

Close-up of LEO.

LEO. All right.

Interior. House. Drawing-room.
MARIAN *is arranging flowers by the window.*
LEO *runs in in cricket flannels.*

MARIAN. Hello. Don't you look marvellous? Are you in the team?

LEO. Well, not exactly. I'm twelfth man. Marcus, you see, is convalescent.

MARIAN. What's twelfth man?

LEO. First reserve.

MARIAN. Ah. Well maybe someone will drop dead and then you can play. (*She pricks her finger on a thorn.*) Blast!

LEO. I've got a message for you from Hugh. He wants to know if you'll sing at the concert.

MARIAN. Oh, does he? Well, tell him . . . that I'll sing
. . . if he sings too.

Exterior. Village street. Day.　　　**PRESENT**
The back of COLSTON *crossing the street towards a
young man who glances at him.*
TRIMINGHAM'S VOICE (OVER)
But I don't sing.

Exterior. Lane.　　　*PAST*
*The house team walking to the ground, dressed in
white. The camera finds* LEO *and* MARCUS.
LEO. Why did you say I couldn't wear my cap?
MARCUS. Because it's a school cap. If it was an England cap,
or a county cap, or a club cap, then, of course, you
could wear it. But to wear a school cap in a private
match simply isn't done.
LEO. Stomach pump!

Exterior. Cricket pavilion.
The village team stands in a line. TRIMINGHAM
leads LEO *along it.*
TRIMINGHAM. Burdock, this is our twelfth man, Colston.

BURDOCK *and* LEO *shake hands and mutter 'how do
you do'. This formula is repeated in all cases, with the
following men :* STUBBS, MERSHAM, TOMS, BLUNT,
HOLLYOAK, BATES, HANDSON, THORBURN,
BOLT *and lastly* TED BURGESS.
Close-up of LEO.
Three shot.
TED *smiles.*
TED. Oh we know each other, m'lord, Master Colston
and I, he comes to slide down my strawstack.
TRIMINGHAM. Of course. He's told us all about it.
LEO. Are you a good batsman?
TED. No, not me. I'm not much of a cricketer, really.

TRIMINGHAM. He can be very dangerous, Leo. We've got to get him out quickly.

TED. I'm not a cricketer. I just hit.

TRIMINGHAM. Well, we're going to get you out before you get the chance.

Exterior. Cricket ground.
Four old men sitting on a bench smoking pipes. The camera pans from them to see the ground filling up with spectators.
TRIMINGHAM *and* BURDOCK *on the field.* BURDOCK *spins a coin.* TRIMINGHAM *calls 'heads'. The coin lands. He looks at the coin, turns to the pavilion, and makes a gesture of batting.*

Exterior. Pavilion.
LEO *jumping across a bench to* MARCUS.
LEO. He's won the toss! We're batting!

Exterior. Ground scoreboard.
A boy approaches the scoreboard with two mugs of tea and hands them to the scorers.
A shout from the spectators. The scorer looks up and takes down the last batsman's score from the board.

Exterior. Pavilion.
The ladies of the house, including MRS MAUDSLEY *and* MARIAN, *walk to the pavilion to their seats. The gentlemen standing. They settle in their seats. The rector sits beside* MRS MAUDSLEY.
MARIAN *sits in front of them with* KATE. TRIMINGHAM *comes out of the pavilion, inclining his head to the ladies as he passes them. Applause.*
The camera pans from the ladies to find DENYS *with* LEO *and the rest of the team.*

DENYS. He's a pretty bat. A very pretty bat. I have great confidence in him.

Exterior. The pitch.
TRIMINGHAM *driving gracefully.*
MARIAN *applauding.*
DENYS *and* LEO.

DENYS. Isn't he fine? Such command and elegance. Don't you think he's fine?

LEO. Yes, I do.

A shout. They lean forward, shocked.
TRIMINGHAM *leaving the wicket. His stumps are down.*
MARIAN *applauding vigorously as* TRIMINGHAM *returns to the pavilion.* MR MAUDSLEY *comes out of the pavilion. Applause.*
DENYS *turns to* LEO.

DENYS. We're in trouble. There's only me to come. I mean that's any good, quite frankly.

Exterior. The pitch.
MR MAUDSLEY *tapping his bat on the ground, waiting for the ball. It is bowled. He places it calmly between two fielders and runs.*
MR MAUDSLEY *steering the ball calmly off his legs. He runs.*

Exterior. Pavilion.
DENYS. He's in some command. But he mustn't tire himself.

A shout. DENYS *jumps up.*

That's me. It's absolutely up to me. But I mustn't tire him. He's not young.

Exterior. Pitch.
MR MAUDSLEY *leaning on bat waiting.* DENYS *comes to arrive at the wicket.*

Shot over DENYS *to* MR MAUDSLEY *batting.*
MR MAUDSLEY *plays the ball and starts to run.*
DENYS's *hand shoots up.*
DENYS (*loudly*). No!

MR MAUDSLEY *looks at him with irritation.*
Long shot. Ground.
MR MAUDSLEY *plays the ball and starts to run.*
DENYS *flings up his hand.*
DENYS (*loudly*). No!

Exterior. Ground. LEO *and* MARCUS.
LEO. Why does he keep saying no?
MARCUS. He wants to save my father's strength. Which is a little unnecessary I think.

Exterior. Pitch.
MR MAUDSLEY *plays the ball and begins to run.*
DENYS *flings up his hand.*
DENYS. No!
MR MAUDSLEY (*shouting*). Come on!

MR MAUDSLEY *runs up the pitch.* DENYS, *late, begins to run. The ball is thrown in.* DENYS *stumbles, falls headlong, flat on his face. The ball has hit the wicket. He is out. He stands, dusts himself, and walks away.*
Close shot. MR MAUDSLEY.
He stands calmly, his hands on his hip.

Interior. Pavilion.
The teams are having tea. The camera tracks down the table.
TRIMINGHAM. Beautifully played, sir.
MR MAUDSLEY. Thank you very much. Now we have to get Burgess out.

The camera tracks. Sandwiches, buns etc.

LEO. What about Burgess? Isn't he dangerous?

DENYS. He's a strong hitter, I grant you. But he's no sense of culture or discipline. Trimingham will be far too cunning for him.

Exterior. Cricket pitch.
TED hitting six.
A tree.
The ball soars into a tree.
Close-up of LEO.
In foreground MARIAN intent. In background MRS MAUDSLEY intent.
They are both watching the game.
TED hitting six.
LEO applauding suddenly. He stops. Looks about him. The camera looks with him towards MARIAN. She is biting her lip.
The back of MRS MAUDSLEY's head in foreground. The back of MARIAN's head in background.
They are both still.
Close shot. TED.
He hits the ball hard.
A FIELDER half stops the ball with his hand, falls. The ball careers on.

Exterior. Pavilion.
The ball hurtling into the pavilion. It lands near the ladies' seats. MRS MAUDSLEY jumps up with a cry. MARIAN puts her hand to her mouth. The other ladies jump up.

RECTOR. Mrs Maudsley! Are you all right?

MRS MAUDSLEY. Yes, yes. Perfectly all right.

RECTOR. That was a close shave.

KATE. What a shock. He's terribly savage.

Close shot. LEO picking up the ball.
He looks up.

TRIMINGHAM'S
VOICE. Where's our twelfth man?

Two shot. MRS MAUDSLEY *and* MARIAN.
MRS MAUDSLEY *leans over.*

MRS MAUDSLEY. Are you all right, Marian?
MARIAN. Yes, Mama. Thank you.
MRS MAUDSLEY. The ball didn't hurt you?
MARIAN. It didn't touch me, Mama.

Exterior. Pitch.
TRIMINGHAM *walking with* LEO.
TRIMINGHAM (*muttering*). We've got to get him out or he'll beat us on his own.

TRIMINGHAM, *tossing the ball, walks to the bowler's end. The camera with* TRIMINGHAM *looks down the wicket at* TED. TRIMINGHAM *runs up to bowl. Bowls.* TED *swings, the ball beats him but misses the wicket.* TRIMINGHAM *flings up his arms.* TED *grins. The ball is returned to* TRIMINGHAM.
Close-up of LEO *watching.*
Close-up of TRIMINGHAM *turning.*
Close-up of TED *waiting for the ball.*
TRIMINGHAM *bowls.*
TED *drives.*
The ball landing in the crowd.
LEO *standing. Biting his thumb.*
TRIMINGHAM *bowls fast.*
Shot over LEO'*s shoulder.*
In background TED *swings. Hits the ball. It hurtles through the air towards* LEO. LEO *jumps up and catches it.*
LEO *on his back on the grass. The ball in his hand. Applause.* TRIMINGHAM *comes into the shot, helps him up, pats him on the back.*
TRIMINGHAM. Magnificent catch.

Shot from behind MRS MAUDSLEY *and* MARIAN. *Their backs are still. In background the players are returning to the pavilion.*
The players.
LEO *runs to* TED *who is walking alone.*

LEO. I didn't really mean to catch you out.
TED. It was a damn good catch. (*He laughs. Then murmurs.*) I never thought I'd be caught out by our postman.

Applause grows. TED *goes forward. Shouts of his name. He goes into the pavilion alone.* TRIMING-HAM *stops the team at the pavilion gates and ushers* LEO *in alone. Applause for* LEO. *As the team follows* LEO *up the steps the camera rests on* MARIAN. *She is still. Her head is bent.*

Exterior. Cricket field. Evening.   *PAST*
The field is silent. As we have just seen it, but empty. Long shadows across it.
COLSTON'S VOICE (OVER)
Isn't it dull for you to live here alone?
MARIAN'S VOICE OLD (OVER)
Alone? But people come in shoals. I'm quite a place of pilgrimage.

Interior. Village hall.
The concert.
Union Jacks, paper streamers etc. Food, wine. MR MAUDSLEY *on the platform.*

MR MAUDSLEY. And last but not least, except in stature, our young David, Leo Colston, who slew the Goliath of Black Farm, if I may so describe him, not with a sling but with a catch.

Close shot of TED. *In high starched collar.*
He winks at LEO.
LEO *surrounded by applause.*
MR MAUDSLEY *on platform.*

And now, I believe, it is time for the music. Who I wonder will be prepared to give us the first song?

The assembly.
A proportion of the assembly is slightly drunk, particularly BLUNT *and* STUBBS. *A number of people turn to look at* TED *and call for him.*

BLUNT. Ted's the one! He's the big hitter!

STUBBS. And he's the best shot with a gun!

BLUNT. But is he the best singer?

Calls of 'Yes, come on, Ted' 'Ted's the one' and 'Give us a song'.
TED stands boldly. A shout of acclaim from the audience. TED walks with confidence up to the platform. Shouts of 'Good old Ted'.
The platform.
TED puts his music down on the piano and grins. He suddenly looks at the piano stool, goes to it and lifts it up, looking at it carefully. He turns to the audience.

TED. I can't see the pianist.

The audience.
Some of the audience laugh and then a murmur begins.
Voices: 'Where's the pianist?' 'What's happened to him?' etc.

VOICE. He's in bed. Ill.

Cries of 'In bed?' 'He should be here'.

He's caught a fatal finger disease.

A laugh and then sudden silence falls on the assembly.

TRIMINGHAM. We can't manage without a pianist.

The platform.
TED holding piano stool uncertain.
The audience from TED's point of view.

BLUNT. Come on, Ted. Don't be shy. You don't need music.

STUBBS. Yes, give us a song.

BLUNT. But take your collar off first! It's going to strangle you!

Medium shot. TED.
He puts the piano stool down and stands dogged and unhappy. He shakes his head.
Close-up of MRS MAUDSLEY.
She sits with a very faint smile in her eyes.

BLUNT'S VOICE (OVER)
Come on, be a gentleman. You're dressed up like one.

STUBBS. A sheep in wolf's clothing.

A sudden rustle. Silence. A murmur from the audience.
The audience from TED's *point of view.*
MARIAN *moving swiftly down the aisle towards the platform. Applause from the audience.*
The platform. Long shot.
MARIAN *climbing the steps to the platform.* TED *still. He moves abruptly to help her up. Ironic applause from some members of the audience. She goes to the piano stool and sits down. She picks up the top sheet of music and holds it up to* TED *questioningly.* TED *nods miserably. She places it on the music rest.* TED *turns to the audience.*

TED (*very low*). Take a pair of sparkling eyes.
BLUNT. What did you say? Speak up.
TED. Take a pair of sparkling eyes.
STUBBS. Well, cheer up it isn't a funeral.

Close-up. TED *begins to sing.*
Close-up of MARIAN *playing the piano.*

Interior. Cottage. The sitting-room. Long shot.
  PRESENT
COLSTON *standing with his back to the camera. A maid comes into the room. She says something unheard.* COLSTON *shakes his head. The maid leaves the room.* COLSTON *stands.*
Over this TED's *voice singing 'Take a pair of sparkling eyes'.*

Interior. Village hall.   *PAST*
Audience clapping.
Close-up of LEO *clapping.*
Shouts of encore.

TED *and* MARIAN *on platform.*
TED *begins to leave the platform. Shouts of encore.*
TRIMINGHAM *smoking, looking up at the platform.*
MR MAUDSLEY *looking across at* TRIMINGHAM.
He glances down.
Applause. MARIAN *rises from her stool. She bows to*
TED. *He jerks his head towards her and away. The*
audience laughs. He slowly turns towards her and
bows. Then they bow to the audience.

Exterior. Cricket field. Early evening. PRESENT
The field is silent. A modern mower stands in the
centre of the field. The shot is held in silence. Suddenly
MARIAN's *voice :*
MARIAN'S VOICE. Well, Leo, what's it to be?

Close-up of LEO. *Quick cut.*　　　　　　*PAST*
LEO *is now on the platform.*
Platform. Long shot.
LEO *approaches the edge of the platform. The audience*
is still. He sings :

Angels! Ever bright and fair,
Take, oh take me to your care.
Speed to your own courts my flight
Clad in robes of virgin white
Clad in robes of virgin white.

During this song the camera gently cuts between
STUBBS *and* BLUNT, *totally sober and attentive,*
TRIMINGHAM, MR MAUDSLEY, MRS MAUDSLEY
and TED. *Close-ups of* MARIAN *and* LEO. *Gleam of*
MARIAN's *white arms and neck from* TED's *and*
LEO's *point of view.*
The final shot of this sequence of shots is from the back
of the hall as LEO *finishes the song, the audience quite*
still, before the applause.

Exterior. Lane. Moonlight. Night.
The party walking back to the house. MARCUS *and*
LEO *straggling behind.*

MARCUS. Well, thank goodness we've said good-bye to the village for a year. Did you notice the stink in that hall?

LEO. No.

MARCUS. What a whiff! I suppose you were too busy mooing and rolling your eyes and sucking up the applause. Still, toadstool, I must admit you didn't do too badly.

LEO. Oh thank you.

MARCUS. Except that it was rather horrific to see your slimy serpent's tongue stuck to the roof of your mouth and your face like a sick cow.

LEO *seizes him.*

LEO. You po-faced pot-bellied bed wetter!

MARCUS. Pax! I'll tell you a secret.

LEO. What?

MARCUS. Marian's engaged to marry Trimingham. It'll be announced after the ball. Are you glad?

LEO *lets him go.*

LEO. Yes, I am. I'm sure I am.

Exterior. House. The long shot. Lawn. Day.
MARIAN *and* TRIMINGHAM *playing croquet. They play slowly and with concentration. He moves towards her and whispers something to her. They laugh. The camera suddenly observes that* LEO *is watching them.*

Interior. House. The hall looking through to dining-room.
The end of luncheon. The house party sitting at the long table eating peaches.
MARCUS *and* LEO *come out of the dining-room.*

MARCUS. Are you going out?

LEO. Yes. Shall we?

MARCUS. I'm afraid I can't.

LEO. Why not, sewer rat?

MARCUS. Nanny Robson isn't well. She lives in the village. Marian says I have to spend the afternoon with her. Isn't it boring? Marian said she was going herself after tea. What will you do? Where will you drag your evil smelling carcase?

LEO. Oh I might hang round the rubbish heap for a bit. And then –

MARCUS. Well, don't get carted away by mistake.

The boys tussle in the hall.

Exterior. Back of house.
LEO *strolling away from the thermometer. He turns in the direction of the rubbish dump.* MARIAN's *voice stops him:*

MARIAN. Hello, Leo. Just the man I was looking for.

She comes into shot.

Will you do something for me?

LEO. Oh yes. What?

MARIAN. Take this letter.

She holds out the letter.
LEO *looks at it and then at her.*

LEO. But . . . who to?

MARIAN. Who to? Why to the farm. You silly.

Close-up of LEO.
He stares at her.
Two shot.

What's the matter?

LEO. But I can't.

MARIAN. Can't? Why not?

Pause.

LEO. Because of Hugh.

MARIAN. Hugh? What has Hugh to do with it?

LEO. He . . . might be upset.

MARIAN. What has Hugh got to do with it? I told you, this is a business matter between Mr Burgess and myself. It has nothing to do with anyone else, no one else in the world. Do you understand? Or are you too stupid?

Close-up of LEO.

LEO. But you and Hugh . . . you and Trimingham . . . you . . .

Close-up of MARIAN.

MARIAN. What are you talking about? You come into this house, our guest, a poor nothing out of nowhere, we take you in, we know nothing about you, we feed you, we clothe you, we make a great fuss of you – and then you have the damned cheek to say you won't do a simple thing that any tuppeny-ha'-penny rag-a-muffin in the street would do for nothing!

Long shot.
MARIAN *and* LEO *alone on the path.*

Nothing!

She raises her hand. LEO *starts back. They are still. Close-up of* MARIAN.

You want paying, I suppose. I see. How much do you want?

Two shot.
LEO *snatches the letter and runs.*

Exterior. Country lane. Very high shot.
LEO, *a tiny figure in the landscape, walking, kicking a stone.*
MARIAN'S VOICE OLD (OVER)
So you met my grandson?

COLSTON'S VOICE (OVER)
Yes. I did.
MARIAN'S VOICE OLD (OVER)
Does he remind you of anyone?
COLSTON'S VOICE (OVER)
Of course. His grandfather.
MARIAN'S VOICE OLD (OVER)
That's it, that's it. He does. Yes, he does.
The stone is kicked against a gate.
Shot over farmyard gate to LEO.
His face is stained with tears.

Interior. Farm. Kitchen.
TED *is sitting alone holding a gun between his knees.*
His chest is naked. The barrel is pressed against it.
The muzzle just below his mouth. He is peering down
the barrel.
The shot holds.
Sound of a knock and a door opening.
TED *looks up.*
TED. Hullo! It's the postman!

Shot of kitchen.
TED *stands.*

How are you?

He comes closer to LEO *and peers at him.*

You've been crying. What's the matter?

TED *takes out a handkerchief and gives it to him.*

Would you like to have a shot with my gun? I was
just going to clean it but I can do that afterwards.

LEO *shakes his head.*

Come and watch me then. There's some old rooks
round here that could do with a peppering.

Exterior. Farmyard.
TED *standing in the yard. Gun at his shoulder.* LEO *by*
the door.

TED *shoots.* LEO *starts.*
LEO's *point of view.*
The bird twirls slowly to earth. TED *picks it up and throws it into a bed of nettles.*
The sky.
Rooks wheeling away.
TED'S VOICE. They won't come back in a hurry.

Interior. Scullery.
TED *putting the kettle on to boil on the grate.*
TED. Have you got a letter for me?

Interior. Kitchen.
TED *walks in with tablecloth and drapes it over the table.* LEO *hands him the letter.*
TED. Looks as though you've been sleeping on it.

TED *reads it quickly, puts it away.*

You'd like some tea, wouldn't you? I'm on my own to-day. My daily woman doesn't come on Sundays.
LEO. Oh, do you have a woman every day?

TED *looks at him.*

TED. No. I told you she doesn't come on Sundays.
LEO. Have you any message for her?
TED. Who?
LEO. Marian.
TED. I might have, but do you want to take it?
LEO. Not very much. But she'll be angry if I don't.

TED *lights a cigarette.*

TED. So it was her. (*Pause.*) It isn't fair to ask you to do it for nothing. What can I do to make it worth your while?

Close-up of LEO.

LEO. The last time I was here you said you'd tell me something.

Close-up of TED.

TED. Did I?

LEO. Yes, you said you'd tell me about . . . spooning.

Close-up of LEO.

I don't know any other word. Is there another word?

The kitchen.
TED *goes to the dresser, brings some teacups and saucers and puts them on the table.*

You'd said you'd tell me.

TED (*collecting plates*). Yes. But now I'm not sure that I shall.

LEO. Why not?

TED. It's a job for your dad, really.

LEO. My father's dead. And I'm quite sure he never did it!

TED. Are you?

Pause.

LEO. You can't break your promise.

Pause.

TED. Well . . . it means putting your arm round a girl, and kissing her. That's what it means.

LEO *jumping out of chair.*

LEO. I know that! But it's something else too. It makes you *feel* something.

TED. What do you like doing best?

LEO. Oh . . .

Hissing of the kettle from the scullery.

TED. The kettle's boiling.

TED *goes into the scullery.* LEO *stands.* TED *comes out with a teapot and a jug of milk and puts them on the table.*

It's like whatever you like doing best, and then some more.

Close-up of LEO.

LEO. Yes, but *what more*? What is lover-like? What does it mean? What is a lover? What does a lover do? Are you a lover? What do you do? You know. I know you know. And I won't take any more messages for you unless you tell me!

TED *from* LEO'*s point of view.*
TED *towers above him, and moves towards him.*

TED. Clear out of here quick.

LEO'*s back darts out of shot.*

Interior. Cottage. Hall and front door. PRESENT The back of COLSTON *walking through the hall, down a step into the sitting-room. The maid closes the door and follows. She leaves the room by another door.* COLSTON *stands.*
Over this LEO'*s voice:*
LEO'S VOICE (*as if writing*).
Dear Mother, I am sorry to tell you I am not enjoying myself here. I would like to come home.

Exterior. Road outside farm.   *PAST*
LEO *running away from farm.* TED *waving and shouting at farmyard gate, receding into the distance.*

Interior. House. Tea. The silver teapot.
The camera withdraws to find MARIAN *presiding over tea.* TRIMINGHAM *sits beside* MARIAN, *on a low stool, half in shadow. She regards her guests with a smile, pouring milk in one cup, a slice of lemon in another and lumps of sugar into some. The cups and plates of cakes are passed round. When it is* LEO'*s turn for tea* MARIAN *drops four lumps of sugar into his cup, giggling.*

This shot is silent. Over the shot hear MARIAN'S *voice as an old lady.*
MARIAN'S VOICE (OLD)
I rarely went to parties. People came to see me, of course, interesting people, artists and writers, not stuffy country neighbours. There *are* stuffy people, aren't there? No, no, interesting people came to see me. Artists and writers. Modern people with modern views.

Interior. House. Hall. Brass postbox.
LEO *popping letter into the postbox.*

Exterior. Back of the house. Early evening.
LEO *and* MARCUS *pushing each other.*
MARCUS. What shall we do? Where shall we go?
LEO. What about the rubbish dump?
MARCUS. Oh no, it's so boring. What about those mysterious outhouses?
LEO. Good idea.
MARCUS. Not that there's anything worth seeing, apart from a lot of dreary old outhouses.
LEO. There's the deadly nightshade.
MARCUS. Oui, le belladonne.
LEO. You mean atropa belladonna.

They begin to walk towards the outhouses. MARCUS's *voice receding.*

MARCUS. I don't mean that at all. I mean deadly nightshade.

MARCUS *and* LEO *walking through the tangled undergrowth.*

Mama is ill in bed.
LEO. Why?
MARCUS. I don't know.

They walk on.

What do you think of my mother?

LEO *glances at him.*

LEO. I think she has a lot to look after . . . with the house and everything, and organizing the ball and everything.

MARCUS. She has, yes. She undoubtedly has.

They walk on.

My sister is very beautiful, isn't she?

LEO. Yes. She is very beautiful.

They walk on.

MARCUS. She's going to London tomorrow.

LEO. What for?

MARCUS. Firstly to buy a dress for the ball, you oaf. The engagement ball, you oaf, and then to get something for you.

LEO. What do you mean?

MARCUS. A birthday present, frog-spawn. Now shall I tell you what it is or shall I not?

LEO. Do you *know* what it is?

MARCUS. Yes, but I don't tell little boys.

LEO *grapples with him and holds him in a firm grip.*

Well swear that you won't tell anyone I told you.

LEO. I swear.

MARCUS. It's a bicycle.

LEO *lets* MARCUS *out of his grip.*

LEO (*with great pleasure*). What?

MARCUS. Do you know what colour it is? It's green, green, you imbecile. Bright green. And do you know why? Because you are green yourself. It's your true colour, Marian said so.

LEO *standing with* MARCUS *dancing round him.*

Green. Green. Green!

LEO. Did she say that?

MARCUS. But of course.

MARCUS *continues to dance around* LEO.

Green. Green. Green!

Close-up of LEO.

LEO (*violently*). Do you know where Marian is at this moment?

Two shot.
MARCUS *stops still.*

MARCUS. No. Do you?
LEO. Yes.
MARCUS. Where?
LEO. I don't tell little boys.

LEO *dances round* MARCUS.

Little boy, little boy, wouldn't you like to know?
MARCUS. Pax!

LEO *walks away.*
LEO *and* MARCUS *walking.*

Do you really know where she is?
LEO. Ah-hah!

They walk on in silence, kicking stones as they go.
Suddenly LEO *stops.*
The deadly nightshade.
It has grown out of its door, and spread. It emerges over the roofless wall. It is heavy, purple, oppressive.
MARCUS'S VOICE
Shall we push past it into the shed?
Close-up of LEO.

LEO. No, you mustn't.

Suddenly the low murmur of a man's voice heard.
MARCUS *and* LEO *freeze. The voice is insistent, cajoling, tender. The words are indecipherable.*
MARCUS *whispers to* LEO.

MARCUS. A loony talking to himself. Shall we go and see?

A second voice heard, low, toneless, light.

There are two of them. They're spooning. Let's go and rout them out.

Quick close-up of LEO.

LEO (*hushed whisper*). No! It would be too boring!

Exterior. Outhouses.
LEO *walks away.* MARCUS *stands a moment, looking back, and then follows. He joins* LEO *in foreground.*

MARCUS. What confounded cheek. Why should they come here? This is private property. I wonder what Mama would say.

LEO. Oh, I shouldn't tell her. What's the point?

MARCUS. What confounded cheek!

They disappear from shot.
The camera holds on the view of the outhouses, including the deadly nightshade.

Interior. House. Hall. The postbox.
LEO *looks through the pane into the postbox. He sees his letter. He fingers the door. It opens. He takes the letter out, looks at it, puts it back quickly. Closes the door.*
The camera pans to watch him run up the centre stairs.

Interior. House. Corridor. First landing.
LEO *appears and sees* TRIMINGHAM *going into the smoking-room. The door closes.*
LEO *hesitates, then walks to the smoking-room door, hesitates, knocks at the door, opens it.*

Interior. Smoking-room.
TRIMINGHAM *picking up a newspaper.* LEO *pokes his head round the door.*

TRIMINGHAM. Hello.

LEO *hesitates at the door.*

Come in.

LEO *closes the door.*

Never been in here before?

LEO. No.

TRIMINGHAM. Sit down. Cigar?

LEO. No thank you.

TRIMINGHAM *sits down and lights a cigar.*

Can I ask you something?

TRIMINGHAM. You can.

LEO. I was reading a book. And in this book . . . two men fought a duel . . . over a quarrel . . . about one of the men's wife. And then . . . in this duel . . . the wife's husband . . . the husband . . . was shot.

TRIMINGHAM. Mmn–hmnm. (*Pause.*) What's your question?

LEO. Well, I thought . . . when I read it . . . that it was probably the lady's fault, but she didn't have to fight the duel and I just thought that it was a little unfair.

Close-up of TRIMINGHAM.

TRIMINGHAM. Nothing is ever a lady's fault.

Close-up of LEO.

LEO. Oh.

Close-up of TRIMINGHAM.

TRIMINGHAM. Does that answer your question?

Shot across TRIMINGHAM *to* LEO.

LEO. Yes.

TRIMINGHAM. Any other questions?

LEO. Er . . . what do you think of Ted Burgess?

TRIMINGHAM (*ruminatively*). What do I think of Ted Burgess? (*Pause.*) He's a powerful hitter.

LEO *chuckles.*

But you had the measure of him.

LEO *smiles*.

You defeated him, didn't you? (*Pause.*) Yes, Ted Burgess is quite a decent fellow. A bit wild.

LEO. Wild? Do you mean he's dangerous?

TRIMINGHAM. He's not dangerous to you or to me. He's a bit of a lady-killer, that's all.

LEO (*baffled*). A lady-killer?

The door opens. MR MAUDSLEY *comes in.*
TRIMINGHAM *and* LEO *rise.*

MR MAUDSLEY. Sit down, please sit down. Ah! A new recruit to the smoking-room. Have you been telling him some smoking-room stories?

TRIMINGHAM *laughs*.

Or showing him the pictures? (*He turns to* LEO.) Have you looked at the pictures?

MR MAUDSLEY *indicates a row of small dark canvases, set deep in heavy frames.*
LEO *turns to look at the pictures.*
Men sitting on tubs, drinking. Women serving them. One woman leaning on the back of a man's chair watching the card game. The chair back pressing against her breasts, which bulge over its rim.
LEO *turns away from the pictures.*
Close-up of MR MAUDSLEY.

He doesn't like them.

Three shot.

TRIMINGHAM. Teniers is an acquired taste, in my opinion. We were talking about Ted Burgess when you came in. I told Leo he was a lady-killer.

MR MAUDSLEY. He has that reputation, I believe.

TRIMINGHAM. I've been talking to him about joining the army. A likely man. Single. No ties. And a pretty good shot too with a rifle, by all accounts.

MR MAUDSLEY. He has that reputation, I believe. (*Pause.*) Do you think he'll go?

TRIMINGHAM. I think he may. He was quite interested.

MR MAUDSLEY. He won't altogether be a loss to the district.

TRIMINGHAM. Why?

MR MAUDSLEY (*vaguely*). Oh, what you were saying just now.

> MR MAUDSLEY *goes to the cabinet to pour sherry from a decanter.*

They say he's got a woman up this way.

LEO. I know.

> *Close-up of* MR MAUDSLEY.
> MR MAUDSLEY, *in the act of pouring sherry, stops and looks over his shoulder at* LEO.
> TRIMINGHAM *and* MR MAUDSLEY *looking at* LEO.
> *Close-up of* LEO.

But she doesn't come on Sundays.

> TRIMINGHAM *and* MR MAUDSLEY.

TRIMINGHAM (*to* MR MAUDSLEY). Cigar?

> *Exterior. Cornfield. Long shot. Day.*
> LEO *stands in foreground looking across the field.* TED *is driving the reaper.* LEO *waves.* TED *does not see him. A labourer sees* LEO *and signals to* TED. TED *stops the horse and dismounts. The labourer gets up on the reaper and continues the work.*
> TED *walks slowly across the fields towards* LEO. *The camera moves with* LEO *as he walks towards* TED. *They stop at a short distance from each other. Silence.*

TED. I didn't think you'd come again. (*Pause.*) I'm sorry I shouted at you. I didn't mean to. I just didn't feel like telling you – what you wanted to know – that's all. But I'll tell you now if you like. (*Pause.*) Do you want me to tell you? Because I'll tell you now. If you want me to.

> *Close-up of* LEO.

LEO. No, no. I wouldn't dream of troubling you. I

know someone who'll tell me. As a matter of fact I
know several people who can tell me.

Two shot.

TED. As long as they don't tell you wrong.
LEO. How could they? It's common knowledge, isn't
it?

Pause.

TED. What are you doing with your bathing suit?

They begin to stroll along the edge of the cornfield.

LEO. I told Marcus you were going to give me a swimming lesson. I've come to say good-bye, you see.

Long shot. Across cornfield.
LEO *and* TED *walking along its rim. Their voices:*

TED. Oh, you're off are you?
LEO. Yes, I'm expecting to hear from my mother by
Friday at the latest. I think I really should go home.
She does miss me, you know.
TED. I'm sure she does.

Pause.

LEO. Is it true you're going to the war?
TED. Who told you that?
LEO. Lord Trimingham. (*Pause.*) Did you know
Marian was engaged to him?
TED. Yes. I did.

Close two shot. TED *and* LEO *stopping.*

LEO. Is that why you're going?
TED. I don't know that I *am* going. That's for her to
say. It isn't what I want, but what she wants.

Close-up of LEO *staring at him.*

Two shot.

LEO. Well, good-bye.
TED. So long, postman.

They shake hands. LEO *turns, turns back.*

LEO. Shall I take one more message for you?

Close-up of TED.

TED. Yes. Say tomorrow's no good, but Friday at half-past five, same as usual.

Close-up of MARIAN.

MARIAN. Did you miss me?

LEO'S VOICE. Well . . . I've been quite busy.

MARIAN. That's the first unkind thing I've ever heard you say.

Two shot MARIAN *and* LEO.
They are sitting in a small writing room.

MARIAN. I've been to London on a special mission.

LEO. Did you enjoy yourself?

MARIAN. No.

LEO. I'm sorry.

MARIAN. No you're not. You couldn't care less if I dropped dead in front of you. You're a hard-hearted boy, but then all boys are.

LEO. What about men?

MARIAN. You're all alike, blocks of granite. Or the beds here. They're *really* hard.

LEO. Mine isn't.

MARIAN. You're lucky. Mine is, harder than the ground.

LEO. I know a boy who slept on the ground once. He said it made his hips sore. Did you find that?

MARIAN *looks at him.*

MARIAN. What makes you think I've slept on the ground?

LEO. Because you said your bed was harder.

MARIAN. Well, so it is. (*Pause.*) I'm sorry I was so nasty to you the other day. I'm not really nasty. I'm a good natured girl, really.

Close-up of LEO.

LEO. Do . . . soldiers have to sleep on the ground?
MARIAN. Yes, I suppose so.
LEO. Will Ted have to?

Close-up of MARIAN.
MARIAN. Ted?
LEO. Yes, when he goes to the war.
MARIAN. Ted going to the war, what do you mean?

Two shot.

LEO. Hugh told me. Hugh asked him to join up and he said he might.
MARIAN. Hugh? Hugh! Do you mean that Hugh has persuaded Ted to enlist?

She stands and goes to the window.
MARIAN *foreground. Window.* LEO *background.*

(*Quietly.*) No. No he won't, he won't go to the war. I'll see to that. I'll tell Hugh . . . that it's out of the question. One word would do it.

LEO *comes to her at the window.*

LEO. No, you mustn't say any word. You see, Hugh doesn't *know.*
MARIAN. Doesn't know? Then why does he want Ted to go to the war?
LEO. He's patriotic. (*Pause.*) Perhaps he *wants* to go.
MARIAN. He couldn't.

Pause.

LEO. Why don't you marry Ted?
MARIAN. I can't . . . I can't. Can't you see why?
LEO. But why . . . are you marrying Hugh?
MARIAN. Because I must. I must. I've got to.

Wide shot. Room.
MARIAN *suddenly cries quietly.* LEO *stares at her and then begins to cry himself.*

They stand, crying. They hold each other. LEO *forces himself to stop.*

LEO. I have a message for you.

She looks up.

Friday at 5.30.

MARIAN. Yes.

LEO. But can you be back in time?

MARIAN. For what?

LEO. For my birthday. For cutting the cake.

MARIAN *takes his hand.*

MARIAN. Of course. Of course.

Exterior. Village street.   **PRESENT**

COLSTON *standing by the car. At the far end of the village the figure of a young man appears. He slowly draws nearer on the other side of the street.* COLSTON *moves a few steps, stops and watches the young man. As the young man comes closer,* COLSTON *begins to cross the street towards him.*

Zoom in to young man's face turning sharply, seeing COLSTON *approach.*

LEO'S MOTHER'S VOICE *over this (as if writing):*

LEO'S MOTHER'S VOICE.

I think it would be ungrateful to Mrs Maudsley after all her kindness to you if you were to leave so suddenly. I think it would be a mistake.

Interior. LEO's *room. Night.*   **PAST**

LEO *at the writing table, erecting a structure like a small altar. Four books form the framework. Within stand four candles, a soap dish drainer rests on the books, on the drainer a silver cup, four boxes of matches, a water bottle and a damp sponge, set at precise intervals on the table.* LEO *looks at his clock. It is 11.15.*

Over this shot the woman's voice continues:

LEO'S MOTHER'S VOICE.

The ten days will soon pass, my darling, and then you'll be home. We can't expect to be happy *all* the time, can we?
He puts on his slippers and his dressing gown over his nightshirt and opens the door.

Interior. House. Staircase. Night.
Through the closed door of the drawing room sounds of a piano and singing. MARIAN *is singing 'Roaming in the Gloaming'.*
The front door is open. LEO *creeps down the main staircase, hesitates a moment and then goes out the door.*

Exterior. Back of the house. LEO *running through the bushes.*
The sky, cloudy, through moonlight.
The outhouse.
LEO *stops dead.*
LEO's *point of view. The deadly nightshade.*
LEO *walks towards it slowly. When he is close to it, he stops.*
He touches it. He moves quickly past it and into the outhouses.

Interior. Outhouse.
Close-up of LEO. *The twigs of the deadly nightshade about him.*
He shifts his position. A berry touches his face. He whimpers, tries to force his way out, hits a wall, turns, nightshade flowers around his face.
LEO *begins to tear at the nightshade. Branches rip and crack. He stumbles, still pulling, out of the outhouse, pulling at the main stem. Leaves fall, the main stem cracks. Roots creak. He pulls with all his might to unearth the plant and suddenly it gives way.*
He falls on his back clutching the stump.

High shot. LEO *lying with stump.*
LEO. Delenda est Belladonna.

Interior. LEO's *room. Close shot silver cup on writing table. Night.*
Diary open beside it. Incomprehensible writing seen.
LEO *is crushing a leaf, flower and two berries from the deadly nightshade in the cup, pouring boiling water into it with his left hand.*
LEO'S VOICE (*whispering*).
Delenda, delenda, delenda.

Interior. Lavatory.
LEO *pouring the mashed contents of the cup into the lavatory.*
COLSTON'S VOICE.
Delenda est Belladonna.
LEO *makes a gesture of exorcism.*

Exterior. House. Lawn. Rain. Day.
The rain sweeps over the lawn and through the cedars.
Close-up of MRS MAUDSLEY.
MRS MAUDSLEY. And now today . . . is Leo's day.

She smiles.
The camera tracks back to find MRS MAUDSLEY *and the others at the breakfast table. In front of* LEO *are opened envelopes and packages. Cards, ties etc.*

You've opened your presents. At seven o'clock you'll cut your birthday cake, and receive a rather special present, so I believe. Now how would you like to spend the day? Unfortunately the weather . . . has changed, but if it clears perhaps you would like to go for a drive to Beeston Castle, after luncheon? You haven't seen it, have you?
LEO. That would be very nice.
MRS MAUDSLEY. Well, we shall do that, if the weather clears. We shall decide at luncheon.

DENYS. What if the weather doesn't clear, Mama?

MRS MAUDSLEY. Then we shall have to think again. We shall make our decision at luncheon. Don't you think, Hugh?

TRIMINGHAM. Quite a fair plan, I should say.

DENYS. But it may not clear.

Exterior. Village street. Over COLSTON *to the young man.* PRESENT
The young man steps back to point to a cottage at the far end of the village. COLSTON *nods to the young man. They shake hands and part.*
Over this the following dialogue:

MR MAUDSLEY. I think it will. The rain seems to have stopped. For the moment anyway.

DENYS. So it has.

MRS MAUDSLEY. There you are then. It seems that all will be well for Leo's birthday.

DENYS. There's still a lot of dark cloud about.

MR MAUDSLEY. What's your opinion, Hugh?

Interior. Hall. Morning. PAST
Guests passing through the hall. MARIAN *stops, alone, and turns.*

MARIAN. Leo, come with me and tell me what the weather means to do.

Exterior. Front of house.
MARIAN *and* LEO *emerge and look up at the sky. They walk along the path and turn by the side of the house into the rhododendrons, the camera watching them.*
MARIAN *and* LEO *amid the rhododendrons.*

LEO. Do you think the summer is over? It's one of the hottest summers on record. You know.

MARIAN. Of course it isn't over. Tell me, would you like to walk?

LEO. Oh yes! Where shall we walk?

MARIAN. I can't, I'm afraid. It's this kind of walk.

Close shot of MARIAN's *hand touching* LEO's. *A letter in* MARIAN's *hand.*
Close-up of LEO.

LEO. Oh no!

Close-up of MARIAN.

MARIAN (*laughing*). Oh yes!

Two shot.
MARIAN, *laughing, tries to thrust the letter into* LEO's *hand.* LEO *resists. They begin to dodge and feint and lunge, both now laughing.*

MRS MAUDSLEY'S
VOICE. Marian! Leo!

They stop still. The camera moves towards them.

What were you fighting about?

MARIAN. Oh I was just teaching him a lesson –

LEO *whose hands are at his sides, suddenly drops the letter.*
The camera dips slowly to look at it. It lies on the ground, crumpled.
LEO *looks sharply into camera.* MARIAN *remains composed.*
Close-up of MRS MAUDSLEY.

MRS MAUDSLEY. Was that the bone of contention?

Three shot.
MARIAN *picks up the letter and puts it into* LEO's *pocket.*

MARIAN. Yes it was, Mama. I wanted him to take this note to Nanny Robson to tell her that I will go and see her some time this afternoon. And would you believe it, Leo didn't want to! He pretended he had something on with Marcus.

LEO *looks at her.*

Yes you did!

MRS MAUDSLEY. I shouldn't let it worry you, Marian. You say she often doesn't remember whether you've been or not. She is certainly growing old, poor Nanny Robson. I think it's about time Leo and I took a walk in the garden. (*She takes* LEO's *hand.*) Come along Leo. I don't believe you've seen the garden properly, have you? (*She turns to* MARIAN.) You can spare Leo now, can't you Marian?

MARIAN. Oh, yes.

Long shot.
MRS MAUDSLEY *with* LEO *walks away from* MARIAN.

LEO. Would you like Marcus to come with us?

MRS MAUDSLEY. Oh no. Marcus isn't interested in flowers. You are though, aren't you?

LEO. Yes, I am.

The backs of MRS MAUDSLEY *and* LEO *walking through the garden.*
They arrive at the flower beds.

MRS MAUDSLEY. The rain has certainly stopped. (*Pause.*) Well, now, here's the garden. What kind of flowers truly interest you?

LEO. Poisonous ones really.

MRS MAUDSLEY. I don't think you'll find many of those.

LEO. Oh there is one in the out –

Two shot.
MRS MAUDSLEY *stops.*

MRS MAUDSLEY. In the what?

LEO. Well . . . I've seen . . .

MRS MAUDSLEY (*smiling*). What have you seen, Leo?

LEO. Well, there is a deadly nightshade in one of the outhouses.

MRS MAUDSLEY. Oh, you mean where the old garden used to be.

LEO. Yes, somewhere there . . .

MRS MAUDSLEY. Do you often go to the outhouses?

LEO. Oh no, not often.

They stop by a magnolia.

MRS MAUDSLEY. This always reminds me of Marian. How sweet of you to say you'd take her note to Nanny Robson. Does she often send you with messages?

LEO. Oh no, just once or twice.

MRS MAUDSLEY. It rather worries me that I stopped you going just now. Perhaps you would like to go? You know the way, of course?

Pause.

LEO. Well, not quite but I can ask.

MRS MAUDSLEY. You don't know the way? But I thought you had taken messages there before.

LEO. Yes, well, yes I have.

MRS MAUDSLEY. But you don't know the way. (*Pause.*) I think perhaps the note should be delivered. You have it in your pocket, haven't you? I'll call one of the gardeners and ask him to take it.

LEO. Oh no, really. It's not a bit important. Please don't bother.

MRS MAUDSLEY. It is important in a way, you see. Stanton, could you come here a minute.

A gardener puts down his tools and comes towards her and into the shot.

We have a note here for Miss Robson, rather urgent. Would you mind taking it?

STANTON. Yes 'm.

LEO *digs his fingers into his pocket.*

LEO. I've . . . lost it. I haven't got it. It must have fallen out of my pocket.

MRS MAUDSLEY. Feel again.

LEO *does so.*

LEO. I must have dropped it.

MRS MAUDSLEY. Very well, Stanton.

STANTON *moves away.*

Close-up of MRS MAUDSLEY.

Take your hands out of your pockets. Has no one

ever told you not to stand with your hands in your pockets?

Close-up of LEO *taking his hands out of his pockets.*

Two shot over LEO *to* MRS MAUDSLEY.

MRS MAUDSLEY. I could ask you to turn your pockets out. But I won't do that. I'll just ask you one question. You say you have taken messages for Marian before?

LEO. Well I –

MRS MAUDSLEY. I think you said so. If you don't take them to Nanny Robson –

Exterior. Village street. No cars. Day.
                                    TIME NEUTRAL
Exterior. House. Garden. Long shot.
MRS MAUDSLEY *and* LEO *standing.*

Interior. House. Lavatory.
LEO *sitting on lavatory lid.*
MRS MAUDSLEY'S VOICE (OVER)
– to whom do you take them?

Exterior. Village street.   PRESENT
Across COLSTON *to the young man. The young man is listening to* COLSTON.

Exterior. House. Garden. Rain sweeping over the garden.   PAST
No one in sight.

Interior. Cottage.   PRESENT
COLSTON *ushered into the room by the maid.*

Interior. House. Lavatory.   *PAST*
LEO *sitting.*
MARIAN'S VOICE OLD (OVER)
So you met my grandson.
COLSTON'S VOICE
Yes, I did.
MARIAN'S VOICE OLD (OVER)
Does he remind you of anyone?
COLSTON'S VOICE
Of course. His grandfather.
MARIAN'S VOICE (OLD)
That's it, that's it. He does.

Close-up of COLSTON.   *PRESENT*

(*NOTE: In the following shots we see the faces of* COLSTON *and* MARIAN *old for the first time.*)

COLSTON. It must be a comfort for you to have him near you.

Close-up of MARIAN *as an old lady.*   *PRESENT*

MARIAN. Yes. But he doesn't come to see me very much. I think he has a grudge against me.

Close-up of COLSTON.   *PRESENT*

COLSTON. Oh surely not.

Close-up of MARIAN.   *PRESENT*

MARIAN (*old*). They tell me that he wants to marry a girl – a nice girl – but he won't ask her . . . he feels . . . I think he feels . . . that he's under some sort of spell or curse, you see. That's just plain silly. Now this is where you come in.
COLSTON. I?
MARIAN. Yes, you. You know the facts, you know what *really* happened. Tell him, tell him everything, just as it was.

Close-up of COLSTON.   *PRESENT*
Shot over COLSTON *to* MARIAN   *PRESENT*

Every man should get married. You ought to have
got married. You're all dried up inside, I can tell
that. Don't you feel any need of love? Speak to
him, tell him there's no spell or curse except an
unloving heart.

Interior. House. Hall. Evening.   *PAST*
MRS MAUDSLEY *descending the stairs.*
MARIAN'S VOICE OLD (OVER)
Tell him that.
MRS MAUDSLEY *walks to the door of the drawing-
room and opens it.*
*From her point of view. See a collection of people
standing at windows looking out.*
Distant thunder.
Interior. Drawing-room. The windows. LEO. *He
turns.*
MRS MAUDSLEY *moving into the room.*

MARCUS. We're watching the lightning, Mama.
TRIMINGHAM. Rather good luck we didn't set out for Beeston
Castle.
MRS MAUDSLEY. Yes, it would have been rather a damp expedition.

The gathering clusters round the tea-table.

Sit here please, Leo, dear. (*She indicates a place.*)
Do you see what's in front of you?

Across table at LEO. *Sitting.*
*In foreground a birthday cake with twelve candles.
Crackers, flowers. A smaller cake with one candle.*
Over LEO *to* MRS MAUDSLEY.
You see I don't like the number thirteen – isn't
it silly of me? So we've put twelve candles round
the big cake, and then when they're blown out, you
shall light this one, and blow this one out.

MRS MAUDSLEY's *hands.*
Over MRS MAUDSLEY *to* LEO.

LEO. When will that be?

MRS MAUDSLEY. When Marian comes. She has a rather special present for you. She wants to give it to you herself, naturally.

Long shot. Room.

Let's all sit down.

Everyone does so.

Marian should be back at about six o'clock from Nanny Robson.

TRIMINGHAM. I haven't seen Nanny Robson for years. How is she?

MRS MAUDSLEY. Remarkably well. Isn't it time that Leo cut the cake?

MARCUS. Yes! If he can do it.

MRS MAUDSLEY. That's unkind. Of course he can do it. He's a man of great capabilities.

TRIMINGHAM. Considerable. And well loved. Didn't you know he was Marian's cavalier?

LEO *blowing the candles out.*
Cries of encouragement. Applause.

MARCUS. He's done it!

The SERVANTS *handing round portions of the cake.*

DENYS. Leave a piece for Marian.

TRIMINGHAM. She ought to be here now.

MR MAUDSLEY. It's still raining. (*Pause.*) We'd better send the carriage down to fetch her. Why didn't we think of it before?

Table in foreground.
MR MAUDSLEY *talking to butler at door in background.*

Exterior. House. Rain. Evening.
The carriage going into the distance down the drive.

Interior. Drawing-room.
Everyone eating cake.
Silence.

TRIMINGHAM. She should be with us in five minutes now.

A GUEST. She may be walking up in the rain. Poor darling, she'll be soaked.

Pause.

MARCUS. What about your thirteenth candle?

TRIMINGHAM. We must light it first.

It is lit.

LEO *blowing the candle out.*

DENYS. Now you must cut a piece for yourself.

LEO *does so.*

He'd rather have his cake than eat it.

DENYS *laughs. No one else does.*
Close-up of LEO.
He nibbles a little at his cake.
Silence.
The room.
Silence.

MR MAUDSLEY. Let's have a round of crackers. Here, Leo, come pull one with me.

LEO *does so. Everyone, with the exception of* MRS MAUDSLEY, *finds partners.*

Now all together!

They pull the crackers. They all put on paper hats and blow whistles.
Medium shot of LEO *turning to look for a cracker.*
A cracker is thrust into his hand. He looks up.
LEO's *point of view.* MRS MAUDSLEY *with cracker.*
Over MRS MAUDSLEY *to* LEO.
They pull. The cracker cracks.
Back of BUTLER *at door.*
The assembly turns to him. MRS MAUDSLEY *in the forefront.*

BUTLER. Excuse me, Madam. The carriage has come back but not Miss Marian. She wasn't at Miss

Robson's. And Miss Robson said she hadn't been all day.

The BUTLER *goes out.*
Silence.

DENYS. Where can she be?

Pause.

MR MAUDSLEY. Well, all we can do is wait for her.

DENYS. I've just found a wonderful riddle. Listen to this.

MRS MAUDSLEY's *chair scraping back. Her skirt.*

Close-up of MRS MAUDSLEY.

MRS MAUDSLEY. No. We won't wait. I'm going to look for her. Leo. you know where she is. You shall show me the way,

Long shot. Room.
MRS MAUDSLEY *seizes* LEO's *hand. A chair falls.*
She takes him to the door.
Close-up of MR MAUDSLEY.

MR MAUDSLEY. Madeleine!

Interior. Hall.
MRS MAUDSLEY *and* LEO *going through hall. They pass a green bicycle standing in the hall, and go out the door.*

Interior. Room.
Silence. Everyone still.

Close-up of TRIMINGHAM *sitting quite still.*

Exterior. House. Night.
MRS MAUDSLEY *and* LEO *come out of the front door. The* BUTLER *follows them swiftly and offers* MRS MAUDSLEY *a lantern and an umbrella. She ignores them both.* MRS MAUDSLEY *and* LEO *walk along the path, she leading. It is raining heavily.*

Exterior. House. Garden. Rain. Night.
MRS MAUDSLEY *and* LEO *moving past the rhododendrons towards the outhouses.*

Interior. Cottage. **PRESENT**
COLSTON *and* MARIAN *sitting. Long shot.
She is speaking, but the words are unheard.
Over this voices:*
MARIAN'S VOICE (YOUNG)
You won't . . . tell anyone about this letter.
You won't . . . will you?
LEO'S VOICE.
Of course I won't.

Exterior. House. Garden. Rain. Night. **PAST**
MRS MAUDSLEY *and* LEO *moving past rhododendrons towards outhouses.*

Exterior. Outhouses. Rain. Night.
MRS MAUDSLEY *and* LEO *approach the outhouses.*

Exterior. Cottage. Through window. **PRESENT**
MARIAN *and* COLSTON *sitting. She is talking,
words unheard. Over this voices:*
MARIAN'S VOICE (YOUNG)
Tell me. Would you like a walk?
LEO'S VOICE
Oh yes! Where shall we walk?
MARIAN'S VOICE (YOUNG)
I can't, I'm afraid. It's this kind of walk.

Exterior. Outhouses. Rain. Night. **PAST**
MRS MAUDSLEY *and* LEO *approach the outhouses.
Medium shot. Stump of deadly nightshade lying on
the path. Camera still. Rain.*

Interior. Deadly nightshade. Outhouse.
MRS MAUDSLEY *standing.* LEO *behind her.*

MRS MAUDSLEY. Not here.

Close-up of LEO *whimpering.*
MRS MAUDSLEY's *face comes into the shot.*

No, you *shall* come.

She pulls him after her.

MRS MAUDSLEY *dragging* LEO *towards the row of outhouses. Rain.*
Light flickering. Their faces.
They stop.

Interior. Outhouse.
A lantern on the ground.
A shadow moving on the wall like an umbrella opening and closing.
Close-up of LEO *mystified.*
The shadow.
Close-up of MRS MAUDSLEY.
The shadow.
Close-up of MRS MAUDSLEY.
Her face contorts. She lets her breath out in a long exhalation and groan.
The shadow ceasing to move.
Close-up of MRS MAUDSLEY. *Her face contorted. No sound.*
Close-up of LEO.
The faces of TED *and* MARIAN *on the ground.*
They are still. TED's *head is buried in* MARIAN's *shoulder.* MARIAN *looks up through half-open eyes.*

Exterior. Lawn. Front of houses. Day.
In foreground a shape of a girl lying in a hammock.
The wide lawn falls away before the house on a gentle slope. Cedars, elms. The hammock, faded crimson

*canvas, swings gently. In background figures in white
playing croquet. Over this* MARIAN'S *voice.*
MARIAN'S VOICE (OLD)
You came out of the blue to make us happy. And
we made you happy, didn't we? We trusted you
with our great treasure. You might never have
known what it was, you might have gone through
life without knowing. Isn't that so?

Close-up of COLSTON *listening.*   *PRESENT*
MARIAN'S VOICE (OLD)
But you see you can tell him, Leo. You can tell him
everything, just as it was.
The camera holds on COLSTON.

Medium shot of TED *dead.*

*He is slumped in his chair, his gun against his leg. His
shirt is bloody. His head cannot be seen.*
Near the end of this shot MARIAN'S *voice begins:*
MARIAN'S VOICE (OLD)
Hugh was as true as steel, he wouldn't hear a word
against me.

Close-up of MARIAN OLD.   *PRESENT*
MARIAN. But everybody wanted to know us, of course. I was
Lady Trimingham, you see. I still am. There is no
other.

*Interior. Car windscreen. Moving towards Brandham
Hall.*   *PRESENT*
MARIAN'S VOICE OLD (OVER)
Remember how you loved taking our messages,
bringing us together and making us happy. Well

this is another errand of love and the last time I shall ever ask you to be our postman.

The car goes down an incline and begins to rise.

Interior. Car. COLSTON's *face impassive.*

                                                    PRESENT

MARIAN'S VOICE OLD (OVER)

Our love was a beautiful thing, wasn't it? Tell him he can feel proud to be descended from our union, the child of so much happiness and beauty. Tell him –

The sound stops abruptly.

The car comes to the top of the hill.

Exterior. Road. Day.   *PRESENT*

The south west prospect of Brandham Hall springs into view.

The elms have been cut down.

The car stops.

Brandham Hall.

A cloud of dust from the car slightly obscures the view.